THE HANDBOOK OF
COUNSELLING
PSYCHOLOGY

The Companion Website

Visit https://study.sagepub.com/handbookcounsellingpsychology to find a range of additional resources for students, including:

- **Videos** and **Podcasts** of the editors in discussion with practitioners and trainees.
- **Further Reading**, **Exercises** and **Case Studies** to further bring the content to life.

THE HANDBOOK OF
COUNSELLING
PSYCHOLOGY

Edited by

BARBARA DOUGLAS, RAY WOOLFE, SHEELAGH STRAWBRIDGE, ELAINE KASKET AND VICTORIA GALBRAITH

FOURTH EDITION

Los Angeles | London | New Delhi
Singapore | Washington DC | Melbourne

Los Angeles | London | New Delhi
Singapore | Washington DC | Melbourne

SAGE Publications Ltd
1 Oliver's Yard
55 City Road
London EC1Y 1SP

SAGE Publications Inc.
2455 Teller Road
Thousand Oaks, California 91320

SAGE Publications India Pvt Ltd
B 1/I 1 Mohan Cooperative Industrial Area
Mathura Road
New Delhi 110 044

SAGE Publications Asia-Pacific Pte Ltd
3 Church Street
#10-04 Samsung Hub
Singapore 049483

Editor: Susannah Trefgarne
Editorial assistant: Edward Coats
Production editor: Rachel Burrows
Marketing manager: Tamara Navaratnam
Cover design: Lisa Harper-Wells
Typeset by: C&M Digitals (P) Ltd, Chennai, India
Printed and bound in Great Britain by Ashford Colour
Press Ltd

First edition published 1996. Reprinted 1997, 1998, 2001
Second edition published 2003. Reprinted 2006, 2007, 2009
Third edition published 2010. Reprinted 2011, 2012, 2014

This Fourth edition first published 2016

Library of Congress Control Number: 2015946617

British Library Cataloguing in Publication data

A catalogue record for this book is available from the British Library

ISBN 978-1-4462-7631-0
ISBN 978-1-4462-7632-7 (pbk)

At SAGE we take sustainability seriously. Most of our products are printed in the UK using FSC papers and boards. When we print overseas we ensure sustainable papers are used as measured by the PREPS grading system. We undertake an annual audit to monitor our sustainability.

CONTENTS

LIST OF FIGURES AND TABLES

FIGURES

TABLES

ABOUT THE EDITORS AND CONTRIBUTORS

ABOUT THE EDITORS

Dr Barbara Douglas is a Chartered and Registered Counselling Psychologist and runs a busy independent practice in Edinbugh. She has recently retired as Registrar for the British Psychological Society's Qualification in Counselling Psychology before which she was Senior Lecturer in Counselling Psychology at the University of the West of England. Prior to that Barbara was Director of the North West Centre for Eating Disorders. She has particular interest in the histories of both psychology and psychiatry and has written chapters for several books and co-authored the 2014 Sage book *Common Presenting Issues in Psychotherapeutic Practice.* Barbara was Chair of the BPS Division of Counselling Psychology (2009–2011) and Chair of the Representative Council in 2011. She was very honoured to receive the British Psychological Society Professional Practice Board's Practitioner of the Year Award in 2011.

Ray Woolfe is a Registered Counselling Psychologist and Psychoanalytical Psychotherapist. A career as a university teacher involved jobs as Staff Tutor in Education and Senior Lecturer in Health and Social Welfare at the Open University and then Senior Lecturer at Counselling Studies at Keele University. He is now semi-retired but operates a small private therapy and supervision practice in Bristol. He was Chair of the Special Group in Counselling Psychology at the time it achieved divisional status and was the first Registrar of the Examination Board for what is now the Qualification in Counselling Psychology. He was a founding member of the Register of Psychologists Specialising in Psychotherapy. In 2001 he received a Special Centenary Award from the Division for the 'Development of Counselling Psychology within the Society'.

Sheelagh Strawbridge is a Chartered Psychologist, Registered Counselling Psychologist and Registered Psychologist Specialising in Psychotherapy (Senior Practitioner). Practising in

Hull, she has experience in university teaching, professional training and examining. She has long been actively involved in the development of counselling psychology within the British Psychological Society and has engaged in committee work in the BPS for many years. She is a Fellow of the British Association for Counselling and Psychotherapy and was, for a number of years, an Associate of The Northern Trust for Dramatherapy. Her publications include *Exploring Self and Society* (with Rosamund Billington and Jenny Hockey) (Macmillan, 1998), book chapters and journal articles. She was one of the editors and a contributor to the third edition of the *Handbook of Counselling Psychology* (Sage, 2009).

Dr Elaine Kasket is a Registered Counselling Psychologist (HCPC) and Chartered Counselling Psychologist (BPS). She maintains a private practice and is Programme Director of the DPsych in Counselling Psychology at Regent's University London. She has supervised or examined dozens of doctoral candidates and is committed to promoting a strong research culture within the counselling psychology profession. Her own research focuses on the psychological and sociological implications of the digital age and social networking. One thread of this research activity focuses on how psychologists function personally and professionally in the digital age. She also studies technologically mediated mourning and memorialisation and regularly speaks on these topics at academic conferences and in the popular press. She has authored several book chapters on research processes within a counselling psychology context.

Dr Victoria Galbraith is a Chartered and Registered Counselling Psychologist, Coaching Psychologist and Associate Fellow of the British Psychological Society (BPS). She is Registrar for the BPS Qualification in Counselling Psychology, serves on the Training Committee for the Division of Counselling Psychology and has an independent practice. Victoria was formerly Programme Director for the PsychD professional training programme at the University of Wolverhampton and delivered the keynote public address at the Division's Annual Conference in Cardiff, 2013. She is committed to raising the profile of counselling psychology, hence she contributes to broadcast, written and social media. Victoria is an active researcher, with various current interests, including attitudes towards mental health and help-seeking; personal development and self-care; coastal and physical activities for mental health; and coastal ecotherapy.

ABOUT THE CONTRIBUTORS

Yesim Arikut-Treece is a Chartered Counselling Psychologist and an HCPC-Registered Counselling Psychologist. Her main role is as a Principal Psychologist at Wolverhampton Healthy Minds and Wellbeing, in the West Midlands. An experienced CBT and EMDR supervisor, she has specialised in helping clients with complex trauma, and leads a team providing Dialectical Behaviour Therapy. Prior to an NHS career, she worked in a residential service for people with severe personality disorders. She uses a range of therapeutic approaches, working towards developing an understanding of how client problems relate to early experiences and are altered by current context.

Sarah Bartlett reached psychology via a tortuous route after careers in teaching and with the British Council. Following qualification via the Independent Route, she worked for fifteen years in the Primary Care service for complex cases of Manchester Mental Health Trust. She was able to develop her interest in Psychodynamic Interpersonal Therapy, going on to teach and supervise trainees specialising in that model on the Manchester Doctorates in Counselling and Clinical Psychology. Since moving to Bristol she resumed her interest in working with adults with a learning disability. She continues to work at the Bridge Foundation for Psychotherapy and maintains a small independent practice supervising trainees. She is enjoying exploring new terrain, in Exmoor and the South-West coast, and the planting of apple trees.

Anja Bjorøy works as a family therapist, couples therapist and mediator. She holds a Master's degree in Health Science from the University of Oslo, and a Master's degree in Family Therapy and Systemic Practice from the University of Diakonhjemmet, where she also functions as a student-supervisor.

Lewis J. Blair is a Registered Counselling Psychologist (HCPC) and Chartered Counselling Psychologist (BPS). He trained at Glasgow Caledonian and Strathclyde Universities and currently works in Adult Psychology in NHS Forth Valley. Lewis contributes to the Doctorate in Counselling Psychology at Glasgow Caledonian University and the NHS South of Scotland CBT Course. He has published a number of articles and his interests include mentoring, masculinity, spirituality and ecopsychology. He is active in the Division of Counselling Psychology (Scotland) and contributes to a peer-mentoring network for counselling psychologists in Scotland.

Dr Michael Carroll is a Chartered Counselling Psychologist with the British Psychological Society. He is an accredited Executive Coach and an accredited Supervisor of Executive Coaches with APECS (Association for Professional Executive Coaches and Supervisors). Michael is Visiting Industrial Professor in the Graduate School of Education, University of Bristol, and the winner of the British Psychological Society Award for Distinguished Contributions to Professional Psychology. He is also a Fellow of the British Association for Counselling and Psychotherapy and APECS. Michael works with individuals, teams and organisations specialising in the theme of learning. He supervises, coaches and trains nationally and internationally and works within the private and public spheres. He has written a number of books, of which the latest are: *Effective Supervision for the Helping Professions* (Sage, 2013) and (with Elisabeth Shaw) *Ethical Maturity in the Helping Professions* (PsychOz, Australia, 2012; Jessica Kingsley, UK, 2013).

Mick Cooper is a Professor of Counselling Psychology at the University of Roehampton and a Chartered Counselling Psychologist. He is author and editor of a range of texts on person-centred, existential and relational approaches to therapy, including *Existential Therapies* (Sage, 2003), (with Dave Mearns) *Working at Relational Depth in Counselling and Psychotherapy* (Sage, 2005) and (with John McLeod) *Pluralistic Counselling and Psychotherapy* (Sage, 2011). Mick has also led a range of research studies exploring the process and outcomes of humanistic counselling with young people. His latest book is *Existential Psychotherapy and Counselling: Contributions to a Pluralistic Practice* (Sage, 2015). Mick lives in Brighton with his partner and four children.

Dee Danchev has worked as a university counsellor for over twenty years, first at Keele University, then as Head of Counselling, Health Advice and Disability at the University of the Arts, London, and finally as Pastoral Advisor at Nuffield College, Oxford University. She has also had a parallel career in counsellor and counselling psychologist training at Keele University, City University and Oxford University. She is currently Chair of the Counselling Psychology Qualifications Board and a member of the Qualifications Standards Committee. She is co-author with Alistair Ross of *Research Ethics for Counsellors, Nurses and Social Workers* (Sage, 2013).

Rachel Davies is a Chartered Counselling Psychologist. She works in private practice offering therapy, supervision and training, and undertakes research. She has held a number of academic positions, is a published researcher and currently teaches on counselling, psychology and psychotherapy programmes. For several years she has practised and supervised in the cancer and palliative care field, including managing an innovative partnership between Macmillan and Relate offering therapy to families. She has particular expertise in working with families and couples where the family system is affected by physical illness. With colleagues in the BPS's Division of Counselling Psychology, she set up a Special Interest Group for Cancer and Palliative Care to build a community of practice for counselling psychologists.

Dr Mark Donati is an HCPC-Registered Counselling Psychologist, a BPS-Registered Applied Psychology Practice Supervisor and a BPC-Accredited Dynamic Interpersonal Therapy practitioner. He has been involved in the training of counselling psychologists for over ten years, and has a particular interest in curriculum design, the development of reflective practice and the therapist's use of self. He is currently Principal Lecturer and Programme Convener for the PsychD in Counselling Psychology at the University of Roehampton. He has also held a number of positions within the NHS, including as Lead Counsellor for the Brent IAPT Counselling Service and Team Leader for the North Lambeth Talking Therapies Service.

Dr Hamilton Fairfax is a Chartered and Registered Counselling Psychologist and Professional Lead for Psychology and Psychological Therapies, Torbay, in the Devon Partnership NHS Trust. He is also the Research Lead for the Counselling Psychology's Divisional Committee. His interests include personality disorder, OCD, mindfulness, neuropsychology and therapeutic process. With a colleague, he developed an integrative approach to complex presentations (Adaptation-based Process Therapy) and has published in these areas. Hamilton was awarded the British Psychological Society Professional Practice Board's Award for Practitioner of the Year in 2014.

Nicola Gale is an HCPC-Registered Psychologist and BPS Chartered Psychologist (Associate Fellow). She is Clinical Lead for the Staff Psychological & Welfare Service at University College London Hospitals NHS Foundation Trust, and Senior Lecturer on the professional Doctorate in Counselling Psychology at City University London. As a member of the British Psychological Society, Nicola has held leadership roles in the Society, including Chair of the Representative Council and Chair of the Division of Counselling Psychology. Nicola has worked in organisational development and training, as a management consultant, and as an accountant. She has experience in fields including strategy, organisational development and change; people selection, development, training and coaching; performance improvement; operational, people and financial management. She has worked in different industries and on international projects.

Dr Stelios Gkouskos is a Chartered Psychologist, a Registered Counselling Psychologist, a Registered Integrative Psychotherapist and a member of the BPS's Register of Psychologists Specialising in Psychotherapy with senior practitioner status. He has been involved in training counselling psychologists and psychotherapists since 2006. For the past three years, he held the position of Senior Lecturer and Course Leader for the Doctorate in Counselling Psychology at Regent's University and this October he took the post of Research Coordinator for the PsychD at the University of Surrey. He has worked in a variety of NHS and private mental health settings and currently he runs a private practice in London. His specialist interests include the integration of psychotherapeutic approaches at the levels of epistemology, theory and clinical practice, developments in contemporary psychodynamic psychotherapy and developments in the training and supervision of counselling psychologists and psychotherapists.

Dr Diane Hammersley is a Chartered Counselling Psychologist practising independently as a psychotherapist, supervisor, trainer and expert witness. Having worked in a clinical and research team concerned with dependence on prescribed medication, she ran workshops on drug withdrawal around the UK. Later her doctoral research explored therapists' experience of clients who had been taking medication, how that impacted on the therapeutic process and how medication might be viewed more realistically and metaphorically. Since then she has given talks and run workshops for counsellors and psychotherapists on understanding and managing psychopharmacology and psychotherapy. She has served on a number of BPS Boards and Committees and is a former Chair of the Division of Counselling Psychology.

Terry Hanley is the Programme Director for the Doctorate in Counselling Psychology at the University of Manchester. He is a Fellow of the Higher Education Academy, an Associate Fellow of the British Psychological Society and was Editor of *Counselling Psychology Review* between the years 2009 and 2015. He has a keen interest in training therapists in research skills and is a co-author of *Introducing Counselling and Psychotherapy Research* (Sage, 2013). His own therapeutic practice and research has primarily focused on work with young people, and he is the lead editor of *Adolescent Counselling Psychology* (Routledge, 2013).

Dr Isabel Henton is a Chartered Counselling Psychologist (BPS) and a Registered Counselling Psychologist (HCPC). She lectures and supervises research within the counselling psychology doctoral programme at London Metropolitan University, and is developing a private clinical practice in London. Isabel studied classics and philosophy at Oxford University, subsequently working in management consultancy for six years. Having re-trained in psychology and counselling psychology, she completed her doctorate at London Metropolitan University in May 2015. Isabel is interested in the philosophy of counselling psychology, and in relational and phenomenological approaches to therapeutic work. Her research interests include counselling psychology research training and identity, the possible relationships between psychotherapy research and practice, and qualitative and practice-based psychotherapy research methodologies.

Andrew Hill has previously worked as a Senior Lecturer in Counselling at the University of Salford. He is currently Head of Research at the British Association for Counselling and Psychotherapy. He has published several systematic reviews and is co-author of a recent text on counselling for depression. He is interested in evidence-based practice and how practitioners can be encouraged to engage in research activity.

Paul Hitchings is a Registered Counselling Psychologist (HCPC), a Chartered Counselling Psychologist (BPS) and Integrative Psychotherapist (UKCP). He has been a staff member at Metanoia Institute for over 25 years where he currently teaches and supervises on the 'Doctorate in Counselling Psychology and Psychotherapy' and on the programme for the 'Certificate in Integrative Supervision'. He is a former Chair of the Division of Counselling Psychology and until recently was the Chief Assessor for the British Psychological Society's Qualification in Counselling Psychology. He practises in both Dublin and London.

Professor Pamela James is a Chartered and HCPC-Registered Counselling Psychologist and a Registered Psychologist Specialising in Psychotherapy (Senior Practitioner). She has been Chair of the BPS Qualification in Counselling Psychology and twice Chair of the BPS Division of Counselling Psychology. She held lecturing and management posts at Liverpool John Moores University for 25 years, where she was awarded Professor of Counselling Psychology in 2000; she also worked in NHS Adult Mental Health for ten years. Currently, she has a private practice in Southport. Her doctoral thesis was in learning and she remains interested in the learning process per se, including the process of change while in the therapeutic relationship. She has recently co-authored *Common Presenting Issues in Psychotherapeutic Practice* (Sage, 2014).

Garrett Kennedy is a Chartered and HCPC-Registered Counselling Psychologist. He currently works as the Programme Director for the Doctorate in Counselling Psychology at the

Institute of Psychology, University of Wolverhampton. He works with regional NHS services in the West Midlands to support Counselling Psychologists in clinical practice. He also works in private practice in Birmingham with clients suffering trauma and the effects of past abuse. Prior experience includes working in psychotherapy settings with clients suffering severe and enduring mental health issues, and in primary care IAPT settings. He has also worked as part of a pilot-team developing new primary care mental health services in the West Midlands. Research interests include LGBT issues, religion and spirituality, critical psychopathology and the social constructs of psychotherapy.

Professor David A. Lane has been providing services within counselling since the early 1970s with children, adults and organisations. He was part of the group that created Counselling Psychology within the British Psychological Society and served on the governing committee of the Association for Behavioural Approaches with Children. He has been a member of BABCP for more than 30 years. He was Chair of the British Psychological Society Register of Psychologists Specialising in Psychotherapy, and has served on committees of the British Psychological Society, the Chartered Institute of Personnel and Development and the European Mentoring and Coaching Council. He convened the Psychotherapy Group of the European Federation of Psychologists Associations. His contributions to counselling psychology led to the senior award of the BPS for 'Outstanding Scientific Contribution'. In 2009 he was honoured by the British Psychological Society for Distinguished Contribution to Professional Psychology.

Jane Lawrence is a Chartered Counselling Psychologist, registered with the HCPC and on the register of applied psychology practice supervisors (RAPPS), and is currently Deputy Programme Leader and placement coordinator for the Professional Doctorate in Counselling Psychology at the University of East London (UEL), where she facilitates reflective case groups and contributes to teaching in supervision and professional practice. She completed her counselling psychology training at UEL after teaching in middle schools, practising as a Relate counsellor, trainer and supervisor, and working as an Open University associate lecturer. Since then she has completed a PhD at UEL, researching the implications for practice of therapists' understandings of intimate partner violence. During the past twelve years Jane has practised in both the NHS and in private practice, and recently completed a Dynamic Interpersonal Therapy training.

Dr Stephen Madigan MSW, MSc, is the Director of the Vancouver School for Narrative Therapy, in Vancouver, Canada. He is the author of the best-selling book *Narrative Therapy: Theory and Practice* (American Psychological Association, 2011). For articles and training information, visit his website at www.therapeuticconversations.com

Professor Martin Milton CPsychol, CSci, AFBPsS, UKCP Reg, is Professor of Counselling Psychology at the School of Psychotherapy and Psychology at Regent's University London. He also runs an independent practice in psychotherapy and supervision. Martin was awarded the BPS award for the promoting of equality of opportunity in 2012.

Paul Moloney is based in an NHS Adult Learning Disabilities Team in Shropshire, UK. Formerly a lecturer for the Open University and a mental health and community social worker, Paul has a longstanding interest in community psychology. He is a founder member of the Midlands Psychology Group – a collection of psychologists dedicated to challenging the assumptions of mainstream psychology. His most recent publications include *The Therapy Industry: The Irresistible Rise of the Talking Cure, and Why it Doesn't Work* (Pluto, 2013).

Dr David Nylund, MSW, is a Professor of Social Work at California State University, Sacramento, and the Clinical Director of the Gender Health Center. He is on the faculty of the Vancouver School for Narrative Therapy. He is the author of three books and several articles on narrative therapy.

Dr Denis O'Hara is Associate Professor of Counselling and Psychotherapy and Deputy Head of School of Counselling at the Australian College of Applied Psychology, Brisbane. He is a Chartered Psychologist and Associate Fellow of the British Psychological Society, and a register member of the Psychotherapist and Counsellors Federation of Australia. He has taught counselling and psychology in Australia, Hong Kong, Malaysia and in the United Kingdom. He is a keen researcher and author in counselling and psychotherapy and has authored and edited several books on hope and psychotherapy. His most recent book is *Hope in Counselling and Psychotherapy* (Sage, 2013). Some of his research interests include hope, spirituality and psychology/psychotherapy, self-differentiation, and chronic problems of the self. He enjoys providing professional development and supervision.

Simon Parritt, BA, BSc(Hon), MSc, CPsychol, AFBPsS, is a Chartered Psychologist, Counselling Psychologist, Psychosexual Therapist and supervisor in independent practice. In addition to his general work as a counselling psychologist, he specialises in psychosexual and relationship therapy, disability and chronic illness. A former Director of the Association to Aid the Sexual and Personal Relationships of People with a Disability (SPOD), he has worked in geriatric medicine, primary care and the voluntary sector. Currently, he is visiting lecturer at the Surrey University doctoral programme in counselling psychology and the Tavistock Centre for Couple Relationships. He is a member of the British Psychological Society and the College of Sexual and Relationship Therapists. He has been a disabled person himself since the age of five.

Dr David Pilgrim is Professor of Health and Social Policy at the University of Liverpool. He trained and worked in the NHS as a clinical psychologist before completing a PhD in psychology and then a Master's in sociology. With this mixed background, his career was split between clinical and academic work as a health policy researcher. His publications include *A Sociology of Mental Health and Illness* (Open University Press, 2005 – winner of the 2006 BMA Medical Book of the Year Award), *Mental Health Policy in Britain* (Palgrave, 2002) and *Mental Health and Inequality* (Palgrave, 2003) (all with Anne Rogers). All of this work is approached from the position of critical realism and so the philosophy of science and social science is an overarching framework in relation to those topics.

Loan Receipt
Liverpool John Moores University
Library Services

Borrower Name: Karen O'Brien
Borrower ID: ********

The handbook of counselling psychology /

31111014848152
Due Date: 02/03/2018 23:59:00 GMT

Total Items: 1
28/02/2018 11:17

Diana Sanders is a Counselling Psychologist and Cognitive Psychotherapist, and Associate Teacher at the Oxford Mindfulness Centre. After many years working in mental health settings in Oxford, she now works independently, teaching mindfulness classes and workshops and supervising staff in end-of-life care settings. She has written a number of books and articles on cognitive therapy and mindfulness-based approaches in health care.

Elisabeth Shaw is a clinical and counselling psychologist, couple and family therapist in private practice in Sydney, Australia. She teaches clinical skills and professional ethics at a postgraduate level, and supervises many health services and practitioners in diverse areas of clinical practice, management, ethics and supervision of supervision. She is past chair of the Psychotherapy and Counselling Federation of Australia ethics committee, and current chair of the Australian Psychological Society ethics committee, and an associate of the St James Ethics Centre. Co-author with Michael Carroll of *Ethical Maturity in the Helping Professions: Making Difficult Life and Work Decisions* (Psychoz, Australia, 2012; Jessica Kingsley, UK, 2013), she has more recently been exploring the application of moral theory to clinical practice and her publications on relational ethics and moral blindness have appeared in the *Australian and New Zealand Journal of Family Therapy*.

Clive Sims is a Chartered Psychologist with a wide range of experience, being professionally registered in five areas of psychology: forensic, counselling, clinical, health and neuropsychology. He also holds professional qualifications in business administration and in IT. Now retired as a Lead Consultant Forensic Psychologist in the NHS, Clive continues his professional involvement through membership of British Psychological Society committees, such as the Training Committee for Counselling Psychology and the Committee on Test Standards, and various professional working parties. He is actively involved in the postgraduate training of counselling and forensic psychologists. Clive's interests range from the neuropsychology of violence through to the psychological impact of the Criminal Justice System. He is Fellow of the Royal Society of Medicine and a Member of the Society of Expert Witnesses.

Gail Sinitsky is a counselling psychologist. Gail is dedicated to highlighting the contribution that the profession makes to work with children, young people and their families. In her own clinical work providing assessment and therapy, Gail has an interest in applying creative modalities in therapy, including play, sand tray and arts. She has also been delivering specialist therapeutic groups to children in primary schools for the last six years. In addition to her clinical work, Gail delivers a range of training workshops to professionals working with children and families, as well as to counselling psychology trainees. She has a particular passion for writing and was delighted to be invited to contribute to this new edition of the *Handbook*.

Edith Steffen is a lecturer in counselling psychology at the University of Roehampton, having previously taught at the University of East London and at the Open University. She is a Chartered and HCPC-Registered Counselling Psychologist and worked in secondary and tertiary care in the NHS until taking up a full-time lectureship in 2015. Her main research interests are in continuing bonds and meaning making in bereavement, anomalous experience and post-traumatic growth, and practice-relevant issues concerning diversity, spirituality and religion and social justice. She is particularly interested in qualitative research and recently completed a funded qualitative research project investigating the peer bereavement support provision of a national charity. Her doctoral research at the University of Surrey, from which she graduated in 2011, focused on the experience of sensing the presence of the deceased in bereavement and incorporated interpretative pluralism as part of its methodological approach. She has co-authored a number of papers with Adrian Coyle and published in journals such as *Death Studies*, *Mental Health, Religion & Cult*ure and *Omega: Journal of Death and Dying*. She has also contributed to a number of book chapters in the fields of counselling psychology, anomalous experience research and (critical) positive psychology. As Associate Editor of *Counselling Psychology Review* from 2012 to 2015, she was responsible for coordinating peer reviews and took editorial leadership on a number of special issues, namely on 'Power and Equality' (2013), 'Existential Approaches' (2014) and 'Positive Psychology' (2015).

Dr Léonie Sugarman is a Chartered Psychologist (BPS) and Emeritus Reader of the University of Cumbria. Her PhD from Birkbeck, University of London, concerned women in early adulthood, with specific reference to their decision of whether and when to have children. She has researched, written and taught in the fields of professional development, transition and change over the life course. She has contributed chapters on aspects of life-span development to the previous three editions of the *Handbook of Counselling Psychology*, and published books in the field for psychologists, counsellors and occupational therapists. She has had a long involvement with the *British Journal of Guidance and Counselling* and is an Honorary Life Fellow and previous Vice President of the British Association of Counselling and Psychotherapy.

Caroline Vermes trained in counselling psychology at Rutgers University in the early 1990s, and has been a full-time practitioner since then. She has also worked in psychological service leadership and development since 2006. Her interests include fostering social entrepreneurship and social action for counselling psychologists, particularly via third-sector clinical programme initiation, management and research.

FOREWORD: THE JOURNEY TO PRACTICE
DAVID A. LANE

It is a pleasure to write a foreword to the fourth edition of what has become firmly established as the key text for the field. Being a key text carries responsibilities both to represent the field and provide guidance to those entering or working in our profession. These responsibilities are grasped and explored in the new edition.

The development of counselling psychology as a distinct area has been mapped through the opening chapters, which situate our practice and address the fundamental themes that inform our work. These are followed by accounts to inform the journey of the practitioner.

What do these explorations tell us about our field? When the field was fledging it was required to demonstrate both its foundations within psychology and its distinctiveness from our sister fields. To some extent that remains – we still find it necessary to say why we are different, yet the differences are not as they were. Our sister fields have adopted ideas that always informed our work. The concept of reflective practice, which was always present in our work from our birth (long before its definition in the literature), has been accepted across professional practice in psychology. The role of supervision throughout a career span, which was highly contested when the Special Group in Counselling Psychology proposed it as part of creating a Division, is now embedded in all practice. So we can be proud of our role as prime movers across several fields of practice within psychology. Many other examples exist where what made us distinctive has disappeared with changes in other fields and our increasing absorption into medicalised work contexts.

So where are we now at this point in our history, marked by the fourth edition of this text?

It is clear from this text that we are looking well beyond ourselves and to the value counselling psychology brings to practitioners in a range of disciplines – we are no longer looking inward to justify our place in psychology's domain. The book presents a discipline that is confident in its beliefs and approaches and which offers leadership to the profession in key areas. We are comfortable engaging with debates about the role of science in our practice but are questioning assumptions about what this means in ways that are consistent with our psychology. We have taken forward debates around the nature of reflective practice to enhance specific approaches to learning that it generates. Thus our science, our craft and our values are debated, contested and strengthened. As a result, we are mapping our world and offer it to clients.

The journey of our discipline is clearly articulated in the opening chapters. So how within that journey do we grow as practitioners? We are presented with a map of our own journey as well as to the fundamentals of becoming a counselling psychologist. This is essential to the nature of counselling psychology; we map the personal, the subjective and a value base that focuses on our humanity and places it within the broader context of our contribution to society. Yet this is placed with the debate about the nature of science as we perceive it and practise our craft.

This provides a grounding for the journey to becoming a counselling psychologist and the way we can best engage with the encounters through mapping our selves, reflective practice, academia, supervision, clinical placement and research. The contributors provide the necessary guidance to this journey but always reflect a sense of why counselling psychology is a journey of personal and well as professional discovery.

In finding our way through the core tasks that underpin our work, the reader is guided to reflect upon understanding the client and the interface with the world they and we inhabit. Getting to grips with formulation is always something that takes time to acquire as a skill and is one that is continually being refined. There is a narrative to that process which incorporates key areas from the contributors. How we form relationships based within an ethically mature understanding, living with and embracing diversity, the boundary with other fields such as pharmacology and our place as researchers are all explored. Undertaking this in a way that cares for others is placed in the context of our own self-care. This issue becomes more important as the contexts in which we work become more demanding and diverse. It is important that it features in the process of finding our way through practice. These themes take us to but also enable our encounters with the differing landscapes of our practice. Emerging developments are introduced and these certainly illustrate the richness of the field and the willingness of counselling psychologists to engage with new and challenging ideas.

This willingness is fully expanded into the territories in which we operate. Counselling psychologists are located within the psychotherapeutic field but in many others besides. The importance of looking beyond medicalised models and contexts of practice is clearly demonstrated. The challenge and potential that this presents is beautifully illustrated in the text. Readers are urged to engage with fields outside their own practice and consider how that might inform their own work. We can learn much from practice outside our own zone of comfort.

So while this volume talks to those beginning the journey to becoming a counselling psychologist, it also provides guidance to those fully embedded in practice to inform, challenge, update and intrigue them. It then talks to our lifetime careers and our work guiding others into the profession. It concludes with an editorial, which embraces the richness of our profession and the themes that have guided us well as we seek to serve our clients and society.

I thoroughly recommend this new edition to colleagues in counselling psychology and beyond. It fully meets its obligation to both represent the field and to be a guide to those who practise within it.

INTRODUCTION: NAVIGATING THIS TEXT

This is the fourth edition of *The Handbook of Counselling Psychology*, the first edition having been published in 1996 in the context of the emergence of a specialism in counselling psychology in the UK. Much has changed since then in the world of psychology generally and in the world of counselling psychology more particularly. Successive editions of the *Handbook* have mirrored these changes. The first edition reflected early debates about the identity of counselling psychology in the UK and was perhaps inevitably somewhat inward-looking. By the time of the second edition a more confident discipline was emerging alongside a number of accredited courses enabling the book to look outwards and to examine traditional therapeutic modalities in more detail. In the third edition there was more of a focus on newer developments and on contemporary issues such as the requirement for evidence-based practice.

Alongside the changing content, the editors have over time sought a broader perspective, looking beyond the UK, and to work towards making the book more relevant to the requirements of teachers and learners. This is at the heart of our thinking about the new edition. In planning the content, we decided that our objectives could best be met through adopting a developmental focus, which involved moving through the stages of training from beginning a course, developing skills, an appropriate ethical demeanour and a sense of a professional identity, through qualifying and entering the world of work to becoming an experienced practitioner contributing to the development of the discipline through research and the training and supervision of colleagues. This is well expressed by Skovholt and Rønnestad (1992). In taking this approach to the process of becoming and developing as a counselling psychologist, we have found the idea of a journey involving a series of transitional stages to be useful and the book is divided into sections that reflect this process.

The 'journey' as a guiding metaphor for this edition of the *Handbook* is richly suggestive. Therapeutic processes are often described as journeys and we can imagine each of us embarking on personal journeys, through our lives and careers. Our individual journeys will interweave with those of others and we can see our discipline as itself on a journey of discovery. The metaphor can conjure ideas of excursions into unmapped territories as well as ambles along well-trodden paths. Journeys can be exciting, challenging and sometimes frightening; they can be enjoyable at times and tedious at others. They involve departures and arrivals but, most importantly, they suggest a process of travelling and exploration. As Cavafy (1911) reminds us, a long road can be full of adventure and discovery and it is what we gain on the way that is worthwhile. Watts (1990: 216), too, contends that a world that only values getting somewhere as fast as possible becomes a world without substance. So it is worth remembering, in the current outcome-focused climate, that exploration, process, discovery and change are key associations central to thinking about counselling psychology.

Prior to a departure it is useful to plan and to consider resources. The personal resources necessary to sustain any significant journey are likely to be similar and include a desire to explore, fuelled by curiosity. However, initial enthusiasm can be dulled as we plod through what seems like familiar territory or as we tire in the face of difficulties. So we need to develop resilience and build relationships with trusted guides and companions who can support, challenge and inspire as well as help to keep us alert to possible dangers. Other key resources are maps and the tools and techniques to negotiate the differing kinds of terrain and the obstacles we are likely to encounter.

Venturing into any new territory can be confusing and somewhat daunting so at the outset it is useful to gain a broad sense of the landscape. With this in mind the first two chapters offer an overview of the field and some of the challenges it presents. Some of the material covered here will undoubtedly make more sense as familiarity grows with experience. Many of the early chapters focus on the knowledge and skills needed to read existing maps and to develop the competence to use available resources and equipment. Later chapters assume growing experience and offer guidance in venturing into less well-known or unexplored territory where we can contribute to map-making and the development of new tools and techniques.

Some chapters foreground the importance of companions on our journeys, as we are supported and in turn support others through training, supervision and management. Indeed, the production of this *Handbook* would not have been possible without the collaboration and support of colleagues with a wide range of knowledge and experience. The passage of time on the journey through four editions has involved changes not only in content but also in personnel. Individuals who were among the early cohorts of trainees are now assuming positions of leadership within the discipline and this is reflected in their inclusion among the chapter authors and in the editorial group. One contribution of our two additional editors has been to take a leading role in developing the new companion website, which aptly symbolises the ability of the discipline and the *Handbook* to be dynamic and move forward.

REFERENCES

Cavafy, C. P. (1911) 'Ithaka', in C. P. Cavafy (1984) *Collected Poems*. London: Hogarth Press.
Skovholt, T. and Rønnestad, M. H. (1992) *The Evolving Professional Self*. Chichester: Wiley.
Watts, A. W. (1990) *The Way of Zen*. London: Arkana.

SECTION I

SITUATING COUNSELLING PSYCHOLOGY

CONTENTS

Have you ever looked for a map online only to discover that what comes up is a detailed localised map of the area highlighting the feature you are after (e.g. a hotel)? I did this recently, looking for a country house hotel, and discovered that while I found the hotel I still had little idea where it was. There were few broader clues to help me locate the hotel in its wider context. Just as we need these clues for geographical understanding, so we also need them to locate ourselves, both personally and professionally, in context. We, and our clients, are all relational beings living in social, historical and cultural contexts which become integral to us, and with which we interact daily.

Our profession – counselling psychology – also exists in relation to, and situated within, the wider contexts with which it interacts. Through this interaction, both the profession and its wider contexts are influenced and changed. This first section of the *Handbook* looks at exactly this. Chapter 1, 'Mapping the world of helping', begins by situating counselling psychology in the world of helping, asking that most fundamental question which can sometimes be overlooked: What is helping? It then considers the nature(s) of professional helping and the languages of helping which act to determine, or influence, how we perceive the values, process and practice of helping. It reviews, for example, the notions of reflective practitioner and scientist practitioner and whether a medical model is an appropriate one in which counselling psychology should sit. It concludes by emphasising the dialectical nature of these processes and how their constantly changing interactions result in mutual influence on both counselling psychology and its related professions.

Chapter 2, 'Science, craft and professional values', follows with a detailed consideration of aspects of the scientific contexts in which counselling psychology is located. We may talk about the scientist practitioner, for example, but what science is, and is not, as well as its socio-historical development, are things that we may overlook, yet they underpin any critical examination of research. Similarly, we may overlook the socio-cultural evolution of a more specific psychological science, its theories and models, and how these have interacted (and continue to interact) with the profession of counselling psychology. The chapter demonstrates a tension between the natural and human sciences in which we sit and discusses how we recognise, give weight to and value knowledge that may be less amenable to some definitions of science; that is the tacit dimension of 'knowing how' rather than 'knowing that'.

The themes put forward in these important first two chapters provide much food for thought. In setting the scene for much of what is contained within the following sections and chapters, they set a course for an evolving internal map of the field of counselling psychology for the reader.

1
MAPPING THE WORLD OF HELPING: THE PLACE OF COUNSELLING PSYCHOLOGY

RAY WOOLFE

INTRODUCTION

The aim of this chapter is to locate counselling psychology within the world of helping. Using the metaphor of this world as a map, where is counselling psychology to be found? The task involves exploring what the world of helping consists of but also in unpicking what we mean when we refer to counselling psychology. Is it a body of knowledge or a discrete discipline or a philosophical approach or a form of practice or, in the final resort, no more than the title of a division within the British Psychological Society (BPS)? These are all variables that enter into the mapping process and the outcome unsurprisingly is not simple or two-dimensional.

What then does it mean to call oneself a counselling psychologist? Individuals enter programmes of training in the subject for a variety of reasons and with a variety of already established personal and professional identities. While it potentially represents a vocational qualification, there may be a greater or lesser commitment, at least initially, to its ethos and philosophy. Even people who complete training may have a less than clear understanding of what their qualification in counselling psychology means or stands for in terms of offering a professional identity or how it differs, if at all, from the identity offered by other programmes of training, such as clinical psychology on the one hand or counselling/psychotherapy on the other. If, in the end, people from a variety of different trainings find themselves working in the same NHS or IAPT settings, for example, and doing the same work, is it logical to assume that their different titles are different in name only?

Perhaps it was easier to differentiate counselling psychology from other therapeutic enterprises in the early days of the discipline. Before the division was established within BPS I described counselling psychology in Britain as 'an idea whose time has come' (Woolfe, 1990). The philosophy and approach to helping seemed to offer a scientific basis to counselling and at the same time a more intuitive, artistic and humanistic basis to psychology than provided by clinical psychology. The ethos and philosophy of humanistic psychology, of an empathic engagement with the client, the importance of the helping relationship and a concern with health rather than pathology seemed to set it apart. But a quarter of a century later, this outlook has collided with the *Zeitgeist* of a less idealistic world focused on performance and outputs. If one works in an organisation such as the NHS, or indeed any organisation, one cannot but be influenced by the culture of that organisation. Cultures are dynamic and subject to change, and a focus on evidence-based practice has become the central theme of helping, certainly within the NHS. I have argued (Woolfe, 2012) that central to the success of counselling psychology up to the present time has been the ability to identify a narrative around which all counselling psychologists, whatever their preferred orientations, could rally. This offered an identity and a statement of difference from other helping practices. It provided a scientific base but at the same time paid allegiance to the relationship between client and therapist. This narrative is of the reflective practitioner and there is a question of whether it can survive in a world of evidenced-based practice. At the same time counselling psychology did not invent this idea, has no copyright on it and it is well represented in other professions. I intend to examine the concept more closely but first I want to step back and think about what is involved in helping.

WHAT DO WE MEAN BY HELPING?

The world of therapy is a coat of many colours (Woolfe, 2011) and consists of a large number of occupational groups with a vast variety of titles. These include counsellors, psychotherapists, psychiatrists, drama therapists, group analysts, clinical psychologists, family therapists, hypnotherapists, occupational therapists, mental health social workers, community psychiatric nurses, and so on. One could go on and on; this list is by no means exhaustive. Were we to engage in an imaginary exercise of constructing the world of therapy from scratch it might look a lot simpler than the patchwork quilt that presently exists. As it is, the boundaries between different categories of therapy are frequently opaque. The few clear ones include psychiatry, for which one has to be a medical practitioner, and counselling psychology and clinical psychology, respectively, which necessitate a psychological qualification. As for counselling and psychotherapy, this is a minefield of complexity. The difference between these two activities, if it exists at all, is not clear. For many years the British Association for Counselling (BAC) resisted including psychotherapy in its title but eventually changed its mind and is now the British Association for Counselling and Psychotherapy (BACP). The reasons are complex but owe as much to politics as to rational debate. Dryden (1996), in discussing this difference, refers to it as 'a rose by any other name' (p. 26) and ends the article in light-hearted fashion by describing the difference between the two as 'about £8000 per annum' (p. 27). Readers interested in a less witty but more detailed exploration of differences between the two concepts will find this in Woolfe (2011, p. 20).

The word 'therapy' is often employed as a commonality binding all these categories together. But of course not all helpers could be accurately described as therapists. For example, someone who works in an advice bureau or human resources department or indeed in any caring capacity would seem to have just as much right to be described as a helper as someone who describes themselves as a therapist. Samaritans are clearly helpers but elect not to describe themselves as therapists. Many counselling psychologists work in sectors such as work or education and their role is not defined as a therapist and many would not think of themselves as therapists. Does this then set them outside the world of helping?

It is instructive to reflect on what is implied by the term 'helping'. If one helps a child to cross the road, one would appear to be performing the role of helper, if only very temporarily. However, this seems to set the definition of helping so wide as to make it almost meaningless. What of the paid carer who looks after a group of people with severe learning disabilities or older adults? Such a person might not be trained as a therapist but might well have training and expertise in key aspects of therapy, such as listening skills or non-verbal communication. Perhaps, then, when we talk about the world of helping we are referring to paid professional roles. But if we do this, we exclude the volunteer counsellor or advice worker. Therefore, a definition of helping and, by implication, the world of helping seems less clear than would at first appear to be the case. It includes professionals and volunteers with therapists as just a sub-set.

WHAT IS A PROFESSIONAL?

For the purposes of this book we need to focus on the professional helper, which raises its own set of questions, most notably what does it mean to be a professional? Does the meaning differ across occupations? At its most basic, professionals profess, but what is it that they profess to? The usual definition is that it is based upon the claim of technical expertise embedded in a body of knowledge. Thus priests are seen to have specialised access to knowledge about the soul, doctors to the body and psychologists to the mind. Professionals have traditionally grouped together in associations, in theory to develop their expertise, but in practice serving to establish firm boundaries to exclude others. Historically, the state has mandated their privileges by allowing them the right to define entry standards and to manage their own affairs. In recent times the state has sought to intervene more actively in the work of professional bodies and to give greater rights to consumers of services.

However, to emphasise technical expertise takes no account of the intersubjective frame in which this expertise is encapsulated. This consists most crucially of a relationship in which one person has a set of needs and the other professes to have the ability to respond to these needs. Thus there is a power imbalance. While some counselling psychology practitioners may emphasise the need for equality between client and practitioner, the reality of their respective positions is inescapable. The fact that one party is more powerful than the other leads to the potential for abuse, which in turn leads to a second characteristic of professional groups, which is a commitment to a set of principles and rules based upon altruism, caring and commitment. Arguably the most important chapter in this book is the one entitled 'Toward ethical maturity in counselling psychology' (Chapter 15). What we do in a relationship matters but this has to be embedded in a particular disposition which all helping professionals are expected to bring to that relationship. While the world of helping is characterised by many different professional groups, what they all have in common is a concern with the ethical basis of their practice.

CODES OF ETHICS

The ethical basis is expressed in codes of ethics and practice drawn up by the respective professional bodies. Different professions have their own subtly different codes of ethics and practice but it is informative to examine those that exist within the professions of psychology, counselling and psychotherapy as they provide us with information about how professionals are expected to approach and attend to their responsibilities and overall duty of care towards their clients. Until relatively recent times, both the British Psychological Society (BPS) (1993) and the British Association for Counselling (BAC) (1993) had ethical codes that could be described as fairly prescriptive, laying down explicit rules about what was regarded as minimum appropriate behaviour. However, more recently these codes have been revised (BPS, 2006) so that they are best described as aspirational rather than prescriptive and guidelines rather than rules. There is an emphasis on ethical awareness and reflection on practice and a focus on thinking about the values underlying practice. 'Thinking about ethics should pervade all professional activity' (BPS, 2006, p. 7). The Division of Counselling Psychology (BPS, 2005, p. 1) built upon the earlier document by seeking to identify what psychologists are expected to do in pursuit not of minimum but of best standards. The document states that 'mention or lack of mention in the guidelines of a particular act or omission shall not be taken as conclusive on any question of professional conduct'. In other words, each individual is expected to be responsible for and to monitor their own ethical practice on an ongoing basis.

This position is presented cogently by Carroll and Shaw (2012), who use the notion of 'ethical maturity' in the helping professions. They argue that too often people are guided by regulations or specified codes laid down by others and thus external to them. Their suggestion is that ethics should be practised internally. Thus the codes represent just the first step on the road to ethical practice. You can read more about this in their chapter in this book (Chapter 15). A similar development of approach can be found in British Association for Counselling and Psychotherapy (BACP) (2013). This document states that 'reliance on principles alone may detract from the importance of the practitioner's personal qualities and their ethical significance in the counselling or therapeutic relationship' (p. 1). It is a moot point as to the extent to which different professions adhere to a more prescriptive or more aspirational code. However, it appears clear that the more a profession commits to the latter and emphasises individual responsibility the more important is the relationship between psychologist and client. Counselling psychology, with its emphasis on the reflective practitioner, seems well positioned in response to the direction in which these developments are moving.

DISCOURSES ABOUT HELPING

The roots of therapeutic practice are complex and differ from profession to profession. Douglas (2010) suggests that there are a variety of discourses that frame attempts to understand therapeutic relationships with people with mental health problems and that these include religious, moral, medical and psychological discourses. Douglas and James (2013) suggest that psychotherapy contains a number of narrative accounts or ideologies of what the practice involves. They suggest that psychological services are largely framed within two competing world views. One they describe as 'psychopathological' while the other they see as emphasising the intersubjective world of client and therapist and the joint construction of meaning. In the latter, consciousness and agency are emphasised. The authors see these two world views as existing in a state of tension.

In practice, the discourse that has historically been of most influence is the former, which has been powerfully taken up by the medical profession. However, this view of the world goes back a long way and has its origins in an interest in and attempt to examine, explore, investigate and explain the natural and physical world. Aristotle argued that nature is understandable, explainable and predictable, while in the sixteenth century, Leonardo da Vinci was able to produce explicit anatomical diagrams of the human body and a century later Newton demonstrated the existence of cause–effect relationships. This process of scientific discovery accelerated during the so-called Enlightenment of the eighteenth century and its dominance developed in the nineteenth century as more recent intellectual giants, such as Darwin and Freud, began to identify and to answer questions about where we sprang from as a species and what psychological processes are at work within us. In the field of human behaviour, discourses about behaviour based upon morality (badness) were replaced by explanations based upon experimentally based scientific knowledge. In particular, the causes and treatment of a variety of diseases were uncovered and what has become known as a natural science model became elevated to its contemporary status. Its underlying philosophy lay in positivism; in the belief that the only valid data were those that could be observed and measured.

THE IMPORTANCE OF LANGUAGE IN DEFINING REALITY

Of course the language we use defines the agenda of any discussion. To talk about formulation, for example, sets up a different agenda from the language of diagnosis. In a challenging and provocative article, Rizq (2013) suggests that the language we use dictates how we work with clients. She points to the overwhelming influence of the philosophy of evidence-based practice. The language it fosters emphasises 'checking, auditing, regulating, measuring, assessing, evaluating and governance' (2013, p. 23). It is required for managers to get funding for services, for academics to get research grants and, above all, to label clients in terms of interventions and outcomes. She suggests that it 'polices the legitimacy of knowledge' (p. 22) and compares it to

Orwellian Newspeak. She suggests that 'it dispenses with the idea of relationship by converting suffering into a satisfying consumer activity' (p. 22). She reserves particular criticism for the English IAPT scheme (Increasing Access to Psychological Treatment).

This point of view is uncomfortable but important to consider. It reminds us that all theories about therapeutic practice situate clients and the conception of their problems in normative discourses. Douglas and James (2013) refer to this model as 'psychopathological'. However, while the word 'psychopathological' can sound rather pejorative in its tone, it encompasses a variety of relatively objectivist practices familiar to counselling psychologists, and to dismiss it out of hand as a kind of metaphorical supping with the devil seems unnecessarily undermining. All helping relationships involve interaction between human beings and to be effective have to create a working alliance. A relatively directive and structured therapeutic method such as found in behavioural protocols still requires that the therapist must get to understand the client sufficiently well to know what he or she will find reinforcing. This demands an ability to be empathic and to enter into the subjective world of the other. This seems a *sine qua non* of any helping relationship. Cognitive behavioural therapy has always emphasised collaborative empiricism but increasingly has taken on board insights from attachment theory and transference (see Parpottas, 2012). On the other side of the coin, professionals could not communicate without some common language and to do this without categories or labels is impossible. We cannot simply refuse to talk about borderline personality disorder, for example, because we disagree about the nature of this condition or, indeed, whether it exists. Language inevitably codifies and while Rizq rightly alerts us to the manner in which some forms of language are more privileged than others and, therefore, become more dominant, thus pushing us into a debate about this, the fact is that we cannot have the debate without first having an agreed language to debate with (see Woolfe, 2013).

THE MEDICAL MODEL IN PRACTICE

In recent times, the concept of a medical model has become the standard terminology for describing this approach to addressing issues about mental and emotional well-being. The model provides the theoretical underpinning for the idea of the scientist practitioner. A central plank is the idea of disease, which of course implies that there exists some sort of norm with disease as a deviation from this. Recognition of the deviation arises through the presence of symptoms and treatment is directed at the reduction and ultimate removal of symptoms thus restoring the organism to its original homeostasis. The presence of symptoms is identified through a process of diagnosis. This model places a heavy emphasis on the expertise of the professional while the role of the patient (as he or she is traditionally described) tends to be passive. It ignores, or at the very least downplays, the responsibility of the client for his or her own well-being. It fails to acknowledge the client's internal subjective experiences and the importance of the relationship between helper and client in responding to the latter's areas of concern.

Applied to mental health, the application of the medical model can be seen to have serious weaknesses. Categories such as depression or anxiety or attention deficit disorder or schizophrenia are not discrete, well-bounded categories in the same way as a broken bone or measles might be identified and treated. Whether a person is labelled as schizophrenic or having a traumatic psychosis disorder, or whether a person is labelled as having a borderline personality disorder or complex PTSD, may depend as much on the helper's professional identity and preferred theoretical orientation or research interests as on anything else. They are not truths but the product of a form of contested discourse which privileges certain accounts of reality at the expense of others. But one way or another, this is what Sanders (2006) refers to as 'the medicalization of distress'. This thesis has been well documented by contemporary British writers (see Johnstone, 2000; Parker, 1999; Pilgrim, 1997; Smail, 1978). However, I wanted to refer here particularly to the seminal work of Thomas Szasz, who writes in his book *The Myth of Mental Illness* (1961, p. 14), 'the question What is mental illness? Is shown to be inextricably tied to the question, What do psychiatrists do?') Szasz is frequently dismissed as a product of the anti-psychiatry movement of the 1960s, but this would be to ignore his insights. More recently he wrote in a manner that would be easily recognised by counselling psychologists that 'only after we abandon the pretence that mind is brain and that mental disease is brain disease can we begin the honest study of human behaviour and the means people use to help themselves and others to cope with the demands of living' (Szasz, 2007, p. 149). It is true that present developments in neuro-psychology are providing us with an outpouring of new knowledge on the relationship between brain function and emotional states but this does not undermine Szasz's basic thesis that we must differentiate between mind and brain.

If one responds to the question 'what do psychiatrists do?' by answering that they largely dispense medication, one immediately begins to point to the vested interest of the drug companies to defining the existence of emotional distress as an illness and as a consequence encouraging the identification of more and more new categories of illness (see Healy, 2004; Johnstone, 2000). The *Diagnostic and Statistical Manual of Mental Disorders – V* (American Psychiatric Association, 2013) has recently replaced DSM-IV as the standard psychiatric diagnostic tool but its creation has generated an enormous amount of impassioned debate. Particular concern lies in its tendency to medicalise normal developmental events such as bereavement. By the definition of DSM-V, normal grieving is assumed to last for two weeks, after which the assumption is that the continued presence of sadness in the individual is indicative of depression and should be treated as such. More generally, psychiatry has been attacked on the basis that its diagnostic categories are based on symptom clusters, not on underlying biological causes. This discussion is taken up in the next chapter of this book. We might also note the lack of emphasis which psychiatry places upon cultural factors (see, for example, Suman, 2010).

The question of where counselling psychology stands in relation to diagnostic categories is taken up by Larsson et al. (2012). They reviewed the counselling psychology literature pertaining to diagnostic categories. They found that a majority of the sources examined 'positioned counselling psychology between two conflicting epistemological positions' (p. 55). One view consistent with the psychopathological model adopted an empirical stance that counselling psychology should engage with the medical model while retaining its critical perspective. The other emphasised the 'phenomenological experience of the client' not making normative assumptions as characterised by the use of diagnoses. They conclude by asking whether counselling psychologists can retain the philosophical value of non-pathologising in an environment dominated by the medical model. This question is a very pertinent one. Counselling psychology exists, as do all other helping occupations, in a real, not a theoretical, world and is intimately entwined in a symbiotic relationship with this world. People's livelihoods are at stake. Does a clinician, for example, refuse to take on medico-legal work (which is reasonably well-remunerated) because this frequently demands making a psychiatric diagnosis for the benefit of the court? Counselling psychologists are not immunised against such dilemmas?

The British Psychological Society has been active in addressing these issues and concerns. A document (2011) looks at formulation-based alternatives to psychiatric diagnosis. The latter, it points out, is deeply embedded in NHS practice:

> Trusts are required to return mental health Minimum Data Sets based on psychiatric diagnoses. The IAPT initiative is based upon diagnostic criteria for depression and anxiety disorders. NICE recommendations and most outcome measures are diagnostically-based, and a diagnosable mental illness is a pre-requisite for access to mental health services. (Division of Clinical Psychology, 2011, p. 24)

The document points out that 'most evidence-based practice is based upon classification by psychiatric diagnosis despite the fact that these terms are not evidence-based themselves; that is they have poor reliability and validity'. More recently, the British Psychological Society has issued a 'Position Statement on Classification' (Division of Clinical Psychology, 2013) which advocates a radical paradigm shift on how we understand mental distress, moving away from a model based on the diagnosis of a disease.

While it is tempting to perceive diagnosis as bad in the sense that it stigmatises individuals, we should not ignore the benefits that it potentially confers, not least the relief felt by some individuals when they are able to put a name onto distressing felt experiences. As emphasised throughout this chapter, it is naïve to talk about counselling psychology and its relationship to diagnostic categories without taking account of the occupational context and the wider world of helping in which counselling psychologists work. The reality is that the NHS and other statutory agencies increasingly represent the main forms of employment for counselling psychologists. Working in this environment, ideological purity is a luxury that may not be affordable.

THE REFLECTIVE PRACTITIONER

The main weapon in the armoury of counselling psychology in responding to this dilemma is through a commitment and adherence to the narrative of the reflective practitioner. This emphasises the role of the counselling psychologist as a self-reflective practitioner with a commitment to personal development work. Such awareness extends not only to technical expertise but also to the ethical, social, political and cultural context of their work. This has helped to give it a discrete and separate identity from clinical psychology. However, it is important in a different way. The basic problem in finding an identity for counselling psychology lies in the multiple forms of therapy practised by counselling psychologists. This is built into the regulations for training in which practitioners are required to be proficient in more than one orientation, frequently encapsulating radically different philosophies. This differs from training requirements in counselling and psychotherapy where a single-model approach is more often than not standard practice. Given this requirement, how can this produce any form of unity or sense of a unified discipline? Put in another way, how can these diverse sources be integrated?

The diversity of practice can be demonstrated in an imaginative fashion through exploring ideas derived from literary criticism (see Frye, 1965), particularly in relation to the work of Shakespeare. Fear and Woolfe (1996, 1999) identify four visions of reality or outlook on the world, namely romantic, tragic, comic and ironic. These can be linked to different therapeutic methods. The romantic vision is that of the humanistic practitioner. Human beings are perceived as basically good and filled with potential, the life drama being of an exciting heroic adventure based upon an optimistic stance. The role of the therapist is to facilitate this move towards self-actualisation or, to paraphrase Carl Rogers, to become what one is capable of becoming. In contrast, the tragic vision is rooted in psychodynamic practice, in which the life drama represents an attempt to come to terms with primitive forces over which the actor has little or no control. Life's journey is less a romantic quest than a painful struggle to access repressed memories. To paraphrase Sigmund Freud, the goal of therapy is to translate neurosis into ordinary unhappiness. Finally, we have what can be described as the comic vision. The term is used here not to refer to comedy in the contemporary sense but to a situation characterised by confusion in which the actor or actors fail to achieve their objectives because of dysfunctional behaviour. The best examples in Shakespeare are *As You Like It*, *Twelfth Night* and *Much Ado About Nothing*. In each of these plays, through a learning experience, a new understanding emerges and social and personal goals are achieved. The equivalent in the world of therapy is CBT.

On the face of it, these three positions seem incompatible and thus there can be no unified discipline of counselling psychology. However, there is an option towards an ironic position which attempts to reconcile all these positions. This involves a willingness to aim at detachment, seeing all sides of an argument and to achieve some form of synthesis. It requires the ability to think dialectically in reflecting upon practice and to work towards a personal integration. Without the ability to think ironically across traditional boundaries, it is doubtful whether there can be a discipline of counselling psychology – just psychologists who work within their own individual paradigms. Dialectical thinking will be discussed further and its importance reinforced in the conclusion to this chapter.

THE SCIENTIST-PRACTITIONER

While clinical psychology owes its early development to its links with medical practice, its modern format and success since the Second World War owes a great deal to the manner in which it has incorporated and internalised a coherent narrative about itself, namely that of the scientist practitioner. This began to take shape in the 1950s after a conference held by the American Psychological Association at Boulder, Colorado, in 1947, when the model was officially endorsed by the American Division of Clinical Psychology. In the model, clinicians are perceived as applied scientists, drawing on the science of psychology.

It has been subjected to considerable scrutiny with both high levels of endorsement and severe criticism (see Blair (2010) for a critical review of the concept). Despite evidence that the model is rarely fulfilled in practice and that scientists and practitioners have different objectives, it remains a potent narrative reinforced by the contemporary emphasis on evidence-based practice defined as empirically supported treatment protocols. The model was, and perhaps still is, well suited to clinical psychology whose origins derive from an experimental and medical background. In contrast, and on the face of it, it appears less well suited to counselling psychology which, coming from a humanistic tradition, has favoured a more multi-dimensional approach in which the relationship between psychologist and client has been emphasised as a critical factor.

However, to polarise the situation in this way runs the risk of over-simplification. An important question is what constitutes evidence and whether randomised controlled trials are the only form of reliable and valid evidence? As Blair (2010) points out, randomised controlled trials offer an indication of what works best for a particular client group, not what is best for an individual client. Thus the challenge for counselling psychology is to expand the definition of what constitutes evidence in a way that retains its credibility as a form of scientific practice. This involves building a bridge between the various positions, a challenge taken up by Corrie and Callanan (2001). They suggest that we can think about the scientist-practitioner model as itself a continuum from a closed model prioritising prediction and control to a more open model where psychological evidence might be used in a more holistic manner according to the needs of a given enquiry. Lane and Corrie (2006) refer to a need to find a 'mid-point between being purely pragmatic and the experimentally rigorous, suggesting a more liberal, flexible and stakeholder focussed basis' (p. 16).

The message is that in applying the scientist-practitioner model to the real world of British psychological practice, there is no virtue in situating counselling and clinical psychology in two opposed camps. While there may be differences of emphasis, we should not create straw men or women that we can then knock down with a flourish. The reality on the ground is that members of the two disciplines frequently work alongside each other, often with very similar client issues. The Division of Clinical Psychology (2011, p. 13) refers to the main therapies used by NHS clinical psychologists as CBT, systemic, psychodynamic and CAT. Add person-centred and existentialist to this list and we probably have a statement of the main therapies used by counselling psychologists. Nevertheless, as already indicated, counselling psychology has chosen to move away from a single-model approach which tends to characterise programmes of training in clinical psychology but also in counselling and psychotherapy.

Given that counselling psychologists employ much the same techniques as clinical psychologists and counsellors/psychotherapists, does the difference reside in the emphasis on reflective practice? It would be absurd to argue that clinical psychologists are not reflective in their practice. Taylor (2003) has deconstructed the use of the reflective-practitioner model within the NHS in the context of nursing. She perceives it as foremost a disciplinary practice that is part of a confessional structure. However, she adds that 'to confess sins of omission or commission is acceptable so long as these are part of a process of learning and development' (p. 248). Commenting on this, Lewis (2008) suggests that the point Taylor is trying to make is that as an account of the client, a reflective account is no more authentic than a case formulation. However, reflective practice for a counselling psychologist 'aligns with practice in a more fundamental way' (p. 64) by 'foregrounding the use of self in the therapeutic process' (p. 63) and it is this fact that puts reflective practice and the reflective practitioner at the heart of counselling psychology. In this context the requirement for personal therapy in approved programmes of counselling psychology training provides some distance from other disciplines.

COUNSELLING PSYCHOLOGY AND HELPING OUTSIDE THE HEALTH SECTOR

Almost inevitably much of this chapter has focused upon the health sector, but of course counselling psychology also exists in fields such as education, employment, organisational development and coaching. While the notion of helping may have slightly different meanings in these contexts, what most have in common is that feature of counselling psychology that emphasises well-being rather than sickness. The growth of coaching psychology is an excellent example with its focus on the development of life skills rather than responding to crisis. The whole positive psychology movement reflects this movement away from helping as a response to pathology towards a focus on helping as a movement towards self-actualisation. It is notable that counselling services within universities now frequently describe themselves using the language of offering support and facilitating well-being.

CONCLUSION: A DIALECTICAL WAY OF THINKING

The map of the world of helping is in a constant state of flux. The bit of that world known as counselling psychology reflects this dynamism. It looks very different in 2013 than it did in 1992 when it became a division, and even more so than in 1982 when it became a section within BPS. At that time, evidence-based practice was just a gleam in the eye, IAPT did not exist, NICE likewise, and HCPC (Health and Care Professions Council) and statutory registration was a long way away. In 2015 or beyond, when you read this chapter, it may have changed even more than in 2013/14 when the chapter was written. It follows that any map has to be flexible enough to offer not just a snapshot at a particular point of time but to take account of movement and change.

The idea of a dialectical process, which derives from the work of Hegel and Marx, offers a framework for this. It has already been adopted in this chapter in the discussion on the role of ironic thinking. In its classical form the basic concept is that ideas that frequently start out as opposites eventually come together in the form of a synthesis. In politics this is reflected in movement of the two main parties towards the middle ground. The end product is more than a sum of its parts. Thus a thesis is opposed by antithesis which eventually coalesce together as a synthesis. This synthesis then forms the new thesis which we can think of as the orthodoxy. In time this generates an antithesis leading to a new synthesis and so on and so on *ad infinitum*. Apply this analysis to counselling psychology and what we find, as this chapter has suggested, is that the discipline developed as an antithesis to the contemporary thesis as represented by key ideas dominating clinical psychology and psychiatric practice. However, over time, the philosophy behind counselling psychology has filtered into and been taken on board by the wider psychological world, while counselling psychology for its part has had to broaden its outlook in order to recognise the imperatives of this wider world. Conceiving of the world map in this manner, the philosophy of counselling psychology is now part of the new thesis/orthodoxy.

Over time a new antithesis will develop and indeed it possibly already exists in the form of a more politicised perspective which emphasises the need for psychologists to work towards social justice and to oppose any use of psychology which might perpetuate inequality or oppression. This is sometimes described as critical psychology. This places the practice of the psychologist within a wider social and political context. This is exemplified in a book by Proctor et al. (2006) entitled *Politicizing the Person-centred Approach*, and the community psychology approach of Kagan et al. (2010).

Looked at this way, counselling psychology can be regarded as a success. While it is unfortunate that the discipline lags behind clinical psychology in terms of resources devoted to it, we need to remember Joseph Stalin's rhetorical question about how many battalions the Pope had. Stalin's empire is long dead but the Papacy, whatever we think about it, remains powerful. Mindful of this, we should not evaluate the influence of counselling psychology by measuring numbers or resources. My view is that it has something good to offer in the form of its philosophy and methods and has succeeded in convincing a wider world of the value of its product. Recent publications referred to in this chapter by the British Psychological Society on formulation and psychiatric diagnosis respectively demonstrate that radical challenge to established positions does not solely exist within the Division of Counselling Psychology.

In 2009, Mollon, a clinical psychologist, wrote about what he saw as the corrupting influence of NICE, with its emphasis on identifying specific protocols for specific diseases replacing 'the nuances of individual experience' (2009, p. 130). He posed the question, 'Why are counselling psychologists not angrier with clinical psychologists?' However, I venture to suggest that this is an overgeneralisation of what differentiates the two divisions and that there is no merit to be had in being envious of clinical psychology or in adopting a defensive posture of splitting the world into good and bad. Counselling psychology is not a passive recipient of the world in which it exists and of the changes which go on all around it. It does have the power of agency to relocate itself. It does have a choice. It can work to further establish itself and strengthen its position within the new thesis as part of the dominant group. Alternatively, it can seek to work to integrate its focus on the reflective practitioner with newer, more radical ideas such as those outlined above.

So where does this take us in terms of defining what is counselling psychology and identifying a role for it? Blair (2010, p. 20) describes it as 'situated at a busy junction of diverse and sometimes competing ideologies, frameworks and paradigms'. It is a body of knowledge but much of it shared with other disciplines. It is a form of practice but again shared with others. At its most basic, it is a division of the BPS with a specific set of principles but the divisional structure may not last for ever. There has been discussion of something akin to a college of all psychologists working in the field of health and incorporating and thus replacing divisions. Perhaps there is an understandable fear were that to happen that all would be lost; what Bion (1962) described as 'nameless dread' (what cannot be spoken about) would come to pass. However, my view is that this fear can be confronted. The possibility, even likelihood, exists that the philosophy and disposition of counselling psychology would not be lost, but on the contrary would enter even more into the practices of other helpers. After all, in the field of helping, if one has something good to offer, the ethical position is surely not to keep it to oneself but to give it away so that its benefits are disseminated as widely as possible.

Visit the companion website to read Mapping the World of Helping.

REFERENCES

American Psychiatric Association (2013) *Diagnostic and Statistical Manual of Mental Disorders – V* (DSM-V). Washington, DC: APA.

Bion, W.R. (1962) 'A theory of thinking', *International Journal of Psychoanalysis*, 43: 306–310.

Blair, L. (2010) 'A critical review of the scientist-practitioner model for counselling psychology', *Counselling Psychology Review*, 25(4): 19–30.

British Association for Counselling (1993) *Code of Ethics and Practice for Counsellors*. Rugby: BAC.

British Association for Counselling and Psychotherapy (2013) *Ethical Framework for Good Practice in Counselling and Psychotherapy*. Lutterworth: BACP.

British Psychological Society (1993) *Code of Conduct, Ethical Principles and Guidelines*. Leicester: BPS.

British Psychological Society (2005) *Professional Practice Guidelines*. Leicester: BPS, Division of Counselling Psychology.

British Psychological Society (2006) *Code of Ethics and Conduct*. Leicester: BPS.

Carroll, M. and Shaw, E. (2012) *Ethical Maturity in the Helping Professions: Making difficult life and work decisions*. Melbourne: PsychOz Publications.

Corrie, S. and Callanan, M.M. (2001) 'A review of the scientist-practitioner model: reflections on its potential contribution to counselling psychology within the context of current health care trends', *British Journal of Medical Psychology*, 73: 413–427.

Division of Clinical Psychology (2011) *Good Practice Guidelines on the Use of Psychological Formulation*. Leicester: BPS.

Division of Clinical Psychology, BPS (2013) *Position Statement on the Classification of Behaviour and Experience in Relation to Functional Psychiatric Diagnosis: Time for a paradigm shift*. Leicester: BPS.

Douglas, B. (2010) 'Disorder and its discontents', in R. Woolfe, S. Strawbridge, B. Douglas and W. Dryden (eds), *Handbook of Counselling Psychology*. London: Sage. pp. 23–43.

Douglas, B. and James, P. (2013) *Common Presenting Issues in Psychotherapeutic Practice*. London: Sage.

Dryden, W. (1996) 'A rose by any other name: a personal view on the differences among professional titles', in I. James and S. Palmer (eds), *Professional Therapeutic Titles: Myths and realities*. Leicester: BPS.

Fear, R. and Woolfe, R. (1996) 'Searching for integration in counselling practice', *British Journal of Guidance and Counselling*, 24(3): 399–411.

Fear, R. and Woolfe, R. (1999) 'The personal and professional development of the counsellor: the relationship between personal philosophy and theoretical orientation', *Counselling Psychology Quarterly*, 12(3): 253–262.

Frye, N. (1965) *A Natural Perspective: The development of Shakespearean comedy and romance*. New York: Columbia University Press.

Healey, D. (2004) *Let Them Eat Prozac: The unhealthy relationship between the pharmaceutical industry and depression*. New York: New York University Press.

Johnstone, L. (2000) *Uses and Abuses of Psychiatry: A critical look at psychiatric practice*. London: Routledge.

Kagan, C., Tindall, C. and Robinson, J. (2010) 'Community psychology: linking the individual with the community', in R. Woolfe, S. Strawbridge, B. Douglas and W. Dryden (eds), *Handbook of Counselling Psychology*. London: Sage.

Lane, D. and Corrie, S. (2006) 'Counselling psychology: its influences and future', *Counselling Psychology Review*, 21(1): 12–24.

Larsson, P., Brooks, O. and Lowenthal, D. (2012) 'Counselling psychology and diagnostic categories: a critical review', *Counselling Psychology Review*, 27(3): 55–67.

Lewis, Y. (2008) 'Counselling psychology training: implications for self', *Counselling Psychology Review*, 23(4): 64–69.

Mollon, P. (2009) 'Our rich heritage – are we building upon it or destroying it? (or why are counselling psychologists not angrier with clinical psychologists)', *Counselling Psychology Review*, 24(3/4): 130–142.

Parker, I. (ed.) (1999) *Deconstructing Psychotherapy*. London: Sage.

Parpottas, P. (2012) 'Working with the therapeutic relationship in cognitive behavioural therapy from an attachment theory perspective', *Counselling Psychology Review*, 27(3): 91–99.

Pilgrim, D. (1997) *Psychotherapy and Society*. London: Sage.

Proctor, G., Cooper, M., Sanders, P. and Malcolm, B. (2006) *Politicizing the Person-centred Approach: An agenda for social change*. Ross-on-Wye: PCSS Books.

Rizq, R. (2013) 'The language of healthcare', *Therapy*, March: 20–23.

Sanders, P. (2006) 'Principled and strategic opposition to the medicalization of distress and all of its apparatus', in S. Joseph and R. Worsley (eds), *Person-Centred Pathology: A positive psychology of mental health*. Ross-on-Wye: PCSS Books. pp. 21–42.

Smail, D. (1978) *Psychotherapy: A personal approach*. London: J.M. Dent.

Suman, F. (2010) *Mental Health, Race and Culture*. Basingstoke: Palgrave Macmillan.

Szasz, T. (1961) *The Myth of Mental Illness: Foundations of a theory of personal conduct*. London: Secker & Warburg.

Szasz, T. (2007) *Coercion as Cure: A critical history of psychiatry*. New Brunswick, NJ: Transaction.

Taylor, C. (2003) 'Narrating practice: reflective accounts and the textual construction of reality', *Journal of Advanced Nursing*, 42(3): 244–251.

Woolfe, R. (1990) 'Counselling psychology in Britain: an idea whose time has come', *The Psychologist*, 12: 531–535.

Woolfe, R. (2011) 'Training routes for counsellors, counselling psychologists and psychotherapists', in R. Bor and M. Watts (eds), *The Trainee Handbook*. London: Sage. pp. 17–32.

Woolfe, R. (2012) 'Risorgimento: a history of counselling psychology in Britain', *Counselling Psychology Review*, 27(4): 72–78.

Woolfe, R. (2013) 'Foreword', in B. Douglas and P. James, *Common Presenting Issues in Psychotherapeutic Practice*. London: Sage.

2
SCIENCE, CRAFT AND PROFESSIONAL VALUES
SHEELAGH STRAWBRIDGE

INTRODUCTION

Much of our thinking is metaphorical (Lakoff and Johnson, 1980), pervaded by images and analogies, and psychological thinking is no exception. For example: moods can be 'up', 'down' or 'swinging'; Freud's theories draw on a diversity of ideas and images from topography, the forces of energy dynamics and the symbolic transformations of meaning; we often describe mental functioning in terms borrowed from computing and information technology; and we invoke medical and warlike imagery in 'battling mental illness' or 'fighting' anxiety and depression. It can be instructive to explore the metaphors that infuse our thinking and Pickering (2006) has examined the metaphorical nature of the concept of 'mental illness' in some depth. Metaphors are powerful; they can fire our imaginations and suggest fruitful lines of inquiry but can also limit us when we lose the all-important sense of 'as if'.

Taking up the journey metaphor, this chapter will focus on the journey of our discipline and examine the kinds of maps that guide our explorations. Like any discipline, counselling psychology has arisen and is shaped within socio-historical contexts. Its guiding metaphors and assumptions, explicit or implicit, about its nature and purpose and about the character of the terrain it explores change over time. These assumptions direct the development of its theories, which can be seen as the maps that define its territory and, in turn, explorations can lead to a re-drawing of current theoretical maps, as their limitations are encountered.

As Macfarlane (2003: 191) notes, maps give meaning and structure to a landscape, placing a territory within a wider matrix of significance and making the unknown known. However, he warns:

> on a map the weather is always good, the visibility always perfect. A map offers the power of perspective over a landscape: reading one is like flying over the countryside in an aeroplane – a deodorized, pressurized, temperature controlled survey. But a map can never replicate the ground itself. (2003: 184)

Indeed, if it could it would no longer be useful. Our sense of 'reality' is always conveyed by perceptions, images and ideas. Metaphors are suggestive of ways of seeing and maps and theories allow us to negotiate complex landscapes by reducing them to features salient to our purposes. A geological map is very different from a road map and so it is with the theoretical maps that help us to navigate and make sense of the complex terrain of human life. While disciplines such as history, anthropology, sociology, politics, linguistics, biology and medicine, alongside psychology, have all usefully charted aspects of the territory, a unified theoretical map is impossible.

Counselling psychology is currently at an interesting point in its journey. It emphasizes well-being and human potential and resists defining psychological distress in medical terms but, as it is increasingly practised in medical contexts, it struggles to maintain its distinctiveness. Nevertheless, while advances in neuroscience pull towards a biologically based view of mental health, controversial revisions to psychiatric categories (American Psychiatric Association, 2013) are revitalizing debates about the dominance of medicalized practice. The territory, then, is contested. Struggles over differing ways of mapping and shaping it reveal differing interests and professional rivalries, so this seems an opportune moment to take stock. Conflicts are valuable in prompting a honing of positions and clarifying ideas. However, they can also result in entrenchment and hardening lines of defence that close off fruitful interaction and cross-fertilization. It is, then, important to maintain the open-minded curiosity, that is the hallmark of genuine exploration, and recognize that the landscape is indeed too complex and diverse for any one map to encompass.

Counselling psychology defines itself within psychology as a science but as Lane and Corrie (2006: 70–89) note, we need to ask what this means and how science relates to practice. Differing conceptions of psychological science shape the character of its explorations and the theories it produces and uses. More specifically, as counselling psychology focuses on human well-being and psychological distress, how these are conceptualized and charted is significant in guiding our practice (see Chapter 9).

WHAT IS SCIENCE?

Our culture is permeated by ways of thinking shaped by science and technology so, remembering that the map is not the territory, it is useful to reflect on how psychology is located within broader mappings of science. The 'modern' scientific world-view that prevailed through the nineteenth and much of the twentieth centuries can be traced to the 'scientific revolution' of the seventeenth century and its development through the 'Enlightenment', interlinked ideas about nature, human beings and society, associated with eighteenth-century France. The Enlightenment is deemed to mark the beginning of the modern period or 'modernity' and characterized by its challenge to the domination of European thought by Christianity and the Church's authority. While the sixteenth-century Copernican revolution dramatically re-conceptualized the universe as heliocentric, this involved a further significant metaphysical shift. Reason and rationality were promoted as the basis of all human knowledge with science increasingly seen as the key to its expansion. The belief in the power of science became coupled with equally strong beliefs in technological and social progress, which would be enhanced by the scientific understanding of human beings and human societies.

Associated with the philosophies of empiricism and positivism, the conception of science that evolved stressed that knowledge claims must be objective and value-free. Importantly, it proposed a rational, empirically based approach to creating knowledge free from religious dogma, although, for the scientists of the seventeenth and eighteenth centuries, nature was God's creation and its study a celebration of his glory. The universe was imagined as a great clockwork mechanism designed and set in motion by God and its permeation by divine reason underpinned the belief in its rational intelligibility. In time, the notion of conscious design by divine reason seemed unnecessary and the more thoroughly materialist metaphysics, characteristic of the modern scientific world-view, emerged. A key aim became to reduce the phenomena of reality to their most fundamental elements and explain wholes in terms of their parts. Unifying principles across the sciences were sought and 'higher level' explanations, such as those of biology, were considered to be ultimately reducible to 'lower level' explanations, with the laws of physics seen as the most fundamental and atoms the basic components of matter.

Some of the most successful scientific ideas of the nineteenth and twentieth centuries were inspired by this powerful idea. For example, it underpinned the spectacular developments in molecular biology arising from the discovery of the structure of DNA (Watson, [1953] 2012) and Crick declared the ultimate aim was the explanation of all biology 'in terms of the level below it, and so on right down to the atomic level', leading to 'a great influx of physicists and chemists into biology' (Crick, [1966] 2004: 14). More recently, Dawkins has described us as survival machines for DNA molecules ([1976] 2006: 21–22), and has evoked the clockwork image of the universe through his metaphor of a 'blind watchmaker' ([1986] 2006). Mapping the human genome has been one of the triumphs of this approach.

The achievements inspired by this mechanistic image of the universe and the reductionist drive to discover its fundamental building blocks and unify the sciences are not to be underestimated. It has, nevertheless, generated intractable problems. Divorcing consciousness from material reality raises persisting questions about the limits of our knowledge, the nature of consciousness (e.g. Velmans, 2009) and the tension between moral responsibility, dependent on free will, and determinism. The realization that our experience is inseparable from our techniques and instruments of observation (including telescopes, MRI scanners and the Large Hadron Collider) and is ordered and made intelligible through our conceptual maps challenged naïve notions of objectivity. Moreover, the image of a stable clockwork mechanism required modification in the light of the theories of evolution and thermodynamics. Additionally, notions of matter, space and time were rendered problematic by theories of electromagnetic fields, relativity, subatomic particles and quantum mechanics.

At least since the 1930s some branches of natural science have espoused various forms of systems thinking, focused on patterns of relationship within an integrated whole not reducible to the sum of its parts. Dynamic self-organizing systems comprising complex webs of relations regulating component parts, such as the balance between atmospheric gases, are of particular interest. Although familiar in the human sciences, where historical processes, social structures and cultures are seen to have determining effects on the lives of individuals, these ideas were innovative in the natural sciences. Alternative holistic metaphors challenged reductionism and the machine image. In physics, for example, Bohm's (1980) notion of an 'implicate order' is infused with holographic imagery and in the life-sciences networks, organic processes and ecosystems became common notions. (For an overview see Capra and Luisi, 2014.) Progress in these branches of science has been facilitated by the development of complexity theory in mathematics where the emphasis is on dynamic processes and forms (Prigogine and Stengers, 1985; Stewart, 1997).

Studies in the philosophy, history and sociology of science have also undermined the notion of a unifying 'scientific method'. Science can no longer be conceived as unitary and socially detached but as characterized by diversity and embedded in communities of scientists guided by shared conceptual maps. These may remain stable for long periods but can undergo significant shifts. Chalmers (1999) usefully introduces differing conceptions of science, continuing controversies and key thinkers, including Popper, Kuhn, Lakatos, Feyerabend and Foucault. So we can no longer think in terms of an all-encompassing 'modern' world-view with rationality defined within a hierarchically ordered but unified science. It now seems appropriate to think more modestly, in 'post-modern' plural terms, of the sciences, alongside other disciplines, including the humanities, as charting important domains of knowledge and inquiry. This is recognized by the recently launched 'Human Mind Project' (http://human-mind.ac.uk/), and resonates with Serres' (1995) contention that no domain is sole arbiter of reason. He sees it as the job of philosophy to negotiate channels of communication between the sciences and humanities (Serres, 1995; and see Brown, 2002).

Sciences, such as molecular biology, chemistry, ecology, sub-atomic physics and climatology, map particular domains of inquiry with sometimes radically different guiding metaphors and metaphysical assumptions. Their research methods, theories and explanations are generated and maintained within the discourses of their relevant scientific communities. So, some post-modern thinkers have taken up extreme relativist positions, seeing all theories as social constructions without foundation in reality. Hacking (1985 and 2000), however, challenges the more uncompromisingly relativist views espousing the notion of 'styles of scientific reasoning', which accepts plurality while maintaining the conviction that there are good and bad explanations. He has examined conceptions of social construction in some detail. Similarly, Serres argues, 'we construct *a* real, among many possibilities, which is *a* rational one, among other possibilities' (1995: 25) and Collins (2014) too, while recognizing the inexact and messy nature of science, strongly defends scientific reasoning and expertise.

Nevertheless, while accepting limits to relativism, acknowledging the sciences as human enterprises, culturally and historically situated, means that they are subject to socio-political influences and must be considered in context. The task, however, is not to devalue science but to understand its complexity and distinguish good from bad science (e.g. Goldacre, 2008, 2014). So, in the light of the above, we must ask what kind of science is psychology, how is its domain of knowledge and inquiry defined, if indeed it is a single domain, and how is it affected by the social and political contexts in which it is practised. As the territory is contested, while it is important to ask the questions, no definitive answers are possible.

PSYCHOLOGICAL SCIENCE AND COUNSELLING PSYCHOLOGY

Modern psychology, emerging in the late nineteenth and early twentieth centuries, positioned itself within the 'modern' technical-rational approach to science. At the beginning of the twentieth century the cultural climate in America was pervaded by the idea of creating a truly modern industrial civilization founded on the practical utility of science and technology (Richards, 1996: 47). This climate was favourable to behaviourism, defined by Watson in 1913, which was nomothetic and deterministic, seeking laws that would allow the prediction and control of human behaviour. Pavlov's research on conditioning, in the Soviet Union, suggested a physiological basis for behaviourism and Richards (1996: 55) notes that, despite ideological differences, both societies were looking to psychology to develop techniques of behaviour control.

Applying behavioural laws to the treatment of criminality and mental illness, the assessment of abilities and aptitudes, the education of children, the organization of the workplace, and so on, would contribute to human well-being through a more rationally organized society. Its focus on the components and laws of behaviour resonated with the reductionist search for basic elements and the demand for objectivity and observability. This conception of psychology, with its focus on possibilities of behaviour change, excluded studies of consciousness and subjective experience. The living brain being inaccessible to scientific study was initially dealt with as a 'black box', though in recent years, with the development of functional neuroscience, it has become possible to study living brains and there are current arguments concerning the potential for understanding consciousness in terms of brain processes. Despite claims to the contrary, far from being value-free, the inherent determinism of this approach is implicitly conformist. It locates control outside those being controlled and its thrust is towards adaptation and adjustment, rather than a critique of social conditions. For a discussion point on working with EAPs see the companion website.

Of course, knowledge evolves and the early stress on behaviour and behaviour modification has shifted significantly towards a re-conceptualization as cognitive-behavioural psychology (Bergin and Garfield, 1994: 824). In the psychological therapies the picture becomes increasingly complex as practitioners of different approaches continue to learn from each other. Nevertheless, the arenas of 'clinical' practice are largely medical and oriented towards a technical-rational model of natural science. In this context, cognitive-behavioural psychology and CBT predominate as, while espousing a specifically psychological approach, they are relatively compatible with psychiatry's goal of diagnosing problems and developing techniques to solve them. They are amenable to research based in this tradition, with randomized controlled trials (RCTs) seen as the 'gold standard' in assessing the effectiveness of interventions. In specifying the 'conditions' to be researched, the psychiatric categories of the

Diagnostic and Statistical Manuals (DSMs) are often used. These are, however, widely criticized and the later editions seem increasingly unscientific in eschewing theory and the search for causal explanations. This fundamental aspect of scientific medicine recognizes that symptoms, like persistent headaches or diarrhoea, have a variety of causes which a failure to investigate can lead to inappropriate treatments and even death.

Although a natural science vision has inspired psychology, particularly in Britain and America, the appropriateness of using the same methods to study both the natural and the human world has always been questioned. As history, psychology, sociology, economics and social anthropology emerged as disciplines, claims were made that their subject matter is significantly different from that of the natural sciences and requires differing methods of study. In Britain, John Stuart Mill adopted the term 'moral sciences' for these disciplines and their distinctiveness was similarly argued by the German philosopher Dilthey. He linked the notion of 'human science' to a theory of understanding and influenced the development of research into human consciousness, subjective experience, meaning and culture (e.g. see Rickman, 1967). Wundt, for instance, in the 1850s saw psychology as the science of consciousness, James (1890) explored conscious experience and Mead (1934) emphasized the social context in which the 'self' is constructed as well as its capacity for self-reflection. In the human sciences it is assumed that the subject matter is meaningfully or symbolically constructed. The aim of inquiry is to penetrate its logic and this applies to expressions of psychological distress as much as to cultural practices.

Such questioning characterized the 'humanistic psychology', emerging in America around 1940. Rogers and Maslow were key figures in this 'third force' in American psychology. It challenged the perceived determinism of behaviourism and psychoanalysis, as well as the biomedical model in psychiatry. Its emphasis on free will and human potential became significant in the context of emerging protest movements (Herman, 1992) and counselling was just one of a range of democratizing practices in humanistic psychology. It stressed the quality of the therapeutic relationship, emphasized the validity of subjective experience and valued the capacity for self-determination and personal responsibility of the person in the client-role. The early ideas of humanistic psychology were peculiarly American and, it can be argued, over-optimistic (e.g. Spinelli, 2005: 179–80). Nevertheless, Rogers, Maslow and others recognized their roots in European existential and phenomenological thought (e.g. Rogers, 1964) dating back at least to the nineteenth century.

By the 1960s existential and phenomenological ideas were gaining ground in a climate of political and intellectual upheaval and were posing a challenge to over-deterministic conceptions of history, social structure, social processes and human behaviour. Consciousness and human agency were re-emphasized and values were seen as inseparable from the assumption that human beings have the capacity for choice and personal responsibility. So the search for methods appropriate to the study of self-conscious, experiencing, reflective and self-determining beings was revitalized and the range of rigorous, qualitative research methods now available owes much to this period. Initially these were more eagerly embraced in sociology and anthropology than in Anglo-American psychology, although there are notable exceptions. Bruner (1986), for instance, made his important distinction between 'paradigmatic' and 'narrative' knowing in the 1980s and drew attention to the significance of stories in human experience.

In addition to phenomenology, structuralist and post-structuralist studies of language and discourses have unlocked possibilities for exploring conscious and unconscious meanings and their social contexts. The study of consciousness and experience by qualitative methods is now seen as important in psychology and much qualitative research is idiographic, more focused on the detail of subjective experience than on general laws and is not amenable to RCTs. From this perspective it is acknowledged that people react to interpretive and explanatory concepts and change in response to being classified or diagnosed. So, in therapeutic work an egalitarian, collaborative relation between practitioner and client is favoured, with a stress on the exploration and understanding of individual experiences. Formulation, in contrast to diagnosis, acknowledges complexity, recognizing that experiences, for example, of abuse, vary, as do individual expressions of the resulting distress. Personal qualities, choices and relationships are seen as central to the work and the therapeutic significance of the personal and intimate nature of the client–practitioner relationship emphasized.

Psychology has, then, been contested territory from the start. Counselling psychology is generally best mapped within the human science tradition but this is not to say it cannot draw on other branches of psychology or on disciplines within the natural sciences or humanities. For instance, an understanding of narrative, which owes much to literature and linguistics, informs narrative approaches within psychology and therapy. Equally, developments in neuroscience offer new insights into brain function that it would be folly to disregard. Moreover, the systems perspectives introduced above, notwithstanding the individual focus of much therapeutic practice, are a valuable source of ideas. Indeed, there is a strong tradition of systems thinking in work with couples, families and groups and Lane and Corrie (2006: 86) argue more generally that the dynamics of therapeutic interventions might be better understood in terms of the non-linear relationships of complex systems than as clear-cut causal relationships.

The tensions and varieties of approach within psychology suggest it may be better to think of it, not as a single domain of knowledge and research, but as comprising a number of related domains requiring the negotiation of paths of communication between them. Given the complexity of the human psyche this could prove fruitful, opening up rather than closing down avenues of inquiry. However, as Lane and Corrie note: 'Re-examining our commitment to one particular model of science may be an uncomfortable prospect in a climate that favours speedy solutions over journeys of discovery' (2006: 88). They go on to contend that a commitment to science and the identity of scientist-practitioner is an ethical stance about having '...an inner professional 'compass', which carries with it a moral injunction to distinguish between sources of knowledge on the basis of their origins' (2006: 98). It implies that not to keep abreast of theoretical debates and research amounts to a violation of a central ethic of our profession.

Science, then, perhaps does not imply adherence to any particular method but more an ethical attitude towards rigorous empirical inquiry, which involves observing, questioning and forming theories that can guide and be tested in further inquiry. The best science depends on the careful framing of significant questions, which may not be amenable to ready-made research methods. Indeed, considerable creativity and ingenuity are often required in designing research. It is the burning questions that drive good science and those specific to counselling psychology arise within the complex challenges of practice. While the demand for evidence-based practice seems reasonable, failure to recognize that complexity can lead to exaggerated expectations and the desire for neat solutions and quick fixes to oversimplification. See also Bem and de Jong (2013) for an overview of some central conceptual issues in psychological science.

THE TACIT DIMENSION

Notwithstanding the variety of approaches within psychology and psychological therapy, there is a central tension between a natural science and a human science orientation. The former largely inclines towards a technical-rational attitude, searching for causal explanations and remedial techniques, whereas the latter favours the exploration of subjective experience and the interpretation of meanings. Nevertheless, both are established 'scientific' traditions. On closer examination we can see that what this means is by no means straightforward, but in the modern world the idea of science can perform an ideological function bestowing legitimacy over and above other domains of knowledge and understanding. Those that cannot be described as scientific are more easily dismissed as, similarly, in the medieval world, knowledge claims incompatible with the dominant religious world-view were deemed heretical. Midgley, for instance, writes about how science can become a 'modern myth of salvation' (1992). Making exaggerated claims does a disservice both to science and to other legitimate domains of inquiry and types of reason. Ethical opinion, for instance, was for a time viewed as emotional expression not amenable to rational argument (e.g. Ayer, 1934).

Accepting that rationality extends beyond the sciences and into the humanities, there is still a tendency to associate knowledge with what can be made explicit. Ryle (1949), however, made an important distinction, significant for practice, between 'knowing that' and 'knowing how'. The latter refers to the fact that skilful action reveals that we can know more than we can tell. Polanyi (1967) termed this 'the tacit dimension' and explored many everyday examples, such as recognizing faces and the moods they express, using tools and riding a bike. From a different perspective Kahneman (2011) has added to our understanding of the tacit dimension, distinguishing fast intuitive from slow deliberative thinking and showing the significance of the former in making judgements and decisions. Polanyi was particularly interested in the role of the tacit dimension in scientific discovery. He argued that creative acts are driven by strong personal commitments, guesses and hunches. Drawing on Merleau-Ponty's work (e.g. [1945] 1981) and Gestalt psychology, he argued that discovery is like perception, going from an awareness of many particulars to grasping their joint meaning in a coherent whole. It involves skilled, imaginative integration rather than formal reasoning and he stressed the value of dialogue within an open community in fostering creativity. In pointing to the importance of scientific communities his work echoed that of Kuhn (1962), and Bohm (1996) has explored further the nature and significance of open dialogue.

Following Polanyi, Collins (1985, 2013) has led research into the part played by the tacit dimension in science. For example, scientists found it impossible to replicate building a laser from research papers or detailed written instructions. Only those who were shown how to do it by others who already had the experience were successful. Collins argues that this kind of research suggests two models of learning. One he terms 'algorithmical' rests on formal instructions, as in a computer program. The other he terms 'enculturational' and likens to learning a new language or culture. Enculturational learning requires personal interaction and guidance, showing rather than telling, involving watching, visualizing and copying bodily movements. So 'knowing how' involves knowing more than we can tell and scientists learn as much from experience and interaction with colleagues as from formal papers.

Schön too, in developing Polanyi's ideas, highlighted the importance of the tacit dimension in experiential learning by examining the work of professionals in a variety of fields. He demonstrated the limitations of the technical-rational approach, contesting the notion of intelligent practice as the application of knowledge to instrumental decisions. In proposing his 'reflective practitioner' model (Schön, 1985), he argues that 'reflection-in-action' is central to the art of dealing well with practice situations of uncertainty, instability, uniqueness and value-conflict and that developing competence requires coaching and dialogue. All of this indicates that, important as scientific knowledge might be in grounding practice in evidence, it is far from the whole story.

Learning from experience within a community of practitioners is crucial for acquiring the competence demanded in complex practice situations of all kinds, including those of science. This suggests the value of the kind of apprenticeship required in learning any skilled craft. Sennett (2009) has explored the tacit dimension in craftsmanship across a wide variety of practices, including pottery, musicianship and medicine. He stresses the intimate connection between head and hand, 'the dialogue between concrete practices and thinking' (2009: 9) and the importance of guidance by experienced teachers. The emphasis on the connection between head and hand, the embodied nature of skill acquisition, challenges the Cartesian conceptual split between body and mind that has bedevilled British education, where academic 'knowing that', the highly valued province of universities, is regularly separated from 'knowing how'. Practice competence is often assumed to derive from the direct application of theoretical knowledge, the assumption Schön has questioned, or, in the case of arts and crafts, to be acquired in specialized schools or apprenticeships and often relatively undervalued. Systems theory, however, suggests a way beyond the split, conceiving mind and consciousness as processes not entities.

Bateson (1973) was one of the first to view mental processes, such as learning, memory and decision making, as systems phenomena characteristic of all living organisms and a consequence of a certain level of complexity, but not dependent on brains and highly developed nervous systems. Maturana and Varela have independently proposed a similar theory of cognition as the organizing activity of living systems at all levels of life (e.g. Varela et al., 1993).

Strongly influenced by Merleau-Ponty's emphasis on embodiment and the primacy of perception, they see cognition as stratified, increasing in complexity along with the evolution of sensory organs. This extends the notion of cognition beyond conscious awareness, recognizing the physicality of a whole organism's learning from interactions with its environment, a brain being one specific, highly evolved, structure through which the process operates. Consciousness is conceived as a particular kind of cognitive process that emerges when a sufficient level of complexity is reached.

These ideas situate cognition in an evolutionary context and have opened up new avenues of research in cognitive science. They resonate with Damasio's (2000) notions of 'core' and 'extended' consciousness and suggest a neuroscientific foundation for understanding embodied learning, unconscious processes and the deeply metaphorical nature of our thinking (Lakoff and Johnson, 1999). They also seem somewhat akin to Rogers' conception of organismic knowing and valuing, which Neville (2012) links with theories of deep ecology, while Rogers himself (1995) makes reference to complexity theory and the process philosophy of Whitehead ([1927–28] 1985). Such ideas suggest a rich field of exploration beyond the scope of this chapter. For an exercise on metaphors see the companion website.

Besides embodiment, work on the tacit dimension recognizes the significance of direct contact between people. It helps to understand the difficulty in being explicit about the crucial interpersonal connection between client and practitioner in counselling psychology, which implies the possibility of 'knowing (and communicating) more than we can tell' and of entering the world of another in a way not amenable to causal explanations or explicit interpretations. Rogers' work has been central in drawing attention to the importance of the therapeutic relationship, 'being-with' rather than 'doing-to', and Buber's distinction between 'I-It' and 'I-Thou'. More recently, Stern (2004) has also explored the profound impact of 'moments of meeting', distinguished from 'moments of interpretation', from a psychoanalytic perspective. Our capacity for knowing from the inside as well as the outside is, as recognized in the human science tradition, a feature of our common humanity. We are the same kind of beings as our clients and research subjects. Comparing the heroic fictional detective Sherlock Holmes and the self-effacing, but equally successful, Father Brown illustrates this well. Holmes is a man of action, amateur scientist and logician. He is an acute observer with remarkable powers of deduction. In contrast, Brown puts himself imaginatively into the minds of criminals and in discovering them through his empathy, grounded in their shared humanity, discovers his own capacity for sin. In disclosing Father Brown's secret, Chesterton (1981: 461–67) tells us something about his art as a writer, excavating his own experience to enter the lives of his characters.

Neuroscience may now be beginning to explain the tacit dimension, including our capacity for deep empathic connection in close relationships, the direct understanding that most of us have experienced but which has proved difficult to explicate (Cozolino, 2006). Moreover, such meetings between persons are rooted in valuing the other. This essentially moral and interpersonal character of psychotherapy is explored in some depth by Lomas (1999) and Gordon (1999) and is as vital as science and craft.

> To interpret human life requires unending observation, profound sympathy, wide reading, the ability to open yourself to strange and unexplored areas of your personality and to penetrate deep into the lives of others. (Callow, 2004: 230)

 No one kind of knowledge is sufficient and this reflection on acting applies equally to counselling psychology. For a discussion point on the use of technology in therapy visit the companion website.

POLITICS AND VALUES IN SCIENCE AND PRACTICE

Practice, then, involves much more than the application of science. Nevertheless, sound scientific research is indispensable in developing best practice, although, as already discussed, the nature of science is complex. It is not value-free but value-full, observations are shaped by theories and it is a social activity. If it implies an ethical stance, it is also culturally situated. It can be mythologized to perform an ideological function and is prone to political influence. We have seen that science emerged historically as a challenge to the prevailing world-view and was guided by a mechanistic metaphor that favoured a technical-rational approach to understanding the natural world, improving human life and solving problems such as disease, famine and other social ills.

Powerful as this mechanistic metaphor has been in Western science, some historians of ideas have linked it to the Promethean myth of a masculine hero who, in his quest for freedom, progress and mastery over the natural world, has 'constantly striven to differentiate himself from and control the matrix out of which he emerged' (Tarnas, 2010: 441). Feminist critiques have noted that its language is infused with sexual imagery. Nature has been imagined as female with knowledge created in a process of interrogation in which she is unveiled, penetrated and forced to reveal her most intimate secrets (Merchant, 1983; Harding, 1986). It has also been associated, from a neuroscientific perspective, with the increasing dominance of left-brain mentality in Western culture (McGilchrist, 2009; see also the RSA Social Brain Project (http://thersa.org)).

Moreover, it has been argued that we ignore the latter part of the Promethean myth at our peril (Neville, 2012: 32). This tells us that our liberation from the gods or nature is illusory. In focusing on resolving specific problems and failing to comprehend the complex interactions of the whole, technical solutions often cause new problems. Mellor (1989) cites Shelley, whose fictional scientist creates a monster he cannot control, as one of the first to highlight the dangers of scientific hubris. Jung too warned:

> our progressiveness, though it may result in a great many delightful wish-fulfilments, piles up an equally gigantic Promethean debt which has to be paid off from time to time in the form of hideous catastrophes. (1980: para. 276)

Current fears for the future, about pandemics, the decreasing effectiveness of antibiotics, and the consequences of climate change, suggest such a debt. In the light of these challenges, the organic, holistic and systemic world-views of some natural scientists are becoming more widely accepted. Indeed, the Promethean myth is countered by Lovelock's alternative of Gaia, which sees the Earth as a self-regulating system unbalanced by the depredations of humanity (e.g. Lovelock, 2006). This is capturing imaginations beyond the confines of ecology and climatology and entering political debates advocating sustainability over exploitation.

Nevertheless, technical rationality still pervades our world-view and is not confined to science. Weber ([1904–05] 1974) linked it to the development of industrial capitalism, associated with the growth of markets and bureaucracy, and termed the process 'rationalization'. This involves the application of criteria of rational decision making, tied to calculable economic efficiency, to widening areas of social life. Its effect is to construct a system geared to the relentless pursuit of profit. This, underpinned by scientific and technological progress, becomes an end in itself, the rationale of the whole system as opposed to a means whereby human needs may be satisfied. Ritzer (1993) argues that rationalization continues to intensify. He coined the term 'McDonaldization' to characterize the highly controlled, bureaucratic and dehumanized nature of much contemporary social life. The fast-food restaurant, built on principles of efficiency, calculability, predictability and control, where quantity and standardization replace quality and variety as indicators of value, serves as a metaphor for the general mania for efficiency. Increasing areas of social life, including education and medicine, are subject to McDonaldization so the stress on grades and league tables in education focuses attention on what is quantifiable in the end product, rather than the quality of the experience, and health care is becoming more impersonal and technological.

Ritzer (1998: 59–70) also considers the organization and experience of work and links his perspective to Braverman's (1974) analysis of the labour process. He recognizes that the deskilling and degradation of labour is characteristic of rationalization. Work is highly routinized, thinking reduced to a minimum and even social interactions are scripted (e.g. Hochschild, 1983) with creativity, critique, higher-level skills (such as planning) and genuine human contact effectively excluded. McDonaldization presents a challenge to counselling psychology by devaluing professionalism (Strawbridge, 2002). Over-simplified notions of science are promoted, the tacit dimension ignored and the richness and unpredictability of practice is endangered by shortened, formulaic, model-based trainings that advocate manualized practice. It thus contributes to a process of de-professionalization that is being experienced across the caring professions through increased 'managerialism', where direct work with service users is devolved to less well-trained and poorly paid workers (Hugman, 1998; May and Annison, 1998). In medicine too, where the benefits of science and technology are clear, rationalization is not without its dangers. As Helman (2006) argues, the stress on the technical aspects of medicine can result in a failure to attend to patients' stories and a loss of caring contact that is detrimental to effective treatment. Indeed, it may be that the technical, reductionist nature of modern medicine contributed to the loss of compassion and disregard for welfare evidenced in recent UK hospital failures. Fortunately, the narrow focus of medical education and practice is the subject of debate, as in the 'Medicine Unboxed Project' (http://medicineunboxed), and some medical schools are broadening their curricula to include medical humanities (Pugh, 2013). To read an original article on the McDonaldization of therapy visit the companion website.

In medical contexts of counselling psychology practice, technical rationality favours the biomedical over the psychosocial dimensions of psychological distress. The use of psychiatric diagnostic categories leads to the recommendation of specific 'treatments' for identified 'disorders'. It directs attention to an individual's internal state and away from interpersonal and socio-economic circumstances to which the distress may be an understandable response. It is nevertheless worth noting that the extensive critical literature attracted by the DSMs is from within as well as outside psychiatry. Burns (2013), for instance, is critical of 'criterion-based' diagnoses and contends that detailed history taking and careful listening are crucial in recognizing a patient's patterns and processes. He draws on Sennett (2009) in stressing the vital part played by experiential learning in psychiatry and argues that experience, more than technical knowledge, is needed in detecting the same signs and symptoms in very different people. Like Sennett, he recognizes the many hours of guided practice it takes to master any skilled art, including medical diagnosis.

Importantly, shifting the stress to psychosocial dimensions focuses attention on why psychological distress, manifest in issues around eating, alcohol and drug use, as well as in anxiety, depression and suicide, appears to be increasing. All of these can be indicators of social problems and classic research, such as Durkheim's study of suicide ([1897] 2006), which associated suicide rates with measures of social cohesion, and Brown and Harris's study of 'depression' in women (1978), still offer insights, as does more recent work (e.g. Smail, 1993; Pilgrim and Rogers, 2002; Wilkinson and Pickett, 2010). A psychosocial emphasis draws attention to socio-political issues concealed by an overly biomedical approach. Burns notes that 'the threshold for diagnosis and treatment has been steadily lowering in all branches of medicine, accompanied by an ever lengthening list of diseases' (2013: 225). So expanding the range of 'disorders', as in successive editions of the DSMs, and conceptualizing psychological distress in terms of individual mental health problems can perform an ideological function manifest in a medicalization of everyday life (see also Horwitz and Wakefield, 2007).

This expansion of medicine is closely associated with the growth of the pharmaceutical industry. Leader (2008: 13–17), for example, links the increasing diagnosis of depression with the development and marketing of antidepressant drugs and Appignanesi notes that the use of antidepressants rose by 234 per cent between 1992 and 2002. She remarks, 'There is nothing like a much publicized set of pills to invoke a mirroring illness' (Appignanesi, 2008: 3). While the effectiveness of antidepressants is now questioned (Healy, 2004; Kirsch, 2009), the diagnostic category, itself problematic, remains the basis for the recommendation of specific treatments.

Of course, many modern drugs are extremely beneficial in reducing suffering and death and, while they can produce enormous profits, they are also very expensive to develop. Drug companies invest hugely in research and often fund whole university departments that then depend on them for survival. This threatens the independence of research and has led to abuse resulting in scandals that damage the reputation of science (Goldacre, 2012; Healy,

2013; Moncrieff, 2013). Of course this is not limited to the pharmaceutical industry. Universities, increasingly expected to run as businesses, widely seek partnerships with industry to fund expensive research. Not only can some of these prove controversial, for example, with tobacco and oil companies, they can also detract from the value of departments that cannot attract commercial backing.

The growth of global capitalism and the expansion of markets into areas where commercial interests are prioritized over ethical issues and the democratic consideration of the common good can be understood in the context of continuing rationalization. Some of the dangers were foreseen by Mills (1959), who identified the power of an elite class of military, business and political leaders driven by mutual interests and beyond democratic control. President Eisenhower (1961) warned about the unwarranted influence of the 'military-industrial complex' and Sandel (2012) has argued that we have drifted from a market economy into being a market society and raised questions about how we can protect 'what money can't buy'. As further dramatic changes are predicted both in the nature of global capitalism (Stiglitz, 2013; Piketty, 2014) and as a result of technological innovation (Brynjolfsson and McAfee, 2014), the contexts of practice will present many novel challenges to our profession.

CONCLUSION

This chapter has sought to locate counselling psychology within a broader scientific, professional and political territory in the belief that our understanding of current and future issues can benefit from a perspective that attempts to comprehend the systems within which we practise. We live in a world beset by complex problems and struggles that, in addition to those of interpersonal and family relationships, generate a good deal of psychological distress. In drawing attention to some aspects of that complexity, the chapter has urged resistance to unrealistic demands for individualized quick fixes. The perspective offered is a personal one, the outcome of one journey of exploration and discovery through an individual career. It will resonate with the perspectives of some other practitioners but will also be contested, at least in some respects. It has raised questions, important for the future of our discipline, which we need to address if we accept that it is the responsibility of a profession to define and map its own territory, albeit in negotiation with others and in a context of conflicting interests and power relations. To meet the challenges ahead, to paraphrase T. S. Eliot ([1934] 1963), we will need to seek the wisdom we can lose in knowledge and the knowledge we can lose in information and be guided by our professional compass in maintaining the integrity of our science, craft and values.

Visit the companion website to watch McDonaldization and Deprofessionalization [10:26] and The Journey Metaphor [10:12].

REFERENCES

American Psychiatric Association (2013) *Diagnostic and Statistical Manual of Mental Disorders*, 5th edn. Washington, DC: APA.

Appignanesi, L. (2008) *Mad, Bad and Sad: A History of Women and the Mind Doctors from 1800 to the Present.* London: Virago.

Ayer, A. J. (1934) *Language, Truth and Logic.* London: Gollancz.

Bateson, G. (1973) *Steps to Ecology of Mind: Collected Essays in Anthropology, Psychiatry, Evolution and Epistemology.* St Albans: Paladin.

Bem, S. and de Jong, H. L. (2013) *Theoretical Issues in Psychology: An Introduction*, 3rd edn. London: Sage.

Bergin, A. E. and Garfield, S. L. (1994) *Handbook of Psychotherapy and Behaviour Change*, 4th edn. Chichester: Wiley.

Bohm, D. (1980) *Wholeness and the Implicate Order.* London: Routledge & Kegan Paul.

Bohm, D. (1996) *On Dialogue.* Ed. L. Nichol. London: Routledge.

Braverman, H. (1974) *Labour and Monopoly Capitalism: The Degradation of Work in the Twentieth Century.* London: Monthly Review Press.

Brown, G. W. and Harris, T. O. (1978) *The Social Origins of Depression.* London: Tavistock.

Brown, S. D. (2002) 'Michel Serres: Science, Translation and the Logic of the Parasite', *Theory, Culture and Society*, 19(3): 1–27.

Bruner, J. (1986) *Actual Minds, Possible Worlds.* London: Harvard University Press.

Brynjolfsson, E. and McAfee, A. (2014) *The Second Machine Age: Work, Progress and Prosperity in a Time of Brilliant Technologies.* New York: W. W. Norton.

Burns, T. (2013) *Our Necessary Shadow: The Nature and Meaning of Psychiatry.* London: Allen Lane.

Callow, S. (2004) *Being an Actor.* London: Vintage.

Capra, F. and Luisi, P. L. (2014) *The Sysyems View of Life: A Unifying Vision.* Cambridge: Cambridge University Press.

Chalmers, A. F. (1999) *What is This Thing Called Science?* Maidenhead: Open University Press.

Chesterton, G. K. (1981) *The Complete Father Brown.* London: Penguin.

Collins, H. (1985) *Changing Order: Replication and Induction in Scientific Practice.* London: Sage.

Collins, H. (2013) *Tacit and Explicit Knowledge.* Chicago: Chicago University Press.

Collins, H. (2014) *Are We All Scientific Experts Now?* Cambridge: Polity Press.

Cozolino, L. (2006) *The Neuroscience of Human Relationships: Attachment and the Developing Social Brain.* New York: W. W. Norton.

Crick, F. ([1966] 2004) *Of Molecules and Men.* New York: Prometheus Books.

Damasio, A. (2000) *The Feeling of What Happens: Body, Emotion and the Making of Consciousness.* London: Vintage.

Dawkins, R. ([1976] 2006) *The Selfish Gene*, 30th edn. Oxford: Oxford University Press.

Dawkins, R. ([1986] 2006) *The Blind Watchmaker.* London: Penguin.

Durkheim, E. ([1897] 2006) *On Suicide.* Trans. R. Buss. London: Penguin.

Eisenhower, Dwight D. (1961) 'Farewell Address'. *The Annals of America 1961–68: The Burdens of World Power, 1–5*. Chicago: Encyclopaedia Britannica 1968.

Eliot, T. S. ([1934] 1963) 'Choruses from the Rock', in *Collected Poems: 1909–1962*. London: Faber and Faber.

Goldacre, B. (2008) *Bad Science*. London: HarperCollins, Fourth Estate.

Goldacre, B. (2012) *Bad Pharma: How Drug Companies Mislead Doctors and Harm Patients*. London: Fourth Estate.

Goldacre, B. (2014) *I Think You'll Find It's a Bit More Complicated than That*. London: Fourth Estate.

Gordon, P. (1999) *Face to Face: Therapy as Ethics*. London: Constable.

Hacking, I. (1985) 'Styles of scientific reasoning', in J. Rajchman and C. West (eds), *Post-Analytic Philosophy*. New York: University of Columbia Press.

Hacking, I. (2000) *The Social Construction of What?* Harvard, MA: Harvard University Press.

Harding, S. (1986) *The Science Question in Feminism*. Milton Keynes: Open University Press.

Healy, D. (2004) *Let Them Eat Prozac: The Unhealthy Relationship between the Pharmaceutical Industry and Depression*. New York: New York University Press.

Healy, D. (2013) *Pharmageddon*. Berkeley, CA: University of California Press.

Helman, C. (2006) *Suburban Shaman: Tales from Medicine's Frontline*. London: Hammersmith Press.

Herman, E. (1992) 'Being and doing: humanistic psychology and the spirit of the 1960s', in B. L. Tischler (ed.), *Sights on the Sixties*. New Brunswick, NJ: Rutgers University Press.

Hochschild, H. R. (1983) *The Managed Heart: Commercialization of Human Feeling*. London: University of California Press.

Horwitz, A. V. and Wakefield, J. C. (2007) *The Loss of Sadness: How Psychiatry Transformed Normal Sorrow into Depressive Disorder*. Oxford: Oxford University Press.

Hugman, R. (1998) 'Social work and de-professionalization', in P. Abbott and L. Meerabeau (eds), *The Sociology Of The Caring Professions*, 2nd edn. Abingdon: Routledge.

James, W. (1890) *The Principles of Psychology*. New York: Henry Holt.

Jung, C. G. (1980) *Collected Works, 9. Part 1: The Archetypes and the Collective Unconscious*, 2nd edn. Princeton, NJ, and New York: Princeton University Press.

Kahneman, D. (2011) *Thinking, Fast and Slow*. London: Allen Lane, Penguin.

Kirsch, I. (2009) *The Emperor's New Drugs: Exploding the Anti-Depressant Myth*. London: Bodley Head.

Kuhn, T. (1962) *The Structure of Scientific Revolutions*. Chicago: University of Chicago Press.

Lakoff, G. and Johnson, M. (1980) *Metaphors We Live By*. Chicago: University of Chicago Press.

Lakoff, G. and Johnson, M. (1999) *Philosophy in the Flesh*. New York: Basic Books.

Lane, D. and Corrie, S. (2006) *The Modern Scientist Practitioner: A Guide to Practice in Psychology*. London: Routledge.

Leader, D. (2008) *The New Black: Mourning, Melancholia and Depression*. London: Hamish Hamilton, Penguin.

Lomas, P. (1999) *Doing Good? Psychotherapy Out of Its Depth*. Oxford: Oxford University Press.

Lovelock, J. (2006) *The Revenge of Gaia*. London: Allen Lane.

Macfarlane, R. (2003) *Mountains of the Mind: A History of a Fascination*. London: Granta.

May, T. and Annison, J. (1998) 'The de-professionalization of probation officers', in P. Abbott and L. Meerabeau (eds), *The Sociology of the Caring Professions*, 2nd edn. Abingdon: Routledge.

McGilchrist, I. (2009) *The Master and His Emissary: The Divided Brain and the Making of the Western World*. New Haven, CT: Yale University Press.

Mead, G. H. (1934) *Mind, Self and Society*. Chicago: University of Chicago Press.

Mellor, A. K. (1989) *Mary Shelley: Her Life, Her Fictions, Her Monsters*. Abingdon: Routledge.

Merchant, C. (1983) *The Death of Nature: Women, Ecology and the Scientific Revolution*. New York: Harper & Row.

Merleau-Ponty, M. ([1945] 1981) *Phenomenology of Perception*. Trans. C. Smith. London: Routledge & Kegan Paul.

Midgley, M. (1992) *Science as Salvation: A Modern Myth and its Meaning*. London: Routledge.

Mills, C. Wright (1959) *The Power Elite*. Oxford: Oxford University Press.

Moncrieff, J. (2013) *The Bitterest Pills: The Troubling Story of Antipsychotic Drugs*. London: Palgrave Macmillan.

Neville, B. (2012) *The Life of Things: Therapy and the Soul of the World*. Ross-on-Wye: PCCS Books.

Pickering, N. (2006) *The Metaphor of Mental Illness*. Oxford: Oxford University Press.

Piketty, T. (2014) *Capital in the Twenty-First Century*. Harvard, MA: Harvard University Press.

Pilgrim, D. and Rogers, R. (2002) *A Sociology of Mental Health and Illness*, 2nd edn. Buckingham: Open University Press.

Polanyi, M. (1967) *The Tacit Dimension*. London: Routledge & Kegan Paul.

Prigogine, I. and Stengers, I. (1985) *Order Out of Chaos: Man's New Dialogue with Nature*. London: Fontana.

Pugh, R. (2013) 'Opening medical minds', *Guardian*, 20 November: 40.

Richards, G. (1996) *Putting Psychology in its Place: An Introduction from a Critical Historical Perspective*. London: Routledge.

Rickman, H. P. (1967) *Understanding and the Human Studies*. London: Heinemann.

Ritzer, G. (1993) *The McDonaldization of Society*. London: Pine Forge.

Ritzer, G. (1998) *The McDonaldization Thesis*. London: Sage.

Rogers, C. R. (1964) 'Towards a Science of the Person', in T. W. Wann (ed.), *Behaviourism and Phenomenology*. Chicago: University of Chicago Press.

Rogers, C. R. (1995) *A Way of Being*. New York: Houghton Mifflin.

Ryle, G. (1949) *The Concept of Mind*. London: Hutchinson.

Sandel, M. (2012) *What Money Can't Buy: The Moral Limits of Markets*. London: Allen Lane.

Schön, D. A. (1985) *The Reflective Practitioner: How Professionals Think in Action*. New York: HarperCollins, Basic Books.

Sennett, R. (2009) *The Craftsman*. London: Penguin.

Serres, M. (1995) *Genesis*. Trans. G. James and J. Nielson. Michigan: University of Michigan Press.

Smail, D. (1993) *The Origins of Unhappiness: A New Understanding of Personal Distress*. London: HarperCollins.

Spinelli, E. (2005) *The Interpreted World*, 2nd edn. London: Sage.

Stewart, I. (1997) *Does God Play Dice: The New Mathematics of Chaos*, 2nd edn. London: Penguin.

Stern, D. N. (2004) *The Present Moment in Psychotherapy and Everyday Life*. New York: W. W. Norton.

Stiglitz, J. E. (2013) *The Price of Inequality*. London: Penguin.

Strawbridge, S. (2002) 'McDonaldization or fast-food therapy', *Counselling Psychology Review*, 17(4): 20–24.

Tarnas, R. (2010) *The Passion of the Western Mind: Understanding the Ideas that Have Shaped Our World View*. London: Pimlico.

Varela, F. J., Thompson, E. and Rosch, E. (1993) *The Embodied Mind: Cognitive Science and Human Experience*. Cambridge, MA: MIT Press.

Velmans, M. (2009) *Understanding Consciousness*, 2nd edn. London: Routledge.

Watson, J. D. ([1953] 2012) *The Double Helix*. London: Phoenix e-book.

Weber, M. ([1904–05] 1974) *The Protestant Ethic and the Spirit of Capitalism*. London: Unwin.

Whitehead, A. N. (1927–28] 1985) *Process and Reality*. New York: The Free Press.

Wilkinson, R. and Pickett, K. (2010) *The Spirit Level: Why More Equal Societies Almost Always Do Better*. London: Penguin.

SECTION II

SETTING OUT ON THE JOURNEY

CONTENTS

Perhaps there is little that is more daunting than being poised at the very start of something. Whether one is travelling to an unfamiliar place, being exposed to a novel situation, or taking initial, tentative steps in the acquisition of a new skill, it is rarely entirely comfortable to feel like a babe in the woods. Alongside the discomfort, however, there is often the thrill of excitement, especially when one is starting out on a significant path, a journey towards a qualification in a rewarding and challenging profession. Whatever the balance of anxiety and anticipation, these are often the moments one feels most in need of a guide. Section II of *The Handbook of Counselling Psychology* aims to serve as that guide, so if you are beginning your own training and embarking on your first steps towards a career in counselling psychology, this section is dedicated to this phase of your development.

Taken as a group, the authors of this section have experienced – as trainees, trainers, or both – over half of the counselling psychology programmes that currently exist in the United Kingdom. While the specific structures of training programmes or the Qualification in Counselling Psychology (QCoP) vary, and will change over time, much remains consistent about the experiences of early-stage trainees, and the authors in this section have a keen sense of their needs. Having this section close at hand, particularly during application for training and during the first year or two on a programme, will be invaluable not just for trainees but for those who support them – trainers, supervisors and placement providers.

The first chapter in this section, 'Designing your life map' (Chapter 3), guides the reader through reflective activities that will help to anchor trainees in their values and to get a sense of the place of training in their lives. Continuing the theme, 'Becoming a reflective practitioner' (Chapter 4) discusses the core counselling psychology value of reflexivity and its manifestation in training and in clinical practice. While every programme is different, 'Engaging with academia and training programmes' (Chapter 5) orientates the reader to the common features of counselling psychology training; importantly, it sensitises the aspirant or early-stage counselling psychology trainee as to how this academic context may differ from those previously experienced.

Finding placement work is often an area of anxiety for new trainees, so 'Entering clinical placements' (Chapter 6) covers not just acquiring placements but getting off to the best possible start. Once on placement, finding a 'good supervisor' becomes the next order of business, but do most supervisees neglect the other side of the equation, that is, what it is to be a 'competent supervisee'? 'Becoming a supervisee' (Chapter 7) explores and guides the reader towards such competence. Finally, 'Engaging with research' (Chapter 8) aims to encourage and inspire trainees to embrace their research and to incorporate it into their training from the outset.

Welcome to the very start of something quite exciting.

3
DESIGNING YOUR LIFE MAP
LÉONIE SUGARMAN

INTRODUCTION

The *Handbook* of which this chapter is a part envisions the process of becoming and being a counselling psychologist as a journey. Take a look at the section headings – they describe you as 'setting out', 'finding your way', encountering different landscapes and territories, and, over time, 'becoming a guide'. Similar metaphors are frequently applied to our journey through the life course (Lakoff, 1993; Lakoff and Turner, 1989) and the title of the present chapter, being concerned with the process of designing your life map, is in similar vein. Located within the 'setting out' section, its focus is on what Rønnestad and Skovholt (2013; Skovholt, 2012) describe as the novice student stage, but it should not be assumed this is a once-and-for-all process. No longer does 'career' denote step-wise, linear progression along a single career path. The notion of an ever-rising career ladder – some sort of 'stairway to heaven' – only ever applied to a minority of generally white, male, professional workers and has, since the latter part of the twentieth century, been replaced by notions of a boundaryless (Arthur and Rousseau, 2001; Sullivan and Arthur, 2006), protean (Gubler et al., 2014; Hall, 2004), kaleidoscopic (Mainiero and Sullivan, 2006; Sullivan and Mainiero, 2008) or portfolio career (Gold and Fraser, 2002; Handy, 2002). We live in an age of change and uncertainty where the future is largely unpredictable.

While the stable organisations and largely secure employment that characterised much of the twentieth century offered a firm basis for building a career and envisioning a future, the changing job market and unsettled economy of the twenty-first century has brought a new social arrangement of work in which temporary assignments and time-limited projects frequently replace permanent jobs (Savickas, 2012). I am sure that many of you have experienced this first hand, and while counselling psychology has the potential to offer a relatively straightforward career path, it is not immune to the shift in focus from career as maturation in a stable medium to a focus on career as adaptation to a changing landscape. 'The 20th-century meta-phor of career as a recognizable path through life has now changed to a 21st-century metaphor of career as carrier of meaning. Today, the metaphor is career as a cart or car that carries the person into uncharted territory' (Savickas, 2013: 150). Rather than 'career paths', it is prefer-able to think of 'life trajectories' in which we progressively design and build our own lives, including our work careers (Savickas et al., 2009). This requires regular reflection on and revaluation of our self and our environment, receptivity to feedback, and the imagination of possible selves (Oyserman and James, 2011). A flexible life map rather than a pre-set route plan is the order of the day.

The 'growth-maintenance-decline' model that has traditionally characterised much devel-opmental psychology does not fit this twenty-first-century notion of career. More appropriate is the notion of the life course as an alternating sequence of change and consolidation, with periods of change, upheaval and transition typically lasting some 3–5 years and periods of consolidation and step-wise progression typically lasting in the region of 5–7 years (Levinson, 1990). During the periods of change and transition key aspects of your current lifestyle are terminated and key decisions are made in one or more significant area of life – for example, relationships, work, living arrangements and personal philosophy. Following the upheavals is a period during which the changes are implemented and their consequences adapted to and lived through. These are not, of course, periods devoid of change, but the changes tend to be in a particular direction along a particular path, rather than the turning upside down of your world with completely new routes and lifestyles up for grabs. It may be that you, at the outset of your counselling psychology training, have a foot in both the change and the consolidation camp (for the boundaries between phases may be far from clear-cut). Having made and implemented key decisions concerning your future career – and also, possibly, about finances, family arrangements and where to live, etc. – you are now entering a phase where you must live through the consequences of your decisions. While the details of your route through your years of counselling psychology training may remain vague, to a significant extent you have, for better or worse, 'made your bed' and are now striving to lie in it. However, by seeing the natural rhythm of the life course as the never-ending sequence of alternating phases, you can be sure that at some point in the future you will move into another period of upheaval. It may be that this constant need for building re-evaluation points into our life feels wearisome, and we may yearn for a future characterised by greater stability and certainty. But such a dream is unsustainable, and the inevitable future periods of upheaval mean that we continue to have the opportunity to make significant changes in our life, and the decisions we make now do not set our future in stone.

Thus, planning a career is not a question of once and for all matching yourself to a par-ticular a job. Rather, it is a process of both searching for work that is compatible with your interests, talents and values, and also developing life preparedness – 'a healthy state of vigi-lance regarding one's career well-being as well as alertness to resources and opportunities on which one can capitalize' (Lent, 2013: 7). Such preparedness encourages us to use proac-tive strategies to manage barriers, build supports and otherwise take control of our own career-life future. The present chapter suggests strategies and concepts that can facilitate the development of such a stance. Its goal is to promote the development of life preparedness by presenting a number of concepts and strategies that you can call on in the design of your life map. These concepts and strategies constitute what Mahrer (2004) calls models of usefulness – that is, conceptual tools that assist us to achieve some goal. They provide ways of developing alternative constructions of events and, as such, can be thought of as convenient fictions (fictions not in the sense of being wrong, but in the sense of being created) that are effective in achieving some purpose – here the design of a life map. These models of usefulness constitute concepts and strategies that I have argued (Sugarman, 2004, 2012) are also relevant to work with clients, and elaboration of this point forms the final section of the chapter.

LIFE-SPACE MAPPING

Near the beginning of their training journey, I have frequently invited fledgling therapists to construct a map of their life space, and I would encourage you to do the same. Life-space mapping (Peavy, 2004; Rodger, 2006, 2010) is a non-linear and potentially non-textual way of exploring the self in context and, as such, is a valuable tool for exploring and facilitating decisions about both your own life course and those of your future clients. It recognises that, while there will undoubtedly be some similarities, for each of you the personal meaning of your training as a counselling psychologist will be unique. Viewing the self in context through the lens of life-space mapping draws back the camera, as it were, from a focus entirely on your training in order to encompass other elements of your self and the context in which you are embedded. A life-space map is a visual representation of the personal niche (Willi, 1999), life structure (Levinson, 1990) or life space – defined here as the self and the networks of personally meaningful people, relationships, experiences and circumstances (social, cultural and material), with the relationships between the different parts of the map hinting at how you make meaning of your world.

There are many ways to construct a life-space map, but, as a start, I suggest that you arm yourself with, at a minimum, a large sheet of paper (at least A3 size) and some felt-tip pens – ideally of various sizes and colours. Your life-space map could possibly be squashed onto a sheet of A4 paper, or the back of an envelope, but you will be able to be more creative and comprehensive if you give yourself a larger canvas to work on. Another valuable tool would be a number of small 'post-it' notes. This means you can use one post-it note for each element within your life space, moving them around on the map until you are satisfied with their location. If you use post-it notes of different colours you can colour code the different factors if you like – one colour for each type of element. These materials are then used to construct a visual representation, or 'map', that depicts the people, activities, plans, and other elements that are important parts of your life at the current time. Stepwise instructions are shown in Box 3.1.

Box 3.1   Life-space mapping

While there are many ways to construct a life-space map – and certainly there are no 'right' or 'wrong' ways – the following procedure is suggested:

- Take your sheet of paper and place your name in the centre of the page.
- Think about your life at this present moment. What are the main factors occupying your time, your thoughts and your energy? What are your main preoccupations, interests, concerns…?
- Write each significant element – particular people, places, experiences, activities, etc. – on a separate 'post-it' note.
- Show the importance of these elements to you and to each other through their physical placement on the sheet of paper. In this way create a map of your personal life space. Move the 'elements' around until you are satisfied with their position.
- Use connecting lines, drawings, words, colours, and shading, etc. to indicate the quality and nature of the interrelationships between the elements and between them and yourself.
- When complete, reflect on your life-space map and the nature of your life space: What are your initial impressions? What do you like about it? How rich a tapestry is it? What is missing? What would you like to change?
- If possible, work with one or two of your fellow students to talk through and compare your life-space maps.
- Note down and reflect on what you have learned from this activity.

While the completion of a map can be immediately instructive, relevant questions to ask of a life-space map include: What type of item or 'element' have I included in the map? It is mainly other people, or does it include more diverse features such activities, places, objects, organisations or personal values? Are the items positive and facilitative, negative and inhibitory – or both? What is the interaction between the elements? In what ways do they impact on other each other? How has the map changed? What might it have looked like six months ago? Two years, ten years ago? How might it change in the future? By addressing these questions life-space mapping can be a foundation for goal planning and life design.

The life space is dynamic and changing, and comparing past and present life-space maps can facilitate the exploration of change and loss. Repeating the life-space mapping at various times during the course of your training can be instructive. I have found that, when used during the early stages of the student journey, life-space mapping (and, crucially, dialogue in pairs or small groups following the activity) can facilitate student induction and sense of group identity, and can contribute to student learning by promoting self-awareness and creativity in learning. When comparing the life-space maps constructed by students in year two of their course with the maps created on entry, it is apparent that the maps are also capable of capturing change and development across time. While most (but not all) students constructed stylistically similar maps on both occasions, typically, the later maps showed greater complexity and awareness of interconnections between elements, greater clarity and less chaos, and more explicit emotional expression. As such, these observations facilitated the students' reflective learning. See the companion website for examples of life-space maps – although preferably only after completing your own.

Of particular relevance to you now, near the outset of your counselling psychology journey, is the fact that life-space mapping can also be used to help imagine and plan for the future. 'Possible selves are the selves we imagine ourselves becoming in the future, the selves we hope to become, the selves we are afraid we may become, and the selves we fully expect we will become' (Oyserman and Fryberg, 2006: 17). From maps of hoped-for selves, specific plans and action strategies can be developed to promote movement towards them. And likewise, we can take concrete actions to avoid or come to terms with feared future selves. In other words, possible selves are constructed rather than given and are never complete (Collin and Guichard, 2011).

The life-space map you are directed to complete in the box above is a snapshot of now – your life space as it currently is. Given that you are, as this section of the *Handbook* assumes, near the beginning of your counselling psychology training, it is likely that your current life space differs in significant ways from how it was one, two or three years ago. It is also likely that three, four or five years from now it will be different again. The next two sections of this chapter introduce models of usefulness that can be called upon to explore change and stability in the life space: first, through the concept of transition, and, secondly, through the notion of stability zones and support convoys.

TRANSITION

Put your current life-space map to one side for the moment, and think about the composition of your life space some two years ago. What has changed? Were those changes planned or unexpected? Welcome, unwelcome, or a mixture of both? Are the changes done and dusted, or are you still in the midst of the change process? It is likely that at least some of these changes constitute psychosocial transitions. From several possible definitions of transition (Ruble and Seidman, 1996), I find that I return most often to an early definition offered by Nancy Schlossberg – a psychologist who went on to devote much of her career to the study of transitions in adult life (Anderson et al., 2012). She defined a psychosocial transition as the process occurring when 'an event or non-event results in a change in assumptions about oneself and the world and thus requires a corresponding change in one's behaviour and relationships' (Schlossberg, 1981: 5). I return to this definition for two reasons. First, it focuses on internal rather than external change, prioritising changes in self-identity rather than in behaviour or social status. This is in keeping with the focus of the chapter on the personal meaning and interpretation of the life space at least as much as its objective characteristics. Secondly, this definition is notable because it includes non-events (that is, hoped for or antici- pated events that did not in fact occur) as possible triggers of transition. This recognises that failure to gain a place on a particular course, obtain an anticipated promotion or conceive a planned baby, for example, may provoke as significant a transition as the course, new job or baby would have done. Look back at your life-space map and, more broadly, think about the key transitions you have experienced in your life, and those you anticipate for the future.

Schlossberg and her colleagues (Anderson et al., 2012) talk of moving out of an old life space, through a period of searching for a new life, and into a new life structure characterised by commitment to a new set of roles, routines and assumptions about oneself. This sequence of disengagement, searching and re-engagement echoes Levinson's sequence of alternating structure-changing and structure-building phases, and also shares much with the work of William Bridges (2004), another long-time worker in the field of transitions. Bridges makes the point that transition is not simply another word for change. Whereas change is situational, transition is psychological. Events such as job change, bereavement or taking a course in counselling psychology do not of themselves constitute transitions. Transition is 'the inner reorientation and self-redefinition that you have to go through in order to incorporate any of those changes into your life' (Bridges, 2004: xiii). Thus, like Schlossberg (1981), Bridges focuses on the internal dynamics rather than the external concomitants of transition. Bridges (2004) goes on to propose that transitions actually begin with an *ending*. This is followed by a period of *confusion and distress*, out of which *new beginnings* emerge. In describing the period of confusion and distress as a zone of fertile emptiness (although 'fertile chaos' might capture the experience more accurately), Bridges offers us an instructive model of usefulness. We can think of the time of fertile emptiness as a liminal zone, existing between an old past and a new future. Is this perhaps where you were before your counselling psychology training place was confirmed and in the days and weeks leading up to the start of your course?

Liminality is a threshold, a state of being betwixt-and-between, neither-this-nor-that, neither me nor not-me. It can be a scary and unnerving place to be, and the temptation is often to rush through the void or else try to return to the security of a former life structure. This, again, may be something you can recognise in the consequences of your own decision to take up your place on your training programme. It may be that some of the endings associated with this new beginning – handing in your notice at work, saying goodbye to colleagues or clients, giving up your evening classes or allotment, moving home, etc. – left you fearful as well as excited. You may have been tempted to give up the course before it began and return to a more familiar and seemingly safer way of life.

But, liminality is also a place full of energy and potential. If we have the courage to stay in this space, we may be able to use it as a moratorium from our everyday routine that allows for personal reflection, reappraisal and redirection. Engaging with life-space mapping can help you to stay within this place of opportunity, whereas a very specific plan can lead to the premature cutting off of other options and opportunities.

STABILITY ZONES AND SUPPORT CONVOYS

As tumults and upheavals cry out and grab our attention, it becomes all too easy to overlook that which might, by remaining constant, hold us steady. Think about the structure of your life space today in relation to how it was two years ago. Whereas the previous section invited you to focus on what had changed, you are now asked to consider what has remained constant.

Elements within the life space that have not been lost or turned upside-down can assume enhanced significance during times of transition. They operate as anchors, or stability zones (Pedler et al., 2013), that we depend on when all else is confused, uncertain and frightening. More or less any element within the personal life space has the potential to operate as a stability zone. Frequently, however, they are associated with other *people* (in the form of valued and enduring relationships); *activities* that offer support or distraction; *ideas and values* that underpin personal standards and commitments; *places*, both large-scale (like a country) and small-scale (for example, a street, a garden or a particular room); *belongings*, in the guise of favourite, familiar, comforting possessions; and *organisations* such as professional bodies, work, social, cultural, spiritual or other organisations with which we identify. Perhaps your identity as a counselling psychologist or your association with a particular training course or university is already, or is in the process of becoming, a significant stability zone for you.

While offering a degree of security and support, it is important to recognise that neither the stability zones themselves nor your requirements of them are static. Needs, situations and roles change over time and stability zones my fade or become unavailable. By the same token, stability zones that are clung onto even when they no longer provide that which is needed may weigh you down rather than hold you up. Thus, stability zones can never be sorted out once and for all. They require regular examination, clarification and nurturing so that some are always available to provide reassurance, security and confidence when others are lost or discarded.

Life-space maps and stability-zone reviews are like snapshots, capturing a picture of the person at a particular moment. Linked to the notion of stability zones is that of a personal support convoy (Kahn and Antonucci, 1980; Levitt, 2005), often an important component in the design of your life map. Support convoys transport the person across time. They consist of networks of relationships that surround each of us and move with us through life, providing continuity of support while also changing in structure over time. As we move through life new relationships will be added to the support convoy and/or become more central, while others will fade in importance or be lost. It can be helpful to visualise your support convoy as a series of concentric circles, with yourself at the centre, with your most consistently important convoy members in the inner circle and the most transient on the periphery. Embarking on your counselling psychology training may well have triggered a change and realignment in the make-up of your support convoy. Friends and colleagues who were central to your support convoy may have moved – temporarily or permanently – towards the periphery, perhaps already being replaced with new members drawn from your fellow trainees.

The process of life-space mapping, with a particular focus on points of change and sources of stability can provide a basis for designing a life map to inform and direct your life trajectory as counselling psychologists. The professional, personal and career issues addressed elsewhere in this *Handbook* are all likely to figure as components in a dynamic and evolving life map to which you can return and reconsider throughout your career. Furthermore, in the therapeutic encounter your life space overlaps and interacts with that of your clients. The concepts and techniques involved in life-space mapping have relevance not only to you as a trainee counselling psychologist and with regard to your own life design, but also in relation to your work with clients. The following sections of the chapter consider some of the ways in which this is the case.

LIFE-SPACE MAPPING WITH CLIENTS

The process of constructing and reflecting on a life-space map with clients can facilitate the development of an effective working relationship and can reveal personal values, assumptions and feelings that the client may have struggled to put into words. In comparison with the spoken word or narrative-style writing, mapping can provide a more creative and less structured way of describing the life space. It is a client-centred method that may be accessible to clients who are not verbally oriented or who find it hard to put their feelings into words. It has been used, for example, to facilitate life-career planning in adolescents (Shephard and Marshall, 1999) and to help clients integrate spirituality into the clinical dialogue (Hodge, 2005), including in a hospice environment (Bushfield, 2010). It has also been developed as a strategy for evaluating the progress and outcome of counselling (Rodger, 2006, 2010).

CLIENTS' TRANSITIONS AND THE ZONE OF FERTILE EMPTINESS

It is likely that many clients will come to you at a point of crisis in their lives and in the midst of transition. Indeed, like ripples from a stone thrown into a pond, one transition may trigger another, such that your clients may experience multiple upheavals in several different areas of their life space. Their experience will frequently have forced them into profound, often involuntary, and possibly sudden reassessments of their self-image – their sense of who they are. Such clients may well be experiencing the chaos and uncertainty that ensues when multiple support structures and stability zones are falling apart. It will be your role to facilitate their journey through this void. In doing this, you would do well to be familiar with accounts of the transition experience that are more detailed than the broadly drawn phases of 'ending', 'emptiness' and 'new beginnings'. Of several candidates, it is Kubler-Ross's (2009) work on death and dying that is perhaps the most influential and widely disseminated. It is a landmark example of a life event being viewed as a long-term process rather than a point-in-time occurrence and proposes five distinct, but overlapping stages in the process of facing and coming to terms with death: *denial, anger, bargaining, depression* and *acceptance.*

Kubler-Ross's formulation has had an immense impact on the attitude and practice of professionals working with the dying, and has been widely popularised in books for those facing terminal illness and their families. The sequence bears a close resemblance to John Bowlby's (1998) phases of grief: *shock or numbness*; *pining, yearning and protest*; *disorganisation and despair*; and *readjustment.* Many other losses have been studied and in the mid-1970s a generalised model of transition dynamics was proposed (Hopson and Adams, 1976; Hopson et al., 1988), suggesting that disruptions to our accustomed way of life trigger a relatively predictable cycle of reactions and feelings: *shock and immobilisation; reaction and minimisation; self-doubt; acceptance of change; testing the new reality; finding meaning;* and *integration.*

Such stage theories of transition have been both widely accepted and widely criticised, with a main and general criticism centring on rejection of what is seen as a 'one-size-fits-all' mentality that denies individual differences and attempts to force people's experience into predetermined categories rather than work with the unique experience of a unique individual. If, however, such frameworks are seen as models of usefulness rather than universal truths, then they can be recognised as indicative patterns rather than rigid prescriptions. As such, accounts of the transition sequence come laden with many qualifications and caveats. It is important to be aware that passage through the cycle is rarely smooth and one-directional. People vacillate between stages and may be working on several stages simultaneously. No definitive guidelines can be given either as to the length of any one phase or to the degree of vacillation of mood. Nor can it be assumed that all individuals will complete the cycle with regard to every transition. We may become 'stuck' – willingly or not – at any stage. It is also important to recognise that in accepting the new reality and moving on, we do not 'put the past behind us' and leave it there. More usually, ties are loosened and renegotiated, rather than broken completely (Klass et al., 1996; Neimeyer, 2001).

Likewise, the timings and specific nature of the transition are also important. For example, Kubler-Ross's sequence was first identified in studies carried out with people in young and middle adulthood with terminal cancer. The timing of their likely death will cut short the normally expected life span, and it is feasible that this could accentuate both the denial and the anger. Among older people who have already lived longer than they expected to, acceptance of impending death without denial may be less difficult. Also, the fact that cancer can go into and out of remission may make denial seem a reasonable and rational response, providing a justification for bargaining rather than resignation to the inevitable. Such nuances may be lost when the memorable sequence of stages is cited without reference to the specific context in which it was developed.

Despite the above caveats and qualifications, the transition cycle offers signposts as to how the emotional concomitants to change – and in particular loss – are likely to pan out for the individual. It serves to suggest how clients' needs may change as they move through its different stages. During the first part of the cycle, clients' preoccupations are primarily emotional, with an increasing involvement of cognitive processes as they move through the stages of testing and the search for meaning. Arguably, the focus of a counselling psychologist's work should similarly change as a client moves through these stages.

While each person's experience of loss is unique, this does not mean it shares nothing with any other experience – either the experiences of other people or other experiences of the same person. There may be occasions where knowledge of the transition cycle can help quell despondency or feelings of being overwhelmed, and facilitate, instead, a sense of hope, direction and reassurance, and recognition that things need not always remain the same. This, in turn, can give clients the courage to remain within their zone of fertile emptiness, thereby allowing for the emergence of new beginnings. Appreciating that the sequence of emotions described in the transition cycle is 'normal' (that is, not inherently pathological) and 'normative' (that is, experienced by others) can be reassuring, helping to lessen the loneliness of clients' suffering.

CLIENT STABILITY ZONES

The concepts of stability zones and support convoys, similarly, have relevance for clients and for the therapeutic relationship, providing a valuable lens through which to explore a client's life-space map. How adequate, for example, are clients' support convoys and repertoire of stability zones? How enduring? What should be retained and what needs changing? Have some stability zones outlived their usefulness?

Clients – especially those in crisis – may have suffered the loss or disruption of many stability zones. It is important to bear in mind that elements in the therapeutic relationship which are familiar to you to the extent that they are part of your own sense of security, stability and identity – the office where you meet, for example, or the whole notion of 'psychology' and 'counselling' – may be alien and frightening for clients, adding to their sense of being 'all at sea' (to continue the journey metaphor). If clients are hospitalised or in some other strange environment, then their loss of familiar anchors is likely to be all the greater. It follows from this that an important question for you to reflect on as a counselling psychologist is the extent to which you could be, are and should be a stability zone for your clients.

The therapeutic relationship has the potential to operate as a stability zone, providing a secure base (Bowlby, 2012) and a holding environment (Winnicott, 1960, 1990) that is able to offer consistency and predictability to the client, and also contain (Bion, 1989) and accept all parts of the client, including those parts of which the client is fearful, ashamed or unaware (Casement, 1985). Such holding and containment acknowledges and accepts the chaos or void of the zone of fertile emptiness can help to provide the space from which new beginnings can emerge.

While the therapeutic bond can, notably in long-term therapy, demonstrate the characteristics of an attachment relationship (Farber et al., 1995; Obegi, 2008; Parish and Eagle, 2003; Skourteli and Lennie, 2011), it is important to be sensitive to the limits on your capacity to operate as a stability zone for your clients, and, indeed, to its appropriateness. You are, it must be remembered, only a temporary presence in clients' life. Clients who see you for one hour a week will still spend the vast majority of their time elsewhere. Of course, the impact of that one hour can be profound and can extend well beyond the actual face-to-face contact, but it is also the case that in many, perhaps the majority, of instances you will not be a long-term member of your clients' support convoy. Endings, in particular, can be hard for clients who are heavily invested in the counselling relationship as a stability zone and/or the counselling psychologist as an attachment figure. It is a dynamic to which you will constantly need to be sensitive.

In reflecting on your role as a stability zone for clients it is also important to consider the flip side of this coin – the extent to which clients might operate as a stability zone for you.

Your professional identity as a counselling psychologist has already been suggested as a possible stability zone, but what about individual clients? It can be important to consider whether there are occasions where you want to 'hang on' to clients with whom you think you work well. Do you feel bereft when clients finish seeing you, especially if they terminated counselling suddenly or unexpectedly? Supervision can be a key stability zone for you in these circumstances, providing a place where you can reflect on the extent to which these emotions are appropriate concomitants of professional commitment and the extent that they may they reflect a desire for the therapeutic relationship to meet your needs rather than those of the client.

CONCLUSION

While you share with your fellow trainees, albeit in your own individual way, the transition into counselling psychology training, it would be risky to make assumptions about other things that you might have it common (Achenbaum and Cole, 2007). You are likely to have reached this point via differing routes. This chapter has proposed life-map design as a strategy for managing your training and career as a counselling psychologist in the twenty-first century. I have suggested the process of life-space mapping, with its interrogation of and evaluation of both change and stability, as an approach to personal reflection that you can return to at decision and re-evaluation points throughout your training and beyond.

I have also argued that the concepts discussed in this chapter resonate with your work with clients. They constitute models of usefulness and contribute to what Gerard Egan, in the preface to one of the many editions of *The Skilled Helper*, described as a working knowledge – a theoretical and research knowledge translated into 'the kind of applied understandings that enable helpers to work with clients' (Egan, 1990: 17). The goal of life-map design is life preparedness, something intimately linked to notions of agency, resilience, prevention and adaptability (Lent, 2013), qualities that, as counselling psychologists, you will wish to promote not only in yourselves, but also in your clients.

Visit the companion website to see examples of life-space maps.

REFERENCES

Achenbaum, W.A. and Cole, T.R. (2007) 'Transforming age-based policies to meet fluid life-course needs', in E.A. Pruchno and M.A. Smyer (eds), *Challenges of an Aging Society: Ethical Dilemmas, Political Issues*. Baltimore, MD: Johns Hopkins University Press. pp. 238–67.

Anderson, M.L., Goodman, J. and Schlossberg, N.K. (2012) *Counseling Adults in Transition*, 4th edition. New York: Springer.

Arthur, M.B. and Rousseau, D.M. (eds) (2001) *The Boundaryless Career: A New Employment Principle for a New Organizational Era*. Oxford: Oxford University Press.

Bion, W.R. (1989) *Learning from Experience*, new edition. London: Karnac Books.

Bowlby, J. (1998) *Loss (Attachment and Loss: Volume 3)*. London: Pimlico.

Bowlby, J. (2012) *A Secure Base: Parent–Child Attachment and Healthy Human Development*. Routledge Classic Edition. Abingdon: Routledge.

Bridges, W. (2004) *Transitions: Making Sense of Life's Changes*, 2nd edition. Cambridge, MA: Da Capo.

Bushfield, S. (2010) 'Use of spiritual life maps in a hospice setting', *Journal of Religion, Spirituality and Aging*, 22(4): 254–70.

Casement, P. (1985) *On Learning from the Patient*. Brighton and Hove: Routledge.

Collin, A. and Guichard, J. (2011) 'Constructing the self in career theory and counselling interventions', in P.J. Hartung and L.M. Subich (eds), *Developing Self in Work and Career: Concepts, Cases, and Contexts*. Washington, DC: American Psychological Association. pp. 89–106.

Egan, G. (1990) *The Skilled Helper: A Systematic Approach to Effective Helping*, 4th edition. Monterey, CA: Brooks/Cole.

Farber, B.A., Lippert, R.A. and Nevas, D.B. (1995) 'The therapist as attachment figure', *Psychotherapy Theory, Research, Practice, Training*, 32(2): 204–12.

Gold, M. and Fraser, J. (2002) 'Managing self-management: Successful transitions to portfolio careers', *Work, Employment and Society*, 16(2): 579–97.

Gubler, M., Arnold, J. and Coombs, C. (2014) 'Reassessing the protean career concept: Empirical findings, conceptual components, and measurement', *Journal of Organizational Behavior*, 35(S1): S23–S40.

Hall, D.T. (2004) 'The protean career: A quarter-century journey', *Journal of Vocational Behavior*, 65(1): 1–13.

Handy, C. (2002) *The Age of Unreason*. London: Random House Business.

Hodge, D.R. (2005) 'Spiritual lifemaps: A client-centred pictorial instrument for spiritual assessment, planning and intervention', *Social Work*, 50(1): 77–87.

Hopson, B. and Adams, J. (1976) 'Towards an understanding of transition: Defining some boundaries of transition dynamics', in J. Adams, J. Hayes and B. Hopson (eds), *Transition: Understanding and Managing Personal Change*. London: Martin Robertson. pp. 3–23.

Hopson, B., Scally, M. and Stafford, K. (1988) *Transitions: The Challenge of Change*. Leeds: Lifeskills.

Kahn, R.L. and Antonucci, T.C. (1980) 'Convoys over the life course: Attachment, roles and social support', in P.B. Baltes and O.G. Brim (eds), *Life-Span Development and Behavior*, Volume 3. New York: Academic Press. pp. 254–83.

Klass, D., Silverman, P. and Nickman, S. (eds) (1996) *Continuing Bonds: New Understandings of Grief*. London: Taylor & Francis.

Kubler-Ross, E. (2009) *On Death and Dying: What the Dying have to Teach Doctors, Clergy, Nurses and their own Families*, 40th Anniversary Edition. London: Routledge.

Lakoff, G. (1993) 'The contemporary theory of metaphor', in A. Ortony (ed.), *Metaphor and Thought*, 2nd edition. Cambridge: Cambridge University Press. pp. 201–51.

Lakoff, G. and Turner, M. (1989) *More than Cool Reason: A Field Guide to Poetic Metaphor.* Chicago: Chicago University Press.

Lent, R.W. (2013) 'Career-life preparedness: Revisiting career planning and adjustment in the new workplace', *Career Development Quarterly*, 61(1): 2–14.

Levinson, D.J. (1990) 'A theory of life structure development in adulthood', in C.N. Alexander and E.J. Langer (eds), *Higher Stages of Human Development: Perspectives on Adult Growth.* New York: Oxford University Press. pp. 35–53.

Levitt, M.J. (2005) 'Social relations in childhood and adolescence: The convoy model perspective', *Human Development*, 48(1): 28–47.

Mahrer, A.R. (2004) *Theories of Truth, Models of Usefulness: Toward a Revolution in the Field of Psychotherapy.* London: Whurr.

Mainiero, L.A. and Sullivan, S.E. (2006) *The Opt-out Revolt: Why People are Leaving Companies to Create Kaleidoscope Careers.* Mountain View, CA: Davies-Black.

Neimeyer, R.A. (2001) 'Meaning reconstruction and loss', in R.A. Neimeyer (ed.), *Meaning Reconstruction and the Experience of Loss.* Washington, DC: American Psychological Association. pp. 1–9.

Obegi, J.H. (2008) 'The development of the client–therapist bond through the lens of attachment theory'. *Psychotherapy Theory, Research, Practice, Training*, 25(4): 431–46.

Oyserman, D. and Fryberg, S.A. (2006) 'The possible selves of diverse adolescents: Content and function across gender, race, and national origin', in C. Dunkel and J. Kerpelman (eds), *Possible Selves: Theory, Research and Implications.* New York: Nova Science. pp. 17–39.

Oyserman, D. and James, L. (2011) 'Possible identities', in S.J. Schwartz, K. Luyckx and V.L. Vignoles (eds), *Handbook of Identity Theory and Research. Volume 1: Structures and Processes.* New York: Springer. pp. 117–45.

Parish, M. and Eagle, M.N. (2003) 'Attachment to the therapist'. *Psychoanalytic Psychology*, 20(2): 271–86.

Peavy, R.V. (2004) *Sociodynamic Counselling: A Practical Approach to Meaning-Making.* Chagrin Falls, OH: Taos Institute.

Pedler, M., Burgoyne, M.J. and Boydell, T. (2013) *A Manager's Guide to Self Development*, 6th edition. Maidenhead: McGraw-Hill.

Rodger, B. (2006) 'Life space mapping: Preliminary results from the development of a new method for investigating counselling outcomes', *Counselling and Psychotherapy Research*, 6(4): 227–32.

Rodger, B. (2010) 'Life space mapping: Developing a visual method for investigating the outcome of counselling and psychotherapy from the client's frame of reference'. PhD dissertation, University of Abertay, Dundee.

Rønnestad, M.H. and Skovolt, T.M. (2013) *The Developing Practitioner: Growth and Stagnation of Therapists and Counselors.* New York: Routledge.

Ruble, D.N. and Seidman, E. (1996) 'Social transitions: Windows into social psychological processes', in E.T. Higgins and A.W. Kruglanski (eds), *Social Psychology: Handbook of Basic Principles.* New York: Guilford Press. pp. 830–56.

Savickas, M.L. (2012) 'Life design: A paradigm for career intervention in the 21st century', *Journal of Counseling and Development,* 90(1): 13–19.

Savickas, M.L. (2013) 'Career construction theory and practice', in S.D. Brown and R.W. Lent (eds), *Career Development and Counseling: Putting Theory to Work,* 2nd edition. Hoboken, NJ: John Wiley & Sons. pp. 147–83.

Savickas, M.L. et al. (2009) 'Life designing: A paradigm for career construction in the 21st century', *Journal of Vocational Behavior,* 75(3): 239–50.

Schlossberg, N.K. (1981) 'A model for analysing human adaptation to transition', *Counseling Psychologist,* 9(1): 2–18.

Shephard, B. and Marshall, A. (1999) 'Possible selves mapping: Life-career exploration with young adolescents', *Canadian Journal of Counselling,* 33(1): 37–54.

Skourteli, M.C. and Lennie, C. (2011) 'The therapeutic relationship from an attachment theory perspective', *Counselling Psychology Review,* 26(1), 20–33.

Skovholt, T.M. (2012) *Becoming a Therapist: On the Path to Mastery.* New York: John Wiley & Sons.

Sugarman, L. (2004) *Counselling and the Life Course.* London: Sage.

Sugarman, L. (2012) 'Age', in C. Feltham and I. Horton (eds), *The SAGE Handbook of Counselling and Psychotherapy,* 3rd edition. London: Sage. pp. 34–8.

Sullivan, S.E. and Arthur, M.B. (2006) 'The evolution of the boundaryless career concept: Examining physical and psychological mobility', *Journal of Vocational Behavior,* 69(1), 19–29.

Sullivan, S.E. and Mainiero, L.A. (2008) 'Using the kaleidoscope career model to understand the changing patterns of women's careers: Designing HRD programs that attract and retain women', *Advances in Developing Human Resources,* 10(1): 32–49.

Willi, J. (1999) *Ecological Psychotherapy: Developing by Shaping the Personal Niche.* Seattle, WA: Hogrefe & Huber.

Winnicott, D.W. (1960) 'The theory of the parent–infant relationship', *International Journal of Psychoanalysis,* 41: 585–95.

Winnicott, D.W. (1990) *The Maturational Processes and the Facilitating Environment: Studies in the Theory of Emotional Development,* new edition. London: Karnac Books.

4
BECOMING A REFLECTIVE PRACTITIONER
MARK DONATI

INTRODUCTION

The concept of the 'reflective practitioner' holds a long-standing and privileged status within the professional history and identity of counselling psychology (Strawbridge and Woolfe, 2009). This is because it is a vital meta-concept that underpins many aspects of what counselling psychologists do, and how they think and learn. Moreover, when combined with other elements of their identity, counselling psychologists' skills as reflective practitioners make them distinctive and potent professionals with much to offer those with whom they work.

In order to *become* a reflective practitioner, it is important to have an understanding of what it means to be one, the kinds of skills and capacities involved, how these might be developed, and in what kinds of situations they are useful. The aim of this chapter is to explore these areas and demonstrate why being a reflective practitioner is so fundamental to the identity of a counselling psychologist. It will begin by considering the meaning and origins of the reflective practitioner concept, and the related notion of experiential learning. The centrality of these concepts to a counselling psychologist's professional development will then be discussed. The role of reflection in understanding the relational processes that underpin psychological change and therapy will also be considered. The relevance of reflective practice in a research context will be illustrated, via the concept of reflexivity, as well as its links to other key aspects of a counselling psychologist's identity. Finally, the need for and challenges to reflective practice in the wider world will be noted, along with the suggestion that counselling psychologists can play an important role in promoting reflective practice through their various domains of professional activity.

ORIGINS OF THE REFLECTIVE PRACTITIONER CONCEPT

Although a variety of definitions and models of reflective practice exist today (Finlay, 2008), the concept is most closely associated with the work of Donald Schön and his book *The Reflective Practitioner: How Professionals Think in Action* (1983). Schön defined reflective practice as 'the capacity to reflect on action so as to engage in a process of continuous learning' (p. 11). The concept emerged from his interest in understanding the processes by which professionals, such as psychotherapists, architects and engineers, think and learn. Based on his research he developed the central thesis that:

> Experienced professionals know more than they can put into words, and ... to meet the challenges of their work, they rely less on formulas and theories learned in graduate school than on the kind of improvisation and knowledge learned in practice. (Schön, 1983, p. 19)

He suggested that through practical experience, professionals develop tacit personal theories, termed 'knowing-in-action' frameworks, which they draw on to guide their actions and solve the problems involved in their work. Moreover, he argued that these implicit theories can be articulated and made explicit through a process of introspection. He developed two key concepts that summarised these ideas: *reflection-in-action*, which refers to the relatively unconscious process of thinking on one's feet based on tacit personal theories derived from experience, and *reflection-on-action*, which refers to the conscious activity of drawing out the underlying principles and processes guiding professional decision making to facilitate learning.

Schön was critical of the limitations of the paradigm of 'technical rationality' (1983, p. 21), which he felt dominated approaches to education at the time. He believed that the core skills of professional practice could not be reduced to a set of techniques or ideas, but are acquired 'on the job' through an individualised process of *experiential* rather than academic learning, under the guidance of a seasoned practitioner. Schön's work was influenced by earlier theorists, such as the American philosopher and educator John Dewey (1938). Dewey viewed learning as an active process of meaning making and interpretation rather than one of passively acquiring knowledge and skills. He viewed the teacher's role as being to facilitate a process of critical enquiry and understanding from personal experience, rather than an authoritative expert who didactically imparts knowledge to the learner.

The ideas expressed in Dewey and Schön's work have gone on to become accepted principles in many fields of educational and professional practice, such as nursing (Bulman and Schutz, 2013), social work (Knott and Scragg, 2013), counselling and psychotherapy (Bager-Charleson, 2010; Stedmon and Dallos, 2009), as well as management and organisational development (Vince, 2001). It is no coincidence that these are all fields that involve human relationships; dynamic evolving systems of knowledge; real-world problems that are not amenable to formulaic solutions; and increasing demands for accountability and evidence. In other words, these are all areas where a complex relationship exists between *theory* and *practice*, and where a process of continual critical evaluation is required to maintain optimal practice.

REFLECTION IN MODELS OF EXPERIENTIAL LEARNING

Schön's emphasis on the role of purposeful reflection in professional practice is consistent with other influential models of experiential learning. For example, Kolb (1976, 1984) posited that experiential learning follows a cyclical process that involves four key stages: (1) having a concrete *experience*, (2) observing and *reflecting* on that experience, (3) developing an abstract *conceptualisation* of the experience, and (4) *experimentation* and testing of new insights and learning (see Figure 4.1). In this process, an individual has an experience within their domain of practice, perhaps one that was significant or challenging in some way. They then engage in a process of *post hoc* analysis and reflection to identify and examine salient features. In the next stage, the individual attempts to create a more abstract theoretical explanation of what took place, in order to produce new insights and implications. In the final step, the individual applies and experiments with the insights gleaned. This produces further experiences that can be reflected on, conceptualised and learned from, thus perpetuating a cyclical process.

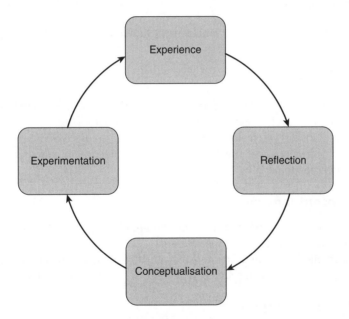

Figure 4.1   Kolb's model of experiential learning

The kind of learning outlined by Kolb is implicit in many of the teaching and assessment methods used in counselling psychology training, such as case studies and process reports (Bor and Watts, 2010: Padadopoulous et al., 2003), where trainees are asked to examine, conceptualise and identify relevant learning from their professional experiences, in order to guide future practice. Such activities help trainees develop core reflective practitioner skills, such as the capacity to explicate and critique the processes guiding their interventions, to link theory effectively to practice, to reflect on learning and identify future development needs.

Reflective exercise: An experiential learning interview

Think of a specific experience or interaction you have had with a client that you feel has been important to your learning and development as a counselling psychologist. It may be an experience that you found particularly difficult, went particularly well, where you made a mistake but learned from this, or where you had to deal with difficult feelings or processes, such as conflict, hostility or aggression, in yourself and/or your client.

Ask a friend or colleague to 'interview' you about the experience, using questions that help you to explore the four stages of the experiential learning cycle. The questions below provide some examples.

Stage 1: Experience

- Can you describe the experience or incident, including when and where it happened and what actually happened?

Stage 2: Reflecting

- What were you thinking and feeling as it was taking place, and immediately afterwards?
- Was anything particularly challenging about the situation for you?
- What assumptions did you make about the client, problem or situation?
- How did your assumptions influence your actions/practice in the situation, i.e. your responses, decision making?

Stage 3: Conceptualising

- How could you have viewed or understood the situation from another perspective? How might someone else have viewed the incident?
- Are there theoretical concepts or literature that might be useful in helping to explain what was going on, e.g. transference and countertransference, schemas, negative automatic thoughts?

Stage 4: Experimentation

- What do you think you learned from this experience?
- How did your learning influence your practice subsequently?
- What learning/development does this incident make you aware is still needed?

Debrief and reflection

- What has it been like to do this exercise?

REFLECTION IN MODELS OF THERAPIST DEVELOPMENT AND TRAINING

The importance of reflection to the process of professional development for psychotherapeutic practitioners is also well supported by research. For example, in their seminal study of therapist and counsellor development, Skovholt and Rønnestad (1995) found that an activity they referred to as 'continuous professional reflection' played a key role in maintaining healthy growth and career satisfaction in the long term. Core reflective activities, such as supervision and personal therapy, were found to be fundamental to enabling practitioners to negotiate the many challenges encountered in their work. Their study highlighted a subtle and evolving relationship between the personal and professional selves of the therapist over time, which they conceptualised in terms of a model of 'professional individuation'. For example, they found that during training therapists become aware of a significant interaction between their personal needs and motivations and their professional practice, which can be experienced as destabilising. They also tend to feel overwhelmed by new knowledge and insecure about their professional competence. However, over time, through purposeful reflective activity, they are gradually able to reach a more secure position, in which practice is guided by clinical experience, and a coherent integration of personal and professional selves.

The inextricable relationship between the personal and professional selves of the therapist is well recognised within the field of counselling psychology, and central to the rationale for personal therapy and development during training. For example, the British Psychological Society's competence standards for counselling psychologists require trainees to:

> understand the experience of therapy through active and systematic engagement in personal therapy, which will enable them to:
>
> (i) demonstrate an understanding and experience of therapy from the perspective of the client, which will be utilised to guide their own practice;
>
> (ii) demonstrate an understanding through therapy of their own life experience, and understand the impact of that experience upon practice;
>
> (iii) demonstrate an ability for critical self-reflection on the use of self in therapeutic process (British Psychological Society, 2014, p. 24)

Although commonplace in counselling and psychotherapy trainings, the requirement to engage in personal therapy is unique to counselling psychology among the family of applied psychologies, illustrating the particular emphasis it has given to reflective practice historically within mainstream psychology (Woolfe and Strawbridge, 2009). Counselling psychology's view of the client–therapist relationship as the primary vehicle of change means that the therapist's self is always regarded as implicated in the therapeutic process, irrespective of the model being used (Orlans and Van Scoyoc, 2009). The therapist's ability to make effective use of their self in the therapeutic process relies on their capacity to be aware of how personal thoughts, feelings, needs and unresolved issues are evoked during the course of their work. Training components such as personal therapy, experiential work and supervision become central activities through which a trainee's understanding of the interaction between their personal and professional selves, and their capacity to make effective use of this in their work, is developed (Donati, 2003).

BECOMING A REFLECTIVE PRACTITIONER: WHERE DOES THE JOURNEY BEGIN?

As noted previously, research suggests that during training therapists tend to become aware of significant personal factors that influenced their choice of profession (Rønnestad and Skovholt, 2012; Skovholt and Rønnestad, 1995). This implies that the relationship between the therapist's personal and professional selves extends back to a point that precedes training.

Aveline (2007, p. 521) has suggested that 'the trainee therapist has long been in the making before he or she formally enters training' to suggest that individuals develop the qualities required for the role of the therapist through prior life experience before they begin a process of professional training. Guy (1987) has proposed a number of personal attributes that constitute constructive motivating forces in the decision to pursue psychotherapeutic training. These include an interest in understanding people, an enjoyment of listening to others, a capacity for self-denial, an ability to tolerate uncertainty and the expression of feelings, and a capacity for warmth and humour.

Guy also collated studies that investigated the early backgrounds of therapists and found that they often came from backgrounds in which they had taken on a helping or care-taking role within their family, for example supporting a parent or relative who had a mental health problem. Another biographical feature identified was that of being a social outsider. This is characterised by the experience of feeling in some way different from others, which fosters a capacity for tolerance of difference in others, as well as a curiosity about the influence of contextual factors on human identity. A third key theme Guy notes in therapists' backgrounds is that of the 'wounded healer'.

Originally from Jungian psychology, the wounded healer concept relates to a commonly observed phenomenon that those who enter careers as therapists have often had their own experiences of psychological difficulty and therapy (Jung, 1985). These experiences generate a capacity to empathise with the suffering of others. Moreover, by helping others who are in difficulty, they remain engaged with their own process of self-healing and understanding. The wounded healer concept challenges a naïve notion that people who go into careers in psychotherapy are altruistic individuals who just 'like helping people'. Moreover, Guy (1987) has suggested that therapists can be motivated by unconscious needs to save, control, be loved by or act vicariously through their clients, which can undermine safe and effective practice.

From a lay perspective, one may well wonder what motivates someone to choose a career that involves listening to other people's emotional problems and being intimately engaged with their suffering on a regular basis. This is a pertinent question for those wishing to enter training to consider, as well those responsible for selecting candidates for training (Donati, 2003; Donati and Watts, 2000). The idea that the practitioner's own emotional needs are being met in an implicit way through their professional work is important as it provides another justification for the need for therapists to engage in reflective practice and personal development.

Reflective exercise: 'What are my personal motivators?'

Read through the list of possible factors below that might attract someone to a role as a therapist. Ask yourself to what extent you think each area could apply to you. Monitor your internal reactions to each statement to identify any strong resonances, positive or negative, and reflect on their meaning. Put a rating next to each statement to indicate its potential relevance to you, for example as follows: 1 low, 2 slight, 3 moderate, 4 quite high and 5 high relevance.

Table 4.1 Personal motivators

I wanted to become a therapist...	Relevance rating (1–5)
To learn more about myself	
To grow as a person	
To work on my own issues	
Because I enjoy helping others	
Because I find other people fascinating	
Because helping others is what I have always done in my life	
Because I feel I am quite different from most people	
Because helping others gives me a way to make up for things that were lacking in my own life or family	
Because I find professional/therapeutic relationships easier to manage than personal relationships	
Because I like the respect and admiration others have for people who are therapists	
Because it enables me to do something about injustices in the world that I have experienced or relate to	
Because I like being in a position of power and authority	

(Continued)

(Continued)

I wanted to become a therapist…	Relevance rating (1–5)
Because I want to share with others the benefits of therapy that I have experienced myself	
Because it gives me a way to challenge the status quo in society	
Because I feel I have a special ability to help people	
Other reason…	

Now ask yourself how any factors you have identified as potentially relevant to you might influence your practice, in helpful or unhelpful ways, and where they have come from in your life. Consider exploring further in personal therapy.

THERAPY AS A PROCESS OF EXPERIENTIAL LEARNING

As noted previously, models of reflective practice and experiential learning were developed primarily as ways of understanding learning processes in professional and educational contexts. However, I would like to suggest that these concepts can also help us understand the basic developmental processes that underpin psychological therapy and the difficulties that many of our clients have encountered.

Clients often come to therapy because of problems in living that have their origins in past experiences, from which they have developed implicit 'personal theories' that have guided subsequent experiences and behaviour. The rationale for these theories (e.g. about the self in relation to others, how to avoid painful affect or get one's needs met) can often be understood logically in terms of the individual's attempts to respond adaptively to challenging situations, using whatever resources, scripts or behavioural models were available to them at the time. Different approaches to therapy all have their own way of referring to these personal theories, whether as core beliefs, schemas, internal working models, object relationships or conditions of worth. But common to all is the idea that over time these theories become unconscious, habitual and self-reinforcing. They then act as lenses that predispose the individual to perceive and interpret their experiences and interactions with others in ways that inhibit their capacity to appraise these accurately and adaptively. Clients entering therapy often have a sense that something is not going right in their lives but feel unable to understand or resolve this for themselves, and this is usually why they come to see us for help.

The suggestion that individuals develop personal theories based on past experiences that help them deal with challenging situations, which then implicitly guide future behaviour, is of course similar to Schön's concept of *reflection-in-action*. Moreover, the idea that in order to promote further learning and development it is necessary to identify and critique the tacit theories that guide behaviour is consistent with Schön's concept of *reflection-on-action*.

Applying Kolb's model of experiential learning to the therapy process, we might also suggest that clients bring to their sessions problematic life *experiences* which the therapist helps them observe and *reflect* on, so that a more nuanced picture of what is going on can be developed. The therapist may contribute to this process by adding their own observations and suggestions, perhaps drawing attention to potentially salient aspects of the narrative (e.g. thoughts, feelings, sensations) that appear more implicit or challenging. A key part of what the therapist then brings to the therapy process is an ability to offer insights and explanations based on a body of psychological knowledge and theory. As Rizq (2006) has suggested, theory enables the therapist to offer more than just an ordinary helping relationship. Through offering formulations and interpretations, the therapist thus helps the client *conceptualise* and understand their experience in a new but potentially helpful way. These new understandings may also indicate what needs to happen in order for change to take place and presenting problems to be addressed. It thus helps the client consider new ways of thinking, feeling and acting, with which they can *experiment* through further contact with the situations they typically find problematic. The insights derived from such a process can bring a sense of relief, hope and autonomy to the client, but they can also be challenging, as they may highlight subtle investments the client has in not changing, or anxieties about what change might involve, which may be a significant part of why the client has not been able to resolve their difficulties up to now.

THERAPY AS A REFLECTIVE RELATIONSHIP

Viewing psychological therapy as a form of experiential learning helps highlight continuities in developmental processes across different contexts, as well as the centrality of reflection to these (Loewenthal and Greenwood, 2005). It also shows how normative models of learning may be applied to understand what happens when difficulties or problems arise in these processes. However, it is important to bear in mind, particularly from a counselling psychology perspective, that therapy cannot easily be reduced to a simple 'learning' process, in which client and therapist work together in a straightforward dispassionate way to figure out what is going wrong in the client's life and how to fix it. Rather, therapy is founded on a human relationship between two individuals involving complex inter-personal processes, unconscious dynamics and implicit forms of communication, which may need to be understood in order for effective therapy to occur.

To work purposefully and effectively in this relationship, the therapist needs to develop a capacity to attend to both the *content* and *process* of sessions. This is not necessarily an easy task, particularly for the novice therapist whose attentional capacities are likely to be taken up with a degree of anxiety. Clients invariably present in varying states of vulnerability, incongruence, distress or distrust, requiring different kinds of emotional responsiveness from the therapist. Some clients may have strong attachment needs that dominate their interactions with others. The therapist may thus be subject to powerful projections and demands, for example to extend a session time or provide definitive answers to a client's questions, which can be challenging but important to recognise. What is communicated by clients at more implicit or non-verbal levels, for example a tendency to intimidate or control others, may reflect unconscious aspects of experience or ways of relating that have not been fully owned or understood by them, but which may be important to addressing their difficulties.

The way the client feels about and relates to us in the therapy process can therefore be useful to reflect on, as it is likely that their characteristic ways of relating will also show themselves in the therapy relationship. In turn, how we feel about and relate to the client may tell us something useful about the dynamics and processes that influence their relationships with others. The client's habitual styles of relating can exert a pull on the therapist to respond or reciprocate in ways that are consonant with the client's implicit expectations and experiences of relationships, potentially reinforcing rather than altering unhelpful patterns of behaviour, what Sandler (1976) termed 'role responsiveness'. Furthermore, how we feel about and react to our clients is not just a product of what the client brings to the therapeutic situation, but also our own personal motivations, needs, biases and blind spots.

In other words, the therapeutic relationship is constituted by a complex matrix of inter-subjective processes (Mitchell and Aron, 1999) to which both therapist and client make active contributions. This means that it is not necessarily easy for the therapist to perceive, disentangle or attribute objectively what 'belongs' to them from what belongs to the client in any given interaction, though it may be important to do so, particularly if working with clients who present with complex relational difficulties. The importance of the issues noted here to counselling psychology practice is reflected in the Health and Care Professions Council's *Standards of Proficiency*, which state that counselling psychologists need to learn to manage 'the … emotional impact of their practice', to understand 'the dynamics present in therapeutic and other relationships' (p. 8), and to be aware of the 'explicit and implicit communications in a therapeutic relationship' (p. 10) (HCPC, 2009).

To work effectively with this relational complexity requires the therapist to be able to process a significant amount of information, external and internal, verbal and non-verbal, cognitive and emotional, manifest and latent. This relies heavily upon the therapist's internal reflective capacity, developed through activities such as personal therapy and supervision. Over time, the therapist becomes increasingly able to *participate* in and *observe* the therapeutic interaction simultaneously. Casement (1985) coined the term the 'internal supervisor' to refer to a process by which the therapist develops an inner observational space that helps them to reflect on what is happening in the therapeutic interaction, while also participating in it. He suggests that clinical supervision provides an auxiliary reflective space which supports the therapist's ability to unpack and conceptualise the complexities of the therapy process *post hoc*, and produce insights that can be taken back into the work with the client. Casement suggests that, with experience, the therapist becomes increasingly able to perform this supervisory function autonomously and in the immediacy of their interaction with clients. Casement also proposes that the therapist's theory base supports their reflective functioning by providing a reference point that enables them to think objectively about emerging clinical material and their subjective experience of being with the client (see Figure 4.2). For example, concepts such as transference, countertransference and projection may provide reference points that help orient and stabilise the therapist during turbulent phases in the therapy or where complex relational process are at play. Personal therapy provides an important context in which the therapist can develop a familiarity with their own emotional landscape and how aspects of their psyche are likely to be triggered in their clinical work (Donati and Legg, 2010; Rizq and Target, 2010).

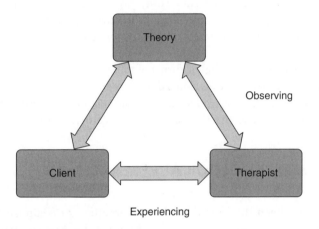

Figure 4.2   The reflective function of theory

For clients who come to therapy in a state of confusion and distress, it could be suggested that they are experiencing a loss or deficit in their capacity to observe or understand their experience more objectively, and thus to modify it. We might therefore suggest that, as well as enabling a process of experiential learning, therapy offers the client a relationship in which their capacity to reflect on, contain and understand their feelings and difficulties is supported and extended by the therapist's capacity to reflect on, contain and understand their difficulties; so that over time the client recovers or perhaps develops for the first time an ability to do this for themselves. Hence, as well offering the client a new way of *conceptualising* their experiences, the therapist also models for them a new way of *relating* to their experience and to themselves. In other words, they help the client not just to develop specific new insights but a core reflective capacity that will enable them to go on processing and managing their experiences more effectively for themselves. This is reminiscent of the old adage that 'if you give a man a fish he can feed himself for a day, but if you give him a fishing rod he can feed himself for life', and consistent with counselling psychology's emphasis on fostering clients' autonomy (Orlans and Van Scoyoc, 2009).

Depicting the core mechanisms of therapy in terms of a relationship that builds reflective capacity is consistent with contemporary psychoanalytic perspectives (Lemma, 2003) and views of developmental psychopathology that emphasise the role of mentalisation and affect regulation (Fonagy and Target, 1997). These theories suggest that an individual's sense of self and capacity to manage their experiences is first developed during infancy through a relationship with a primary caregiver who is attuned to and able to contingently mirror the infant's subjective experience. Over time, through repeated contact with adequately attuned caregiving, the child internalises a capacity to contain and regulate their experiences for themselves. This reflective function and capacity to 'mentalise' helps the individual to perceive and understand their own and others' mental states and intentions clearly (Fonagy and Target, 1997), and is thought to be directly implicated in healthy psychological development and resilience. It has been found to be impaired in individuals who have experienced neglectful or abusive early caregiving environments and implicated in problematic psychological states, such as depression and anxiety.

As the foregoing discussion highlights, forms of reflection appear to be fundamental to the processes of experiential learning, professional development, psychological therapy and psychological development. Moreover, it is evident that human relationships provide the fundamental context in which individual reflective skills and capacities are developed and passed on.

REFLECTION IN PSYCHOLOGICAL RESEARCH

Up until now we have been thinking of 'reflective practice' for a counselling psychologist primarily in terms of *therapeutic* practice, but of course the range of activities a counselling psychologist engages in extends beyond clinical work (Milton, 2010). Reflective practice underpins the way a counselling psychologist engages with *all* aspects of their professional activity, including research (Kasket, 2012). Just as a relationship exists between the personal and professional selves in clinical practice, the same is true in research. For example, practitioners' personal needs, biases and agendas can also enter into the way they view, critique, use or undertake research, as well as the kinds of research topics that spark their interest.

In my experience as a research supervisor, counselling psychology trainees frequently choose research topics with which they have a salient personal relationship, and are invested in some way. Often the trainee is not fully aware of this relationship or its implications for their research, but it usually becomes evident during supervision and as the research process unfolds (Kasket and Gil-Rodriguez, 2011). For example, it may become clear that, before the trainee has even carried out a literature review, they are making all sorts of assumptions about what they will find, which reflect tacit beliefs or wishes. Researcher bias can enter into the research process in all sorts of ways, from choice of topic, selection and critique of papers for review, construction of a research question, choice of methodology, interpretation of data and conclusions drawn. There can be powerful personal needs that drive trainees to want to understand something about a particular topic, or to use their research to change the views of others based on their own agenda, rather than a more open dispassionate study of the topic. It may therefore be useful to reflect on the extent to which we act as 'wounded researchers' as well as wounded healers (Bager-Charleson, 2010; Romanyshyn, 2013).

The personal relationship between a researcher and research topic is something that is well recognised in contemporary literature, primarily through the concept of 'reflexivity'. This concept represents the idea that the observer and observed cannot be separated and that a reciprocal relationship exists between the two. In a research context this means that it is not possible for a researcher to position themselves 'outside' the subject matter of their research and to view it 'objectively' (Finlay and Gough, 2003). Reflexivity is a concept that is not identical to reflection but is related to it in that it implies the necessity of reflective activity in order to identify the impact of tacit aspects of a researcher's own subjectivity on the research process.

The role of reflexivity in research was first emphasised by anthropologists and subsequently in feminist critiques of research. It is now a significant concept within the qualitative research paradigm as a whole, where the centrality of the researcher's subjectivity and meaning making to the research process is explicitly recognised. This is likely to be one of the reasons that many counselling psychologists find qualitative research appealing (Kasket, 2012). However, this does not mean that the influence of the researcher's self only operates in qualitative research and that reflexivity is not relevant to quantitative research. Rather, the concept of reflexivity suggests that subjective and co-constructive processes are inherent in the development of *all* forms of knowledge, whatever methods are used; just as we might say that the self of the therapist, and significant relational processes, are implicated in all models of therapy, irrespective of the extent to which they are emphasised in the model. Taking up such an epistemological position also enables us to critique research processes and outcomes more broadly. For example, the notion of reflexivity sensitises us to considering how underlying assumptions or biases may be operating in the way a particular topic has been constructed or studied to date, what kinds of research questions or methods have been prioritised over others and what the implications might be for the knowledge base that has been produced.

This more reflexive view of research is consistent with the way science has been critiqued and deconstructed over the last century by philosophers of science (Chalmers, 2013). It could be suggested that there is now a greater recognition of the role of reflexivity in good science. This is certainly a position that counselling psychologists would generally endorse and seek to incorporate into their identities as 'scientist-practitioners' (Corrie and Callahan, 2000; Lane and Corrie, 2006). If we think about the classical definition of the scientist-practitioner as someone who produces (does), consumes (uses) and evaluates (critiques) research, it is possible to see how a reflexive stance can help us to appraise the theory, evidence and recommendations produced by research, and hence the independent critical judgement we are able to exercise in making decisions about how we are influenced by that research in our own practice. This constant critical eye and reflective viewpoint permeates the way counselling psychologists approach all aspects of their work, whatever the task at hand (Orlans and Van Scoyoc, 2009).

Reflective exercise: 'Where am I in my research?'

Consider the following questions to help develop your personal reflexivity as a counselling psychology researcher:

- What is my personal relationship to the research topic(s) that interests me?
- What kinds of personal assumptions do I hold about this topic(s)? Where do these come from?
- Do I have a personal agenda or bias as a researcher?
- How might my own personal beliefs, biases and motivations shape or affect the process and outcomes of any research I do in this area?
- How can I monitor/regulate the impact of my own subjectivity on the research process and outcomes?

REFLECTIVE PRACTICE AND COUNSELLING PSYCHOLOGY

As the preceding sections have sought to illustrate, reflective practice is central to counselling psychology because it represents a 'way of being' that underpins and supports other key functions of its professional identity (Figure 4.4). These include things like:

- The *scientist practitioner* model and the need for a critical awareness of the individual, methodological and contextual factors that influence research processes and outcomes
- The *inter-subjective* foundations of human communication, development and knowledge
- *Reflexivity* and the notion that it is impossible to engage with the world in a way that is free from personal subjectivity or bias
- The inevitable *co- and social construction* of meaning and reality, and the fluid and pragmatic nature of knowledge or understandings derived from these processes
- The *humanistic* valuing of individual phenomenology, uniqueness, difference and meaning-making processes
- *Pluralism* and the valuing of and respect for multiple ways of being, knowing and acting in the world.

All of the above, in different ways, rely on a capacity to maintain an open and observing stance in relation to our experience and knowledge, rather than to settle for unified or final positions in relation to ours and others' understandings. In this sense, reflective practice for a counselling psychologist sustains a valuable capacity to recognise, understand and work with the *complexity* inherent in the problems and experiences with which they engage in the course of their work. Becoming a reflective practitioner thus requires an openness to all of these facets, and how they are interconnected, within one's identity as a counselling psychologist.

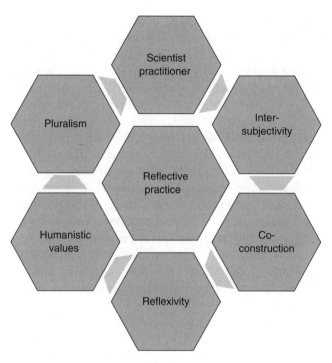

Figure 4.4   Reflective practice as an underpinning concept in counselling psychology

CONCLUSIONS: REFLECTIVE PRACTICE IN THE WIDER WORLD

As I hope I have demonstrated in this chapter, being a reflective practitioner is at the heart of what it means to be a counselling psychologist. Moreover, as the popularity and need for reflective practice has proliferated in recent years, professionals skilled in this way of working are very much needed. It is interesting to note that 'reflective practice groups' have come to be increasingly used in health-care settings to support the work of a range of clinicians involved in psychologically demanding work (Johnston and Paley, 2013; Riordan, 2008). These use the reflective capacity of the group to contain and make sense of complex clinical experiences, as well as help teams better understand their own processes and functioning.

At the same time, mounting pressures on health-care providers to deliver accountable and cost-effective services can make it more difficult for clinicians to practise in an emotionally responsive, relational way. As Oelofsen (2012a, p. 1) points out, the escalating costs of health care have led to an increased rationalisation and manualisation of treatments that risk overlooking 'the less tangible aspects of health care that rely on human interaction'.

This is consistent with critiques Rizq (2012, 2013) has put forward regarding what she regards as the defensive and perverse functions of discourses like Improving Access to Psychological Therapies (IAPT) and National Institute for Health and Care Excellence (NICE) guidelines in the National Health Service in the United Kingdom. Oelofsen argues that 'a whole systems approach to reflective practice' is needed within health-care organisations to support 'better decision making, more humane patient care and staff wellbeing' (2012a, p. 1).

However, it is perhaps worth remembering that there are reasons why reflective practice may be resisted rather than welcomed. Engaging in reflective practice is effortful and requires time and space to do effectively (Finlay, 2008). In the today's tough, target-driven economic climate, spaces for reflection can be few and far between. Moreover, reflective practice can bring with it an awareness of complexity, which once acknowledged may be hard to ignore, though not easy to respond to. For example, reflective practice may be experienced as unhelpful or idealistic in contexts where practitioners are under pressure to deliver brief interventions to large numbers of clients who present with significant psychological need. In such instances, the pull to simplify and minimise engagement with complexity may seem like a rational response to an inherently problematic set of expectations, driven more by economic constraints than clinical ideals.

In this sense, the challenges to maintaining reflective practice in the wider world have perhaps never been greater. However, counselling psychologists are well placed to make a distinctive contribution in settings where reflective practice and psychological understanding are needed, whether in their roles as clinicians, researchers, supervisors, trainers or managers. Counselling psychologists can therefore play a significant role in maintaining and promoting reflective practice through the various domains of their professional expertise and activity.

 Visit the companion website to listen to Reflective Practice.

REFERENCES

Aveline, M. (2007) The training and supervision of individual therapists. In W. Dryden (ed.), *The Handbook of Individual Therapy* (5th edn). London: Sage. pp. 515–548.

Bager-Charleson, S. (2010) *Reflective Practice in Counselling and Psychotherapy*. Exeter: Learning Matters.

Bor, R. and Watts, M.H. (eds) (2010) *The Trainee Handbook: A Guide for Counselling and Psychotherapy Trainees* (3rd edn). London: Sage.

Bulman, C. and Schutz, S. (eds) (2013) *Reflective Practice in Nursing* (5th edn). London: Wiley-Blackwell.

British Psychological Society (2014) *Standards for the Accreditation of Doctoral Programmes in Counselling Psychology*. Leicester: BPS.

Casement, P. (1985) *On Learning from the Patient*. London: Routledge.

Chalmers, A.F. (2013) *What is this Thing Called Science?* (4th edn). Maidenhead: Open University Press.

Corrie, S. and Callahan, M.M. (2000) 'A review of the scientist-practitioner model: Reflections on its potential contribution to counselling psychology within the context of current health care trends', *British Journal of Medical Psychology*, 73: 413–427.

Dewey, J. (1938) *Experience and Education*. London: Collier Macmillan.

Donati, M. (2003) 'Personal development in counselling psychology training: A critical investigation of the views and experiences of trainers and trainees'. Unpublished PhD thesis, City University, London.

Donati, M. and Legg, C. (2010) 'Getting the most out of personal therapy', in M. Watts and R. Bor (eds), *The Trainee Handbook: A Guide for Counselling and Psychotherapy Trainees* (3rd edn). London: Sage. pp. 261–276.

Donati, M. and Watts, M.H. (2000) 'Personal development in counselling psychology training: The case for further research', *Counselling Psychology Review*, 15(1): 12–21.

Finlay, L. (2008) *Reflecting on 'Reflective practice*. PBPL paper 52. A discussion paper prepared for PBPL CETL (www.open.ac.uk/pbpl).

Finlay, L. and Gough, B. (eds) (2003) *Reflexivity: A Practical Guide for Researchers in Health and Social Sciences*. London: Wiley-Blackwell.

Fonagy, P. and Target, M. (1997) 'Attachment and reflective function: Their role in self-organization', *Development and Psychopathology*, 9: 679–700.

Guy, J.D. (1987) *The Personal Life of the Psychotherapist*. London: Wiley.

Health and Care Professions Council (2009) *Standards of Proficiency: Practitioner Psychologists*. London: HCPC.

Johnston, J. and Paley, G. (2013) 'Mirror mirror on the ward: Who is the unfairest of them all? Reflections on reflective practice groups in acute psychiatric settings', *Psychoanalytic Psychotherapy*, 27(2): 170–186.

Jung, C.G. (1985) *The Practice of Psychotherapy: Essays on the Psychology of the Transference and Other Subjects*. Princeton, NJ: Princeton University Press.

Kasket, E. (2012) 'The counselling psychologist researcher', *Counselling Psychology Review*, 27(2): 64–73.

Kasket, E. and Gil-Rodriguez, E. (2011) 'The identity crisis in trainee counselling psychology research, and what to do about it', *Counselling Psychology Review*, 26(4): 20–30.

Knott, C. and Scragg, T. (2013) *Reflective Practice in Social Work* (3rd edn). Exeter: Learning Matters.

Kolb, D.A. (1976) *Learning Style Inventory: Technical Manual*. Boston, MA: McBer.

Kolb, D.A. (1984) *Experiential Learning: Experience as the Source of Learning and Development*. Englewood Cliffs, NJ: Prentice-Hall.

Lane, D. and Corrie, S. (2006) *The Modern Scientist-Practitioner: A Guide to Practice in Psychology*. London: Routledge.

Lemma, A. (2003) *Introduction to the Practice of Psychoanalytic Psychotherapy*. Chichester: John Wiley & Sons.

Loewenthal, D. and Greenwood, D. (2005) 'Counselling and psychotherapy as a form of learning: Some implications for practice', *British Journal of Guidance and Counselling*, 33(4): 441–456.

Milton, M. (ed.) (2010) *Therapy and Beyond: Counselling Psychology Contributions to Therapeutic and Social Issues*. London: Wiley-Blackwell.

Mitchell, S.A. and Aron, L. (eds) (1999) *Relational Psychoanalysis: The Emergence of a Tradition*. New York: The Analytic Press.

Oelofsen, N. (2012a) 'The importance of reflective practices', *Health Service Journal*. Available at http://m.hsj.co.uk/5048994.article (accessed October 2015).

Oelofsen, N. (2012b) *Developing Reflective Practice: A Guide for Students and Practitioners of Health and Social Care*. Banbury: Lantern Publishing Ltd.

Orlans, V. and Van Scoyoc, S. (2009) *A Short Introduction to Counselling Psychology*. London: Sage.

Papadopoulous, L., Cross, M. and Bor, R. (2003) *Reporting in Counselling and Psychotherapy: A Trainee's Guide to Preparing Case Studies and Reports*. London: Routledge.

Riordan, D. (2008) 'Being ordinary in extraordinary places: Reflective practice of the total situation in a total institution', *Psychoanalytic Psychotherapy*, 22(3): 196–217.

Rizq, R. (2006) 'Training and disillusion in counselling psychology: A psychoanalytic perspective', *Psychology and Psychotherapy: Theory, Research and Practice*, 79: 613–627.

Rizq, R. (2012) 'The perversion of care: psychological therapies in a time of IAPT', *Psychodynamic Practice*, 18(1): 7–25.

Rizq, R. (2013) 'IAPT and thought crime: Language, bureaucracy and the evidence-based regime', *Counselling Psychology Review*, 28(4): 111–115.

Rizq, R. and Target, M. (2010) '"If that's what I need, it could be what someone else needs": Exploring the role of attachment and reflective function in counselling psychologists' accounts of how they use therapy in clinical practice: A mixed methods study', *British Journal of Guidance and Counselling*, 38(4): 459–481.

Romanyshyn, R.D. (2013) *The Wounded Researcher: Researcher with Soul in Mind* (2nd edn). New Orleans, LA: Spring Journal Books.

Sandler, J. (1976) 'Countertransference and role responsiveness', *International Review of Psychoanalysis*, 3: 43–47.

Schön, D.A. (1983) *The Reflective Practitioner: How Professionals Think in Action*. New York: Basic Books.

Skovholt, T.M. and Rønnestad, M.H. (1995) *The Evolving Professional Self: Stages and Themes in Therapist and Counselor Development*. New York: Wiley.

Stedmon, J. and Dallos, R. (2009) *Reflective Practice in Psychotherapy and Counselling.* London: Open University Press.

Vince, R. (2001) 'Power and emotion in organizational learning', *Human Relations*, 54(10): 1325–1351.

Woolfe, R. and Strawbridge, S. (2009) 'Counselling psychology: Origins developments and challenges', in R. Woolfe, S. Strawbridge, B. Douglas and W. Dryden (eds), *Handbook of Counselling Psychology* (3rd edn). London: Sage. pp. 3–22.

5
ENGAGING WITH ACADEMIA AND TRAINING PROGRAMMES
VICTORIA E. GALBRAITH

You will either step forward into growth or back into safety. (Abraham Maslow)

This chapter aims to draw the reader into the world of becoming a 'counselling psychologist in training', from the initial thought of entering professional training to the training itself. This may begin with the thrill of being admitted onto a university-validated professional training programme or the BPS's Qualification in Counselling Psychology (QCoP), and the associated feeling of being 'accepted' or 'good enough', but later may include the sense of being de-skilled and negative concerns such as imposter syndrome creeping in. In this chapter, the fears, uncertainties, hopes and expectations will be captured along with the personal and professional investment that accompanies training at this level. Alongside this will be a window into the mind of the trainer in order to gain some understanding of roles and responsibilities, as well as the dynamics that come into play. The chapter will focus upon three distinct essential elements – academic, professional and personal – and the ingredients within these realms that are necessary to become a fully-fledged counselling psychologist.

BEGINNING THE JOURNEY

For some, the journey towards qualified counselling psychologist status may have begun a long time ago, perhaps decades ago, possibly with a constant push towards this end goal of training, gaining all the necessary prerequisites. Others may have engaged in a completely different career path only to find that the role of a counselling psychologist was beckoning. For others, the journey may have been more recent and straightforward: school, university degree in psychology, and application to a course of study (in the UK this would be either a university course or the British Psychological Society (BPS) Qualification in Counselling Psychology (QCoP)).

For many, the invitation to interview may be the first hurdle of many, filled with anxiety, anticipation and excitement, and accompanying thoughts may be 'I *am* good enough to have been offered an interview'. Then there is the interview itself: an opportunity to be assessed for suitability and compatibility with the profession of counselling psychology. While you might feel that you truly fit with the profession and hope that the interview will go well as a consequence, you may also worry about whether you have enough experience, whether you will be too anxious to express yourself clearly and, importantly, how you can best 'sell' yourself. Selling oneself in a counselling psychology interview can be a minefield, as a counselling psychology interview is quite a unique beast in that sense. While of course it is important to be able to present oneself in the best light possible with regards to academic knowledge and, on many courses, therapeutic experience, it is arguably of equal importance to demonstrate a good level of self-awareness and reflexivity. The problem here is that self-awareness is often demonstrated through acknowledging the less marketable areas of oneself or, rather, areas in need of development. Hence there is certainly a level of humility that goes hand in hand with the counselling psychology interview, which could be considered 'at odds' with most other interviews. Furthermore, some interviewees may overplay the need to focus upon vulnerability and struggle, which would not be considered desirable either. There is therefore a fine line for applicants to draw, in order to ensure that they demonstrate the necessary self-awareness and focus upon areas in need of development while also ensuring that they are portrayed in a positive light and demonstrating suitability for the profession.

For programme teams on UK-based university training courses, the role of professional gate-keeping begins here. Can we see this person as a member of the profession of counselling psychology? Do they demonstrate the necessary level of academic knowledge and therapeutic skills commensurate with our entry requirements? Do their personal characteristics demonstrate a commitment to the ethos of the counselling psychology profession? Does this person have the capability of developing into a counselling psychologist? Would I feel comfortable with this person as my therapist? These are just some of the questions that *may* cross a trainer's mind when they enter into the interviewer role, while at the same time being mindful of the interviewee's potential anxiety and aiming to enable them to perform as best as they can. This is not an easy feat!

Co-ordinating supervisors (CS) for the QCoP route to training will be facing similar pressure, as their role reflects that of a programme director or tutor for individual candidates. Their initial meeting will be an opportunity to decide whether to take on a particular candidate or not (and vice versa), based on whether the CS can see this person as a future member of the profession and whether the independent route to training seems suitable for the candidate. Once both parties have decided to proceed, the candidate submits an enrolment portfolio, which includes a plan for the whole training. If an applicant requests that any prior learning be considered towards meeting a particular competence(s), then an accredited existing competence (AEC) application must be submitted detailing the existing competence and providing evidence for it (for example, relevant certificates). A competence mapping procedure (in the form of a unit mapping document) then takes place. The training plan must ensure that all competences will be met by the end of training and once the plan is approved, candidates are then officially registered onto the programme.

ACADEMIC ENGAGEMENT

Once accepted onto a training programme, the hard work really begins, and initial feelings may include elation, anxiety or a mixture of both surrounding the prospect of beginning the journey of training. And then comes the first day, which Kidd recalls as follows:

> The first day of the [counselling] course is etched firmly in my memory as one of blind terror. There were shades of schooldays, in my conviction that everyone else would be more intelligent, more competent, more articulate than I was. I felt tongue-tied and inadequate in the warm up exercise and asked myself, why do the others all seem so at ease, so able to talk readily to others in this assembled group of strangers? (2004: 59)

Kidd goes on to note that although she may experience similar feelings if she were to begin therapeutic training again, having personally developed during the training process, she would now have a better way of coping with these emotions.

While trainees may have similar experiences to Kidd, it is important to remember that by following a rigorous recruitment process, the staff team believe that selected trainees have what it takes to succeed on the programme. However, this should by no means encourage complacency. All the life experience and academic qualifications that have been gained to date stand candidates in good stead to begin this journey towards doctoral-level qualification and this can be seen as 'entering a new phase of personal and professional development' (Taylor-Smith, 2004: 25), but while the prerequisites may have been met prior to acceptance onto a course, the academic and professional work of a counselling psychologist, together with continuous review of suitability, begins here.

Before embarking on counselling psychology training, some trainees' previous courses may have provided incoming students with every piece of the jigsaw from the lecture to the reading material and beyond. However, counselling psychology training is far from an exercise in spoon feeding. In keeping with the humanistic framework, counselling psychology training provides the trainee with the opportunity to explore, to grow, to learn, and to develop not only the theory and skills essential for the work, but also to develop as a person – 'to become'. This requires a different approach to learning and teaching than may have been experienced in previous education, which trainees may find difficult to swallow at first. The safety of responsibility lying with the tutor team is replaced with a two-way contract, a spirit of co-operation between trainee and trainer, and an atmosphere of reciprocal reflection (Schön, 1987) between trainer and trainee. This may come as a surprise for many who are more familiar with a more didactic form of learning and teaching. According to the Health and Care Professions Council (HCPC) guidance on conduct and ethics for students (2010: 10), 'you are responsible for your own learning'. Programme teams may therefore aim towards fostering a level of equality with trainees, but this comes with its own difficulties, as trainers assume a professional gate-keeping role together with the authority that resides with assessing submitted pieces of work. This balance of equality alongside the professional gate-keeping therefore provides an inherently contradictory position. For trainers, this can be perceived as a double-edged sword. While equality can engender empowerment and autonomy, the para-dox lies with both parties being fundamentally aware that the ultimate power resides with the trainer. However, in many ways the contradiction clearly reflects the client–therapist relation-ship, and as trainees begin to experience this early on in their training, it may serve to assist them in their practice. As complex as these situations may be, trainers are ever-mindful that eradicating such issues, perhaps through adopting a purely didactic approach to teaching, may not be as developmentally helpful as being open to them and aiming to work through them (Totton, 2009).

Teaching styles and delivery within counselling psychology training programmes vary con-siderably, whether trainees are registered on a university programme, the BPS qualification or an international programme. However, according to the UK-based Quality Assurance Agency (QAA) (2011: 7), 'most professional and practice-based doctorates have always included struc-tured elements such as lectures and seminars and have had an emphasis on acquiring professional skills in addition to conducting original research'. There will be huge variation between courses, modules and lecturers or tutors, but most will attempt to cater for the types of learner outlined by Honey and Mumford (1986). They manifest as shown in Table 5.1.

Table 5.1 Types of learner (Honey and Mumford, 1986)

Activists	Those who enjoy the here-and-now and are keen on teamwork and games.
Reflectors	Those who prefer to sit back and reflect on behaviours and events. Reflectors are often thinkers.
Theorists	Those who like to be presented with theory in order to analyse and synthesise information.
Pragmatists	Those who like to apply learning or theory to practice in the real world.

As well as catering for the various learning styles, many tutors will adopt a 'theory Y' approach to learning and teaching (Biggs, 2002), which espouses that people, specifically trainees and trainers in this instance, can be trusted to direct, drive and shape their own train-ing experience. This reflects the humanistic ethos of the counselling psychology profession and facilitates a supportive, formative, systemic and qualitative learning climate that also encourages responsibility in trainees, which many can find disconcerting. While individual training programmes will retain their own distinct qualities and philosophical foundations, Tran (2004: 13) provides the following observation of his own humanistic counsellor training: 'one of the first things about the course that really impacted upon me, and on others, was the person-centredness of it all. It was both really challenging and really irritating! I had not experienced this style of education before, and was unused to having so much freedom to shape things.' He goes on to note that his own course handbook said: '[A] further aspect of the centrality of respect for the person is the expectation that course members will take responsibility for their own learning.'

All of the above being said, there is of course a great deal of responsibility that lies with the training programme. In the UK, HCPC-approved and BPS-accredited counselling psychology training programmes consist of various distinct elements that aim to ensure that, upon qualification, trainees are conferred eligibility to register with the HCPC as Counselling Psychologists and as Chartered members of the BPS. Therefore various standards of competency and proficiency are required. A link to the full standards for competency and proficiency for counselling psychologists can be found on the companion website.

In developing doctoral-level training programmes, trainers refer to the Quality Assurance Agency (QAA) (2011) *Doctoral Degree Characteristics*, the HCPC (2012a) *Standards of Proficiency* and the BPS *Standards for Doctoral Programmes in Counselling Psychology* (2014). The key aims of accredited programmes in counselling psychology are set by the BPS (2014: 7) and outlined in Box 5.1.

Box 5.1   BPS Standards for Doctoral Programmes in Counselling Psychology (2014)

[T]he key aim of an accredited programme is to produce graduates who will:

1. be competent, reflective, ethically sound, resourceful and informed practitioners of counselling psychology able to work in therapeutic and non-therapeutic contexts;
2. value the imaginative, interpretative, personal and collaborative aspects of the practice of counselling psychology;
3. commit themselves to ongoing personal and professional development and inquiry;
4. understand, develop and apply models of psychological inquiry for the creation of new knowledge which is appropriate to the multi-dimensional nature of relationships between people;
5. appreciate the significance of wider social, cultural, spiritual, political, and economic domains within which counselling psychology operates;
6. adopt a questioning and evaluative approach to the philosophy, practice, research and theory which constitutes counselling psychology; and
7. be able to develop and demonstrate communication, influencing, teaching and leadership skills by applying psychological knowledge and skills in a range of professional, clinical, organisational, and research contexts.

Integral to these competences are skills such as critical understanding and evaluation, synthesis of knowledge, critical reflection and provision of an original contribution to literature that merits publication. This can be quite a step-up for many trainees when they embark on such training, and gauging the level required can be difficult. Previously high-flying students may find that the modular learning outcomes are difficult to meet. However, there is a benchmark that needs to be met by the end of training, and the QAA provides this as follows.

Doctoral degrees are awarded to students who have demonstrated:

- The creation and interpretation of new knowledge, through original research or other advanced scholarship, of a quality to satisfy peer review, extend the forefront of the discipline, and merit publication;
- A systematic acquisition and understanding of a substantial body of knowledge which is at the forefront of an academic discipline or area of professional practice;
- The general ability to conceptualise, design and implement a project for the generation of new knowledge, applications or understanding at the forefront of the discipline, and to adjust the project design in the light of unforeseen problems, and a detailed understanding of applicable techniques for research and advanced academic enquiry. (QAA, 2011: 32)

These characteristics, together with the HCPC standards of proficiency and the BPS standards of competency, must all be evidenced at the end of training. It is therefore no wonder that, at times, trainees feel de-skilled and doubt their capabilities, for example, putting their successes down to good fortune or timing as opposed to competence and proficiency. However, while this level is the highest academic level that can be achieved, upon entering professional training, courses generally require that only Level 7 (or master's level) outcomes are met in the first year for full-time programmes (or part-time equivalent). Level 8 (or doctoral level) outcomes must be met in subsequent years. So for trainees, this often requires a jump from Level 6 (final year of undergraduate study) to Level 7 at the beginning of training in year one, and on to level 8 for the remainder of training.

The transition between these levels can be difficult to negotiate. Nevertheless, there are strategies that trainees can employ in order to counteract these feelings of vulnerability. While trainees *may* be familiar with relying solely on lectures to provide information, trainees should engage with academic literature early on in order to deepen their understanding of various concepts and theories. Rather than taking information at face value, reading around an area of interest can assist trainees in conceptualising from a variety of different standpoints. What we have come to know and understand about much of psychology literature is that there is often no right and wrong, but rather a variety of ways of looking at an issue, theory or scenario. Wide reading will therefore assist in understanding an idea from different frames of reference. In turn, this reading will enable trainees to gain further understanding of the expected level of submitted work. Trainees should always be working towards a publishable standard of work, and reading widely early on in their careers can help facilitate this aim. Training to become a counselling psychologist is, arguably, as much about becoming an academic as it is about becoming a therapeutic practitioner, and of course a lot more besides. As aforementioned, the BPS requires trainees to adopt a questioning and evaluative approach;

therefore critical evaluation of self, practice and academic writing is key. However, in order to develop a critical approach, it is imperative that an underpinning knowledge is gained through reading broadly and through deeper exposure to information and perspectives. In ensuring that these outcomes are met, whenever trainees are engaging with the literature for coursework or research they may wish to pursue the following strategy:

- Choose an area of interest;
- Conduct a keyword search;
- Retrieve current texts and academic papers;
- Read papers for both breadth and depth;
- Do not just settle for one perspective. Consider alternative viewpoints and continue reading for breadth and depth until all avenues have been explored.

Attendance at critical writing courses may assist with this endeavour. Such courses may be offered as part of a university's skills training or could be accessed by external trainees through various universities. There are also several texts focusing upon critical writing that could be of benefit to trainees or indeed to qualified practitioners who hope to develop these skills further (for example, Cottrell, 2011; Wallace and Wray, 2011).

The development of critical writing skills is essential for the various assessments throughout training and particularly significant for the research thesis, which forms part of the qualification. There are various chapters within this book dedicated to the counselling psychology researcher (Chapter 8 for the beginning of the research journey; Chapter 14 for carrying out research; Chapter 32 for moving from being a consumer to a producer of research; and Chapter 38 for researching across the career span) but suffice to state that the research journey should begin very early on in training, with areas of interest preferably identified within the first year. Historically, many counselling psychology trainees have attended training programmes expecting to be trained predominantly in therapeutic method and delivery. However, counselling psychology's two dominant models are that of scientist practitioner and reflexive practitioner (Martin, 2010), with evidence-based practice and practice-based evidence providing the backdrop to everything that we do as professionals.

BECOMING A PROFESSIONAL

Authors have suggested that becoming a professional therapist is complex, and although researchers such as Rønnestad and Skovholt (2003, 2013) have investigated the developmental processes involved, it is still not yet fully understood (Koltz and Champe, 2010). Rønnestad and Skovholt (2003) developed a six-phase model of the process of professional development of 100 counsellors and therapists. These phases incorporated the lay helper, the beginning student, the advanced student, the novice professional, the experienced professional and the senior professional. The lay helper refers to the assistance that the trainee may have provided to others prior to training (for example, to parents, children, friends and colleagues). The beginning student, 'who finds the start of professional training to be exciting, but also intensely challenging' (Rønnestad and Skovholt, 2003: 11), realises that the lay way of helping others is no longer deemed acceptable. Openness to new experiences and to learning is required at this stage in order for professional development to be effective.

Towards the end of training trainees feel more capable and responsible for the work undertaken. The novice professional recognises that they are now out on their own, embraces this new step but also feels the associated anxiety. There almost seems to be a sense of 'not knowing enough' taking place here and concern over not meeting expectations. The experienced professional has typically gained experience in different settings. 'A central developmental task for most experienced professionals is to create a counselling/therapy role which is highly congruent with the individuals' self-perceptions (including values, interests, attitudes), and which makes it possible for the practitioner to apply his/her professional competence in an authentic way' (Rønnestad and Skovholt, 2003: 20). The senior professional has a wealth of experience and is training others and/or supervising others, and perhaps leading services, and therefore requires a change to identity in some way. One participant disclosed 'they [trainees] get brighter all the time: I feel that I learn as much from the interns as I teach them. They have become my teacher' (Rønnestad and Skovholt, 2003: 25). This statement echoes the aforementioned comments regarding the movement towards equality between trainer and trainee.

While professionalism can be considered difficult to define, the HCPC (2012b) conducted a piece of research to determine the views of three HCPC-registered health professionals (paramedics, chiropodists/podiatrists and occupational therapists) on the concept of 'professionalism'. Although the findings did not incorporate the views of psychologists, they did indicate that professionalism is a concept that holds different meanings for different people, rather than there being one sole definition. The health professionals understood professionalism as incorporating 'an holistic construct', 'good clinical care', 'an expression of self', 'attitudes and behaviours' and 'appearance'. As counselling psychologists, we do not ordinarily subscribe to the medical way of working. However, the Royal College of Physicians defines medical professionalism as 'a set of values, behaviours, and relationships that underpins the trust the public has in doctors', which strikes a chord with the 'trust' underpinning the therapeutic relationship (2005: 14). Furthermore, fundamental attributes of professional counselling psychologists include that practitioners can be trusted to apply theory to practice in a competent manner, that they are accountable for their actions and that they also display characteristics such as honesty, integrity, respect for others, self-awareness and emotional intelligence. The notion of professionalism therefore is not only restricted to working life but also extends to one's personal characteristics too. However according to Dinwoodie (n.d.), 'professionalism can be hard to define and even harder to teach'.

Many trainees do work in a professional *capacity* prior to counselling psychology training but the beginning of training may provide the initial phase of a transition to assuming a professional identity (Rønnestad and Skovholt, 2003) which can be a fairly daunting prospect. They must feel comfortable with working autonomously and within levels of competence, yet also make good use of tutors, trainers and clinical supervisors. The University of Wolverhampton's *Professional Doctorate in Counselling Psychology Course Guide* (2013–14: 26) states that 'professional standards of behaviour apply to all aspects of the course: relationships with the course team, visiting lecturers, other trainees and on placement must be conducted with respect and integrity'. Trainees are ambassadors for the profession as well as for their training institution. The BPS and HCPC provide guidance on such matters for UK-based trainees, and it is essential that trainees are familiar with these guidelines, specifically the BPS's *Professional Practice Guidelines for Counselling Psychology* (2007), the BPS's *Code of Ethics and Conduct* (2009), and the HCPC's *Guidance on Conduct and Ethics for Students* (2010).

The BPS's *Professional Practice Guidelines for Counselling Psychology* (2007: 2) were developed to ensure that practitioners were aware of their 'responsibilities and obligations to (1) self and to clients; (2) to self and to colleagues; and (3) to self and to society'. While qualified counselling psychologists – to include trainers – are required to be 'responsible for the maintenance of adequate standards in the application of psychological principles and ethics, especially in promoting the welfare and rights of clients and in preserving the confidentiality of their case material' (2007: 6), trainees too have responsibility here, as advised by the Health and Care Professions Council's *Guidance on Conduct and Ethics for Students* (2010). While the word 'responsibility' is not used within the guidance, the document outlines how trainees should conduct themselves. This guidance includes the material outlined in Box 5.2.

Box 5.2   HCPC Guidance: Trainee Conduct

- you should always act in the best interests of your service users,
- you should respect the confidentiality of your service users,
- you should keep high standards of personal conduct,
- you should provide any important information about your conduct, competence or health to your education provider,
- you should limit your study or stop studying if your performance or judgement is affected by your health,
- you should keep your professional knowledge and skills up to date,
- you should act within the limits of your knowledge and skills,
- you should communicate effectively with service users and your education provider and placement providers,
- you should get informed consent to provide care or services (as far as possible),
- you should keep accurate records on service users,
- you should deal fairly and safely with the risks of infection,
- you should behave honestly,
- you should make sure that your behaviour does not damage public confidence in your profession.

Aside from the professional and ethical issues highlighted here, there are also more practical ways of demonstrating professionalism, which can stand trainees in good stead for their future. One of the strengths of counselling psychology training is that rather than being required to undertake specific clinical placements, trainees can tailor their training towards their areas of interest. Of course there are stipulations around this provided by the BPS, HCPC and course providers, yet there is some flexibility around short-term/long-term placements, mode and modality of work, client group and general placement type. In many ways, therefore, the world is your oyster, and it is certainly worth considering ways to make the training work for you. Given this breadth of possibility, trainees can benefit from some forward planning and thinking, while also bearing in mind that during training, learning and reflection may precipitate a change of direction. The answer is to embrace reflexivity, to think ahead in terms of placement needs and areas of specialism, and to consider employability and career progression, yet to also allow for options to be left open. Communication with others, whether via face-to-face networking or virtual connection, can provide a catalyst for professional learning, support and development. Further comprehensive discussions around clinical placements can be found in Chapter 6.

PERSONAL LEARNING AND DEVELOPMENT

> [C]ounselling psychologists' distinctive identity is reflected in their high levels of competence to work both with structure/content and with process/interpersonal dynamics as they unfold during the therapeutic encounter. Moreover, they bring aspects of themselves to their work, derived from their training, wider knowledge, and lived experience. (BPS, 2014: 4)

In the practice of counselling psychology, there is a distinct need for the awareness of interpersonal dynamics and the use of self; therefore, training routes reflect this in their provision of the personal development components of training. Indeed, the BPS (2014: 13) training standards for counselling psychology require this as well, as shown in Box 5.3.

Box 5.3   BPS Standards: Trainee self-awareness

8.2 strive to do no harm by recognising their personal limitations, appropriate boundaries and understanding of the dynamics present in therapeutic and other relationships, including dynamics of power;

8.3 understand the experience of therapy through active and systematic engagement in personal therapy, which will enable them to:

(Continued)

(Continued)

    i. demonstrate an understanding and experience of therapy from the perspective of the client, which will be utilised to guide their own practice;

   ii. demonstrate an understanding through therapy of their own life experience, and understand the impact of that experience upon practice;

  iii. demonstrate an ability for critical self-reflection on the use of self in therapeutic process.

Wilhelm Wundt, who formed the first psychology laboratory in Leipzig, Germany, believed that the inner consciousness could be investigated through researchers' analysing their own inner thoughts and feelings, and thus the term 'introspection' was coined. Introspection is a personal and subjective process, and only the individual can examine his or her own psychological processes. Within the profession of counselling psychology it is understood that clients and therapists have the capacity to engage in introspection, and therefore the history of introspection not only affects the therapeutic work encountered but also impacts upon the training of counselling psychologists, with self-awareness, self-reflection and personal development being continually encouraged. The belief that self-analysis was crucial to therapeutic efficacy originated within the time of Freud and specifically within psychoanalysis. Subsequently, an understanding has formed that suggests that by addressing vulnerabilities, therapists are in an improved position to assist others in their quest for growth. According to Wilkins, 'it is only by addressing their own conditions of worth or repressed and suppressed early experiences or irrational beliefs that therapists become fit persons to accompany others on the sometimes fearful and painful journey of personal growth' (1997: 63).

Interestingly, Donati and Watts (2000) and Williams and Irving (1996) assert that personal development is a poorly articulated area of counselling psychology training; yet, personal psychological therapy is an essential component on every HCPC-approved and BPS-accredited counselling psychology training course and 'it distinguishes the training of counselling psychologists from that of other formal bodies of psychological practice' (Woolfe, 1996: 6). In addition to mandatory attendance at personal therapy, the personal development component of training often includes additional forums for the facilitation of self-awareness, for example: regular personal development groups composed of trainee counselling psychologists and a facilitator; journaling, which involves a written account of a trainee's reflections on their personal and professional life; mindfulness; and other creative techniques that vary by training programme.

The mandatory personal therapy requirement ensures that counselling psychology trainees attend a minimum of 40 hours of personal therapy during the course of their training, although the specific number of hours differs between training programmes. While this requirement is still a contentious issue given its mandatory status, there are studies suggesting that personal therapy benefits trainees. For example, Williams et al. (1999) performed a large-scale study (N = 192) investigating how counselling psychologists view their personal therapy. Results indicated that 88 per cent were in favour of personal therapy as a training requirement, and most participants rated the outcome and process of their personal therapy as positive. However, 27 per cent also reported some negative effects. These negative effects have not been elaborated upon in their research paper, but apparently 'those who reported negative effects were still in favour of mandatory therapy for trainees' (Williams et al., 1999: 552), suggesting that the benefit outweighs the cost, at least for this sample of participants.

Richards (1999) investigated cross-cultural (in)sensitivity of the personal development component of training and argued that the more traditional forms of personal development (for example, personal therapy) are not adequate for all cultures. Richards' position is that personal therapy may not be as meaningful for cultures that have a more collectivist standpoint, and that there should be more of a package of personal development options that recognises and celebrates the diversity of trainees. In fact, most current training programmes do encourage continuous personal and professional development via a range of different means, for example personal development exercises, reflexive journals and the sharing of oneself within a group situation. While teaching delivery styles vary from tutor to tutor, there will generally be a heavy emphasis on group work within counselling psychology training, whether that is structured group work or personal and professional development groups, and there is certainly a great deal of learning that can take place through training relationships and within the group environment.

Robinson's (1974) learning model suggests that learners move through four stages, from unconscious incompetence, to conscious incompetence, to conscious competence, to unconscious competence. According to Johns (1996), stages two and three are the most difficult as they involve giving up a specific self-image and, as such, can involve huge transitions for trainees, yet, at the same time, these are considered essential for new learning to take place. Trainees' perspectives on group work differ from person to person based on their own individual expectations and experiences, and Keys (2004) has articulately captured her perspective, which illustrates the move through the stages:

> At the beginning of the course I spent a lot of time feeling isolated because I did not feel 'heard': I imagined that no-one could understand or respond to me adequately, and perversely I pushed away any attempts to do so. Gradually, with help, I began to recognise that this was a self-destructive pattern that alienated me from what I most desperately wanted. ... Much of our work on the course took place in a group in which there was nowhere to hide and where an awareness and acceptance of difference was paramount. I was challenged to accept myself; my uniqueness, my right to a voice, my inevitable weaknesses and strengths. It was hard to show myself unconditional positive regard and accept, for example, that I had prejudices. It did not fit with my view of myself as open-minded and non-judgemental. (Keys, 2004: 75)

Keys goes on to note, 'I am slowly, however, learning to chastise myself less' (2004: 75), which could be considered a change in levels of self-acceptance and therefore indicative of new learning and development.

Various researchers have investigated the impact of group work and personal development groups in psychotherapeutic training, yet there still appears a paucity of outcome research available (Galbraith and Hart, 2007; Lennie, 2007). Lennie (2007: 118) conducted a mixed-methods investigation to explore the factors that contribute to the development of self-awareness within such a group, including the 'comfort fit' (which was defined as 'the relationship between the perceived "help" of each factor in developing self-awareness and its "presence" within the current group'), and the relationship between this fit and self-awareness. Themes that occurred most commonly fell within 'interpersonal' (for example, group cohesion, group involvement, group conflict), 'intrapersonal' (for example, courage, fear, humour, confidence) and 'environmental' (for example, personality of facilitator, student support, comfort of physical surroundings) factors, and findings indicated that trainees were more comfortable in their personal development group at the beginning of their training as opposed to the end; and there was no obvious relationship between their 'comfort fit' and an increase in self-awareness.

Galbraith and Hogan (2006) utilised a grounded theory methodology to investigate trainees' experiences of personal development groups, developing an illustrative model of the transition that takes place over time. The model (Figure 5.1) indicates that trainees begin the group with goals for personal development and that, over the course of the group, there are various intervening conditions that determine whether a trainee will develop personally or professionally as a result of the group. These include the ability (or not) to take a risk within the group and the uneasy feelings associated with taking that risk, which may trigger difficulty in expressing emotions, as opposed to feeling at ease when expressing emotions.

When a trainee takes a risk, they may experience and express certain emotions, resulting in further emotional connection to other members of the group. However, this is all dependent upon the response of the facilitator and the rest of the group. In the presence of therapeutic elements such as safety, acceptance, support and empathy, and when the facilitator guides exploration, a trainee is more likely to develop than in the presence of impeding elements, such as feelings of threat/danger within the group, non-acceptance, lack of empathy, support and lack of guidance from the facilitator. In a therapeutic (as opposed to impeding) group environment, the outcomes may then include inter- and intrapersonal learning, such as professional learning, accepting others, learning from interaction with others, self-acceptance, self-confidence, self-awareness and congruence. This model of transition over time in a personal development group highlights ways in which trainees can make the experience as valuable as possible, both for themselves and for their colleagues. By sharing oneself and providing the necessary conditions, as outlined within the model, this could encourage a safe environment for disclosure, support, personal and professional learning to take place.

The Galbraith and Hogan (2006) model indicates that facilitator style can either support or impede the process of personal development, and that when facilitators guide the process, this can be deemed supportive. It also details that more valued facilitative roles would include the provision of safety within the group, monitoring the progress of the group and offering guiding behaviours and actions. Furthermore, trainees identified facilitators as

**Personal development group model
of transition over time**

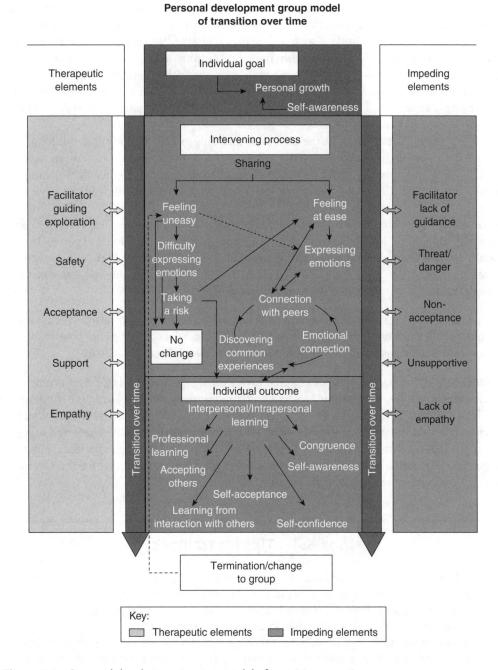

Figure 5.1   Personal development group model of transition over time

useful when they had some level of constructive involvement within the group rather than purely observing the group in action or collusion. According to Irving and Williams (1995), the individual's learning style also impacts on facilitator preferences. They investigated experiences of group work in psychotherapeutic training, and it was found that theorists prefer facilitators to provide a firm framework, while both theorists and pragmatists expect arbitration to be a fundamental role of the facilitator, in addition to challenging (the latter also being a view shared by reflectors). Activists and reflectors valued feedback as an integral component of facilitation.

The trainees participating in the Galbraith and Hogan (2006) study had not long completed their personal development (PD) group, and it would therefore have been useful to conduct a follow-up study with this group in order to determine whether the learning outcomes from their PD group remained the same over time and, indeed, whether their perception of the role of the facilitator remained the same. Thomas suggests that "'transference issues' can have a particular recognisable flavour ... trainees' expectations, fears, anxieties and, often, low self-esteem stemming from previous educational experiences ... as adults are likely to regress at times into dependent child states, where they both request and resent firm guidance from their tutors' (1998: 105–106). Of course, this can translate to the role of trainer, as demonstrated in the following quote:

> [I]n fact I really hated sharing responsibility (with my peers) for the self-selection of tutorial groups. It felt like we were doing the tutorial staff's jobs. Why could they not have made it easier for us and sorted out the tutorial groups themselves? (Alred, 2006: 290)

Smith (2011) conducted a piece of research investigating the student–tutor relationships and their impact on learning within counselling programmes. In line with the findings of Galbraith and Hogan's research on personal development group facilitators, Smith found that these relationships have a significant impact on learning experience, with a safe and supportive tutor-facilitated environment being integral to an effective learning experience. However, regardless of tutoring and facilitation style, trainees *can* take responsibility for their learning. Box 5.4 outlines some ways they can do this.

Box 5.4   Tips for trainees

- Adopting a sense of responsibility from the beginning of their training;
- Being forward thinking in terms of placement choices and research interests;
- Being in a position to increase their learning outcomes through awareness of their own individual learning styles and engaging in wide and critical reading;
- Increasing their personal development through providing a safe and supportive environment for one another to take risks and being mindful that the roles of tutor and facilitator continue to retain their impact, in some ways reflecting the client–therapist relationship.

THE FUTURE

Counselling psychology training is demanding. One former counselling trainee described it as follows:

> [It is] one of the most dramatic periods of my life. I sometimes think the course directors should issue a health warning to prospective trainees! A facetious observation this may be, but on a more serious note, several of my fellow trainees have (like me) undergone dramatic lifestyle changes as a result of the course. (Kidd, 2004: 60)

And this is only the beginning. In a profession such as ours, many have a thirst for learning and are continually striving to learn more and to continue to develop both personally and professionally. In essence, training never really ends, and the more we know, the more we realise we do not know. For this reason, continual professional development (CPD) is not only needed but is also a requirement for maintaining professional registration. The Health and Care Professions Council (HCPC) (2005: 4) has specific CPD requirements for registrants, as shown in Box 5.5.

Box 5.5   The Health and Care Professions Council's CPD requirements

Practitioner psychologists must:

1. maintain a continuous, up-to-date and accurate record of their CPD activities;
2. demonstrate that their CPD activities are a mixture of learning activities relevant to current or future practice;
3. seek to ensure that their CPD has contributed to the quality of their practice and service delivery;
4. seek to ensure that their CPD benefits the service user; and
5. upon request, present a written profile (which must be their own work and supported by evidence) explaining how they have met the standards for CPD.

In conclusion, training and academic work is a lifelong pursuit, and the first year of training is just a continuation of the journey that may have begun a long time ago. Trainees can take advantage of the training opportunity by taking responsibility for learning rather than sitting back to absorb knowledge, making good use of the 'self' in the learning process, and thinking critically and outside the box. In essence, engagement with academia during training can act as a catalyst for change and for making a difference to the profession of counselling psychology.

Visit the companion website for the following:

- QCoP Independent Route.
- A Conversation with Trainees.
- Engaging with Training and Academia.

REFERENCES

Alred, G. (2006) 'A trainee's perspective', in R. Bor and M. Watts (eds), *The Trainee Handbook: A Guide for Counselling and Psychotherapy Trainees* (2nd edn). London: Sage. pp. 284–296.

Biggs, J. (2002) 'The reflective institution: Assuring and enhancing the quality of teaching and learning'. Retrieved on 29 July 2014 from http://webcache.googleusercontent.com/search?q=cache:6Yr2X4v8jwUJ:www.medev.heacademy.ac.uk/assets/documents/resources/database/id109_The_Reflective_Institution_Assuring_and_enhancing_the_quality_of_teaching_and_learning.rtf+&cd=1&hl=en&ct=clnk&gl=uk

British Psychological Society (BPS) (2007) *Professional Practice Guidelines for Counselling Psychology*. Leicester: BPS. Retrieved on 22 February 2015 from www.bps.org.uk/sites/default/files/documents/professional_practice_guidelines_-_division_of_counselling_psychology.pdf

British Psychological Society (BPS) (2009) *Code of Ethics and Conduct*. Leicester: BPS. Retrieved on 22 February 2015 from www.bps.org.uk/system/files/documents/code_of_ethics_and_conduct.pdf

British Psychological Society (BPS) (2014) *Standards for Doctoral Programmes in Counselling Psychology*. Leicester: BPS. Retrieved on 22 February 2015 from www.bps.org.uk/system/files/Public%20files/PaCT/counselling_accreditation_2014_web.pdf

Cottrell, S. (2011) *Critical Thinking Skills: Developing Effective Analysis and Argument* (2nd edn). London: Palgrave Macmillan.

Dinwoodie (n.d.) 'How to encourage professionalism in your trainees'. Retrieved on 1 August 2014 from www.medicalprotection.org/uk/practice-matters/issue-6/how-to-encourage-professionalism-in-your-trainees

Donati, M. and Watts, M.H. (2000) 'Personal development in counselling psychology training: The case for further research', *Counselling Psychology Review*, 15 (1): 12–21.

Galbraith, V.E. and Hart, N.M. (2007) 'Personal development groups in counselling psychology training: The case for further research', *Counselling Psychology Review*, 22 (4): 49–57.

Galbraith, V.E. and Hogan, N.M. (2006) 'A grounded theory model of personal development groups in counselling psychology training'. Unpublished doctoral thesis, University of Wolverhampton.

Health and Care Professions Council (HCPC) (2005) *Continuing Professional Development and Your Registration*. London: HCPC. Retrieved on 10 August 2014 from www.hcpc-uk.org.uk/registrants/cpd/

Health and Care Professions Council (HCPC) (2010) *Guidance on Conduct and Ethics for Students*. London: HCPC. Retrieved on 22 February 2015 from www.hpc-uk.org/publications/brochures/index.asp?id=219

Health and Care Professions Council (HCPC) (2012a) *Standards of Proficiency: Practitioner Psychologists*. London: HCPC. Retrieved on 22 February 2015 from www.hpc-uk.org/assets/documents/10002963sop_practitioner_psychologists.pdf

Health and Care Professions Council (HCPC) (2012b) 'Research report: Professionalism in healthcare professionals'. Retrieved on 4 December 2014 from www.hcpc-uk.org.uk/assets/documents/10003771Professionalisminhealthcareprofessionals.pdf

Honey, P. and Mumford, A. (1986) *The Manual of Learning Styles*. Maidenhead: Peter Honey.

Irving, J.A. and Williams, D.I. (1995) 'Experience of group work in counsellor training and preferred learning styles', *Counselling Psychology Quarterly*, 8(2): 139–144.

Johns, H. (1996) *Personal Development in Counsellor Training*. London: Cassell.

Keys, S. (2004) 'Singing out', in V. Harding Davies, G. Alred, K. Hunt and G. Davies (eds), *Experiences of Counsellor Training: Challenges, Surprise and Change*. London: Palgrave. pp. 71–79.

Kidd, C. (2004) 'A new world', in V. Harding Davies, G. Alred, K. Hunt and G. Davies (eds), *Experiences of Counsellor Training: Challenges, Surprise and Change*. London: Palgrave. pp. 58–70.

Koltz, R. and Champe, J. (2010) 'A phenomenological case study: The transition of mental health counseling interns from students to professionals'. Retrieved on 4 December 2014 from http://counselingoutfitters.com/vistas/vistas10/Article_31.pdf

Lennie, C. (2007) 'The role of personal development groups in counsellor training: Understanding factors contributing to self-awareness in the personal development group', *British Journal of Guidance and Counselling*, 35(1): 115–129.

Martin, P. (2010) 'Training and professional development', in R. Woolfe, S. Strawbridge, B. Douglas and W. Dryden (eds), *Handbook of Counselling Psychology* (3rd edn). London: Sage. pp. 547–568.

Quality Assurance Agency (QAA) (2011) 'Doctoral Degree Characteristics'. Retrieved on 10 August 2014 from www.qaa.ac.uk

Richards, G. (1999) 'The cultural (in)sensitivity of personal therapy for trainee counselling psychologists'. Paper presented at Annual Counselling Psychology Conference, Brighton.

Robinson, W.L. (1974) 'Conscious competency: The mark of a competent instructor', *Personnel Journal*, 53: 538–539.

Rønnestad, M.H. and Skovholt, T.M. (2003) 'The journey of the counselor and therapist: Research findings and perspectives on professional development', *Journal of Career Development*, 30(1): 5–44.

Royal College of Physicians (RCP) (2005) 'Doctors in society: Medical professionalism in a changing world'. *Report of a Working Party of the Royal College of Physicians in London.* London: RCP.

Schön, D. (1987) *Educating the Reflective Practitioner: Toward a New Design for Teaching and Learning in the Professions.* San Francisco, CA: Jossey-Bass.

Skovholt, T.M. and Rønnestad, M.H. (2013) *The Developing Practitioner: Growth and Stagnation of Therapists and Counselors.* New York: Routledge.

Smith, V.J. (2011) 'It's the relationship that matters: A qualitative analysis of the role of the student–tutor relationship in counselling training', *Counselling Psychology Quarterly,* 24(3): 233–246.

Taylor-Smith, H. (2004) 'The consequences of clarity', in V. Harding Davies, G. Alred, K. Hunt and G. Davies (eds), *Experiences of Counsellor Training: Challenges, Surprise and Change.* London: Palgrave. pp. 24–35.

Thomas, A. (1998) 'Groups in counselling training', in H. Johns (ed.), *Balancing Acts: Studies in Counselling Training.* London: Routledge. pp. 96–109.

Totton, N. (September, 2009) 'Power in the therapy room', *Therapy Today,* 20(7): 16–19.

Tran, V.-A. (2004) 'Picking up the gauntlet', in V. Harding Davies, G. Alred, K. Hunt and G. Davies (eds), *Experiences of Counsellor Training: Challenges, Surprise and Change.* London: Palgrave. pp. 8–23.

University of Wolverhampton (2013–14) *Professional Doctorate in Counselling Psychology Course Guide.* Wolverhampton.

Wallace, M. and Wray, A. (2011) *Critical Reading and Writing for Postgraduates* (2nd edn). SAGE Study Skills Series. London: Sage.

Wilkins, P. (1997) *Personal and Professional Development for Counsellors.* London: Sage.

Williams, F., Coyle, A. and Lyons, E. (1999) 'How counselling psychologists view their personal therapy', *British Journal of Medical Psychology,* 72(4): 545–555.

Williams, D.I. and Irving, J.A. (1996) 'Personal growth: Rogerian paradoxes', *British Journal of Guidance & Counselling,* 24: 165–172.

Woolfe, R. (1996) 'The nature of counselling psychology', in R. Woolfe and W. Dryden (eds), *Handbook of Counselling Psychology.* London: Sage. pp. 3–20.

6
ENTERING CLINICAL PLACEMENTS
JANE LAWRENCE

INTRODUCTION

An important phase of the journey to becoming a counselling psychologist begins when trainees meet their first client on placement. However, the importance of systematic preparation, before even entering clinical placements, should not be underestimated. As with any journey, it is essential to know the 'destination', map the route and have appropriate resources to meet any challenges along the way. At the point of successful completion of training on programmes approved by the Health and Care Professions Council (HCPC, 2012a), trainees will have acquired requisite core academic knowledge and competencies, and will have demonstrated that they are 'fit to practise' in accordance with the HCPC standards of education and training, and the standards for doctoral programmes in counselling psychology (BPS, 2014). The acquisition of knowledge and skills, and their application in practice, is facilitated by clinical teaching on a doctoral programme, though some trainees may choose the Independent route, also known as the Qualification in Counselling Psychology (QCoP). Integral to either mode of training are: private study, placement experience, the completion of academic assignments and the requirement to undergo their own personal therapy, which provides an additional resource for trainee self-development. In common with clinical psychology trainees, more than half of counselling psychology trainees' learning will occur on their placements (Falender and Shafranske, 2004).

Placement learning is, therefore, a fundamental component of counselling psychology training programmes, integrating other aspects of trainees' learning and development (see Figure 6.1), and represents a seminal step in the journey to becoming a competent, reflective practitioner with transferable skills. Good placement experiences enable trainees to develop their clinical skills, to apply theoretical knowledge, and to practise safely and ethically under supervision from experienced practitioners, and they provide a bridge between academic and workplace learning (Rodger et al., 2008). Moreover, it is on placement, working alongside counselling psychologists and having exposure to other professionals, that they begin to embrace their identity as trainee counselling psychologists as they learn about the practical aspects of the role.

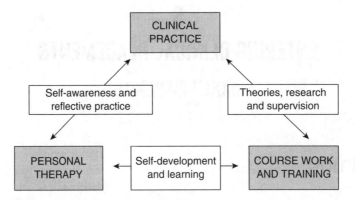

Figure 6.1   Personal and professional development

Counselling psychology bridges two different disciplines, that is counselling and psychology, and with its strong commitment to a diversity of approaches to research and therapy, this contributes to a construction of the profession as set apart from more 'schoolist' traditions of psychotherapy (Moore and Rae, 2009, p. 381). Increasingly, the profession is adopting a more explicit social justice perspective, highlighting the importance of delivering therapy to marginalised service users/clients (Cutts, 2013) and a need to consider the implications of culture, gender and disability as applicable to trainees, staff and clients (Siggins Miller Consultants, 2012). Adopting a postmodern, critical stance towards traditional approaches, while at the same time developing a coherent professional identity, can be challenging for new trainees. However, the experience of providing services to clients can play an important role in fostering a positive sense of a professional identity, and of belonging to a professional community, particularly where the clinical setting embraces the values of counselling psychology (Gazzola et al., 2011).

It is important, therefore, that trainees begin their training well prepared to secure the kind of placements that will support their learning on the training course they have chosen. This chapter provides guidance on how to prepare for finding the first clinical placement and what the respective perspectives of training programmes and placement providers are. It also goes on to map out what the trainees' responsibilities are when on placement and how best to navigate the various expectations of the training programme and placement providers.

TRAINEE PERSPECTIVE: WHAT TO EXPECT AND HOW TO PREPARE FOR ENTERING PLACEMENTS

Planning ahead

The BPS (2014) sets core standards for doctoral programmes in Counselling Psychology, leading to eligibility for Chartered Membership of the Society (CPsychol) and full membership of the Division of Counselling Psychology on successful completion of the training. Nevertheless, training programmes vary in the emphases they place on gaining experience with particular clinical groups and therapeutic modalities, and their curriculum content and training methods may also differ. Similarly, potential applicants will differ in their experience and training; they may have been assistant psychologists and will typically have experience of working one to one in a helping capacity with clients in mental health settings. Relevant experience includes support-work, generic counselling/training and the role of an Improving Access to Psychological Therapy (IAPT)-trained Psychological Wellbeing Practitioner (PWP), providing low-intensity Cognitive Behaviour Therapy (CBT) interventions, or acting as a High Intensity (HI) practitioner. There is, therefore, scope for trainees to develop their own training pathway in the context of the requirements of a particular training programme, their own preferences, previous experience, strengths and competencies. The selection of appropriate and varied practice placements to create a coherent profile of practice experience will be instrumental in building on these competencies and enhancing employability.

Before applying to a particular training programme it is essential, therefore, that potential applicants not only have the relevant experience and academic qualifications required (BPS, 2014), but also an awareness of their own preferences, in order to achieve a good fit between what is offered and what they are seeking. By the end of their programme, trainees will have demonstrated competence to postgraduate level of the theory and practice in at least one specific model of psychological therapy and a working knowledge and supervised practice in one other (BPS, 2014). However, as the particular modalities are not prescribed, it will be important for prospective applicants to be clear as to the theoretical model and requirements of their chosen programme (e.g. CBT/Psychodynamic/Integrative). They will also need to be realistic about the financial implications of a training that requires them to work in a voluntary or honorary capacity, cover the costs of training and associated expenses, such as therapy and supervision, and manage the logistics of getting to the training institution and their placements (Bor et al., 1997). Additionally, it is important to bear in mind that programmes may differ in terms of their placement and supervision requirements, what count as 'clinical practice' hours and the placement opportunities they have access to, or provide.

Securing the first placement

Each programme will have particular specifications but, in general, a suitable placement is one that meets the threshold standards set out by the HCPC in the *Standards of Education and Training* (2012a), in conjunction with the requirements of the training institution. These standards (SET 5) encompass health and safety policies and procedures, ethical practice, trainees' rights and the responsibilities of placement managers and supervisors. These aim to ensure appropriate governance of placement procedures and enable trainees who successfully complete their training to be eligible to apply for registration with the HCPC.

The point at which trainees will be seeking their first placement will depend on the requirements of each training programme. It is essential to find out what this will involve as soon as a training place has been offered and accepted, and to be guided by the requirements of the programme and the programme placement co-ordinator, or co-ordinating supervisor if trainees are on the Independent route. Training programmes may have organised placement opportunities or a list of recommended placement organisations to which trainees can apply, or trainees may have to begin their own search. Whatever the requirement, trainees will need to be proactive in the process, particularly if they have to find their own placement.

Securing placements, particularly the first one, is a competitive process and can be a lengthy one, as it is likely to include several applications and interviews before reaching the stage of the taking up of references, the completion of an honorary contract, Disclosure and Barring Service (DBS) check (formerly Criminal Records Bureau (CRB) check), or Scottish or Northern Ireland equivalent, and an induction. The sooner a trainee starts, the better positioned they will be to choose a placement rather than feel they have to take anything that is offered, whether or not it is suitable (Clark, 2004). Concerns about achieving the required number of supervised clinical practice hours can start to override other considerations if the securing of a placement is left to the last minute.

The primary aim for all trainees, whether on training programmes or on the Independent route, will be to match the placement experience to the therapeutic modality in which they are seeking competence (Gazzola et al., 2011). Another major consideration is whether the placement can provide an experience that amounts to more than the trainee just attending to achieve their target of supervised practice hours in a particular modality. Trainees will initially be guided by tutors on the programme, or their co-ordinating supervisor (QCoP), in the selection of suitable placements. A suitable placement is one that offers experience of working in an organisation, while providing the level of individual support that will best enable trainees to achieve the learning outcomes and relevant clinical competencies. Ideally, this would aim to build on their current experience and interests.

Even when programmes have some existing arrangements with nearby placement providers and/or provide opportunities for trainees to apply for, trainees may need, or choose, to find their own placements, particularly if they live at some distance from the training institution and want to be on placement in a more convenient location. Indeed, trainees who take the initiative to secure placements that interest them can find this contributes to their personal and professional development, as Sarah, a trainee on a part-time programme, reflected:

> The first year I felt that I did a lot of the work in finding a placement. The placements suggested by the university didn't come to much for me, so I approached organisations that I found of interest and had success that way. In many ways, this was beneficial for my confidence and I had a sense of my own autonomy as a result. (Sarah, second-year trainee)

The initial search for a suitable placement can be a somewhat daunting process given the diversity of potential providers, including: the NHS; third sector and social care; primary, secondary and tertiary care; in-patient units and community services; and organisational, educational and forensic settings. The degree of support different services can provide will vary, as will trainees' needs and their current skill set and level of competence. Another London-based trainee, Raj, compared her experience of a third sector placement and one in the NHS:

> Charities often lack resources and time, so they cannot always provide enough support to first years but this is where they are more likely to end up. ... NHS placements are more containing and there is support and clear protocols compared to placements in charities. (Raj, second-year trainee)

As this quote suggests, NHS placements may require applicants to have some counselling experience. Those trainees without practical experience may need to begin their search in third-sector organisations, which may be more flexible but lack the resources to provide a comparable level of support. So, it is important that a trainee's approach is realistic, persistent and, above all, systematic in making a plan and initiating a search, treating the process just like a job hunt.

When searching for potential placements, it is a good idea to make an initial call to identify and arrange to speak to the placement manager, either to check if they are offering placements or to find out more about the placement and to check its potential suitability before proceeding with an application. Trainees will be asked to complete an application form or send a curriculum vitae (CV) and covering letter, setting out the reasons they are applying to the placement and why they are suitable for it. It is a good idea to prepare a CV and covering letter in advance, and then adapt these to the particular organisation. It is important to neither underplay nor overplay past experience, rather to identify existing transferable skills. References will be taken up by placement providers, so it is important to establish in advance who can provide a reference, for example a tutor, placement co-ordinator, or co-ordinating supervisor (QCoP), and then to inform referees before submitting the formal application (Clark, 2004).

The questions in Box 6.1, taking into account the particular programme's requirements, need to be considered when beginning the search for a suitable placement.

Box 6.1 Finding a suitable placement: Key questions

- Does the academic institution have existing placement partnerships? If not, what help is available from the programme to guide the search?
- By which date must a placement be secured?
- What would be a manageable distance to travel and how will the trainee get there?
- How many days on placement are required by the programme and which days does the trainee have available?
- How many clients or client hours are required?
- What category of clients (e.g. adults, children)?
- What kind of presenting problems and level of complexity are appropriate (e.g. mild-to-moderate anxiety)?
- What therapeutic modality does the programme teach and is experience of a particular modality required for assessment purposes (e.g. CBT, integrative, psychodynamic)?
- What are the arrangements for supervision and who holds clinical responsibility for the work? Is supervision provided on placement or by the programme, or do trainees find their own supervisors? If so, what qualification should supervisors have to comply with programme requirements?
- Should the placement experience include group work and other non-clinical work (e.g. presentations, meetings, leadership experiences)?
- What placement documentation must be completed for the programme and the placement (e.g. a contract, personal liability insurance)?
- What health and safety issues need to be considered (e.g. physical environment and personal security)?
- Who is responsible for arranging a Disclosure and Barring Service check (DBS), or Scottish or Northern Ireland equivalent?

Attending interviews

When offered an interview, trainees should approach this as they would a job application and respond promptly. It is often the case that trainees make multiple applications resulting in multiple interviews, which may coincide. It is important to behave professionally, communicate clearly and attend interviews on time. Trainees should dress appropriately, bearing in mind the setting, the role they are applying for and the client group.

The interview itself provides an opportunity for both the placement and the trainee to establish whether there is a good fit between the requirements of each. So, trainees should ensure that they have done their research about the organisation and its client group in advance, and be clear about what their programme's specific requirements are, for example: the ratio of supervision to client hours; the qualifications of a potential supervisor; the number of clinical hours needed to successfully complete the placement; the year-specific learning outcomes; and procedures for placement assessment. It is also a good idea to take along some questions, to establish whether what the trainee is able to offer will match with the expressed needs of the placement (Clark, 2004). These may include the placement days offered and level of experience required by the placement. If they are expected to record client sessions, trainees should ensure that they check whether this is permissible, as not all placements will agree to this.

Post-interview considerations

It is vital to establish whether there is a good fit between what the placement is offering and what the trainee needs, with regard to the number and suitability of client referrals they can expect. This is key to the likely success of the placement experience, as Raj reflects:

> Learning objectives are more easily met if placements match the therapeutic orientation of the service. This should be emphasised early on. In my experience of counselling organisations, they do not always allocate appropriate clients in terms of their complexity and suitability. (Raj, second-year trainee)

A common dilemma is for trainees to find they receive more than one offer at the same time, or receive one offer while waiting to hear from their preferred placement. It is important to be realistic about what is a manageable workload and, if in doubt, to discuss this with a tutor on the programme, or the QCoP supervisor, rather than to take on more than one placement and risk being overwhelmed.

Checking what paperwork needs to be completed for the placement and the programme before the placement begins, and being conscientious about ensuring this is done in a timely fashion, reduces stress for the trainee. Questions commonly arise with regard to supervision arrangements. Trainees should check whether supervision is provided on the placement and whether additional supervision is needed to meet the programme requirements, requiring liaison and negotiation between programme and placement (see Hitchings, Chapter 7 in this volume). The majority of a trainee's supervision should be provided by a counselling psychologist with two years' post-qualification experience, but programmes may be flexible depending on the supervision available and the context of the specific placement. Similarly, some placements require all supervision to be 'in-house', while others may be flexible about trainees having external supervision if the placement is unable to provide supervision by a counselling psychologist and if this is a programme requirement. Trainees will need to be both persistent and patient throughout this process, as it can take up to three months to complete all the necessary paperwork to set up a placement.

Getting started on placement

Before assigning clients, placements should provide trainees with an induction, which will inform them about placement protocols and procedures to do with the day-to-day running of the service, health and safety matters, and risk management. The provision of information at the beginning of the placement was reported as a top priority by clinical psychology trainees (Hughes and Byrne, 2011). Similarly, for counselling psychology trainees, being oriented to the service context is important, including the opportunity to ask questions and familiarise themselves with the setting and practical matters such as where they will see clients, administrative procedures, how clients are referred, what client measures must be completed at each session, and how client data are recorded.

As with any job, trainees should be clear as to what time they are expected to start each day, what is appropriate dress and what exactly their responsibilities are with regard to attending team or other meetings, supervision and training events at the placement. It is important for their professional development and understanding of the role of a counselling psychologist in practice, that trainees make the time and effort to engage in activities additional to providing therapy sessions, and learn about the responsibilities of working in a team. The following comments by three trainees on a part-time London programme highlight this:

> [C]linical placements rarely have the necessary induction/training needs for a trainee. I could come in simply for client hours then leave, not feeling integrated or contained. (Second-year trainee)

> I strongly feel that all effort should be made to ensure trainees are in placements which develop us as psychologists and therefore requires that we work closely with other psychologists within the placement. (Fourth-year trainee)

> [T]rainees sometimes only attend placement specifically for the time we are actually seeing clients, but in doing so we miss the other aspects of the role of the psychologist in the workplace. Report writing, multidisciplinary team meetings, communication with the team – all [are] important skills to have for the role of psychologist. (Fourth-year trainee)

Where placements do not offer or encourage participation in their wider activities, it is important that trainees are proactive in voicing their training needs in discussion with placement manager, supervisor and placement co-ordinator. Setting developmentally appropriate goals for the placement that reflect the learning outcomes of the programme and the trainee's particular needs is essential in facilitating both trainees' confidence in the assessment procedures and the likelihood that the placement experience will be successful.

As mentioned, an important part of this process is the negotiation of the number and level of complexity of the cases allocated to the trainee (Keary and Byrne, 2013). This should be a collaborative process, between the trainee and supervisor, to which the placement manager may contribute. It is usual that an inexperienced trainee will be given one case to begin with and then be allocated another when the supervisor considers that the trainee is ready. While some trainees can find this frustrating as they are concerned about achieving their clinical hours, trainees would be well advised not to take on too many cases initially. Placement managers may welcome an enthusiastic trainee's wish to take on a large caseload, but it can lead to trainees feeling overwhelmed and having insufficient time to reflect on their learning, and put them at risk of burn-out. On the other hand, taking on too few cases during a placement means that there may be insufficient opportunity to consolidate learning, build confidence and fulfil the required number of practice hours. Such concerns should be raised in supervision as soon as they arise and, with the supervisor's agreement, discussed with the placement manager. Trainees should similarly raise such matters with their placement co-ordinator, or QCoP co-ordinating supervisor, as joint discussion between training institution and placement may be helpful in expediting a mutually beneficial solution.

Making good use of the placement experience: Managing anxieties

Research exploring the potential stressors of counselling psychology training indicates that placement-related matters, such as fitting placements in around other commitments, finding suitable placements and achieving the clinical hours, figure as key concerns for trainees, alongside issues that might be considered intrinsic to a postgraduate clinical training (Kumary and Baker, 2008). Indeed, Skovholt and Rønnestad (2003) conceptualise the trainee therapist's journey as an 'arduous' one and identify seven potential stressors for new trainees: performance anxiety, the scrutiny of gatekeepers, porous or rigid emotional boundaries, fragile practitioner-self, inadequate conceptual map, glamourised expectations and need for positive mentors. They highlight the inherent ambiguity and complexity of the work of a therapist, which may only become apparent to a new trainee when they encounter their first client and realise that developing therapeutic relationships and conceptualising client problems is more difficult than they imagined. While this anxiety cannot be removed, knowing that there are struggles ahead can normalise the experience and encourage discussion of their doubts with tutors and supervisors as they arise, so contributing to self-awareness (Truell, 2001).

Developing a capacity to tolerate this ambiguity will help trainees to focus on what they can learn from placement experiences and, in particular, to embrace the tensions that arise within the trainee in relation to the many perspectives they encounter: clients', supervisors', tutors' and, not least, their own subjectivity. These tensions are perhaps heightened by counselling psychology's commitment to diversity and the requirement to be trained in at least two therapeutic models (BPS, 2014). As Rizq (2006, p. 618) points out, counselling psychology trainees are faced with 'constant dialogue with, and accommodation to, differing voices, opinions and minorities'. They are expected to manage this in the context of counselling psychology's philosophical and epistemological position of postmodern pluralism, which does not align itself to any one model of therapy and indeed values critical engagement with multiple theoretical perspectives. While having different perspectives on their client work can be experienced as enriching, the lack of certainty this generates can also be experienced as confusing and anxiety-provoking for new trainees (Scott and Hanley, 2012):

> Often it is very overwhelming having one (or more) internal supervisors and an external supervisor (if the internal supervisor is not a counselling psychologist or the supervision to clinical hours does not meet the programme requirements). While it can be helpful to get different perspectives, it can also be confusing and overwhelming when a trainee, especially in the early part of training. (Sue, third-year trainee)

Understandably, this can leave trainees unsure which is the 'right' approach, and without a conceptual map to understand and guide the work. Being told that they need to learn to manage this uncertainty may only engender further frustration! This is reminiscent of Raimy's (1950, p. 150) somewhat paradoxical description: 'Psychotherapy is an undefined technique applied to unspecified problems with an unpredictable outcome. For this we recommend rigorous training.' Nevertheless, uncertainty about how to help their first client is a common experience for new trainees and can generate intense disappointment with their training programme and their supervisors. It can also induce self-doubt and anxiety, particularly if trainees hold perfectionist beliefs and believe they have fallen short of their idealised view of what they 'should' be able to achieve (Truell, 2001).

So, it is common for trainees to feel anxious when entering their first placement. Self-doubt and fears about whether they will know what to say to a client and whether they will be able to keep talking for the therapy hour may preoccupy trainees; they may wonder whether they have 'the personal characteristics needed for this kind of work, the resourcefulness needed to complete the studies and the ability to bridge the felt chasm between theory and practice' (Rønnestad and Skovholt, 2003, p. 12). Trainees may hold unrealistic expectations of what the training placement requires of them and may be anxious about voicing such concerns to a supervisor, a programme tutor, or QCoP supervisor, aware that they are being assessed by each. Regular communication between programme tutors and the placement can help to normalise performance anxiety and self-doubts, particularly when trainees are included in three-way meetings, as this trainee suggests:

> Constant evaluation can be overwhelming and anxiety-provoking, particularly when this comes from placement supervisors, and this might sometimes hinder what is/isn't disclosed in supervision. It might be helpful to have a face-to-face meeting between personal tutor/ placement supervisor and trainee once a year. (Sue, third-year trainee)

Programmes recognise that trainees need extra support and encouragement from supervisors as they start seeing clients, and so it is usual for trainees to be required, initially, to receive weekly supervision, to support their learning and provide case management and guidance. This may take the form of individual and/or group supervision at the placement, with additional external supervision organised by the trainee or the programme, depending on the programme requirements. Being given the opportunity to observe a more experienced practitioner, or to be observed by a supervisor, can be helpful where these experiences provide supportive, positive feedback and clarify trainees' expectations of the placement:

Having the opportunity to observe a supervisor/more experienced practitioner in a session with a client would be really helpful. Perhaps this could be encouraged/suggested. I had the opportunity to be observed and to do joint sessions with my supervisor and the feedback from this was very helpful. (John, fourth-year trainee)

Having access to mentors, supervisors and tutors who can provide support and act as role models is crucial. Ideally, they should offer trainees both the certainty of their professional experience, knowledge and competence and a reflective space in which the uncertainty of there being many alternatives can be explored. Experiencing this kind of guided learning is instrumental in enabling trainees to embrace ambivalence and make the most of their placement experience (Rizq, 2006). Additionally, the role of the placement co-ordinator as a positive mentor in providing a supportive reflective space for problem-solving will be particularly important should difficulties arise on placement.

TRAINEE RESPONSIBILITIES: RECORD-KEEPING AND MAINTAINING FITNESS TO PRACTISE

Trainees are responsible for negotiating the practical issues to do with managing their own study time, their placement commitments and fitting all of this, including their therapy and supervision, around their days on the programme and the other demands of their personal life (Kumary and Baker, 2008). Trainees will have specific administrative responsibilities with regard to record-keeping on the placement, keeping appropriate client records and communicating in writing with other professionals and the client, as required by the placement. Trainees will also be expected to maintain accurate records of their clinical hours, supervision and non-clinical activities on placement and submit these to their programme, or co-ordinating supervisor (QCoP), as specified.

Most importantly, trainees have ethical responsibilities to their clients and to themselves in terms of recognising the limits of their competence and when they may not be fit to practise; developing their professional skills and knowledge; and maintaining high standards of personal conduct. The HCPC (2012b, pp. 9–12; 2012c) requires that both registrants and those applying for registration (including trainees and graduates of training programmes) should adhere to a set of minimum standards of conduct, performance and ethics to ensure that those providing services do so in the best interests of service users, communicate appropriately, respect confidentiality and do not behave in any way that damages confidence in their profession. Trainees should also ensure they are familiar with the BPS's *Code of Ethics and Conduct* (2009) and HCPC's *Guidance on Conduct and Ethics for Students* (HCPC, 2012b) and have their own professional liability insurance.

Regulating one's emotional response to clients is critical to maintaining fitness to practise, but can be challenging for a relatively inexperienced trainee. Trainees may, for example, be influenced by a strong inclination, drawing on their experience as a helper in other contexts, to give advice and sympathise. Skovholt and Rønnestad (2003) identify three ways trainees can respond, each with different implications for the trainee's capacity to differentiate between client and therapist responsibilities and to maintain appropriate boundaries. These are premature closure (feeling overwhelmed and then detaching); insufficient closure (experiencing an inability to stop thinking about the client, or over-identifying); and functional closure (feeling able to reflect, not becoming stuck, and acting therapeutically). Finding the balance between over- and under-involvement can take time and experience and requires an ability to engage emotionally while not taking responsibility for clients' emotions. Caring for the self is an important part of this process of learning to recognise 'what is ours and what is not' (Barker, 2010, p. 45).

Identifying and addressing problems on placement

For new trainees, meeting clients for the first time can constitute a critical incident and they may be particularly sensitive to negative feedback from their clients or supervisors (Rønnestad and Skovholt, 2003). Uncertainty as to how assessment criteria are applied can also interfere with trainees' ability to reflect on their client work and contribute to disillusionment and loss of confidence (Skovholt and Rønnestad, 2003). It is important that trainees consult their supervisor and programme tutor/placement co-ordinator if they have concerns that they are not progressing towards the achievement of the learning outcomes and required hours. Trainees are advised to bring concerns first to their supervisor, although in some instances they might consult tutors/placement co-ordinator first, particularly if the concerns are about supervision. Examples of issues of concern are listed in Box 6.2.

Box 6.2   Issues that might cause concern for a trainee

- Placement management issues, such as organisation of rooms, administration, level of support with regard to placement procedures
- Too much or too little involvement with other activities on placement, such as trainings and meetings
- Availability of manager/supervisor/mentor
- Lack of opportunity to observe experienced staff
- Lack of contact with, or opportunity to meet, other trainees on the placement
- Caseload that does not support the achievement of learning objectives in some way: too complex, not complex enough, too large, too small
- Regularity, amount and/or quality of supervision
- The extent to which differences in style of trainee and supervisor or relationship difficulties can be discussed in supervision
- Lack of clarity as to what is expected to pass the placement
- Negotiating an appropriate level of dependence/independence with supervisor

---

Placement failure

Concerns about professional competence should be discussed with the trainee and other relevant individuals, for example the supervisor and clinical tutor, as soon as issues arise and/or at a mid-year review, or quarterly review for QCoP. In such a meeting, a plan would be agreed with the trainee setting out new learning objectives and/or actions required to address the concerns identified, with copies of any agreements shared with supervisor, placement manager and trainee. However, when concerns are serious, for example contravening BPS Code of Ethics or HCPC standards, a placement manager or supervisor may end the placement contract immediately, and the trainee may not be permitted to continue training.

A trainee may fail a placement because he/she has not met the learning objectives or outcomes and/or because of fitness to practise issues, including those outlined in Box 6.3.

Box 6.3   Reasons for placement failure

- Evidence of insufficient learning or progress during the placement contract
- Failure to make use of supervision
- Poor reliability/time management
- Major and/or persistent interpersonal difficulties with clients, colleagues or other staff members on the placement
- Failure to disclose relevant personal information that could impact detrimentally on client care
- Gross incompetence or negligence resulting in potential harm to themselves, patients/clients, or to the public, including failure to inform supervisor, programme team, or co-ordinating supervisor of critical actions or situations when this could be expected
- Abuse of clients, supervisors, or other staff members
- Other gross or unprofessional conduct, including contravention of placement policy, the BPS *Code of Ethics and Conduct* (2009). Trainees should ensure they are familiar with these standards and the BPS codes of practice (2009) and have their own professional liability insurance.

Following the guidance above, and making effective use of the available support, can help ensure that trainees successfully navigate their first placement experience, managing the concept of practising within the boundaries of their competence and pre-empting potential issues, as outlined above.

Thus far, the focus has been on the trainee perspective, and we now move to a consideration of a key stakeholder in this process, the training institution.

PROGRAMME RESPONSIBILITIES

For those psychologists engaged in the teaching of trainees who will be undertaking clinical practice, alongside their developmental role there is an ethical responsibility to act as gatekeepers of the profession, whether in the UK or elsewhere (Brear et al., 2008; Johnson et al., 2008). Successful completion of an approved programme of training in counselling psychology allows trainees to meet the BPS standards for chartership and the HCPC standards of proficiency and makes them eligible to apply for registration. This requires programmes to make decisions about trainees' ability to practise ethically and effectively and to make judgements about trainees' academic ability and suitability for professional practice, in the interests of protecting the profession and the public. Though 'gatekeeping' is a widely used construct, there is little agreement as to how this is defined or implemented in practice, with evidence in the counselling and psychotherapy field that encountering unsuitable trainees is a common occurrence, and one which presents a challenge to those involved in the teaching and assessment of trainees. For example, a US study of psychologists in training found that 72 per cent of programmes and 10 per cent of internship sites reported having current trainees with significant psychological problems (Huprich and Rudd, 2004). Brear et al. (2008) explored these issues in Australia and offer this definition:

> Gatekeeping is the evaluation of student suitability for professional practice. It is a mechanism that aims to ensure the health of the profession by controlling access to it. It involves the identification of evaluative criteria and process, and the accountability of the gatekeeper to apply the criteria and take responsibility for the evaluative decisions. (Brear et al., 2008, p. 93)

Trainees' professional competence is regularly assessed by supervisors and monitored by programme tutors, and QCoP supervisors, in relation to developmentally appropriate learning outcomes agreed at the start of a placement. Professional competence is itself a complex construct which is assessed against a range of criteria, not least an ability to deliver ethical and effective therapy, but also self-understanding, psychological fitness to practise, interpersonal skills, awareness of diversity and difference, and personal qualities such as honesty and integrity (Johnson et al., 2008). It is incumbent upon the different stakeholders in this process that a transparent framework exists for early identification and management of competence issues on placement, which is both fair to trainees and ensures that trainee performance is properly evaluated. Programmes must ensure that they provide appropriate training to placement providers who will be completing assessments of trainees. Financial pressures on programmes and placement providers to keep numbers up, or a desire to avoid conflict, should not influence decisions as to a trainee's suitability or cause programmes to ignore evidence that a trainee is struggling. Psychologists have a duty of care to the public and to the trainees they teach and supervise (BPS, 2009; HCPC, 2012c).

Approval and monitoring of placements

The HCPC requires all programmes to ensure that trainees take up suitable placements, and to provide training for placement providers, so that providers know how to assess trainees in accordance with the required standards of the programme. There is similar governance of QCoP by the BPS, ensuring that procedures are in place to regularly monitor placements and each trainee's placement experience. These should include the following:

- Approval of the placement by placement co-ordinator or QCoP registrar before it starts, ensuring there are appropriate health and safety regulations, and equality and diversity policies and procedures, in place, as well as an adequate number of appropriately qualified staff and supervisors who are appropriately registered and have undertaken practice placement training. This comprises placement documents detailing the contracted agreement between trainee, placement and training programme, or co-ordinating supervisor for QCoP, for example, setting out the dates of the start and completion of the placement, days on placement, number of hours of clinical practice the trainee will undertake and arrangements for supervision, including who takes clinical responsibility for the trainee's work. (This is in addition to the honorary contract between placement and trainee in NHS settings.)
- Reviews of trainee learning outcomes/competencies/goals and progression. This will involve QCoP quarterly reviews or mid-year programme placement reviews with the placement supervisors, monitoring whether the trainee's placement goals, client hours and year-specific learning outcomes are on track to be met by the programme's assessment schedule or the trainee's plan of training (QCoP). This can then be used to formulate an updated plan to provide additional support for a trainee and/or set new placement goals. Timings will vary depending on whether programmes are part-time or full-time.
- End-of-year summative assessment reports from placement managers and placement supervisors, or annual plan of training updates (QCoP) which assess the trainee's progress in relation to the agreed learning outcomes and determine whether the trainee passes the placement.
- Where there is a failure to progress, there should be a clear procedure that identifies any fitness to practise concerns and provides for consultation and communication with the placement manager, supervisor, training institution and the trainee, and explains how a trainee can appeal or make a formal complaint. This process should identify what support is needed and lead to the implementation of a plan and review.
- Annual submission of a log of clinical, supervision and therapy hours, and non-clinical activities on placement, including practice reports/reviews as required by the programme or QCoP, verified by placement manager and/or supervisor and trainee. There should be opportunities for both placement providers and trainees to give feedback about the placement experience, recognising that placement providers are stakeholders, with a vested interest in the delivery of successful placements.

We now turn to a consideration of the placement perspective.

PLACEMENT RESPONSIBILITIES

While most placement experiences are mutually beneficial to the trainee and placement provider, there may be times when either one may not be satisfied with the conduct of the other. Placement managers and supervisors, as accredited professionals, must adhere to a code of ethics and thus have a duty of care to trainees, but their primary responsibility is to their clients and to the protection of their clients' confidentiality. They have a responsibility to inform a member of the programme team if they have concerns regarding a trainee's conduct on placement, in case this might put a service user or the trainee at risk of harm, even if no action needs to be taken. When completing trainee assessments they are required to do so honestly and to ensure that they are familiar with the programme, or QCoP learning outcomes, and how to assess these.

Placement providers are required to have their own documented procedures to deal with health and safety issues, and matters of compliance. These include protocols for the completion of contracted placements and their ethical management, and responding to complaints by a trainee. Placement managers and supervisors also need to be familiar with relevant training information advising them of assessment and fitness-to-practise procedures followed by the training institution. Additionally, where supervision is, by agreement with the placement and the programme, or QCoP co-ordinator, provided externally to the placement, procedures should be put in place to ensure regular communication between placement, supervisor and the programme, in order to provide appropriate support for the trainee's development. It is also important that placements are kept informed as to trainees' academic progress should this put at risk the continuation of their training and/or their placement. Box 6.4 outlines some potential issues.

Box 6.4   Issues that might cause concern for placement providers

- A mismatch is apparent between a trainee's skills and the needs of the client group
- A trainee does not demonstrate the level of competence expected
- A trainee does not progress as expected
- A trainee is unprofessional/inappropriate in their dress or in their behaviour with clients or colleagues
- A trainee does not attend supervision or responds defensively to feedback
- A trainee is under- or over-confident
- A trainee's attendance is unreliable
- A trainee appears to have health problems that have not previously been disclosed

---

If placement providers or supervisors have concerns about a trainee's engagement with service users/clients, supervisor or colleagues, or their well-being, this should be raised as soon as possible with the trainee, in the first instance, and the placement co-ordinator, programme team or co-ordinating supervisor should be informed. Some difficulties may arise through a misunderstanding to do with what either a trainee or placement provider expects of the other, so the early involvement of the programme's placement co-ordinator, or QCoP co-ordinating supervisor, may be helpful in resolving this and, where appropriate, implementing a revised set of learning objectives.

CONCLUSION

Placement experiences are likely to represent one of the most stimulating and both personally and professionally rewarding aspects of training. They provide a structured opportunity to observe, consult and work with other more experienced professionals, and in so doing develop awareness of the ethical dimensions of clinical work, its complexities and contradictions. They also help create an understanding of a professional practitioner's responsibilities, across a range of client groups and in different organisational contexts. Systematic preparation before entering placements will enhance trainees' enjoyment of what will undoubtedly be a challenging and influential learning experience, and provide a firm foundation for the further development of their competence, confidence and capacity for reflective practice.

Visit the companion website to listen to Entering Clinical Placements [12:01].

REFERENCES

Barker, M. (2010) 'Self-care and relationship conflict', *Sexual and Relationship Therapy*, 25(1): 37–47.

Bor, R., Watts, M. and Parker, J. (1997) 'Financial and practical implications of counselling psychology training: A student survey', *Counselling Psychology Quarterly*, 10(1): 69–75.

Brear, P., Dorrian, J. and Luscri, G. (2008) 'Preparing our future counselling professionals: Gatekeeping and the implications for research', *Counselling and Psychotherapy Research*, 8(2): 93–101.

British Psychological Society (BPS) (2009) *Code of Ethics and Conduct*. Leicester: British Psychological Society [Online]. Available at: www.bps.org.uk/system/files/documents/code_of_ethics_and_conduct.pdf (accessed 21 November 2014).

British Psychological Society (BPS) (2014) *Accreditation through Partnership Handbook: Guidance for Doctoral Programmes in Counselling Psychology*. Leicester: British Psychological Society [Online]. Available at: www.bps.org.uk/careers-education-training/accredited-courses-training-programmes/useful-accreditation-documents/use (accessed 21 November 2014).

Clark, P. (2004) 'Trainee placements: A manager's perspective', *Counselling & Psychotherapy Journal*, 15(7): 29–31.

Cutts, L.A. (2013) 'Considering a social justice agenda for counselling psychology in the UK', *Counselling Psychology Review*, 28(2): 8–16.

Falender, C.A. and Shafranske, E.P. (2004) *Clinical Supervision: A Competency-based Approach*. Washington, DC: American Psychological Association.

Gazzola, N., De Stefano, J., Audet, C. and Theriault, A. (2011) 'Professional identity among counselling psychology doctoral students: A qualitative investigation', *Counselling Psychology Quarterly*, 24(4): 257–275.

Health and Care Professions Council (HCPC) (2012a) *Standards of Education and Training*. London: HCPC [Online].Available at: www.hpc-uk.org/assets/documents/1000295EStandardsofeducationandtraining-fromSeptember2009.pdf and www.hpc-uk.org/Assets/documents/10003E0FUpdatedfurtherinformationsectionofSETsguidance.pdf (accessed 21 November 2104).

Health and Care Professions Council (HCPC) (2012b) *Guidance on Conduct and Ethics for Students*. London: HCPC [Online]. Available at: www.hpc-uk.org/assets/documents/10002D1BGuidanceonconductandethicsforstudents.pdf (accessed 21 November 2014).

Health and Care Professions Council (HCPC) (2012c) *Standards of Conduct, Performance and Ethics*. London: HCPC [Online]. Available at: www.hcpc-uk.org.uk/assets/documents/10003B6EStandardsofconduct,performanceandethics.pdf (accessed 21 November 2014).

Hughes, A. and Byrne, M. (2011) 'Clinical psychology trainee perceptions of what facilitates a good placement start', *Clinical Psychology Forum*, 226: 42–47.

Huprich, S.K. and Rudd, D.M. (2004) 'A national survey of trainee impairment in clinical, counseling and school psychology doctoral programs and internships', *Journal of Clinical Psychology*, 60: 43–52.

Johnson, W.B., Forrest, L., Rodolfa, E., Elman, N.S., Robiner, W.N. and Schaffer, J.B. (2008) 'Addressing professional competence problems in trainees: Some ethical considerations', *Professional Psychology: Research and Practice*, 39(6): 589–599.

Keary, E. and Byrne, M. (2013) 'A trainee's guide to managing clinical placements', *The Irish Psychologist*, 39(4): 104–110.

Kumary, A. and Baker, M. (2008) 'Stresses reported by UK trainee counselling psychologists', *Counselling Psychology Quarterly*, 21(1): 19–28.

Moore, T. and Rae, J. (2009) '"Outsiders": How some counselling psychologists construct themselves', *Counselling Psychology Quarterly*, 22(4): 381–392.

Raimy, V.C. (ed.) (1950) *Training in Clinical Psychology*. Upper Saddle River, NJ: Prentice-Hall.

Rizq, R. (2006) 'Training and disillusion in counselling psychology: A psychoanalytic perspective', *Psychology and Psychotherapy: Theory, Research and Practice*, 79: 613–627.

Rodger, S., Webb, G., Devitt, L., Gilbert, J., Wrightson, P. and McMeeken, J. (2008) 'Clinical education and practice placements in the allied health professions: An international perspective', *Journal of Allied Health*, 37(1): 53–62.

Rønnestad, M.H. and Skovholt, T.M. (2003) 'The journey of the counselor and therapist: Research findings and perspectives on professional development', *Journal of Career Development*, 30(1): 5–44.

Scott, A.J. and Hanley, T. (2012) 'On becoming a pluralistic therapist: A case study of a student's reflexive journal', *Counselling Psychology Review*, 27(4): 28–40.

Siggins Miller Consultants (2012) *Promoting Quality in Clinical Placements: Literature Review and National Stakeholder Consultation*. Health Workforce Australia, Adelaide.

Skovholt, T.M. and Rønnestad, M.H. (2003) 'Struggles of the novice counselor and therapist', *Journal of Career Development*, 30(1): 45–58.

Truell, R. (2001) 'The stresses of learning counselling: Six recent graduates comment on their personal experience of learning counselling and what can be done to reduce associated harm', *Counselling Psychology Quarterly*, 14(1): 67–89.

7
BECOMING A SUPERVISEE
PAUL HITCHINGS

INTRODUCTION

Your development as a 'counselling psychologist in training' is usually both an exciting and challenging process. In early training there is a range of roles to negotiate: that of student, colleague, client in therapy and then that of therapist and of supervisee. Each role calls for specific skills and knowledge, and this chapter focuses on the questions and issues that surround your development in becoming a competent supervisee. What might be meant by 'a competent supervisee'?

To answer this question fully we need to visit definitions of the term 'supervision', supervisory requirements, practical issues, including finding a supervisor, challenges and tensions to be managed, contracting, models of the process, self-supervision and self-care.

WHAT IS SUPERVISION?

Supervision can be a misleading term with everyday connotations of being overseen from a 'parental' perspective as a barely competent beginner. However, the term in our professional context does have a much broader meaning.

The question of definition

There are perhaps no precise definitions to which we can all subscribe, but all of the various definitions will tend to embrace two main aims: first, protection of and delivering the best possible service to the client, and secondly, enhancing the learning of practitioner. When one is foreground, the other is always contextualised as essential background. The process through which these aims are achieved is within a supervisory relationship characterised by a 'working alliance' that reflects mutual energy, collaboration and respect.

These two aims can be seen in the following definition:

> A working alliance between the supervisor and counselor in which the counselor can offer an account or recording of her work; reflect on it; receive feedback and, where appropriate guidance. The object of this alliance is to enable the counselor to gain in ethical competence, confidence, compassion and creativity in order to give her best possible service to her client. (Inskipp and Proctor, 2001: 1)

Devising your own definition

How you define supervision will affect your expectations and how you engage with the process. Your definition of supervision will almost certainly change over time and be influenced by the literature, by your development as a practitioner, and as a consumer of supervision. Take some time to record some of the key concepts in your current definition and note how they change over your training. Try not to censor yourself and record these in a learning journal. Include images as well as words. A simple example is given in Box 7.1.

Box 7.1   Devising your own definition of the supervisory process: An example

Words:

Reflection-on-action, consultation, assessment, support, confirmation, role model, direction, creating accountability

Images:

Two mirrors facing each other

An oasis

Crossing the canyon together on a rope bridge

SUPERVISORY REQUIREMENTS

Programmes of training (course routes and the British Psychological Society's Qualification in Counselling Psychology, the latter often referred to as the 'Independent Route' or QCoP)

have a range of requirements concerning supervision, which are likely to be outlined in the relevant course documentation. These requirements usually include reference to:

- Frequency of supervision (typically at least fortnightly), which may hold across times even when your caseload is temporarily reduced.
- Ratio of supervision to client contact (typically one supervision session to six client sessions).
- Mode of supervision allowed. This is usually face to face. Some programmes may allow some Skype/telephone contact while others may not. When group rather than individual supervision is undertaken, this raises the question of how many of the hours attended can be claimed towards the supervision requirements. For example, if three supervisees attend a two-hour supervision group, some programmes allow each supervisee to accrue the whole two hours while others would allow a more limited ratio claim.
- Indication of how many supervisors can be simultaneously involved. There is commonly more than one supervisor involved at any one time; for example, there may be supervision from a supervisor who may be privately engaged, and additional supervision offered as part of a placement. Some supervision may also be conducted as part of the course itself, but may not count towards the supervision hours requirement.
- Requirements for change of supervisor. Some programmes require more than one supervisor to have been involved over the time of your training.
- Total hours of supervision accrued for programme completion (typically around 60 hours). The cumulative total is usually indicated in supervisory reports (commonly at approximately six-monthly intervals), and it is advisable practice to maintain your own ongoing log of supervisory and client hours.

IMPLICATIONS OF SUPERVISORY REQUIREMENTS

It is clearly wise to familiarise yourself with the programme requirements for supervision, as they will have financial and time implications (preparation, travel and attendance). While programmes vary, the current client contact requirement is 450 hours, with an overall supervision ratio of 1:6. Assuming that client contact hours are accrued over a three-year period, this would require 25 supervisory sessions per year, which means a minimum of fortnightly supervision. Time should be allowed for preparation, travel, attendance in supervision, and later note writing. Fees for supervision can vary greatly by area and supervisor.

FINDING, INTERVIEWING AND CHOOSING A SUPERVISOR

It is possible that you have an allocated supervisor (see later section), and in many training settings in the UK, you may also be required to find and engage with a clinical supervisor as a private arrangement. You may be directed to use an 'in-house' list, which will usually have the advantage that the supervisor will to some extent 'know' the programme and will likely have a supervision qualification and philosophical stance that is acceptable to and compatible with your training programme.

If such an 'in house' list is not available or there is no supervisor on it that is available or geographically near, then recourse to a broader list such as those on the BPS Register of Applied Psychology Practice Supervisors (RAPPS) can be useful. There are some pitfalls to avoid here. You need a supervisor who will satisfy any criteria given by your training arrangement and who holds a philosophy of practice that is compatible with your training. Course staff may be useful here to help direct your search.

It is wise to establish your supervisory arrangements before you see your first client. Your first task is to identify a number of potential supervisors with regard to location. You do not want to involve yourself in considerable journey times unless perhaps you live rurally and this cannot be avoided.

To make contact with potential supervisors, email is probably the most efficient means as you can convey essential information quite succinctly in a manner that makes it easy to respond to. Include in your request the programme you are on, your likely placement(s), the amount and frequency of supervision sought, limits to your availability, and briefly any supervisory obligations involving third parties, for example an annual report to the training institution. You might also request a brief meeting for a mutual informal assessment. Occasionally, potential supervisors may be willing to offer this for free.

Having secured potential supervisors to meet, ensure that you make this a mutual interview. It probably is wise to be unashamedly transparent that you are 'shopping' for a supervisor.

Carroll and Gilbert (2011) outline a series of questions that may help in choosing a supervisor. Examples of such questions might be:

- What is your philosophy of supervision?
- What challenges you about this process?
- How do you think about and manage conflict in supervision?
- Do you have a written supervisory contract?

At the close of this brief meeting let them know when and how you will inform them that you wish to (or do not wish to) further your engagement with them.

For reflection after the initial meeting/interview, Carroll and Gilbert (2011) also suggest a list of reflective questions that may help. Examples of such questions might be:

- Were the answers I received largely open and non-defensive?
- Did I get a sense that I could trust this person?
- Was I made to feel welcome?
- Did they seem to strike a balance of friendliness and role-holding as reflected in their boundary management?

If you are fortunate enough to find more than one potential supervisor to choose from, consider how you felt with each. Be curious and reflect on this before you make your choice.

ALLOCATED SUPERVISOR

In many circumstances you may have a supervisor that you are allocated to on your placement. This might be your only supervisor but more likely will be additional to other supervisor(s) external to the placement. You are likely not to have chosen them, nor them you. This allocation to one another does not, however, preclude you from asking the kinds of questions listed in the previous section. This can help lay the foundation for developing a good supervisory working alliance. While most arrangements do work well, there will potentially be some conflict to manage. This is true of 'chosen' supervisory relationships too, but difficulties may be magnified when choice has not been part of the process. This leads us to consider the issue of managing both complexity and potential relational difficulties in the supervisory process.

MANAGING TWO SUPERVISORS

As mentioned above, it is not uncommon in training arrangements in the UK to have both a supervisor that is centred in the counselling placement, who is usually allocated, and a supervisor who is chosen by you and satisfies the conditions of your training programme.

How might supervision from two supervisors be managed? Clearly this is an area for the management of complexity. Often within the placement supervisory setting there is a greater focus on safety and administrative issues (often addressed within group supervision), and within the academic/programme establishment supervisor there is a greater focus on the development of the individual supervisee. While this arrangement appears complex, in my experience most supervisees manage this arrangement well.

A common question for supervisees in this arrangement is what to do if both supervisors give contradictory messages. While there is no formula to resolve this situation, be as transparent as possible with both supervisors about any dilemma(s) that you face.

INDIVIDUAL OR GROUP SUPERVISION?

Sometimes a supervisor has a space in (or is setting up) a small group (for example, three supervisees over two to three hours) that you might join. Assuming that you have such a choice, what are the relative merits of individual versus group supervision? There are both advantages and disadvantages to supervision in a group setting.

Group supervision does have the benefit of providing the opportunity of learning from the presentations of others and the commonality of experience that others too struggle with similar issues, which can be enormously reassuring. It also may provide a greater opportunity to further develop your own internal supervisor (see later section). Two potential disadvantages are the restriction of choice of time/day and the greater complexity of the dynamics that are likely to be generated among the participants (although, when well managed, this can be a source of rich learning). For further discussion see Carroll and Gilbert (2011) and Van Ooijen (2013).

MANAGING RELATIONAL DIFFICULTIES

Carroll and Gilbert (2011), drawing upon research in this area, outline the more common sources of potential conflict that can lead to unexpected supervisory relationship difficulties. Among these are theoretical orientation, style of supervision, contract issues, evaluation issues, group issues and personality issues.

Managing conflict is unlikely to be comfortable or easy, and may be especially challenging given the power disparity inherent in being a 'beginner'. However, the majority of causes of difficulties have sources that are relatively accessible to awareness by both parties, and some non-defensive discussion and negotiation can often resolve the problem. Contracting, re-negotiating and frequent checks on the relationship should limit difficulties. The question 'How might we manage any difficulties in our relationship?' needs to be addressed, preferably by the supervisor, at the start of the relationship.

Being open about difficulties is important. Undisclosed and unresolved issues are likely to drain energy away from the real work of supervision. Paradoxically, good management of relational difficulties can constitute a significant part of the tasks and goal of supervision. The outcome can be the enhanced relational ability (Yontef, 1991) of the supervisee (and supervisor!), who is then better equipped to work with conflict in the therapeutic dyad.

One way of conceptualising such conflict can be thought of as *psychological contracts*, sets of beliefs that both bring to the encounter, which lie partially outside awareness (Sills, 2006). When these are unmet, conflict is probable.

Examples of beliefs inherent in such psychological contracts, from the supervisee's perspective, might be:

- Supervision will give me the answers I need to get it right.
- My supervisor will always be there for me/will not be there for me much.
- My supervisor will not challenge me too much.
- Supervision should always be comfortable and supportive.
- Supervision should be a place where I always feel safe.
- If I keep on the right side of my supervisor, then I will get a good report.
- Some things are too risky to bring to supervision and are best kept secret.
- If my supervisor really knew my work, they would…
- My supervisor should remember everything I've told them.
- If my client does not improve, the supervisor will think I'm doing something wrong.

Supervisors too have their own versions of these!

What 'good housekeeping' guidelines might help prevent and, if needed, resolve such difficult events?

- Do not too easily discount your 'gut' experiences.
- Hold the courage to tell your supervisor of issues concerning your supervisory experience – possibly even seemingly minor ones.
- Express your feelings.
- Assume your supervisor's goodwill to resolve issues.
- Accept that conflict is an ordinary part of all human relationships and that it may be magnified in this relationship where there is a power differential.
- Be willing to meta-talk, that is to talk non-defensively about your process as you perceive it.
- Embrace a co-created philosophy – you both made some contribution to a difficult event. This stance can help avoid blaming and getting caught in 'who is right and who is wrong'.
- Stay with the discomfort initially rather than immediately rushing to a solution.

You may want to consider what your usual style is in dealing with relational difficulties. What challenges to these are posed by client work? How may your usual style influence your becoming a 'competent supervisee'?

These guidelines can help to resolve rather than polarise a conflict, which in turn can strengthen your relationship and have a positive impact on your work with clients. However, some conflictual relational events might be at the higher end of the scale, involving ongoing transferential happenings, which significantly and enduringly impact on the supervisory work. What happens if issues simply cannot be resolved despite genuine repeated attempts? Sometimes our 'buttons' or those of the 'other' activate an impasse. Perhaps then the best thing is to move on with as much good grace as can be mustered and accept that this is part of the human condition.

THE INITIAL SESSION(S)

Once you have chosen a supervisor and are ready to meet for supervision, you need a session to 'settle in' to the supervisory relationship, negotiate diary issues and pay attention to the broad contract between yourselves. Thus the main task of this initial session or two will be mutual contract understanding, negotiation and clarification.

THE LAYERS OF CONTRACTING

The contract might be viewed as a series of 'onion layers': the outer layer, the working layer, the session layer and the inner layer.

The outer layer: This includes broad agreements and administrative issues. Topics should cover stakeholder party agreements (e.g. training programme, placement setting), confidentiality and limits, ratio of supervision to client contact, fees, diary limits to availability of both parties for sessions, duration of sessions, cancellation notice, limits to re-scheduling of sessions, lateness to sessions, contact between sessions and guidelines for emergency discussions. It is advisable that these are in written format. For an example format, see Carroll and Gilbert (2011: 153–155).

The working layer: Here the expectations of both parties may be negotiated. Issues are likely to include means of presentation in supervision, whether written assignments for course work can be brought to supervision, and exam-focused supervision (e.g. viva preparation). In terms of presentation, negotiation may focus around frequency of audio recordings being brought (each time? six monthly? with or without a transcript?); what client notes are presented (e.g. a formulation); and what balance of verbal and written presentation is likely to work for both parties. The frequency of formal review as well as the frequency of less formal ongoing feedback may also be agreed. An initial review might be agreed upon to ensure that you both feel that you are a 'good enough' fit. Dates and times of meetings may well be booked up ahead, especially as there are usually diary restrictions for both parties.

The session layer: How are sessions structured? The importance of preparation is likely to mean that session time is used optimally. Usually a 'session agenda' is brought and time allocated accordingly. Typically you might bring a number of issues that you wish to have consultation on, and it is wise to prioritise these with the option that the least important could be left for a subsequent session. This layer, together with the working layer, might be thought of as the 'business contract'.

The central layer: The previous layers act to create a solid supervisory relationship to protect the space for engagement. Proctor (2008) refers to this central layer as the heart of the matter, the *reflective space*.

MAIN WORKING PHASE AND MODELS OF THE PROCESS

You have had one or two supervision sessions, largely to consolidate your working agreement, and mutually decide that this supervisory relationship is viable for both parties. What models might provide some maps for you both to navigate together?

Experiential learning

Supervision is in large part an activity where we can reflect on experience to generate new ideas and learning. Here we can draw upon the familiar model of experiential learning (Kolb, 1984) shown in Figure 7.1.

There is a range of ways in which this model can be useful. It can be used as a way to recognise the elements involved in learning from experience, our weak and strong areas and

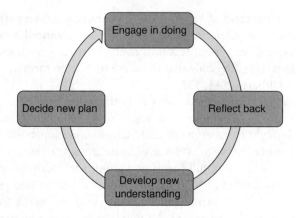

Figure 7.1   Model of experiential learning (Kolb, 1984)

places we may become 'blocked'. See Carroll and Gilbert (2011: 21–23) and Hawkins and Shohet (2012) for a fuller discussion. As experiential learning is at the core of the supervisory endeavour, then models of the supervisory process act as maps to guide us around the circle. While we know that the map *is not the same as* the territory (Korzybski, 1994) and there will be no perfect fit, nevertheless they can be very useful guides.

Many models of the supervisory process were developed at a time when the focus was based largely on the activity of the supervisor. As supervision has moved to a much more collaborative activity, with an emphasis on a two-person approach, these models have required some shifts to accommodate this. This chapter is aimed at the supervisee, and this is reflected in the way that they are elaborated on below.

Three such models have been chosen for discussion, with each offering a different but compatible frame for analysis. They are also generic in the sense that they are not bound to any particular counselling orientation. Such models can be used to guide practice, reflect on the supervision done, help choose supervisory priorities and reflect on practice over time. The first model discussed is that of Clarkson (1992), which offers some of the likely *ingredients*, and two further models are drawn from Hawkins and Shohet (2012), with one offering a *map of the process* and another the *potential areas of focus*. At the end of the discussion of these three models, a vignette of a supervisory scenario is offered that integrates these models in practice.

MODEL 1 – 'BRIEF SUPERVISION CHECKLIST' MODEL (CLARKSON, 1992)

The strength of this model is that it offers a guide to the *ingredients* of an individual supervision session. This is an eight-item model: six items originally with two further items added by Tudor and Worrall (2004). This provides a framework to reflect on the strengths and limitations of given supervisory event(s). Under each item I have added reflective sub-questions. Clarkson's checklist is shown in Box 7.2, and each item is discussed below.

Box 7.2   Clarkson's Brief Supervision Checklist

- Contract fulfilled?
- Key issues identified?
- Possibility of harm (to client) reduced?
- Developmental direction of supervisee increased?
- Process modelled by supervisor?
- Relationship equal?
- Context?
- Ethics?

Contract fulfilled?

The contract refers to a mutually agreed outcome to the supervision, for example 'I want help to complete a client formulation' or 'I want to understand what I am doing in this transcript from a theoretical perspective'. Sometimes you may arrive at supervision not knowing precisely what you want from presenting an issue, and so then the contract becomes one to 'explore' for a time until the 'want' emerges. My experience is that when supervision is impaired it is often because no contract was ever agreed or both parties have held differing implicit contracts.

Some useful sub-questions might be:

- Was a contract explicitly and mutually agreed?
- Was it mutually and explicitly re-negotiated at some appropriate point?
- Was it too ambitious for the time frame?
- Was a different contract pursued and was this acceptable/efficient?
- Was an exploratory contract made?
- On what basis might we say it was or was not fulfilled?
- What feelings were involved in this process?

Key issues identified?

Key issues might range from the more 'ordinary' to the more 'personal'. The question that is engaged is: 'What broader issue might underlie this particular supervisory focus?'

Examples here might be for the supervisee: to develop a more personal understanding of countertransference (experiential); to widen their theoretical understanding through further reading (educational); or to develop assertive skills in time management of the session (a self-esteem issue). Identification of a key issue might allow a greater transfer of learning from the particular issue to more generally applicable learning.

Some useful sub-questions might be:

- Was a key issue identified?
- By whom was it identified?
- Does it seem useful to reflect on?
- What might I do with this?

Possibility of harm (to client) reduced?

'Harm' is the term that Clarkson (1992) used, which might be considered somewhat too focused at one end of a continuum. Such a continuum might be conceptualised as ranging from a 'missed opportunity' at one end to 'harm' at the other. Issues here might include reflection on the stability of the therapeutic working alliance; an evaluation of the robustness of a client to manage a particular challenge/intervention; the need to involve a broader team in the work; and risk assessment or safety between sessions. This reflection might also be extended to those in the client's life and indeed yourself as the supervisee. This criterion clearly overlaps with ethical reflexivity.

Some useful sub-questions might be:

- How might the client benefit from this piece of supervision?
- Has a safety issue emerged/been emphasised?
- Has something that has been missed/neglected been noted?
- Has potential 'harm'/risk to myself been considered?
- Is there anyone in this client's life who needed to be and was taken into account?

Developmental direction of supervisee increased?

Supervision needs to balance both ends of a continuum of support and challenge. In the early phase of your experiences in supervision, it is likely that your supervisor offers more support than challenge to consolidate your growing confidence. It is possible, however, for both parties to resist moving further along the continuum towards 'challenge' and so limit opportunity for critical reflection and 'learning for further learning'.

Some useful sub-questions might be:

- Was this supervision piece challenging to me in some way?
- Can I transfer learning from this to other client issues?
- Did I actively contribute in this supervision?

Process modelled by supervisor?

Was the process of supervision created in the supervisory relationship congruent with the content arrived at? This criterion relates closely to the issue of the 'parallel process' (see Eye 5 in Hawkins and Shohet's (2012) model). For instance, a difficulty with maintaining the time boundary with a particular client might be brought to supervision. Congruence of supervisory process with content would require that time management in the supervisory frame was well managed.

Some useful sub-questions might be:

- Did we enact a process in the supervisory relationship that was congruent with the supervision outcome?
- Was there a parallel process (see further discussion later) between us that reflected the client– therapist process and was this noted?

Relationship equal?

While the relationship between supervisee and supervisor is not equal in terms of power, nevertheless in a particular supervisory event(s) was it one where mutual respect was present and communicated?

Some useful sub-questions might be:

- Was mutual respect held in this process?
- Was shame avoided in this learning process? If not, what was the source?
- Was I respected and respectful in the relationship?

Context?

Within the triad of supervisor–supervisee–client, were contextual issues (both those inherent to the parties and pertaining to the environment) taken into some account? This might be more relevant in some supervision scenarios than others; however, it is likely to always have some relevance.

Some useful sub-questions might be:

- What contextual factors did we take account of (e.g. a NHS setting)?
- Were issues of 'difference' in the triad paid attention to? If not, how might they have been relevant in retrospect?

Ethics?

Was awareness of any actual or potential ethical complexities made overt? This criterion may be more obviously present in some supervisory issues than in others, but it will always have a presence.

Some useful sub-questions might be:

- What actual or potential ethical issues were noted?
- Does anything need to be done?

MODEL 2 – 'CLEAR' MODEL (HAWKINS AND SHOHET, 2012)

This model describes the typical *stages* that a supervision session might progress through.

- Contract – includes establishing the focus and the 'working alliance' for a particular supervisory episode.
- Listen – includes the dyad further clarifying the issue.
- Explore – includes exploring impacts and feelings, and the visiting of different possibilities and options.
- Action – involves the dyad choosing the option or direction for the issue at hand.
- Review – includes reflecting on the process between them and an agreement for feedback in future sessions on the effect of this decision on the supervisee and the client. The latter is rare in models and is an often-neglected area.

This model clearly aligns very closely with Kolb's (1984) experiential learning model shown in Figure 7.1. This can be used as a guide for the supervisee to reflect back on a particular supervision session and also on how the various elements were used across supervision sessions. The achievement of the 'contract' element might require some listening and exploration.

Reviewing this model can aid reflection on whether any elements were missed, rushed, routinely left out, over-emphasised or overly directed.

MODEL 3 – 'SEVEN-EYED SUPERVISION MODEL' (HAWKINS AND SHOHET, 2012)

The first version of this model emerged in 1985, so it has been in use for almost 30 years. It easily lends itself to an integrative approach and so continues to appear in many supervision texts. In part its strength lies in being able to accommodate preferences; it can aid in choosing what to bring to supervision, and those 'eyes' that are mostly ignored or that have become habitual can be noted. It offers a choice of which 'process' to primarily focus on. The model does not imply that a supervisory session should be limited to any one eye, or that all eyes should be contained in any one session. It is a process map that can offer a range of choices and awareness. (For a fuller discussion see Hawkins and Shohet (2012).) Table 7.1 offers a summary of each eye and the associated aim, with possible discussion areas.

Table 7.1   The Seven-Eyed Supervision Model (Hawkins and Shohet, 2012)

EYE – focus on...	Aim	Examples of possible discussion areas
Eye 1: Client	Gather information for making a formulation	What is their presenting issue?
		Who and what is in their current life?
		General situation – stressors and level of functioning?
		Strengths and resources?
		History? Expectations?
Eye 2: Interventions	Making a therapeutic plan	What do I have in my 'toolbag'?
		What might I need to learn?
		What is the strength of the 'working alliance'?
		What might be appropriately challenging or too challenging for this client?
		What might I do next?
		What theories am I using?
Eye 3: Therapeutic relationship	Reflecting on and understanding the dynamics	What is the transference/countertransference relationship here? Are there any boundary disturbances?
Eye 4: Therapist reactions	Reflection on 'personal' reactions	What is being triggered for me? How do I make sense of this?
Eye 5: Supervision relationship	Reflecting on and understanding the dynamics	What is happening between us? Does this mirror myself and the client (parallel process)?
Eye 6: Supervisor reactions	Reflection on 'personal' reactions to client	Disclosure of responses to the client – understanding if this has meaning for the therapeutic work.
Eye 7: System/context	Reflection on impact of context on each and all members of the triad	How does the broader system impact on us all?
		What issues of power and difference in the triad sit here?

The Seven-Eyed Supervision Model is well described by the originating authors. There are, however, some comments that are worth noting concerning the movement from the early eyes to the later eyes, and specifically about Eye 5.

The use of certain models of therapy align themselves more comfortably with certain eyes; for example, a CBT approach might align most comfortably with Eyes 1 and 2 and a psychodynamic approach with Eyes 3 and 4. It is also true that the lower eyes are often a natural place to begin a supervision session; for example, Eye 1 to confirm a formulation and Eye 2 to consider how to proceed. However, it is all too easy for supervisees to limit themselves to these foci. These lower eyes can, if focused on predominantly, become a too-safe place and so limit the involvement of the person of the therapist and consequently your development as a practitioner.

Eye 5 deserves special mention as it contains a process that might be quite unfamiliar to some readers, that of 'parallel process'. Carroll (1996: 103) states that it 'refers to the process whereby aspects of the counselling relationship are expressed in the supervisory relationship'. The theoretical mechanism of its occurrence may be unclear, although the existence of it seems widely agreed. While it can be overused as an explanation, it can also be a valuable guide to the dynamics of the therapeutic relationship, vividly reproduced for the supervisory pair to engage with. It can also go both ways, both positively and negatively; a healthy (or unhealthy) process in the supervisory relationship can be healing (or limiting) for the therapeutic relationship. A simple example from my own practice as a supervisor is offered in Box 7.3.

Box 7.3   Example of a parallel process

Amanda presented her client and talked mostly uninterrupted for ten minutes. My inner experience was that although I had been listening diligently, whatever she had said was a complete blur in my mind. I wondered whether I was distracted that day and I also felt uncomfortable. Aware that we had a solid supervisory relationship, with some hesitation, I shared with her the experience of having listened but not having retained much of what she had said.

She responded with surprise and relief: 'That's exactly how I feel with this client!'

This then provided the basis for the remains of the supervision session unpacking and making sense of the dynamic with her client.

The main lesson here is for both to be open to the possibility of the parallel process, to be curious about our responses, and to bracket our negative self-judgements.

HOLDING THE MODELS TOGETHER: A VIGNETTE

The following supervisory vignette illustrates the synthesis of the above models.

Madjid brings to supervision his difficulty in maintaining the time boundary with a client; he knows boundaries are important but cannot seem to end on time. Madjid wants to make sense of this so that he can find a way to manage this. Madjid and his supervisor agree to pursue this as a supervisory focus. This equates to the 'Contract' stage in the CLEAR model.

The supervisor further listens to the issue, establishes that this is the only client that this seems to happen with, asks some clarifying questions, finds out what Madjid has tried and listens to the feelings of anxiety that this problem creates for him. This equates to the 'Listen' stage in the CLEAR model.

In further unpacking this issue, it emerges that the client is very anxious and appears not to be particularly sensitive to interpersonal cues. Madjid is concerned that if he is 'too' boundaried in his work, the client might be offended. From further discussion it emerges that Madjid is often concerned with being seen as warm and caring, and that this was the main message given to him in his childhood. The supervisor notes the likely therapeutic issue but merely flags it rather than opening it up, as they both know that this would not be appropriate in a supervisory relationship. They generate a range of options, and Madjid chooses one of them. This equates to the 'Explore' stage in the CLEAR model.

The intervention that Madjid chose was to use the last five minutes of the counselling session to review the session with the client and at the same time alter his body position and language to indicate the closing phase of the session. With the supervisor he did a mini-practice of this, which had the effect of increasing his confidence. This equates to the 'Action' stage in the CLEAR model.

In the last few minutes of this supervision session they reviewed this work together, checked for any unfinished business and noted that Madjid would bring back to the next supervision session the effects of his planned intervention. The supervisory session ended elegantly and on time. This equates to the 'Review' stage in the CLEAR model.

This scenario can also be reflected upon using Clarkson's (1992) Brief Supervision Evaluation checklist and Hawkins and Shohet's (2012) Seven-Eyed Supervision Model.

Reflecting using Clarkson's model (1992), the contract was made and achieved. The key issue of Madjid's countertransference and the historical source was noted. Potential harm to the client from loosened boundaries was reduced. The developmental direction of the supervisee had likely been increased, as the supervisor encouraged him to reflect and choose for himself rather than tell him what to do. There was congruence between what was brought and the manner in which the supervision session was conducted, especially the time-frame maintenance. The relationship was mutually respectful throughout. The contexts of Madjid, his client and the setting were considered, and both supervisor and supervisee were aware that this was a professional and an ethical issue.

Had one or more criteria that are part of this model not been achieved, this should not be taken to conclude that a piece of supervision does not have value, rather that attention should be given by both parties to any pattern of missing ingredients emerging across supervisory sessions.

The issue Madjid brought was primarily located in Eye 2; he wanted to know how he might differently intervene. In working with this focus, Eye 1 was also involved, in that he made sense of this issue in terms of the conceptualisation of the client as very anxious and so not responsive to interpersonal cues. Eye 3 and 4 were also touched upon in terms of the personal issues that were stimulated for him and the countertransference that Madjid brought to the situation.

All the models support the experiential learning process as described earlier. Events were reflected upon, new understandings were generated, and a plan of action was devised ready for implementation at the next client session. Both agreed that Madjid would bring back the impact of this to the next supervision session, so entering the next phase of the learning cycle.

SELF-SUPERVISION AND DEVELOPING YOUR INTERNAL SUPERVISOR

The effective use of supervision requires some self-supervision. Your ability to self-supervise starts from the beginning of client work. It is largely you who will choose what to bring to supervision and what to leave out. Hawkins and Shohet (2012) argue that this kind of self-supervision is always relevant, even if you are already receiving good supervision from somewhere else. How might you support your developing ability to self-supervise? There are a number of ways that you can do this.

Becoming a consultant to yourself

Casement (1985) made the distinction between the *internalised supervisor* and the *internal supervisor*. In your early training you will likely take on board understanding derived from your tutors, texts (including this!), your supervisor and likely your own therapist. You are likely to model yourself on these significant 'others' and this, of course, is a natural phase in any learning process.

Over time you will develop your own nuanced understandings, ways of integrating theory and an ability to assess your own work. This is the stage of developing your internal supervisor. What thwarts this process is a belief in having to get it 'right' and the experience or fear of shame. As most of us have been shamed at some point in the learning process, this is a considerable challenge. Given such a challenge, what may support you in your development?

Reflective journal-keeping

It is good practice to keep a reflective journal, and this can be an excellent aid to increasing your competence as a supervisee. In writing this, quieten the great enemy of learning – self-criticism – and increase the volume on curiosity. Carroll and Gilbert (2011: 74) state: 'Start with curiosity and then move to evaluation, not the other way around.' Make a note of any patterns, questions, theory used, choice points, ethical questions/dilemmas and supervision learnings.

Working with a peer

An excellent system for peer working is to use audio (or video) recordings and to utilise the system of Interpersonal Process Recall (IPR), as developed by Kagan (1984). This allows you to (re)capture some of the missed thoughts, feelings, body sensations and other processes at particular moments of client interaction and so widens your phenomenological field. This process involves replaying a recording, from as recent a time as possible, with a peer and then pausing the replay at points where there was an impactful moment. Such moments are likely to have been subtle and not fully paid attention to at the time. At such points your peer offers questions to act as an 'inquirer'. Such questions might include:

- What were you feeling at that moment?
- What were you thinking?
- Any sensations?
- Any images, pictures, fantasies or associations?
- What did you do?
- Any bodily sensations that accompanied this?

Clearly, a confidentiality contract needs to be agreed with your peer. A good brief guide to the use of IPR is provided by Allen (2004).

SELF-CARE

In beginning supervision and client work, good self-care can help you keep a sense of perspective and support you in this new learning process. Each of us knows what supports us.

Some ideas include:

- Recalling earlier learning challenges and knowing that you met them.
- Nurturing your sense of humour and having a friendly laugh at yourself.
- Developing relationships that support you both generally and especially with your peers as they too embark on this supervisory journey.

BECOMING A COMPETENT SUPERVISEE

In the first paragraph of this chapter the question posed was: What might be meant by a 'competent supervisee'? In supporting you with this aim this chapter offers the following suggestions:

- To become familiar with definitions of the term 'supervision' and to develop your own.
- To be fully aware of the supervisory requirements of your training programme and consider their practical and financial implications.
- To be considered in finding and choosing a supervisor.
- To reflectively manage more than one supervisor.
- To consider the merits of group versus individual supervision.
- To know about layers of contracting in the supervisory relationship.
- To reflect on and manage relational difficulties in supervision.
- To know generic models of the supervisory process as an aid to preparing and reflecting.
- To develop self-supervision and your own 'internal supervisor'.
- To use peer working and to ensure self-support throughout training.

If you have read this before entering supervision, it is hoped that this will have been useful preparation. If you have already been in supervision, you might find that it consolidates what you have done well and offers some challenges.

Visit the companion website for the following:

- QCoP Co-ordinating Supervisor.
- QCoP Trainee.
- Being Supervised.

REFERENCES

Allen, P. (2004) 'The use of Interpersonal Process Recall (IPR) in person-centred supervision', in K. Tudor and M. Worrall (eds), *Freedom to Practice: Person-Centred Approaches to Supervision*. Ross-on-Wye: PCCS Books.

Carroll, M. (1996) *Counselling Supervision: Theory, Skills and Practice*. London: Cassell.

Carroll, M. and Gilbert, C. (2011) *On Being a Supervisee: Creating Learning Partnerships* (2nd edn). London: Vukani Publishing.

Casement, P. (1985) *On Learning from the Patient*. London: Tavistock.

Clarkson, P. (1992) *Transactional Analysis Psychotherapy: An Integrated Approach*. London: Routledge.

Hawkins, P. and Shohet, R. (2012) *Supervision in the Helping Professions* (4th edn). Milton Keynes: Open University Press.

Inskipp, F. and Proctor, B. (2001) *Making the Most of Supervision: Part 1* (2nd edn). London: Cascade.

Kagan, N. (1984) *Interpersonal Process Recall: A Method of Influencing Human Interaction. Instructor's Manual.* Houston, TX: Mason Media.

Kolb, D. (1984) *Experiential Learning.* Englewood Cliffs, NJ: Prentice-Hall.

Korzybski, A. (1994) *Science and Sanity* (5th edn). Englewood, NJ: The International Non-Aristotelian Library Publishing Company.

Proctor, B. (2008) *Group Supervision: A Guide to Creative Practice* (2nd edn). London: Sage.

Sills, C. (ed.) (2006) *Contracts in Counselling and Psychotherapy* (2nd edn). London: Sage.

Tudor, K. and Worrall, M. (eds) (2004) *Freedom to Practice: Person-Centred Approaches to Supervision.* Ross-on-Wye: PCCS Books.

Van Ooijen, E. (2013) *Clinical Supervision Made Easy: A Creative and Relational Approach for the Helping Professions* (2nd edn). Ross-on-Wye: PCCS Books.

Yontef, G. (1991) 'Recent trends in Gestalt therapy in the US and what we need to learn from them', *British Gestalt Journal,* 1(1): 5–20.

8
ENGAGING WITH RESEARCH
ISABEL HENTON

The mind ... works on the data it receives very much as a sculptor works on his block of stone. In a sense, the statue stood there from eternity. But there were a thousand different ones beside it, and the sculptor alone is to thank for having extricated this one from the rest. Just so the world of each of us ... the world we feel and live in will be that which ... we, by slowly cumulative strokes of choice have extricated out of this, like sculptors, by simply rejecting certain portions of the given stuff. Other sculptors, other statues from the same stone! Other minds, other worlds from the same monotonous and inexpressive chaos! (James, 2013 [1890], pp. 288–289)

INTRODUCTION, AIMS AND AUDIENCE

This chapter is addressed to you if you are about to embark upon counselling psychology training, and you are therefore beginning to contemplate the question of engaging (or re-engaging) in research, and, in due course, in your own research question. It discusses research as a process, and as something (an object, if you like) to relate to, including philosophically. This object may, for some, at least initially, seem something like a Mr Darcy to an Elizabeth Bennet – grand, difficult, intimidating, perhaps even an anathema. Yet in Jane Austen's story (2003 [1813]), Miss Bennet gradually overcomes her pride, and her prejudice, becoming seduced, then engaged, and finally entering into a state of marriage. My aim, similarly, is to persuade you that research may not be as forbidding as you (might) imagine, and to romance you, if romance you need, into some kind of union (well, at least for the time being; perhaps it will be life-long for one in three of you). I hope you will find it encouraging and useful.

THE DOCTORAL GATEWAY

Developing critical research knowledge is a requirement for practitioner psychologists (Health and Care Professions Council [HCPC], 2012). Since the HCPC set a doctoral threshold for entry into counselling psychology in 2009, professional doctoral training within UK training institutions now culminates in a D-level thesis, while the Qualification in Counselling Psychology (or independent route) involves D-level assessments and an M-level thesis. And yet ... between January 2010 and December 2012, 1.4 per cent of UK counselling psychologists published research (Gordon and Hanley, 2013). In a survey of 3,000 British Psychological Society (BPS) Division of Counselling Psychology members' views on future counselling psychology research, only 2.8 per cent of recipients responded (85 members), 41 per cent of whom were trainees (James and Kasket, 2013). While neither of these data equate to a full picture of counselling psychologists' research activity, they do at least imply that many UK counselling psychologists may currently be more involved in other professional fields, such as teaching, consultancy or practice-based careers.

A complex picture seems likely to lie behind this. In a recent mixed-methods study among qualified UK and Greek counselling psychologists, Apostolopoulou and Skourteli (2015) found that males, practitioners with more years of experience, and (predictably) those in academic posts reported higher levels of research activity. The gender aspect is particularly striking given the relatively high numbers of women in the profession. Factors facilitating or hindering research activity post-qualification related to the presence or lack of funding, samples, instruments or support, time or energy, knowledge, skills or confidence, previous positive research experiences, appreciation of or passion for research, and financial or professional benefits. Overall, Apostolopoulou and Skourteli emphasised the interplay between intrinsic motivations (for instance, passion for research), which significantly predicted research activity, especially in early-stage careers, and extrinsic professional or cultural contexts, which might either sustain or overwhelm. It seems helpful to highlight the fuzziness of the intrinsic and the extrinsic in relation to doing (or not doing) research. I have noticed, in the context of counselling psychology training, and elsewhere, that research often seems to be the extra thing there is not enough time or energy left, at the end of the day, to do. But it is hard to say where time and energy are located – are they on the inside, the outside, or somewhere in between?

Anecdotally, UK professional doctoral trainees' motivation to enter programmes often rests on a wish to pursue a therapeutic career (Kasket, 2011). If A (doctoral research) is a compulsory gateway for B (a wished-for non-research career), the prospect of A seems likely to be met with ambivalence, or as a means-to-an-end, at least for some. US counseling psychology has an older doctoral tradition, and a long history of ambivalence towards research among trainees (Gelso, 1979). Within family therapy training, a similar structure to counselling psychology, US trainees expressed their ambivalence towards their doctoral gateway, using poems or metaphors (Piercy et al., 2005). One read: 'Roses are red, violets are blue, research is a thorn in my side, but it will help my dreams come true' (p. 369). Research is an invasive, potentially poisonous experience, an ever-present, itching, nagging, bodily experienced pain, until it can be plucked out, healed over or forgotten. Perhaps it is the central problem of the training fairy-tale, whose happy ending lies not in academia, but somewhere else – the therapy room?

In September 2013, 12 first-year counselling psychology trainees spent half an hour with me[1] discussing their thoughts and feelings about engaging in doctoral research at the start of their training. Ten of the 12 expressed a wish for a future practice-based career. Regarding the prospect of the doctoral thesis, their comments seemed to draw on previous research experiences as 'schemas', and gave the sense of 'a big deal' in choosing what research to do (see Box 8.1).

Box 8.1   First-year counselling psychology trainees' thoughts and feelings about engaging in doctoral research

'I still feel absolutely traumatised from my third-year project at uni … so I'm a bit scared that feeling is going to come back.'

'It's the biggest thing you have to produce in your life – it's daunting.'

'What do counselling psychologists research and where do you start? I have no idea!'

'It's a big opportunity … but it's also kind of a lot of decision-making.'

Training in counselling psychology and allied disciplines is often characterised as a journey involving stages, difficulties *en route* and personal transformation. In the counselling psychology training journey, you may begin wanting one thing (practice), but realising you need first to survive something else (research). It is interesting that research, especially qualitative research, is often cast in similar terms, as a journey involving unchartered territory, adventure or quest (e.g. Finlay, 2006; Willig, 2008). A journey is a kind of story: Russian narratologist Vladimir Propp (1968 [1928]) proposed that most stories begin with a character leaving their safe environment to embark on a dangerous journey. This character's initial attitudes are relevant to, but not dictated by, the main story event – a threat to 'an implicit canonical script' (Bruner, 1991, p. 11). In other words, something anxiety-provoking (unwanted, uncertain, uncontrollable) comes along, and we do not initially know how, or whether, we will overcome it.

THE TRADITIONAL GAP BETWEEN RESEARCH AND PRACTICE

In the wider field, among practitioners, research and practice are sometimes seen as dichotomous: research is 'objective, hard, cold, scientific, factual, time-consuming, difficult, prestigious,

---

1 Some of their responses are produced in this chapter with their kind permission.

tedious, expert', while practice is 'subjective, busy, messy, difficult, soft, warm, pressured, and flexible' (Darlington and Scott, 2002, p. 5). Moreover, survey research traditionally suggests practitioners find clinical experience, supervision, personal therapy and theoretical literature more useful for their practice than research findings (Morrow-Bradley and Elliott, 1986; Orlinsky et al., 2001). However, in recent decades, the concept of 'evidence-based practice' within psychotherapy has changed this dialectic. Evidence from randomised controlled trials (RCTs), which experimentally pit one brand of therapy against another in a horse-race, is currently the gold standard in a methodological hierarchy dominating the UK National Institute of Clinical Health and Excellence (NICE) guidelines, the Improving Access to Psychological Therapies (IAPT) programme, US empirically supported treatments (ESTs), and corollary systems of commissioning, insurance and employment on both sides of the Atlantic.

This development begins from the political and economic need for some basis on which to allocate resources in healthcare settings: evidence of therapies' results, or outcomes, has become the criterion. RCTs are defended as the only valid test of efficacy; that is, cause-and-effect relationships between particular therapies' ingredients and their outcomes. However, epistemologically speaking, can we really know how therapy works, and, if we think we can, does it work like this? Are therapies like drugs, and their active ingredients, techniques? Can these techniques be experimentally isolated, and other variables (relating to therapists' and clients' experiences together in the therapy room) be controlled for, or statistically removed? Do we even believe in such a thing as cause-and-effect? Even if we do, we can't be sure that treatments are causes in the complex web of local factors: RCTs only tell us that something works somewhere, but not that it works per se, or that it will work where we are sitting (Cartwright, 2007).

The over-reliance on RCT evidence has been thoroughly criticised both as epistemological myopia and as socio-economic exclusion (Holmes et al., 2006; Westen et al., 2004). RCTs are characterised as modernist research-speak, a form of ideological colonisation and dominance (Loewenthal, 2011; Toulmin, 1990), reflecting mid-twentieth-century modernism's assumption of an underlying order of deep, transcendental truths or structures, emancipating to discover. Their research practices are, arguably, far away from the artful, tacit, or context-dependent ontology of therapeutic work (Polkinghorne, 1992). Therapeutic communities and practices, including within counselling psychology, are less represented within this form of research and are increasingly disenfranchised, as, for example, bodies such as the UK's Centre for Workforce Intelligence contribute to the re-shaping of the employment landscape (cf. Centre for Workforce Intelligence, 'Defining a psychological therapist', 2013, p. 12).

In the background, there are the broader arguments against positivism. Nineteenth-century French sociologist Auguste Comte (1988 [1844]) coined the term 'positive science', suggesting that all phenomena, from physics to human behaviour, could be explained by a single set of natural laws. Positivism has come to refer to a singular methodological ideal or standard, and to the idea that the external world shapes the one and only view that can be taken of it – our subjectivities are not really involved (Robinson, 2010). The realm of positivistic psychological research, Kvale (2003) has enigmatically suggested, is a psychology of strangers: a world of brief encounters in the laboratory, in which, paradoxically, 'in order to behave like scientists, we must construct situations in which our subjects … can behave as little like human beings as possible, and we do this in order to allow ourselves to make statements about the nature of their humanity' (Bannister, 1966, p. 24).

How has the evidence-based practice controversy been reflected or constructed within *The Handbook of Counselling Psychology* since its inception 18 years ago? At its first edition (Woolfe and Dryden, 1996), counselling Psychology had become a BPS division only two years before; professional entry was achieved through an Advanced Practitioner Diploma or equivalent. Yet, the *Handbook*'s first chapters described quantitative, qualitative and service evaluation research methodologies respectively. The second edition (Woolfe et al., 2003) retained these chapters, but expressed a growing tension between counselling psychology's relational practice and the demand for technical expertise in healthcare settings.

By the third edition (Woolfe et al., 2010), and the advent of IAPT, this tension seemed more urgently felt. There was a more thorough-going critique of positivism and the natural sciences model of psychological helping. The research methodology chapters were replaced by one chapter entitled 'What is evidence?' (Corrie, 2010). Ironically, one year after the doctoral criterion was established, information about *doing* research was absent. Perhaps this expressed an anxiety, or a feeling of being at a loss over how to guide prospective doctoral students, given the apparently increasing conflict between counselling psychology's values and the evidence-based agenda.

COUNSELLING PSYCHOLOGY RESEARCH POSITIONS

The title of this chapter might seem to imply that incorporating research into counselling psychology training is obviously a good idea – trainees just need to agree and get more enthusiastic about it. However, nothing, not even research, is essentially good and everything needs to be argued for – the doctoralisation of training has not been universally welcomed. Loewenthal (2011) suggests trainings have incorporated research not because it is deemed essential, but from a need to stay in the game. Without care, engagement in research may encourage trainees towards narrow notions of evidence or truth, or an over-valuing of techniques or methods, influences which, if imported into practice, might diminish criticality, open inquiry and paying attention. What may be more helpful in developing thoughtful practice is a non-empirical approach to research, focusing on our impressions of phenomena, and the sources of our preoccupations (ibid.).

However, the practice of research is also conceived as a form of social action, which attempts, ultimately, not unlike therapeutic work, to alleviate human suffering through increased understanding. Additionally, it can be argued that therapy needs research for its explication – without research, ethical issues of accountability to funders, and equity for those seeking help, seem inevitably to arise (McLeod, 2003). As therapists, even if we live in a world of socially constructed meanings, we arguably have a moral obligation to listen and to learn outside therapy as well as inside it. Without at least considering available forms of knowledge (including, but certainly not limited to, research), there might be a danger of veering too far towards omnipotence or narcissism.

'As a liminal discipline, counselling psychology occupies a position in between established orthodox psychologies and other domains such as psychotherapy, rhetoric, poetry, anthropology and philosophy … uncomfortable but fertile meeting ground for diverse knowledges and practices' (Davy, 2010, p. 79). Counselling psychology's between-ness, or openness to possibility, places it on an anxious but potentially powerful edge, where uncertainty may be the only foundation, particularly since dynamical systems (chaos) theory has changed what it seems possible to know (Spinelli, 2013). Our worlds may be based on the simplest of underlying natural orders, but how these will play out is infinitely uncertain. Embracing this uncertainty might be both anxiety-provoking and invigorating, in life, in practice and in research. The concept of uncertainty sets the scene for further positions taken up by counselling psychology in relation to research, explored below as a loose, interrelated confederation of ideas.

Reflexivity (subjectivity)

Loewenthal's argument (above) might work equally well as an argument for reflexivity in research. What is reflexivity? It is a 'bending back upon oneself' (Finlay and Gough, 2003, p. ix): an awareness of and reflection on the presence of one's own mind or subjectivity, as the first context for the beginning and the doing of any research. This subjectivity involves the personal, the epistemological, and everything in between (Willig, 2008). To be reflexive means working with subjectivity, and intersubjectivity, throughout the process, staying aware of how these contribute to the evolving field of researcher and researched, and ultimately limit what can be found, or constructed. To recall the words of William Morris (1974 [1880]), what we sculpt, or carve out, through our research, may be useful, or beautiful, or not, but either way, we must try to acknowledge our own contributions, which begin before the research has begun, and are implicated in every word we read, hear or use along the way.

Postmodernism, and the in-*différance* of research and practice

Counselling psychology is a postmodern endeavour in its attention to context, discourse, philosophy and power relations. Valuing local or little narratives, postmodernism might argue for the primacy of practice in research, or that research should be practice-led (Strawbridge and Woolfe, 1996). However, postmodern *différance* between research and practice might also suggest that the meaning of each word is deferred and defined in binary opposition to the other (Derrida and Bass, 1982). By emphasising the play of meaning, *différance* potentially implies the in-difference or alikeness of apparently dichotomous or opposing phenomena, such as research and practice. On this basis, research and practice might be more ecumenically related to each other than practice-led or practice primacy implies, ideally existing in some form of 'live dialectic relationship' (McLeod, 2003, p. 9). Freud was an early proponent of a similar idea: in his psychoanalyses, research and practice proceeded 'hand-in-hand' (1963, p. 120). Likewise, counselling psychology proposes a marrying of research and practice (British Psychological Society, 2006), calling for increased dialogue or relationship between these two discovery-oriented activities.

Postmodernism suggests, paradoxically, that all dichotomies may be both completely inevitable and completely questionable. What if research and practice were more alike than is sometimes conceived? Clearly research and practice are not equivalent in their domains or aims: for instance, research usually has wider ambitions towards communicating knowledge and effecting change. However, in some ways, research and practice activities do seem significantly similar. Like research, therapeutic practice is also a form of social action attempting to reduce suffering, and an open system of interdisciplinary enquiry (McLeod, 2003). Etymologically, (re)search suggests repeated, mutual exploring or seeking – processes also evident in therapeutic work (Moodley, 2001). Barker et al.'s (2002) research cycle (have ideas, interact with the world, interpret what we find, compare with previous ideas, modify ideas) perhaps resembles assimilative processes within therapy. This model implies a mode of relating, relevant to practice and research, which is flexible (willing to absorb new information) and open (willing to modify ideas given new information). To summarise (and including from my own experiences), research and practice may both involve helping, new knowledge creation, thinking critically, exploring patterns or relationships, telling or re-telling stories, subjectivity and intersubjectivity, uncertainty, complexity, creativity, emotion, investment, mess, difficulty and exhaustion.

Pluralism, and against methodolatry

Isaiah Berlin (1953) suggested there are two types of people: hedgehogs, who wish to relate everything to a single system, and foxes, who pursue many paths without trying to fit them together. Pluralism is fox-oriented epistemology, proposing that 'any substantial question admits a variety of plausible but mutually conflicting responses' (Rescher, 1993, p. 79). Pluralism is compatible with postmodernism's rejection of grand narratives, and is often characterised as an ethical stance, since it prioritises the other or 'otherness'. Similarly, methodological pluralism is methodology determined by and continually re-negotiated in relation to its object (Slife et al., 2005). Methodological pluralism implies that no form of research should be taken as having privileged access to truth, but equally no form should be automatically rejected. Pluralism can be applied at the level of epistemology, methodology or interpretation. With respect to the latter, it is worth saying that our interpretations (in research, practice, or otherwise) may say as much about our own subjectivity than those who have participated with us. Multiple diverse interpretations of the same data are not only possible but inevitable – to acknowledge this is also to research ethically (Willig, 2012).

Counselling psychology might argue, pluralistically, that all research knowledge is contingent, relational, subject to subjectivity and context. Such an argument has also been characterised as a qualitative stance towards all forms of research (Marecek, 2003), regardless of methodology, and might be characterised as a distinctly scientific idea. In choosing a form of inquiry, perhaps what is more at stake than methodology for pluralistic counselling psychology researchers is epistemology and ontology (two sides of the philosophy-of-science coin – 'what can I know and what's out there to know?') and values ('what might be important to explore?'). Gergen (1985) argued for prioritising research questions over the enthronement of methods (or methodolatry) in psychology; and there may be further ways in which distinctions between qualitative and quantitative methodologies break down. Arguably, all research starts from experience, and all experience is qualitative, that is, based on qualities, even imagined ones, which are the sources our senses pick up as we relate to our environments (Eisner, 2003). Additionally, perhaps all research is some kind of response to variation (or uncertainty). Scientist Stephen Jay Gould (1996) reminds us that variation was deemed accidental in Plato's world – essences (forms) were the true reality. However, with the advent of Darwin, variation became the one irreducible property of natural phenomena, the 'defining and concrete earthly reality, while averages, our closest operational approach to essences, became mental abstractions' (Gould, 1996, p. 41). Might we argue that quantitative research attempts to control variation, isolating statistical relationships between constructed 'variables' in order to make general claims about groups, while qualitative research embraces variation, and explores or constructs various-ness?

Praxis, position and politics

Praxis means philosophy-in-action – a process through which a theory or a skill is practised, realised or embodied. Aristotle's Πραξις was about living or practising to be good. Unlike Plato, but like William James, Aristotle did not argue for absolute forms of goodness. Instead, to be pragmatic, we must focus on the object at hand, and try to discriminate, to discern what the right thing to do might be, in ever-shifting, uncertain circumstances. However, one person's pragmatism may be another's oppression (Spinelli, 2013). This exploration of counselling psychology research positions implies it is important to be open to all forms of research as potentially meaningful sources of knowledge, and to carefully consider one's own position in thinking about research, and deciding what kind of research to do.

I once heard schools counsellor and researcher Susan McGinnis (2012) describe the challenges of developing a pilot RCT of play therapy for children with severe emotional and behavioural needs. It was moving to hear that her motivation to do this came from a deeply compassionate place – to improve the help available to a disadvantaged, vulnerable group. At times like this, the distinction between tender-minded practice and tough-minded research (to borrow another idea from William James, 2014 [1907]) seems to disintegrate, and the possibility of a both–and position, taking up the tools of outcome research from the standpoint of humanism, seems more real. Although it is likely not wanted or possible for everyone or every circumstance, such a research involvement may represent a form of philosophical doing or a praxis. In similar vein, it emerges that there may be many ways of doing RCTs that are more philosophically congruent with counselling psychology (Cooper, 2011).

Engaging with research means engaging with the politics and economics of our profession – issues of social justice, professionalisation and earning a living. In December 2012, incoming NICE Chair, Professor David Haslam, suggested criteria for developing psychological therapy guidelines must be reviewed. This announcement was welcomed since it offered cautious hope for an epistemologically broader, more democratic evidence system in the future, which better reflects complexity and uncertainty, asks wider-ranging questions, and prioritises clients' voices (Midgley, 2011). Such a system would inevitably give greater space to a wider variety of approaches to psychotherapy research – including practice-based and qualitative research methodologies. Counselling psychology is well placed to argue for such an agenda, and to contribute towards a wider research base for psychotherapy. But where to begin, especially in the early stages of training? What kinds of psychotherapy research topics and methodologies are out there, from which one might choose?

As a starting-point, Midgley (2004) offers a useful rubric for psychotherapy and psychotherapy-relevant research, which I have adapted here (Box 8.2). His framework is like a set of concentric circles, zooming in, ever closer, to the moment-to-moment experiencing of therapeutic work.

Box 8.2   Midgley's (2004) framework for psychotherapy research

1. *Research that is relevant to psychotherapy but not about psychotherapy*: basic or pure research about experiences, meanings, symptoms, epidemiology, social and cultural contexts, co-factors, discourses, aetiologies or other explanatory frameworks or trajectories, communities, or life-stages.
2. *Psychotherapy research:*
   i. *Large-scale, quantitative outcome research* in experimental or routine settings (efficacy or effectiveness research, respectively).
   ii. *Smaller-scale qualitative accounts of psychotherapy*, gathered retrospectively (from clients, therapists, or both) through interviews or focus groups, which might focus on any aspect of therapy, and be analysed in wide-ranging ways. Such research gives voice to the participants of therapy and deepens understandings of the various-ness of therapeutic work.

iii. *Case studies*, describing a single case or series of therapy cases. Case studies have a long heritage in psychotherapy, dating back at least as far as Freud and Breuer's early 'Studies on Hysteria' (1991 [1895]). While they may vary in epistemology (from more narrative to more systematic forms), at best case studies capture complexity, draw on multiple sources, are longitudinally sensitive (describing process and outcome changes over time) and tell a contextualised story (McLeod, 2010).

iv. *Process research*, exploring the micro-level interior of therapy as 'text'. Process research originated in the 1950s and 1960s from influences including Carl Rogers' therapy events paradigm (Timulák, 2008). Process research aims to describe therapeutic processes, or link particular processes to therapeutic change or outcome. Contemporary process research is an exciting, epistemologically broad field of research, often co-constructed with clients, using narrative, constructivist or dynamic systems methods (e.g. Gelo et al., 2012).

READING RESEARCH

Beyond philosophy, politics and economics, the business of counselling psychology training involves many and various research processes, not least the development of an appropriate counselling psychology research question and design (for which, see Chapter 14). In what remains of this chapter, I return to research as something to relate to, and a process of relating to others, highlighting, in particular, the processes of reading and writing research.

How do we feel about the idea that we read research, then use it, or apply it, in our practice? In the landscape of 'evidence-based practices', the relationship between research and practice is reified into a thing, or things – institutionally sanctioned treatments for diagnostically constructed clinical problems. However, evidence-based practice has more than one meaning. It was originally coined from the term 'evidence-based medicine', indicating a process, a verb: what do practitioners, using judgement, do with what they know, circumstantially (Sackett et al., 1996)? This emphasis on practitioners combining or mediating what is 'known' from research (in this case), with something else (here, clinical judgement), converts evidence-based practice not only into a process, but into a complex, intersubjective process, far removed from institutionalisation of evidence-based practices. Indeed, counselling psychology, encompassing, for instance, phenomenological, person-centred or psychoanalytic ways of thinking, might particularly embrace this second version of evidence-based practice, since it implies that no form of knowledge has, or should have, the last word on the therapeutic exchange (Castonguay, 2011). The question may be less about what (we think) we know or want to know, more about how we relate to whatever this is in practice: how much we can, or want, to achieve what psychoanalyst Wilfred Bion (1962) called 'negative capability' – tolerating uncertainty and putting aside preconceptions, in order, mindfully, to be present and listen to the other person, before applying anything at all (cf. Lee and Prior, 2013).

Having said this, reading research, like reading theory or technique, or learning from experience, may be one way of questioning our assumptions about what to do or how to be within our therapeutic work. A recent large-scale mixed-methods study among practitioners of various theoretical orientations suggested a link between therapists scoring higher on a mindfulness scale (and engaging in mindful activities such as yoga, meditation, swimming, walking and running) and effective outcomes. More effective therapists were also more likely to emphasise the use of humour in their therapeutic work (Pereira, 2014). Conversely, what do we assume about the kinds of things that might lead therapy to go awry? Persisting with theory-driven techniques when clients seem reluctant has been linked to drop-out in more than one kind of therapy (Castonguay et al., 1996; Piper and Ogrodniczuk, 1999). A recent study asked therapists and clients who reported problems in therapy what had gone wrong (a refreshingly negative research question!). Generally, on a scale of 1 to 10, clients characterised therapy as more harmful than therapists did, while therapists were more likely to emphasise potential longer-term gains for clients, despite problems that emerged during therapy. Clients attributed problems to: (a) opening up a Pandora's Box of problems; (b) negative labels; (c) therapy not addressing their issues; (d) feeling blamed; (e) confirmation of negative self-perceptions; and (f) a loss of hope or confidence (Parry, 2014). This is sobering, and worth reflecting on, not just for us as individuals, but in terms of what might be going on more systemically that such phenomena even arise. Perhaps, in the marketised systems in which we might be working, the sense of loss, or anxiety, gets amplified, as it is cascaded down the line (Bell, 2010).

WRITING RESEARCH

A researcher needs to be a writer, and writing well is an art. There is much talk in research about rigour and relevance; however, when it comes to writing research, Linda Finlay (2009) emphasises rigour and *resonance*. Writing research, she suggests, is a poeticising project – research that 'doesn't break your heart just isn't worth doing anymore' (p. 15). The impact on readers is all-important: in writing research, ensure you give sufficient credit to the art of persuasion, that is, to the role of rhetoric – when people are interested, or better still, moved, they pay attention.

Research writing has to believe in itself, to have a certain amount of omnipotence, even if balanced with the modesty of relating to what has gone before, and to what may come after. Writer Joan Didion (1976, p. 1) suggests:

in many ways, writing is the act of saying I, of imposing oneself upon other people, of saying listen to me, see it my way, change your mind. It's an aggressive, even a hostile act. You can disguise its qualifiers and tentative subjunctives, with ellipses and evasions – with the whole manner of intimating rather than claiming, of alluding rather than stating – but there's no getting around the fact that setting words on paper is the tactic of a secret bully, an invasion, an imposition of the writer's sensibility on the reader's most private space.

In another sense, writing might be a form of thinking, or even, of coping. Pelias (2011) suggests that in research, it is often a case of 'writing ourselves into position': writing is inherently therapeutic, bringing order or recognisable shape to the sadness or chaos we may experience. He writes brilliantly about what distinguishes a 'flat' from an inspired piece of writing ('I'm sitting at my desk, trying', pp. 666–667) – an energising read for anyone feeling tired. From personal experience,[2] I would add, prioritise developing speed and flow with your writing (for example, try writing a précis of your research findings in an hour). There is much more at top of mind than you think; and whatever words come out might be what's important. If you are passionate enough about what you are writing, the energy will come (back). Write in the first person as much as you can: it helps to distinguish your subjective involvement, while not separating this from what you have researched or found.

CONCLUSION

Box 8.3   A final word from first-year counselling psychology trainees

'You meet so many interesting people in the field, completely different fields, it's a great way to see the world, research comes from everywhere, such different communities and different ways of thinking, so it's good to keep your mind open…'

To conclude, you will know already that doing research involves energy, time, effort, commitment and, often-times, anxiety. It rarely goes according to plan, there will be factors outside your control, unexpected turns-of-events, and it all takes much longer than you think (Hodgson and Rollnick, 1996). So for what it is worth, Box 8.4 offers some final ideas in advance of your doctoral endeavour from a battle-weary person.

---

2 Thank you to Dr Elena Manafi and Dr Nick Midgley for inspiration and support in developing my own writing.

Box 8.4   Some final ideas for your doctoral endeavour

1. Be very, very planful.
2. Corner-shop research: start early, keep your research open and don't close up too often or too long. Large gaps in time are scary – being open all hours is surprisingly easy.
3. If you can scrimp, steward, win bursaries, book advance fares, or sleep on the floor, etc., go to a research conference or two – it will be sociable and it might be inspiring.
4. Talk to and seek support from your peers, your department, and more widely. Try to click into other people's interests and find mutual benefits.
5. Balance omnipotence and modesty: write at speed, then re-write slowly…

The main aim of the chapter has been to persuade you that research is a rich, broad and exciting domain, eminently relevant to, and perhaps eminently like, therapeutic work. Like the best therapeutic practice, research may involve:

1. Thinking critically and questioning your assumptions.
2. Listening carefully to others (clients, participants, the wider world).
3. Acknowledging multiple possibilities.
4. Paying attention mindfully.
5. A sense of humour.
6. Embracing uncertainty.

In respect of the latter, McLeod (2003) asks us to imagine what kind of totalitarian world we would live in if we always knew the answer to Paul's often-cited question (1967, p. 111): 'What treatment, by whom, is most effective, for this individual, with that specific problem, and under which set of circumstances?' Maybe all we can do, he suggests, and all we want to do, is to find a temporary clearing in a forest of not-knowing, and so retain some curiosity within our therapeutic work. It may be that your engagement with research, in all its complexity, diversity and uncertainty, is what will help to distinguish you as a reflexive and ethical practitioner. Good luck.

 Visit the companion website to watch Engaging with Research.

REFERENCES

Apostolopoulou, A. and Skourteli, M. (2015) 'An investigation into counselling psychologists' research activity: Motives, facilitators and barriers – a contextual perspective', *Counselling Psychology Review*, 30(2): 47–66.

Austen, J. (2003) *Pride and Prejudice*. London: Penguin. (Original work published 1813.)

Bannister, D. (1966) 'Psychology as an exercise in paradox', *Bulletin of the British Psychological Society*, 19: 21–26.

Barker, C., Pistrang, N. and Elliott, R. (2002) *Research Methods for Clinical Psychologists* (2nd edn). Chichester: John Wiley.

Bell, D. (2010) 'Psychiatry and psychoanalysis: A conceptual mapping', in A. Lemma and M. Patrick (eds), *Off the Couch: Contemporary Psychoanalytic Applications* (pp. 176–193). London: Taylor & Francis.

Berlin, I. (1953) *The Hedgehog and the Fox: An Essay on Tolstoy's View of History*. London: Weidenfeld & Nicolson.

Bion, W. (1962) *Learning from Experience*. London: Karnac Books.

British Psychological Society (BPS) Division of Counselling Psychology (2006) *Professional Practice Guidelines*. Leicester: BPS.

Bruner, J. (1991) 'The narrative construction of reality', *Critical Inquiry*, 18: 1–21.

Cartwright, N. (2007) 'Are RCTs the gold standard?', *BioSocieties*, 2: 11–20.

Castonguay, L.G. (2011) 'Psychotherapy, psychopathology, research and practice: Pathways of connections and integration', *Psychotherapy Research*, 21(2): 125–140.

Castonguay, L.G., Goldfried, M.R., Wiser, S., Raue, P.J. and Hayes, A.M. (1996) 'Predicting the effect of cognitive therapy for depression: A study of unique and common factors', *Journal of Consulting and Clinical Psychology*, 64: 497–504.

Centre for Workforce Intelligence (2013) *Improving Workforce Planning for the Psychological Therapies Workforce: A Review*. Retrieved 15 March 2014 from www.cfwi.org.uk/publications/improving-workforce-planning-for-the-psychological-therapies-workforce.

Comte, A. (1988) *Introduction to Positive Philosophy*. Trans. F. Ferre. Indianapolis, IN: Hackett Publishing. (Original work published 1844.)

Cooper, M. (2011) 'Meeting the demand for evidence-based practice', *Therapy Today*, 22(4): 10–16.

Corrie, S. (2010) 'What is evidence?', in R. Woolfe, S. Strawbridge, B. Douglas and W. Dryden (eds), *Handbook of Counselling Psychology* (3rd edn, pp. 44–61). London: Sage.

Darlington, Y. and Scott, D. (2002) *Qualitative Research in Practice: Stories from the Field*. Buckingham: Open University Press.

Davy, J. (2010) 'Interpreting case material', in R. Woolfe, S. Strawbridge, B. Douglas and W. Dryden (eds), *Handbook of Counselling Psychology* (3rd edn, pp. 62–82). London: Sage.

Derrida, J. and Bass, A. (1982) *Margins of Philosophy*. Trans. A. Bass. Chicago: University of Chicago Press.

Didion, J. (1976) 'Why I write', *The New York Times Magazine*, 5.

Eisner, E.W. (2003) 'On the art and science of qualitative research in psychology', in P.M. Camic, J.E. Rhodes and L. Yardley (eds), *Qualitative Research in Psychology* (pp. 17–29). Washington, DC: American Psychological Association.

Finlay, L. (2006) '"Going exploring": The nature of qualitative research', in L. Finlay and C. Ballinger (eds), *Qualitative Research for Allied Health Professionals: Challenging Choices* (pp. 3–8). Chichester: Wiley.

Finlay, L. (2009) 'Debating phenomenological research methods', *Phenomenology & Practice*, 3(1): 6–25.

Finlay, L. and Gough, B. (eds) (2003) *Research Reflexivity: A Practical Guide for Researchers in Health and Social Sciences*. Oxford: Blackwell.

Freud, S. (1963) *Therapy and Technique*. New York: Collier.

Freud, S. and Breuer, J. (1991) 'Studies on hysteria', in A. Richards (ed.) and J. Strachey (trans.), *Penguin Freud Library* (Vol. 3). London: Penguin Books. (Original work published 1895.)

Gelo, O.C.G., Salcuni, S. and Colli, A. (2012) 'Text analysis within quantitative and qualitative psychotherapy process research: Special issue', *Research in Psychotherapy*, 45.

Gelso, C.J. (1979) 'Research in counseling: Methodological and professional issues', *The Counseling Psychologist*, 8(3): 7–35.

Gergen, K.J. (1985) 'The social constructionist movement in modern psychology', *American Psychologist*, 40(3): 266–275.

Gordon, R. and Hanley, T. (2013) 'Where do counselling psychologists based in the UK disseminate their research? A systematic review', *Counselling Psychology Review*, 28(4): 7–17.

Gould, S.J. (1996) *Full House: The Spread of Excellence from Plato to Darwin*. New York: Harmony Books.

Health and Care Professions Council (HCPC) (2012) *Standards of Proficiency for Practitioner Psychologists*. London: HCPC.

Hodgson, R. and Rollnick, S. (1996) 'More fun, less stress: How to survive in research', in G. Parry and F. Watts (eds), *Behavioural and Mental Health Research: A Handbook of Skills and Methods* (pp. 75–89). Hove: Psychology Press.

Holmes, D., Murray, S.J., Perron, A. and Rail, G. (2006) 'Deconstructing the evidence-based discourse in health sciences: Truth, power and fascism', *International Journal of Evidence Based Healthcare*, 4: 180–186.

James, P. and Kasket, E. (2013, July) The Nature of Counselling Psychology Research. Workshop at the BPS Division of Counseling Psychology conference, Cardiff.

James, W. (2013) *The Principles of Psychology*. New York: Cosimo Books. (Original work published 1890.)

James, W. (2014) *Pragmatism*. New York: Cambridge University Press. (Original work published 1907.)

Kasket, E. (2011, July) 'Motivations and (mis)perceptions in applicants seeking training in counselling psychology'. Paper presented at the BPS Division of Counselling Psychology conference, Bristol.

Kvale, S. (2003) 'The psychoanalytic interview as inspiration for qualitative research', *Social Psychological Review*, 5(2): 20–42.

Lee, B. and Prior, S. (2013) 'Developing therapeutic listening', *British Journal of Guidance & Counselling*, 41(2): 91–104.

Loewenthal, D. (2011) 'Research, ideology, and the evolution of intersubjectivity in a post-existential culture', in D. Loewenthal (ed.), *Post-existentialism and the Psychological Therapies: Towards a Therapy without Foundations* (pp. 157–174). London: Karnac Books.

Marecek, J. (2003) 'Dancing through minefields: Toward a qualitative stance in psychology', in P.M. Camic, J.E. Rhodes and L. Yardley (eds), *Qualitative Research in Psychology* (pp. 49–69). Washington, DC: American Psychological Association.

McGinnis, S. (2012, May) 'Development of an RCT for person-centred play therapy with children with SEBN'. Paper presented at the British Association of Counselling and Psychotherapy's annual research conference, Edinburgh.

McLeod, J. (2003) *Doing Counselling Research.* London: Sage.

McLeod, J. (2010) *Case Study Research in Counselling and Psychotherapy.* London: Sage.

Midgley, N. (2004) 'Sailing between Scylla and Charybdis: Incorporating qualitative approaches into child psychotherapy research', *Journal of Child Psychotherapy*, 30(1): 89–111.

Midgley, N. (2011, November) 'Talking therapies: What count as credible evidence?' Contribution to panel session at the fifth annual New Savoy conference, London.

Morris, W. (1974) *The Beauty of Life.* London: Brentham Press. (Original work published 1880.)

Moodley, R. (2001) '(Re)Searching for a client in two different worlds: Mind the research-practice gap', *Counselling and Psychotherapy Research*, 1(1): 18–23.

Morrow-Bradley, C. and Elliott, R. (1986) 'Utilization of psychotherapy research by practicing psychotherapists', *American Psychologist*, 41: 188–197.

Orlinsky, D.E., Botermans, J.F. and Rønnestad, M.H. (2001) 'Towards an empirically grounded model of psychotherapy training: Four thousand therapists rate influences on their development', *Australian Psychologist*, 36(2): 139–148.

Parry, G. (2014, May) 'When the special relationship goes wrong: Headline results from a research project on understanding and preventing adverse effects of psychological therapy (AdEPT)'. Paper presented at the British Association of Counselling and Psychotherapy's annual research conference, London.

Paul, G.L. (1967) 'Strategy of outcome research in psychotherapy', *Journal of Consulting Psychology*, 31(2): 109–118.

Pelias, R.J. (2011) 'Writing into position: Strategies for composition and evaluation', in N.K. Denzin and Y.S. Lincoln (eds), *The SAGE Handbook of Qualitative Research* (pp. 659–668). Los Angeles: Sage.

Pereira, J. (2014, May) 'The art of practice: Examining common factors that contribute to effective practice'. Paper presented at the British Association of Counselling and Psychotherapy's annual research conference, London.

Piercy, F.P., McWey, L.M., Tice, S., James, E.J., Morris, M. and Arthur, K. (2005) 'It was the best of times – it was the worst of times: Doctoral students' experiences of family therapy research training through alternative forms of data representation', *Family Process*, 44(3): 363–378.

Piper, W.E. and Ogrodniczuk, J.S. (1999) 'Therapy manuals and the dilemma of dynamically oriented therapists and researchers', *American Journal of Psychotherapy*, 53(4): 467–482.

Polkinghorne, D.E. (1992) 'Postmodern epistemology of practice', in S. Kvale (ed.), *Psychology and Postmodernism* (pp. 146–165). London: Sage.

Propp, V. (1968) *The Morphology of the Folktale* (2nd edn). Houston, TX: Texas University Press. (Original work published 1928.)

Rescher, N. (1993) *Pluralism against the Demand for Consensus*. Oxford: Clarendon Library of Logic and Philosophy.

Robinson, M. (2010) *Absence of Mind: The Dispelling of Inwardness from the Modern Myth of the Self*. New Haven, CT: Yale University Press.

Sackett, D.L., Rosenberg, W.M.C., Muir Gray, J.A., Haynes, R.B. and Richardson, W.S. (1996) 'Editorial. Evidence-based medicine: What it is and what it isn't', *British Medical Journal*, 312(7023): 71–72.

Slife, B.D., Wiggins, B.J. and Graham, J.T. (2005) 'Avoiding an EST monopoly: Toward a pluralism of philosophies and methods', *Journal of Contemporary Psychotherapy*, 35(1): 83–97.

Spinelli, E. (2013, July) 'Embracing uncertainty: Counselling Psychology as a human and humane enterprise'. Keynote paper presented at BPS Division of Counselling Psychology annual conference, Cardiff.

Strawbridge, S. and Woolfe, R. (1996) 'Counselling psychology: A sociological perspective', in R. Woolfe and W. Dryden (eds), *Handbook of Counselling Psychology* (pp. 609–620). London: Sage.

Timulák, L. (2008) *Research in Psychotherapy and Counselling*. London: Sage.

Toulmin, S. (1990) *Cosmopolis: The Hidden Agenda of Modernity*. Chicago: University of Chicago Press.

Westen, D., Novotny, C.M. and Thompson-Brenner, H. (2004) 'The empirical status of empirically supported psychotherapies: Assumptions, findings, and reporting in controlled clinical trials', *Psychological Bulletin*, 13(4): 631–663.

Willig, C. (2008) *Introducing Qualitative Research in Psychology: Adventures in Theory and Method* (2nd edn). Maidenhead: Open University Press.

Willig, C. (2012) *Qualitative Analysis and Interpretation in Psychology*. Maidenhead: Open University Press.

Woolfe, R. and Dryden, W. (eds) (1996) *Handbook of Counselling Psychology*. London: Sage.

Woolfe, R., Dryden W. and Strawbridge, S. (eds) (2003) *Handbook of Counselling Psychology* (2nd edn). London: Sage.

Woolfe, R., Strawbridge, S., Douglas, B. and Dryden, W. (eds) (2010) *Handbook of Counselling Psychology* (3rd edn). London: Sage.

SECTION III

FINDING YOUR WAY

CONTENTS

As we continue on the journey the complexity of the landscape becomes more apparent and this can be confusing. It is perhaps at this stage that we really begin to sense what it means to become a professional practitioner taking responsibility for our own practice, decision-making and development.

One thing that we have to contend with from the start is the realisation that we are not alone. There are other practitioners exploring and laying claim to terrain that we might see as ours. There maybe counsellors, psychotherapists, arts therapists, psychiatrists, physicians, social workers, coaches, mentors and, of course, clinical, health, forensic, occupational, child and educational psychologists. We often find ourselves in teams of people with differing conceptual maps, tools, resources and priorities with differing ideas about who should lead. Even within our own territory of counselling psychology there are alternative maps that define its key features differently. So it is important, if we are to make our own distinctive and useful contribution, that we are both able to remain open to ideas and to negotiate effectively.

For this we need the confidence that comes with a deepening understanding of the territory and its inhabitants as well as a rooted sense of our own identity and values. The authors in this section offer guidance through some of the complex challenges this presents without offering ready-made answers. We are, after all, on an expedition not a packaged trip and, while there is support and companionship in abundance, there is hard but exciting work to be done.

Chapter 9 considers the very nature of conceptual maps and how they may guide us usefully without excluding alternative possibilities, whereas Chapter 10 focuses on a central tension between medical and psychological mapping. For all the alternative maps of differing professions and approaches Chapter 11 draws our attention to the central emphasis that counselling psychologists place on making relationships and explores what this involves, while Chapter 12 focuses on the diversity of the people we may work with and the challenges this brings. In Chapter 13 we are reminded of the personal demands of our discipline and the importance of self-care and developing resilience. Attention is then turned to the need for continuing exploration and Chapter 14 offers guidance in carrying out research. The centrality of values and ethical practice are the concern of Chapter 15 and we are asked to consider what is meant by ethical maturity in our profession. Finally, in this section, Chapter 16 challenges us not to be daunted when encountering the terrain of psychopharmacology.

9
CONCEPTUALISING IN CLIENT WORK
BARBARA DOUGLAS

INTRODUCTION

The word 'conceptualisation' sounds very academic, implying a layer of thinking that is rather abstract. Indeed, conceptualisation is usually considered to be about forming an idea of something. But if we stop to consider what it really conveys, it is simply a need to make sense of experience, to place some order on what might otherwise be chaotic and random experiences within which we would flounder, unable to act in any meaningful way. Consider, for example, that you are standing in the street on a dark evening looking up at the sky. On one occasion you see a whitish crescent-shaped object, on another a whitish ball-shaped object, and on another there is no shape there at all. How do you know these are different views of the same structure we know as the moon, rather than different structures seen on each occasion? It is because you have learnt in childhood to make sense of the moon within a scientific conceptualisation of the universe and stars. From this you learn to take some reassurance in the cycle of light and dark, seasons, tidal activity and the continuity of your world.

This is a very different conceptualisation of the cosmos from, for example, the Mayans, a sophisticated Mesoamerican society that flourished roughly from 500 BC to AD 900. The Maya conceptualised the cosmos as an interplay between the Gods and their people with existence on three planes. The world was flat and supported by the Gods; below this was an underworld where they went after death, via caves in the world; and above was the world of the Gods, through whom all cycles of existence were controlled. The Sun, Moon and Venus, for example, passed below the horizon to the underworld every evening, needing help from the Gods to return the next day. Within this world view the infant learned to make sense of their world, their actions and effects within a framework of interrelationship between the Gods and humans.

So, conceptualisations are a necessary means of establishing order out of chaos. As the above examples demonstrate, they are also formed within particular socio-historical environments, are premised on the dominant world view of the time, and act as cultural maps of the world, making sense of experience and guiding action.

From our births we are launched into trying to make sense of ourselves, other people and the worlds we inhabit in order to impose some structure on the vast array of information that our senses experience. Much of developmental psychology involves examining how children do this. How, for example, does the new-born infant come to recognise where they end and the carer begins? How does the toddler learn that in a game of peek-a-boo the hiding person has not simply disappeared but remains present but out of sight; or how does a child acquire language? Might this be about innate structures within the human brain that predispose the child to make sense of language rules and/or does the child learn by imitation or reinforcement? In each of these examples theoretical frameworks provide a way of conceptualising aspects of children's development and generate questions against which further research can be tested.

In counselling psychology practice too we conceptualise our work. Indeed, much of our training, as well as that of other therapeutic practitioners, is concerned with framing our work with clients through the lenses of particular conceptualisations. Conceptualisations of therapeutic work have different levels of abstraction and our client work is informed at these various levels. So, for example, models of therapy are premised on underpinning philosophical stances that contain different notions of truth and different models of the person. These lead to different practice principles and actions and research methodologies. Then again, there are conceptualisations for understanding the experiences of human distress that may bring clients to the therapy room. Do we, for example, conceptualise distress normatively as categories of disorder with specific criteria for their diagnosis or might we understand clients' distress more ideographically, particular to the individual and their context, requiring a more fluid understanding, as in the process of formulation?

This chapter will focus on conceptualisation as a means of creating and developing meaning in the therapy room; of considering the fundamental question of what is therapeutic about therapy and, hence, in navigating our work with clients. The extent to which conceptualisations direct and guide the intersubjective therapeutic process, and *whose* conceptualisations therapist and client are working with, vary between philosophies, values, approaches and individuals, but they each provide a means for therapist and client to make sense of the client's world. The chapter examines these issues in the following sections:

Section 1: Philosophical bases of therapeutic approaches.

Section 2: Conceptualisations of therapeutic approaches premised on the above.

Section 3: Conceptualisations of distress.

Section 4: Conceptualisations of assessment, diagnosis and formulation.

SECTION 1: PHILOSOPHICAL BASES OF THERAPEUTIC APPROACHES

Approaches to client work have evolved theories and practices to explain what is therapeutic, and why, on the basis of (arguably) very different conceptualisations of the person. Their frameworks of knowledge, science and the person have arisen from, and found sustenance for growth within, particular socio-cultural world views, as outlined in the following examples. Firstly, consider early psychoanalytic approaches that suggested that the psyche is made up of interacting parts; that intrapsychic conflicts occurred as a result of childhood difficulties and that these would result in particular psychological difficulties. Implicitly contained within this framework are notions that there is a psyche or mind which is active; that this psyche comprises different parts that are related and that these parts are located within the individual. It suggests that understanding the origins of difficulties comes from an understanding of child development and how this may influence the individual's manifestation of particular conflictual intrapsychic relationships.

So where did such notions come from? Late nineteenth-century European psychiatry and neurology was enveloped within a landscape of profound social psychiatric despair, and of Social Darwinism with its concepts of tainted heredity and degeneration. Alternative perspectives of magnetism, mesmerism, hypnotism, hysteria and the power of the unconscious offered alternative optimistic and individualistic discourses, ones within which Freud, Jung and psychoanalytic theories could emerge and flourish (Ellenberger, 1970). The model of science propounded by dynamic theories was based on the notion that dysfunctional behaviour and experience was the result of conflict between the various aspects of the psyche, which was largely unconscious and inaccessible to awareness. Bringing these conflicts to awareness would resolve them by overcoming the defences that were operating unconsciously and hence result in the person's recovery from symptoms. The favoured scientific presentation of the approach was therefore the case study, which evidenced the process by which the psychoanalyst brought the person's conflicts to awareness and resolution.

But while the early emergence of psychoanalysis was firmly located within the medical profession, the subsequent growth of psychotherapy was influenced by the growing discipline of psychology which, by the 1930s, had rejected introspection and the unconscious in favour of the study of observable behaviour. Conceptualisation of science and the person within such a framework was premised on learning theories that suggested that many adult behavioural difficulties were learnt patterns resulting from the child's stimulus, reward and conditioning environments. Thus, behaviours could be changed by similar means (see Bandura, 2013).

The behaviourist tradition lent itself to a very different form of psychotherapy, one that emphasised behaviour change through various programmes of conditioning and modification. These first took root in practice through the development of training programmes for children, psychiatric patients and those contemporaneously referred to as 'mental defectives'.

Similarly, its scientific principles favoured the randomised controlled trial in which behavioural change could be controlled for and evidenced.

But learning theories produced disquiet both about the principles of addressing only observable behaviour, and its research and practice ethics (of, for example, aversion therapy) and the behaviourist tradition was seriously challenged by humanist philosophies. Just as dynamic psychotherapy arose out of a need to find an alternative to the social psychiatry of the day, so humanistic psychologies arose partly in response to dissatisfaction with the rigidities and limitations of learning theory conceptualisations. Humanistic approaches to therapy flourished in the fertile soil of mid-twentieth-century western individualism, which emphasised subjective experience and the capacity of the individual for growth.

American psychologist Carl Rogers worked within the positivist framework of contemporaneous psychological research and experimentation but was also influenced by European phenomenology. His emphasis on the fundamental importance of the conditions of empathy, congruence and acceptance was an expression of the therapeutic need to understand the subjective experience of the individual and trust the inherent capacity of each person towards growth. Hence, he argued, when offered the facilitating conditions, the individual would find their own growth-directed solutions. Clinician-directed notions of shaping behaviours, as in therapy premised on learning theories, were redundant. Scientific principles within this framework favoured a strong emphasis on illuminating and examining the psychotherapeutic process between therapist and client, asking such questions as what were the conditions of growth, how could these be offered and received, and how could we learn more about such processes between people?

Reflecting an emerging western cultural and epistemological focus on co-created meaning and intersubjective experience, Rogers, towards the end of his life, grappled with a concept of presence, in which the inner spirit of the therapist touches that of the client (Kirschenbaum and Henderson, 1990). This formed part of a broader movement towards a shared meaning and a relational attitude within the therapeutic relationship, emerging as part of a 'narrative turn' in conceptualisations of knowledge, both within psychology and across other disciplines within the social sciences and humanities (Polkinghorne, 1988). The emergence of UK counselling psychology in the 1980s and 1990s, with its framework and values of shared meanings and co-created understanding within psychotherapeutic journeys of change, was integral to this shifting emphasis. Subjective experience and co-creation of meaning were seen as valid research arenas underpinned by appropriate qualitative methodologies that were suited to such a conceptualisation (see, for example, Greenberg and Pinsot, 1987).

So time and context sit side by side with theorists and practitioners as co-creators of any conceptualisation of psychotherapeutic endeavour. As Potter et al. (1999: 88) state, 'truth, certainty and evidence may be seen as situated practices'. Each therapeutic approach has evolved its theories, practices and research bases in order to adapt to changing conceptualisations of knowledge and science and Section 2 examines these approaches.

SECTION 2: CONCEPTUALISATIONS OF THERAPEUTIC APPROACHES

The approaches to knowledge and science discussed above contain conceptualisations of the person and associated theoretical frameworks to explain the development of life difficulties, rationales for therapeutic intervention and models of the process by which change takes place. In this section these will be illustrated with reference to the anonymised, composite case study below.

Case study

Alesha was the youngest (by six years) of three girls. Her parents ran their own business and Alesha's early childhood care was shared with her maternal grandmother. When Alesha was six, her grandmother, with whom she reported having a very close relationship, died, and Alesha described the next few years as being rather lonely at home. Her sisters were either out or had been reluctantly pressured to look after her after school. But she enjoyed primary school where she excelled at both hockey and netball. On transferring to secondary school Alesha continued her interest in sport, playing competitively and being accepted for the junior county hockey team and the school netball team. She had a small friendship group that included friends from primary school as well as others she had met at secondary school.

When she was 13, Alesha developed glandular fever and post-viral fatigue, which resulted in low mood and weight loss. She missed several months of schooling over the next year and lost her places in both the netball and hockey teams. In addition, her friendship group had re-formed to include others she didn't know and she felt on the edge of the group rather than central to it. Having missed so much school she was also behind in work and experienced gaps in her knowledge and understanding of several subjects which resulted in her grades dropping. Alesha was aware that she had lost weight and decided to cut back a bit further. Initially folk made flattering comments about her weight loss, which felt good, and she cut back further. After several months she had lost two stone and refused to eat with her family. She and her parents argued about her health and weight and her mother took her to the GP. Alesha was referred to the local Child and Adolescent Mental Health Service (CAMHS) unit where she began four years of cycling outpatient and inpatient treatment during the course of which she gained weight while in hospital and lost it again following discharge. Despite this she achieved good results in all her school exams and secured a place at her university of choice.

At university Alesha moved into the halls of residence and initially felt a sense of freedom and relief, but after some months found that she did not know how to manage the lack of structure and was unable to create her own. She felt chaotic and frightened and her eating

(Continued)

(Continued)

was less under control. She began binging and vomiting and was self-deprecating about being unable to restrict her eating anymore, something on which she had placed a high personal value. She began to cut herself on a regular basis, along her arms, her stomach and the tops of her legs, and began to have thoughts about whether she could carry on anymore. She arranged an appointment with her GP who prescribed her medication for low mood and referred her to the local eating disorders service.

So how might therapists from different therapeutic approaches conceptualise and work with Alesha's difficulties?

Person-centred approach

Based on research evidence, Rogers concluded that 'it is the attitude and feelings of the therapist, rather than his [sic] theoretical orientation, which is important in the process of constructive change' (1961: 44). In focusing on the attitudes of the therapist, and offering the therapist-provided conditions, a person-centred therapist seeks to be accurately attuned to the client's own process of change, so facilitating the client's actualising tendency towards fluidity of experience of self and others. He suggested that incongruence, that is a greater reliance on external locus of value than an organismic internal process, results from the development of internalised conditions of worth. In essence, our awareness of ourselves (self-concept), rather than the totality of our being, develops out of our childhood experience of relationships with others. Change, Rogers argued, involves a movement through seven stages of a process from internal stuckness to movement, through an increasing sense of one's internal life and its trustworthiness and of an acceptance of the complex natures of oneself and others. How this process is facilitated is the core of therapy. An empathically attuned therapeutic relationship acts as a facilitative step to experiencing self as of intrinsic worth, with trust in one's own internal locus of evaluation.

Alesha expected to be given a lot of information about her eating and self-harming, with a programme of actions designed to change these. She felt surprised when the therapist seemed not to offer this. She experienced the therapist as being interested in her and began to relax a bit, talking about her childhood and how things changed so much when her grandmother died. She described having wondered what was wrong with her that her family seemed not to want to spend time with her anymore. Describing her experience of glandular fever and its consequences, she indicated that she had felt a sense of pleasure in the associated weight loss but that the consequences of missing school, on friendships and academic and sporting opportunities had left her feeling very lonely and out of control. The therapist experienced a pervading feeling of something wrong with her and reflected on this with Alesha, who began to cry. She said that was exactly how she felt and that losing weight had given her a sense of being OK at something. Now that was gone she knew there really was something wrong with her as a person. Alesha said she was surprised that talking about all this had been a relief and she left feeling that maybe somebody might be able to hear and help her.

Although this was likely to be only the beginning of a long, and sometimes very bumpy, road towards a more comfortable way of living, it illustrates the importance of being empathically attuned to where in the process of change a client is when they arrive in the therapy room. Alesha's self-concept had become one of being deeply unworthy, or of 'something wrong with me'. Her eating problem offered a means of dealing with a damaged self-concept, a means of having a 'reliable' relationship (with food rather than person). In this respect, the eating behaviour was not the source of the problem, rather, it was a response that reflected Alesha's internalised sense of self. Addressing the addictive properties of her eating problems may well be necessary but a symptom-orientated approach alone was unlikely to facilitate Alesha's movement towards a more comfortable self-concept (Douglas, 2012).

Dynamic approaches

Psychodynamic approaches also offer a developmental understanding of the person that provide a framework within which therapeutic work can be understood and guided. Consider object relations theory. This refers to a psyche or mind with different parts that are in active relation. The parts are in relation within the individual, with internal representations of others and with others themselves. This inner and outer relatedness is called 'object relations'. Therapeutic change is considered to be about understanding the origins of difficulties, which are likely to be about some aspect of our object relatedness, understanding unconscious conflicts, gaining insight to the ways in which change may be possible through re-experiencing the conflicts experienced in a past relationship in the present therapeutic relationship, so enabling change and offering a safe context and relationship in which to do the above.

Listening to Alesha, the therapist reflected on the possible main underlying conflicts. It appeared that, at age six, Alesha had lost a central attachment figure. With parents focused on their business and older siblings reluctant to look after her, Alesha experienced a relational emptiness combined with a profound sense of loss. Her friends and school work therefore became the focus for her sense of belonging. The therapist realised that Alesha's defences had been sorely challenged when she developed glandular fever and her relational strengths were subsequently lost. He understood that Alesha was again vulnerable to the sense of loss and abandonment she had experienced at the age of six. As a teenager, however, the defensive strategies and relationship patterns deployed to manage these were different. Anorexia had effectively (initially) given Alesha a sense of control and of having a reliable 'friend' who would not abandon her. The problem was that her relationship with this 'friend' had a strong detrimental impact on her health, which resulted in what she perceived as recurring, unwanted and unwarranted interference from others. Alesha's battle had been transferred from anorexia towards these perceived hostile external relationships.

Only on going to university did Alesha experience her 'friend' turning on her. Her therapist felt Alesha had lost her secure base, with cutting becoming a way of anaesthetising her unmanageable and overwhelming feelings. For Alesha to find a more comfortable way of living, therapy would need to provide her with a (likely fairly long-term) safe contained relationship within which she could re-experience feelings of loss and abandonment. These could then be articulated, shared and managed within the therapeutic relationship rather than in the self-contained relationship to food and cutting. In this way Alesha could begin to trust herself in other current relationships without the need to resort to eating problems and self-harm.

Discussion point

This section has examined how two broad therapeutic approaches might conceptualise the person and/or therapeutic change. Of course there are very many nuances within each approach and there are other approaches, for example CBT and existential approaches, to name but two. How might you understand Alesha's distress, the rationale for therapeutic intervention and likely process of this in an approach other than those highlighted above?

SECTION 3: CONCEPTUALISATIONS OF DISTRESS

Clients often come to therapy seeking help to alleviate levels of psychological or relational discomfort or distress. Where causing significant problems in day-to-day living, such distress may be termed mental health problems and the person is referred to specific psychological services. These services are likely to include staff who work within a range of conceptualisations of distress which frame subsequent interventions, as is highlighted by James (Douglas and James, 2014: 6):

> The UK field of mental health could be perceived as a stage on which there are many players. Currently these include psychiatrists, general practitioners, clinical and counselling psychologists, psychotherapists, counsellors, psychiatric social workers, psychological well-being practitioners, high intensity workers and mental health nurses. This multi-professional group do not all share the same understanding and explanation of the concept of mental health.

What we may term psychological distress has historically given rise to a variety of discourses that frame attempts to understand such experiences. These include the religious, supernatural, moral, medical and psychological. Such discourses frame the way societies attempt to make sense of difference and each gives rise to its own classificatory systems and research directions as a way of imposing order and understanding on the unfamiliar, the different, the frightening and the distressing (Douglas, 2010). Some recent and current conceptualisations of distress and mental health include:

- Biomedical models
- Social models
- Critical models
- Biopsychosocial models

These models are outlined below and are illustrated by work in the field of eating problems.

Biomedical models

Why, we might ask, does the current, and arguably dominant, framework for understanding psychological distress centre on a medical model. The answer begins largely with early twentieth-century German psychiatrist Emil Kraepelin (1856–1926). Kraepelin developed a classification of psychiatric illness underpinned by a framework of aetiology and disease process based upon the twin axes of manic depression and dementia praecox (Greene, 2007). Emphasis on the physicality of mental disease process was given further weight by the discovery of syphilis as the cause of general paralysis of the insane (GPI), a common and devastating condition found in all psychiatric institutions of the time. These, and similar events, led over the course of the twentieth century to the development of many experimental physical treatments for psychological distress as well as research based on categorical classifications of mental disorder. Current iterations of classificatory systems, designed originally to further research agendas, include the *Diagnostic and Statistical Manual of Mental Disorders–5* (American Psychological Association, 2013) and the *International Classification of Diseases–10* (World Health Organization, 2010). Such criterion-based systems describe the various signs and symptoms of a particularly defined disorder plus the numbers and duration of these criteria that must be experienced or displayed to warrant a diagnosis.

Within a biomedical model, areas of research into eating problems may include focus on genetic causality. Evidence suggests, for example, that the concordance rate for anorexia in monozygotic twins is higher than for dizygotic twins (Bulik et al., 2000). Equally, such a framework may research links between abnormal brain chemistry and anorexia (Kaye et al., 2005). Research on treatment or therapeutic intervention may be based on randomised controlled trials within research clinics where participants are diagnosed with, and treated for, specific eating disorders.

Social models

Social models of distress argue that medical models locate disorder firmly within the individual and do not adequately take into account the relational, social or political worlds where the locus of distress may actually belong (see, for example, Russell-Mayhew, 2007). Social models of distress have evolved over time and with different emphases. These have ranged from the Mental Hygiene Movement, founded in 1908, which focused on strengthening the social fabric of the population, to current work, which includes examination of the links between unemployment and mental distress, and cultural studies, which examine cultural understandings, experiences and treatment of mental distress. In studies of depression within general practice, for example, research by Ostler et al. (2001) demonstrated that neighbourhood social deprivation accounted for 48.3 per cent of the variance in those experiencing depression.

Illustrating social models of distress, we find research on eating problems focusing on low self-esteem stemming from personal, familial and cultural experiences such as adverse childhood experiences or the impact of bullying (see, for example, Womble et al., 2001). Alternatively, as Russell-Mayhew (2007: 5) suggests, a social justice emphasis on eating problems and their treatment requires research questions to expand beyond the intrapsychic nature of inquiry and that 'societal issues related to health status are addressed because differential health status across diverse communities is the focus rather than the intrapsychic nature of the problems'.

Critical models

Critical models of psychiatric and psychological distress were highly influenced by the work of Michael Foucault (2001 [1961]). Foucault argued that the construction of deviance is culturally linked, with each historical period having its own deviants who are segregated from society. Only in the age of reason did madness specifically become considered a form of unreason and therefore deviance. This resulted in the mentally ill being separated out from society and the consequent need for an extensive programme of psychiatric institution building, most of which took place during the nineteenth century.

Critical approaches to emotional distress suggest that reality is co-created through shared knowledge and language. Categorisation of forms of mental illness therefore reflect, and further develop social acceptance of, the current dominant cultural explanation of understanding distress. Such a view takes a stance to truth that it is not something out there to be discovered but is socially, politically and culturally created within the interaction of people, culture and language. Labelling someone as psychotic, for example, may or may not have a basis in 'truth' but does serve social purposes. Firstly, it has an epistemological purpose based on a need to try to make sense of human distress. Secondly, it serves to provide a service provision route map, with its implicit notion that the organisation of service delivery may also be considered a co-construction of our notion of disorder(s).

So, to illustrate with reference to eating difficulties, the concept of disorder itself may be seen as historical, cultural and/or gendered (e.g. McVittie et al., 2005), and the question may be asked, for example, why have we constructed a gendered disorder category that emphasises a drive for thinness rather than a drive for muscularity? That this is not simply an academic question but something that centrally impacts on therapeutic intervention is evident in men regularly reporting difficulty asking for help for body and food issues that may be considered a female problem. Where they do ask for help, there is evidence that the referrer is more likely to seek an explanation of their difficulties in other disorders so that access to therapeutic intervention may take longer (Räisänen and Hunt, 2014).

Biopsychosocial model

The conceptualisations detailed above are based on different notions of 'truth' concerning human distress. However, common sense tells us that therapeutic understanding is likely to benefit if we can integrate understandings into a model that captures different aspects of distress. Such a model was introduced as a biopsychosocial approach by American psychiatrist George Engel in his seminal paper of 1977. As Borrell-Carrio et al. (2004: 576) put it:

> The biopsychosocial model is both a philosophy of clinical care and a practical clinical guide. Philosophically, it is a way of understanding how suffering, disease and illness are affected by multiple levels of organization, from the societal to the molecular. At the practical level, it is a way of understanding the patient's subjective experience as an essential contributor to accurate diagnosis, health outcomes, and humane care.

There is the suggestion, however, that in our medicalised world not all levels of this organisation are given equal weight, as Strawbridge (2008) argues:

> Increasing numbers of people are being 'diagnosed' with 'mental health disorders' expressed within a framework of psychiatric categories and counselling psychologists are increasingly being drawn into this framework. ... If counselling psychology is to maintain its radical edge it needs to develop its theoretical framework in a way that remembers the social within a truly biopsychosocial model of understanding and practice.

Discussion point

How might you conceptualise Alesha's difficulties within each of the frameworks of distress outlined above?

SECTION 4: CONCEPTUALISATIONS OF ASSESSMENT, DIAGNOSIS AND FORMULATION

So far, this chapter has looked at various forms of conceptualising in client work, namely epistemological positions underpinning therapeutic approaches, followed by these approaches

themselves, and then understandings of human distress. This section now turns to conceptualisations of assessment in client work. What does it means to assess, why assess, what and
who is being assessed and how, what is the purpose of it and for whom? This section will focus
on three conceptualisations of assessment: diagnosis, formulation and assessment of process.
Of course assessment in therapy is broader than the conceptual, for example risk assessment.
However, for the purposes of this chapter the focus in this section is on diagnosis, formulation
and assessment of process. While diagnosis typically leads on to certain activities, such as
testing, categorising, service provision and/or medication prescription, formulation typically
offers a fluid, collaborative understanding of individual distress and therapeutic intervention.
Humanistic approaches, particularly a person-centred approach, on the other hand, are more
likely to adopt a position of assessing the process occurring between therapist and client
rather than the client or their problems *per se*.

Table 9.1 outlines certain characteristics of both diagnosis and formulation, although these
may be questioned; for example, can categories really be described as simply descriptive?

Table 9.1   Characteristics of diagnosis and formulation (adapted from Mace and Binyon, 2005)

Characteristic	Diagnosis	Formulation
Format	Descriptive label	Explanatory summary
Standpoint	What is shared?	What is unique?
Derivation	Structured examination	Interactive interview
Use of theory	Theory neutral stance	Explicitly informed by theory
Predicts	Course of problem	Responses to problems
Treatment	Identifies therapy	Informs therapy

Diagnosis

Diagnosis is premised on a medical narrative to psychological difficulties, as articulated by
Woolfe (2014: xiii), who suggests that it:

> Offers a vocabulary in which mental and emotional health is seen as essentially consisting
> of two discrete states: health or illness. It relies on a philosophy whose roots lie in positivism
> and natural science in which it is held that the only truth resides in scientific knowledge. In
> turn, this leads into an emphasis on the experimental method in which the notion of a
> cause-effect relationship is powerful. The outcome of such an epistemological position is
> that aspects of the human condition can be identified objectively and then labelled through
> diagnosis.

There continues to be much debate about the notion of diagnosis; for example, as to whether
diagnostic categories actually exist as clinically recognisable sets of symptoms or behaviour.

For the practitioner one of the key arguments concerning diagnosis is that, in providing only a descriptive label, a diagnosis is static and unable inform or guide an ongoing collaborative therapeutic intervention that enables both client and therapist to make sense of the client's experiences and process of change (Johnstone et al., 2011).

Some clients experience a diagnosis as helpful, for example relief from a sense of self-blame, or as leading to service access. Other clients experience a diagnosis as humiliating, or demeaning. For example, the term 'borderline personality disorder' is often considered pejorative and stigmatising by both clients and clinicians alike; a term that acts to deny access to services (Markham, 2003).

Discussion point

Consider the following questions and discuss how these relate to your practice with clients.

- Are clusters of symptoms pre-existing and waiting to be recognised?
- Discuss the idea that increased number of diagnostic categories in recent iterations of the DSM indicates clinicians and researchers are becoming progressively more knowledgeable about what they are seeing?

Formulation

Competence in formulation is required of all counselling psychologists and the British Psychological Society's Standards of Education Section 3 (British Psychological Society, 2014) include the following:

3.5 construct collaborative formulations utilising theoretical frameworks and the clients' subjective experience aiming at an empathic understanding of their predicament;

3.6 ensure that formulations are expressed in accessible language, culturally sensitive, and non-discriminatory in terms of, for example, age, gender, disability, and sexuality;

3.7 reflect on and revise formulations in the light of on-going feedback and intervention and use them as a basis for decision making with regards to an appropriate therapeutic plan;

3.8 lead on the implementation of on-going formulation in work settings, utilised in order to enhance teamwork, multi-professional communication and psychological mindedness in those settings.

But what does the term 'formulation' mean? Consider the following two definitions:

It makes a statement about the nature of the patient's problems or difficulties, usually in terms of repeated maladaptive patterns occurring in relationships. ... Makes an inference as to how these are related to the patient's internal world, including unconscious conflicts. Links the above (if possible) with historical information in an explanatory model. (McGrath and Margison, 2000: 2)

[Its] purpose is both to provide an accurate overview and explanation of the patient's problems that is open to verification through hypothesis testing, and to arrive collaboratively with the patient at a useful understanding of their problem that is meaningful to them ... the case formulation is then used to inform treatment or intervention by identifying key targets for change. (Tarrier and Calam, 2002: 312)

As is evident from the language used, each of these definitions frames the clients' difficulties and process of therapy within conceptualisations of person and therapeutic change, and as a result offer both an explanation of the client's difficulties and also a framework for therapeutic process that can be fluid and collaborative during therapy, taking into account evolving and new information and understandings. Formulation is not new; indeed, in its use of interpretation, psychodynamic approaches have been formulating client issues and the process of therapy for the last hundred years. But the more formal acknowledgement and development of the *concept* of formulation evolved in the mid-twentieth century, and involved psychological, political and professional issues and understandings. Early psychology, in its clinical applications, had been considered largely a technical profession that carried out testing as determined by the psychiatric profession. However, during the Boulder conference on graduate education in clinical psychology (Boulder, Colorado, 1949), a more powerful defining framework for the profession developed as that of the scientist-practitioner model. Nevertheless, its continued reliance on a medical model was contentious and as Albee (2000: 247) stated: 'The flaw was not the insistence on scientific training for clinicians. It was the uncritical acceptance of the medical model, the organic explanation of mental disorders, with psychiatric hegemony, medical concepts and language.'

In Britain too there was a reaction to the continued predominance of a medical framework in American applied psychology's conception of psychological problems. Perhaps most influential in this at the time was Hans Eysenck (1975: 4–5), who considered that such difficulties 'are not to be construed as diseases. The subject which is fundamental to an understanding of behavioural disorders is psychology, not medicine.' So in Britain, behavioural therapy, and subsequently CBT training and practice, developed the notions of functional analysis and case formulation (see Persons, 1989).

As the kind of working knowledge developed by therapist and client using this model does not pathologise, stigmatise or diagnose in a static segment of time, it was increasingly considered a helpful conceptual tool that could inform both client issues and therapeutic process. Further developments saw, among others, the emergence of integrative formulation in the 1990s with Weerasekera's 'Four Ps Scheme' (1996) and more recently a narrative approach (Corrie and Lane, 2010). For further information on formulation, as conceptualised and practised. the reader might look at the individual chapters in Johnstone and Dallos (2006).

Visit the companion website to read formulations from three therapeutic approaches based on the case example of Alesha above.

However, research on the relationship between formulation and outcome is, to date, limited and, as Dudley and Kuyken (2006) remind us, formulation is a process whose effectiveness should not be taken for granted. Not only that, but there are arguments that both diagnosis and formulation arise from the therapist's frame of reference and do not necessarily reflect the experience and needs of the client, as discussed below.

A person-centred approach to assessment

Although Mearns (1997) suggests that the whole question of client 'assessment' runs entirely counter to person-centred theory, Tolan (2004) points out that however one conceptualises the process of assessment, some judgements have to be made. Within a person-centred approach, she argues, these will be about the process between therapist and client, not about client characteristics or behaviours. This view is elaborated by Wilkins (2005), who argues that in order for therapeutic change to occur an assessment of the process between therapist and client will be made that:

- Is based on Rogers''necessary and sufficient conditions' and seven stages of process.
- Focuses on features of the relationship between client and therapist and not on the client alone.
- Takes the necessary and sufficient conditions as a series of questions that a responsible therapist must ask at the beginning of (and throughout) the therapeutic endeavour. (Adapted from Wilkins, 2005: 142)

So within this conceptualisation of therapeutic work it is the process between client and therapist that is the focus for decisions as to whether and how therapy proceeds. As Wilkins (2005: 142) continues: 'If the answer to one or more of these questions is "no" and the "necessity" is not met by definition, therapeutic change will not occur. Making this judgement (which may very well be much more about the therapist's abilities and limitations than the client) is an assessment.'

In conclusion, each of these forms of assessment, that is diagnosis, formulation and process assessment, are framed by different conceptualisations of person and therapeutic intervention. In our client work we are inevitably engaging with such frameworks in attempting to understand. Awareness of how these conceptualisations influence, contribute to and/or interact with therapeutic engagement and processes of change is the very stuff that the reflective practitioner is made of.

Discussion point

Consider the following questions and discuss how these relate to your practice with clients.

- Are clusters of symptoms pre-existing and waiting to be recognised?
- Discuss the idea that increased number of diagnostic categories in recent iterations of the DSM indicates clinicians and researchers are becoming progressively more knowledgeable about what they are seeing?

Consider the BPS Standards, Section 3, regarding formulation.

- Discuss in relation to your own client work.
- Go to the companion website resources for this chapter and consider the different examples of formulation and assessment based on the case study of Alesha.

CONCLUSION

This chapter has demonstrated that at all levels of our client work we are conceptualising, whether we are aware of it or not. From philosophies of mind, feelings and behaviour, to models of the person based on these, to notions of distress and how we assess these (or not), nothing is conceptually neutral. Perhaps, however, one of the clearest expositions of experienced differences in understanding the world comes not from psychologists or philosophers, but from the poet William Wordsworth. His poem entitled 'The Idiot Boy' (Wordsworth, 2008 [1888]) reminds us all that individuals understand and experience the world in very different ways.

REFERENCES

Albee, G. (2000) 'The Boulder model's fatal flaw', *American Psychologist*, 55(2): 247–248.

American Psychological Association (2013) *Diagnostic and Statistical Manual of Mental Disorders* (5th edn). Washington, DC: American Psychiatric Association.

Borrell-Carrio, F., Suchman, A. and Epstein, R. (2004) 'The biopsychosocial model 25 years later: Principles, practice, and scientific inquiry', *Annals of Family Medicine*, 2(6): 576–582.

British Psychological Society (2014) *Standards for Doctoral Programmes in Counselling Psychology*. Leicester: BPS, www.bps.org.uk/system/files/user-files/Society%20Member/dcounspsy_standards_approved_may_2014.pdf (accessed 12 June 2014).

Bulik, C., Sullivan, P., Wade, T. and Kendler, K. (2000) 'Twin studies of eating disorders: A review', *International Journal of Eating Disorders*, 27: 1–20.

Corrie, S. and Lane, D. (2010) *Constructing Stories, Telling Tales: A Guide to Formulation in Applied Psychology*. London: Karnac Books.

Douglas, B. (2010) 'Disorder and its discontents', in R. Woolfe, S. Strawbridge, B. Douglas and W. Dryden (eds), *Handbook of Counselling Psychology* (3rd edn). London: Sage. pp. 23–43.

Douglas, B. (2012) 'Working with clients who have eating problems', in J. Tolan and P. Wilkins (eds), *Client Issues in Counselling and Psychotherapy*. London: Sage. pp. 131–144.

Douglas, B. and James, P. (2014) *Common Presenting Issues in Psychotherapeutic Practice*. London: Sage.

Dudley, R. and Kuyken, W. (2006) 'Formulation in cognitive-behavioural therapy: There is nothing either good or bad but thinking makes it so', in L. Johnstone and R. Dallos (eds), *Formulation in Psychology and Psychotherapy*. London: Routledge. Chapter 2.

Ellenberger, H. (1970) *The Discovery of the Unconscious: The Evolution of Dynamic Psychiatry*. New York: Basic Books.

Engel, G. (1977) 'The need for a new medical model', *Science*, 196: 129–136.

Eysenck, H. (1975) *The Future of Psychiatry*. London: Methuen.

Foucault, M. (2001 [1961]) *Madness and Civilisation* London: Routledge Classics.

Greenberg, L. and Pinsot, W. (1987) *The Psychotherapeutic Process: A Research Handbook*. New York: Guilford Press.

Greene, T. (2007) 'The Kraepelinian dichotomy: the twin pillars crumbling?' *History of Psychiatry*, 18(3): 361–379.

James, P. (2014) 'Exploring dilemmas, evidence and practice', in B. Douglas and P. James, *Common Presenting Issues in Psychotherapeutic Practice*. London: Sage. p. 6.

Johnstone, L. and Dallos, R. (2006) *Formulation in Psychology and Psychotherapy*. London: Routledge.

Johnstone, L., Whomsley, S., Cole, S. and Oliver, N. (2011) *Good Practice Guidelines on the Use of Psychological Formulation*. Leicester: British Psychological Society.

Kaye, W., Guido, K., Frank, U., Bailer, U. and Shannan, E. (2005) 'Neurobiology of anorexia nervosa: Clinical implications of alterations of the function of serotonin and other neuronal systems', *International Journal of Eating Disorders*, 37: 515–519.

Kirschenbaum, H. and Henderson, V. (eds) (1990) *The Carl Rogers Reader*. London: Constable.

Mace, C. and Binyon, S. (2005) 'Teaching psychodynamic formulation to psychiatric trainees: Part 1. Basics of formulation', *Advances in Psychiatric Treatment*, 11: 416–423.

Markham, D. (2003) 'Attitudes towards patients with a diagnosis of "borderline personality disorder": Social rejection and dangerousness', *Journal of Mental Health*, 12(6): 595–612.

McGrath, G. and Margison, F. (2000) 'The dynamic Formulation', in L. Johnstone and R. Dallos (eds), *Formulation in Psychology and Psychotherapy*. London: Routledge.

McVittie, C., Cavers, D. and Hepworth, J. (2005) 'Femininity, mental weakness and difference: Male students account for anorexia nervosa in men', *Sex Roles*, 53(5): 413–441.

Mearns, D. (1997) *Person-Centred Counselling Training*. London: Sage.

Ostler, K., Thompson, C., Kinmonth, A., Peveler, R., Stevens, L. and Stevens, A. (2001) 'Influence of socio-economic deprivation on the prevalence and outcome of depression in primary care: The Hampshire Depression Project', *British Journal of Psychiatry*, 178(1): 12–17.

Persons, J. (1989) *Cognitive Therapy in Practice: A Case Formulation Approach*. London: W.W. Norton & Co.

Polkinghorne, D. (1988) *Narrative Knowing and the Human Sciences*. Albany, NY: State University of New York Press.

Potter, J., Edwards, D. and Ashmore, M. (1999) 'Regulating criticism: Some comments on an argumentative complex', *History of the Human Sciences*, 12(4): 79–88.

Räisänen, U. and Hunt, K. (2014) 'The role of gendered constructions of eating disorders in delayed help-seeking in men: A qualitative interview study'. Available online at www.bmjopen.bmj.com/content/4/4/e004342 (accessed 7 June 2014).

Rogers, C. (1961) *On Becoming a Person: A Therapist's View of Psychotherapy*. London: Constable.

Russell-Mayhew, S. (2007) 'Eating disorders and obesity as social justice issues: Implications for research and practice', *Journal for Social Action in Counseling and Psychology*, 1(1): 1–13.

Strawbridge, S. (2008, July) 'Social amnesia: Losing sight of the social in the biopsychosocial model of mental distress'. Paper presented at the Division of Counselling Psychology Conference, Dublin.

Tarrier, N. and Calam, R. (2002) 'New developments in cognitive-behavioural case formulation', *Behavioural and Cognitive Psychotherapy*, 30: 311–328.

Tolan, J. (2004) *Skills in Person Centred Counselling*. London: Sage.

Weerasekera, P. (1996) *Multiperspective Case Formulation: A Step Towards Treatment Integration*. Malabar, FL: Krieger.

Wilkins, P. (2005) 'Assessment and diagnosis in person centred therapy', in S. Joseph and R. Worsley (eds), *A Positive Psychology of Mental Health*. Ross-on-Wye: PCCS Books.

Womble, L. et al. (2001) 'Psychosocial variables associated with binge eating in obese males and females', *International Journal of Eating Disorders*, 30(2): 217–221.

Woolfe, R. (2014) 'Foreword', in B. Douglas and P. James (eds), *Common Presenting Issues in Psychotherapeutic Practice*. London: Sage.

Wordsworth, W. (2008 [1888]) *The Major Works*. London: Oxford Paperbacks. pp. 67–79.

World Health Organisation (2010) *International Statistical Classification of Diseases and Related Health Problems*. Geneva: WHO, http://apps.who.int/classifications/icd10/browse/2010/en#/V (accessed 12 June 2014).

10
DIAGNOSIS AND FORMULATION IN MEDICAL CONTEXTS

DAVID PILGRIM

INTRODUCTION

This chapter explores the challenges facing counselling psychologists when trying to make sense of people and their presenting mental health problems. It will begin with a framework, which has pre-emptively construed, and seemingly solved, this dilemma by offering a checklist approach to psychiatric diagnosis. The rationale of psychiatric positivism embodied in nosological systems like DSM (American Psychiatric Association, 2013) and ICD (World Health Organization, 1992) will be summarised. I will explain why this rationale is both anti-humanistic and anti-scientific and argue that psychologists should reject its premises. This early and explicit recommendation is made in the knowledge that some counselling psychologists (not just psychiatrists) at times embrace diagnosis or are uncritical of its shortcomings.

The chapter then turns to some fundamental theoretical and philosophical challenges for consideration. If psychiatric positivism is abandoned, then this is the start and not the end of the matter. Psychologists are still then informed by competing bodies of knowledge from their own background, from, for example, phenomenology, existentialism, depth psychology, behaviourism, cognitivism and variants of constructivism. Thus, a preference for formulation rather than diagnosis, if indeed we should prefer the former over the latter, still requires critical reflection, if for no other reason than psychological alternatives patently are not of one voice, a point that began to be obvious in the 1960s and has remained unaltered since (Wann, 1964).

With this plurality of models and the contestation and forms of eclecticism and integration they spawn, three overarching questions recur for us all about psychological formulations. First, is it legitimate to attribute *causation* when making sense of people and their problems and if so how is this achieved persuasively? Second, how do we make plausible knowledge claims about *meanings* in psychological formulations and which of these options about meaning attribution should be privileged in psychological opinion? Third, what role is played by *values* when psychological formulations displace psychiatric diagnoses?

These three questions are already (or should be) important for counselling psychologists because their core discipline, psychology, is a *moral science* (Brinkman, 2011; Harré, 2002). That is, if we engage with the human world, then being systematic (in its broadest sense, 'scientific') in the service of others is necessarily a value-led not value-free process.

One of the contradictions in Western Anglophone psychology, but especially British psychology with its history of naïve empiricism, has been its attempt to deal with the inevitable and obvious co-existence of facts and values. Even strong advocates of that tradition of British empiricism, such as Hans Eysenck, though he tried his best, failed to keep these apart in practice. Initially, he argued that psychologists should *not* be therapists, on the grounds that this undermined the detached or disinterested assessment or experimental stance required by an applied science (Eysenck, 1949). But before too long, and maybe inevitably, he was advocating that psychologists should be experts in behaviour therapy (Eysenck and Gwynne-Jones, 1958).

I will return to these questions in the third part of the chapter by drawing upon a dissenting version of British empiricism (critical realism) as a framework for integrating causes, meanings and values within our efforts to formulate, rather than diagnose. I start, though, with the shortcomings of psychiatric positivism.

THE FAILURE OF DIAGNOSTIC PSYCHIATRY

Any adequate medical diagnosis should comply with certain expectations. However, its critics (e.g. Bentall, 2010; Pilgrim, 2007; Van Os, 2010) have argued that functional diagnoses in psychiatry fail in these expectations and I now suggest this checklist for the reader to consider:

1. *Measurement/empirical validity.* A valid medical diagnosis entails the demonstrable presence of measurable phenotypes. These reflect a proven natural disease entity. A diagnosis accurately describes an empirical reality about that disease in the patient diagnosed. The disease becomes clearly manifest in an embodied form in the patient sitting before us.
2. *Construct validity.* A category must be coherent and clear and separate from other categories; clear conceptual boundaries should exist between one disease and another.
3. *Prognosis/predictive validity.* A diagnosis should provide a predictive advantage beyond guess work. The diagnostician should be able to make accurate judgements about the future trajectory of an embodied disease if it remains untreated or treated.
4. *Inter-rater reliability.* Diagnosticians should agree with one another about a diagnosis in a particular case being considered before them. If they are trained in the same protocols of diagnosis, then they should agree on the diagnosis of a particular patient. If they fail to do so, then this form or reliability falls.

5. *Test–retest reliability.* A diagnosis should reflect a stable clinical state over sufficient time that it cannot be simply ignored as a transient variation in the functioning of the patient. If the diagnostic label keeps changing, then this undermines this form of reliability. However, cure or full and permanent recovery would also bring the stable clinical state to an end.

6. *Aetiology and pathogenesis.* A reasonable agreement is made by diagnosticians about the original causes (aetiology) and mediating causal processes (pathogenesis) in the patient underlying a disease. A good diagnosis brings with it some plausible professional authority about relevant causal antecedents. Without this, diagnosis is just name-calling.

7. *Treatment specificity.* A particular treatment should match and target a particular diagnostic state and not another one. A diagnosis should be a logical guide to treating this particular disease and not another one.

8. *Acceptability.* Patients receiving a diagnosis should find that it actually helps them. They should be informed of their diagnosis and, when informed, it should be experienced as a helpful communication. If it is not experienced as helpful by the patient, then the worthiness of diagnosis is undermined in principle.

This checklist of an ideal or good enough medical diagnosis highlights a range of problems with psychiatric labelling. However, some other medical diagnoses are vulnerable to some legitimate criticisms arising from the list. For example, some physical conditions, such as multiple sclerosis, are not always easy to diagnose and the prognosis in particular patients is difficult to estimate on diagnosis. Some other conditions have poor treatment specificity. For example, musculo-skeletal problems might be treated with analgesics, anti-inflammatories or even anti-cancer agents, case by case.

It is only the *degree* of uncertainty about the above criteria in psychiatric medicine that marks it off from the rest of the discipline and this is why I disagree with the dichotomous reasoning of those like Szasz (1961) (cf. Bentall and Pilgrim, 1993). Szasz designated mental illness to be a myth but thereby uncritically accepted the scientific descriptions in physical medicine, when in fact they are not beyond criticism in relation to the above checklist.

Of greatest importance for us here, and what Szasz himself correctly emphasised, is the absence of true signs in psychiatry; there is no blood test for 'depression' or 'schizophrenia'. This means that measurement has been problematic in principle for psychiatry in relation to its bread and butter work ('functional disorders'). Instead, measurement has been replaced by tautology in the following logic. Q. How do we know that this woman has 'schizophrenia'? A. Because she habitually hears voices and talks incoherently. Q. Why does she talk and act in this strange way? A. Because she is suffering from 'schizophrenia'.

Even the staunchest critics of psychiatric diagnosis concede the real existence of specific symptoms or complaints, for example the patient reporting low mood or hearing voices others cannot hear. Thus maybe some confidence in diagnostic categories could be gained by ensuring that even a symptom-based, though tautological, diagnosis has both validity (it identifies using an empirical method what it is supposed to identify and not something else) and reliability (it is used consistently between diagnosticians and over time). However, both validity and reliability are found lacking, even when common symptom checklists, such as

DSM, are deployed. Despite professionals allegedly adhering to such a common frame of reference, psychiatric diagnosis remains inconsistent (Kirk and Kutchins, 1994).

Also test–retest reliability is poor in clinical samples with chronic patients accruing many diagnoses during their 'career' of service contact and 'dual diagnosis' is common to rationalise this predicament. But even if inter-rater reliability were to be perfected, reliability is not validity. A reliable concept may or may not be a valid one. We can reliably agree on what a unicorn looks like. However, unicorns do not exist, except in the shared imagination of those socialised in cultures describing them to children. Psychiatric diagnoses are like unicorns.

Predictive validity is also important for good decision-making about individual cases. It also helps plausible research into epidemiology and service planning. However, psychiatric diagnosis fails in this regard. Statistical analyses of symptoms identified in community samples do not map on to the diagnostic categories used from DSM and so are not helpful (Mirowsky and Ross, 2003). And when treatment decisions are made upon the basis of prognosis (the implication and calculated risk of leaving a case untreated), both psychotropic medication and psychological treatments have proved to be problematic. In individual cases the person may be helped or left unaffected by interventions. Also they might even be harmed ('clinical iatrogenesis'). The latter is the case in psychological treatments where 'deterioration' effects can emerge at the hands of incompetent or abusive therapists. A common cultural assumption is that only drugs can harm us; 'talking treatments' can as well.

As far as aetiological specificity is concerned, psychiatrists are divided in their views. Competing aetiological theories have come and gone in fashion. They have included: genetic cause or pre-disposition; season of birth vulnerability; various neurochemical abnormalities; various neuropathological abnormalities; dysfunctional learned attachment styles; dysfunctional learned cognitive habits; intra-psychic conflicts; intra- and inter-generational family dysfunction; childhood maltreatment; recent environmental insults of loss and trauma; and differential social stress in relations to the life events inflected by class, race, gender and age. All of these are of course plausible but the point is that none on the list has proved to be unequivocally pre-eminent when we look for hard evidence.

As for the final criterion of the acceptability of psychiatric diagnosis to patients, this is ambiguous from what we know to date. Some patients embrace the process and feel some subjective or objective benefit from it (such as access to treatment services or extra welfare benefits) but many patients complain that diagnosis does not exactly cause stigma, but certainly contributes to it. Patients surveyed do not typically construe their problems in diagnostic terms. Instead, they put forward accounts about their personal histories, current social conditions and even their spirituality (Rogers et al., 1993). The latter authors found that only 10 per cent of psychiatric patients interviewed framed their difficulties in diagnostic terms.

A US survey found that attempts to de-stigmatise mental disorder by emphasising that it is 'a disease like any other' have failed. While the general public have been persuaded by professional campaigns to emphasise the biological ontology of mental disorders, they have retained similar levels of fear and distrust of psychiatric patients as before the anti-stigma campaigns (Pescosolido et al., 2013). According to the latter survey, bio-medical determinism may 'excuse', and even appear to explain, mentally disordered action. At the same time, though, it may also confirm the ineluctable incorrigibility of those with a psychiatric diagnosis. In the public imagination, it seems to invite fatalism, and so prejudice, not compassion, then ensues.

CONTESTATION ABOUT FORMULATION

The celebration of a formulation-driven rather than diagnosis-driven approach to client assessment is now on record (Bruch and Bond, 1998; Johnstone and Dallos, 2006). In the current British context, the Division of Clinical Psychology now offers a clear approach to the classification of mental health problems, which is formulation-based and rejects diagnosis (British Psychological Society Division of Clinical Psychology, 2011 and 2013). A formal professional separation is beginning to appear then between psychiatric diagnosis and psychological formulation, posing challenges for the training curriculum in applied psychology, where trainers have ambivalently held on to systems such as DSM (Carey and Pilgrim, 2010). Now the onus is upon them to explicitly reject a diagnosis-based approach.

However, each solution brings with it new problems or challenges. So now I turn my critical attention to *psychological not psychiatric accounts* of mental abnormality. Formulations have three main advantages over diagnoses.

First, they emerge from a dialogue between the client and the professional. In diagnosis there is the semblance of a dialogue but it is basically a medical monologue: the professional starts with an a priori set of categories (codified in DSM or ICD) and then 'elicits' symptoms from the patient to establish which category fits the symptom profile. This is a Procrustean Bed supplied in advance by the medical profession to identify embodied examples of assumed disease states. By contrast, a psychological formulation starts from what the client tells the professional about their life, past, present and maybe even future. Those biographical details contain a mixture of events, processes and the client's view of them. In response, using their preferred model of stasis and change, the professional negotiates a shared understanding with the client about what is going on in their life and what resources might exist to ameliorate the particular complaint being presented. Thus the process of negotiation is consensual and not seemingly professionally dominated, though it undoubtedly remains profession-centred (see below).

Second, in diagnosis the meaning of the illness to the patient is of little relevance. The priority for the professional is to get the diagnosis right (a primary duty drilled into medical practitioners during their professional socialisation). What the patient makes of it is a secondary consideration and becomes only subsequently relevant to case management or treatment. This deferred medical concern is about 'compliance'. Interestingly, in psychiatry the term 'mental illness', not 'mental disease', tends itself to concede a slippery experiential element. Generally in medicine 'disease' refers to the objective characteristics of pathology and 'illness' refers to the patient's subjective experience of the disease. Because functional diagnoses rely on symptoms, not signs (see below), then psychiatry is largely dealing with illness, not disease, even within its own traditional medical frame of reference.

In formulation, a shared commitment to change is established, or tested out, from the outset by the client being afforded the right and the responsibility (n.b.) to be a co-author of the formulation. Indeed, because most forms of psychological intervention imply a form of re-socialisation or re-learning (I come on to their differences below), then the assessment period is an initial testing ground for the professional's grasp both of the biographical challenge being reported *and* the capacity of the client to re-set or re-author their lives hereafter.

But the germane issue here is the professional's respect for the agency of the client. Psychological models of all varieties accept the existence and central role of human agency; Skinner's radical behaviourism is the exception that proves this rule (Skinner, 1971). A medical model of diagnosis has little or no interest in this core aspect of being human, instead the agency of the professional is emphasised alone. It is his or her authority to describe the world that is primary. As Bentall (2010) notes, 'phenomenology' in Karl Jaspers' diagnostic psychiatry referred primarily to the appearance of reality of significance to the diagnostician not to the patient. For example, Jaspers always privileged the doctor's view over that of the patients, if they did not concur on reality (as in paranoia). Within the diagnostic medical framework, only matters of 'insight' and 'cooperation' or 'compliance' become relevant to ensure an untroubled process of 'treatment' or 'management'.

Third, personal accounts from clients are sufficiently open-textured for any psychological model, potentially at least, to frame or process the communications being offered within the context of a relationship. The latter then becomes the vehicle for change, just as much as the content of the account and the dialogue it then triggers with the professional and their preferred psychological model. Formulations, then, establish the start of a process of change with the client rather than a disinterested form of labelling (claimed or aspired to by diagnosis).

This is all good news about formulations, when we compare them to diagnoses, on both scientific and humanistic grounds. However, we also need to consider their limitations as well.

First, formulations arise from contestation in human science. The formulation offered by a psychoanalyst is clearly different from that of a cognitive therapist. A credibility problem for models of psychotherapy is that their variegated and sometimes mutually hostile character might be perplexing to outsiders. Which model should be believed (if any) given that they seem to be so wide-ranging in their epistemological preferences? Can the formulation of the psychoanalyst and that of the cognitive therapists both be correct? How is that possible logically?

Second, although all psychological models of formulation might offer the advantages I note above, compared to the medical monologue of a psychiatric diagnosis, it is misleading to characterise them in a wholesale way as being client-centred, rather than professional-centred. All psychological accounts are versions of biographical description mediated by professionals; they are not raw and unmediated forms of autobiography. Indeed, with the exception of a pure person-centred model in the tradition of Rogerian counselling, all the other models have an a priori set of professionally generated assumptions about human functioning. Moreover, even the Rogerian model imports its own assumptions of sorts (about the nature of human growth) and these notably were the focus of early studies of the effectiveness of psychotherapy (investigations of 'the central therapeutic triad').

Third, psychological models vary in the degree to which they follow the unfolding process of the client's account and adopt a permissive versus directive approach to that account. For example, CBT uses homework whereas psychoanalysis does not. Some approaches emphasise questioning, whereas others do not. Some ignore or play down problems (such as Solution Focused Therapy, which largely ignores 'problem talk') whereas others explore particular problems in more and more depth. Again, this suggests that psychological formulations are highly discrepant, which might be a reason to question their collective credibility, thereby reinforcing my first point above.

Fourth, the mode of therapy will shift the focus of the formulation. For example, some of the key models of formulation are individualistic (e.g. Rogers' model of growth potential within a dyad or the emphasis on transference interpretations in psychoanalysis). But once the setting of therapy shifted to groups and families, then *what* was being formulated shifted with it. For example, in psychoanalysis when soldier patients could not be treated individually, for cost reasons, then new frames of formulation were invented that were less about individuals and more about group dynamics (Bion, 1959). Similarly, General Systems Theory was imported into family work to describe interconnectivity rather than to formulate individual aspects of presenting problems of 'the identified patient'. My point here is that when we talk about 'formulation' in psychological terms it is not self-evident that this is any longer about understanding individuals; it may or may not be.

Fifth, because counselling psychologists are psychologists, then they conceptualise psychologically. This is obvious but it has consequences for formulation. The latter will be about intra-psychic or interpersonal functioning. The boundaries of disciplinary comfort for psychologists range from physiology on one side to social psychology on the other. Examples of those limits of conceptualisation are learning theory informing behaviour therapy and field theory informing group work. General Systems Theory informing family therapy is a more ambitious trans-disciplinary application to formulation, but if the boundaries of its application to understanding are those of a family alone (a natural rather than created group), then a closed, not open, system is the focus. By contrast, sociology studies open systems and so always places human experience and mental health problems specifically in social context (Rogers and Pilgrim, 2014).

This limited disciplinary focus from psychologists means that they may lack the confidence and competence to consider the role of macro-social, or even for that matter neurobiological, factors within a formulation. Because personal problems *are* personal, psychology is the most obvious starting point of expertise for their understanding. But supposing that such a starting point does not exhaust the field of inquiry, and we need to understand the role or salience of non-psychological factors. A psychological formulation (of whatever type preferred) may then be an incomplete account. Moreover, as I noted in relation to the contestation about etiological specificity in relation to psychiatric diagnosis, for now no one knows for certain about how particular problems in particular people emerge in particular circumstances in their particular lives at this point in time rather than another. A psychological formulation is at best a provisional glimpse and piece of very partial guess work. This caution is a cue for my next section.

THE CHALLENGE OF INTEGRATING CAUSES, MEANINGS AND VALUES

In this section I approach the above set of points about the failure of psychiatric diagnosis on the one hand, and the strengths and weaknesses of psychological formulations on the other, by addressing some deeper considerations about the philosophical underpinnings of psychology. Unless we deal with these matters, then we are left with the 'undecidability of propositions', to use a phrase favoured by postmodernists, which implies a version of nihilism in the wake of Nietzsche (Bull, 2014). This philosophical tradition, reinforced in the past 20 years by the popularity of French post-structuralism, refers to unending representations of reality or perspectives ('perspectivism'), a position that has captivated many psychologists in the recent past (e.g. Parker et al., 1995).

By contrast, here I adopt a position from critical realism about diagnosis and formulation. This philosophy provides us with an opportunity to integrate causes, meanings and values in psychology (Pilgrim, 2013). Its three main premises are epistemological relativism, ontological realism and judgemental rationality (Archer, 2002). The first refers to the fact that in human sciences all phenomena might be construed in a variety of ways by different people (or even the same person over time) and our collective ways of understanding the world will vary over time and space. However, the second refers to a commitment to reality. Reality exists in ways which we currently understand to some extent but by and large the real is beyond our immediate grasp. Reality is mind-independent and so precedes our birth and will post-date our death individually and as a species. The third refers to knowledge being about fair judgement; educated guesswork in good faith which is always inflected by our values.

Given the first two points, we do our best to make fair judgements but must always remain sceptical or in a state of doubt (another term for critical realism is 'sceptical realism'). Moreover, we cannot achieve a disinterested or purely objective form of knowledge. Thus critical realism rejects the premise of positivism about 'disinterested' science, which claims to separate facts from values, but it does retain its Popperian emphasis on the fallibility of science.

Epistemological relativism is aligned with contructivist or postmodern theories. However, critical realism is only a weak form of constructivism. More radical versions argue instead that 'everything is socially constructed' and thereby reject the second premise of critical realism (ontological realism). The recent tradition from French post-structuralism, which has spawned a commitment to unending epistemological relativism, is thus *anti-realist*. By contrast, positivism is realist but it has a 'flat' or single view of reality and so rejects epistemological relativism in favour of claims about the universal nature of knowledge. For critical realists, this is naïve and tends to confuse reality with empirical knowledge alone and gives no credence to reality being complex, deep and for the most part beyond our current knowledge. The emergent consequences of real forces ('generative mechanisms') may be blocked from empirical expression. These mechanisms are multiple and may be *in potentia* and so reality is far more than the empirical.

Critical realism accepts that there are universal 'demi-regularities' but these are always expressed in emergent new ways in particular circumstances ('concrete universals'). Whereas positivism depicts the world as there and fixed and awaiting understanding (via the discovery of permanent and universal laws), critical realism understands the world as being real but in constant flux (a feature of open systems). All human activity is part of an open system and therefore predictions are always difficult to establish accurately. Everything exists (it is not merely 'constructed' by the language we use) but it keeps changing over time and space. This makes reality difficult to understand and so we should approach it with humility but without rejecting it nihilistically as being completely unknowable (cf. the radical constructivism noted above which replaces reality with the social construction of reality).

Having now explained the premises of critical realism, which is a middle way between the linguistic or postmodern turn in psychology on the one hand and positivism or traditional empiricism on the other, what implications do they have for our understanding of diagnoses and formulations? The following points answer that question.

First, psychiatric diagnoses are flawed because they aspire to establish fixed and singular ways of describing distress, madness and incorrigible egocentricity. These spurious and misleading claims about abstract universals commit the fundamental error of the 'epistemic fallacy'.

Second, the epistemic fallacy refers to the tendency within positivism to confuse the map with the territory (Bateson, 1972). So, for example, under DSM a map of 'schizophrenia' is developed using a checklist of two of any five symptoms to make the diagnosis. But schizophrenia does not exist – what exists are professionally-preferred ways of *describing* people, who are unintelligible to those who are sane by common consent. The latter make decisions about psychological abnormality *before* it is medically codified by psychiatric experts. Thus professionals invent concepts to suit their own theoretical preferences or interests and then, misleadingly, broadcast them as being naturally occurring phenomena existing 'out there'. However, they are not 'out there' but in the heads or collective awareness of the professionals. Some people hear voices but they do not 'have schizophrenia'. Some people are profoundly sad but they do not 'have major depression'. Some people are incorrigibly egocentric across settings but they do not 'have a personality disorder'.

Third, the epistemic fallacy can also be found in some psychotherapeutic formulations. A lesser known paper of Thomas Szasz, about transference rather than the 'myth of mental illness', pointed out that transference interpretations (which are central components of psychodynamic formulations) are not about the natural world of facts but about the therapist's needs. Freud invented transference because he could not cope with the raw feelings of desire and hatred he encountered from his patients. He could argue that the patient did not want to have sex with (or kill) their therapist but this 'really' was about other parties instead (the patient's parents) (Szasz, 1963).

Fourth, thus when we assess people, and their presenting complaints about their life and relationships, the caution of the epistemic fallacy needs bearing in mind, whether we diagnose or formulate. However, from a critical realist perspective we also need to consider ontology not just epistemology. If we *only* focus on concepts or language, then this does not exhaust our cautious and sceptical task. There is also the matter of psychologists putting forward some variety or other of putative causal processes in relation to *why* this person is presenting with these particular problems at this time in his or her life. These legitimate proposals do require some notion of causality and so allude to real events and processes in the current or past circumstances of the patient. (Occasionally they might even refer to future circumstances, when the person is worried about what is looming in their life.) As with any other form of investigation (for example, detective work or journalism), we need to check our facts and put forward reasonable grounds for trusting them. Here, then, when creating formulations, there is a professional need to attend to the interplay of ontological realism and judgemental rationality. Faced with the overall picture presented by the client, in terms of what has happened to them in their life and how they understand those occurrences, what is the fairest way to work out what is going on for them psychologically? Answering that question is an exercise in judgemental rationality.

Fifth, because we are dealing with particular people as moral agents living within a particular moral order (of their time and place) we need to attend to a deeper ethical dimension to formulation. Values, not just facts, require our attention. Eysenck spotted that psychological therapy was a moral or value-led process (and could not hold the untenable separation within positivism of facts and values). If we are trying to encourage mental health gain or reduce distress or dysfunction, then this requires value judgements, which compare a current unsatisfactory state of existential affairs for the client (A) with a prospective improved situation for them (B). The negotiation of movement from A to B is necessarily normative; both professional and client are embarking on a shared commitment to human improvement. This is why psychological formulations and interventions are an expression of scientific humanism; they are not purely matters of science, nor are they purely matters of humanism. They are a proportionate combination of the two. The notion of proportionality is part of the professional judgemental rationality noted in the previous point. Counselling psychologists are not friends in a natural social network. However, they are also not dispassionate and uncaring experimenters, when faced with a person in need of help. This is a socio-ethical scenario *par excellence* and so it cannot be reduced to a dispassionate experiment. A formulation is a stock-taking part of that proportionate response of scientific-humanism-in-action, both at the start of the relationship and on an ongoing basis, as it becomes a revisable live document, co-authored by counselling psychologist and client.

Sixth, that contingent socio-ethical scenario of a helping relationship itself emerges, then, in one particular context and not another. The counselling psychologist temporarily joins the biographical circumstances of the client as part of an open system. This alerts us to two cautions. First, the professional is only one input to that open system. Enabling and disabling inputs are also present, some of which are known to the client and professional and some not. The danger of a profession-centred discourse is that the practitioners will tend to over-value their influential role and personal salience. Erroneously, they may attribute change to their input alone. Equally, when change does not occur this might be over-attributed to 'resistance' in the therapy, when other contextual influences might explain stasis. The second caution is that the professional's own motives for formulating the client's complaint in this way and not another are driven from their side of the relationship and so should be part of a wider lens for formulation. In this contingent socio-ethical scenario, what assumptions about epistemology and ontology are operating and what power is in play within the asymmetry of the relationship? I have commented elsewhere that psychotherapy can be framed as a set of secular cults or tribes vying for a claim to pre-eminence, in one branch of applied human science (Pilgrim, 1997). With this sceptical framing in mind, being joined by those who are more actively hostile to the 'talking treatments' broadly conceived (e.g. Masson, 1987; Smail, 1996), at the very least counselling psychologists need to consider their *own* role, powers and preferred ways of understanding that are shaping the formulation process. A credible formulation is, in part at least, an aspect of rhetoric of justification for professional authority (Simons, 1985). The professional needs to be aware of that process of rhetoric generation. Formulations describe client functioning but they are also rhetorical devices to help claim and maintain professional status and salaries.

DISCUSSION

I have used this chapter to pursue three main aims. First, I argued that psychiatric diagnosis is part of a pseudo-science (medical positivism) that psychologists would now be wise to reject. Second, I rehearsed the strengths and weaknesses of psychological formulations as alternatives to psychiatric diagnosis. Third, I offered critical realism as a philosophical solution to the pitfalls on one side of positivism (or naïve realism) and on the other of radical constructivism (or perspectivism).

In that middle way, as I understand it, we operate as applied human scientists in a constant state of ambiguity (this is why psychologists need to be people who can tolerate uncertainty in their work). On the one hand, we might tentatively offer causal suggestions within any formulation we offer. On the other hand, we are part, with the client, of an open system and so at best those suggestions are based upon our unfolding and very partial understanding of the client's complex life (past, present and future). Formulations are versions of detective work and so are fallible and that work, we must remember, could be pursued differently but quite legitimately by another 'detective'.

Such educated guesswork (because that is what formulation is ultimately) is always incomplete and always open to alternative emphases and framings. But, to remind the reader of the legs of the milking stool of premises from critical realism: we choose to formulate in this way and not another (epistemological relativism), while being faced with and reporting likely causal processes in the particular and real material conditions of the client's life (ontological realism) and then we have to come to a conclusion about what is more likely to be true, in our opinion, about that complexity in this particular case (judgemental rationality).

In formal philosophical terms, psychological formulations operate at the ambiguous borderline between confident explanations in natural science (*erklären*) and more diffident descriptions and interpretations in social science (*verstehen*). Models of psychological therapy have ranged in the balance they strike about this tension. At one extreme reductionist explanations can be found in some forms of behaviourism, for example neurosis is simply a product of classical conditioning (Pavlov, 1941), but also psychoanalysis, for example all mental health problems are reducible to schizoid phenomena (Guntrip, 1985). At the other extreme, pure phenomenological accounts would do little more than report a rich description of the client's view of their life and their noted resources to cope and change (Rogers, 1962). Such a description would be evident, for example, in a letter written by a client-centred counsellor. Some other models, such as cognitive analytical therapy, would be a shared record of work together and thus reflect a middle way on the continuum between authoritative professional explanations and reports of sense-making from the client's viewpoint alone (Ryle, 1990). And so it goes on from model to model.

A related consideration here relates to what we mean by 'interpretation'. This has a particular meaning within the psychodynamic tradition but the original notion of *verstehen*, proposed by Max Weber and Wilhelm Dilthey, simply argued that the human sciences should provide descriptions of sense-making from the individual social actor's point of view. As *all* psychological formulations are within that definition, then in their own way they are all hermeneutic exercises and so part of this process of *verstehen*. But because this is about sense-making from the viewpoint of the individual, we need to tease out case by case and from one psychological model to another, whether the individual professional's or the individual client's viewpoint is being privileged and in what way a balance is being struck between the two. Moreover, I would argue that the (warranted) interpretation of personal sense-making also needs to be augmented with tentative attempts at causal reasoning (Pilgrim, 2014). Without that detective work about historical causes we would not trace such important processes as the impact of childhood adversity on adult mental health.

As I noted in my first caution about the limitations of psychological formulations, an inherent weakness in advocating them is that they are not of one voice for the very reason that they theorise the balance of causes and meanings in different ways and codify them using different types of language. Applied psychology is always contested and so it generates many models, which at times vie for pre-eminence within the politics of bids for professional legitimacy. This may be rather confusing for onlookers and may even provoke their cynicism at times.

Psychologists (not surprisingly) are prone to psychological reductionism, a tendency amplified within applied psychology. The latter can only work with client agency and so its practitioners are prone to ignoring that which they cannot control (the client's environment, past and present). This understandable pragmatic focus on what is achievable individualistically, along with a relative lack of sociological knowledge, can disable the psychologist from being familiar with the full role of social context for intelligibility in their formulations. And a fuller contextual appreciation would reveal that many mental health problems are a function of the intersection of multiple historical and current social forces beyond the control and often knowledge of the client (Brown and Harris, 1978; Stockdale et al., 2007; Teghtsoonian, 2009). This disciplinary limitation is my final caution about our confidence in psychological accounts of mental abnormality.

CONCLUSION

Psychological formulations represent scientific and humanistic progress for applied psychologists, once the latter knowingly reject psychiatric diagnosis. However, their own credibility about their preferred professional assessments is open to doubt for a range of reasons. The preference for formulations itself has emerged in a context of competing professional bids for legitimacy. I have offered critical realism as an overarching philosophy to appreciate our understanding of what might be incorporated sensitively and intelligently in formulations and to guide their use by counselling psychologists. In particular, we need to retain a respectful balance between meanings, causes and values. There is no proven or provable single correct way of striking this balance, while attending at all times to the biographical context of the client and the professional context of the psychologist offering to help them with their problems in life. However, I hope that the considerations offered in this chapter help the reader to reflect on that challenge in their particular work setting.

Visit the companion website to read Evaluating the Adequacy of a Psychological Formulation.

REFERENCES

American Psychiatric Association (APA) (2013) *Diagnostic and Statistical Manual of Mental Disorders* (5th edition). Washington, DC: APA.

Archer, M. (2002) *Realist Social Theory: The Morphogenic Approach*. Cambridge: Cambridge University Press.

Bateson, G. (1972) *Steps to an Ecology of Mind*. New York: Chandler Press.

Bentall, R.P. (2010) *Doctoring the Mind*. London: Penguin.

Bentall, R.P. and Pilgrim, D. (1993) Thomas Szasz, crazy talk and the myth of mental illness. *British Journal of Medical Psychology*, 66(1): 69–76.

Bion, W.R. (1959) *Experiences in Groups*. New York: Basic Books.

Brinkman, S. (2011) *Psychology as a Moral Science*. New York: Springer.

British Psychological Society Division of Clinical Psychology (2011) *Good Practice Guidelines on the Use of Psychological Formulation*. Leicester: BPS.

British Psychological Society Division of Clinical Psychology (2013) *Classification of Behaviour and Experience in Relation to Functional Psychiatric Diagnosis: Time for a Paradigm Shift*. Leicester: BPS.

Brown, G.W. and Harris, T.O. (1978) *The Social Origins of Depression*. London: Tavistock.

Bruch, M. and Bond, F.W. (1998) *Beyond Diagnosis: Case Formulation in CBT*. London: Wiley.

Bull, M. (2014) *Anti-Nietzsche*. London: Verso.

Carey, T. and Pilgrim, D. (2010) Diagnosis and formulation: What should we tell the students? *Clinical Psychology & Psychotherapy: Theory, Research and Practice*, 17(6): 447–454.

Eysenck, H.J. (1949) Training in clinical psychology: An English point of view. *American Psychologist*, 4: 173–176.

Eysenck, H.J. and Gwynne-Jones, H. (1958) The psychiatric treatment of neurosis. Paper presented to the Royal Medico-Psychological Association, London.

Guntrip, H. (1985) *Psychoanalytic Theory, Therapy, and the Self*. London: Karnac Books.

Harré, R. (2002) *Cognitive Science: A Philosophical Introduction*. London: Sage.

Johnstone, L. and Dallos, L. (2006) *Formulation in Psychology and Psychotherapy: Making Sense of People's Problems*. London: Taylor & Francis.

Kirk, S.A. and Kutchins, H. (1994) The myth of the reliability of DSM. *The Journal of Mind and Behavior*, 15(1&2): 71–86.

Masson, J. (1987) *Against Therapy*. London: HarperCollins.

Mirowsky, J. and Ross, C.E. (2003) *Social Causes of Psychological Distress*. New Brunswick, NJ: Transaction.

Parker, I., Georgaca, E., Harper, D., McLaughlin, T. and Stowell-Smith, M. (1995) *Deconstructing Psychopathology*. London: Sage.

Pavlov, I.P. (1941) *Psychopathology: Lectures on Conditioned Reflexes*. Vol. 2: *Conditioned Reflexes and Psychiatry*. Trans. W.H. Gantt. London: Lawrence & Wishart.

Pescosolido, B.A., Medina, T.R., Martin, J.K. and Long, J.S. (2013) The 'backbone' of stigma: Identifying the global core of public prejudice associated with mental illness. *American Journal of Public Health*, 103(5): 853–860. doi: 10.2105/AJPH.2012.301147. Epub 14 March 2013.

Pilgrim, D. (1997) *Psychotherapy and Society*. London: Sage.

Pilgrim, D. (2007) The survival of psychiatric diagnosis. *Social Science & Medicine*, 65(3): 536–544.

Pilgrim, D. (2013) The failure of diagnostic psychiatry and the prospects of scientific progress offered by critical realism. *Journal of Critical Realism*, 12(3): 336–358.

Pilgrim, D. (2014) *Understanding Mental Health: A Critical Realist Exploration*. London: Routledge.

Rogers, A. and Pilgrim, D. (2014) *A Sociology of Mental Health and Illness*. Buckingham: Open University Press.

Rogers, A., Pilgrim, D. and Lacey, R. (1993) *Experiencing Psychiatry: Users' Views of Services*. London: Macmillan.

Rogers, C. (1962) *Toward Becoming a Fully Functioning Person*. Washington, DC: A.W. Combs.

Ryle, A. (1990) *Cognitive-Analytical Therapy: Active Participation in Change*. Chichester: Wiley.

Simons, H. (ed.) (1985) *Rhetoric in the Human Sciences*. London: Sage.

Skinner, B.F. (1971) *Beyond Freedom and Dignity*. New York: Alfred A. Knopf.

Smail, D. (1996) *Getting By without Psychotherapy*. London: HarperCollins.

Stockdale, S.E., Wells, K.B., Tang, L., Belin, T.R., Zhang, L. and Sherbourne, C.D. (2007) The importance of social context: Neighbourhood stressors, stress buffering mechanisms and alcohol, drug and mental disorders. *Social Science & Medicine*, 65: 1867–1881.

Szasz, T.S. (1961) The uses of naming and the origin of the myth of mental illness. *American Psychologist*, 16: 59–65.

Szasz, T.S. (1963) The concept of transference: A logical analysis. *International Journal of Psychoanalysis*, 44: 432–435.

Teghtsoonian, K. (2009) Depression and mental health in neoliberal times: A critical analysis of policy and discourse. *Social Science & Medicine*, 69: 28–35.

Van Os, J. (2010) Are psychiatric diagnoses of psychosis scientifically useful? The case of schizophrenia. *Journal of Mental Health*, 19: 305–317.

Wann, T.W. (ed.) (1964) *Behaviorism and Phenomenology: Contrasting Bases for Modern Psychology*. Oxford and Chicago: University of Chicago Press.

World Health Organization (1992) *The ICD-10 Classification of Mental and Behavioural Disorders*. Geneva: WHO.

11
FORMING A RELATIONSHIP: A PHENOMENOLOGICAL ENCOUNTER
MARTIN MILTON

For many people within the profession, counselling psychology's privileging of the therapeutic relationship is both well known and highly valued. It is one of the first things that trainees are asked to start thinking about and it is something that we proudly base in the research evidence – we know that therapies of all kinds work best when based in robust therapeutic relationships (Gelso and Carter, 1995). But what is a 'relationship'? What does a therapeutic relationship look like? How is it distinct from any other relationship that we enjoy or is good for us and that enhances our well-being? How do we put effort into creating such a relationship?

This chapter will look at a range of information and bodies of knowledge that can inform counselling psychologists about the importance of developing good relationships with clients and guide us in our attempts to form strong relationships wherever we might work – as therapist or researcher.

BACKGROUND

Before trying to define 'relationship' specifically for our professional purposes (the consulting room or for research contexts maybe), it is important that we think about what we already know about relationships, and to do this counselling psychologists draw on a wealth of experience and information. This includes reflection on personal experiences (counselling psychologists are, after all, as embedded in relationships as clients are and we engage in our own personal therapy); scholarly work in the various sub-disciplines of psychology (developmental, social, evolutionary psychology, group psychologies, and neuropsychology, etc.); and related disciplines such as philosophy, sociology and politics. I would suggest that it is also fruitful to draw on information from other, often overlooked, sources, such as zoology, comparative psychology, literature, drama and economics – anything, in fact, that can help us understand the range of relationships in which we engage.

SO WHAT DO WE KNOW?

Human history shows that at our core we are a social species and seldom thrive in isolation (Diamond, 2005; Pimm et al., 1988). From our species beginnings, humans have gathered together for safety and security, fun and obligation, feeding, socialising and reproduction. Economics, sociology, anthropology and archaeology all confirm this and neuroscientists and psychologists offer insights into the ways in which we have evolved to strengthen this capacity. It seems that our brain developed to facilitate this (Diamond, 1991), the development of language thrust our social abilities forward enormously (Dunbar, 2010), and our cultural and technological talents fast-track this even further (Diamond, 1998; Dunbar, 2010). At an ontological level, our hard-wired abilities to attach, to empathise and to care facilitates this, so we are frequently engaged in this without even knowing it. We are, as the philosophers brought into focus, 'Being-in-the-world' (Heidegger, 2010). We cannot *not* be in relationship.

For the purposes of this chapter, primacy is given to human–human relationships and what they can tell us about therapeutic relationships. However, readers should not think that this is the only form of relationship that is important to our psychological well-being. While this may be our culture's current preoccupation, these same bodies of knowledge also attest to the fact that our natural affinity for relationship is *not* just to other people; we are affected by the relationship we have with our wider planetary environment (Jordan, 2014), to the place we call home and to other, non-human animals (Hicks, 2008; Louv, 2006; Steyn, 2008). This is elaborated later in Chapter 23.

THE REALITY OF RELATIONSHIPS

Unfortunately there is a trend, culturally and in some therapeutic circles, to romanticise 'relationships', and we therefore tend to limit our thinking to such positively constructed experiences as respect, love, care and concern. These are desired for themselves, but also as a way to deal with some more difficult experiences, such as sadness, anxiety and distress. We also see a privileging of such themes in our culture and therapeutic profession, for example 'love can conquer all', or that a 'therapeutic relationship' can work wonders. Our theoretical, cultural and personal systems prioritise these too. We see that one of the first statements of the Health and Care Professions Council (HCPC) is that practitioner psychologists 'understand the need to respect, and so far as possible uphold, the rights, dignity, values and autonomy of every service user, including their role in the diagnostic and therapeutic process and in maintaining health and wellbeing' (Health and Care Professions Council, 2012: 6), and one of the first things that the British Psychological Society's *Generic Professional Practice Guidelines* (2008: ii) notes is that 'the professional practice of applied psychologists is underpinned by four key ethical values – Respect, Competence, Responsibility and Integrity'. Of course, we would not want to argue with this as most of us value the respect we receive from others; any of us who have been in love know that to look into your lover's eyes can be a powerful and transformative experience, and as clients and therapists will attest, the unburdening of our long-held anxieties to a person we trust can be both cathartic and also an empowering experience. So, if this is such a well-known experience, why did I start this section with the word 'unfortunately'?

The 'unfortunate' aspect is that this perspective is only partial, and too ready an acceptance of the positive overshadows the reality of relationships. There is the fact that positive feelings are not always straightforward and can present dangers – we see over-identification or over-involvement at the root of such problems as inappropriate sexual encounters with clients and trainees (Pope and Vasquez, 2011; Russell, 1993). And of course, like virtually any other relationship, therapeutic ones are vital, multi-dimensional and nuanced. The over-focus on the positive means that there is often a misconception that therapeutic relationships are 'nice' relationships; always valuable and important, exclusively characterised by respect and warmth. On the contrary, therapeutic relationships can also include, or even be dominated by, other feelings too – boredom, resentment, disgust, rage, disappointment, hate, and the like. Of course these are *not* aspects we would deliberately invoke, but they are ones that may need attention as they may be a core part of the client's experience and they may be part of the difficulties that bring clients to therapy. In that case, they may *need* to be experienced, or at least heard, witnessed and engaged with in the therapeutic relationship. If therapists cannot engage with these, what hope is there that clients can come to understand and manage them through therapy?

A vignette may be helpful in illustrating just one example of this.

In sessions, little six-year-old Charlotte[1] is not hesitant in verbally abusing her psychologist. The therapist has been called a bitch and a c*nt on several occasions. While trying to remain calm and professional, the psychologist has recognised that she herself feels angry and some choice phrases come to her mind too.

Interactions such as this, and the associated feelings, can be trying in the best of relationships. In other types of relationship people might retaliate or they might remove themselves. However, for the therapist, it is not so straightforward. Rather than walk away, counselling psychologists need to notice, reflect upon and consider these interactions.

---

1 'Charlotte' is a disguised and anonymised client example.

A therapeutic relationship requires, whether positive or negative feelings abound, that we engage with all aspects of the client as possible. That may mean receiving the client's joy and exhilaration, their sadness and tears. It may mean bearing witness to anxiety. It may also mean, and this can feel more difficult, that we have to be present and help them recognise, feel and come to understand their rage, their disgust and their aggressive impulses. This is hard to do as it may mean that we can become targets of such feelings, and we are no more immune to the impact of such feelings than anyone else.

We will return to this later, but now to consider the concepts and practices that counselling psychologists have available to them when trying to develop effective therapeutic relationships.

HOW DO WE OPTIMISE RELATIONSHIPS?

Basic human skills

Some of what creates good relationships are our core, human, social skills. People often simply have a sense of 'knowing' what to do – it feels intuitive and 'natural'. A range of disciplines highlight that our species has a talent for relating: evolutionary theory reminds us that this is a use of hard-wired social talents that has evolved over aeons for survival (Dunbar, 2010; Gillies, 2010); a review of the comparative psychology literature shows that this is a talent that we share with other mammals (Ulfstrand, 2002) and this is also a reason why animal-assisted therapy is also a useful relational possibility (Favali and Milton, 2010); and existential philosophers shed light on our relational essence and that while inauthentic relationships are unavoidable, we benefit from our efforts to create authentic relationships (van Deurzen, 2008).

Core basic counselling skills, such as verbally paraphrasing and reflecting on words and process, and mirrored body language, also help counselling psychologists attune to, and engage with, clients and can be very important. Through these interpersonal skills, people tend to feel better and even function better as they feel liked and sense that others are interested in them. This applies to friendships, romantic relationships and therapeutic relationships too. So when we are able to listen closely, to communicate our interest in getting to know the client and are able to slow down any need to instruct or direct a client, we are opening up a possibility of finding strong relational ground.

Listen, listen and listen some more

One way of consciously and deliberately building on our innate relational abilities is to recognise that relationships are enhanced by a sense of closeness – in essence, this is through the attempt to move from what Buber termed an 'I–It' relationship to an 'I–Thou' relationship (Buber, 2004 [1937]). To do this the counselling psychologist tries to get an attuned sense of the person they are with. This is not always as easy as it sounds as people are so embedded in assumptions – both cultural and clinical – that a second or third hearing is required before we can begin to grasp the more apt understandings of a communication. Of course, one can ask for clarification and paraphrase in order to get a sense of what has been grasped and what hasn't. However, a counselling psychologist would not *instruct* a client to tell the story over and over again as this would, firstly, run the very real risk of avoiding what was experienced in the moment for the sake of a story about another point in time and, secondly, it is unnecessary – important stories tend to get told several times over a number of sessions.

More than just words – our Being speaks volumes

It would be wrong to assume that the previous section equated 'listening' with just 'hearing' or 'words' – *meaning* is a much richer, more complex communication than simply words (as any user of email or social media sites will probably confirm). Of course, the counselling psychologist will be listening closely to the content of what the client talks about, but more than that, they will be listening to the style and tone of the communication, to the 'feel' of it and to the emotions being expressed by the client and by their own subjective experience. They will be seeing how the body confirms or disconfirms the verbal content and the ways in which metaphors offer multiple ways to understand the client and what it is they are communicating. The issue of 'words' is worth elaborating a little further.

No matter whether we have had a wonderful weekend or a rotten one, many of us still answer the familiar Monday morning question 'How was your weekend?' with the same speedy 'Fine thanks' and usually finish off our part of that interaction with 'And yours?' In doing so we engage in a social process that the novelist Alexander McCall Smith's character Mma Precious Ramotswe sums up well. She muses that these are:

> the polite enquiries that form dictated were made – *You are keeping well, Rra? Yes, and you, Mma?* There were no surprises in the answers such questions elicited – there never were – but these conversations still had to take place: It was not what was said that counted, but the fact that it was said. (McCall Smith, 2014, Kindle edition, 38%)

The function of the question about our weekend is, firstly, a recognition of presence and, secondly, a confirmation that one is ready to work (an I–It relationship), and this may well be fine – whether the statement is 'true' in any absolute sense is almost irrelevant.

However, should you have had a rotten weekend and be asked that same question by someone who knows you more intimately or cares for you more deeply, you face a dilemma – to offer the same speedy and automatic response is likely to be unconvincing or to actually *trigger* their concern. They will 'know' it doesn't feel or look right. They know you are less forthcoming, less present than normal. It may not be possible to state categorically why this is known, but it carries a great sense of certainty and you are likely to face further questioning – 'Are you sure?' or 'Is everything OK?'

This everyday illustration has a parallel in therapy, as client and therapist alike, are tuning in to words, to posture, gesture and tone all the time and it is the gestalt of this that carries enormous meaning and thus warrants curiosity and consideration. Counselling psychologists will have studied the literatures on the role of non-verbal communication. For example, some research has shown that 45 per cent of communication is affected by tone, inflexion and other voice elements, 50 per cent by body language (e.g. movements, eye contact) and only 5 per cent by the actual words (Knapp et al., 2014).

Blending our thinking and talking ... multi-tasking

Contrary to the gendered stereotypes about 'multi-tasking', the comments above highlight that relating is never a single action or single task process. We are always listening, watching and sensing. We are trying to react and we are trying to monitor the other and much of this occurs outside our reflective awareness (van Deurzen, 2008).

Counselling psychologists, however, learn to complement any natural ability in this domain with conscious and deliberate attention to the full communicative milieu. To do this counselling psychologists try to balance both spontaneous being-in-the-moment and post-hoc reflection. During the interaction (and after) it is helpful to think about what is being said by the client about the topic itself and separately from that, what it means about the client, and what it might mean about the client–therapist interaction (maybe even in coded form).

This curiosity about meaning extends beyond the narrow constraints of the consulting room. We are cultural beings in relationship with place and context. Because of this, the counselling psychologist also considers what is being communicated at a more cultural/discursive level (see Langdridge, 2014; Strawbridge, 1999). Do the genders of the therapeutic relationship make some things easier or more difficult to be direct about? How do class, wealth, status, education level, or physical abilities affect the ways in which things can be communicated? What about first- or second-language issues? What was the response to disclosure of this type of material in earlier attempts and is that affecting how the client discusses these issues now? These are important issues to be considering while at the same time engaging with the client in the moment. Meaning straddles class, gender, identity, culture and time.

As well as these broader ways of enhancing the relationship with clients, counselling psychologists draw on their humanistic values and, associated with that, the phenomenological method to enrich their relationships with clients. It is to this that we now turn.

OUR UNDERPINNING PHENOMENOLOGICAL PERSPECTIVE

While counselling psychology, as a profession, has a pluralistic engagement with a range of theories (see Draghi-Lorenz, 2010; Milton, 2010) and the meanings they have for our work, our fundamental humanistic values mean that the phenomenological stance is at the basis of our practice – whether one might later come to identify as primarily working from an existential, psychodynamic, systemic or other model.

Phenomenological method as a way of getting to know the client

Phenomenology helps us understand phenomena in deep and rich ways. In our therapeutic endeavour, the 'phenomenon of choice' is often the personhood of the client and their relationship to their difficulties, their world and, in therapy, to their therapist.

As Spinelli (1989: 17) notes, 'whatever its primary goal, … the phenomenological method is carried out in much the same way. It is composed of three distinguishable, though interrelated, steps'. Spinelli (1989) describes these as the rule of epoche, the rule of description and the rule of horizontalisation. This method helps us, firstly, to bracket as many of the pre-existing, personal, contextual and cultural assumptions as possible, freeing us up somewhat to experience the other as they disclose themselves; secondly, to prioritise the description of the client and their experience rather than explanations of who or what they are; and thirdly, not to assume that any single piece of information is more or less important than anything else. In essence, our therapeutic effort is to continually be curious about and ponder with the client – who are you right now, and what has the experience been for you to come to be this way? What possibilities are there and how might you enter into those so that you live the best life you are able to?

This sensitive, modest, yet curious stance is often facilitated by a focused curiosity on the part of the therapist about the client. Core relational skills, such as those outlined above (the use of paraphrasing, reflections and clarifications), are often evident. Such an approach has a strong resonance with client-centred therapy, and Rogers himself noted that 'this theory is basically phenomenological in character' (Rogers, 1951: 532).

The place of words in a relationship

A focus on paraphrasing, reflections and clarifications can sometimes lead people to think that the relationship is formed by a close reading and comment on the *words* of the client. That our intent is to capture what is spoken as closely as we can. While there is much to be gained with a clear and accurate grasp of what someone utters, the phenomenological stance itself and the core relational skills go well beyond words. Relationships are enhanced when we can reflect and paraphrase what is felt but not yet been pulled together, what is present but may not have been spoken but what is being communicated in other ways; sometimes clarification is made by an attuned and empathic response, such as an appropriate smile, a well-timed nod of the head or a simple 'I can see that'.

In order to free oneself up and go beyond a slavish following of words, and to avoid becoming an annoying caricature of the parroting therapist, the counselling psychologist aims to have a particular type of openness to the client – one characterised by interest and un-knowing (Spinelli, 2007). Such a stance can be helpful in facilitating intellectual attention as well as an openness to one's own process, what thoughts, feelings, day-dreams and physical sensations inhabit the experience of being with this client at this point in time in this place.

While there may be some tensions between schools in how this is understood, it seems many approaches recognise this important relational quality. Psychoanalytic theory offers us the idea of 'free floating attention' (Smith, 1999) and at the other end of the historical continuum, mindfulness practitioners also suggest such an orientation (Nanda, 2005). Of course different approaches offer different understandings and glean different insights from these encounters, but the recognition of such an open and receptive stance to the full experience of the encounter is very common.

The centrality of meaning

The phenomenological stance upon which counselling psychology is based notes that it is *meaning* that is central to our relational lives – whether that's the relationship with ourselves, with others or with the wider world (Spineli, 2007). So another concept that is important to consider, and relates to the points made above, is the importance of elaboration or amplification. As we speak with another, as we relate to another, we are not simply following each word but looking for what it means and how it enhances or shifts our grasp of their *overall* Being. It is this aspect that means 'I'm fine' can mean 'I am content and well' on some occasions, but the same words might *mean* 'I am distressed and don't trust myself to feel the distress, or share it with you' on another occasion. Despite the words being spoken, tone, pace, physiology and other cues will inevitably amplify our state of being so the other has a sense of what it means.

We often amplify consciously questioning the different meanings that specific words have, why specific words might be used and the personal and cultural implications that those words have. Gendered language, for instance, often gives clues as to wider meanings, which may be less than conscious for us as we speak. Catching a glimpse of the value applied to assumed 'male' characteristics and less to assumed 'female' qualities might offer us insight into the meaning that a client sees in themselves, their relationships and the social and other opportunities available or denied them (Langdridge, 2014). While a question about such language can sometimes lead to nothing, equally, it is often questions like this that clarify and amplify meanings which stops us in our tracks. We can feel surprised, excited and uncomfortable, and realise that there are more profound meanings than we had known.

The notions of 'truth' and interpretation

Counselling psychology has evolved with a postmodern sensibility, where claims to absolute truth are questioned. Our phenomenological roots are helpful as they assist in our ability to enter into a range of encounters and sustain both interest and our ability to listen to the obvi-ous, but also to be open to other possibilities. One way we do this is by a natural but also considered linking between different aspects and experiences of the encounter. Tone and pace might enhance or contradict the obvious meaning, and preoccupation with different topics alongside throw-away lines might help us understand previously unseen meanings, etc. The linking and the voicing of what is evident can be part of what enhances a relationship as it not only captures intellectual fact, but carries an emotional impact of being seen and being under-stood – at least to some degree. And the isolation involved in our suffering is sometimes part of what exacerbates it and makes it even worse.

In eschewing radical positivism, counselling psychology has aligned itself to perspectives that recognise that meanings vary from context to context and person to person. In light of this, interpretation is an important aspect of all relationships. Of course, in the psychological literature the term 'interpretation' can mean many things, including, within psychoanalysis, a specific 'technique'. I am using the term here deliberately to bring home the fact that coun-selling psychologists recognise that we can never completely grasp the subjective experience of another, or, as Sartre (1956) noted, the complete knowing of the other is 'unrealisable'. This is because, as Hyslop (2014) notes:

> there are (at least two) problems of other minds. There is the epistemological problem, con-cerned with how our beliefs about mental states other than our own might be justified. There is also the conceptual problem: how is it possible for us to form a concept of mental states other than our own.

Therefore, the closest we can get to fully knowing another is an attuned interpretation of their being. But this is not to be underestimated – a parent interprets their child's needs, lovers interpret their partners' desires and counselling psychologists recognise that we are always interpreting the meanings that are trying to be expressed in our work with clients. So relation-ships are always vehicles for interpretation.

The recognition of these aspects of 'interpretation' allows us to consider the role of 'direc-tiveness' in therapy. To be too non-directive (i.e. to be experienced at refusing to offer our understanding of the unclear and confusing process) can be as problematic as offering too concrete (or directive) a view. There has long been debate in the broader psychological and psychotherapeutic literature about directive and non-directive therapies and the rationale for each. Whether or not therapists recognise it, our 'reflections' can be as much of an interpreta-tion as a formally structured analytic interpretation of a dream. While counselling psychologists may consider the issues involved and make different decisions depending on the client and the context, at the core of a strong relationship is a recognition that being directive has its limits. Therapeutic gain is often experienced more positively when a client feels their role in the change, they have a sense of agency and understand the possibilities and limitations in which they live. Van Deurzen and Adams (2011) have suggested that the 'directive–non-directive' debate is limited and unhelpful (it is another example of our split, dichotomous thinking, after all). Their suggestion is that we recognise the fact that therapy should be 'directional' (van Deurzen and Adams, 2011) but that this comes out of a phenomenological engagement.

The fluid self

Unlike some strands of psychology, medicine and science (and some of our own research questions) that offer overarching trends in population characteristics, when in the consulting room, the counselling psychologist is more usually trying to understand a specific, subjectively unique person. They may be understood as a member of a certain gender or cultural group, but the issues they faced tend to be more at the level of their own, ontic and subjective dilemmas. A phenomenological approach helps counselling psychologists recognise the fact that our way of being can – and does – vary enormously. We are never static; we are not just one 'thing'. When we act as though we are, we fall into 'bad faith' (Sartre, 1956). Bad faith is Sartre's term that 'describes a condition whereby we live in denial of our "true nature" and our essential freedom' (Pearce, 2014: 95). While these are inevitable states, simply a part of one's experience, they can be seen to allow some experiences that can be considered positive. But we must not overlook that in our Being and in our relationships we wax and wane, flow, and change on a minute-to-minute, context-to-context basis. The same way that we try to facilitate children learning how to balance love and hate in their relationship to their parents, and lovers enjoy the pleasure that aggression and care, force and gentleness, can bring to a relationship, we have to think of such flow in the development of therapeutic relationships.

As well as working to understand the clients' movements and associated dilemmas, counselling psychologists engage with their own need and ability to master the tension between being active and passive, conversational and quiet, and at times liking and disliking their client. The relationship with a client is not 'therapeutic' simply because one has a licence to practise. It is therapeutic to the degree that one can enter into the world and engage with the needs of the client, and where abuse, shame, distrust, violence, oppression and other difficult experiences have been endured, the relationship must be open to the possibility of some of that being brought to therapy in a live fashion.

So far, I have outlined basic fundamental human ways of relating and some concepts and styles of encounter that are born out of our phenomenological allegiance. Once we have established the beginnings of a therapeutic relationship, or once therapy has been established, this leads to such questions as: How *do* we assess the way the therapeutic relationship is developing and whether it makes sense? How *do* we decide whether the difficult relationship is a problem and that the client and therapist are not well matched and a reallocation should be made? Or how *do* we decide that these difficulties are manifestations of the core relational, psychological and existential difficulties the client has and, as such, their presence in therapy is actually a *useful* thing, indicative that actual relational issues are being confronted?

At this point I want to consider the ways in which we translate our own personal understandings into something more professional in nature. This is central to counselling psychology practice and is shared with both the client and referrers, and that is psychological formulation. In the next section I reflect on the advantages and effects of formulation on our practice from a somewhat different perspective from that in Chapter 10.

MAKING SENSE OF RELATIONSHIP DYNAMICS: EVOLVING FORMULATIONS

When engaged in the complex relationships outlined above, counselling psychologists do more than simply proceed on a course of doggedly using the core 'skills' outlined above, as this can lead to a pressure for everyone to conform to a benevolent (yet sometimes tyrannical) norm. Whether or not these practices – or this therapeutic relationship – are useful should be assessed by thinking about the formulation that has been developed. When things feel that they are going well, it may feel less urgent or less gruelling, but when a client brings aggression or mistrust, or we feel bored in their presence, we may struggle. Once we understand that the process is related to something, whether that be experiences of abuse, betrayal or other relational trauma, we can start to make sense of what was previously confusing and we are able to bear the onslaught that little bit better. After all, why would we expect a client with those difficult interpersonal experiences to be able to, or even think it possible to, like and trust us immediately?

So let us revisit 'little Charlotte', who we met briefly earlier and who verbally abused her therapist.

The scenario

In sessions, little Charlotte is not hesitant in verbally abusing her psychologist. The therapist has been called a bitch and a c*nt on several occasions. While trying to remain calm and professional, the psychologist has recognised that she herself feels angry and some choice phrases come to her mind too.

Reflections on the relationship

Rather than simply trying to repress her reaction, the psychologist recognises that she doesn't understand the outbursts, and she also realises that she is not happy with her own feelings when she is called these names. She finds herself wondering 'what have I ever done to deserve this?'

In supervision, the psychologist voices her concern and her feelings of being exasperated, confused and sometimes angry. She is encouraged to relax a bit and to take her time. The psychologist explains to her supervisor that 'little Charlotte' was referred to her in her role as the school psychologist and that the identified problems were that Charlotte is often aggressive and violent (to children and to her teacher) and her mother feels she is at her wits' end. The psychologist notes that she, too, is quickly feeling adrift and unsure of how to assist. At this point she starts to notice some relational parallels.

The psychologist reflects on the information offered in the referral letter, which is that Charlotte's parents have recently experienced an acrimonious divorce and Charlotte was witness to physical violence from both parents. Like the parents and the teacher, the psychologist is concerned that the other six-year-old children are starting to avoid her and that she has recently hit her teacher. The psychologist remembers feeling very pleased when informed that Charlotte wants to come to sessions (she told the teacher that the psychologist is the 'nice lady'), and she wonders whether this has led her to 'expect' a warmer, friendlier child. Her experience with Charlotte has confused her, as Charlotte clearly isn't always 'nice'; nor does she use 'childlike' language all of the time. The psychologist comes to realise that it is not the insult that offends her so much as the shock that such a 'pretty little blonde girl', as 'cute as a button', can talk like that!

As she outlines the issues, the psychologist and supervisor together start to consider what is known, and they come to realise that while unpleasant, this isn't just some arbitrary outburst. Together, the psychologist and the supervisor realise that the escalation in violent behaviour may actually be meaningful, offering insight to both her recent experience but also as to what it is that she needs. While the world seems to be intent on infantalising her (calling her 'Little Charlotte', expecting her to be some pretty little 'princess', all 'sweet and nice'), Charlotte's recent experience has actually been one of huge uncertainty about her place in the world. The two people closest to her have problems, and this takes attention away from her needs and her sense of being understood and cared for. Once the psychologist and the supervisor start to consider this and what that might indicate about Charlotte's relational needs, the psychologist recognises that as well as being angry, Charlotte could well be terribly scared. The exacerbation of distress may be a sign of just how much containment is needed. As well as that, the outbursts highlight the dilemma Charlotte may be facing. If she really allows herself to feel close to someone, however 'nice', she may also feel the fear that they may be violent or abandoning.

The psychologist begins to recognise how her own assumptions had affected the relationship. Rather than an openness to the client in her entirety (i.e. sweet but scared, wanting to be liked yet also fearful of that, powerless but also powerful), the psychologist recognises that she had been seduced by a gendered stereotype of a sweet little blonde girl, who was more likely to be passive and fearful than angry and forceful. Because of this, the nature of the outbursts had taken her by surprise and she caught herself thinking: 'It's normally teenage boys that talk like that'. Her assumption that Charlotte would be a certain way may have created an obstacle to fully knowing Charlotte as she is and as she needs to be understood. The psychologist starts to perceive Charlotte as both scared and angry, as both powerless but also experiencing a desperate urgency to find some power.

Once the supervisor and psychologist were able to piece together the basics of an understanding, the psychologist reported that she not only felt closer to Charlotte, but she felt more able to think about being with her in a more fruitful and therapeutic manner. She realises that she did not feel at any physical risk in Charlotte's presence – the risk had been a sense of not finding a way to 'get' Charlotte. Now she had recognised her own biases and obstacles, she felt more able to engage with the 'sweet' persona and the other angry (and potentially quite powerful and robust) capacities. By being open to the meaning of the difficult aspects of the relationship, the psychologist felt much more able to engage and work therapeutically.

CONCLUSION

This chapter has offered some insights into a variety of theoretical and philosophical per-spectives, and associated relational practices, that the counselling psychologist can avail themselves of in an effort to enhance what they can offer each client. However, it is clear that there are limitations on what can be achieved. One cannot hope, in one chapter, to offer complete or conclusive insight of the full range of styles of relating that people are able to have. My hope is that, by being explicit about this, readers will use this chapter as a trigger to their thinking and learning, and go on to become even more curious about the relational aspects of their work. My hope is that rather than shy away from the confusing and difficult aspects of relationships, readers will feel able to engage imaginatively with these aspects of the client–therapist relationship, both in their reading and learning and also explicitly with their clients in the therapeutic process.

 Visit the companion website to watch Forming a Relationship.

REFERENCES

British Psychological Society (2008) *Generic Professional Practice Guidelines*. Leicester: BPS.

Buber, M. (2004) *I and Thou*. Trans. R. Gregor-Smith. London: Routledge. (First published in 1937.)

Diamond, J. (1991) *The Rise and Fall of the Third Chimpanzee: How Our Animal Heritage Affects the Way We Live*. London: Vintage.

Diamond, J. (1998) *Guns, Germs and Steel: A Short History of Everybody for the Last 13,000 Years*. New York: Viking.

Diamond, J. (2005) *Collapse: How Societies Choose to Fail or Succeed*. New York: Viking.

Draghi-Lorenz, R. (2010) Different theoretical differences and contextual influences. In M. Milton (ed.), *Therapy and Beyond: Counselling Psychology Contributions to Therapeutic and Social Issues*. Chichester: Wiley-Blackwell. pp. 105–122.

Dunbar, R. (2010) *The Human Story: A New History of Mankind's Evolution*. London: Faber and Faber.

Favali, V. and Milton, M. (2010) Disabled horse-rider's experience of horse-riding. *Existential Analysis: Journal of the Society for Existential Analysis*, 21(2): 251–262.

Gelso, C.J. and Carter, J.A. (1995) Components of the psychotherapy relationship: Their interaction and unfolding during treatment. *Journal of Counseling Psychology*, 41(3): 296–306.

Gillies, F. (2010) Being with humans: An evolutionary framework for the therapeutic relation-ship. In M. Milton (ed.), *Therapy and Beyond: Counselling Psychology Contributions to Therapeutic and Social Issues*. Chichester: Wiley-Blackwell. pp. 73–88.

Health and Care Professions Council (HCPC) (2012) *Standards of Proficiency: Practitioner Psychologists*. London: HCPC.

Heidegger, M. (2010) *Being and Time*. Trans. J. Stanbaugh. Albany, NY: State University of New York Press.

Hicks, C. (2008) Interview: Dr Colin Hicks. *Counselling Psychology Review*, 23(2): 7–8.

Hyslop, A. (2014) Other Minds. *Stanford Encyclopedia of Philosophy*, http://stanford.library.usyd.edu.au/entries/other-minds/ (accessed 29 October 2014).

Jordan, M. (2014) *Nature and Therapy: Understanding Counselling and Psychotherapy in Outdoor Spaces*. Hove: Routledge.

Knapp, M., Hall, J. and Hogan, T. (eds) (2014) *Non-verbal Communication in Human Interaction* (8th edition). Boston, MA: Wadsworth.

Langdridge, D. (2014) Gay affirmative therapy: The power of the social world. In M. Milton (ed.), *Sexuality: Existential Perspectives*. Ross-on-Wye: PCCS Books. pp. 160–173.

Louv, R. (2006) *Last Child in the Woods: Saving Our Children from Nature-Deficit Disorder*. Chapel Hill, NC: Algonquin Books.

McCall Smith, A. (2014) *The Handsome Man's De Luxe Café*. London: Little Brown.

Milton, M. (ed.) (2010) *Therapy and Beyond: Counselling Psychology Contributions to Therapeutic and Social Issues*. Chichester: Wiley-Blackwell.

Nanda, J. (2005) A phenomenological enquiry into the effect of meditation on therapeutic practice. *Counselling Psychology Review*, 20(1): 17–26.

Pearce, R. (2014) Sexual expression, bad faith and authenticity. In M. Milton (ed.), *Sexuality: Existential Perspectives*. Ross-on-Wye: PCCS Books. pp. 92–118.

Pimm, S., Jones, H.L. and Diamond, J. (1988) On the risk of extinction. *The American Naturalist*, 132(6): 757–785.

Pope, K. and Vasquez, M. (2011) *Ethics in Psychotherapy and Counselling: A Practical Guide*. Hoboken, NJ: John Wiley & Sons.

Rogers, C.R. (1951) *Client-Centered Therapy*. Boston, MA: Houghton-Mifflin.

Russell, J. (1993) *Out of Bounds: Sexual Exploitation in Counselling and Therapy*. London: Sage.

Sartre, J.-P. (1956) *Being and Nothingness: An Essay on Phenomenological Ontology*. New York: Philosophy Library. (First published 1943.)

Smith, D.L. (1999) *Approaching Psychoanalysis: An Introductory Course*. London: Karnac Books.

Spinelli, E. (1989) *The Interpreted World: An Introduction to Phenomenological Psychology*. London: Sage.

Spinelli, E. (2007) *Practising Existential Psychotherapy: The Relational World*. London: Sage.

Steyn, V. (2008) Interview: Villiers Steyn. *Counselling Psychology Review*, 23(2): 60–61.

Strawbridge, S. (1999) Counselling and psychotherapy as enabling and empowering. In C. Feltham (ed.), *Controversies in Psychotherapy and Counselling*. London: Sage. pp. 294–303.

Ulfstrand, S. (2002) *Savannah Lives: Animal Life and Human Evolution in Africa*. Oxford: Oxford University Press.

van Deurzen, E. (2008) *Psychotherapy and the Quest for Happiness*. London: Sage.

van Deurzen, E. and Adams, M. (2011) *Skills in Existential Counselling and Psychotherapy*. London: Sage.

12
WORKING WITH DIFFERENCE AND DIVERSITY
SIMON PARRITT

INTRODUCTION

The terms 'diversity' and 'difference' should not necessarily be viewed as problematic or the cause of conflict and difficulty, but be seen as positive and enriching. However, at an organisational and socio-political level, promoting diversity has become concerned with issues and policies addressing the experience of marginalised, disadvantaged and oppressed people and groups who face discrimination at a structural and personal level. These policies aim to redress the power imbalance and bring minorities within the core of an organisation as citizens, employees, consumers and users. However, the emphasis in this chapter will be on how we, as counselling psychologists, can actively address the individual's experience of being different or from a diverse group within our work and individual practice, and acknowledging that the therapeutic relationship does not take place within a cultural or political vacuum. This is especially relevant in today's world where '[h]uman migration and immigration connected to political oppression, economics, poverty, and the need for employment bring challenges for everyone involved' (Gerstein et al., 2011).

The aim of this chapter will be to bring together some aspects and issues of difference and diversity and highlight that although oppressed and minority groups are, by their very nature, distinct and uniquely different, they share much in relation to their experience of the dominant culture and ideology and the underlying issues that confront them. Further, the chapter will explore how counselling psychology may be uniquely placed to meet this challenge because of its philosophical underpinning and how this can facilitate working effectively to empower those who are often silent, quiet, ignored or 'voiceless', not just at a socio-cultural level but also in relation to therapy itself, as they are often 'positioned outside the masculine cultural metaphors and conventional theoretical epistemologies of counselling, psychology and psychotherapy' (Moodley, 2009: 299). Moodley (2009) suggests that the history of psychotherapy sits within a Eurocentric, ethnocentric, individualistic and masculine cultural discourse, which places minority groups in an invidious position where they can only articulate their experience with a narrative embedded in a kind of cultural hegemony. The aim here, then, is examine how to build upon counselling psychology practice in order to address some of these barriers.

Diversity and difference exist within a complex matrix that involves various levels and overlapping concepts. The feminist stance that 'the personal is political' has significance for all oppressed and minority groups and any action addressing oppression and liberation requires attention at many levels, the personal/individual, the socio-cultural and the wider political and ideological. Increasingly, attention and research has looked at the links and 'socio-political synergies' (Moane, 2010) between diverse oppressed groups and, while an in-depth discussion of the political is outside the scope of this chapter, working as a counselling psychologist involves reference to, and reflection upon, these aspects and facets of both clients' and our own lives and relationships. How we experience and work with difference when we encounter the 'other' is fundamental to working in a modern, pluralistic and culturally diverse society. Much can be gained from reflecting upon the pluralist viewpoint, as Cooper and McLeod (2011: 7) state, 'a pluralist holds that there can be many "right" answers to scientific, moral or psychological questions which are not reducible down to any one, single truth'.

The interpersonal and relational are central to counselling psychology, whatever technique or model is employed. The interaction between a dominant majority and a marginalised minority is played out and reflected in the therapeutic relationship itself and as such 'it is not just therapists who should decide on the focus and course of therapy – rather, therapists should work closely with their clients to decide on how the work should proceed' (Cooper and McLeod, 2011: 7). While applicable to all client/therapist therapeutic relationships, this is particularly pertinent when working with marginalised and oppressed groups, such as black and minority ethnic (BME), gender, sexuality and disability. This approach is not without its challenges, as counselling psychologists work within, and often belong to, the dominant cultural and ideological group and, as will be addressed later, the work environment and context can become problematic for counselling psychologists who may also feel marginalised and isolated within their workplace.

DIFFERENCE AND THE DOMINANT CULTURE

Therapy is a special kind of intense contact and a client who identifies as lesbian, gay, bisexual and transgender (LGBT), BME or disabled, lives, works and will have daily contact with those from the dominant culture in which traditional psychology and psychotherapy have their roots. As far back as the 1950s, Allport (1954), in looking at the nature of prejudice between groups, proposed a 'contact hypothesis' in which, given optimal conditions, intergroup contact can have a beneficial effect. However, the effect is limited, especially in changing attitudes and beliefs of those from, or within, the dominant power group, who usually have little or no access to the lived experience of the 'other'. It appears the majority find it hard to conceptualise how those from the oppressed and marginalised groups actually feel, think or view the world. This may explain why even though in 'non-optimal conditions' contact can improve intergroup relations (Pettigrew and Tropp, 2006), there is evidence that 'quality of contact is especially relevant for the majority group' (Vezzali et al., 2010). This suggests it is the majority who must learn from the 'other' and this is about developing real understanding and empathy. Yet even within the profession, a minority group such as disabled psychologists 'may challenge the underlying perceptions of clinical and health psychologists and members of other health professions. The professional role of a disabled colleague clashes with stereotypes of disability which are firmly linked to patients' (Levinson and Parritt, 2005: 180).

For this reason, counselling psychologists need to pay attention to, and acquaint themselves with, the world in which their client lives and breathes, adopting a proactive stance and informing themselves, at all levels. There is considerable merit in the British Psychological Society (BPS) guidelines for working with sexual and gender minority groups: 'Psychologists are encouraged to be knowledgeable of the diversity of sexual and gender minority identities and practices' (British Psychological Society, 2012: 7). It is worth noting that the implied 'proactive' nature of 'knowledgeable' is used here and not the more passive implications of 'awareness'.

Taking the above into consideration, given the particular constraints of workplace settings, session and time limitations, exploration of difference can be challenging but all the more effective and meaningful within the safety of the relational space of therapy. The idea that it is the quality of the 'therapeutic relationship' that is central in the outcome and progress of therapy, irrespective of other variables, has gained increasing acceptance (Asay and Lambert, 1999; Cooper, 2005; Lambert and Barley, 2001). Empathy, genuineness and acceptance are three of the core conditions (Rogers, 1957) that form the basis of an effective therapeutic alliance. Empathy developed out of the German '*Einfuhling*', meaning 'feeling into', which has an implied sense of active moving, rather than a passive state of being. Its role cannot be overstated as it offers the foundations of an alternative to the traditional positivism of the relationship between science and psychology. It suggests, along with the aforementioned pluralist approach, 'a practice led model based on: co-operative inquiry; the valuing of feelings; a respect for the reality of differing universes of experience and meaning; and, the preserving, fostering and releasing of potential' (Strawbridge, 1994: 5–12).

Working in this way with oppressed and minority groups can be uncomfortable as well as rewarding, as barriers and resistances arise, not only from within the client and the counselling psychologist's own different personal histories and identities, but from the surrounding working, socio-economic, cultural and political environment. For these reasons alone it is almost inevitable that the client and the psychologist come together with different values and experiences. As Aung San Suu Kyi is quoted as saying: 'The value systems of those with access to power and of those far removed from such access cannot be the same. The viewpoint of the privileged is unlike that of the underprivileged.'

COUNSELLING PSYCHOLOGY AND DIFFERENCE

In a modern, pluralistic, complex and internationally mobile society, counselling psychologists increasingly work in many types of setting and with diverse groups of people.

Therefore, reflecting upon our relationship to the place and setting is centrally important. Whether as trainees, experienced practitioners, lecturers or researchers, we need to be part of, work within and contribute to such organisational policies and practices around diversity that aim to meet these modern challenges. As applied psychologists, we practise within certain ethical and practice guidelines that assume a common philosophical and ethical framework, integral to which is a socially inclusive practice (British Psychological Society, 2008).

There is, however, always a gap between policies and guidelines and the day-to-day experience of those working with clients 'at the coalface', and this can sometimes be lonely, stark and problematic. Counselling psychologists can experience themselves in a place where they find their own identity is shaken or challenged by being 'different'. This is particularly the case when being the sole person, or one of very few, representing counselling psychology within a corporate enterprise such as the National Health Service or the increasingly larger number of private healthcare providers and agencies. We might do well to reflect upon this hidden sense of difference, what it means, how it feels, and how it influences our own relationship with colleagues and organisations. Before we work with those who struggle with their own lived experience of difference, how free do we feel to celebrate our own difference, as counselling psychologists, as unique, positive and valued professional members of a team? Many years ago in the early days of our profession a very prominent psychologist suggested that I drop the term 'Counselling' and just refer to myself as a Chartered Psychologist. Hopefully such attitudes have progressed. Nevertheless, what are the hidden assumptions about us, how we work and what we believe in? How powerful or powerless do we feel in our work context as counselling psychologists? Just like our clients, what barriers exist for us to be openly proud of what we bring and be different and equal?

Early in our professional journeys as trainee counselling psychologists, reflecting upon our thoughts and feelings around our identity can be problematic and troubling. We often work in unpaid and voluntary positions, feeling undervalued and even, at some level, exploited but powerless to challenge or effect change. This may offer a very small window into a client's sense of being valued within the relationship, of being placed alongside the trainee's feeling of being valued and seen for who they are. How far does this inform the therapeutic space? Even though this is still an unavoidable economic and political reality, it does not diminish the importance of recognising and naming this power dynamic and its impact upon and within the process. When a client is referred to a counselling psychologist in training or a trainee, how do they feel, think and experience this in terms of their status and value? When a disabled client is referred to a trainee, are both feeling 'less than' and, if so, in what ways?

This issue is no less pertinent later, as qualified and increasingly experienced counselling psychologists, whether we work alone or work where our philosophical approach, experience and beliefs could, if voiced confidently and assertively, bring us into conflict with a mental health team, social system or even family and cultural beliefs. We can feel powerless, frustrated and even angry but resigned using a quiet subordinate voice or be silent outside the therapy room, if not also inside.

LOCATING PRACTICE IN CONTEXT

Before a client enters the room, we need to ask where and how this service is located philo-sophically, socially and geographically? Why and how does it exist and what are our expectations, as well as those of our clients? In mainstream UK society and most of Western Europe it is less socially acceptable for prejudice and oppression to be as blatant and openly in evidence as it has been historically. All the same, homophobia, sexism, disablism, racism, etc. still run deep in many parts of the world, including in UK society. Underlying structural oppression and unacknowledged negative thoughts and feelings are nonetheless powerfully present in varying degrees and at many levels both personal and structural. Recognising and owning this within ourselves, at an individual and societal level, is essential.

Some clients have access to low-cost or free counselling exactly because they are categorised as belonging to a particular minority, or an at risk or vulnerable group, which is often targeted and defined by national policy as a consequence of economic and political agendas. They target issues such as addiction, sexual abuse or domestic violence, rather than the individuals per se. As a result, agencies grow to meet these specific, socially defined and funded groups. Those who fall outside such defined groups may lose out, as may many who feel unable to see themselves as defined by only one aspect of who they are. Despite this, there can be benefits, as clients are offered a setting where there is more opportunity for an informed, empathetic and experienced response. This is in contrast to a primary care setting or GP practice, where potential clients are drawn from a general local demographic and currently may be offered a single-model approach. The danger is that a 'difference', in its broader social context, is downgraded, or worse ignored, to address symptom relief and outcome measures where the focus is upon 'cost-effective treat-ment'. While effective for some, there can be a problem for minority and marginalised groups, and for disabled clients in particular, as this strengthens a medical model approach where 'depression' or 'anger' are conceptualised as having their roots in the individual's cognitive pro-cesses and of 'coming to terms' with impairment. It also avoids and fails to adequately address the social model, marginalisation and the experience of powerlessness and being a 'passive recipient' of charity or care, as well as the impact of their impairment. The focus upon treating, curing or repairing, is perhaps why there are few specialist disability counselling services, while there is more, though still little, support for those who 'care for' disabled people. Some disabled people have expressed the desire for more dedicated services (Parritt, 2005), but there is little evidence for lobbying for such a service, reflecting perhaps powerlessness, made more problem-atic due to 'internalised oppression', discussed later in the chapter.

DIFFERENCE, DISABILITY AND THE SOCIAL MODEL

In looking for an approach to working with difference and diversity in general, the primary example chosen will be disability. One reason is that disability is probably the largest, most diverse, oppressed and marginalised group of people in the world at around 15 per cent of the world's population or 1 billion people (World Health Organization, 2011). While there is a unique physical impairment dimension to disability, which will be addressed later, by taking 'the social model' stance (Finkelstein, 1980; French, 1993; Oliver, 1996), there is a shared experience with other oppressed and minority groups. Despite the increasing recognition that counselling is, in part, a power and socio-political act (Katz, 1985), counselling and psychotherapy has been slow to encompass disability within a social model in the same way that it has other groups, such as feminist, ethnic and cultural minorities. This is unfortunate, as although there are inherent and fundamental differences and problems with the early social model of disability (Shakespeare and Watson, 2001), it offers unique opportunities and challenges which highlight an often uncomfortable relationship between the reality of the physical, the psychological and the social world. The social model goes back nearly 40 years and attempted to differentiate between the two concepts: disability and impairment. It emerged from the ideas of the Union of Physically Impaired Against Segregation (UPIAS), and it is still worth noting the original distinction:

Impairment: lacking part of or all of a limb, or having a defective limb, organ or mechanism of the body; and

Disability: the disadvantage or restriction of activity caused by a contemporary social organisation which takes no or little account of people who have physical impairments and thus excludes them from participation in the mainstream of social activities. Physical disability is therefore a particular form of social oppression. (UPIAS, 1976)

Like other marginalised and oppressed individuals, many disabled people are born as a 'disabled person' but, unlike other groups, anyone can instantly, without warning or choice, become a disabled person. In this respect it offers a view of difference from different perspectives within the same individual's lived experience of the self in relation to society.

Most minority and oppressed people are located at the edges of society. Disabled people are no different but, unlike those from other groups such as black, minorities ethnic or LGBT groups, they have little or no access to political and social groups and individuals who offer an alternative and positive identity. The value of identifying resources and opportunities to work with, and alongside, therapy to repair a damaged sense of self is an integral part of the wider social context and action employed by groups such as feminist and sexual minorities. The disability movement has incorporated some of these groups' experiences and philosophies in an attempt to secure a position where disability can be seen, and internalised, as a positive identity with its own cultural values, social history and human rights. Attempting to place disability within a social context rather than a medical healthcare model has met with some resistance and criticism and, as stated earlier, there are problems:

'It is harder to celebrate disability than it is to celebrate blackness, or gay pride or being a woman. 'Disability Pride' is problematic because disability is difficult to recuperate as a concept, as it refers either to limitation and incapacity or else to oppression and exclusion or else to both dimensions.' (Shakespeare, 2013: 220)

As counselling psychologists we need to work with the individual's diversity within difference, as disabled people themselves still struggle with who and what they are in relation to each other, let alone to the dominant and powerful majority. Society still struggles to break free of stigmatising (Goffman, 1963) where shame and contamination run as a cultural undercurrent and therefore need to be openly discussed and confronted within the therapeutic space, as well as in a wider work context. It is a requirement to understand the social and personal impact of disability between you and your client, the relationship with disabled people as a group and further with the wider dominant society. For this reason, working with disabled clients raises issues that are inherent in, and across, all diversity and difference. It places the counselling psychologists at the heart of ethical, moral and professional dilemmas and debates about the boundaries of the therapeutic relationship. Later illustrations of disabled clients will highlight some of these 'difficult' dilemmas, involving all three aspects of difference – physical, psychological and socio-political – and invoke echoes and resonances linking all those of difference and diversity and those who experience oppression and exclusion.

Assigned, acquired or inherent

Recognising we are different may be a slow or sudden process of realisation. Being born into a marginalised group such as LGBT, black or disabled, of which in the UK 17 per cent are born with their impairments (Regan and Standley, 2011), is a different process from those who acquire, or discover, their difference later in life. Those with acquired or inherent impairments are, or become, members of a minority group experience, but within each person there will be different experiences and awareness levels of oppression. There is also difference, both emotionally and psychologically, between the two groups as attitudes and values around difference and disability among those with acquired impairments will have been formed as a non-disabled person, where there is perhaps a difference in the internalised oppression. The impact of personal histories and emotional development cannot be understood by reference to the group experience of oppression and exclusion alone, but by discovering it within an open, trusting and creative therapeutic relational journey that recognises the power of counselling psychology's prioritising individual formulation above that of diagnosis and categorisation.

Disability demonstrates that a minority group can have very distinct internal diversity within it and yet also share important similarities with other oppressed groups. This common ground, or overlap, is particularly evident when looking at difference in relation to power, oppression and discrimination. Holding both internal and external diversity in mind, we need to look at the individual experience within context as it is rarely a simple difference between client and psychologist or client and the prevailing culture but a result of a number of interlinking, overlapping and conflicting 'differences' (Reynolds and Pope, 1991).

Born different

Difference, then, for many people involves having multiple, overlapping identities of two or more groups. Being LGBT and disabled, black or from a minority culture is just one example of many.

Maria was born with cerebral palsy, in rural Eastern Europe, to an English mother and a locally born father, and initially her birth was seen as a tragedy and the loss of 'the hoped for child' by her parents. While cultural and traditional attitudes are changing, in the past many disabled children were placed in schools or homes for 'handicapped' children. Her mother, being brought up in the UK, resisted and devoted herself to helping Maria develop as much as possible physically, as part of the world around her. When Maria was eight, her parents separated and she returned to rural England with her mother. This rupture in cultural, educational and family relationships had a profound impact as being different was now not only about being a disabled child but also about being ethnically and culturally different. Achieving a level of independence, Maria learnt to 'pass' as non-disabled, attended mainstream schools, university and eventually work. However, after a few years she found herself increasingly tired, struggling with full-time work and feeling excluded. Despite many acquaintances, she failed to develop close friends and intimate relationships. She finally left her job and returned home with depression.

Maria talks about 'missing her cousins' and being around an extended family where she felt 'different, but part of the world'. Her still vivid memories of her childhood may be idealised but suggest that despite her 'difference' she had a place within the community as a disabled child. Nevertheless, memories also include struggling with day-to-day activities and she now shares her feelings, as an adult: 'I have to push myself all the time, push myself to do things or explain why I can't do what others do without thinking.'

Born a disabled female child, it was not until Maria arrived in England that her ethnic and cultural difference became entwined with her identity as a disabled child and later a disabled woman. Now in her late thirties, Maria feels isolated and angry, and she has no place to be herself, despite or because of her diverse identities. Over the years she has had private individual and group psychotherapy within an NHS psychotherapy service. She feels psychotherapists dismiss her status as a disabled woman, ignore her cultural loss and are 'not telling me the truth' and avoiding or dismissing what she feels.

Counselling and therapy was not a positive experience for Maria and, as her therapist, the initial task is to redraw a relationship of trust and empathy. She has had little or no contact with other disabled people or those from her childhood culture. However, unlike her ethnic and cultural identity, being a disabled person and different from birth meant there was no mirroring from others to lay the foundations of a positive identity. Parents and siblings, those around her, struggled with the 'unwanted' or at least 'less than wanted' part of her. Disability is nearly always negative and stigmatising, and resistance to adopting this identity is deeply rooted in society and therefore also in many disabled people themselves. Social reactions to disability in terms of 'stigma' suggest that 'fear of difference' has archaic origins in society's need to discriminate and exclude to protect itself in evolutionary terms from disease and contamination. This is then reinforced by rewarding, with affection and praise, actions, feelings and behaviours that treat, reduce and ideally cure the 'defected part'. When this inevitably fails, there is little option but to deny and/or ignore a core part of their identity. This is evident in high-profile and successful individuals, from politicians to sport personalities, who have significant impairments but choose not to identify themselves as disabled people. How far this parallels people from BME and LGBT groups is perhaps an indication of how individuals see themselves in relation to their particular group identity, powerlessness and oppression.

In the beginning

When a disabled client enters the room, how different are they from any other client from a minority group? Maria has a visible physical impairment, but whether you identify her as a 'disabled woman' will depend upon your personal and professional experience of disability and how you weigh impairment and social identity. For some, working with disability in the same way as any other difference, such as black and white, male and female, and less visible cultural differences, such as English and Spanish, may seem counterintuitive. The non-disabled therapist can be personally affected by the physicality of impairment as well as the imagined life of restriction. It is inevitable that early sessions raise questions, anxieties and thoughts for the counselling psychologist but exploring them with candour and honesty with the client and addressing this and countertransference in supervision is important. It has been shown that initial feelings, such as pity, helplessness and an association with tragedy, can emerge even in experienced therapists who have little training or contact with disability (Parritt and O'Callaghan, 2000). Maria's life has been one of difference and distance, geographically, culturally and emotionally, and the loss of personal, social and intimate relationships. Prioritising and managing overlapping roles of difference, such as disability, culture, sexuality and gender, can be complex and time consuming.

While formulation is central for counselling psychologists, as opposed to a diagnostic approach, we can still fall victim to unconscious social assumptions and prejudices. Clients may arrive with negative, or at best, defensive and wary attitudes towards us, and psychological therapies in general, where there has been little attention to, or understanding of, being different and excluded. Poor social skills and difficulty in engaging with others and society can be pathologised in those who live as different rather than understanding the impact of social exclusion and pervasive prejudicial and negative attitudes and projections of the dominant culture.

Becoming different

John was born and grew up as a non-disabled white male within mainstream UK culture. Ten years ago he sustained a spinal chord injury and today, now a full-time wheelchair user in his early thirties, he lives in adapted accommodation with direct payments (managing his own support with a budget from social services). He has been referred as depressed and not coping. Difference is evident – as a wheelchair user he will experience all the physical and social barriers of which non-disabled people have no experience. He must allow medical and social care professionals access to and scrutiny over not just his daily life, finances and space, but also his body. How and to what extent has becoming a disabled man changed his identity and sense of self?

What do you, as a psychologist, represent to John? Just another health professional whom he must now allow access to his thoughts and feelings, as others have access to his physical world? What are his relationships with others, disabled and non-disabled, as well as professionals? Consider that when a black British person sees a white British therapist, the difference is one of lived experience and not just skin pigmentation. So it is with John, the difference is not just impairment but his experience of being and becoming a young disabled man in a non-disabled world. However, as discussed earlier, the impact of living with his impairments is real, and removing all social barriers and negative attitudes will not remove the personal experience of impairment. It is important to give permission to explore that a wheelchair may provide mobility in an accessible world, but it cannot easily recover the non-disabled physical experience and freedom of walking independently. Equally, assuming that impairment is the cause of John's distress can be a trap for the non-disabled therapist to tumble into. The counselling psychologist can feel anxious or even de-skilled by the 'other' when this is outside their experience and John may collude in a formulation that only focuses upon loss and tragedy. Siller suggested that lack of experience may result in anxiety when a person is confronted with something outside their construct system, and in inadequacy and uneasiness when in the company of a 'disfigured person' (Siller, 1976). It would seem logical that this process is at work when therapists fall back on familiar psychological models rooted only in a medical model. Dealing with John's distress by emphasising behavioural and cognitive 'coping strategies' that deal with 'loss' and treating 'lack of' function conceptualises 'the problem' and 'solution' within the individual excluding the wider social perspective. By acknowledging a narrative of oppression and incorporating the social model, the possibility that impairment is not the only, or largely John's, problem, an enriched formulation develops, recognising that access, lowered income, status and sexual identity all play a major role.

Internalised oppression

John, like most psychologists, was brought up within, and internalised, a non-disabled culture, where disability is usually seen as a tragedy and a medical condition that individuals 'suffer from'. A new unwelcome identity has been thrust upon him where he is part of a social narrative that is marginalising, desexualising, and often leads to exclusion, discrimination and oppression.

He did not choose to be, nor was he born, part of an oppressed or marginalised community. However, as a disabled man, society and those around him react differently towards him. Therapeutically, though, it is what it means to him to be 'a disabled man', and how internalised negative attitudes and beliefs as that non-disabled person still contaminate his value, self-esteem and identity. These issues have direct parallels for counselling psychologists when working with other oppressed and marginalised groups, such as LGBT and BME groups. Brauner suggests 'It is necessary for white therapists to explore and work through their guilt and defensiveness with regard to racism and internalised homophobia or biphobia' (Brauner, 2000).

It is therefore not only you the psychologist but John himself that represent the non-disabled world and the negative narrative of difference within the dominant culture. Who, therefore, in the room represents, holds or argues for a positive, equal identity for disability or difference? Taking this on is important, but it places the non-disabled or counselling psychologist without difference in a difficult position where they are in conflict with the client's current belief system and identity, when not actually being part of, or experiencing, the reality of living with an impairment and being a disabled person themselves.

The power of words and language

Words and language are the main building blocks of a culture. The narrative and discourse around diversity and difference reflects and is impacted by this. The language we employ reveals and contributes to the therapeutic relationship and its relationship within a wider social context. Referring to an individual as a 'person with a disability' rather than a disabled person or as 'wheelchair bound' rather than 'wheelchair user' is one example where meaning is embedded in language. These were common descriptions some years ago, even among disabled people themselves. Being sensitive to the client's frame of reference, while also setting the parameters in early sessions by using appropriate language, is an important step towards empowerment. Using the term 'wheelchair bound' is an explicit example where language reinforces powerlessness and restriction. There are many examples spanning the gamut of diverse and different groups, from black and ethic minority groups, gender and the LGBT community. Indeed, using words such as 'queer' and 'crip' as self-descriptors has been an attempt to reclaim language from the oppressor by minority and oppressed groups.

Counselling psychologists should be sensitive to how often ordinary words and descrip-tions are imbued with 'loss', 'tragedy' or 'less than', and ensure they use words carefully while also demonstrating empathy and acknowledging what the client feels. The elephant in the room can, ironically, become what is outside the room, where there is a narrative of oppression and exclusion in everyday language. Reflecting upon and, when appropriate, adopting a language that challenges some of these unspoken assumptions draws into the room these feelings and beliefs in order to engage in a mutual dialogue and exploration.

WORKING IN SPECIALISED SERVICES

The existence of specialist services for particular disadvantaged and oppressed groups, delivered by those with difference themselves, has been important in improving access and value for women, the BME and the LGBT community. There are still few psychologists who are disabled, but how would it have been if John or Maria had seen a counselling psychologist who was a disabled person? Studies have shown that where black therapists work with black clients there is less countertransference and better empathy development (Sue and Sue, 1990). It is, however, not without difficulties as the therapist is in danger of colluding and over-identifying with the client's situation (Comas-Diaz and Jacobsen, 1991). Having said that, working together and developing a narrative that pays attention to social exclusion, isolation, stigma or tragedy are important and valuable aspects of this work. Working collaboratively with a disabled person or a person with difference, while identifying and challenging each other and society's negative attitudes and reactions to difference, can be painful, and not just for the client. Difficulties can arise where there is a shared difference, so close attention needs to be given to issues around transference and countertransference, and these need to be addressed in supervision.

APPROPRIATE SUPERVISION

Much could be said about the use of an appropriate supervisory relationship, as it is crucial when working in this area. It is important to have a safe place to reflect upon and explore your own attitudes and beliefs with someone who has extensive experience or knowledge of difference and diversity. In the case of both John and Maria, supervision, underpinned by a social model perspective, is an effective way to meet the challenges and questions that arise, otherwise there is a danger of avoidance, minimising or even perhaps denial of structural and social aspects of the client's experience.

CONCLUSION

In an increasingly mobile world, working with difference and diversity is an integral part of everyday practice. It presents particular challenges but offers a potentially rewarding and enriching experience for both the client and counselling psychologist. The philosophy that underpins counselling psychology also offers opportunities to counter some of the negative experiences of psychological therapies that have tended to place responsibility on the individual to 'fit in' or accommodate to society, while not addressing the oppressive and pathologising context in which they live.

This chapter has pointed less to a range of skills, techniques and models but rather to active self-reflection and questioning, while also adopting a collaborative, pluralist therapeutic approach. It has been the aim to point to examining the relative contribution of social barriers, the physiological reality of impairment in the case of disabled people, and the psychological and emotional impact of an individual's life story. It calls for a kind of bravery that incorporates the wider socio-political dimension of difference as well as questioning some of the traditional boundaries of therapy models, which can be challenging for counselling psychologists, organisations and clients alike. Working in this wider, more socially aware and inclusive manner requires looking critically at our place and responsibility in society, not just as psychologists, but as fellow human beings. We need to be clear who we are in relation to our clients' difference, be that gender, ethnicity, culture or sexuality. In order to achieve this, supervision plays a key role in examining wider aspects of our practice, while always remaining grounded and located at practice level when working with individual clients.

The prime example has been disability, as it shares and sharpens aspects of the common experiences of many diverse and different groups. In addition, disability remains an area that counselling and psychotherapy has continued to avoid or ignore. Where this has not been so, it has usually failed to incorporate the social model or pays lip service to it within a health or medical speciality. Anecdotal reports often portray psychological interventions as unhelpful, individualising and even pathologising, something that echoes past experiences of groups, such as the BME and LGBT communities. Perhaps this is confounded by there being so few openly disabled counselling psychologists compared to other minority groups.

The thrust of this chapter has been to stimulate reflection upon and a questioning of not only what we do, but how we do it at a practice level, particularly with disability as an example. It has indicated that identities are rarely one-dimensional, and that the emotional, cognitive, physical and socio-political weave around each other, creating an individual's uniqueness. The reality of impairment and its very personal impact exposes how difference is embedded within the social and psychological. Ignoring this reality is a recipe for failure, as is assuming identity from a client's sexuality, ethnicity or gender. The chapter stressed the importance of a relational approach in tandem with accepting the reality of the physical and social experience. It proposes an approach which incorporates permission-giving that goes beyond the therapy room, offering, without demanding, a rights and social model perspective, suggesting that this has a central and essential part to play.

While we are all individuals with unique lives and identities, the lived experience of being an 'outsider' or 'the other', of being or feeling 'less than', resonates across all marginalised peoples, be they BME, LBGT, women or disabled. It is worth noting that belonging and sharing is key, and sometimes connecting with other oppressed and marginalised peoples can be a positive step towards confronting, mitigating and finally removing the shame and stigma that social and internalised oppression brings and which is experience by all at some level.

Finally, the chapter attempted to widen the scope of how we work, stressing the importance of becoming aware of our own difference, place and participation within the profession and how we can help challenge the dominant social and political agenda inside our own profession and practices. However, it is not intended that this should in any way detract from, but enhance and enrich, the core of the counselling psychologist's work, which is embodied in the one-to-one therapeutic relationship with another human being, our client. It is only here, together, that the tangled web can safely be examined, unpicked and rethreaded, paying respect and doing justice to an individual's diversity within a group where we may all be different but equal human beings.

Visit the companion website for the following:

- Towards Anti-Oppressive Practice in Counselling Psychology.
- Considering Difference and Discrimination.

REFERENCES

Allport, G.W. (1954) *The Nature of Prejudice*. Cambridge, MA: Addison-Wesley.

Asay, T.P. and Lambert, M.J. (1999) The empirical case for the common factors in therapy: Quantitative findings. In M.A. Hubble, B.L. Duncan and S.D. Miller (eds), *The Heart and Soul of Change: What Works in Therapy* (pp. 33–56). Washington, DC: American Psychological Press.

Brauner, R. (2000) Addressing, race, culture and sexuality. In D. Davies and C. Neal (eds), *Pink Therapy: Issues in Therapy with Lesbian, Gay, Bisexual and Transgender Clients*. Buckingham: Open University Press.

British Psychological Society. (2008) *Professional Practice Board Social Inclusion Group*. Leicester: BPS.

British Psychological Society. (2012) *Guidelines and Literature Review for Psychologists Working Therapeutically with Sexual and Gender Minority Clients*. Leicester: BPS.

Comas-Diaz, L. and Jacobsen, F.M. (1991) Ethnocultural transference and countertransference in the therapeutic dyad. *American Journal of Orthopsychiatry*, 61: 392–402.

Cooper, M. (2005) Working at relational depth. *Therapy Today*, 16(8): 16–20.

Cooper, M. and McLeod, J. (2011) *Pluralistic Counselling and Psychotherapy*. London: Sage.

Finkelstein, V. (1980) *Attitudes and Disabled People*. New York: World Rehabilitation Fund.

French, S. (1993) *Disability, Impairment or Something in Between*. London: Sage.

Gerstein, L.H., Heppner, P., Ægisdóttir, S., Leung, S.A. and Norsworthy, K.L. (2011) *Essentials of Cross-Cultural Counseling*. Thousand Oaks, CA: Sage.

Goffman, E. (1963) *Stigma: Notes on the Management of Spoiled Identity*. Englewood Cliffs, NJ: Prentice-Hall.

Katz, J.H. (1985) The sociopolitical nature of counseling. *The Counseling Psychologist*, 13(4): 615–624.

Lambert, M.J. and Barley, D.E. (2001) Research summary on the therapeutic relationship and psychotherapy outcome. *Psychotherapy: Theory, Research, Practice, Training*, 38(4): 357–361.

Levinson, F. and Parritt, S. (2005) *Against Stereotypes: Experiences of Disabled Psychologists*. Basingstoke: Palgrave Macmillan.

Moane, G. (2010) Sociopolitical development and political activism: Synergies between feminism and liberation psychology. *Psychology of Women Quarterly*, 34(4): 521–529.

Moodley, R. (2009) Multi(ple) cultural voices speaking 'Outside the Sentence' of counselling and psychotherapy. *Counselling Psychology Quarterly*, 22(3): 297–307.

Oliver, M. (1996) *Understanding Disability: From Theory to Practice*. New York and Basingstoke: Palgrave Macmillan.

Parritt, S. (2005) Time to talk: Sex survey. *Disability Now*, May: 4–5.

Parritt, S. and O'Callaghan, J. (2000) Splitting the difference: An exploratory study of therapists' work with sexuality, relationships and disability. *Sexual & Relationship Therapy*, 15(2): 151–169.

Pettigrew, T.F. and Tropp, L.R. (2006) A meta-analysis test of intergroup contact theory. *Journal of Personality and Social Psychology*, 90: 751–783.

Regan, S. and Standley, K. (2011) Work for disabled people. *New Economy*, 10: 56–61.

Reynolds, A.L. and Pope, R.L. (1991) The complexities of diversity: Exploring multiple oppressions. *Journal of Counseling & Development*, 70(1): 174–180.

Rogers, C.R. (1957) The necessary and sufficient conditions of therapeutic personality change. *Journal of Consulting Psychology*, 21(2): 95–103.

Shakespeare, T. (2013) *The Social Model of Disability*. London: Taylor & Francis.

Shakespeare, T. and Watson, N. (2001) The social model of disability: An outdated ideology? *Exploring Theories and Expanding Methodologies: Where We Are and Where We Need to Go*. Amsterdam and New York: Emerald. pp. 9–28.

Siller, J. (1976) Attitudes towards disability. In H. Rusalem and D. Malikin (eds), *Contemporary Vocational Rehabilitation*. New York: New York University Press.

Strawbridge, S. (1994) Towards anti-oppressive practice in counselling psychology. *Counselling Psychology Review*, 9(1): 5–12.

Sue, D.W. and Sue, D. (1990) *Counseling the Culturally Different: Theory and Practice* (2nd edn). New York: John Wiley.

UPIAS. (1976) *Fundamental Principles of Disability*. London: Union of the Physically Impaired Against Segregation.

Vezzali, L., Giovannini, D. and Capozza, D. (2010) Longitudinal effects of contact on intergroup relations: The role of majority and minority group membership and intergroup emotions. *Journal of Community & Applied Social Psychology*, 20(6): 462–479.

World Health Organization. (2011) *World Health Report on Disability*. Geneva: WHO and The World Bank.

13
DEVELOPING SELF-CARE AND RESILIENCE
VICTORIA E. GALBRAITH

INTRODUCTION

Personal development within counselling psychology training programmes has been a contentious issue for many years: first, due to the lack of research evidence for its inclusion and, secondly, due to its mandatory requirement within training programmes. While this remains a valid argument to be having (Malikiosi-Loizos, 2013), this chapter will not be delving into this debate as Rizq eloquently captured much of the narrative within the previous edition of the *Handbook of Counselling Psychology* (Rizq, 2010: 569–589) and further coverage of personal development is included within Chapter 5 of this edition. Suffice to state that while the recently reviewed and approved Standards of Competency for Counselling Psychologists indicate that trainees must 'understand the experience of therapy through active and systematic engagement in personal therapy' (British Psychological Society, 2014: 13), further research is still required in order to determine the efficacy of personal therapy (Donati and Watts, 2000) and personal development groups (Galbraith and Hart, 2007) for counselling psychologists in training. However, whether or not one is in agreement with the inclusion of personal development, self-care is not only integral to our personal and professional well-being but also forms part of the Society's *Code of Ethics and Conduct* (see British Psychological Society, 2009: 18). This chapter therefore focuses upon resilience and self-care across the career trajectory and considers the potential benefits together with the health hazards associated with utilising our self within psychotherapeutic work. While the chapter is UK-focused, the general principles discussed within the chapter apply globally and across the profession (including counselling, psychotherapy, and other helping roles). The chapter begins with the concept of the wounded healer, which has existed for over 2,500 years (Zerubavel and O'Dougherty Wright, 2012) and which was popularised by Carl Jung (1981 [1929]) in the 1920s.

WOUNDED HEALER

> The doctor is effective only when he himself is affected. Only the wounded physician heals.
> (Jung and Jaffe, 1962: 134)

The wounded healer concept suggests that psychological therapists are motivated towards their choice of profession as a consequence of their own difficult life experiences (Barnett, 2007; Farber, Manevich, Metzger and Saypol, 2005; Guggenbuhl-Craig, 1999; Martin, 2011; Sedgwick, 1994; Sussman, 2007; Zerubavel and O'Dougherty White, 2012) and it is through this experience of caring for our own wounds that enables us to care for the wounds of others (Vachon, 2010).

Let us focus initially on the first component of this, the experience of pain or suffering leading towards a profession such as counselling psychology. While there is limited literature in relation to the chosen profession of counselling psychology, DiCaccavo (2002) reports on several studies that have focused upon the motivations of other caring professions, such as social workers (Vincent, 1996), doctors (Johnson, 1991; Vaillant et al., 1972) and psychotherapists (Fussell and Bonney, 1990). According to DiCaccavo (2002), studies such as these suggest that helping professionals are more likely to report childhood deprivation and emotional trauma than those in non-caring professions. It has been further suggested by various authors (for example, Barr, 2006; Goldberg, 1986; Sussman, 2007) that caring professionals are drawn towards careers that meet their own needs. I am reminded at this point of Siegel's (1998) story of 'the patient who cured his therapist...' (visit the companion website for a link). None of us are invincible or superhuman; we experience the vicissitudes of life in the same way as every other mortal.

So, it has been recognised that counselling psychologists and other psychological therapists, together with their clients, may experience emotional injury and authors report that these wounds might lead to a specific choice of career. To add to this, it has been further argued by Rice (2011) and Zerubavel and O'Dougherty White (2012) that the wound itself is not necessarily the catalyst for healing others but rather that the recovery process allows for an awareness and understanding of one's own vulnerabilities in addition to the pain of others and thus enables the facilitation of our clients' journey towards recovery.

However, according to Martin (2011: 10), 'For many therapists woundedness is a hidden secret. This deceit is sometimes masked as "professionalism"'. While one might hope that counselling psychologists would be at ease with such disclosure, it remains a difficult subject for many. The reality is that, first and foremost, we are human beings and, as humans, we are not immune to the affects of life and living and, furthermore, we are also affected by the social (Vogel et al., 2009; Zerubavel and O'Dougherty White, 2012) and personal stigma (Vogel et al., 2006; Zerubavel and O'Dougherty White, 2012) associated with mental health difficulties. Yet others may believe that psychologists are beyond personal pain due to their professional role (Callahan and Ditloff, 2007). Barnett et al. (2007: 605) argue that psychologists need to be wary of unintentionally endorsing such views due to their own 'professional blind spots'. 'Rather than facilitating change and address-ing the problem, the reported literature suggests that practitioners may be feeding into the problem by keeping their own mental health issues undisclosed' (Galbraith and Galbraith, 2008: 57).

Zerubavel and O'Dougherty White (2012) argue that disclosure can be frightening for some therapists if they have an internalised self-stigma and/or if they hold the perception that colleagues hold stigmatising beliefs. They go on to note that while psychologists might not adopt stigmatising views when considering their clients' wounds, their own difficulties together with those of their colleagues may be consistent with a more general social stigma. In fact, they propose that the move from a therapeutic milieu to that of professional gate-keeper may increase the social stigma of mental health difficulties. The aforementioned gatekeeping responsibilities can be viewed in the Society's Standard 2.4 for recognising impairment (British Psychological Society, 2009). This relates to monitoring 'one's own per-sonal and professional lifestyle in order to remain alert to signs of impairment' and taking responsibility to act accordingly (Standards 2.4 (i), (ii) and (iii)), in addition to:

> Encourage colleagues whose health-related or other personal problems may reflect impair-ment to seek professional consultation or assistance, and consider informing other potential sources of intervention, including, for example, the Health [and Care] Professions Council, when such colleagues appear unable to recognise that a problem exists. Psychologists must inform potential sources of intervention where necessary for the protection of the public. (Standard 2.4 (iv)) (British Psychological Society, 2009: 17)

Although Zerubavel and O'Dougherty White (2012) provide a valid argument, it must be said that in comparing three studies investigating psychiatrists' (White et al., 2006), doctors' (Hassan et al., 2009) and psychologists' (Galbraith et al., in preparation) attitudes towards mental health and help-seeking, chartered psychologists' responses appear more favourable with regards disclosure and motivations for disclosure. White et al.'s (2006) study investi-gated 370 psychiatrists' attitudes to mental health and help-seeking and found that they would be reluctant to disclose mental health difficulties to colleagues (319/370 – 86.2 per cent) and professional organisations (323/370 – 87.3 per cent). Similarly, in a study of 2,462 Birmingham doctors (70 per cent response rate), Hassan et al. (2009) found that they were more likely to disclose to family or friends (1,807 – 73.4 per cent) than to professional/gov-ernmental institutions (317 – 12.9 per cent) or to colleagues (159 – 6.5 per cent) and 178 (7.2 per cent) would not disclose at all. Galbraith et al. (in preparation) conducted a national survey of 257 chartered psychologists – clinical psychologists (159 – 55.2 per cent), counsel-ling psychologists (79 – 25.8 per cent), and both (19 – 6.2 per cent). Although psychologists were also unlikely to disclose to professional/governmental institutions (13 – 5 per cent) or to colleagues (12 – 4.6 per cent), over half (166 – 63.6 per cent) would choose to disclose to family and friends and nearly a quarter would disclose to a personal therapist or supervisor (64 – 24.5 per cent). Psychologists also rated personal well-being as the most influential fac-tor in choosing whether to disclose whereas stigma was the least influential reason.

Psychiatrists, however, cited confidentiality, followed by career implications, as the most influential factors in choosing whether to disclose. The factors influencing disclosure in these studies can be found in Table 13.1.

Table 13.1   Summary statistics from Galbraith et al. (in preparation), Hassan et al. (2009) and White et al. (2006)

	Doctors (2,462 participants) Hassan et al. (2009)	Psychiatrists (370 participants) White et al. (2008)	Psychologists (157 participants) Galbraith et al. (in preparation)
Personal well-being	Not measured	Not measured	59.8%
Career implications	32.5%	35%	5.5%
Professional integrity	29.7%	Not measured	14.5%
Client safety	Not measured	Not measured	8.6%
Stigma	19.9%	22%	5.1%

Given the reported lack of focus on stigma within these figures, it could be suggested that psychologists, and in particular counselling psychologists, could be leading the de-stigmatisation campaign through their arguable openness and honesty surrounding woundedness (Galbraith and Galbraith, 2008). However, we must not become complacent. There is still much work to be done around moving towards greater openness and support for the wounded healer (Zerubavel and Dougherty White, 2012). Further transparency, together with empathic communication and support for others within our profession and indeed for ourselves, is needed. Not only could this level of support assist other counselling psychologists but '[i]t is contended that we stand a better chance of making an authentic relationship with those we seek to help if we are prepared to celebrate our scarred, glorious, mis-shapenly successful, and often faulty selves for what we are' (Martin, 2011: 10).

Given that in psychotherapeutic work our *self* is the tool, it is imperative that we are in a position to take care of ourselves (Barnett et al., 2007). While it may appear outwardly selfish, there is a necessity for us to embody the humanism that we espouse – the first step to taking care of my client is taking care of me!

IN-TRAINING: THE STRESSES AND STRAINS OF TRAINING

Following a thorough investigation of the stress experienced by clinical psychology trainees performed by Cushway (1992), Kumary and Baker (2008) conducted a similar study to investigate the stresses associated with counselling psychology training. Their explanation for conducting a similar study with a comparable group was due to the potential extra stressors placed upon counselling psychology trainees, given that counselling psychology training is not currently publicly funded. This leaves most trainees to finance their course independently (unless they are employer-sponsored) and also to consider their associated living costs, which may add additional pressure for trainees. Furthermore, trainees may also need to work in order to fund their course or living costs, leaving less time for course-related activity. Finally, clinical placement and supervision arrangements are sometimes left to the trainee to organise, rather than the course staff, thus leaving the trainee with further stressors (Kumary and Baker, 2008). Their study indicated that stress levels appear to remain steady over time and they cite Cooper and Quick's paper (2003) which claims that this 'goes with the territory' of success. They go on to note that being offered a position on a postgraduate professional training programme is one measurement of success. Furthermore, since 2009, university-based counselling psychology training programmes in the UK are exclusively at doctoral level, the highest-level qualification that can be achieved, therefore acceptance onto such a programme can certainly be deemed a success.

According to Kumary and Baker (2008: 25–26), 'the study's main, obvious and repeated feature is that counselling psychology trainees report stress levels and associated distress levels that are unacceptably high' and this leads to questions such as 'do training programmes expose trainees to unacceptable stress levels while simultaneously promoting high levels of vulnerability/openness to experience?'. This piece of work was conducted with the assistance of staff and participants of several university-based counselling psychology programmes. It is less clear whether there were participants on the 'Qualification in Counselling Psychology' participating in this study. Nevertheless, it has been well reported that an additional stressor for trainees studying the Qualification route may be that they find their experience to be isolating (Hall, 2010; James, 2010).

Anecdotal reasons for stress gleaned from working as a university trainer for many years, together with speaking to trainees from other institutions at accreditation visits, include the commute to and from training/clinical placement (indeed, many will travel a great distance to their nearest training course and/or placement); the financial pressures, which are also mentioned in the Kumary and Baker (2008) study; the sheer volume of work involved and the academic standard required; experiencing the feeling of being de-skilled and 'impostor syndrome' creeping in; the struggle with the personal development component of training; course organisation and communication; the impact on family life; change in personal circumstances; and, last but certainly not least, personal relationships.

> Almost all trainees at some stage of their training are likely to experience periods of distress or bewilderment and may even at times become subject to incapacitating anxiety or depression. Notoriously, too, relationships with spouses and other family members are liable to undergo considerable upheaval or even to flounder altogether. (Dryden and Thorne, 1991: 4)

A commonly asked question at interview for potential trainees rings in my ears: 'This course can be academically, professionally and emotionally challenging. What do you think may be the main challenges for you?' and 'what support mechanisms do you have in place?'

Through immersing oneself in psychological theory and gazing inwardly with constant self-reflection and self-assessment, trainees can often find that their very 'being' is challenged. They may question 'who am I?' and 'what am I hoping to achieve with my life?' and this may come as quite a surprise for many. Although some may be somewhat prepared for this, no one quite knows the potential impact that intense psycho-therapeutic training may have on each individual. It stands to reason that when you are asking yourself these sorts of questions, inevitably they will have an impact on those around you. Trainers therefore have a responsibility to their trainees to ensure that they are provided with a form of informed consent, that they know what they are getting themselves into and that the rose-tinted spectacles of being offered a sought-after place on the course might soon turn a shade of grey when reality sets in.

One significant way of overcoming this dilemma is that trainees and more experienced practitioners engage in reflective practice and regular clinical supervision (see Chapter 7 for 'Becoming a supervisee' and Chapter 35 for 'Becoming a supervisor'); and further emphasis on the need to engage in personal therapy might be beneficial. The BPS *Standards for Doctoral Programmes in Counselling Psychology* (2014: 13) indicate that

> trainees will continuously evaluate their practice in the light of the following principles and, by the end of their programme, will:
>
> 8.3 understand the experience of therapy through active and systematic engagement in personal therapy, which will enable them to:
>
> > i. demonstrate an understanding and experience of therapy from the perspective of the client, which will be utilised to guide their own practice;
> > ii. demonstrate an understanding through therapy of their own life experience, and understand the impact of that experience upon practice;
> > iii. demonstrate an ability for critical self-reflection on the use of self in therapeutic process.
>
> 8.6 develop strategies to build resilience to handle the emotional and physical impact of practice and seek appropriate support when necessary;
>
> 8.7 have the capacity to recognize when their own fitness to practice is compromised and take steps to manage this risk as appropriate.

While this is a prerequisite of qualification, the requirement clearly goes beyond the training experience and to life after training.

HOW DOES THIS TRANSLATE INTO SELF-HELP PRACTICE?

The reality of life, whether a person is in training or qualified, is that living brings obstacles. We will all encounter some level of personal difficulty during our careers and the likelihood is that this may impact on our ability to care for others at that time, and possibly to vulnerability in caring sufficiently for ourselves. For this reason, self-awareness during training and beyond is essential, not least in order to assess personal psychological functioning, recognition of individual needs and vulnerabilities to stress, burnout and other difficulties. A valuable accompaniment to self-awareness in these instances is the ability to adequately look after oneself. Authors (such as Orlans, 1993; Wilkins, 1997) have written about ways in which catering for their own personal, spiritual, physical, social and emotional needs have made them better therapists. Wilkins writes: 'I can ensure that I meet my clients in a refreshed state and without danger of meeting *my* needs in the therapeutic encounter or failing to offer my clients my full attention and all my skills and abilities' (1997: 122, original italic). And I am inclined to agree. I am also conscious of the impact that not giving myself personal time and space can have on my therapeutic work, and in the stressful, fast-paced twenty-first century this can be a difficult prospect, but if I do not give time to myself freely, then how can I offer my time fully to my clients? As Orlans states, 'only when I am prepared to take care of me can I authentically take care of others' (1993: 67).

In the course of our careers, it is inevitable that we will be touched by the stories of our clients. Such a reaction may be due to over-identification with the client or their difficulty, a countertransference reaction, advanced empathic attunement, vicarious trauma and compassion fatigue (Baker, 2003), secondary trauma, feeling de-skilled with particular client(s), discomfort with the characteristics or behaviours that clients engage in, or through something else entirely. Furthermore, authors (Shapiro et al., 2000) have found that stress may impact upon trainees' effectiveness and success by reducing attention, concentration and decision-making.

Various authors have discussed the impact of working therapeutically with traumatised individuals (for example, Jenkins and Baird, 2002; Trippany et al., 2004), and O'Brien (2011) eloquently and movingly describes the effect that a client's death had on him. Needless to say, as human beings with an emotional thermometer, there are periods during our working lives when our mercury levels will rise and lower in tune with the feelings and experiences of our clients. What is important during these less positive moments is to try to ensure that we regain equilibrium as opposed to being suffocated by the affect, even though this might not always be feasible.

Maintaining 'fitness to practice' (British Psychological Society, 2014: 13) is integral to our profession and therefore taking time out of practice when personal circumstances necessitate the need for self-care is essential. However, dependent upon working practices and policies, this can come at a cost for many. Within our current economic climate and the associated job insecurity that prevails alongside fear of redundancy, the pressures faced may be exacerbated further as job concerns can affect our mental health. Cooper (2014) refers to the concept of 'presenteeism' whereby employees arrive at work earlier than usual and stay later, they continue to work at the weekends, remain in touch while on annual leave, and send emails in the evening. By engaging in these behaviours, employees are attempting to demonstrate to their manager(s) that they are committed to their work. However, the cost of this relentless behaviour can often be exhaustion. Excessive workloads can be perpetuated by job insecurity, colleagues' redundancy or sickness absence leading to subsequent additional demands, the sheer caseload (Maslach and Jackson, 1981; Pines and Maslach, 1980) and additional strain of initiatives to reduce waiting lists. This can have a significant impact on the way in which we function. It is well demonstrated that too much stress can increase the risk of both physical and mental health problems (such as burnout). Cooper (2014) offers some advice on ways of combating these pressures, which are highlighted in the companion website resources that accompany this chapter.

Further significant challenges can be faced by those working in private practice when personal difficulties may lead to potential 'fitness to practice' issues. One's livelihood can be endangered, with loss of income being the major threat. The ethical conflict between personal and professional survival versus the needs to protect clients can be profound, and for this reason reflective practice, clinical supervision and other avenues of support are paramount. As well as professional indemnity insurance being a necessity, it is also advisable to consider a loss of earnings policy due to ill health, in addition to seeking expert advice (Syme, 1997).

TAKING CARE AND DEVELOPING RESILIENCE

Resilience has been described as the ability to maintain mental health or return promptly to mental health during times of adversity (Wald et al., 2006). Resilience research shows that while people encounter difficulties in their life, such as grief and sadness, people with resilience have more mature coping and self-management skills. Joseph and Lindley (2006) suggest that intellectual functioning, flexibility, social attachment, positive self-concepts, emotional regulation, positive emotions, spirituality, active coping, hardiness, optimism, hope, resourcefulness and adaptability are associated with resilience. Herrman et al. (2011) add that social support, including relationships with family and peers, is correlated with resilience; secure attachment to mother, family stability, secure relationship with a non-abusive parent and good parenting skills are associated with resilience. Resilience building ideally begins to take place as early as childhood but, if not, it is argued by Palmer (2013) and Rutter (2008) that this is something that could continue to be developed over time. So, in the lifecycle of the counselling psychologist, the development of resilience could begin as early as the commencement of training and entering into a self-care contract might be a great starting point.

Palmer (2013) explains how coaches can utilise various resilience-building strategies within their practice and extends this to incorporate other practitioners, including counselling psychologists. And what better way to develop resilience in others than by developing it in ourselves in the first instance, perhaps during training?

Padesky and Mooney (2012) have developed a four-step model to building resilience: Step 1: search for strengths; Step 2: construct a personal model of resilience (PMR); Step 3: apply the PMR; Step 4: practise resilience. The 'key practitioner message' within this model is that:

> therapists [are] helping clients identify existing strengths that are used to construct a personal
> model of resilience; client-generated imagery and metaphors are particularly potent to help

the client remember and creatively employ new positive qualities; behavioural experiments are designed in which the goal is to stay resilient rather than to achieve problem resolution; [and] therapists are encouraged to use constructive therapy methods and interview practices including increased use of smiling and silence. (Padesky and Mooney, 2012: 283)

Christopher and Maris (2010) are well aware of the impact of stress on trainee therapists and discuss how self-care has been consistently incorporated into several training programmes in the USA and, given our standards of competency (BPS, 2014), self-care is clearly also being addressed within UK training programmes. Wilkins (1997) includes a useful chapter ('Resourcing Yourself') that outlines ways in which therapeutic practitioners might consider taking care of themselves. Christopher and Maris further suggest that training in mindfulness is a forward-moving way of enhancing self-care and, in turn, preventing the aforementioned stresses, such as burnout, compassion fatigue and vicarious traumatisation. Kabat-Zinn (1993), the founder of mindfulness-based stress reduction programmes, claims that mindfulness cultivates awareness to assist people in living every moment of their lives as completely as possible, even the more difficult and painful moments; and 'mindfulness has been found to boost resilience' (Williams and Penman, 2010: 53). Hardiness was first investigated by Kobasa (1979), who found that three psychological traits could determine hardiness. These were control, commitment and challenge. Antonovsky (1987) found that manageability, meaningfulness and comprehensibility were markers of ability to withstand extreme pressure and he termed this 'a sense of coherence', which he believed was related to hardiness. Both Kobasa and Antonovsky developed scales of measurement and the higher a score on these scales, the more resilient a person may be considered to be (Williams and Penman, 2010). 'There is a common agreement that resilience emerges when individuals faced with negative life events or strains have the capacity to mobilise protective factors or internal and external resources and stay well' (Erikkson and Lindstrom, 2010: 342).

So let us return to the work of Christopher and Maris (2010), who claim that incorporating mindfulness into the training of counsellors and psychotherapists may enhance self-care. Jon Kabat-Zinn (Kabat-Zinn et al., 1982: 46) investigated his ten-week mindfulness training course to assess whether this could increase hardiness in a group of chronic pain patients. His findings indicated that 'deep personal insights, greater patience, a new ability to relax in daily life situations, and a willingness to live more in the present moment were commonly reported, as were increased awareness of stressful situations and improved ability to cope successfully'. Kabat-Zinn and others have conducted further investigations across a range of populations, resulting in findings being replicated. For further detail about mindfulness, please refer to Chapter 18. Visit the companion website for additional references.

Christopher and Maris (2010) investigated counselling and psychotherapy students' experiences of a 15-week elective class that ran for 2.5 hours per week. The course was entitled 'Mind-Body Medicine and the Art of Self-Care', and included mindfulness techniques throughout. Various studies were conducted over the period of nine years and the authors published a summary of these qualitative investigations. Their findings demonstrate that trainees 'became more aware of their own sensations, emotions and thoughts, many indicated that they were beginning to notice some significant shifts in their interpersonal relationships' (Christopher and Maris, 2010: 122). As well as impacting on their personal lives, trainees also reported that the mindfulness training affected their work with clients in several ways. For example, they were more at ease with silence, more attentive to the therapeutic process, and felt less pressure to act upon their own negative feelings within the session, as their feelings were less threatening to them. Furthermore, they recognised their own internal fears of feeling de-skilled, and instead felt more present focusing upon the here and now rather than 'what should I do next?' Due to this increased sensitivity, participants in this study indicated that they became more adept at containing their clients and their emotions, with an increased ability in facilitating the shift away from negative evaluation.

In addition to engaging in mindfulness techniques, there are a range of other personal and professional self-care strategies that trainees and qualified practitioners can adopt. These might include: clinical supervision; professional liability insurance; networking with other professionals and gaining support from them; enjoyable/stimulating training and further training (CPD); personal therapy; managing time effectively, saying no and meaning it!; taking time off when feeling unwell; taking care of personal safety; doing the work out of choice rather than compulsion; consideration of support and where to gain appropriate support from others (for example, partners, parents, children, colleagues, tutors); and also ensuring a healthy work–life balance. Research evidence is also accumulating which suggests that health and well-being can increase as a result of physical activity (Penedo and Dahn, 2005) and proximity to certain surroundings, for example, natural (Gatersleben, 2008, see Chapter 23 of this text) and coastal environments (Wheeler et al., 2012; Nichols, 2014). Therefore, attending to these factors and taking regular breaks may further assist in promoting both physical and/ or psychological health. Finally, if feeling isolated, lost or de-skilled, draw on your own personal philosophy.

TO CONCLUDE

While there will be times when it might be considered advisable to refrain from practice in order to take care of yourself and also to prevent any adverse affects on clinical work, the reality of having experienced emotional injury does not impair a counselling psychologist. To the contrary, Martin (2011) views our woundedness as something to celebrate and as a metaphor for making us more human. And Wheeler (2007: 245–246) claims that the term 'is not reserved for 'damaged' therapists who are inferior to others, but is attributed to all who open themselves to engaging in psychotherapeutic practice'. Nevertheless, when we are struggling to cope with our emotional wounds, it is imperative that we take the time to consider whether we ought, at that time, to be assisting others with theirs. Making use of clinical supervision, personal reflection and personal therapy can be a vital resource here. Self-care is vital in our chosen profession and this can begin as early as childhood, later in life, or perhaps when embarking upon the training process or beyond. Research indicates that mindfulness practice can not only make a significant impact on well-being after only a short period of time (eight weeks), but that parts of the brain associated with happiness, empathy and compassion become stronger and more active too (Williams and Penman, 2010). So it is never too late to develop a self-care contract, and that journey can begin today!

Visit the companion website for the following:

- Self-Care.
- NHS guidance on building up emotional resilience.

REFERENCES

Antonovsky, A. (1987) *Untraveling the Mystery of Health: How People Manage Stress and Stay Well*. San Francisco, CA: Jossey-Bass.

Baker, E. (2003) *Caring for Ourselves: A Therapist's Guide to Personal and Professional Well-being*. Washington, DC: American Psychological Association.

Barnett, J., Baker, N., Elman, N. and Schoener, G. (2007) In pursuit of wellness: The self-care imperative. *Professional Psychology: Research and Practice*, 38: 603–612.

Barnett, M. (2007) 'What brings you here? An exploration of the unconscious motivations of those who choose to train and work as psychotherapists and counselors', *Psychodynamic Practice*, 13: 257–274.

Barr, A. (2006) 'An investigation into the extent to which psychological wounds inspire counsellors and psychotherapists to become wounded healers, the significance of these wounds on their career choice, the causes of these wounds and the overall significant of demographic factors'. Unpublished MSc thesis at the University of Strathclyde, Scotland.

British Psychological Society (2009) *Code of Ethics and Conduct*. Leicester: BPS.

British Psychological Society (2014) *Standards for Doctoral Programmes in Counselling Psychology*. Leicester: BPS.

Callahan, J. L. and Ditloff, M. (2007) 'Through a glass darkly: Reflections on therapist transformations', *Professional Psychology: Research and Practice*, 38: 547–553.

Christopher, J. C. and Maris, J. A. (2010) 'Integrating mindfulness as self-care into counselling and psychotherapy training', *Counselling & Psychotherapy Research*, 10(2): 114–125.

Cooper, C. (2014) *NHS Choices: Redundancy Fear*. Retrieved on 17 June 2014 from www.nhs.uk/Livewell/Onabudget/Pages/Redundancyfear.aspx

Cooper, C. and Quick, J. (2003) 'The stress and loneliness of success', *Counselling Psychology Quarterly*, 16: 1–7.

Cushway, D. (1992) 'Stress in clinical psychology trainees', *British Journal of Clinical Psychology*, 31: 169–179.

DiCaccavo, A. (2002) 'Investigating individuals' motivations to become counselling psychologists: The influence of early caretaker roles within the family', *Psychology and Psychotherapy: Theory, Research and Practice*, 75: 463–472.

Donati, M. and Watts, M. H. (2000) 'Personal development in counselling psychology training: The case for further research', *Counselling Psychology Review*, 15(1): 12–21.

Dryden, W. and Thorne, B. (eds) (1991) *Training and Supervision for Counselling in Action*. London: Sage.

Erikkson, M. and Lindstrom, B. (2010) 'Bringing it all together: The salutogenic response to some of the most pertinent public health dilemmas', in A. Morgan, M. Davies and E. Zigglio (eds), *Health Assets in a Global Context: Theory, Methods and Action*. New York: Springer. pp. 339–351.

Farber, B. A., Manevich, I., Metzger, J. and Saypol, E. (2005) 'Choosing psychotherapy as a career: Why did we cross that road?' *Journal of Clinical Psychology: In Session*, 61: 1009–1031.

Fussell, E. W. and Bonney, W. C. (1990) 'A comparative study of childhood experiences of psychotherapists and physicians: Implications for clinical practice', *Psychotherapy*, 27: 505–512.

Galbraith, N. D., Galbraith, V. E., Hogan, N., Stevens-Gill, D. and Davies, S. (in preparation) 'Psychologists' attitudes to mental health and help-seeking'.

Galbraith, V. E. and Galbraith, N. D. (2008) 'Should we be doing more to reduce stigma?', *Counselling Psychology Review*, 23(4): 53–61.

Galbraith, V. E. and Hart, N. (2007) 'Personal development groups in counselling psychology training: The case for further research', *Counselling Psychology Review*, 22(4): 49–57.

Gatersleben, B. (2008) 'Humans and nature: 10 useful findings from environmental psychology research', *Counselling Psychology Review*, 23(2): 24–23.

Goldberg, C. (1986) *On Being a Psychotherapist: The Journey of the Healer*. London and New York: Guilford Press.

Guggenbuhl-Craig, A. (1999) *Power in the Helping Professions*. Putnam, CT: Spring Publications.

Hall, A. (2010) 'Section 3: Being Independent: On Independence: An exploration of the Independent route towards qualification as a counselling psychologist', *Counselling Psychology Review*, 25(3): 48–53.

Hassan, T., Ahmed, S. O., White, A. C. and Galbraith, N. (2009) 'A postal survey of doctors' attitudes to becoming mentally ill', *Clinical Medicine*, 9(4): 1–6.

Herrman, H., Stewart, D. E., Diaz-Granados, N., Berger, E. L., Jackson, B. and Yuen, T. (2011) 'What is resilience?', *Canadian Journal of Psychiatry*, 56(5): 258–265.

James, P. (2010) 'Section 3: Being Independent: A reply from the Chair of the Board of Assessors in Counselling Psychology to the issues raised in a survey of trainees on the qualification in counselling', *Counselling Psychology Review*, 25(3): 54–56.

Jenkins, S. R. and Baird, S. (2002) 'Secondary traumatic stress and vicarious trauma: A validational study', *Journal of Traumatic Stress*, 15(5): 423–432.

Johnson, W. D. K. (1991) 'Predisposition to emotional distress and psychiatric illness amongst doctors: The role of unconscious and experiential factors', *British Journal of Medical Psychology*, 64: 317–329.

Joseph, S. and Linley, P. A. (2006) 'Growth following adversity: Theoretical perspective and implications for clinical practice', *Clinical Psychology Review*, 26(8): 1041–1053.

Jung, C. G. (1981 [1929]) 'Fundamental questions of psychotherapy', in H. Read, M. Fordham and G. Adler (eds), *The Practice of Psychotherapy: Essays on the Psychology of the Transference and Other Subjects: Collected Works of C. G. Jung* (Vol. 16). Trans. R. F. C. Hull. Princeton, NJ: Princeton University Press. pp. 111–125.

Jung, C. G. and Jaffe, A. (1962) *Memories, Dreams, Reflections*. London: Collins.

Kabat-Zinn, J. (1993) 'Mindfulness meditation: Health benefits of an ancient Buddhist practice', in D. Goleman and J. Gurin (eds), *Mind/Body Medicine*. New York: Consumer Reports Books. pp. 259–276.

Kabat-Zinn, J., Massion, A. O., Kristeller, J., Peterson, L. G., Fletcher, K. E., Pbert, L., Lenderking W. R. and Santorelli, S. F. (1992) 'Effectiveness of a meditation-based stress reduction program in the treatment of anxiety disorders', *American Journal of Psychiatry*, 149(7): 936–943.

Kobasa, S. C. (1979) 'Stressful life events, personality, and health: Inquiry into hardiness', *Journal of Personality and Social Psychology*, 37(1): 1–11.

Kumary, A. and Baker, M. (2008) 'Stresses reported by UK trainee counselling psychologists', *Counselling Psychology Quarterly*, 21(1): 19–28.

Malikiosi-Loizos, M. (2013) 'Personal therapy for future therapists: Reflections on a still debated issue', *The European Journal of Counselling Psychology*, 2(1): 33–50.

Martin, P. (2011) 'Celebrating the wounded healer', *Counselling Psychology Review*, 26(1): 10–19.

Maslach, C. and Jackson, S. E. (1981) 'The measurement of experienced burnout', *Journal of Occupational Behaviour*, 2: 99–113.

Nichols, W. J. (2014) *Blue Mind: The Surprising Science that Shows How Being Near, In, On, or Under Water Can Make You Happier, Healthier, More Connected and Better at What You Do*. New York: Little Brown and Co.

O'Brien, J. M. (2011) 'Wounded healer: Psychotherapist grief over a client's death', *Professional Psychology: Research and Practice*, 42(3): 236–243.

Orlans, V. (1993) 'The counsellor's life in crisis', in W. Dryden (ed.), *Questions and Answers in Counselling in Action*. London: Sage.

Padesky, C. A. and Mooney, K. A. (2012) 'Strengths-based cognitive-behavioural therapy: A four step model to build resilience', *Clinical Psychology and Psychotherapy*, 19: 283–290.

Palmer, S. (2013) 'Resilience enhancing imagery: A cognitive behavioural technique which includes resilience undermining thinking and resilience enhancing thinking', *The Coaching Psychologist*, 9(1): 48–50.

Penedo, F. J. and Dahn, J. R. (2005) 'Exercise and well-being: A review of mental and physical health benefits associated with physical activity', *Current Opinion in Psychiatry*, 18(2): 189–193.

Pines, A. and Maslach, C. (1980) 'Combatting staff burnout in a day-care centre: A case study', *Child Care Quarterly*, 9, 5–16.

Rice, Cecil A. (2011) 'The psychotherapist as "wounded healer": A modern expression of an ancient tradition', in R. H. Klein, H. S. Bernard and V. L. Schermer (eds), *On Becoming a Psychotherapist: The Personal and Professional Journey.* New York: Oxford University Press. pp. 165–189.

Rizq, R. (2010) 'Personal development', in R. Woolfe, S. Strawbridge, B. Douglas and W. Dryden (eds), *Handbook of Counselling Psychology* (3rd edn). London: Sage. pp. 569–589.

Rutter, M. (2008) 'Developing concepts in developmental psychopathology', in J. J. Hudziak (ed.), *Developmental Psychopathology and Wellness: Genetic and Environmental Influences.* Washington, DC: American Psychiatric Publishing. pp. 3–22.

Sedgwick, D. (1994) *The Wounded Healer: Countertransference from a Jungian Perspective.* Brighton and Hove: Routledge.

Shapiro, S., Shapiro, D. and Schwartz, G. (2000) 'Stress management in medical education: A review of the literature', *Academic Medicine*, 75: 748–759.

Siegel, S. (1998) *The Patient Who Cured His Therapist and Other Stories of Unconventional Therapy.* New York: Marlowe & Co. Extract retrieved 24 August 2013 from www.psychologytomorrowmagazine.com/achieving-failures-the-patient-who-cured-his-therapist/

Sussman, M. B. (2007) *A Curious Calling: Unconscious Motivations for Practicing Psychotherapy* (2nd edn). Northvale, NJ: Jason Aronson.

Syme, G. (1997) *Counselling in Independent Practice.* Buckingham: Open University Press.

Trippany, R. L., Kress, V. E. and Wilcoxon, S. A. (2004) 'Preventing vicarious trauma: What counsellors should know when working with trauma survivors', *Journal of Counselling & Development*, 82: 31–37.

Vachon, W. (2010) 'Honouring the wounded: Inviting in our successes and mistakes', *Relational Child and Youth Care Practice*, 23(2): 54–62.

Vaillant, G. E., Sobowale, N. C. and McArthur, C. (1972) 'Some psychological vulnerabilities of physicians', *New England Journal of Medicine*, 287: 372–375.

Vincent, J. (1996) 'Why ever do we do it? Unconscious motivation in choosing social work as a career', *Journal of Social Work Practice*, 10: 63–69.

Vogel, D. L., Wade, N. G. and Ascheman, P. (2009) 'Measuring perceptions of stigmatization by others for seeking psychological help: Reliability and validity of a new stigma scale with college students', *Journal of Counseling Psychology, 56*: 301–308.

Vogel, D. L., Wade, N. G. and Haake, S. (2006) 'Measuring the self-stigma associated with seeking psychological help', *Journal of Counseling Psychology*, 53: 325–337.

Wald, J., Taylor, S., Asmundson, G., Jang, K. L. and Stapleton, J. (2006) *Literature Review of Concepts, Final Report: Psychological Resilience.* Toronto: Defense Research and Development Canada.

Wheeler, B. W., White, M., Stahl-Timmins, W. and Depledge, M. H. (2012) 'Does living by the coast improve health and wellbeing? *Health & Place.* Available online 30 June 2012. ISSN 1353-8292. 10.1016/j.healthplace.2012.06.015.

Wheeler, S. (2007) 'What shall we do with the wounded healer? The supervisor's dilemma'. *Psychodynamic Practice: Individuals, Groups and Organisations*, 13(3): 245–256.

White, A., Purushottam, S., Hassan, T., Galbraith, N. and Callaghan, R. (2006) 'Barriers to mental healthcare for psychiatrists', *Psychiatric Bulletin*, 30: 382–384.

Wilkins, P. (1997) *Personal and Professional Development for Counsellors*. London: Sage.

Williams, M. and Penman, D. (2010) *Mindfulness: A Practical Guide to Finding Peace in a Frantic World*. London: Piatkus.

Zerubavel, N. and O'Dougherty Wright, M. (2012) 'The dilemma of the wounded healer', *Psychotherapy*, 40(4): 482–491.

14
CARRYING OUT RESEARCH[1]
ELAINE KASKET

INTRODUCTION

Carrying out high-quality psychological research, suitable for publication, is a requirement for entering the profession of counselling psychology. The first official step in setting a universal doctoral standard occurred in 2005, at which point the British Psychological Society (BPS) stipulated that a practitioner would henceforth need to gain a doctoral-level qualification to become chartered as a counselling psychologist. In 2009, when the Health and Care Professions Council (HCPC) assumed responsibility for the statutory regulation of all professional psychologists, the threshold for qualification for counselling psychology was also set at doctoral level. These shifts did not instantly create a strong 'doctoral culture' on training programmes, and nor did the advent of HCPC automatically produce new generations of trainee counselling psychologists uniformly enthusiastic about, knowledgeable about and skilled in the business of research. Until recently, there were few resources that spoke directly to the doctoral-level counselling psychologist researcher, and to those who support their work. This chapter aims to guide, inform and inspire during this phase of a counselling psychologist's research life.

READERSHIP AND SCOPE

This chapter's primary audience is the trainee counselling psychologist researcher pursuing a doctorate within the UK. While it primarily speaks to candidates on the taught-course route to qualification, it may also assist QCoP candidates, including those who must produce a reflexive essay on a piece of research that may have been previously conducted. It may also benefit researchers from other fields who are undertaking an investigation within a counselling

1 In observance of copyright, I acknowledge that some of this material was originally published in Kasket (2012).

psychology context. Supervisors, examiners for counselling psychology dissertations or theses, and trainers on counselling psychology training programmes may also find it useful. Finally, as doctoral standards in the UK aim to be commensurate with doctoral benchmarks world-wide, much of the material within this chapter will be useful for international readers as well.

The scope of this chapter extends from the research proposal through the viva and the immediate post-viva period. It provides practical guidance and support for some of the frequently encountered challenges in carrying out research, particularly at the doctoral level. Overall, it aims to help readers in giving their research a counselling psychology 'identity'.

PUTTING VALUES INTO ACTION

Most aspirant counselling psychologists are aware of the 'values' on which the profession is based: to include prioritisation of individuals' subjective and intersubjective experiencing; a focus on facilitating growth; an orientation towards empowering people; a commitment to democratic, non-hierarchical relationships; and an appreciation of individuals as unique (Orlans and van Scoyoc, 2008). These values chime with the humanistic principles on which this field is partially founded. However, trainees sometimes find it difficult to recall these values or to articulate how they are personally salient. 'If you ask a roomful of counselling psychology trainees what counselling psychology is or how it's distinctive,' a student once said to me, 'you can hear a pin drop.'

This pin-dropping silence may have something to do with a failure to consider how these values are made manifest. Counselling psychology, after all, is not merely a set of values. It is the *application-in-practice* of those values that moves them from the realm of abstract concepts into more meaningful and tangible realities (Cooper, 2009). *Clinical* practice, however, is not the only arena in which these values are set into motion, and counselling psychology values translate readily into the research context. Certainly, many a trainee counselling psychologist has justified investigating a certain topic or utilising a particular methodology by saying that these research choices are 'in line with counselling psychology values'. Unfortunately, all too often researchers make this statement in an automatic or tokenistic fashion, and leave it at that. The following sections consider how researchers can more *mindfully* and *meaning-fully* integrate a counselling psychology sensibility within their research. This starts at the beginning, when identifying a research question.

IDENTIFYING A RESEARCH QUESTION

In the United Kingdom, the postgraduate courses that lead to qualification as a counselling psychologist are exclusively professional or practitioner doctorates. In comparison to the traditional PhD, which has been with us since medieval times, professional doctorates are quite new, having arrived on UK shores in the 1990s and having since burgeoned in popularity across a variety of professions (Lee, 2008). Rather than having academics as its primary audience, the professional or practitioner doctorate aims to address real-world challenges and issues encountered by professionals in the field. It answers a need in the field by producing knowledge that practitioners can readily use. The Quality Assurance Agency, which sets out the benchmarks for higher education qualifications in the United Kingdom, describes how the research projects produced for this type of doctorate may often have very immediate implications for practice, perhaps directly engendering organisational and policy-related changes (Quality Assurance Agency, 2015). In short:

> The practitioner doctorate provides a way forward for developing the highest levels of university awards in a way that is both academically robust, and directly relevant to professional practitioners who are concerned with leading practice and initiating change rather than [solely] being researchers. (Lester, 2004: 10) (see www.professionaldoctorates.co.uk for more information)

Although the goal of producing practice-applicable research is central to the professional doctorate, the newly doctoral profession of counselling psychology is still catching up with this concept. A goodly proportion of the research questions investigated in this field, particularly at doctoral level, has been described as being focused on the personal preoccupations of individual researchers, or as involving counselling psychology trainees investigating various aspects of what it is like to be a counselling psychology trainee. Although the quote below refers to American practitioners, the warning applies to us in the UK and to the research we produce: 'The myopia induced by navel-gazing on the part of organized counseling psychology has had a pronounced negative effect on the growth and acceptance of the field' (Blocher, 2000: 143).

Why might some doctoral researchers fail to situate their projects within a practice context? Part of the explanation may involve pragmatic considerations. Faced with the task of completing a significant piece of research alongside the placement work, academic modules, supervision and personal development activities that are also required on a three- or four-year jam-packed training programme, some trainees avoid the additional ethical clearance that may be needed in practice contexts, such as the National Health Service (NHS), despite the fact that many have cleared this additional ethical hurdle successfully and within time (refer to the stories at the end of this chapter, as well as the Concluding Editorial). They may also steer clear of populations that might be trickier to obtain ethical approval to access, such as potentially vulnerable clients, instead choosing a research question that merely requires participants that are close to hand and likely to be uncontroversial to university ethics committees, for example other counselling psychology trainees, or participants from non-clinical populations. While investigations within these populations may yield knowledge of use to the field and to society, to exclude research within clinical settings is to avoid gathering the kinds of information that will be of most use to the majority of practitioners.

Another influential factor in some trainees' not investigating practice-applicable research questions is the above-described situation of the qualification threshold's only recently having been set at doctoral level. Trainee researchers may be aware of the need to demonstrate methodological skills, or to showcase their in-depth knowledge of a particular subject area (both of which are required of a degree at master's level), but may not realise the additional, higher remits of a doctoral qualification: to produce knowledge that is not only original but that is considered to be at the forefront of an area of professional practice (Quality Assurance Agency, 2011). Without this realisation, a trainee may feel at liberty to undertake a research project on a topic he or she fancies, failing to tie it to the needs of the profession. As the profession as a whole becomes ever more *au fait* and aligned with doctoral frameworks and expectations, however, examiners are likely to scrutinise candidates far more keenly on the contribution their research will make to the profession of counselling psychology.

While it is true that a strong integration of your research question with professional practice will considerably strengthen your chances of success at viva, there are other benefits. Many a trainee has faltered or lost enthusiasm for their research because they sense that answering their research question does not really matter, that other professionals are not interested in it, that it will not enhance practice significantly, and that in the end it is unlikely to do much beyond moldering on a shelf. When there is a clear interest in the field about a topic, on the other hand, the experience of research can be quite different, and far more vital and exciting. When delegates at conferences, reviewers for journals and colleagues in your practice settings are eager to hear your findings, it is easier to retain passion for and a sense of meaning in your research process. You may immediately see scope for translating your findings into practice, and so your research write-up may devote substantial space to this.

Box 14.1   Suggestions for determining and interrogating your research question

- Found your research in professional practice: Remember the remit of a *professional doctorate*. Are there gaps in service provision? Holes in your own and colleagues' knowledge or capabilities? Areas in which existing therapies, guidelines and service provisions seem to fall short? Remember too that 'professional practice' does not only mean 'psychotherapy' but can refer to any context or role that counselling psychologists assume: clinical work with diverse populations across a wide variety of settings, management/leadership, supervision, assessment, training, research, writing, policy development, social justice work and community intervention.
- Be original: Be thorough in determining that there is a need for your research and that it will meet the doctoral hallmark of originality. Ensure that it responds to a meaningful gap in the literature and does not merely represent a personal curiosity or preoccupation.

(Continued)

(Continued)

- Make a contribution: Actively pursue the question of whether your research is likely to make a perceived contribution, another hallmark of doctoral-level work. Before committing to a research question, 'road test' it with stakeholder practitioners in the field – those who have an interest in the particular area of professional practice you propose investigating. Are they excited by it? Are they eager to know the eventual results? Or do they seem unsure of the relevance of the research to their practice? Thinking forward to a time when your research is completed, do you imagine your results as enabling people to become better practitioners, to do better work and to become more effective counselling psychologists?
- Aim neither too low nor too high: Although you need and want to make a contribution, take care not to aim *so* high that your project becomes practicably impossible. A good mantra to live by is 'It's a [doctorate], not a Nobel Prize' (Mullins and Kiley, 2002: 369). Given the limited timeframe and resources likely to be available to you, an appropriately narrowly focused research question increases your chances of success. It also helps enormously with *thematising* (i.e. formulating of the purpose of the investigation and describing the concept of the topic to be investigated) and with arriving at a manageable design (Kvale, 2007). 'The client's experience of therapy choice in the context of Improving Access to Psychological Therapies (IAPT) services' is an infinitely more manageable question than one that is far too woolly and wide, like 'the experience of being in therapy'.
- Grow your research from the right ground: The ultimate research question is defined, refined and discovered through the process of critical engagement with the literature and perhaps the input of professionals in the field, as described above. If you have a strong commitment to asking and answering a particular question before you have fully, critically engaged with the literature, you may have an insufficiently examined personal agenda.

THINKING PLURALISTICALLY

Two of the counselling psychology values, listed above, were the prioritisation of individuals' subjective and intersubjective experiencing and an appreciation of individuals as unique (Orlans and van Scoyoc, 2008). These values have typically been translated into counselling psychology research in a very literal way. When asked about research interests, many applicants to counselling psychology training programmes espouse their loyalty to or interest in qualitative approaches, believing that this increases their chances of admission. Those approaches that emphasise subjective, idiosyncratic, individually situated experience, such as Interpretative Phenomenological Analysis (IPA), have become enshrined as virtually *de rigueur* for the counselling psychologist researcher. Given that the epistemological assumptions of such methodologies concord very well with the values named above, it is perhaps understandable that this has happened, and training programmes have tended to subtly or overtly encourage the choosing of qualitative methodologies. Additionally, when former doctoral candidates become research supervisors themselves, they tend to nudge supervisees towards those methodologies with which they are best acquainted, and thus the tradition continues.

It could be argued, however, that this equating of counselling psychology research with qualitative methodologies has hobbled the profession in myriad ways. First, it positions counselling psychologists – in their own minds and those of others – as 'one trick ponies' with restricted research abilities, potentially limiting employability and involvement in other types of research studies. Second, it limits the number of journals in which counselling psychologists publish, confining the research they produce to those publications friendly to qualitative methodologies and diminishing the influence and reach of their work. Third, given the hierarchies of evidence employed by bodies such as the National Institute for Health and Care Excellence (NICE), which place single qualitative studies towards the bottom of the barrel, it limits the contribution of counselling psychologists to the guidelines that govern mental health care in the United Kingdom. Fourth, it encourages a cart-before-horse, method-led approach to choosing research questions and designing projects, leading many a trainee to select their methodology before they determine a research question. The method-led approach also removes the incentive to develop a sophisticated understanding of how to select a methodology, for if the selection of IPA is a foregone conclusion, why work to deeply understand the reasons for one's choice? Finally, and interestingly, qualitative 'methodolatry' is not as consistent with 'counselling psychology values' and the humanistic roots of the field as some might imagine. Carl Rogers himself, one of the humanistic founding fathers of counselling psychology, was a clear advocate of methodological pluralism, emphasising the need for 'the method of testing to be appropriate to the hypothesis' and remarking that 'phenomenological methods are not the best tool of research, but simply one tool appropriate to some kinds of situations' (Rogers, in Kirschenbaum and Henderson, 1996: 274, 284–285).

A pluralistic attitude in the research context involves the recognition that 'divergent research methodologies can be equally valid in exploring important questions' (McAteer, 2010: 8). The recent increase of talk about methodological pluralism in our field (see, for example, Rafalin, 2010) could be viewed cynically, as a strategic move to make counselling psychologists more competitive in an era of evidence-based practice, where the most valued evidence is quantitative. It could be seen as making them more employable in the de-professionalised, competitive era of Improving Access to Psychological Therapies (IAPT). Less cynically, however, it can be viewed as representing the heart of the counselling psychology perspective.

The counselling psychologist recognises that there are many ways of conceptualising and approaching a client's difficulties; analogously, there are many ways of conceptualising a research question, many avenues to exploring a research topic, many ways of engaging with the literature and developing an argument, and many methods that may be useful. Being a counselling psychologist researcher can mean openness to all the paradoxes, divergences and different perspectives we may encounter in the empirical literature and in the methodologies we ourselves employ. This is the opposite of clinging to one method of investigation as a one-size-fits-all approach.

Box 14.2   Suggestions for thinking about methodology

- Do not reject methodologies out of hand: When critically reviewing the literature, resist the temptation to rubbish previous studies just because they were quantitative. Ask yourself what value each study brings and how it can inform practice, whatever the methodology. When considering the essential quality/trustworthiness of each research study, consider it based on the quality criteria *for that methodology*.
- Avoid putting the cart before the horse: First determine precisely what the object or focus of your inquiry is. Only then consider the ways in which this may be explored: the research question should point to the methodology, rather than the other way around. If the research question you identify is best answered by a quantitative or mixed methodology you have two alternatives: (1) stick with the question and go with the methodology that the question asks for; or (2) if you are just not willing to undertake the methodology suggested by the research question, choose another question. Whatever you do, however, do not blindly forge ahead with an unholy union of a quantitative-type research question with a qualitative methodology.
- Understand the underpinning frameworks for your research: In order to make the above decisions in a well-informed way, you need to understand epistemology, methodology and method. If you are unclear, read more (see, for example, Carter and Little, 2007) and discuss with your supervisors.
- Unhook methodology choice from personal preference: Your *personal* theoretical or epistemological stance need not prevent you from getting something useful from a piece of research that does not demonstrate that stance. A social constructionist may undertake a quantitative methodology or run a randomised controlled trial; however, he or she may present and contextualise the study and the findings differently than a positivist. One should never select a methodology based on personal preference *irrespective of the research question*.
- Question the need for purity: If you undertake a mixed methodological or 'multi-strategy' research design, you may worry about the philosophical or epistemological consistency between the various elements of your research project. Remember that it is possible to take a pragmatic approach without getting hung up on notions of epistemological purity, and that in fact there may be very good arguments for doing so in terms of the usefulness, applicability, and robustness of your research (see Robson, 2011).

CONSIDERING THE FULL RANGE OF VALUES-IN-ACTION

When one thinks deeply and creatively about counselling psychology values, it becomes apparent just how much they can apply to research. The section above challenged the notion that privileging individual experience means carrying out an IPA study. It is additionally important to note that in any case, the prioritisation of individuals' subjective and intersubjective experiencing would not be automatically achieved by choosing IPA. Any supervisor or examiner will have seen many leading interviews, clearly driven by the researcher's presuppositions and agenda.

A counselling psychologist cares about an individual's experience of research and the researcher, and is aware that this may affect the data. Attention to this is therefore required at every step of the process: the design of the interview schedule, the gaining of informed consent, the handling of the interview, the debriefing and (when relevant) in participant validation and/or the sharing of findings. Recognition of and care for your participants' subjective and intersubjective experience can be seen in write-ups of quantitative research as well, when you discuss ethics, the protection of participants, the concern for their experience, and generally the impact of aspects of the research process and the self of the researcher.

The counselling psychologist researcher, ever mindful of his or her subjectivity, responds to it by engaging in reflexive practices throughout the process (Etherington, 2004). Reflexive practices can take a number of forms:

- writing a reflexive statement, which identifies your positioning relative to the research question, considers how that positioning might affect the research, and plans for how you will manage your biases and foreunderstandings;
- keeping a reflexive research journal, to include entries made after each interaction with participants and each round of data collection;
- attending a reflexive research group, where you discuss your research with peers and receive feedback;
- including methodological reflexivity in the write-up, where you speak about how you interacted with participants at all stages of research and the impact this may have had;
- incorporating epistemological reflexivity in the write-up, in which you consider how your research design helped construct and frame the knowledge gained, and how different designs could have produced different knowledge.

The other values listed above can also be mindfully observed in research. For example, commitment to a democratic, non-hierarchical relationship (in so far as this is achievable) should be visible in informed consent, transparency about the research, and continued participant involvement through participant validation or sharing of findings. Within some methodologies, participants may even have the relatively non-hierarchical status of 'co-researchers' and are actively involved in shaping the design of the study and/or the analysis of results. Focus on facilitating growth, actualisation of potential, and empowering clients can all be related to application to practice, to our keeping in mind what the research is ultimately for. In the ideal case, we see our research as something that will ultimately make a positive difference in people's lives. These values can also be related to our participants' ideal experience of the research process, which has the potential to be empowering and facilitative of understanding and growth.

Appreciation of our participants' uniqueness also relates to applicability. If we interview eight individuals with a common experience, and the themes are consistent among all of them, we keep in mind that we cannot necessarily expect the same from a client that we meet who has also had that experience. If we are using a tightly controlled quantitative approach, with a high participant number and good power, and we have findings that achieved statistical significance, we still remember that we cannot automatically apply these findings to an individual client with that problem who is sitting in front of us.

As counselling psychologists, we remember that while all knowledge may be valuable, even more precious is the ability to bracket our presuppositions and foreunderstandings in order to hear the client. In writing about the practice-applicability of what we have found, therefore, we offer up our findings with a degree of tentativeness: '[T]here is no longer the illusion that we can gain certain knowledge. Instead, by a variety of means and methods, we can gain new knowledge and this new knowledge has a degree of truth value that depends on the methods and circumstances of the particular research study' (Rogers, in Kirschenbaum and Henderson, 1996: 284).

WRITING UP AND DEFENDING THE COUNSELLING PSYCHOLOGY DOCTORATE

After identifying and clearly conceptualising a professionally relevant question, arriving at an appropriate methodology, and carrying out the research in a manner consistent with counselling psychology values, one might consider the battle as good as won. The processes of writing up and viva examination are hurdles at which many trainees falter or fall, however. While this territory is well covered by the cross-disciplinary 'surviving your doctorate' genre (e.g. Lee, 2008; Matthiesen and Binder, 2009; and Trafford and Leshem, 2008), a more specific focus is also helpful. At the field level, doctoral candidates should consider how the counselling psychology context shapes the structure and content of the finished research product. At the institutional level, they should always follow the regulations and guidelines of their programme. In the suggestions below, both general and specific considerations are included.

Box 14.3   Suggestions for doctoral write-up and defence

- Demonstrate relational agency: On a professional doctorate, research vies for space and time with multiple other elements of training. Typically, a trainee on a professional doctorate receives far fewer hours of one-to-one supervision than a PhD candidate whose degree is more heavily focused on research. While a supervisor or supervisory team provides guidance, facilitation, and varying degrees of feedback, ultimately the onus is on the doctoral candidate to demonstrate a high degree of independent work, self-directed learning and autonomous marshalling of additional sources of support that lie beyond formal supervision – administrators, librarians, IT staff, peers, family, other academics, and so on.

One academic uses the phrase *relational agency* (Hopwood, 2010) to describe how a doctoral candidate should identify support sources and should proactively tap into whichever is the most important at a given phase of research. The candidate who expects their supervisor to be all things (therapist, parent, cheerleader, copy editor, administrator), and who needs scrutiny and approval of every paragraph, is not only failing to function at a doctoral level – he or she is almost certain to have difficulty moving forward with the work.

- Account for your decisions: The process of research can be thought of as a series of decisions, and your examiners want to ascertain that you have well-reasoned arguments for making the choices you did. Anticipate this by including clear accounts of the research decisions you undertook. For example, why did you take that research focus? Why did you employ those particular search terms? Why did you use this theoretical framework and not that one? Why was that methodology the best? Why did you discard that bit of the dataset?

- Sell the doctoralness of the work: Doctoral researchers are expected to critique their own research, which is part of demonstrating a 'detailed understanding of applicable techniques for research and advanced academic enquiry' (Quality Assurance Agency, 2011: 33). While researchers often write extensively about perceived weaknesses in the work, they may do little to highlight how the research hits the doctoral mark. Do not hide your light under a bushel! Rather than presenting results non-hierarchically, strongly highlight those aspects of the findings that are particularly novel and useful in the abstract, discussion and conclusion. Beyond this, being aware of the generic doctoral descriptors will orientate you to the broad criteria your examiners will be using.

- Explicitly consider counselling psychology competencies: The BPS lays out its expectations in its *Standards for the Accreditation of Doctoral Programmes in Counselling Psychology*. That document outlines the specific learning outcomes that any graduate of a doctoral counselling psychology programme should meet, including ten outcomes to do with 'Research and Inquiry' (BPS, 2014: 22–23). In your doctoral research submission, attempt to clearly demonstrate your achievement of these.

- Include reflexivity: One of the learning outcomes in the above document is 'develop[ing] the ability to reflect … on [the] experience of being a researcher' (British Psychological Society, 2012: 16). A high degree of reflexivity – personal, methodological and epistemological – is usually expected of counselling psychologist researchers. Although personal reflexivity in particular may not form part of research reports in other disciplines, omitting it in a counselling psychology thesis will often invite examiner inquiry and a requirement for it be incorporated into an amended submission.

- Know what to expect in the viva examination: General references on handling your viva are important (e.g. Ryder, 2013), but it will be additionally helpful to consult discipline-specific guidance. The BPS pamphlet *Guidelines for Assessment of the PhD in Psychology and Related Disciplines* (2008) provides a general outline of best-practice psychology viva procedures within UK universities. These guidelines are primarily aimed at doctoral examiners but, used in conjunction with information from the individual institution, these guidelines will also help the viva candidate orientate to and understand viva processes and procedures.

DISSEMINATING DOCTORAL KNOWLEDGE

As previously noted, counselling psychology is an applied discipline, and its practitioners are particularly interested in creating and consuming research that is relevant to some area of professional practice. Because they are often juggling multiple roles, it is essential that published research findings be both accessible to their target audience and presented in a clear and compelling way that will help a busy professional to easily absorb the research's results and implications. When a significant proportion of a published research article is devoted to how the research findings might inform practice, the usefulness and 'absorbability' of the research is greatly enhanced, and it stands a better chance of making a real impact.

You will remember from the beginning of this chapter that one of the QAA's (2015) criteria for doctoral-level research is that it makes a contribution to an area of professional practice. Obviously, professional practice will hardly be influenced if your doctoral research is not disseminated, and you will essentially have failed to fulfil the doctoral remit. When considering how your research results can best be made accessible, you may immediately think of publication within professional journals, but there are many other ways for research results to be heard and to make a difference.

Box 14.4   Suggestions for disseminating your doctoral research

- Break it down: While ethical publishing behaviour dictates that you not submit the same research to multiple journals simultaneously, remember that a large doctoral thesis may yield more than one research article. While adaptations to the writing will always be required to translate a thesis to a journal article, it remains true that journal articles may be 5,000 to 7,000 words, while doctoral theses range from 25,000 to 60,000 words. For example, a substantial, innovatively designed mixed-methods study could conceivably yield one article based on the literature review; one article about the exciting methodology used; one article devoted to the quantitative data; one article focusing on a subset of the themes from the qualitative portion; and one article focusing on another subset.
- Communicate your research within the field: If your doctoral thesis is strongly situated within a counselling psychology framework and has relevance to the field, which it should, it is likely that you will want to disseminate it in those forums that counselling psychologists are most likely to access. Dare to think beyond the United Kingdom when farming out your articles! *Counselling Psychology Review* is currently the primary journal in the UK, but you should also consider the *Counselling Psychology Quarterly*, which is an international journal; *The Counseling Psychologist*, which is associated with Division 17 of the American Psychological Association (APA); the APA's additional journal *The Journal of*

Counseling Psychology; and *The Australian Journal of Counselling Psychology*. (See Chapter 32 for a deeper discussion and more information on publishing your work.)

- Extend the reach: Although your doctoral research should be relevant to counselling psychologists, it should by no means be relevant to *just* them. If a wider range of allied professionals can benefit from your work, so much the better. To that end, consider publishing in journals that are not explicitly within the field but that have an interest in research that impacts professional practice, such as *Journal of Psychotherapy Practice and Research*.
- Contribute to therapeutic knowledge: While the professional practice of counselling psychologists is not limited to the therapeutic consulting room, your doctoral thesis may very well arise from and be relevant to this context. Remember those academic and professional practice journals that are geared towards particular kinds of therapies or populations.
- Trumpet your methodology: As highlighted above, your research may be interesting on methodological grounds, and methodologies evolve alongside the shifting needs and paradigms of the social and health sciences. Remember that there are many journals dedicated to methodology.
- Conference your work: There is no need to wait for viva or qualification to present your work at conferences. Some conferences will even accept work in progress, either as a poster or as an individual paper. If your research is linked in some way with the works of others (because you are all from one training programme, or because the content areas or methodologies are linked), consider submitting an abstract for a symposium instead of for an individual paper. Be aware of and take advantage of any postgraduate bursaries that may be available from the conference you are attending; your university: the Postdoctoral Conference Bursary Scheme and the International Conference Symposium Scheme (both funded by the Research Board of the British Psychological Society); or the Division of Counselling Psychology.
- Network towards collaboration: At the conferences you attend, take full advantage of the opportunity for networking, particularly if you plan to do more research post-qualification. Once the doctorate is finished, researching can be a lonely business, and collaboration with others can be a powerful factor in keeping you going (see Chapter 38).
- Go public: You may have opportunities to disseminate your research findings to the popular media, via radio, print, television and the internet. Sometimes this comes about because you are presenting at a conference and your abstract is perceived, perhaps by the press officer for the conference, to have potential interest for the masses. Your university's press office or the British Psychological Society's press centre may also play a role in connecting you with a journalist from the popular media. Speaking to the public about your work can be tremendously exciting; when you are good at it and do it on a frequent basis, you may assume the role of a 'public intellectual' – someone who translates your academic knowledge for the lay public and relates developments in your discipline to the wider social, political and/or cultural world. The receptivity of that non-academic world is an indication that your research is of interest and use beyond the consulting room. Be aware, however, of the pitfalls in extending your research findings beyond the academic context (see Atcheson, 2010).

(Continued)

> *(Continued)*
>
> - Use your thesis as the basis for a book proposal: It is entirely possible to parlay the expertise you have developed during your doctorate into the beginnings of a book. Guidance for submitting book proposals is on most academic publishers' websites, and it is also useful to consult someone who has experience. On a smaller scale, if you are doing a good job of networking and getting your work published in journals, you may be approached about contributing a chapter to an edited book. If you possess editorial talents yourself, and would consider putting together a book yourself, approach other practitioners who have written and researched in your subject area.
> - Inhabit the blogosphere: Research blogs are increasingly popular and while they can be a good way of disseminating your research findings or other material related to your research and practice interests, they can also enhance your profile as an expert in a particular area, increasing your visibility, employability and influence.
> - Develop trainings: As noted elsewhere in this chapter, research for a professional doctorate makes a contribution to professional practice. Writing is not the only way to reach your intended audience. Your doctorate can form the basis for seminars, workshops and/or training sessions. Other practitioners in your workplace could be your first audience. Many conferences like to incorporate in-conference workshops. The BPS's training and development portal, the Learning Centre, welcomes proposals for trainings.
> - Guide policy development: With initiative you may find yourself advising organisations and other professionals. Inform the Consultations Response Team at the BPS, which collates responses to consultation documents from governmental and non-governmental organisations, about your particular areas of expertise.

FINAL THOUGHTS AND A CASE EXAMPLE

This chapter closes with the account of one recently qualified counselling psychologist's doctoral research journey. His story chimes well with the themes of this chapter, and it makes clear that while mistakes and hurdles are all part of learning to become a researcher, knowledge is power, and forewarned is forearmed. It is hoped that this chapter has offered both some useful knowledge, and some salutary warnings.

What I learned from my doctoral research experience

Dr Brian Sreenan

The research question for my doctoral thesis emerged from my placement in an Improving Access to Psychological Therapies (IAPT) service. I was fascinated with the emphasis on disorders, 'caseness', throughput and statistics, and noticed that the relational aspect of therapy seemed under-emphasised in that setting. I was eager to approximate some of the pre-existing quantitative research about the therapeutic relationship, to see if the IAPT setting was different; I also wanted to explore the lived experience of IAPT. I thought mixed methods would fit well with the question and with counselling psychology's emphasis on pluralism.

My research questions, though, were not very clear when I started collecting data. I realised that the term 'therapeutic relationship' is pretty all-encompassing. My project would have been more focused if I had worked this out from the start, but I had to refine my research question after the project was already in process, focusing it on the therapeutic alliance in particular.

Looking back, picking an area that had a tighter definition (e.g. alliance) rather than a broad topic (e.g. relationship) would have helped a lot, but there is more that I wish I had done at the start. First, if I had discussed the topic more with my research supervisor, or my peer group, I might have realised how diffuse the area was. Second, replicating research that was in top journals might have been a little too ambitious for a two-year research project. Third, I could have sought more help with NHS ethics procedures. I felt like it was all totally up to me, but by consulting more with various others I could have identified problems and adjusted the focus and scope of the project.

Aside from the research focus, the methodology was an issue for me. It was like getting on a boat that was one degree off course at the start of the journey, and as time went on I was getting into unfamiliar waters. I hadn't thought enough about how the components of the mixed-methods project should inter-relate. The last two months of the project was about survival and battling through rough seas. Because there were issues with conceptualisation from the start, it was like navigating with a faulty sextant or compass. Luckily, I had enough data to analyse. If I hadn't, I would have had to start over.

When writing up and preparing for examination, I also realised that I had not been very aware of the doctoral criteria when setting off. The main message that had been given to us was that the research needed to make an original contribution, be this by subject, methodology or population sampled. Both my examiners were counselling psychologists. There were multiple questions about how the research added to the counselling psychology knowledge base specifically and how my identity as a counselling psychologist impacted on the choice of methodology. My examiners also asked me about pluralism and counselling psychology. Although I was aware that counselling psychology would be a topic of conversation throughout the viva, the extent that it was woven in throughout was a surprise.

I was successful at my viva, but it was a hard road getting there, and there is a lot that I learned from the process. The first tip is that mixed-methods research isn't like doing two smaller projects combined into one! It is two sets of analyses, results and discussions, but most of all it involves integrating two very different methods of research to address the same question. Although I would encourage people to do mixed-methods research, make sure you get extra support if you need it.

(Continued)

(Continued)

The rest of the tips I have apply whether or not you are doing mixed methods. Keep doctoral standards in mind at all times. Defining your question clearly before starting helps massively! If you are applying for NHS ethics, make sure to include every possible question you might ask in an interview – limiting this may limit your project and your ability to collect relevant information. Always base your method on your research question, not the other way around. Think about your sample and about how easy it will be to collect participants. And finally, you *can* get your research finished in the allocated time!

Visit the companion website for the following:

- Engaging in Research, with a doctoral student.
- Carrying out Research and Top Tips, with a doctoral candidate.
- A conversation with recently qualified counselling psychologists.

REFERENCES

Atcheson, Lucy (2010) 'Counselling psychology and the media: The highs and lows', in Martin Milton (ed.), *Therapy and Beyond: Counselling Psychology Contributions to Therapeutic and Social Issues*. London: Wiley. pp. 277–291.

Blocher, Donald (2000) *The Evolution of Counseling Psychology*. New York: Springer.

British Psychological Society (2008) *Guidelines for Assessment of the PhD in Psychology and Related Disciplines*. Leicester: BPS, www.bps.org.uk/sites/default/files/images/inf12_phd_web.pdf (accessed 21 September 2015).

British Psychological Society (2014) *Standards for the Accreditation of Doctoral Programmes in Counselling Psychology*. Leicester: BPS. Available at www.bps.org.uk/system/files/Public%20files/PaCT/counselling_accreditation_2014_web.pdf (accessed 21 September 2015).

Carter, S.M. and Little, M. (2007) 'Justifying knowledge, justifying method, taking action: Epistemologies, methodologies and methods in qualitative research', *Qualitative Health Research*, 17(10): 1316–1328.

Cooper, Mick (2009) 'Welcoming the other: Actualising the humanistic ethic at the core of counselling psychology practice', *Counselling Psychology Review*, 24(3/4): 119–129.

Etherington, Kim (2004) *Becoming a Reflexive Researcher: Using Our Selves in Research*. New York: Jessica Kingsley Publishers.

Hopwood, Nick (2010) 'A sociocultural view of doctoral students' relationships and agency', *Studies in Continuing Education*, 32(2): 103–117.

Kasket, Elaine (2012) 'The counselling psychologist researcher', *Counselling Psychology Review*, 27(2): 64–73.

Kirschenbaum, H. and Henderson, V.L. (eds) (1996) *The Carl Rogers Reader*. Boston, MA: Robinson Publishing.

Kvale, Steiner (2007) *Doing Interviews*. London: Sage.

Lee, Nancy J. (2008) *Achieving your Professional Doctorate*. Milton Keynes: Open University Press.

Lester, Stan (2004) 'Conceptualising the practitioner doctorate', *Studies in Higher Education*, 29(5): 1–10 (www.sld.demon.co.uk/pracdocs.pdf).

Matthiesen, J. and Binder, M. (2009) *How to Survive your Doctorate*. Milton Keynes: Open University Press.

McAteer, Donal (2010) 'Philosophical pluralism: Navigating the sea of diversity in psycho-therapeutic and counselling psychology practice', in Martin Milton (ed.), *Therapy and Beyond: Counselling Psychology Contributions to Therapeutic and Social Issues*. London: Wiley. pp. 5–19.

Mullins, G. and Kiley, M. (2002) "It's a PhD, not a Nobel Prize': How experienced examiners assess research theses', *Studies in Higher Education*, 27(4): 369–386.

Orlans, Vanja and van Scoyoc, Susan (2008) *A Short Introduction to Counselling Psychology*. London: Sage.

Quality Assurance Agency (2015) *Characteristics Statement: Doctoral Degree*. London: QAA. Available at www.qaa.ac.uk/en/Publications/Documents/Doctoral-Degree-Characteristics-15.pdf (accessed 21 September 2015).

Rafalin, Deborah (2010) 'Counselling psychology and research: Revisiting the relationship in the light of our "mission"', in Martin Milton (ed.), *Therapy and Beyond: Counselling Psychology Contributions to Therapeutic and Social Issues*. London: Wiley. pp. 41–55.

Robson, Colin (2011) *Real World Research* (3rd edn). London: John Wiley & Sons.

Ryder, Nathan (2013) *Fail your Viva: Twelve Steps to Failing Your PhD (and Fifty-Eight Tips for Passing)* (eBook). Available at www.nathanryder.co.uk/fail-your-viva/ (accessed 23 October 2015).

Trafford, Vernon and Leshem, Shosh (2008) *Stepping Stones to Achieving Your Doctorate: By Focusing on Your Viva from the Start*. Milton Keynes: Open University Press.

15
TOWARDS ETHICAL MATURITY IN COUNSELLING PSYCHOLOGY
ELISABETH SHAW AND MICHAEL CARROLL

Maturity is not just longevity but, in the context of ethics, suggests a quality of judgment akin to wisdom … maturity suggests a quality of engagement in how we respond to the challenges of professional life. (Bond, 2013: 9–10)

INTRODUCTION

Terri has just completed her training in counselling psychology. Her first job is as one of two counselling psychologists in a large and busy GP practice, a job she shares with Mick, a much older counselling psychologist who has worked there for two years. She is greeted by Mick and the practice doctors who are enthusiastic about her arrival; she also meets and has talks with the practice nurse, the general manager and the administrative staff. Her first few days are both exciting and confusing. She had undertaken advanced studies in psychometric testing during her training – she wonders how well such training might work in this GP setting. After three days she sees no way of using her psychometric expertise for the clients she has just seen, and Mick is rather dismissive of her even trying. She also wonders about the value of short-term versus long-term counselling provision. Her initial experience is that some of her patients need long-term therapy but will have to settle for the agreed six sessions (there is already a waiting list). She was surprised to learn that the administrative staff know a lot about the patients' material that she thought would have been confidential to the doctors. The receptionist said she would be happy to type up Terri's notes, as she did for one of the doctors who was too busy to do them herself. In her first few days she saw a number of older people whom she felt needed social support and friends rather than counselling – they just loved having someone to talk to and their initial sessions with Terri were more social chat than dealing with personal issues in their lives. One patient has already asked her if Terri could see her privately when she finished her allocated six sessions (she would pay for extra sessions).

Effective counselling psychology practice requires us to be:

1. Therapeutically, clinically and emotionally competent as well as
2. Capable in areas of professional practice: the latter being the ethical, legal and administrative aspects of our work.

Complex as the above example is, it is only the beginning of a range of ethical, legal and practice issues Terri will encounter over the course of her career. Terri is experiencing what Schön (1983) described as the difference between the lofty highlands of theory and the swampy lowlands of practice. She is caught in a no-man's land between the two. She is bogged down in the swampy lowlands in experiencing daily dilemmas, problems and issues, and realising that the lofty highlands of theory she had learned on her course are not particularly helpful at the moment. How can Terri prepare herself to respond well to such myriad issues?

The increasing involvement of government and third parties into what was once perceived to be a more 'private' arrangement between counselling psychologist and client/s has added relational and contractual complexity to counselling psychology. Community and professional standards are such that counselling psychologists can struggle to attend to what appear to be competing calls on their time: clients, administration and professional development, at the same time as attending to self-care and home–work balance. Our education and ongoing professional development understandably focuses strongly on the clinical competencies, those reflecting the core interests of the clinician: the art of the work. We also have our codes to hand as helpful guides to some of the determined 'rules' of practice. However, not only do the situations we face seem to be an incomplete fit with our guides, increasingly counselling psychologists are facing situations of relational complexity that seem to warrant higher-order decision making, that demand more from us in terms of knowledge, practice wisdom and emotional intelligence. Today there are complex issues of *diversity* (how do we work with clients who are racially, culturally, sexually different?), *technology* (when do we text and receive texts from clients? How might we use social media in the delivery of services? How to make use of the internet or Skype in counselling psychology provisions?), *service provision* (how do we balance the need to cut essential services to save costs and still provide the service needed by clients?) and using *evidence-based practice* (how do we build a bridge between evidence from research and the application of that evidence to individual need?) Questions such as the following continually arise:

- Am I getting it right?
- Am I making competent ethical decisions?
- How do I balance the needs of the community and the wider systems with the needs of individual clients?

It is so easy in the light of this to over rely on ethical codes or frameworks (which are often insufficient) or outsource our ethical responsibilities to others, such as our supervisors, asking them to make our decisions for us. However, in the example of Terri, most of her concerns are not explicitly listed in professional codes of practice. They require more nuanced clinical judgement and immediate decision making. How can she do this well? How can she know she has done this well?

There can be a belief that counselling psychologist = ethical practitioner. Yet we know from reviewing the complaints made against psychologists that this is a dangerous and defensive assumption to make. It would be equally erroneous to assume that it is the most junior of the profession that transgress; in fact, senior people can also be at risk (e.g. Grenyer and Lewis, 2012). Research also tells us that while we might like to believe that we practice what we preach, therapists can be no better at self-care than anyone else (Adams, 2014; Norcross and Guy, 2007). Finally, Dunning (2005) points out how poor we are as self-psychologists: others often know us better than we know ourselves. This all means that we cannot fool ourselves that we will be clear and robust in our response to ethical decision making just because we are well trained psychologists.

MORAL ALERTNESS

Our reactions to ethical situations vary, depending on our upbringing, life experience and opportunities to consciously develop moral identity. What is a moral 'red alert' to one person may barely resonate with another. This does not automatically mean one is right and one is wrong. It instead requires us to listen to our own disquiet about issues *and* be continually curious about the reactions of others: what can their experience teach us?

Using rules, principles and duties to guide us will always be a valuable part of ethical decision making. However, in this chapter we make the challenge to extend our ethical considerations beyond a straightforward problem-solving method of ethical decision making to consider an ethics of relationship and caring. We propose that ethical maturity in professional practice involves engagement in a journey with ethics rather than a focus on destinational ethics; this journey extends throughout our lifetime. *We will move from an ethics of duty and obligation to an ethics of empathy, compassion and caring within the context of relational fidelity.* Further, we will look at how counselling psychologists not only learn the *skills* of ethical relationship practice, but can increase the emotional competence and empathic attunement required to do this with authenticity.

We ask three questions:

- What is ethical maturity within the field of counselling psychology?
- How can we develop the personal skills, attributes and characteristics of an ethical practitioner, and in particular foster greater readiness and capacity to approach ethical problems? How is this sustained over the course of a career?
- How can we educate ourselves and others to make ethically mature decisions as counselling psychologists?

Ethical maturity is not a given that once achieved remains for ever. What has been hard-won over time can be lost in a moment; we also know that context can so easily overpower character (see Carroll and Shaw, 2013: Chapter 2). Beyond the professional resources available to us, we will look at how to develop ethical practice through self-knowledge, reflection, learning from mistakes and relational connectedness in the service of developing professional wisdom. Our philosophy of ethics is that there is usually no one 'right answer' to the ethical questions we face but that we have to look at a number of factors: intention, context, behaviour, relationships, responsibilities, and most of all what is best for the welfare and good of our clients. At times one or other of these factors moves into the foreground and becomes the main player in making an ethical decision; at other times that factor fades into the background and another consideration becomes more important in influencing the ethical outcome. Moving towards ethical maturity as a counselling psychologist is a constant challenge in 'finding your way' as a professional, in being flexible and being able to fill the gap between theory and practice (Schön, 1983).

THE PROBLEMS WITH ETHICAL PROBLEMS

1 Mind over matter

Terri joined an existing peer supervision group with three other counselling psychologists who worked in GP surgeries, one of whom was Mick. All were more senior to her and had lots of experience. One day, during her lunch break, Terri saw Mick at a café having coffee with a client. She asked him about it later and he told her he always went out for coffee with clients when they finished work to 'equalise' the relationship and acknowledge the growth that had occurred. Terri accepted the decision but was not entirely comfortable with it. About a month later Terri saw a female client go into Mick's counselling room brandishing a bottle of expensive champagne saying, 'our last session so I thought we'd have a toast!' She heard Mick say, 'I'll get the glasses!' She went to one of the other members of their peer supervision group to discuss her concerns, and was told, 'Mick is pretty out there. But I am sure he knows what he's doing. He has one of the best evaluation rates in the service and is very experienced. I wouldn't bother mentioning it.' Terri is now not sure what to do. It doesn't feel like she has endorsement to bring it to the group. Do more senior people know better than herself? Is she making a mountain out of a molehill?

One way we learn about ethics is to test ourselves against vignettes: what should I do in this situation? This common approach in educating ourselves to the nuances of ethical dilemmas is frequently used in professional training in counselling psychology, and makes a lot of sense. It is, after all, easier to see the problems in others' behaviour than our own. Sharing therapy stories, whether it be via case studies or among peers, can be valuable in rehearsing what we might do ourselves were we to encounter something similar. However, this approach has limitations in that it inadvertently reinforces the pervasive notion that in order to make good ethical decisions we must be rational, emotionless and objective. It reflects the dominant philosophical traditions of much of the last two centuries and has been described well by Hinman (2013: 283):

> The starting point of moral modern theory ... is the isolated individual, separate from everyone else and seemingly independent. ... It is, essentially, an ethics of strangers – that is, a set of rules for governing the interactions of people who neither know nor care about one another.

The more formal name given to this approach is 'Quandary Ethics' (Appiah, 2008), which typifies how we try to resolve and make decisions about situations from the lives of others, or situations thought up beforehand. Lawrence Kohlberg (1982) used this approach in his seminal research on moral development.

While this approach helps to sensitise people to ethical issues and to play with possible resolutions, the concern is that we can begin to see ethics as simply the resolution of a problem. Problems are 'out-there' issues about which we can be dispassionate and rational. The people involved are not known to us, do not have a relationship with us, and so we have to deal with what Appiah (2008) calls the 'umpire fantasy' – that we are judges searching for the right answer. 'To turn to them for guidance in the arena of ethics', writes Appiah, 'is like trying to find your way around at night with a laser pointer' (2008: 194). Certainly, psychological and emotional objectivity and distance from a problem can be useful in making good decisions. That is why discussing issues with supervisors or colleagues can help us stand back and consider elements outside our awareness. Of course, turning to others, as Terri did above, does not always guarantee that ethical decision making occurs. We might also tap into others' blind spots or receive incorrect or confusing information.

At the other end of the spectrum, unethical behaviour emerges when we move from trying to distance ourselves from the subjective elements (do I know these people?) to these people are not only not-known by me, but are not human like me (Seabright and Schminke, 2002). Robbed of humanity, objectified others become easily dismissed or invalidated. Ethical decision making is then only a set of *problems* to be resolved rather than *relationships* to be considered. Typically, this process might follow the following format:

1. What is the problem? Clarify it; ensure you are clear about what the real problem is.
2. Look at the options you have. Get them all out on the table.
3. Evaluate these options one by one (you can look at the needs and responsibilities of various stakeholders if you want to at this stage, as well as codes, frameworks, etc.).
4. Choose the best one for the situation.
5. Implement it.

This dispassionate approach to ethical problem solving is out of step with the reality of life, where much more is going on than can be rationally analysed. What research tells us is that most often, qualified psychologists know the right outcome according to relevant codes, but may not implement their decision due to other considerations, such as their emotional reaction (is my level of emotion telling me I am being irrational?) or their relationships (how do I face a colleague I have reported for misconduct?) (e.g. Betan and Stanton, 1999; Smith, McGuire, Abbott and Blau, 1991). In the case of Terri, there are facts, circumstances and relationships to consider in her decision making, which ultimately might affect the decision she makes.

2 Debriefing to death

Good ethical decision making is inherently practical in nature and results in action (even if the action chosen is deliberate non-action!). Often practitioners realise there is an ethical problem, and 'debrief' with colleagues or in supervision. Debriefing is highly valued in our profession, with good reason. A good debriefing can make us feel 'better'; we have shared the problem and been validated for our concerns. However, this is not ethical decision making and it does not resolve the ethical problem at hand. Ultimately, if nothing else happens, debriefing might have simply distracted from and diffused the problem. Even if the debriefing does involve a more structured approach to organising the experience, Kohlberg himself made the point that moral reasoning does not equate to moral action. Moral action requires another level of commitment on our parts. If, as Peter Singer (2000) argues, we are responsible for what we can prevent as well as responsible for what we do, then there is an imperative to act when we see the potential for unethical practice as well as addressing it when it does occur. Debriefing can sometimes be part of establishing readiness to act, and sometimes it takes the issue off the boil altogether (Heubner et al., 2008).

3 Caught on the hop: fast and slow ethical decision making

Every day we make a number of ethical decisions: mostly we make them automatically without thinking about them. Roy Disney, nephew of the famous Walt Disney, puts it succinctly: 'It's not hard to make decisions when you know what your values are' (in Eliot, 2007). We stay within the speed limit even when there are no speed cameras to catch us; we fulfil duties at work even when our boss isn't around; we don't keep our clients or supervisees longer than needed in counselling or supervision because we need the money to pay the mortgage. Unthinkingly, we just do these things – they emerge from the well-embedded values that are part of who we are. Most of the actions above, along with the multiple other ethical ones that feature in your day and ours, come to mind and into action without much deliberation.

Automatic ethical actions occur when we are in familiar territory. In new situations, where memory is not a good guide, we have to be more considered, thoughtful and deliberate (Kahneman, 2011). Now, we have to think about what we do. Novel situations have a way of alerting us to possible dangers and with those dangers we often move from an inner guide to reliance on outer support. Ethical maturity quickly dissolves when fear enters the practice room. This fear can be based on our own ignorance, our biases, a sense of helplessness, or perhaps feeling trapped in some way with seemingly limited options. When the stakes are high, such as when we feel great empathy for a client, where they seem more vulnerable or at risk, when powerful and influential colleagues pressure us, or where we believe in the moment that our future as a professional could be compromised, anxiety can come to dominate.

Terri has been seeing Jody, who is suffering from depression. Jody was raised as a Jehovah's Witness. Still new to her role in the GP practice, Terri has little experience of religious issues and religion has played a very limited role in her own life. Jody has come to discuss the realisation that she is lesbian, and says that this will have huge ramifications within her family and community. For example, she expects to be excommunicated. Terri is wondering how to best assist her. She takes Jody to her peer supervisor group and looks in particular to Frank for some insights. Frank is openly gay and strongly anti-religion. Terri explores the tightrope she sees Jody walking and how to manage her own reactions to parents who would reject their child over being lesbian. Frank is incensed about the situation and strongly encourages Terri to work with Jody on a more political level, linking her in to gay and lesbian groups, helping her to start to critique her religion and become an advocate for religious tolerance. Frank has many years' experience as a counselling psychologist, but Terri is not sure whose interests this strategy would serve.

When faced with an ethically complex situation most individuals quickly seek out safety. *What is the safe thing to do in this instance?* Terri could do what she is told by Frank or she could also ask Frank to take over the case. Both options avert the crisis. However, these decisions could also be seen to be made from fear or insecurity. What if fear had been banished and instead of being anxious about what might happen, Terri continued to put the welfare of her client at the centre of her decision? This decision would lead Terri to stay closely aligned to her client's goals; in the end this may involve the client's own decision to take this up at a political level (or it may not). However, more is in view now, and more is at stake. Terri also has to look at her relationship with Frank and how her decision might impact that relationship. *Safe decisions* can seem better because they often reflect black and white thinking: follow the client or follow Frank – that is the only thing to be considered. They might also limit the problem to something that feels more manageable, but which might exclude important contextual issues that are crucial to good decision making, and this may result in additional ethical issues, such as poorer service delivery. With an *ethically mature decision* Terri analyses the situation from a number of angles. This can be more complex initially. However, in the end Terri will have worked her way through many of the fundamental issues in counselling psychology in relation to clients, management of self, working effectively with colleagues, management of power, and so the list goes on. If Terri had run with her 'safe decision', how might she have felt with time and distance? Would the justification 'Frank made me do it' stack up over time, or would Terri be left with the strong feeling that she had made a safe decision but knew it was not the best ethical decision for her client? Complexity can occur before and after a decision is made and implemented.

4 Multiple imperatives and stakeholders

Counselling psychology is about relationships: with our client/s, within organisations, with the social, cultural and political worlds we inhabit. There is ethical complexity within each layer of the relationship. For example, between the counselling psychologist and client we have considerations around competency, about negotiation of treatment, informed consent, what constitutes an appropriate challenge to move the work along, what level of self-disclosure is appropriate, and the need to define the boundaries of the relationship.

Then there is the relationship between the counselling psychologist and their context. What does the organisation or service situation demand of the practitioner? What service is reasonable in that context? What is allowed (e.g. model of service, short-term or long-term work)? How will other requirements (e.g. supervision, administration, data entry) be managed in the schedule? What voice will the practitioner have to influence the system or to advocate for the client?

The counselling psychologist may also be involved in other relationships involving the client, for example in dealing with their interpreter, lawyer or another treating practitioner. By providing a report to court, attending to subpoenas, intervening with the school, work or other social/service system, we are always working with matters of ethics, legalities and the need for clinical judgement.

When we assess and attempt to resolve ethical dilemmas, we take into account the web of relationships in which we, our clients and our organisations live. We assess whether the problem is even ours to resolve, or whether we feel the issue we face sits somewhere else in the system: with the client, the organisation and/or society. Consider how relationships and systems influence the following scenarios.

Scenario 1: Under a particular mental health programme, doctors must do a comprehensive mental health assessment before referring on to a psychologist. The psychologist must have documentation from the doctor on file in order to provide the service. If audited, the psychologist would be in breach of the service agreement should the required paperwork be missing.

Terri receives referrals from the doctors in the GP practice where she works. However, she often receives paperwork with little on it except the name of the client; certainly no evidence of an assessment. A few times the doctors have put their heads around her door and said, 'I am going to do an assessment next week, but could you see the client in advance and date

(Continued)

(Continued)

the invoice to line up with the paperwork so the client is not out of pocket? She is really financially strapped.' Last week a new client arrived for a session with the paperwork again not sufficiently completed, but on this occasion the client said, 'I didn't actually see the doctor. He just posted me the paperwork after a chat on the phone.'

Scenario 2: Terri works from a 'strengths-based' position and is strongly influenced by Humanist counselling traditions. She has just started working with a client – Peter – who attended after an injury at work, and who will be lodging a claim for compensation. She sees that Peter has taken great strides in his recovery in terms of managing pain and increasing emotional resilience, although it is unlikely that he will work in his previous role again. The employer's insurer has written asking for a report that requires Terri's diagnosis and prognosis. She is unsure how to marry up her approach with a medical model, and how to assess Peter in relation to permanent loss and injury when she spends every session looking at increasing capacity and growth. If her prognosis is 'negative', will Peter be devastated and give up? However, will he also get more compensation? If she records his achievements, will that disadvantage him?

In each of these situations there are implications for relationships: the client's relationships, the client–therapist relationships, and the client and therapist and their wider systems and networks. Counselling psychology requires us to be systems thinkers.

WHAT IF WE INCLUDED RELATIONSHIPS IN ETHICS?

While our philosophical forefathers might focus on singular, rational man (and yes, this has been gendered work over hundreds of years), by this point in the chapter and after reading each of the Terri vignettes, perhaps a better question here might be: 'How do we include relationships in ethics?'

Inevitably, ethical decisions in counselling psychology will have a relational dimension. It is precisely because we are in relationship with individuals, groups and organisations that we think and act the way we do. Horrible human crimes happen because we move 'out of relationship' and see individuals and groups as different from ourselves or as objects or even enemies. The following example illustrates this:

I finished him off in a rush, not thinking anything of it, even though he was a neighbour, quite close on my hill. In truth it came to me only afterwards: I had taken the life of a neighbour. I mean, at the fatal instance I did not see in him what he had been before. (Kassimeris, 2006, from an interview with a participant in the Rwandan genocide who killed a Tutsi neighbour)

Relationships are at the heart of ethics and yet so often it's the very thing that is overlooked when we make ethical decisions in our lives. Get out of relationship and we are then reduced to an over-reliance on codes and frameworks for guidance because our internal relational compasses get blocked or are not to be trusted. We agree with Critchley (2010: 1), who writes:

> 'Relational' in this context means acknowledging the inherently mutual nature of all social processes, and therefore prioritising the importance of the co-created, 'here and now' relationship as the central vehicle for development and transformation *and ethical decision making*. (with our addendum emphasised in italic)

It is possible that if you know already what you are going to do in a relationship, then you are not dealing with the here and now, co-created, mutual situation before you. There are 'ethical fundamentalists' who have an answer for every conceivable ethical issue in advance of it happening. Our sense is that this is a bit like instruction books that come with washing machines or computers – anticipating and having an answer for future problems or situations. People are not machines and yet it is easy to read our ethical codes and ethical frameworks as instructional manuals of how to behave ethically as if people and situations can be reduced to a set of procedures and protocols. For example, adopting an ethical principle such as 'never touch a client' to every counselling psychology relationship irrespective of person or context may contravene the here-and-now relationship, which asks for some therapeutic contact. Not touching this client may in fact be unethical if the here and now, mutually, co-created relationship honestly calls for 'touch'. A code of 'dos' and 'don'ts', except for some non-negotiables, such as sexual contact, can easily move our clients into objects rather than flesh-and-blood individuals, here-and-now individuals with whom I have a counselling relationship and to whom I want to respond from within that present relationship. 'What is needed now?' or 'How might I approach this?' can be better ethical questions to ask than having a clear ethical programme worked out in advance. This is 'journey ethics' rather than 'destinational ethics'. Even when we have clear principles and rules (destinations), we still have to think through how those principles are applied in different situations. The tradition of moral philosophy that says we must divorce ourselves from relationship, context, and emotion has been challenged irrevocably by our current understanding of the brain and social influence (e.g. see Haidt and Kesebir, 2010; Lewis et al., 2003).

There will, inevitably be relational imperatives and principles to guide us. 'Do no harm' is one. Sometimes we know what not to do in advance. For example, whatever ethical decision I come to, you can be assured it will not result in killing or harming you, abusing my power over you, involving you in sexual activity, etc. There is a sense that from the immediacy of the ethical relationship the only thing we can know for sure is what we won't do. What we *will* do depends: on us, on the relationship, on the other, on the situation.

WHAT IS ETHICAL MATURITY IN COUNSELLING PSYCHOLOGY?

What, then, is ethical maturity in counselling psychology? We (Carroll and Shaw, 2012, 2013) present six components of ethical maturity to guide us not only in making ethical decisions but in becoming ethically sensitive to the complexity of ethical decision making. These components are *not* sequential stages in a process; rather, they are conditions that make for good ethical decision making. Figure 15.1 presents these six and shows their interrelatedness.

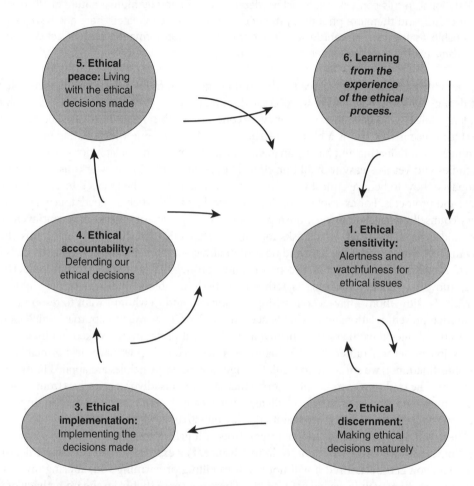

Figure 15.1   The six components of mature ethical decision making

1. **Fostering ethical sensitivity and watchfulness.** At the forefront of ethical development is the growth of ethical antennae that keep us alert to ethical issues/dilemmas as they arise. Our alertness to issues both reflects and further fosters our moral compass and moral character. Ethical sensitivity, that 'gut response' that something is wrong, provides the first alert that there is an ethical issue at stake. Not to be ethically sensitive is to miss the signs of ethical presences and thus abort further stages in the ethical decision-making process. Helping practitioners to develop their ethical compass in relation to professional matters should take place from the point of their

initial training (lectures, supervision, placements) both through structured learning and modelling by people who are themselves ethically aware. The twin anchors of ethical sensitivity are empathy and compassion. Ethical sensitivity is about what we might do as well as awareness about what we haven't done. Singer (2000: xvi) makes this point: 'Where so many are in such great need, indulgence in luxury is not morally neutral and the fact that we have not killed anyone is not enough to make us morally decent citizens of the world.' Translated into counselling psychology terminology, this means that minimum standards (e.g. keeping to the codes) is insufficient to attain ethical maturity.

2. **Discerning ethical decisions** and being able to make an ethical decision aligned to our ethical principles and our values. Once our awareness of an ethical issue is triggered, we need the capacity to slow down, to pause, reflect, consider and decide on a mature course of action. Training programmes and supervisors help budding practitioners at this stage of ethical development by enabling them to reflect in widening ways and consider what values (personal, professional) are at the heart of their decision-making processes. Experienced practitioners also need professional development opportunities and peer relationships that hone and attune ethical radar via continued learning and reflection on ethical issues. Sometimes, despite experience, we only know we have entered ethically compromised territory after events have occurred. Ethical maturity puts the values of relational care and fidelity central to ethical decision making (see British Association of Counselling and Psychotherapy's *Ethical Framework* (2013), British Psychological Society's *Code of Ethics and Conduct* (2006), and Australian Psychological Society's *Code of Ethics* (2007) for other values that will inform mature ethical decision making, for example, integrity, respect for the person, awareness of culture, etc.).

3. **Implementing ethical decision/s.** Having made a decision is only part of the way towards ethical maturity. Decisions need to be implemented and not all ethical decisions are. There is evidence that knowing what to do ethically does not always end in enacting that decision for many reasons (Darley and Batson, 1973; Smith et al., 1991). Implementing action may demand moral courage and perseverance/resilience to see a difficult task completed; it may involve withstanding consequences that seem too high, on a personal and relational level, as we know from the literature on whistleblowing (see, for example, Ethics Resource Centre Report, 2010). Betan and Stanton (1999: 296) conclude from their studies that inadequate ethical decisions can be made in part because professionals are not well attuned to the influential role of emotions, values and context in their processing and procedures. High levels of emotion can render us afraid to act, or can mean we can't trust our own judgement. Instead, we now understand that emotion is a way to understand the ethical issue further (Fine, 2007; Gilligan, 1982; Haidt, 2013) and, through a process of reasoned deliberation, we can move forward to action.

4. **Being able to articulate and justify to stakeholders** why the ethical decisions were made and implemented. Honesty and transparency are required for an ethical explanation. Reason, logic and being able to clearly defend our decision are skills needed at this stage. Knowing ourselves helps us articulate why actions were decided upon, and to be able to catch ourselves out when we move from a reasoned defence to being defensive. This ethical component is not about justification, defensiveness or superficial understandings of our actions, but about knowing ourselves in depth and being able to own up to what is required – always difficult in the area of ethics. However, as professionals we must be accountable for our actions.

5. **Ethical peace and sustainability** is achieving closure on the event, even when there were other possible decisions or 'better' decisions that could have been made. Living peacefully with the consequences of ethical decision making is crucial to ongoing well-being. Letting go of what has been and done is important in ethical closure. Practitioners learn to accept who they are, be compassionate towards themselves, be honest and make restitution when needed.
6. **Learning from what has happened** and 'testing' the decision through reflection. Integrating what we have learned into our lives develops our moral character and extends our ethical wisdom and capacity. Part of the process of developing ethical maturity is learning from experience (Carroll, 2014: Chapter 8).

Ultimately, these six components result in ethical maturity. The six components come together in a definition or description of ethical maturity, which we present as:

Having the reflective, rational, emotional and intuitive capacity to decide if actions are right and wrong, or good and better; having the resilience and courage to implement those decisions; being accountable for ethical decisions made (publicly or privately); and being able to learn from and live with the experience. (Carroll and Shaw, 2013: 28)

Codes and frameworks are starting points for ethical decisions and not end points. They rarely tell us what to do, but do provide overarching principles to help us make decisions. Sticking only to codes results in an ethics of duty, but not always an ethics of fidelity; it is this relational ethics of trust that is our aim. Bond (2006: 436) defines this type of ethical stance: 'Trust is a relationship of sufficient quality and resilience to withstand the challenges arising from difference, inequality, risk and uncertainty.' This kind of relationship in counselling psychology helps create ethically mature practice.

CONCLUSION

Ethics is not about problems to be solved; ethics is about relational issues to be lived. That means the final answer to the question asked by practitioners, 'How do I make ethical decisions?' is: it depends. Claxton and Lucas (2007: 80) provide a wonderful image when they portrayed ethical problems as 'more like tangled fishing nets than ... mathematical equations'.
What is the point of writing a chapter on ethical maturity and ethical decision making in counselling psychology if we end up with the conclusion that 'it all depends ... sometimes I rely on one approach, and sometimes another?' Doesn't this end with a rather chaotic and unstructured approach to ethical navigation? While this position is unsatisfactory in not offering clear answers to specific questions, we believe this approach is more in keeping with modern life and contemporary living. Life and work are complex, complicated and, at times, chaotic. In that context we have more options from which to choose, and that can make decision making seem more difficult. Not having one definitive way means our focus is not on the answers, but on *how*

we make decisions. It challenges us to let go of certainty and immerse ourselves in 'real-time' ethics where often there are few 'givens'. However we make them, good ethical decisions are defensible by reason and need to be justifiable. Making ethical decisions is one step on the road towards ethical maturity. Ethics is not just about doing right or wrong, good or bad. It is more than that – it is about how faithful you are to the relationships in your life and work.

Ethical maturity is a state of being, not a book to pull from a shelf, and it will resource us more effectively for the moment-to-moment responsiveness so often demanded of frontline clinical work. Counselling psychologists need to balance an ethics of duty and an ethics of relational fidelity, learning to trust our inner guides as well as external supports such as ethical codes and frameworks. Ultimately, the greatest tool counselling psychologists can have is their own wise mind: conscious awareness, moral radar, emotional intelligence and reflective practice, as well as gathering strong ethical relationships and resources to assist them when needed.

Visit the companion website to explore Terri's Dilemmas – Cross Cultural Issues and Competence.

REFERENCES

Adams, M. (2014) *The Myth of the Untroubled Therapist*. Brighton and Hove: Routledge.

Appiah, K.A. (2008) *Experiments in Ethics*. Cambridge, MA: Harvard University Press

Australian Psychological Society (2007) *Code of Ethics*. Melbourne: Australian Psychological Society.

Betan, E.J. and Stanton, A.L. (1999) Fostering ethical willingness: Integrating emotional and contextual awareness with rational analysis. *Professional Psychology: Research and Practice*, 30(3): 295–301.

Bond, T. (2006) Intimacy, risk, and reciprocity in psychotherapy: Intricate ethical challenges. *Transactional Analysis Journal*, 36(2): 77–890.

Bond, T. (2013) Foreword. In M. Carroll and E. Shaw, *Ethical Maturity in the Helping Professions: Making Difficult Life and Work Decisions*. London: Jessica Kingsley.

British Association for Counselling and Psychotherapy (2013) *Ethical Framework for Good Practice in Counselling and Psychotherapy*. Lutterworth: BACP.

British Psychological Society (2006) *Code of Ethics and Conduct*. Leicester: BPS.

Carroll, M. (2014) *Effective Supervision for the Helping Professions*. London: Sage.

Carroll, M. and Shaw, E. (2012) *Ethical Maturity in the Helping Professions: Making Difficult Life and Work Decisions*. Melbourne: PsychOz Publications.

Carroll, M. and Shaw, E. (2013) *Ethical Maturity in the Helping Professions: Making Difficult Life and Work Decisions*. London: Jessica Kingsley.

Claxton, G. and Lucas, B. (2007) *The Creative Thinking Plan*. London: BBC Books.

Critchley, B. (2010) Relational coaching: Taking the coaching high road. *Journal of Management Development*, 29(10): 851–863.

Darley, J.M. and Batson, C.D. (1973) 'From Jerusalem to Jericho: A study in situational and dispositional variable in helping behaviours', *Journal of Personality and Social Psychology*, 27(1): 100–108.

Dunning, D. (2005) *Self Insight: Roadblocks and Detours on the Path of Knowing Thyself*. New York: Psychology Press.

Eliot, S. (2007) *Everything You Need to Know from Your Backyard to the Galaxy*. Crow's Nest, NSW: Allen & Unwin.

Ethics Resource Centre (2010) *Blowing the Whistle on Workplace Misconduct*. Arlington, VA: Ethics Resource Centre, www.ethics.org (downloaded 1 June).

Fine, C. (2007) *A Mind of its Own: How Your Brain Distorts and Deceives*. Cambridge: Icon Books.

Gilligan, C. (1982) *In a Different Voice, Psychological Theory and Women's Development*. Cambridge, MA: Harvard University Press.

Grenyer, B.F.S. and Lewis, K. (2012) Prevalence, prediction, and prevention of psychologist misconduct. *Australian Psychologist*, 47: 68–76.

Haidt, J. (2013) *The Righteous Mind: Why People are Divided by Politics and Religion*. New York: First Vintage Books.

Haidt, J. and Kesebir, S. (2010) Morality. In S. Fiske, D. Gilbert and G. Lindzey (eds), *Handbook of Social Psychology* (5th edition). Hoboken, NJ: Wiley. pp. 797–832.

Heubner, B., Dwyer, S. and Hauser, M. (2008) The role of emotion in moral psychology. *Trends in Cognitive Sciences*, 13(1): 1–6. doi: 10.1016/j.tics.2008.09.006. Epub 6 December 2008.

Hinman, L. (2013) *Ethics: A Pluralistic Approach to Moral Theory* (5th edition). Boston, MA: Wadsworth Cengage.

Kahneman, D. (2011) *Thinking Fast and Slow*. London: Allen Lane.

Kassimeris, G. (2006) *Warrior's Dishonour: Barbarity, Morality and Torture in Modern Warfare*. Aldershot: Ashgate.

Kohlberg, L. (1982) *The Philosophy of Moral Development*. San Francisco, CA: Harper & Row.

Lewis, T., Amini, F. and Lannon, R. (2003) *A General Theory of Love*. New York: Vintage Books.

Norcross, J.C. and Guy, J.D. (2007) *Leaving It at the Office: A Psychotherapist's Guide to Self Care*. New York: Guilford Press.

Schön, D. (1983) *The Reflective Practitioner: How Professionals Think in Action*. New York: Basic Books.

Seabright, M.A. and Schminke, M. (2002) Immoral imagination and revenge in organisations. *Journal of Business Ethics*, 38: 19–31.

Singer, P. (2000) *Writings on an Ethical Life*. New York: Ecco Press.

Smith, T.S., McGuire, J.M., Abbott, D.W. and Blau, B.I. (1991) Clinical ethical decision making: An investigation of the rationales used to justify doing less than one believes one should. *Professional Psychology: Research and Practice*, 22(3): 235–239.

16
THE INTERFACE BETWEEN PSYCHOPHARMACOLOGICAL AND PSYCHOTHERAPEUTIC APPROACHES

DIANE HAMMERSLEY

INTRODUCTION

This chapter outlines some of the assumptions, constructs and implications of the psycho-pharmacological and psychotherapeutic approaches based upon different paradigms of the medical model and the psychological model, and how they may interact with each other. This is set within the social and political context of the influence medicine has within the NHS and wider society, and how the concept of mental illness has evolved as a way of explaining and categorising psychological distress.

In the companion website resources linked to this chapter there is a brief outline of psy-chopharmacological drugs, their uses and the guidelines for their prescription, and a discussion of how they may affect the individual's thinking, feelings and behaviour. The implications for therapy, the therapeutic process, the meaning of symptoms and motivation are explored as well as the psychodynamic literature.

TRAINING AND QUALIFYING

The transition from trainee counselling psychologist to being professionally qualified and recognised represents a significant shift in professional authority and personal autonomy. In the field of combining a therapeutic practice with medical approaches that use pharmaco-logical treatments, this requires a shift from the belief that medication is only the domain of the medical practitioner to the belief that these treatments must be subject to critical scrutiny and scientific rigour by counselling psychologists. However, that requires acquiring new knowledge and the acceptance of greater responsibility. It is no longer enough to leave it up to the doctor.

While in training it is possible that a number of myths, which are widely held and often articulated, have become part of the counselling psychologist's landscape. The first is that the whole field of pharmacology is very complicated and therefore requires extensive training, although what we need to know is only a small part of it and we can acquire that knowledge as we go along if we adopt a questioning attitude. So leaving it to other people, who must know better, and thinking it is not my business to question what the doctor has decided are abdications of responsibility. There is also the myth that medication is a more scientific approach that is well researched and well proven. Divorcing symptoms from their causes and leaving the doctor to deal with the symptoms while the counselling psychologist deals with the underlying issues are also a simplistic splitting of the connection between the two.

There is a popular strategy of talking about the patient's choice when, in reality, there may be very little choice, and the patient may be subjected to false reassurance, the myths held by the doctor, the pressure to do something to help quickly, or the belief that something is always better than nothing. If the counselling psychologist ignores the medication and leaves it all up to the client, the client may believe it is unimportant, that it is not relevant to psychotherapy and their beliefs about medication may remain unchallenged. When the issue of medication is frankly and honestly discussed, the client may then have information that leads to realistic expectations of what each approach might provide and how one might impact on the other.

It is important to consider the context within which the counselling psychologist is practising, whether as part of a team in an NHS service, collaboratively or independently, and the level of difficulty of the client and their problems. Working alongside others from different professions requires respect and understanding of the position adopted by them while being able to put forward a reasoned case for the opinions and preferences of the psychotherapeutic practitioner. A further difficulty found by independent practitioners is the frequent failure to consult them about medication issues when the client is already in therapy outside NHS contexts.

Historically, pharmaceutical companies have suppressed the adverse results of clinical trials, withheld information from regulatory bodies, and engaged in dubious marketing practices, particularly in other countries where direct advertising to patients is permitted. As a general practitioner himself, Goldacre (2012) highlights these issues and goes on to describe how 'Big Pharma' influences medical training, drug information and the funding of CPD events for doctors to promote their company's products. Antidepressant prescribing has increased from 15 million items in 1998 to 40 million items in 2012, half of that increase occurring during the four years since the start of the financial crisis in 2008 (Spence et al., 2014). Goldacre admits to not being aware that a drug was ineffective until he saw the evidence, and neither can we rely on our impressions and what the client says.

THE TWO PARADIGMS

In many settings in which psychotherapy is offered, medical treatments often sit alongside psychological interventions. There is widespread tacit acceptance of this, although psychologists sometimes express concern about whether these two approaches are compatible, complementary, or inevitable and beyond question. Perhaps it is more worrying when there is no concern or it appears difficult or dangerous to express those concerns. It is, however, part of a counselling psychologist's approach to maintain a critical stance in relation to evidence, and to question thoroughly what is in a client's best interest from a position that takes into account different and sometimes competing realities. It is equally important, but less often stated, that the psychologist offering therapy needs to consider what is in their own best interests; that is, not to allow themselves and their interventions to be undermined.

THE MEDICAL MODEL

The medical model, as a way of explaining problems or psychopathology, has a number of assumptions around a faulty mental mechanism characterised as a disease (Freeth, 2007). This tends to offer explanations of biochemical imbalance as the faulty mechanism, and such an assumption fits comfortably with concepts of illness, diagnosis, expert interventions and medication as a means of alleviating symptoms, and hence cure. It also has assumptions around the relationship between the doctor and the patient where the helping doctor is seen as expert and knowledgeable and the patient accepting the explanations as facts and complying with the treatment. As Freeth points out, these assumptions are taken for granted in the NHS and the NICE guidelines for mental disorders use the same language for psychological therapies as for medical treatments. Treatments are thought to be disorder-specific and can be evaluated by results which can be measured in randomised controlled trials.

Freeth then goes on to describe therapy as a developmental process, outlining assumptions about the conditions within which the client can explore their subjective realities and meanings. Sanders argues strongly that counselling and psychotherapy must separate themselves from the medical model of mental distress, which he claims 'does not work, and in practice is iatrogenic' (Sanders, 2007: 35). He makes the point that 'illness is a metaphor for distress' (2007: 36) and not a fact, and such a metaphor is in need of revision, although it is still taken for granted by the general public and the majority of practitioners in psychology, psychotherapy and counselling. A similar critique of the dominance of the biological explanation, to the exclusion of the psychological and social, is offered by Read (2005: 596), who illustrates the point that psychiatry is dominated by the drug companies who influence their conferences, journals and research agendas through gifts he calls 'kickbacks and bribes'.

While psychologists may argue against the medical model, there is widespread agreement that it is the dominant model in the NHS and is likely to remain so within the 'psychological therapies', and practitioners must find a way to bridge the divide. In an attempt to find a highway between the worlds of therapy and psychiatry, Pointon (2006) interviewed two psychiatrists with therapeutic training. They agree that therapists need to have a basic template of psychiatric diagnosis, and need to be able to spot symptoms that indicate when to refer on people who need more specialist help. They think it is crucial therapists understand about the drugs doctors are prescribing and need to be confident in communicating with doctors and learn to speak their language. If only similar recommendations could be outlined for what doctors need to be able to do to bridge the gap from their side! Maybe they need to have a basic template of psychological processes, and need to recognise when a psychological problem is beyond their competence and they need to refer on for more specialist help. Perhaps one might add to the list a psychological understanding of the drugs they prescribe.

Resnick (2003), who works with attention deficit disorder, argues that psychologists should be allowed to prescribe medication on the grounds that medication is effective for some patients and can then be combined with other psychological programmes. Given that psychologists would be trained in both models, he and colleagues argue that prescribing rights would also confer the authority to discontinue medications that have been inappropriately prescribed by others, sometimes because they lack sufficient training in understanding psychiatric problems. Johnstone (2003a) argues that there is no such thing as a pharmaceutical 'treatment' for any form of mental distress, because the biological basis of any form of mental distress has not been established. The assumption that a change in brain chemistry is the cause of mental distress remains untested and unproven. In a separate article on the use of electroconvulsive therapy, Johnstone (2003b) makes the point that while all psychological states have their physiological correlates, this does not imply causality, and until we have established causality we cannot make claims about cure.

THE SOCIAL AND POLITICAL CONTEXT

As we have seen above, when therapy is offered within the context of the NHS, the political reality is that psychological problems are usually framed by the medical model, and organisational policies about what can be offered at a particular service level have been determined in advance and are generalised rather than allowing people to be treated as a single case. Time-limited therapy is the norm and assumptions are made about which treatments are possible in the short term, which are cost-effective and readily available. What is measurable and predictable is usually preferred by managers, accountants and politicians, who might regard open-ended therapy that is not structured as a bottomless pit that will soak up valuable resources. There may be some truth in that, as there may be a grain of truth in the claim that what the NHS offers is a sticking plaster until the patient comes through the door again. 'Customer satisfaction surveys' speak for themselves, but as reliable evidence for effectiveness they have their limitations.

Within this context, prescribing medication seems predictable, at least as far as cost is concerned, and has been categorised as being for specific conditions, for specific time-frames, with specific populations, with specific symptom control. In addition, medicine has an established reputation that therapy has not yet attained. Referral processes both in the NHS, in medical insurance provision and, more recently, in occupational health settings have tended to rely on medical practitioners to act as gatekeepers, just as have government benefit agencies. This has given medical diagnosis and opinions enormous power to define problems and prescribe solutions. In legal contexts there has been a tradition of relying on medical opinion because of the medical profession's high level of regard in the eyes of the public.

As well as the influence of the NHS, with its emphasis on cost efficiency and the social power of the medical profession in influencing prescribing and therapy provision, there has been a growing awareness of the influence of the marketing strategies of pharmaceutical companies. Quite apart from their control of clinical drug trials, evidence that only studies that show the effectiveness of drugs are published and the suppression of adverse studies, the companies have been very effective in influencing a climate of opinion through their direct marketing to the public in the USA. Lacasse and Leo (2005) show that a suggestion in advertising to consumers in the USA that SSRI antidepressants may correct a serotonin deficiency which causes depression has gradually been translated into a 'fact' and picked up by the medical profession, much of whose post-qualifying training is sponsored by pharmaceutical companies. It did not take long to cross the Atlantic Ocean and become established as a 'fact' in the UK, in spite of consumer-directed advertising of medication not being permitted in the UK.

THE CONCEPT OF MENTAL ILLNESS

The medical model relies upon diagnosis; that is, the ability to define and describe illness or disease in the organic body and psychopathology of the mind. Reference is usually made to the Diagnostic and Statistical Manual of the USA, DSM-5 (American Psychiatric Association, 2013). Kutchins and Kirk (1997) make the point that there are two major problems with the DSM, namely validity and reliability. You can have agreement among experts without validity, since that does not establish the truth, as those who promoted theories of a flat earth have shown us. While some psychiatrists would agree that some disorders may not be valid, many believe that there is agreement that schizophrenia and depression are examples of mental illness. However, there is a large body of literature that questions the validity of even these categories (Bentall, 2003; Boyle, 1990).

There are also problems about getting agreement between experts as to what constitutes mental illness. Kutchins and Kirk refer to a study (Williams et al., 1992) in which seven studies were conducted in the USA and Germany to test whether pairs of experienced and specially trained clinicians could interview patients and make accurate diagnoses. They interviewed 600 patients in a supervised research setting so that this should have produced the best possible level of reliability. The study showed that the pairs of clinicians frequently disagreed, even though the standard of agreement was very generous, in that diagnosing a personality disorder, even if a different disorder, counted as agreement. This shows that mental health clinicians are as likely to agree or disagree that a person has a disorder and as likely to agree or disagree about which of over 300 DSM disorders it is.

The widespread belief that DSM diagnoses are scientific and accurate contributes to the myth that pharmacological treatments are also scientific and specific, but this is much more questionable than many people believe. One example of this is the widespread myth that depression is caused by serotonin deficiency. 'In fact, there is no scientifically established ideal chemical balance of serotonin let alone an identifiable pathological imbalance' (Lacasse and Leo, 2005: 2). Lacasse and Leo point out that backward reasoning, which allows assumptions about the cause of disease to be based upon the response to treatment, is illogical, in the same way that we cannot infer that headaches are caused by aspirin deficiency because aspirin is an effective treatment for headache.

Recent studies (Kirsch, 2005) call into question the efficacy of SSRIs when evidence of the clinical trials showed that placebo duplicated about 80 per cent of the response and 57 per cent of these trials failed to show a statistically significant difference between SSRIs and placebo. These high rates of placebo response are not found in the treatment of well-studied imbalances such as insulin deficiency, which casts doubts on the serotonin hypothesis.

Another problem is that some treatments for depression do not target serotonin levels and no major difference has been shown between SSRIs and tricyclic antidepressants (TCAs). St John's Wort and placebo have outperformed SSRIs in some studies and exercise was found to be as effective as an SSRI in one trial. In addition, SSRIs are approved for the treatment of eight separate psychiatric diagnoses, such as social anxiety disorder and obsessive compulsive disorder, but serotonin deficiency is not claimed to be the cause of these disorders.

In conclusion, Lacasse and Leo (2005) state that there is no rigorous corroboration of the serotonin hypothesis and there is a significant body of contradictory evidence. Further, there is no peer-reviewed article that directly supports serotonin deficiency in any mental disorder, nor does DSM list serotonin as a cause of any mental disorder. Nevertheless, popular public and medical opinion still promotes serotonin deficiency as a 'cause' of depression and drugs are widely prescribed to correct it.

BELIEFS AND EXPECTATIONS

The medical model and a psychological model which result from different paradigms do not really fit well together, although in practice they are often combined. Different paradigms have different sets of assumptions but often the prescriber, the patient and the therapist have different expectations and beliefs about the part that medication or therapy might play in helping people resolve psychological distress. Where medication and therapy are both offered to the patient, conflicting messages may be implicitly given. It is important to recognise that frequently within the NHS, the first consultation will have been with a prescriber, although in other settings this may not have taken place and the psychologist may be conducting the first consultation.

Examples of implicit messages:

- Prescribing:
  - You have an illness/deficiency which can be cured/corrected by medication.
  - You are not coping therefore you need something from outside to help you cope.

- ○ Drugs will control your symptoms, so that you can sort yourself out.
- ○ You should not be upset or distressed; drugs will make you feel better.

- Therapy:

  - ○ You are not ill but have upset feelings which can be understood.
  - ○ You have the resources within you to sort out your life.
  - ○ Your symptoms are not the real problem but they may point you to what is.
  - ○ Facing up to issues may be painful but it helps to resolve them.

A further set of expectations which a client may hold when first seeking therapy may be around combining these two approaches. It may not have occurred to the client that medication might affect therapy in any way, that there may be unwanted side-effects, that the medication might not be making any difference, that feeling worse may not be evidence of getting worse but may be due to medication, that all drugs are the same, that all therapy is the same, and so forth. Given the powerful position that medical practitioners hold, it may be difficult for clients to realise that the decision about whether to take medication or not is usually theirs and not the role of the doctor or the therapist. If the doctor is sympathetic and caring, as most probably are, it could seem churlish or ungrateful not to accept the help offered or to question it overtly. Just because a doctor offers drugs does not mean he or she is recommending them.

Finally, therapy might seem rather vague or imprecise and the therapist may not be able to state clearly what will happen, how soon the client will feel better and how it works. Beliefs about medication being a scientific treatment and therapy being a bit 'alternative' might undermine a client's willingness to engage in what appears to be 'only talking'. While it may be wise to consider whether the doctor had enough time in the first consultation to discuss the implications of medication in order for the client to make an informed decision, it may be wise to consider what messages about therapy might have been conveyed either overtly or covertly. As alternatives, or in combination, the choice of medication and/or therapy is not a clear-cut issue and the relationship between them is at best uneasy.

PHARMACOLOGICAL APPROACHES

Having a clear idea of what drugs are prescribed and for what is the starting point for psychologists who want to begin to build a bridge between pharmacology and psychotherapy. Put simply, most psychotropic drugs alter moods and are either 'uppers' or 'downers'; that is, they are stimulants or sedatives. The second point is to understand that psychotropic drugs belong to a number of groups of similar drugs, so that knowing which group a drug is included in immediately conveys quite a lot of information about the drug. A third point to bridge building is to realise that drugs are known by their generic name by prescribers and pharmacists and in the literature, although they also have brand names which relate to the name given to them by the manufacturer. The one major point of reference is the British National Formulary (British

Medical Association and The Royal Pharmaceutical Society, 2008), which gives both generic and brand names and such information as the group, what it is prescribed for (indications), what it should not be prescribed for (contraindications), side-effects, dosage and advice.

Kahn (1993) refers to the Boston–New Haven Collaborative Study of Depression, which produced four negative hypotheses. First, they propose that drugs are a negative placebo, increasing dependency and prolonging psychopathology. Secondly, they point out that drug relief of symptoms could reduce motivation for therapy. Thirdly, they suggest that drugs could eliminate one symptom but create others by substitution if underlying conflicts remain intact. And fourthly, they propose that drugs decrease self-esteem by suggesting that people are not interesting enough, or suited to, or capable of insight-oriented work.

THE PSYCHOLOGICAL MODEL

Whatever the therapeutic approach, first, the client needs to experience the relationship with the therapist as fully as possible. Secondly, the re-experiencing of past events and working through them or noticing the emotional effects of changing cognitive distortions might be crucial to therapeutic work. Rosin and Köhler (1991), in exploring psychodynamic aspects of psychopharmacology, suggest that drugs reduce the intensity and alter the quality of the observation of inner and outer experience. This seems to be highly significant to therapists whose clients may be taking drugs and suggests that therapeutic work cannot be really finished until the client is abstinent. Only then can the client judge whether they have really engaged in the therapeutic relationship and been able to reflect on the understandings gained and experience changes in their emotions.

WHEN MEDICATION IS USEFUL

However, drugs are sometimes necessary or helpful in a person's life and combining medication and psychotherapy may involve using drugs sensitively and intermittently to support extreme distress and symptoms, reducing drugs when possible to allow therapy. Ostow (1993) recognises the two treatment approaches and defines them essentially as psychoses needing medication and neuroses needing psychotherapy. He then describes two situations where he advocates combining treatments. The first is in treating depression with antidepressants and following soon with psychotherapy, and the second is for the control of excessive affect in borderline, manic or attention deficit disorder patients. He further notes that medicated patients display rigidity in analysis, that the process is affected, and there is nominal compliance, superficial insight and limited behaviour change in combined treatment patients. He suggests that medication seems to affect the depth at which therapy operates. This may mean that the goals of therapy may have to be limited by what is realistic and possible.

COMBINING APPROACHES

In a systematic review of 52 studies of treatment for depression (Cuijpers et al., 2012), which compares studies of (1) medication versus psychotherapy, (2) medication versus combined approaches, and (3) psychotherapy versus combined approaches, the authors start with the assertion that medication and psychotherapies are both effective and combined treatments are slightly more effective than either alone. The studies use the Beck Depression Inventory and the Hamilton Rating Scale as measures but treatments range from six to 56 sessions of all kinds of therapeutic approaches and all three types of antidepressants, and only look at short-term outcomes, so, as the authors state, the task of identifying patterns for personalised treatments has only just begun.

These types of studies do not address the causes of depression, or even that it might be appropriate following bereavement or other losses, or result from suppressed emotion, such as anger. In addition, medication is now among a range of options that may be offered by a general practitioner and is often seen as first aid which will tide people over until some form of therapeutic treatment is available. Khalsa et al. (2011) examined the relationship between people's beliefs about the causes of depression and their treatment preferences and considered whether people may change their beliefs to be consistent with the treatment they receive or even with those of their therapist. Past experience of therapy or medication that was not helpful may influence both beliefs and treatment choice.

These studies seem to indicate that the quality of the therapeutic relationship plays little part in both choice of treatment and outcome, and the medical contexts imply people do not choose their therapist but are assigned treatments. Where therapists have greater freedom and professional autonomy they may explore people's beliefs about causality, previous treatment experiences and preferences as well as devising a therapeutic approach that is an individual and personalised treatment. In individual practice or voluntary agency settings, the therapeutic approach is less prescriptive and is focused more on long-term outcomes that may contribute to greater client satisfaction.

WHEN MEDICATION MAY BE USEFUL AND WHEN NOT

Long-term antipsychotic medication may be essential for clients with a diagnosis of schizophrenia. Therefore the depth of therapy is likely to be limited. The client can still benefit from therapy related to managing their lives and coping with the illness/condition.

Antipsychotics are not useful in the treatment of anxiety because they interfere with the process of therapy and have side-effects that mimic the symptoms of anxiety.

Long-term medication with lithium may be useful to control the manic-depressive mood swings in a person with a diagnosis of bi-polar disorder. The client can benefit from therapy related to managing their lives and coping with the illness/condition. Clients may be able to work at greater depth.

In severely depressed clients who are dysfunctional, antidepressants may lift the mood sufficiently to allow the therapy to start and the client to engage in the relationship. Severe depression may make people inaccessible to therapy. Clients on antidepressants can engage in therapy, but the depth of work may be limited. Since these drugs have no effect in some cases, therapy may not be affected. Clients cannot be sure the therapeutic work is completed until the drugs are withdrawn.

When clients are dependent on them, benzodiazepines must be continued until the client has made the decision to withdraw. Gradual withdrawal should be integrated with the therapy (Hammersley, 1995). Clients taking benzodiazepines cannot fully engage in therapy. Therapy can be directed towards motivating the client to come off drugs, but the underlying issues cannot be fully dealt with until after the client is abstinent.

EXAMPLES OF ADVANTAGES OF MEDICATION COMBINED WITH THERAPY

Medication is useful or necessary in order to control extreme psychotic symptoms.

Antidepressants may sometimes improve therapeutic access when clients are very depressed.

Continuing the prescribing is essential in order to prevent a withdrawal syndrome when clients are dependent on their drugs. Drug withdrawal should be very gradual and at the client's own pace.

Medication may be necessary to control fits in epilepsy.

Benzodiazepines are used to prevent convulsions in alcohol withdrawal.

Methadone and subutex are used to stabilise mood and reduce harm for clients who are addicted to opiates.

EXAMPLES OF DISADVANTAGES OF MEDICATION COMBINED WITH THERAPY

Removal of symptoms may give false hope or false evidence of change.

Antipsychotics, benzodiazepines and antidepressants may limit therapeutic access, interfere with cognitive and affective processing and increase distance in the therapeutic relationship.

All medication may have unwanted or unrecognised side-effects.

Some medication promotes physical and psychological dependence.

Medication may increase psychological defences of denial, avoidance and splitting.

Continuing medication may reinforce the assumptions of the medical model.

There is a risk that the prescriber may act independently thus undermining the therapy.

HOW MEDICATION AFFECTS THE PROCESS OF THERAPY

Accessibility

In a qualitative research study (abstract on the companion website) exploring how a variety of therapists viewed the therapeutic process with their clients who were taking drugs (Hammersley, 2002), all the participants had noticed an effect of some kind. Many of them identified problems around therapeutic accessibility, either internal accessibility of material for the client or external accessibility in the relationship between the client and the therapist. In the first case, they identified interference of thinking processes or emotional depth. Given that many psychotropic drugs, and in particular the benzodiazepines, have been thought to interfere with grieving (Committee on Safety of Medicine, 1988), I selected this topic to explore with participants what they had noticed about internal accessibility. There were four outcome propositions: (1) that benzodiazepines suppress emotional processing; (2) that loss of memory affects narrative competence; (3) that grieving is inhibited, prolonged or unresolved; and (4) that it is only after withdrawing from their medication that clients realised what life experience they had lost while taking drugs.

Examples:

'I had a client who was her mother's carer and when her mother died she'd lost her identity in life. She was given benzodiazepines and then years later she still hadn't gone through the grieving process. It's like they're in a coma ... like they're asleep.'

'It seems to not exactly block people's feelings ... they actually don't have the feelings so much. They contain them and then they don't need to talk about them.'

'And they could feel sadness, but it was not a good grief; it was more like sadness. Not deep as grief in those circumstances should have been.'

Engagement

Therapists referred to clients not really 'letting them in' or 'getting stuck' or clients not turning up, or not returning to therapy. Some felt that clients did not want any challenge to their view of their internal world, and poor motivation was mentioned. Others mentioned a reduced potential for insight, and a slower and harder process. For those therapists who used the relationship between them and the client, they noticed that clients seemed to depend on the drugs rather than the therapist and eventually themselves.

Examples:

'I feel you cannot counsel someone non-directively and if you try you get stuck. In fact you may not even get to being stuck.'

'There is a reduced motivation to do psychological work because they invest the drug with the power to make them better.'

'Therapy is less effective. There is a feeling of not going forward together, the feeling of marching on the spot.'

'I think the thing that stands out for me is they were depending on it, and how it can feel safer than depending on the therapist or the therapy.'

Reinforced defences

Respondents mentioned drugs increasing a client's defences, which might at first seem useful to them in managing their lives, but which can prove to be a hurdle in therapeutic work. Denial, avoidance, resistance, splitting, anger, disowning and disconnecting, intellectualisation, rationalisations were all mentioned.

Examples:

'They're just not in touch with their suffering. It's a kind of denial.'

'Everything is "you this, you that" and I have endeavoured to get him to personalise statements, but there is just this enormous resistance.'

'People say, "I don't know what I'm doing here", and "there are a lot of people and I know you have a long waiting list", and "am I wasting your time?" I would interpret that as a defence mechanism, resistance.'

Adjustments to therapy

Therapists commented that the focus of therapy had to be on the drugs first and that might mean giving advice and guidance to the client and being more directive than they otherwise might be. Myths about drugs needed to be confronted, clients might need guidance over drug withdrawal rates, or they need to be forewarned about withdrawal syndromes and withdrawing at a much slower pace than they had first thought. There is often an issue over who is in control of the process, with clients having the same expectation of the therapist that they have of their doctor being in control. Sometimes clients are more demanding or more challenging of the boundaries and there may be more conflict.

Examples:

'Coming off becomes the focus of the work to start with, so that is different because they are bringing a very concrete problem into therapy.'

'I think it's probably harder for people who work in a person-centred or psychodynamic way, because it's to do with being directive. The counsellor has to set the agenda when they believe that the client should set the agenda.'

'There's more potential in these circumstances for therapy to be sabotaged. I don't think doctors were knowingly trying to sabotage the kind of relationship you have with the client but it wasn't very helpful and you have to deal with it very diplomatically.'

'I think there was a danger of me colluding with them, partly because of my fear of rejection, and therefore I lower or raise my threshold to challenge. In other words, I would challenge less often or allow escape on a challenge, which I don't think I would allow with other clients.'

In another study of the experiences of psychotherapists conducted in Sweden, Schubert (2007) used two opinion surveys to ask respondents who were either psychotherapists or trainees about different aspects of psychotherapy combined with antidepressant medication. For very depressed patients, antidepressants were seen as an aid to functioning before therapy could be started. Surprisingly, some respondents thought medication made some less-depressed clients more accessible and better motivated, but others thought it impaired the patients' motivation. Medication was seen to obstruct the psychotherapy process as well as making it difficult to evaluate progress, particularly if patients were still taking medication when therapy ended. Using only surveys limited a deeper exploration of some of these issues.

ASSESSMENT OF THE CLIENT TAKING DRUGS

It is important to include questions about medication in any assessment session so that the implications can be discussed with the client before therapy starts. This assessment will allow for the diagnosis to be discussed in relation to the client's past and present life, a reformulation of the presenting issues if this is appropriate, and may provide the client with an opportunity to seek further information about the drugs and how they might impact on therapy. If the client needs antipsychotic drugs to maintain stability and a better quality of life, then the depth of therapy can be adjusted accordingly.

If benzodiazepines have been taken for more than a few weeks, then physical dependence is a real possibility and the client should be made aware of the withdrawal syndrome and a discussion about gradual withdrawal during the course of therapy can take place. If the client is taking antidepressants, a discussion may provide an opportunity to review whether they have been helpful or not and whether to continue them during therapy. Of course it is possible that a client may decide to continue taking medication and decline therapy once the implications have been explored.

MOTIVATION AND READINESS

Readiness for change is an important issue in working with clients who use illegal drugs (Prochaska and DiClemente, 1984) and can usefully be imported into work with clients using prescribed ones. Addressing drug issues in a complete way with the client gives the message that they are an important component in the client's treatment or process and the psychologist is interested in them. Many clients are surprised at first, perhaps thinking that drugs are in a separate medical domain, and have nothing to do with therapy. If that assumption is present, it is important to question it; it may reflect an assumption made by the prescriber. Of course that may have been an assumption made by the therapist too.

As a result of a thorough discussion, some clients may decide to stay on the drugs they are taking and not embark on any therapy either now or in the future. Mostly, people who decline therapy may leave the door open in case their circumstances or views change. The assessment may reveal that this is not the right time or people may need to do some other things in their life first. Some clients will decide to do some brief preliminary work, and perhaps return at a later date. This is a much better outcome than fudging the decision or agreeing to therapy and then dropping out.

Another outcome may be that the client decides to continue with their drugs and engage in therapy, either in the long term or the short term. If the two are to be combined for some reason, either of the client's choosing or out of therapeutic necessity, then the goals and strategies or the therapeutic approach may need to be varied. If the client decides to start therapy and discontinue drugs after therapy has been established, then the pace and mode of withdrawal needs to be discussed. This is not the moment to refer the client back to the doctor to sort it out, because drug withdrawal needs to be an individual process that is integrated within therapy.

THE PSYCHODYNAMIC PERSPECTIVE

 A discussion of some of the key issues from this perspective may be found on the companion website resources associated with this chapter. These include the psychodynamic meaning of drugs from an object relations perspective, and a discussion of the three key relationships: the client–therapist, the patient–doctor and the doctor–therapist.

PROFESSIONAL AND ETHICAL RESPONSIBILITY

Recognising the problems that may appear as cracks in the interface between the medical paradigm and the psychological paradigm is an important professional and ethical responsibility. Those cracks may at times only be hairline cracks but at other times they may become vast crevasses and any friction between these two paradigms will not be soothed by the oil of complacency. With other professionals with whom clinical responsibility for patients is shared, counselling psychologists have an ethical responsibility to ensure that any treatment benefits the client and minimises harm and risks to safety. This is where the evidence base is important. Given that a meta-analysis of the clinical trial data shows that adults given SSRI antidepressants are five times more likely to commit suicide than those given placebo (Healy, 2003) and that the response to SSRIs is largely a placebo effect not a drug effect (Kirsch, 2005), it is irresponsible not to use that knowledge in the consultation and supervision that leads to ethical decision making. That knowledge, if it is integrated with clinical experience, needs to be shared with medical practitioners rather than leaving them to guess at it or flounder on their own.

Respect for the client means that they too need to be informed about the sometimes complex issues around medication and therapy that will allow them to achieve self-determination and make a choice. Leaving it up to the client without engaging in the debate and the decision is not respecting the client's autonomy. Reliance on codes of conduct that are 'rules', procedures such as referring to psychiatrists when people are considered to be at risk and following guidelines such as NICE recommendations are often more a defence against complaints and litigation than a commitment to ethical practice. It is inevitable that at times when two paradigms are close together, there will be some friction. What is needed is greater honesty and openness on all sides about our search for understanding of psychological distress and the limitations of both approaches.

Visit the companion website for the following:

- Psychotropic Drugs.
- Questions to discuss with clients.
- Case Examples.
- Implications for practice.
- Psychodynamic perspectives.
- Summary of Research.

REFERENCES

American Psychiatric Association (2013) *Diagnostic and Statistical Manual of Mental Disorders* (5th edition). Washington, DC: APA.

Bentall, R.P. (2003) *Madness Explained: Psychosis and Human Nature*. London: Penguin Books.

Boyle, M. (1990) *Schizophrenia: A Scientific Delusion?* London: Routledge.

British Medical Association and The Royal Pharmaceutical Society (2008) *British National Formulary*. London: The Pharmaceutical Press.

Committee on Safety of Medicines (1988) 'Benzodiazepines, dependence and withdrawal symptoms', *Current Problems*, 21: 1–2.

Cuijpers, P., Reynolds, C.F., Donker, T., Li, J., Andersson, G. and Beekman, A. (2012) 'Personalised treatment of adult depression: medication, psychotherapy, or both? A systematic review', *Depression and Anxiety*, 29: 855–864.

Freeth, R. (2007) 'Working within the medical model', *Therapy Today*, November: 31–34 (BACP).

Goldacre, B. (2012) *Bad Pharma*. London: Fourth Estate.

Hammersley, D.E. (1995) *Counselling People on Prescribed Drugs*. London: Sage.

Hammersley, D.E. (2002) 'An exploration of how therapists view therapeutic process in relation to clients who are taking benzodiazepines', Unpublished PhD thesis, Regent's College & City University, London.

Healy, D. (2003) 'Lines of evidence on the risks of suicide with selective serotonin reuptake inhibitors', *Psychotherapy and Psychosomatics*, 72(2): 71–79.

Johnstone, L. (2003a) 'Back to basics', *The Psychologist*, 16(4): 186–187.

Johnstone, L. (2003b) 'A shocking treatment', *The Psychologist*, 16(5): 236–239.

Kahn, D.A. (1993) 'Medication consultation and split treatment during psychotherapy', in M. Schachter (ed.), *Psychotherapy and Medication*. Northvale, NJ: Jason Aronson.

Khalsa, S., McCarthy, K.S., Sharpless, B.A., Barrett, M.S. and Barber, J.P. (2011) 'Beliefs about the causes of depression and treatment preferences', *Journal of Clinical Psychology*, 67(6): 539–549.

Kirsch, I. (2005) 'Medication and suggestion in the treatment of depression', *Contemporary Hypnosis*, 22(2): 59–66.

Kutchins, H. and Kirk, S. (1997) *Making us Crazy: DSM – The Psychiatric Bible and the Creation of Mental Disorders*. London: Constable.

Lacasse, J.R. and Leo, J. (2005) 'Serotonin and depression: A disconnect between the advertisements and the scientific literature', *PLoS Med*, 2(12): e392 DOI: 10.1371/journal.pmed.0020392. (www.tinyurl.com/8vywy).

Ostow, M. (1993) 'On beginning with patients who require medication', in M. Schachter (ed.), *Psychotherapy and Medication* Northvale, NJ: Jason Aronson.

Pointon, C. (2006) 'Gulfs and bridges', *Therapy Today*, May: 16–18 (BACP).

Prochaska, J.O. and DiClemente, C.C. (1984) *The Transtheoretical Approach: Crossing Traditional Boundaries of Therapy*. Homewood, IL: Dow-Jones-Irwin.

Read, J. (2005) 'The bio-bio-bio model of madness', *The Psychologist*, 18(10): 596–597.

Resnick, R. (2003) 'To prescribe or not to prescribe-is that the question?' *The Psychologist*, 16(4): 184–186.

Rosin, U. and Köhler, G.K. (1991) 'Psychodynamic aspects of psychopharmacology in functional somatic complaints', *Psychotherapy and Psychodynamics*, 56(3): 129–134.

Sanders, P. (2007) 'Decoupling psychological therapies from the medical model', *Therapy Today*, November: 35–38 (BACP).

Schubert, J. (2007) 'Psychotherapy and antidepressant medication: scope, procedure and interaction. A survey of psychotherapists' experience', *European Journal of Psychotherapy and Counselling*, 9(2): 191–207.

Spence, R., Roberts, A., Ariti, C. and Bardsley, M. (2014) 'Focus on: Antidepressant prescribing', *Qualitywatch programme*. London: Nuffield Trust.

Williams, J.B. et al. (1992) 'The structured clinical interview for DSM-III-R (SCID): II. Multi-site test-retest reliability', *Archives of General Psychiatry*, 49: 630–636.

SECTION IV

ENCOUNTERING THE LANDSCAPE

CONTENTS

Imagine encountering a landscape for the first time. What do you notice? The framework from which that landscape has developed? The way in which it has formed its current structure? One might consider whether this landscape is similar to other, more familiar, landscapes. Personal thoughts about the landscape may include questions such as: How smooth is the terrain? Does it sit comfortably with me and with the way in which I view the world or how I like to travel? Might I struggle with some of its more complex elements or demands? One may hold certain preconceived ideas about particular landscapes. For example, an urban landscape may be considered to be busy and fast-paced, a mountainous terrain for some may be considered an uphill battle whereas for others it may be a personal challenge, while the ocean may be thought of as a place of calm and tranquillity. This fourth section of the book moves towards encountering the landscapes of counselling psychology and, to remain with the ocean metaphor, it also demonstrates how the profession is navigating society's increasingly turbulent times and embracing the winds of change (James, 2011).

The first three chapters within this section introduce readers to the various key psycho-therapeutic approaches within the field of counselling psychology and other allied disciplines. They reflect the contemporary world of the profession but also touch on the rich history and traditions of the discipline. They engage the reader in a developmental journey by drawing attention to the central approaches, yet the chapters focus upon ways in which the terrain has traversed into new and exciting landscapes of understanding and meaning. With the traditional theories blossoming into more contemporary fields of view, these first three chapters demonstrate how theory, research and practice have evolved with the times to create the vision that we have in today's counselling psychology practice.

The remaining chapters within this section navigate readers towards the more contemporary ways of applying our knowledge and understanding. The addition of the therapeutic letter writing, neuropsychology, community psychology and ecopsychology chapters reflect the emergence of new territories of work. The fast-paced twenty-first century is consistent with the evolution of our profession and this section outlines some of the ways in which developments within psychology, society and the wider world impact upon the work that we do and the way in which we practise. As well as focusing on our practice in the therapy room, the latter two chapters draw upon wider contexts, alluding to ways in which our practice and profession may evolve into the future.

The subtle shifts in the landscape of our profession and practice have been captured within this section. Trainees, who may be encountering the landscape for the first time, together with the more experienced practitioner, who may be traversing from the more familiar to less acquainted territories, may benefit from the knowledge that the authors of this section have to impart.

REFERENCE

James, P. (2011) The centrality and consistency of counselling psychology: Before, during and after 2008. *Hellenic Journal of Psychology*, 8: 374–387.

17

PERSON-CENTRED THERAPY IN THE TWENTY-FIRST CENTURY: GROWTH AND DEVELOPMENT

ANDREW HILL AND MICK COOPER

INTRODUCTION

Person-centred therapy (PCT) offers a radical, non-pathologising vision of how to help people heal and grow (Cooper et al., 2013). It is consistent with the strengths-based philosophy of counselling psychology, holding that clients – as with all human beings – have the potential to self-right, to actualise, to become more fully human and to develop their capacities for a deep caring of others (Cooper et al., 2013). The person-centred approach also shares with counselling psychology a belief in the power of the therapeutic relationship to provide a crucible for personal growth and transformation. More than that, the therapeutic relationship itself is seen as having the capacity to be a powerful agent of change.

From a person-centred standpoint, all organisms have an innate tendency to move towards greater complexity and differentiation (Rogers, 1959), and the same can be said of the person-centred *approach* itself. Today, the person-centred 'nation' is generally considered to consist of a number of different 'tribes' (Sanders, 2012). These range from the classical non-directive client-centred approach to the more process-directive Emotion Focused Therapy (EFT, see below), and include such contemporary developments as 'pre-therapy' (Prouty et al., 2002), person-centred expressive arts therapy (Rogers, 2000), focusing-oriented psychotherapy (Gendlin, 1996), and integrative person-centred approaches (e.g. Cain, 2010). There have also been some important theoretical developments emerging from the person-centred field, including new thinking on dialogue and relationality (e.g. Schmid, 2011), the role of the client as an active agent of therapeutic change (Bohart and Tallman, 1999) and experiential, non-pathologising models of 'difficult' client processes (Warner, 2013).

As with all organisms, however, the person-centred approach is also facing some significant external challenges. In many parts of the world, such as Germany and Japan, the approach is in decline, and this is primarily due to the growing dominance of an empirically supported treatments (EST) perspective. The basic principle behind this approach is that therapies are only considered valid to the extent that they have been proven efficacious: through experimental studies (primarily randomised clinical trials, RCTs), with particular groups of clients, with specific diagnoses (Cooper et al., 2013). This is the viewpoint held by many powerful clinical organisations, such as England's National Institute for Health and Care Excellence (NICE), whose recommendations on clinical treatments for specific psychological difficulties has informed the commissioning and funding of publicly available therapies and trainings.

Here, the problem for PCTs is *not* that they have been proved ineffective. Indeed, what evidence there is suggests that they may be efficacious in treating a range of psychological problems, equivalent to CBT and other therapeutic approaches (Elliott et al., 2013). Rather, the problem is that there are not enough of the kinds of studies that organisations like NICE endorse to *prove* their effectiveness. To a great extent, this is because members of the person-centred community tend to reject the principles and practices underlying such research. An RCT, for instance, 'requires categorisation of clients into specific diagnostic groupings; random allocation to different 'conditions'; the delivery of standardised, 'manualised' therapies; and analysis of data that reduces clients' lived-experiences down to de-contextualised, de-individualised averages' (Cooper et al., 2013: 4). Nevertheless, the EST movement carries on unabated (Cooper, 2011), and presents the person-centred field with some difficult choices over whether to 'Render unto Caesar' (Elliott, 2002) or to stick to its principles and risk decline into obscurity.

In this chapter, we present some of the key contemporary developments within PCT, in the face of these challenges. Our focus is particularly on developments of relevance to the UK, and for the field of counselling psychology. The chapter begins by looking at EFT – a new, and well-evidenced, form of person-centred/experiential therapy – that is now being taught on counselling psychology trainings in the UK. It then goes on to discuss the new humanistic psychological therapies competence framework, which has the potential to provide an evidence-based underpinning for the training and delivery of person-centred therapy. From this, the chapter discusses the development of Counselling for Depression (CfD), an evidence-based form of person-centred/experiential therapy specifically tailored to an NHS context; and school-based humanistic counselling, an equivalent competence and evidence-based person-centred therapy for young people. The chapter then looks at the emergence of integrative and pluralistic models of person-centred practice, which are closely aligned to the values and practices of the counselling psychology field.

EMOTION-FOCUSED THERAPY

Emotion-focused therapy (EFT), also referred to as *process-experiential therapy*, is an integrative form of humanistic therapy that begins with the genuinely prizing and empathic relationship, as described by Rogers (1951), and adds to this task-focused and process-guiding therapeutic methods more typical of gestalt therapy (Perls, 1969) and focusing (Gendlin, 1981). The origins of the approach lie in the work of Rogers and Gendlin in the late 1950s when they moved their attention from the therapeutic conditions offered by the therapist to the client's process (Elliott, 2012). The therapeutic practice of focusing emerged from this work and with it the development of an 'experiential' branch of person-centred therapy. Such is the importance of this development that the family of PCTs are sometimes referred to as the 'person-centred and experiential approaches'.

As with the classical client-centred approach (Rogers, 1951), EFT emphasises the primacy of emotional experiencing in human functioning, the importance of authentic human relationships, working with the whole person, self-determination and the innate tendency towards growth. These principles are supplemented with emotion theory (Elliott et al., 2004), which views emotion as fundamentally adaptive, helping people to process information and take action in order to meet needs.

In its theory of human functioning, EFT uses the concept of *emotion schemes* (cf. cognitive schema) to explain how experience is organised. These are conceived as mutable, highly idiosyncratic networks of component elements that, although not immediately available to awareness, are constantly being synthesised into a person's experience (Greenberg and Pascual-Leone, 1997). The networked elements that comprise emotion schemes exist in an interactive and dynamic relationship. Hence, change in one element will quickly spread to other aspects of the emotion scheme. The component elements can be categorised as follows:

- The experienced emotion (e.g. fear, hurt, anger).
- Perceptual/situational elements (e.g. immediate awareness of current situation, together with episodic memories of past situations).
- Bodily/expressive elements (e.g. the physical manifestation of an emotion within the body, such as 'butterflies' in the stomach).
- Symbolic/conceptual elements (e.g. verbal or visual representations of the emotion, such as the phrase 'I'm in trouble', or a visual image of being punished).
- Motivational/behavioural elements (e.g. associated needs, wishes, intentions or actions, such as the need to protect oneself).

EFT recognises that optimal emotional processing involves all of these elements. Additionally, EFT theorises a number of characteristic ways that people respond emotionally:

- *Primary adaptive emotion responses* are natural emotional reactions to a situation that help us take appropriate action and get our needs met. An example of this would be when a fear response to a situation activates a fight or flight reaction that allows us to keep ourselves safe and protected.
- *Maladaptive emotion responses* are where a situation activates a learned response based on previous rather than immediate experience. For example, people with past experiences of physical or sexual abuse may respond to intimacy with fear or anger.
- *Secondary reactive emotion responses* are where a secondary emotion replaces the original emotional response to a situation. For example, where fear may be replaced with anger, as the former is experienced as an unacceptable feeling.
- *Instrumental emotion responses* are displays of emotion intended to elicit a particular effect from others. For example, using anger to bully and intimidate others.

EFT aims to help clients access the primary adaptive emotions that often underlie the other emotional response modes, thus supporting their ability to react naturally and spontaneously to situations and take appropriate action.

Emotion regulation is likewise a key concept in EFT. For emotions to be experienced and processed in a functional way, it is argued that they need to be experienced at an optimal level. The ability to regulate emotion is seen as being moderated by early attachment experiences which, if not satisfactory, can lead to one of two extremes: either perceiving emotions as being painful and threatening and so trying to keep them blocked out of awareness; or viewing emotions as overpowering and so becoming quickly overwhelmed by them. Both of these extremes render a person unable to process their emotions. Effective emotional regulation involves both an ability to *access and amplify* emotion when necessary, such as when preparing for an important performance, or, conversely, *containing* the level of emotional arousal, such as when feeling nervous at the prospect of attending an interview or sitting an exam.

EFT views the self as composed of many different sub-selves, or *self-aspects*, that interact continually to produce experience and action. From this standpoint, problems can occur where a hostile relationship exists between different aspects of the self. For instance, one self-aspect may be punishingly critical of another, and this leads to an internal dialogue that produces psychological distress and emotional pain. In this respect, psychological problems are seen as resulting, to a large extent, from hostile or critical relationships between different self-aspects. EFT has developed a range of methods that seek to make explicit problematic internal dialogues and, in doing so, create opportunities for their transformation.

As with all forms of person-centred therapy, EFT practice is underpinned by the need to establish a therapeutic bond, mutual collaboration and empathic attunement. In addition, however, the client's problems – as presented in therapy sessions – are seen as suggesting different therapeutic *tasks*. From an EFT perspective, therapists need to be able to identify and articulate these tasks and offer clients opportunities to work on them. In this respect, the EFT therapist's empathic responding is supplemented with *process guiding*.

Tasks fall into different categories, indicated by a problem *marker*.

- *Empathy-based tasks* are indicated where a client wishes to explore a particular emotional experience, empathic exploration being the appropriate response from the therapist. Similarly, where a client is feeling vulnerable, empathic affirmation may help them stay with and work through the feelings.
- *Relational tasks* include the need to build a collaborative therapeutic relationship and attend to any challenges to the relationship, such as the client expressing discontent with the therapist or therapy.
- *Experiencing tasks* are where clients need to access and symbolise their emotional experiences. In these contexts the therapist may help the client to clarify how they feel and moderate emotional arousal, for example, if the client is feeling emotionally overwhelmed.
- *Reprocessing tasks* are indicated where a client may present problematic experiences that may be traumatic or simply puzzling. Here the therapist would help the client to narrate the difficult experience, deepening their awareness and contact with underlying feelings. At times, life events may challenge clients' strongly held beliefs, leading them into a state of emotional protest. Therapeutic work here needs to help clients reflect, on the one hand, upon beliefs about self and

the world and, on the other, upon the significance of the troubling life event in order to move towards a greater sense of integration.

- *Active expression tasks* are often indicated where a client is conflicted and particular self-aspects are at odds with each other. The therapeutic task here is to enact dialogue between self-aspects (often using 'two-chair work', in which people move between different chairs to vocalise different self-aspects) in order to transform the dialogue and reduce the degree of self-conflict. Similarly, where a client experiences lingering bad feelings towards a significant other, chair work can be used to enact a dialogue with the significant other, allowing unresolved feelings to be expressed and a sense of resolution achieved.

The development of EFT is supported by a programme of process and outcome research stretching back over the last 25 years. The therapy has been the subject of at least 18 separate outcome studies with a variety of clinical populations. Its effectiveness in the treatment of depression has been evidenced in a number of studies (e.g. Goldman et al., 2006; Greenburg and Watson, 1998; Watson et al., 2003). Several researchers are currently evaluating the effects of EFT with anxiety, including generalised anxiety and social anxiety, with promising preliminary results (Elliott, 2013; Timulak and McElvaney, 2012).

THE HUMANISTIC PSYCHOLOGICAL THERAPIES COMPETENCE FRAMEWORK

EFT, and the work of Elliott and colleagues, played a significant part in the development of competences for humanistic/person-centred therapies in 2009. The resulting competences were used as statements of evidence in the development of National Occupational Standards for humanistic psychological therapy. The background to this work was the Improving Access to Psychological Therapies (IAPT) programme, launched in May 2007 and gradually rolled out across England only; Scotland, Wales and Northern Ireland have their own programmes for the delivery of psychological services. This initiative provided the impetus for the first wave of work on the development of competences for psychological therapies. Initial work identified the competences needed to deliver good quality CBT (Roth and Pilling, 2007) and this CBT competence model was used as a prototype for developing the competences for other psychological therapies (Roth and Pilling, 2008). The humanistic psychological therapies competence framework drew upon a number of sources of evidence:

- A Cochrane review of counselling conducted by Bower and Rowland (2006).
- A database of humanistic psychological therapy trials collated by Robert Elliott and colleagues at the University of Strathclyde.
- A search of databases held by the British Psychological Society's Centre for Outcomes Research and Effectiveness[1] (used as part of NICE guideline development), identifying any additional humanistic trials not identified by the above sources of information.

---

1 www.ucl.ac.uk/clinical-psychology/CORE/core_homepage.htm

A review of these sources resulted in a final list of trials that met, or came close to meeting, the standards of evidence required for clinical recommendation guidelines, such as NICE and SIGN (Scottish Intercollegiate Guidelines Network). Competences from the interventions used in these trials – as articulated in the intervention manuals – were then extracted, to give an indication of the understandings and practices that showed evidence of efficacy.

The framework that emerged (Figure 17.1) included a breadth of humanistic understandings and practices. This included those associated with PCT (both classical and contemporary), with EFT, and with a more psychodynamically informed integrative practice.

The framework organises competences into five domains.

Generic therapeutic competences

Generic competences are those employed in any psychological therapy, reflecting the fact that all therapies share common features. For example, all therapists would be expected to be able to build a trusting relationship with clients, relating to them in a manner that is warm, encouraging and accepting. The building of a solid therapeutic relationship provides a basis for the successful introduction of more technical interventions. These common therapeutic factors sit alongside professional knowledge and skill, such as an understanding of ethics and the ability to manage ethical issues.

Basic humanistic psychological therapy competences

This category of competences underpins the provision of more specific humanistic methods and is viewed as *basic* not because the competences are easy to implement but because of their foundational nature. Humanistic approaches privilege a focus on the therapeutic relationship, based on the proposition that this is the primary vehicle for change. As a consequence, it makes sense for competences in this domain to detail the activities that contribute to the cycle of developing, maintaining and concluding the therapeutic relationship.

Specific humanistic psychological therapy competences

While the competences listed in the basic domain are assumed to be fundamental to all humanistic approaches, the specific competences set out a number of areas of theory and practice that will be approached selectively by humanistic or person-centred practitioners according to their particular orientation. These broad areas of practice are: experiential humanistic therapy, classical client-centred therapy and humanistic-integrative therapy. The assumption is that all humanistic practitioners would implement the basic competences but would be unlikely to use all the specific competences.

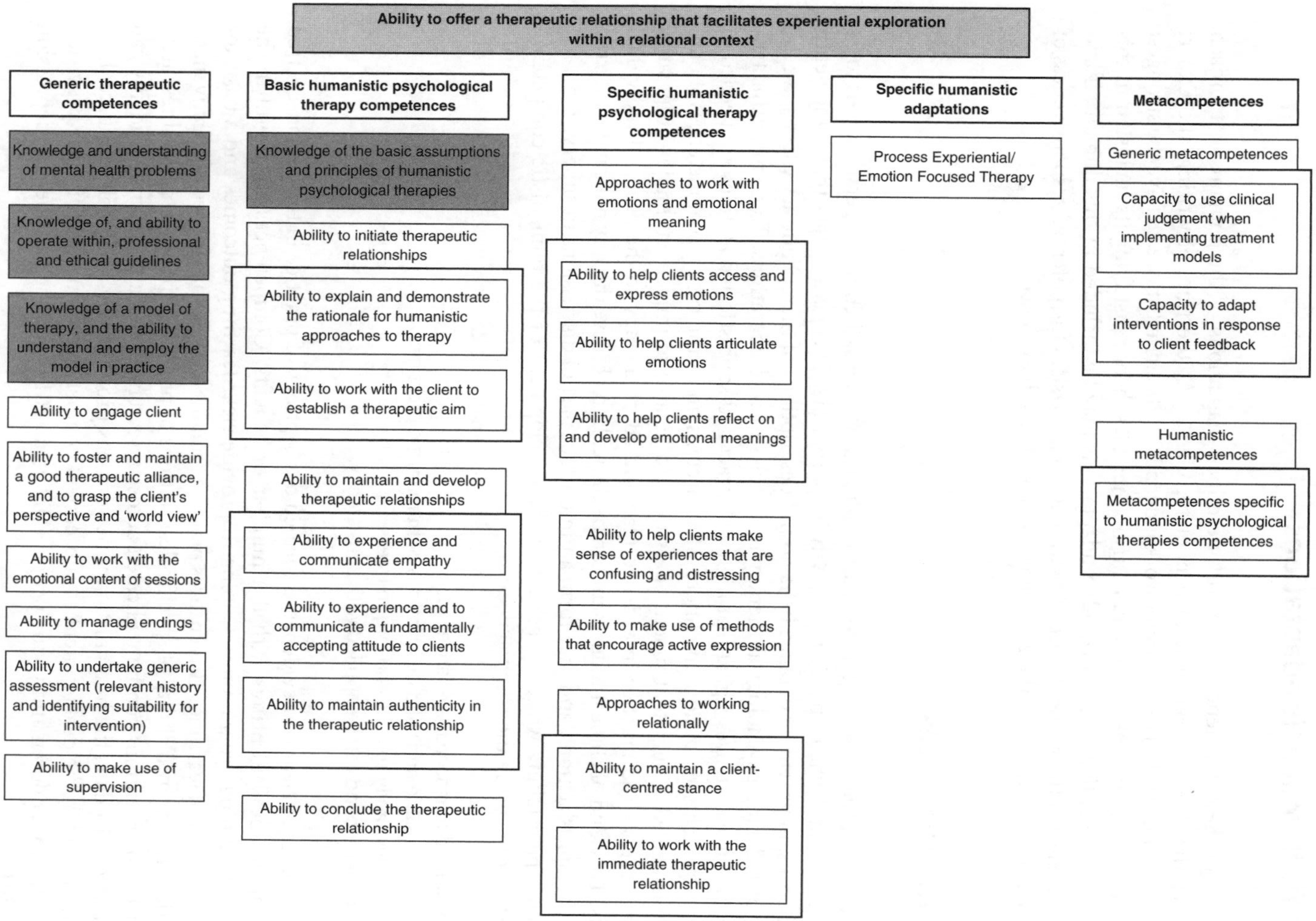

Ability to offer a therapeutic relationship that facilitates experiential exploration within a relational context

Generic therapeutic competences

Knowledge and understanding of mental health problems

Knowledge of, and ability to operate within, professional and ethical guidelines

Knowledge of a model of therapy, and the ability to understand and employ the model in practice

Ability to engage client

Ability to foster and maintain a good therapeutic alliance, and to grasp the client's perspective and 'world view'

Ability to work with the emotional content of sessions

Ability to manage endings

Ability to undertake generic assessment (relevant history and identifying suitability for intervention)

Ability to make use of supervision

Basic humanistic psychological therapy competences

Knowledge of the basic assumptions and principles of humanistic psychological therapies

Ability to initiate therapeutic relationships

Ability to explain and demonstrate the rationale for humanistic approaches to therapy

Ability to work with the client to establish a therapeutic aim

Ability to maintain and develop therapeutic relationships

Ability to experience and communicate empathy

Ability to experience and to communicate a fundamentally accepting attitude to clients

Ability to maintain authenticity in the therapeutic relationship

Ability to conclude the therapeutic relationship

Specific humanistic psychological therapy competences

Approaches to work with emotions and emotional meaning

Ability to help clients access and express emotions

Ability to help clients articulate emotions

Ability to help clients reflect on and develop emotional meanings

Ability to help clients make sense of experiences that are confusing and distressing

Ability to make use of methods that encourage active expression

Approaches to working relationally

Ability to maintain a client-centred stance

Ability to work with the immediate therapeutic relationship

Specific humanistic adaptations

Process Experiential/ Emotion Focused Therapy

Metacompetences

Generic metacompetences

Capacity to use clinical judgement when implementing treatment models

Capacity to adapt interventions in response to client feedback

Humanistic metacompetences

Metacompetences specific to humanistic psychological therapies competences

Figure 17.1 The humanistic psychological therapies competence framework

Note: Shaded boxes indicate areas of knowledge; unshaded boxes, areas of application. Boxes grouped together using larger boxes indicate areas of commonality.

Specific humanistic adaptations

This area of the competence framework describes adaptations of the humanistic approach that have the strongest evidence of benefit for clients. At the time of writing, the Expert Reference Group (ERG) for the framework judged EFT, discussed above, to have the strongest evidence base among the various humanistic therapies, hence justifying its inclusion in this domain. The fact that, over time, other adaptations may be included in this domain, if and when evidence of their efficacy becomes available, emphasises the potential responsiveness of competence frameworks to the emergence of new research evidence.

Metacompetences

This section of the framework recognises that to carry out a skilled task a person needs to be aware of why and when a particular activity is appropriate. There is a danger that competence frameworks, in providing detailed behavioural descriptions of therapeutic activities, have the effect of reducing psychological therapy to a series of rote operations. To counter this tendency, metacompetences signal that highly abstract and sophisticated abilities are needed to make judgements about how and under what circumstances the various competences should be implemented. Competent practitioners need to be able to implement higher-order links between theory and practice in order to plan and adapt therapy to the needs of individual clients. This kind of clinical judgement can be difficult to observe directly but can be inferred from therapists' actions, and may form an important part of discussions in supervision.

Much painstaking work has gone into the development of the humanistic competence framework to ensure the competences:

- are aligned to research evidence;
- are recognisable and valid descriptions of humanistic practice;
- are behaviourally specific and jargon free;
- are coherent and can be applied with consistency.

The existence of clear and evidence-informed descriptions of practice in the person-centred and humanistic field brings with it a number of benefits. Competences are useful in the design of training programmes, helping to provide clear learning outcomes and a basis for the assessment of learning. This ensures practice remains aligned to evidence of effectiveness. Additionally, the availability of specific descriptions of practice supports empirical research, ensuring interventions can be replicated across research studies and treatment fidelity can be assessed. To date, the humanistic framework has proved to be a valuable resource, having been used in the development of subsequent competence frameworks for the provision of therapy for children and young people (Hill et al., 2014) and the treatment of depression (Hill, 2010).

HUMANISTIC COUNSELLING FOR YOUNG PEOPLE

Drawing on both the competence framework for humanistic psychological therapies (Roth et al., 2009), and the competence framework for child and adolescent mental health services (Roth et al. 2011), the competences required to deliver effective humanistic counselling for young people (Hill et al., 2014) was developed in 2012–14. This identified a range of understandings and methods, primarily derived from PCT, that have been shown effective in bringing about positive change for 11–18-year-olds.

Given its person-centred foundations, the framework describes ways of working that reinforce and validate spontaneous and immediate experiencing, and encourage self-awareness and contact with emotion. The practitioner's role is one of helping young people to extend their awareness of their subjective world and supporting their natural striving towards self-awareness and personally determined solutions. However, the framework is also open to the flexible and personalised integration of additional, non-humanistic therapeutic methods that have been evidenced as effective for young people.

Although not attempting to provide a comprehensive description of play therapy, the framework does include competences for specific creative therapies, recognising that these may be particularly relevant for working with children whose capacity for expressing thoughts and feelings is limited by their developmental stage. Additionally, knowledge of and the ability to work effectively within the organisational context are viewed as important areas of competence, based on the assumption that counsellors working with young people would be unlikely to be operating independently of an organisational structure (e.g. schools, third-sector organisations).

COUNSELLING FOR DEPRESSION

Counselling for depression (CfD) is a manualised form of psychological therapy as recommended by NICE (2009) for the treatment of depression. It is based on a person-centred, experiential model and is particularly appropriate for people with persistent sub-threshold depressive symptoms or mild to moderate depression. Clinical trials have shown this type of counselling to be effective when 6–10 sessions are offered. However, it is recognised that in more complex cases which show benefit in the initial sessions, further improvement may be observed with additional sessions up to the maximum number suggested for other NICE recommended therapies such as CBT, that is, 20 sessions. (Sanders and Hill, 2014: 28)

CfD has been developed as an evidence-based therapy, approved for delivery in the English National Health Service (Sanders and Hill, 2014). Its development has drawn upon both EFT theory and practice and the humanistic psychological therapies competence framework, detailed above. The focus of the therapy is to address the emotional problems underlying depression along with the intrapersonal processes, such as low self-esteem and excessive self-criticism, which maintain depressed mood. It aims to help clients contact underlying

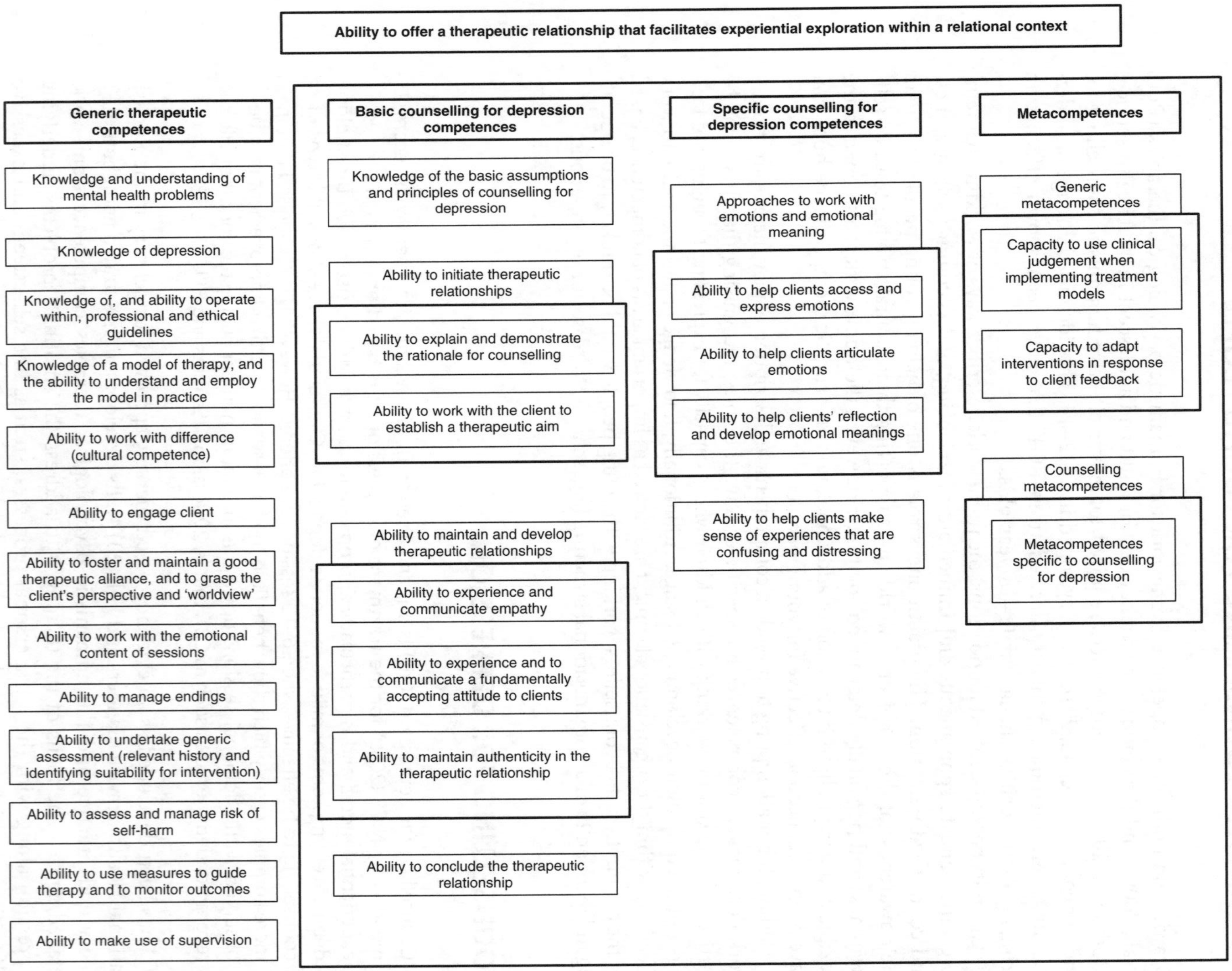

Ability to offer a therapeutic relationship that facilitates experiential exploration within a relational context

Metacompetences

Generic metacompetences

Capacity to use clinical judgement when implementing treatment models

Capacity to adapt interventions in response to client feedback

Counselling metacompetences

Metacompetences specific to counselling for depression

Specific counselling for depression competences

Approaches to work with emotions and emotional meaning

Ability to help clients access and express emotions

Ability to help clients articulate emotions

Ability to help clients' reflection and develop emotional meanings

Ability to help clients make sense of experiences that are confusing and distressing

Basic counselling for depression competences

Knowledge of the basic assumptions and principles of counselling for depression

Ability to initiate therapeutic relationships

Ability to explain and demonstrate the rationale for counselling

Ability to work with the client to establish a therapeutic aim

Ability to maintain and develop therapeutic relationships

Ability to experience and communicate empathy

Ability to experience and to communicate a fundamentally accepting attitude to clients

Ability to maintain authenticity in the therapeutic relationship

Ability to conclude the therapeutic relationship

Generic therapeutic competences

Knowledge and understanding of mental health problems

Knowledge of depression

Knowledge of, and ability to operate within, professional and ethical guidelines

Knowledge of a model of therapy, and the ability to understand and employ the model in practice

Ability to work with difference (cultural competence)

Ability to engage client

Ability to foster and maintain a good therapeutic alliance, and to grasp the client's perspective and 'worldview'

Ability to work with the emotional content of sessions

Ability to manage endings

Ability to undertake generic assessment (relevant history and identifying suitability for intervention)

Ability to assess and manage risk of self-harm

Ability to use measures to guide therapy and to monitor outcomes

Ability to make use of supervision

Figure 17.2 The counselling for depression competence framework

feelings, make sense of them and reflect on the new meanings that emerge, providing a basis for psychological and behavioural change.

The origins of the approach lie in PCT (Rogers, 1951) and in EFT (Elliott et al., 2004). What is distinctive about CfD is its development as a specific treatment for depression, its integration of PCT and EFT, and its alignment with England's NICE guidelines. The IAPT programme, with its initial aim to implement the NICE guidelines for depression and anxiety, provided the backdrop for CfD's development. NICE guidance is officially for England only, although decisions as to how their guidance applies in Wales, Scotland and Northern Ireland are made by the devolved administrations.

The process used to translate into practice NICE's recommendation of counselling for the treatment of depression followed principles outlined by Roth and Pilling (2008), and made use of the humanistic competence framework (Roth et al., 2009) described earlier in this chapter. Additionally, data were gathered on UK counsellors, which indicated that over 70 per cent of members of the British Association for Counselling and Psychotherapy had trained in humanistic therapy, and in particular person-centred therapy. This provided the rationale for selecting the humanistic framework as a starting point for developing the counselling model. The humanistic framework proved to be a valuable resource with its description of a broad range of humanistic therapies, but was ultimately too diverse to use in its entirety. It was necessary to scope the framework in order to produce a narrower and more coherent description of counselling that remained aligned with the NICE depression guideline. The evidence supporting the inclusion of counselling in the depression guideline consists mainly of RCTs of either PCT or EFT (Bedi et al., 2000; Friedli et al., 1997; Goldman et al., 2006; Greenberg and Watson, 1998; Marriott and Kellett, 2009; Watson et al., 2003). This suggested that a focus on these two areas of practice would describe counselling as recommended by the guideline. Hence, competences from the humanistic framework describing PCT and EFT were drawn down to form the basis of a new framework that was termed *counselling for depression* (CfD) (see Figure 1.2). The CfD framework was then used to devise a training curriculum to train therapists to provide evidence-based counselling in the IAPT programme for clients with depression.

The CfD approach recognises the limitations inherent in using diagnostic terms such as 'depression' and the tendency for such terminology to medicalise human distress. However, despite the fact that the underlying experience of their depression is subjective and unique, clients with low mood often experience a range of common symptoms. CfD aims to work with the emotional problems and depressive processes associated with low mood, while at the same time taking a flexible, relational approach that adapts to individual needs. Working both interpersonally and intra-personally, the approach focuses both on the relationship between client and therapist and the client's relationship with themselves.

The CfD conceptualisation of depression derives from both PCT and EFT theory. Watson and Bryan (2010) operationalised Rogers' (1951) concept of incongruence as self-discrepancies; for example, the difference between a person's sense of who they are and who they would like to be. The authors found that measures of self-discrepancy and measures of anxiety and depression were correlated, theorising that a therapeutic approach that reduces self-discrepancy will likewise impact anxiety and depression. Clients inevitably experience depression as a state of being rather than a process, often expressed in statements such as 'I'm not myself' or 'I want my old self back'. Feelings of powerlessness and hopelessness often lead clients to feel 'stuck' in this depressed state of being.

Aspects of EFT theory are brought into CfD to complement person-centred theory. EFT identifies a number of micro-processes (such as self-critical inner dialogues) that are seen as maintaining a state of depression. This introduces the idea that clients are actively, albeit unintentionally, holding themselves in a depressed state of being. It also implies a foregrounding of the client's agency and the notion that clients have the capacity to exercise control over their problems: they can maintain them, make them worse, or reduce them. This suggests that what may be experienced as an intractable depressed state of being can be changed by attending to smaller issues that are more specific and manageable. These theoretical ideas point a way through the stuckness of depression.

Examples of micro-processes particularly associated with depression fall into two areas: emotional processing and problematic self-dialogues. An example of emotional processing is where clients experience core maladaptive emotions such as helplessness or worthlessness as regular responses to situations and life events. These are often learned emotional responses resulting from early experiences of neglect or abuse which serve to keep clients in a state of depression. Problems with moderating emotional arousal (i.e. being consistently emotionally out of touch or, conversely, emotionally overwhelmed) also fall into this category. Examples of problematic self-dialogues, as suggested earlier, are where one self-aspect is excessively critical of another, constantly suppresses another, regularly interrupts another, or experiences the absence of another. The sequelae of these processes can be low self-esteem, lack of access to feelings, inability to think clearly or make decisions, lingering feelings of sadness, anger or resentment, all of which contribute to the more generalised experience of depression.

The central plank of CfD practice – in working with both the generalised experience of depression and its underpinning micro-processes – are the person-centred relational conditions, with a particular emphasis on empathy. In responding empathically, the therapist helps the client to deepen their awareness of their depression, while at the same time being alert to markers that are indicative of problematic micro-processes. Once a micro-process has been identified (e.g. a problematic self-dialogue), the therapist's empathy helps the client to alternately in-dwell in each self-aspect involved in the internal dialogue, facilitating a greater awareness of the underlying thoughts, feelings and behaviour and supporting the articulation of these. As the client experiences a softening of the problematic dialogue, there is a shift in their generalised experience of depression, a reduction in the sense of stuckness, and a movement towards greater congruence. The therapist's ability to work equally effectively with both the general (e.g. the state of depression) and the particular (depression-maintaining micro-processes), and to move seamlessly between the two, integrates PCT and EFT theory and practice to produce a robust and coherent therapeutic approach.

A contrast between EFT and CfD is that, whereas EFT uses process-guiding interventions and therapeutic activities such as two-chair work, CfD remains more rooted in the person-centred relational stance. The reasons for this are both philosophical and pragmatic.

Philosophically, CfD seeks to position itself within the mainstream of counselling practice in the UK, which is heavily influenced by PCT and tends to privilege what the client brings to the therapeutic relationship in terms of their motivation for change and their subjective reality. An empathic stance is viewed as the best way to build on the client's sense of agency and their potential for psychological growth, as opposed to a more process-guiding approach which may be seen as having the potential to get in the way of the client's growth process. On a more pragmatic note, CfD has been developed as a strategic and time-limited therapy. Therapeutic activities such as two-chair work are not recommended in the early stages of therapy and some clients may need significant preliminary work in areas such as emotional regulation before this method can proceed. For these reasons, two-chair work has not been included in CfD, as it does not easily fit with CfD's time-limited structure.

The development of a form of counselling for depressed clients, recommended by NICE for use in the IAPT programme, is a significant step forward for the person-centred community. Training in CfD is now widely available and an adherence measure, the Person-Centred and Experiential Psychotherapy Scale (PCEPS), has been developed at the University of Strathclyde (Freire et al., 2014). The scale can be used to assess both counsellor adherence in research studies and counsellor competence in the training context. Additionally, routine outcome measurement using standard measures has been a feature of IAPT since its inception. Bringing all these developments together, the prospect of conducting RCTs and large-scale cohort studies of CfD now becomes much more feasible, with the longer-term aim of building a robust evidence-base around a specific model of person-centred therapy that has wide currency in the UK context.

SCHOOL-BASED HUMANISTIC COUNSELLING

Alongside the development of CfD, *school-based humanistic counselling* (SBHC) was established in 2009 as a standardised form of person-centred therapy for young people (Cooper et al., 2013). The humanistic orientation of this approach reflects the predominantly person-centred/humanistic style of British school-based counsellors (Cooper, 2009a; Hill et al., 2011). As with CfD, SBHC was based on the humanistic psychological therapies competence framework (Roth et al., 2009), and subsequently the competences for humanistic counselling with young people (Hill et al., 2013).

The assumption underlying SBHC is that young people have the capacity to successfully address difficulties in their lives if they have an opportunity to talk through these problems with an empathic, supportive and independent adult. School-based humanistic counsellors use a range of techniques to facilitate this process, including active listening, empathic reflections, inviting clients to access and express underlying emotions and needs, and helping clients to reflect on and make sense of their experiences and behaviours. Clients are also encouraged to consider the range of options that they are facing, and to make choices that are most likely to be helpful within their given circumstances.

Four pilot trials have now been conducted of SBHC against waiting list conditions for young people experiencing moderate to severe levels of emotional distress (Cooper et al., 2010; McArthur et al., 2013; Pearce et al., 2013; Pybis et al., 2014). Total numbers of participants in each of these trials ranged from 32 to 64, with the SBHC intervention delivered weekly for up to ten weeks. Auditing of the adherence to person-centred/humanistic competences has been with the PCEPS measure, described above. Recruitment was through the school's pastoral care system. A pooled analysis of data across these four pilot studies suggests that SBHC brings about medium to large reductions in psychological distress as compared to pastoral care as usual, up to three months from assessment. This suggests that person-centred practice may have an important place in delivering psychological interventions to young people within an educational context.

PLURALISTIC AND INTEGRATIVE THERAPIES

With the proliferation of person-centred and experiential therapies, a number of authors within the person-centred field have proposed specifically integrative or eclectic forms of person-centred practice. In reality, integrative methods have probably been central to person-centred work for many years. Cain (2010: 62), for instance, writes: 'I suspect a substantial portion of person-centred practitioners are, in fact, integrative, as relatively few adhere to a strictly classical, client-centred model.' However, what is newer is attempts to develop integrative therapies that are *specifically* based on person-centred principles and values, and to establish frameworks whereby these practices can be developed and expanded through research and theory.

The starting point for each of these integrative approaches is that clients are the principal agents of therapeutic change, and that different clients are likely to want – and need – different kinds of input from their therapists (Bohart and Tallman, 1999; Cain, 2010; Cooper and McLeod, 2011b). On this basis, it is argued that it is legitimate for person-centred therapists to go beyond both classical and experiential ways of responding, and instead draw on a wider repertoire of therapeutic practices, if and where they are skilled in such methods. In contrast to a syncretic integrationism, however, the emphasis here is very much on orientating such practices around clients' individual wants and needs, such that the practice retains a strongly *client*-centred emphasis.

An example of this, which is closely aligned to the values and practices of counselling psychology (Cooper, 2009b), is Cooper and McLeod's pluralistic approach (Cooper and McLeod, 2011a, 2011b). This perspective places particular emphasis on an understanding of clients as unique, nonstandardisable 'othernesses', whose therapeutic wants and needs are likely to be highly heterogeneous and unknowable in advance. Based on this idiographic standpoint, it argues that a person-centred understanding of therapeutic change necessitates an openness to, and appreciation of, the many different ways in which clients may benefit from therapy, including, but not limited to, established person-centred and experiential practices. To translate such pluralistic principles into practice, it is suggested that therapists should specifically orientate their work towards clients' goals, and enhance their levels of dialogue and metatherapeutic communication with clients regarding the goals, tasks and methods of therapy. This pluralistic approach to person-centred therapy challenges a 'dogmatic person-centredness', and encourages person-centred practitioners to be aware of the limits of their work. It also provides a coherent, 'client-centred' framework through which person-centred therapists can incorporate a wide body of practices, research findings and theories into their work.

CONCLUSION

In the face of very real threats to its existence, the person-centred approach in the UK has developed and evolved in a range of ways. The challenge of the empirically supported therapies movement and NICE have brought to the fore a more structured, evidenced and targeted person-centred therapy in the form of EFT. The person-centred field has also responded by developing evidence-based competences for its approach, and by systematising and explicating its way of working with depressed adults and young people. The development of integrative and pluralistic forms of therapy, based on person-centred principles, is another recent attempt to re-configure person-centred values and practices to the contemporary therapeutic landscape.

  For some, these developments may seem a betrayal of the very foundations of the person-centred approach: the belief that human beings can grow and evolve from 'within', without the need for external structures or proofs. However, these developments can also be seen as a very person-centred means of keeping the approach alive, fresh and continually evolving in response to its external circumstances. As Carl Rogers (1986, cited in Cain, 2010: 42), himself, put it:

> There is only one way in which a person-centred approach can avoid becoming narrow, dogmatic and restrictive. That is through studies – simultaneously hard-headed and tender-minded – which open new vistas, bring new insights, challenge our hypotheses, enrich our theory, expand our knowledge, and involve us more deeply in an understanding of the phenomena of human change.

REFERENCES

Bedi, N., Chilvers, C., Churchill, R., Dewey, M., Duggan, C., Fielding, K., Gretton, V., Miller, P., Harrison, G., Lee, A. and Williams, I. (2000) Assessing effectiveness of treatment of depression in primary care. *British Journal of Psychiatry*, 177: 312–318.

Bohart, A. C. and Tallman, K. (1999) *How Clients Make Therapy Work: The Process of Active Self-Healing*. Washington, DC: American Psychological Association.

Bower, P. and Rowland, N. (2006) Effectiveness and cost effectiveness of counselling in primary care. *Cochrane Database of Systematic Reviews*. Issue 3, Art. No.: CD001125.

Cain, D. J. (2010) *Person-Centered Psychotherapies*. Washington, DC: American Psychological Association.

Cooper, M. (2009a) Counselling in UK secondary schools: A comprehensive review of audit and evaluation studies. *Counselling and Psychotherapy Research*, 9(3): 137–150.

Cooper, M. (2009b) Welcoming the Other: Actualising the humanistic ethic at the core of counselling psychology practice. *Counselling Psychology Review*, 24(3&4): 119–129.

Cooper, M. (2011) *Development of a Randomised Controlled Trial of Counselling for Depression*. Lutterworth: British Association for Counselling and Psychotherapy.

Cooper, M. and McLeod, J. (2011a) Person-centered therapy: A pluralistic perspective. *Person-Centered and Experiential Psychotherapies*, 10(3): 210–223.

Cooper, M. and McLeod, J. (2011b) *Pluralistic Counselling and Psychotherapy*. London: Sage.

Cooper, M., O'Hara, M., Schmid, P. and Bohart, A. C. (2013) Person-centred therapy today and tomorrow: Vision, challenge and growth. In M. Cooper, P. F. Schmid, M. O'Hara and G. Wyatt (eds), *The Handbook of Person-Centred Psychotherapy and Counselling* (2nd edn). Basingstoke: Palgrave.

Cooper, M., Rowland, N., McArthur, K., Pattison, S., Cromarty, K. and Richards, K. (2010) Randomised controlled trial of school-based humanistic counselling for emotional distress in young people: Feasibility study and preliminary indications of efficacy. *Child and Adolescent Psychiatry and Mental Health*, 4(1): 1–12.

Elliott, R. (2002) Render unto Caesar: Quantitative and qualitative knowing in research on humanistic therapies. *Person-Centered and Experiential Psychotherapies*, 1(1&2): 102–117.

Elliott, R. (2012) Emotion-focused therapy. In P. Sanders (ed.), *The Tribes of the Person-Centred Nation* (2nd edn) (pp. 103–130). Ross-on-Wye: PCCS Books.

Elliott, R. (2013) Person-centred/experiential psychotherapy for anxiety difficulties: Theory, research and practice. *Person-Centered and Experiential Psychotherapies*, 12(1): 16–32.

Elliott, R., Greenberg, L. S., Watson, J. C., Timulak, L. and Freire, E. (2013) Research on humanistic-experiential psychotherapies. In M. J. Lambert (ed.), *Bergin and Garfield's Handbook of Psychotherapy and Behavior Change* (pp. 495–538). Hoboken, NJ: John Wiley.

Elliott, R., Watson, J. C., Goldman, R. N. and Greenberg, L. S. (2004) *Learning Emotion-Focused Therapy: The Process-Experiential Approach to Change*. Washington, DC: American Psychological Association.

Freire, E., Elliott, R. and Westwell, G. (2014) Person-Centred and Experiential Psychotherapy Scale: Development and reliability of an adherence/competence measure for person-centred and experiential psychotherapies. *Counselling and Psychotherapy Research*, 14(3): 220–226.

Friedli, K., King, M. B., Lloyd, M. and Horder, J. (1997) Randomised controlled assessment of non-directive psychotherapy versus routine general-practitioner care. *Lancet*, 350: 1662–1665.

Gendlin, E. T. (1981) *Focusing* (2nd edn). New York: Bantam Books.

Gendlin, E. T. (1996) *Focusing-Oriented Psychotherapy: A Manual of the Experiential Method*. New York: Guilford Press.

Goldman, R. N., Greenberg, L. S. and Angus, L. (2006) The effects of adding emotion-focused interventions to the therapeutic relationship in the treatment of depression. *Psychotherapy Research*, 16: 537–549.

Greenberg, L. S. and Pascual-Leone, J. (1997) Emotion in the creation of personal meaning. In M. Power and C. Brewin (eds), *The Transformation of Meaning in Psychological Therapies* (pp. 157–74). Chichester: John Wiley & Sons.

Greenberg, L. S. and Watson, J. C. (1998) Experiential therapy of depression: Differential effects of client-centred relationship conditions and process experiential interventions. *Psychotherapy Research*, 8: 210–224.

Hill, A. (2010) *The Competences Required to Deliver Effective Counselling for Depression (CfD)*. Lutterworth: British Association for Counselling and Psychotherapy, www.ucl.ac.uk/pals/research/cehp/research-groups/core/pdfs/Counselling_for_Depression/Depression_Counselling_for_depression_clinician_s_guide.pdf (accessed 1 October 2015).

Hill, A., Cooper, M., Pybis, J., Cromarty, K., Pattison, S., Spong, S. and Maybanks, N. (2011) *Evaluation of the Welsh School-Based Counselling Strategy*. Cardiff: Welsh Government Social Research.

Hill, A., Roth, A. and Cooper, M. (2014) *The Competences Required to Deliver Effective Humanistic Counselling for Young People*. Lutterworth: British Association for Counselling and Psychotherapy, www.bacp.co.uk/admin/structure/files/pdf/12841_cyp-counsellors-guide.pdf (accessed 1 October 2015).

Marriott, M. and Kellett, S. (2009) Evaluating a cognitive analytic therapy service: Practice-based outcomes and comparisons with person-centred and cognitive behavioural therapies. *Psychology and Psychotherapy*, 82: 57–72.

McArthur, K., Cooper, M. and Berdondini, L. (2013) School-based humanistic counseling for psychological distress in young people: Pilot randomized controlled trial. *Psychotherapy Research*, 23(3): 355–365. doi: http://dx.doi.org/10.1080/10503307.2012.726750.

National Institute for Health and Clinical Excellence (2009) *Clinical Guideline 90: Depression in Adults: The Treatment and Management of Depression in Adults*. www.nice.org.uk/guidance/cg90/resources/guidance-depression-in-adults-pdf (accessed 1 October 2015).

Pearce, P., Sewell, R. and Osman, S. (2013) The ALIGN project: A randomised controlled trial of school-based person-centred counselling. Paper presented at the BACP Research Conference 2013, Birmingham.

Perls, F. S. (1969) *Gestalt Therapy Verbatim*. Moab, UT: Real People Press.

Prouty, G., Pörtner, M. and Van Werde, D. (2002) *Pre-Therapy: Reaching Contact Impaired Clients*. Ross-on-Wye: PCCS Books.

Pybis, J., Cooper, M., Hill, A., Cromarty, K., Levensley, R., Murdoch, J. and Turner, N. (2014) Pilot randomised controlled trial of school-based humanistic counselling for psychological distress in young people: Outcomes and methodological reflections. *Counselling and Psychotherapy Research*. doi: 10.1080/14733145.2014.905614.

Rogers, C. R. (1951) *Client-Centred Therapy*. Boston, MA: Houghton Mifflin.

Rogers, C. R. (1959) A theory of therapy, personality and interpersonal relationships as developed in the client-centered framework. In S. Koch (ed.), *Psychology: A Study of Science* (Vol. 3, pp. 184–256). New York: McGraw-Hill.

Rogers, N. (2000) *Creative Connection: Expressive Arts as Healing*. Ross-on-Wye: PCCS Books.

Roth, A. D., Calder, F. and Pilling, S. (2011) A competence framework for child and adolescent mental health services. NHS Education for Scotland, www.ucl.ac.uk/pals/research/cehp/research-groups/core/pdfs/CAMHS/CAMHS_Clinician_Competences_Framework_V1__2_.pdf (accessed 1 October 2015).

Roth, A., Hill, A. and Pilling, S. (2009) *The Competences Required to Deliver Effective Humanistic Psychological Therapies*. London: University College London, www.ucl.ac.uk/pals/research/cehp/research-groups/core/pdfs/Humanistic_Therapy/Humanistic_clinicians_guide.pdf (accessed 1 October 2015).

Roth, A. D. and Pilling, S. (2007) *The Competences Required to Deliver Effective Cognitive and Behavioural Therapy for People with Depression and with Anxiety Disorders*. London: Department of Health, www.ucl.ac.uk/pals/research/cehp/research-groups/core/pdfs/cbt/Backround_CBT_document_-_Clinicians_version.pdf (accessed 1 October 2015).

Roth, A. D. and Pilling, S. (2008) Using an evidence-based methodology to identify the competences required to deliver effective cognitive and behavioural therapy for depression and anxiety disorders. *Behavioural and Cognitive Psychotherapy*, 36: 129–147.

Sanders, P. (ed.) (2012) *The Tribes of the Person-Centred Nation: An Introduction to the Schools of Therapy Related to the Person-Centred Approach* (2nd edn). Ross-on-Wye: PCCS Books.

Sanders, P. and Hill, A. (2014) *Counselling for Depression: A Person-Centred and Experiential Approach to Practice*. London: Sage.

Schmid, P. F. (2011) The anthropological, relational and ethical foundations of person-centred therapy. In M. Cooper, P. Schmid, M. O'Hara and A. C. Bohart (eds), *The Handbook of Person-Centred Psychotherapy and Counselling* (pp. 66–83). Basingstoke: Palgrave.

Scottish Intercollegiate Guidelines Network (SIGN), www.sign.ac.uk (accessed 1 October 2015).

Timulak, L. and McElvaney, J. (2012, July) Emotion-focused therapy for generalised anxiety disorder. Paper presented at the conference of the World Association for Person-Centred and Experiential Psychotherapy and Counseling, Antwerp.

Warner, M. S. (2013) Difficult client process. In M. Cooper, P. Schmid, M. O'Hara and A. C. Bohart (eds), *The Handbook of Person-Centred Psychotherapy and Counselling* (2nd edn, pp. 343–358). Basingstoke: Palgrave.

Watson, J. C., Gordon, L. B., Stermac, L., Kalogerakos, F. and Steckley, P. (2003) Comparing the effectiveness of process-experiential with cognitive-behavioural psychotherapy in the treatment of depression. *Journal of Consulting and Clinical Psychology*, 71(4): 773–781.

Watson, N. and Bryan, B. C. (2010) Relations of self-discrepancies to anxiety and depression in the change process in psychotherapy. Paper presented at the meeting of the Society for Psychotherapy Research, Pacific Grove, California.

18
THE EVOLVING WORLD OF COGNITIVE AND MINDFULNESS-BASED INTERVENTIONS

DIANA SANDERS

INTRODUCTION

Cognitive therapy has undergone enormous changes in the last decade or so. With its roots in both psychoanalytic psychotherapy and behaviourism, cognitive therapy started life as a pragmatic, present-centred and short-term therapy for people struggling with depression (Beck et al., 1979). From these early models of depression, cognitive therapy evolved for the many different problems we experience, linking diagnoses such as anxiety, panic and obsessive compulsive disorder with specific cognitive and behavioural formulations and interventions, along with research to clarify the mechanisms of perpetuation and change. These models and interventions have been shown in many clinical trials to be highly effective. Cognitive therapy, also known as cognitive behavioural therapy (CBT), is a valuable and established approach, recommended and widely used in many clinical settings. Although originally seen as the prerogative of psychology and psychiatry, cognitive approaches are now adopted widely in education and occupational as well as health settings. Basic approaches to cognitive models and CBT are the starting point for many trainee counselling psychologists entering the professions, and are widely used in IAPT programmes.

While the CBT revolution appears to be set to take over the world, serious questions arise about those people for which the model was proving less valuable. Is CBT just a short-term fix, a glamorous and efficient means of producing enough change to satisfy the auditors but missing out the essence of being human? Is changing thinking and behaviour enough to make lasting changes in human despair? And how does CBT fit with what we can now see going on in our brains, the neurophysiological processes identified from neuroimaging? Far more is understood about psychological processes, such as attention, acceptance versus avoidance, rumination and worry, and how these feed into maintaining distress and difficulties – ideas of 'metacognition', thinking about thinking, and 'mindfulness', bringing attention and acceptance to the present moment in order to learn to respond rather than react to the challenges of our complex lives. Buddhist psychology now sits comfortably alongside cognitive psychology and psychotherapy, in a move that would, twenty years ago, have been unthinkable in mainstream psychology.

In this chapter, I describe the journey of CBT, from its basic forms to newer models of mindfulness-based cognitive psychotherapies and metacognitive therapies. Rather than evolving a single form over time, CBT now provides a richness of options – the initial models being highly effective and relevant to many people, and to many of those clients that counselling psychologists will meet during their training and practice. The newer models are exciting and attractive, but are in development, and the chapter will urge caution for those beginning their career in CBT methods to leap in before the basic models are fully understood and experienced.

ORIGINS OF THE COGNITIVE BEHAVIOURAL PSYCHOTHERAPIES

Aaron Beck, originally trained in psychoanalysis, developed the first, and essentially core, models and methods of cognitive therapy (see Beck et al., 1979), encompassing how and why people develop emotional problems, how to alleviate and eliminate disturbance, and how further problems might be prevented. These models, supported by what was, for the psychotherapy field, an impressive range of research validation for both its processes and its outcomes, provide the bedrock for modern cognitive psychotherapies, along with substantial evolution. The cognitive behavioural therapies evolved from introducing elements from behaviour therapy, such as exposure to feared and avoided situations and specific behavioural tasks in the form of behavioural experiments (Bennett-Levy et al., 2004). Change in behaviour in itself does not lead automatically to emotional change, but the means by which cognitive change mediates between behaviour and emotion is better understood. For example, a person with agoraphobia may go through the motions of going out of the house, in a series of graded behavioural exposure tasks, but still believe at some level that the outside world is highly dangerous and therefore remain fearful. However, if she also learns 'I can go out because the world is much safer than I believed', and experiences feeling safe, long-term cognitive and behavioural change is possible.

Further evolution and development leads to the wealth of CBT therapies we see today – with applications in physical and emotional health, short-term and long term methods, and applications in many different settings (Westbrook et al., 2012; Wills with Sanders, 2013). CBT is closely informed by evidence-based, scientific research, in its understanding of psychological processes such as cognition, attention, memory and decision-making, linking theory, experimental research and outcome studies. We are now seeing neurophysiological studies through brain scanning and fMRI, enabling greater understanding of the psychophysiology of distress.

THE COGNITIVE MODEL

The cognitive model is a coherent theoretical framework which forms the core of therapy, and is a basis for individual formulations for each unique person we see. It helps to map the development of problems, our beliefs about ourselves, others and the world we form as a result of often difficult early experience, what triggers distress and why problems persist. The model guides what kind of interventions may be helpful and is built up throughout initial assessment meetings and during therapy: a thorough assessment helps client and therapist to understand what created vulnerability to difficulties, why problems started at the point they did, and what kind of environmental, psychological and social factors are preventing recovery.

The following dialogue (Wills, 2008) illustrates the model:

Therapist: I'd like to explain how CBT works by telling a story. A large computer software company was facing financial difficulties, and had to make people redundant. Our two men in the story, A and B, were similar ages and did similar jobs. A, hearing about his redundancy, thought, 'Oh no, this is a disaster. I might never work again. What will my wife think of me? I won't be able to look after the family'. How do you think he felt?

Client: Desperate, I'd guess. Very upset, low. Scared.

Therapist: That's right. And what might he do?

Client: He'd want to give up, I guess. He'd be sort-of paralysed.

Therapist: I'd guess that as well. Our other man, B, same age, same skills, had a different reaction. He thought, 'What a shock. This will be a huge change. But I've not been happy for a while. It might be a chance to get something better, more interesting.' How would he feel? And what might he do?

Client: He'd feel quite shocked for a bit, but then might feel a bit excited, like getting on with the next stage of life.

We can see from the dialogue that two people have very different reactions to the same event, depending on their interpretation of the event or the meaning given to the situation. We can then think about why people have different interpretations, how their circumstances, background and experience determine their beliefs or rules about themselves, others or the world. We may speculate that A did not get enough support and encouragement in his early years, and was picked on and bullied at school. He never felt very confident in himself, but did well in his career by hard work and what he called 'luck'. His beliefs included: 'To be OK, I must do well at my work. If others criticise me, it means I'm a failure.' He interpreted the redundancy as a criticism. B, in contrast, was a more resilient soul, not putting a huge amount of importance on his job, feeling satisfied with his family and life beyond work. His beliefs might be along the lines of 'Life can be tough but something else always turns up'.

The thought–emotion cycle and negative thoughts

One of the aims in cognitive therapy is to look at the meaning the client gives to situations, emotions or biology, often expressed in the client's 'negative automatic thoughts'. The essence of the model shows there is a reciprocal relationship between emotional difficulties and seeing events as exaggerated beyond the available evidence. These exaggerated ways of seeing things tend to exert further negative influences on our feelings and behaviour. Thoughts affect emotions, but also vice versa. For example, depression leads to a negative bias in our thought, emotions and behaviour, and therefore when depressed, we think negative thoughts. When anxiety and fear levels are raised, the mind automatically becomes focused on danger, and we think fearful thoughts. Thoughts and feelings are often experienced as a unitary phenomenon and our labelling of 'thought' and 'feeling' is more a useful heuristic device for therapy than a truly knowable reality.

From thoughts to beliefs and schema

Cognitive therapy has traditionally distinguished between 'core beliefs' or 'schema', 'unhelpful assumptions' and 'negative thoughts', which form layers of meaning which we unpeel during therapy. CBT usually starts with identifying and working with the layer of thoughts, which are easily accessible, then working downwards to uncover and examine unhelpful assumptions. For example, for those who have core belief about badness, wrongness or shame, with maybe difficult or abusive backgrounds, work on core beliefs will be far more important and central in therapy compared with people with relatively helpful central beliefs.

The role of behaviour

What we do in response to our thoughts, feelings and beliefs links in the chain, locking the sequence of thought–feeling–behaviour into persistent, repetitive and unhelpful patterns. Some of these patterns are life-long, such as long-standing anxiety and low self-esteem leading to chronic avoidance, agoraphobia and other problems; others may be in response to short-term depression, such as a temporary withdrawal from normal life.

Mary was five when her mother died of cancer. When Mary was 29, the same age as her mother had been when she died, Mary became convinced she also was going to die, and became extremely anxious about her health. She started to avoid 'taking any risks', including driving and coming into contact with friends in case they had any infections, and focused so much on her body that she began to interpret any slight twinges as evidence of illness. She repeatedly visited her GP for reassurance. Her anxiety made her feel ill and exhausted most of the time, and she was off sick so much, she lost her job. She spent hours at home worrying about her health, lost contact with friends and became extremely low.

We can see from Mary's example that her belief, 'I am going to die young', led to a number of behaviours that maintain health anxiety: avoiding situations that might be dangerous (driving, seeing other people), focusing on her body and seeking reassurance. Her responses also maintain her low mood and depression: withdrawal from life, social isolation, spending time ruminating, and so on. In other problems, such as obsessive compulsive disorder, behaviours such as repeated hand washing, house cleaning and rituals to neutralise 'bad' thoughts are flagrant manifestations of thoughts and beliefs.

KEY FEATURES OF CBT

The basic principles of the cognitive-behavioural approach are as follows:

- A collaborative relationship in which client and therapist work together to understand and resolve problems.
- Cognitive formulation of the individual client, based on a general understanding of the problems brought to therapy.
- The method is structured, educational and focused, using Socratic enquiry and experimentation to promote change.
- CBT is a parsimonious therapy.
- CBT uses a variety of techniques developed in cognitive and other disciplines.
- Homework is a central feature.

Collaborative therapeutic relationship

CBT has always stressed the importance of establishing a strong collaborative relationship between client and therapist, with the therapist playing an active role. Collaboration means therapists are open about their way of working, giving rationales to the client and being open to feedback from the client, which further strengthen the relationship.

Newer understandings of the therapeutic relationship are influenced by mindfulness, discussed below, particularly the 'beginner's mind', encouraging therapists to be intensely curious about one's inner experience as it unfolds –counselling psychology's ethos of reflective practice. Such work is much more in tune with counselling and psychotherapy in general, whereby the process of forming, and healing, the relationship with the therapist is in itself a valuable aspect of therapy. I may, for example, be aware of shutting off in therapy, my moment of 'empathy bypass', when a client is describing events or emotions in a manner devoid of actual emotion. Alternatively, I may feel extremely emotional listening to a client's story, whereas the client's description is devoid of emotion. Both reactions are valuable indicators of the relationship, suggesting the client is either avoiding or is unaware of the emotional impact of what they are saying.

Formulation

A cognitive formulation (also known as conceptualisation) is a means of making sense of the origins, development and maintenance of an individual's difficulties, bearing in mind the theoretical cognitive model. Working in cognitive therapy, our understanding of, and therapy with, each person is shaped by a specific theoretical model of emotional difficulties, such as models for depression, anxiety, OCD and so on, which is individualised into a unique map for our particular client. With skill, theoretical models and treatment protocols are transformed into individual therapy without being formulaic or theoretical (Wills with Sanders, 2013). While the cognitive model for depression may be universal, each client's formulation is unique. The formulation develops in collaboration with the client and leads to a plan for intervention and therapy (Grant et al., 2012).

David had worked for years in education, was well regarded by his colleagues and felt he had 'always done a good job'. He had been well for most of his life, had hardly taken any time off sick, but was knocked off his bicycle and suffered a nasty leg fracture requiring several months off work. When he returned, he was shocked to find how anxious he had become: he had episodes of feeling like he was 'losing it', which 'wasn't like him' – his GP had diagnosed panic attacks. During our first meeting, we drew a vicious cycle to make sense of his panic attacks. We also discussed David's background, which he had 'not thought about for years'. Although, on the whole, David had a 'happy childhood – no problems', he was in intense competition with his older brother, and always felt slightly inferior. David had failed his 11 plus, and gone to the local comprehensive, whereas his 'clever clogs' older brother had passed and as a result went to grammar school. David set out to 'prove himself', which he had certainly done through his job. He had not, however, realised failure had a high price. Two of his beliefs were 'I'm OK so long as I do well' and 'I must keep up my standards at all time'. The accident and subsequent problems had activated these beliefs, so going back into situations where he had to perform made him feel like 'an eleven year old kid, not as good as my big brother'.

Structure

One of the characteristic features of cognitive therapy is the structured, focused approach. Each session has a formal structure, with an agenda which is worked out between client and

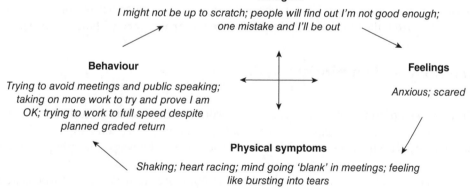

Early Experience
Happy childhood, but competitive relationship with brother
Bullying from brother
Failed 11 plus exam
Went to comprehensive instead of grammar school
Hard work and achievement valued in family

Development of beliefs about self, others and the world
I'm thick, not as good as the rest of them
Others are better than me
The world only values high achievers

Assumptions or rules for living
If I prove myself and do well, I'll be OK
I have to work to my full potential all the time
If I don't do my best, I'll be found out

Critical incident which triggers the problem
Illness and slow recovery from surgery; Getting older;
Going back to work after time off

Thoughts
I might not be up to scratch; people will find out I'm not good enough;
one mistake and I'll be out

Behaviour
Trying to avoid meetings and public speaking;
taking on more work to try and prove I am
OK; trying to work to full speed despite
planned graded return

Feelings
Anxious; scared

Physical symptoms
Shaking; heart racing; mind going 'blank' in meetings; feeling
like bursting into tears

Figure 18.1   Cognitive formulation for David

therapist, a review of 'homework', the main topics for the session, agreeing new 'homework' and ending the session with a review.

The structured approach of CBT is one factor with which therapists from other disciplines have the most difficulties, with concerns about being dictatorial and not relationship-focused. In my experience, the vast majority of clients are happy to work in a structured way, and in good CBT the structure is implicit rather than laboured.

Socratic method and guided discovery

One of the characteristic features of CBT is the use of Socratic questioning, or guided discovery, an investigative process whereby client and therapist work together in a collaborative way to explore different ways of viewing things. Using Socratic questioning, we aim to help clients become aware of different perspectives, or information which they already know but have forgotten.

Socratic questioning is used in many different stages of therapy. For example, when low, anxious, depressed, we tend to think in a way which is quite narrow, and often unhelpful and limited. Using Socratic questions, we encourage clients to broaden their vision, think through alternatives and throw light on strengths they may not realise they have: '*What does that mean to you? If that happened, what then? What would you say to a friend in this situation? If you were not feeling so low, how might you interpret this?*'

Visit the companion website for links to further resources on mindfulness.

Guided discovery encourages a sense of curiosity in both client and therapist, as though we are detectives looking for the bigger picture. Throughout the process, we use empathic reflection and summarising to check we have fully understood. Once we have discovered information, synthesising questions, such as 'What do you make of that?', 'How does this information fit with you saying you're useless?' or 'How might these ideas make a difference to you?', enables the client to learn from the process (Padesky, 1993 – see www.padesky.com/clinical-corner).

Parsimony and empiricism in CBT

CBT aims to be parsimonious, that is, the most work for the least effort. It therefore aims to be as short as necessary to help the target problems and meet goals, an aim which has been snapped up by NHS management, who strive to find ever shorter ways of meeting targets, and integrated into stepped care services.

Empiricism implies we measure what is going on. Once we have defined where we are going, it is very helpful to also have a clear idea about how we will know when we have got there. Obviously, what our clients tell us and what they are doing is one of the most important measures, but, in addition, formal measurement helps both parties to evaluate progress (Westbrook et al., 2012; Wills with Sanders, 2013).

Methods in CBT

The variety of methods used in CBT aim to help clients feel better by becoming more aware of their patterns of thinking and meanings given to experience, to think and assign meaning in a different, more helpful or realistic way and to make changes in behaviour. In some ways, this sounds relatively simple, and reading some CBT texts, one could be forgiven for thinking CBT can somehow offer a magic switch to enable people to literally change their minds. In practice, it is much more complex, and for some clients, an extremely difficult thing to do. Simply working cognitively does not work, and we need a range of cognitive, behavioural and emotional means in order to change minds, behaviour and feelings. Therefore, the methods used in CBT are many and varied, some unique to CBT, such as thought records and behavioural experiments, others borrowed or stolen from other disciplines, such as two-chair Gestalt methods (Westbrook et al., 2012; Wills with Sanders, 2013).

Homework

Although the term 'homework' does not go down well with all clients or practitioners, working on therapeutic tasks between sessions is an essential part of cognitive therapy, as well as mindfulness-based approaches, and is related to good outcome (Mausbach et al., 2010). The concept of homework has to be sensitively introduced. A very negative reaction can provide useful material for therapy, such as the need to do homework 'perfectly', or strong reminders of having to perform at school.

Homework tasks are varied and include:

- Listening to recordings of the session
- Reading information specific to the client's difficulties
- Keeping a diary of symptoms
- Thought diaries
- Behavioural experiment tasks (Bennett-Levy et al., 2004).

COGNITION AND META-COGNITION

A major part of the evolution of cognitive therapies has been changing the focus from the *content* of thinking ('I'm going to make a mess of everything') to the *processes* of thinking, worrying and rumination, such as continual repetitive thoughts that go round and round in the mind with no easy way out. Cognitive processes, not entirely neglected in even early cognitive models, have now moved centre stage, with interest in neurological correlates to worry and rumination, and how they can maintain problems through processes of avoidance. Worry and rumination are patterns of thinking, made up of chains of verbal thought and a pattern of focusing attention on threat and coping strategies that have paradoxical effects. Rather than terminating negative thinking, they extend it. Such metacognitive thinking is driven by underlying beliefs about thinking which fall into broad categories of positive beliefs (e.g. I must worry in order to cope) and negative beliefs (e.g. Some thoughts are dangerous). Mental control is often used as a means of coping with emotional experience: *'If I stop myself thinking about this, I'll feel okay'*, *'These thoughts are doing damage'*.

Understanding of metacognitive processes is central to facilitating change in thinking styles and patterns. Metacognitive therapy aims to raise awareness of the underlying processes and change the way they work, helping people to be more flexible in the way they respond to difficulties (Wells, 2011).

COMPASSION-BASED THERAPY

Fortunately, it is difficult to think of any talking therapy that does not assume the central importance of practising with compassion, and at the very least we are all familiar with Rogers' core conditions of unconditional positive regard, empathy and congruence. Equally, it is hard to imagine a therapist not motivated by caring, kindness and sympathy for the suffering of our clients. As part of the development of CBT, the specific qualities of compassion are gaining attention in their own right (Bueno, 2011). Compassion is a broad cloth, a powerful feeling, an 'orientation of mind' and 'capacity to respond' (Feldman and Kuyken, 2013). Compassion includes kindness, empathy, generosity and acceptance, and, given it is central to caring for our young and living in social groups, compassion is 'hard wired'. Paul Gilbert's compassion-focused therapy combines cognitive behavioural interventions with compassionate mind training, which directly works with self-criticism and shame, developing an attitude of caring and concern to the self as well as to others (Gilbert, 2010).

THIRD WAVE AND MINDFULNESS-BASED INTERVENTIONS

One of the driving forces in developing mindfulness approaches was in the search for ways to help those people for whom standard CBT or other therapies were not helpful in the long term. Although CBT is very effective for episodes of depression, relapse is a significant problem and many people who have experienced one episode of depression are particularly vulnerable to repeated episodes. People with long-standing complex and profoundly painful difficulties may not find CBT helpful, and physical problems such as severe, chronic pain require different models. Cognitive processes of rumination, worry and avoidance are not easily tackled by standard approaches.

Third-wave therapies involve, at their core, changing an individual's relationship to thoughts and experience through acceptance, compassion and mindfulness. The newer approaches include Mindfulness-Based Stress Reduction (MBSR), Mindfulness-Based Cognitive Therapy (MBCT), Acceptance and Commitment Therapy (ACT) and Dialectical Behaviour Therapy (DBT), which includes mindfulness as a means of helping people to regulate emotion. In this chapter I focus on MBCT, my own core training, with further approaches on the companion website.

Visit the companion website for further material on cognitive and mindfulness based interventions.

MINDFULNESS-BASED THERAPIES

The ideas embodied in mindfulness, acceptance, moving towards experience rather than trying to control or change it, are hardly new. Many spiritual traditions, primarily Buddhism, have long known how meditation, and awareness of the present, can reduce suffering. The new models are taking on such ideas and methods, without specifically adopting Buddhist terminology or traditions (Williams and Kabat-Zinn, 2013), and offering an integration of Buddhist concepts and methods with modern psychological principles and approaches. The journey to the vast interest in mindfulness we see today started with Jon Kabat-Zinn's seminal work on mindfulness for people with chronic physical illnesses (Kabat-Zinn, 2013) followed by the search for a way of helping people with recurrent episodes of depression, described in the opening chapters of Segal et al. (2013).

Key themes of mindfulness-based approaches

Decentring

Decentring – the ability to step back from experience and thoughts – is a central process within many eastern traditions and Buddhist practices, and was identified by Mark Williams and colleagues as a salient process in preventing relapse in depression (Segal et al., 2013). In mindfulness, we attend *to* feelings, thoughts and sensations as mental events in the field of awareness, rather than *from* them as aspects of the self. Rather than feeling upset following an argument, and ruminating about the causes and meaning of the upset, mindfulness places the feelings, emotions, sensations and thoughts as objects of enquiry and interest – *here is that familiar tightness in my belly, here's lots of thoughts racing around my head.*

Experiential avoidance causes more problems

One way of coping with difficult experiences, feelings, bodily sensations, pain and adverse events is to try to shut off from them. It makes sense that we are hard-wired to get away from dangers, such as threats to our life or health. However, the mechanism that keeps us safe is over-applied to internal experience in the form of unwanted moods, thoughts or difficult bodily sensations, and to try to avoid these only creates secondary suffering and additional layers of problems. We can see from Figure 18.2 that primary pain, arising from our experiences, lives, bodies or internal world, is then made worse by our attempts to get rid of it, to escape.

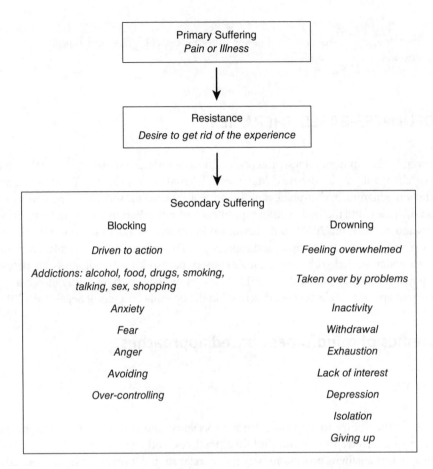

Figure 18.2   Primary and secondary suffering

Source: Adapted from *Living Well with Pain and Illness. The Mindful Way to Free Yourself from Suffering* by Vidyamala Burch (Piatkus, 2008).

Acceptance involves deliberately and intentionally turning towards and inviting in our difficulties rather than pushing them away or striving to make things different, such as using safety behaviours as a means of coping with anxiety.

Simon had experienced panic attacks for years following a period of illness. He would feel, out of the blue, as though he was about to die – his heart raced, he became cold and sweaty and he felt completely detached from everything around him. He went to great lengths to cope by avoiding being on his own, only going out of the house with his girlfriend, asking her for reassurance when he felt so bad. Using mindfulness, he began to turn towards these feelings when they occurred rather than trying to run from them. Initially, this was terrifying for him, and he was concentrating on controlling his breathing under the guise of mindfulness. Very gently and for only a moment at a time, he turned his attention to the feelings of his breath without controlling it. He noticed that his breathing calmed itself down without him trying to control it. He then began to investigate, with a curious rather than fearful stance, the other sensations – sweating, dissociation – and found, again, that they passed as mysteriously as they arose. He began to be less fearful of his body and was able to allow the sensations to come and go without, as he put it, 'powering into them'.

Being more open to experience, whatever it is, leads to a reduction in avoidance of experience, and so the necessity to try to control or get rid of unpleasant or difficult experience. For example, when traumatic memories come to mind, when we habitually try to push them away, or think of something else, or ruminate about them, they can stay stuck and be allowed a great deal of potency over life. Also, if our thoughts and memories become truths, then we might allow them to predict the future, in a way that is not helpful – 'I remember last time I told a friend how upset I felt and she wasn't really interested. I felt so rejected and stupid. I had better avoid letting other people know how I am feeling, never show my feelings and put on a brave face all the time.' By being able to take our experience moment by moment, being aware of the upset at the time rather than generalising into the future, such predictions become just thoughts and therefore not valid realities.

Doing versus being mode

Most of the time, we are in 'doing' mode, focused on tasks, goals, plans, the future. Doing mode is necessary to life, to fulfilment and achievement. When in doing mode, we are using particular areas of our brains as well as our bodies, which are essential to solving problems. It works by looking at where we are now (e.g. reading a novel) and where we want to be (e.g. sitting at the computer getting on with writing this chapter), registering the discrepancy and taking action to meet our goals – using so-called 'discrepancy-based processing' (Segal et al., 2013).

However, we cannot easily 'solve' our emotions and moods using the 'doing' mode. For example, thinking styles, when depressed, are often extremely negative and self-critical. Trying to solve these thoughts, by thinking about them even more and trying to sort them out in our heads, can lead not to solutions but to further rumination and lowering of mood (see Segal et al., 2013: Chapter 4, for full description of these mechanisms).

Being mode, on the other hand, allows things to remain as they are, seeing thoughts as mental events, experience as experience, facilitating the ability to live alongside problems, pain and discomfort. In one study of MBCT for recurrent depression (Allen et al., 2009), half the participants reported that the approach led to a 'new perspective on their depression-related thoughts and feelings that can be summarised as "these thoughts and feelings aren't me"'.

Compassion and kindness

Compassion-focused therapies, described above, identify the central role of compassion in depression and other problems, and how, through learning compassion, people can change their perspective on and become free from long-standing and disabling difficulties. Compassion is central to Buddhist theories and practice, and to mindfulness teaching and practice. The instructor embodies compassion in the teaching, practices and process of enquiry, enabling participants to develop compassion towards themselves and their own difficulties. The extent to which participants are able to cultivate compassion, where before there was self-criticism, underlies the effectiveness of MBCT in reducing relapse in depression (Kuyken et al., 2010).

STRUCTURE OF MBCT

MBCT is taught in eight, weekly classes of two hours, with a one-day workshop half-way through the course. Each group comprises 8–15 people, and they commit to regular, 45-minute daily home practice as well as attending all the groups. The sessions combine psycho-education, cognitive therapy and mindfulness meditation practices. The process of learning in the groups is experiential and dynamic, using enquiry as part of an ongoing cycle of learning (e.g. Kolb's model of adult learning, see Segal et al., 2013).

 Visit the companion website to see Kolb's learning cycle applied to teaching MBCT.

The meditation practices have been drawn from Buddhist meditative traditions (Williams and Kabat-Zinn, 2013), practising careful and steady observation of the breath, sensations from the body, sounds, eating or walking, without judging what is noticed. Participants are invited to notice when the mind wanders off, as it very quickly does, into memories, fantasies, plans or other thoughts, then escort the attention back to the chosen focus, over and over again. Any urges to move or wriggle or scratch or give up the practice are also observed without being acted on. Practitioners are invited to hold an attitude of interest, curiosity and non-judgemental awareness, and when we inevitably rate our experience as 'pluses' and 'minuses' ('*Oh no, I'm thinking again, I'm not doing this right*'), then treat such judgements as thoughts and return to focus. The practice of mindfulness moves on from specific focus, on breath or sounds, to a non-judgemental awareness of the constantly changing nature of experience – thoughts, sensations, urges, emotions come and go.

In order to facilitate the use of mindfulness in everyday life, a three-minute breathing space is a brief and portable meditation, which can be practised regularly throughout the day, and at difficult points, such as times when thoughts or feelings threaten to take over. The three-minute breathing space facilitates the move from 'reacting' to 'responding', enabling better choices about how to cope with what is going on (http://oxfordmindfulness.org/learn/resources/).

Although many people come along with problems in how they are feeling, the ability to use mindfulness to look at what can be overwhelmingly difficult is gradually built up across the first weeks of the course. For example, being able to focus on sensations in the body and sensations of breathing are the first steps towards learning to stay with and accept experience. Emotion is worked with by observing the effect on the body, and allowing feelings to come and go.

Shaida had been looking after her elderly mother for several years, and often found herself getting very angry with her, but tried not to show it. She felt drained by the continual demands and struggled with her mother's frustration and irritability. She tried to keep the anger at bay, finding it unacceptable, but allowed herself to focus on it in meditation. Expecting to notice the strong churning in her stomach and a 'fight or flight' anxious feeling, she was surprised to find tears welling up and her chest tightening, as she experienced a big hollow feeling inside. She sat and watched her body respond, sensing a huge feeling of loss in her heart. Tears flowed down her face and she recognised her feelings of grief, having lost her active and independent mother. She noticed a sense of relief, too, in allowing her sadness and grief to express themselves, and she could sit quietly with these feelings for the rest of the meditation.

Visit the companion website for a PowerPoint presentation about mindfulness in end of life care.

TEACHING MBCT

Training in cognitive psychotherapies, as for all psychotherapeutic models, requires understanding theoretical and clinical principles, rigorous standards, supervision and reflective practice and a training trajectory that can take several years. Learning to teach mindfulness is no different, requiring an in-depth understanding of the theoretical principles and practice of mindfulness meditation and a long period of personal practice as well as supervised teaching experience (Crane et al., 2012; Teasdale and Chaskalson, 2013). Unfortunately, it is not unusual for people who are highly experienced in their field, such as counselling psychology or psychotherapy, to attend a few workshops or an eight-week course and then start the process of teaching themselves. Many questions might be asked about competence and ethics of such teaching. If CBT therapists simply add on mindfulness meditation techniques to their repertoire without full training, the techniques themselves may be of benefit, but the clients are not being offered MBCT. Conversely, highly experienced meditation practitioners, who are skilled in teaching mindfulness, also need a thorough grounding in cognitive and behavioural theory and practice in order to teach MBCT. Training is in the order of years not months.

 Visit the companion website to read good practice guidelines on teaching mindfulness.

MINDFULNESS AND COUNSELLING PSYCHOLOGY

Practising mindfulness ourselves may not only be of benefit to us and our personal lives, it may well impact positively on our clinical work (Hick and Bien, 2010; O'Driscoll, 2009; Siegel, 2010). Mindfulness is no doubt a means to improve our therapeutic relationships, to increase our ability to empathise with and tune into our clients, to listen fully without distraction and to impart acceptance, all of which are essential to fostering strong and effective therapeutic alliances. It may be that mindfulness is an active ingredient in therapy across a range of therapeutic methods. Mindfulness enables us to self-reflect, seeing our thoughts and interventions as they arise, allowing mindfulness about the suitability of our work, moment by moment (O'Driscoll, 2009).

The impact of MBSR on healthcare professionals has been looked at in a four-year study (Schure et al., 2008). Results have shown positive physical, emotional, mental, spiritual and interpersonal changes, with an increased ability to deal with negative emotions, increased clarity of thought, and improved self-reflection (Schure et al., 2008). Although it sounds almost too good to be true, my own experience is that during periods of active use of mindfulness on a regular basis, I feel more in touch with what is going on, more in tune with my clients, and more able to sit and listen and stay with their experience in a clearer way and less muddied by the stress of life impinging all the time. Mindfulness does not prevent pain or self-inflicted suffering, and stressful outbursts when trying to juggle all the various demands of life or get to work on time, but it gives me the tools for moving in that direction.

EFFECTIVENESS OF MBCT

Mindfulness-based therapies have been shown to be effective across a broad range of chronic disorders and problems (DARE, 2014; Hoffman et al., 2010; Khoury et al., 2013; see www.oxford mindfulness.org/mbct/publications for up-to-date references on research), with consistent and relatively strong levels of effect size across different studies. Improvements are shown in measures of both physical and psychological health and quality of life, such as depression, anxiety, coping style, pain and physical impairment. Several studies have replicated the original research looking at the efficacy of mindfulness-based psychological interventions in preventing relapse of major depression (see Segal et al., 2013; Williams et al., 2013). Although research is proliferating, the methods are still in their infancy compared with other psychotherapeutic models.

There is great potential, but mindfulness is not for everyone. MBCT is not a quick fix. It takes time, energy and effort and may be so different from individuals' expectations of what psychological therapies should look like that it may be impossible to engage certain groups of people. The process of seeing and staying with experience can be overwhelmingly painful in the case of highly aversive experience or memories, such as trauma and abuse. One partici-pant with severe health anxiety described being asked to be aware of his physical sensations as 'like being tied to a railway line when the express train is due'. He felt overwhelmed, even at the thought of having to take a peep at his experience without being able to run away by using an array of safety behaviours.

Groups do not suit everyone. The methods can be used with individuals, and it will be inter-esting to see case studies regarding how effective this is compared to the group programme. Mindfulness may well 'leak' into psychotherapy as a whole, becoming a common factor across different models that is taught as part of training in the complexities of working in psycho-therapy, and thus move away from the current model of teaching and regular practice.

CONCLUSION

This chapter has given a brief introduction to cognitive behavioural psychotherapy and mindfulness-based approaches and MBCT. CBT has been around a long time, and has a sub-stantial body of research and experience to back it up. It is a flexible and evolving form of psychotherapy, evolving into new forms such as acceptance and commitment therapy, meta-cognitive therapy and other models. Training in and using CBT requires a comprehensive understanding of its theoretical and clinical principles and evidence base, fostering ethical practice and ensuring that therapy is tailored to the individual, and is efficient and relevant. Without a firm foundation, therapists may drift into the latest models and theories regardless of their proven value (Waller, 2009). Mindfulness-based therapies may prove a seduction too far – being highly fashionable, the flavour of the month in the press, celebrity- and Twitter-driven and increasingly accessible. At a one-day workshop introducing mindfulness to palliative care staff, one participant told me that she was expected to start teaching the methods to patients on the basis of the workshop, such is the pressure on training budgets. CBT is of proven efficacy for many difficulties – anxiety, depression, panic attacks, phobias, obsessive compulsive disorders – and has and still is evolving to help a wider range of peo-ple. Mindfulness is the new kid on the block and, however sexy and tweeted-about, it remains at an early stage. How sound is the evidence? How applicable is it to wider populations?

There are many questions, many uncertainties. It is not a first-line treatment for depression – we already have those. It would be unethical to offer mindfulness as a treatment for phobias when CBT therapies work well.

How might cognitive models and mindfulness look for counselling psychologists of the future? Fitting with the ethos of counselling psychology, cognitive therapy is moving away from a 'diagnostic' approach of understanding people having problems such as 'anxiety' or 'depression'. There is now a greater understanding of how we all, to greater or lesser degrees, struggle with suffering inherent in being humans living in an imperfect, and often stressful, world. Combining our ability to think our way out of difficulties with the need to bring a quiet, non-judgemental mind to the complexity of our lives could see a merging of different models of psychotherapy as well as a merging of cognitive therapy with mindfulness.

In conclusion, CBT and mindfulness interventions all have their place, and neither is a substitute for the other. They both offer a choice of methods and approaches. CBT is essentially a first-line therapy for depression, and MBCT can strengthen the foundations and offer ballast against future storms. In terms of outcome, both MBCT groups and CBT can be effective for treating depression, but giving people a choice in their preference for treatment-mode may in itself prove to be therapeutic.

REFERENCES

Allen, M., Bromley, A., Kuyken, W. and Sonnenberg, S. J. (2009) Participants' experience of mindfulness-based cognitive therapy: 'It changed me in just about every way possible'. *Behavioural and Cognitive Psychotherapy*, 37: 413–430.

Beck, A. T., Rush, A. J., Shaw, B. F. and Emery, G. (1979) *Cognitive Therapy of Depression*. New York: Guilford Press.

Bennett-Levy, J., Butler, G., Fennell, M., Hackmann, A., Mueller, M. and Westbrook, D. (2004) *The Oxford Guide to Behavioural Experiments in Cognitive Therapy*. Oxford: Oxford University Press.

Bueno, J. (2011) Promoting wellbeing through compassion. *TherapyToday*.net, 22(5), www.therapytoday.net/article/show/2515/ (accessed September 2015).

Crane, R. S., Soulsby, J. G., Kuyken, W., Williams, J. M. G. and Eames, C. (2012) *The Bangor, Exeter & Oxford Mindfulness-Based Interventions Teaching Assessment Criteria (MBI-TAC) for Assessing the Competence and Adherence of Mindfulness-Based Class-Based Teaching*. Bangor University, www.bangor.ac.uk/mindfulness/documents/MBI-TACJune2012.pdf (accessed September 2015).

DARE (2014) Effectiveness of Mindfulness-based Therapies in Reducing Symptoms of Depression: A Meta-Analysis. *University of York Centre for Reviews and Dissemination*, www.ncbi.nlm.nih.gov/pubmedhealth/PMH0054830/ (accessed September 2015).

Feldman, C. and Kuyken, W. (2013) Compassion in the landscape of suffering. In J. M. G. Williams and J. Kabat-Zinn (eds), *Mindfulness: Diverse Perspectives on its Meanings, Origins and Applications*. London: Routledge. pp. 143–155.

Gilbert, P. (2010) *Compassion-Focused Therapy: Distinctive Features*. Brighton and Hove: Routledge.

Grant, A., Townend, M. and Mill, J. (2012) *Assessment and Case Formulation in Cognitive Behavioural Therapy*. London: Sage.

Hick, S. F. and Bien, T. (2010) *Mindfulness and the Therapeutic Relationship*. New York: Guilford Press.

Hofmann, S. G., Sawyer, A. T., Witt, A. A. and Oh, D. (2010) The effect of mindfulness-based therapy on anxiety and depression: A meta-analytic review. *Journal of Consulting and Clinical Psychology*, 78(2): 169–83.

Kabat-Zinn, J. (2013) *Full Catastrophe Living: How to Cope with Stress, Pain and Illness using Mindfulness Meditation*. London: Piatkus.

Khoury, B., Lecomte, T., Fortin, G., Masse, M., Therien, P., Bouchard, V. and Hofmann, S. G. (2013) Mindfulness-based therapy: A comprehensive meta-analysis. *Clinical Psychology Review*, 33: 763–771.

Kuyken, W., Watkins, E. R., Holden, E. R., White, K., Taylor, R. S., Byford, S., Evans, A., Radford, S., Teasdale, J. D. and Dalgleish, T. (2010) How does mindfulness-based cognitive therapy work? *Behaviour Research and Therapy*, 48: 1105–1112. doi.org/10.1016/j.brat.2010.08.003.

Mausbach, B. T., Moore, R., Roesch, S., Cardenas, V. and Patterson, T. L. (2010) The relationship between homework compliance and therapy outcomes: An updated meta-analysis. *Cognitive Therapy Research*, 34(5): 429–438.

O'Driscoll, A. (2009) The growing influence of mindfulness on the work of the counselling psychologist: A review. *Counselling Psychology Review*, 24: 16–23.

Padesky, C. A. (1993) Socratic questioning: Changing minds or guided discovery? www.padesky.com/clinical-corner (accessed September 2015).

Schure, M., Christopher, J. C. and Christopher, S. E. (2008) Mind/body medicine and the art of self-care: Teaching mindfulness to counseling students through yoga, meditation and qigong. *Journal of Counseling and Development*, 86: 47–56.

Segal, Z. V., Williams, J. M. G. and Teasdale, J. D. (2013) *Mindfulness-Based Cognitive Therapy for Depression* (2nd edn). New York: Guilford Press.

Siegel, D. (2010) *The Mindful Therapist: A Clinician's Guide to Mindsight and Neural Integration*. New York: W. W. Norton & Co.

Teasdale, J. D. and Chaskalson, M. (2013) How does mindfulness transform suffering? In J. M. G. Williams and J. Kabat-Zinn (eds), *Mindfulness: Diverse Perspectives on its Meanings, Origins and Applications*. London: Routledge. pp. 89–124.

Waller, G. (2009) Evidence based treatment and therapist drift. *Behaviour Research and Therapy*, 47: 119–127.

Wells, A. (2011) *Metacognitive Therapy for Anxiety and Depression*. New York: Guilford Press.

Westbrook, D., Kirk, J. and Kennerley, H. (2012) *An Introduction to Cognitive Behavior Therapy* (2nd edn). London: Sage.

Williams, J. M. G. and Kabat-Zinn, J. (eds) (2013) *Mindfulness: Diverse Perspectives on its Meanings, Origins and Applications*. London: Routledge.

Williams, M., Crane, C., Barnhofer, T. et al. (2013) Mindfulness-based cognitive therapy for preventing relapse in recurrent depression: A randomized dismantling trial. *Journal of Consulting and Clinical Psychology*, 82(2): 275–286.

Wills, F. (2008) *Skills in Cognitive Behavioural Counselling and Psychotherapy*. London: Sage.

Wills, F. with Sanders, D. (2013) *Cognitive Behaviour Therapy: Foundations for Practice* (3rd edn). London: Sage.

19

PSYCHODYNAMIC INTERPERSONAL MODEL: A PERFECT FIT FOR COUNSELLING PSYCHOLOGY?

SARAH BARTLETT

What's so special about Psychodynamic Interpersonal Therapy (PIT)? It is a model that I have found fascinating and illuminating but, more importantly, there are many aspects of it that I see as resonating with counselling psychology, in its philosophy, its integration of a number of influences to establish a coherent new whole and its emphasis on practice-based evidence. Currently, PIT is offered in a number of NHS mental health trusts; from its 'home' in Manchester, where it is offered in a number of services, to Leeds, Birmingham and Oxford, encompassing complex cases in primary care, in-patient and specialist services and in both brief and longer formats. It is being introduced into the IAPT programme in the North West of England. There is also a long established service in Melbourne, Australia.

Psychodynamic Interpersonal Therapy integrates concepts and practice from psychodynamic, Jungian and Humanistic writers; it integrates psychology and philosophy and draws upon Romantic literature, paying particular attention to the language used in the therapy. At the same time it embeds a requirement for the therapist to adopt a 'scientific attitude' while maintaining an experiential, responsive approach (Margison, 2002). I have been captivated by this model since first reading its seminal text, *Forms of Feeling* (Hobson, 1985). I was lucky enough to be supervised by a colleague of Robert Hobson, and to work in the model both as a practitioner and supervisor myself. I will provide a brief overview of the concepts from psychodynamic theories that constitute the core components of PIT and consider how these are integrated within its overall framework. In describing how PIT is used in practice, I hope to illustrate this with some adapted, clinical material. I will briefly outline the research base and hope to show how this has contributed to further developments. My primary concern in this chapter is not 'how to do' PIT; indeed the skills of PIT, although important, are of less significance than the spirit of the therapy (Moorey and Guthrie, 2003). Rather, I hope to offer an additional way of thinking about therapeutic practice, linking in a number of perspectives.

WHERE DOES PSYCHODYNAMIC INTERPERSONAL THERAPY FIT?

Freud did not, of course, invent the concept of the unconscious. We need only look at Shakespeare's portrayal of Lady Macbeth's 'madness' or read Coleridge's *Kubla Khan* for confirmation that writers had long recognised the phenomenon of our 'out-of-awareness'. Freud brought together a number of concepts, including the unconscious, establishing a particular way of working within a conceptual framework that was essentially biological but that was also and, crucially, an intrapsychic model that placed great weight on instinctual drives in its description of our development from infancy to adulthood. The unconscious is seen as offering the possibility for us to create and hold on to representations of those who have been significant in our early lives; it acts as storage, protecting us from painful memories. Freud wrote of the effort we put into avoiding difficult feelings or internal conflicts, often repeating the same behaviour in our attempts to resolve these.

Since Freud's introduction of psychoanalysis, psychodynamic therapies have evolved following a number of different trajectories, depending on the theoretical allegiance of the practitioner. It makes for a fascinating story, but for the purposes of this chapter I want to start with the movement known as Object Relations, which shifted the focus of understanding human behaviour from biological drives to relationships. Within the diverse perspectives of the tradition of Object Relations the common premises are our primary need for relationships with others and that the self is constructed of internal relationships, at both conscious and unconscious levels. It is hard to overestimate the impact of Winnicott's writing about the centrality of the mother/caregiver – the infant's relationship for the person's subsequent sense of self. From him we have the concepts of 'attunement' and 'holding' but also the suggestion that with 'good-enough' care the infant develops a sense of coherence and integration. The integration extends to enable the infant to 'bring together' sensation and emotion, allowing her later to see as connected her emotional, mental and bodily states (Gomez, 1997). Within Object Relations the 'self' can only develop within a relational context, reflecting our essential social nature.

With his development of attachment theory, Bowlby underpinned with scientific rigour the Object Relations principle of the primacy of our need for relationships. 'Intimate attachments to other human beings are the hub around which a person's life revolves' (Bowlby, 1980: 422). Attachment theory places the emphasis on external relationships, rather than the Kleinian concept of internal dynamics. Bowlby observed the damaging impact of separation on children and demonstrated the need for healthy attachments for emotional maturity. He also saw a connection between the loss felt from separation and depression, linking these with mourning. Attachment theory demonstrated our need for security in order to develop a sense of independence. Both Winnicott and Bowlby saw the origins of secure attachment in sensitive, responsive parenting, itself a necessary precursor to the development of a robust sense of self and the capacity to tolerate being alone.

Interpersonal psychoanalysis developed further in the United States with Sullivan's emphasis on the self. Sullivan saw the low self-esteem of those with schizophrenia to be the result of neglectful parenting. Sullivan also adopted an approach to his patients that was radical in the psychiatric treatment of schizophrenia, establishing and maintaining a close involvement with his patients, seeking meaning in their experience of schizophrenia, rather than dismissing it as a manifestation of their madness (Holmes, 2000).

The concepts of self and self-esteem are similarly at the centre of Kohut's work (1971) with responsive parenting seen as providing the essential ground for the development of self-esteem. Kohut's work was with those who do not have a diagnosis of psychosis but whose distress is seen as beyond that of neurosis, placing them in what has come to be labelled as 'borderline' pathology. Kohut extended Winnicott's recognition of 'mirroring' in early childhood as a key interpersonal theme. For Winnicott, parental mirroring allows the child to develop a sense of herself and to 'see' her emotions, thereby developing an ownership of them. Kohut, however, sees mirroring as a necessary reflection of parental admiration contributing to a positive self-regard. Where the early environment is unempathic and mirroring deficient, the child's 'fragile grandiosity' is crushed and self-absorption and a sense of fragility of self are likely to persist beyond childhood (Holmes, 2003).

With the establishment of the interpersonal aspects of psychodynamic therapies the analyst, or psychotherapist, becomes a joint participant in the therapeutic process. There has also been a shift towards psychodynamic therapies as seeking hermeneutic explanations, placing value on exploring meaning, rather than establishing objective truths. Several interpersonal therapies have subsequently developed, some, such as Psychodynamic Interpersonal Therapy and Cognitive Analytic Therapy (Ryle, 1990), drawing explicitly on these psychodynamic theories, and others, equally explicitly, rejecting these.

Counselling psychology has, as a core principle, placed the therapeutic relationship as central to the therapeutic endeavour. In PIT, the relationship between the therapist and client *is*, in essence, the therapy (Moorey and Guthrie, 2003). PIT is constructed around furthering understanding of how each person develops a sense of self and how, in some instances, this might have been disrupted, thereby damaging the person's sense of self and self-value. The concept of 'self' has been criticised by post-structuralists as reinforcing a culture of individualism – see, for example, Pilgrim (1997) or Parker et al. (1995). Their challenge raises important concerns and has brought the social context firmly into psychotherapeutic thinking. However, when we feel despair or are overwhelmed it is often our sense of ourselves that is shaken and it is this that we seek to repair.

ORIGINS OF PSYCHODYNAMIC INTERPERSONAL THERAPY

Initially called the Conversational Model, PIT developed from the clinical work of Robert Hobson and Russell Meares, both psychiatrists working in the 1960s at the Bethlem Royal

Hospital with people who had diagnoses of serious mental illnesses. Many were considered beyond therapeutic help, presenting with profound distress and often a history of trauma resulting in severe psychological damage. They might now be given the label of 'personality disorder' or 'borderline personality'. Hobson's aim was to establish a way of working that followed in the footsteps of '"humanistic" psychologists who have recognised the limitations of a positivist, mechanistic, atomistic view of human behaviour' (Hobson, 1985: 228). Hobson, in particular, was profoundly influenced by Jung's writing and incorporated Jung's principles of the immediate experience and symbolical attitude into the Conversational Model (Margison, 2002).

From detailed scrutiny of tape recordings of clinical sessions, Hobson and Meares started to identify both 'systems of destruction of the sense of personal being, but also "moments of aliveness" that are the seeds of self' (Meares, 2012: 120). Listening to recordings of sessions, with close attention to the tiny specifics, the 'minute particulars' remain a key aspect of the supervision of PIT. This scrutiny draws out the details of what worked within the therapeutic encounter, and what blocked understanding or interrupted the relationship, allowing the model to respond accordingly. The work was subsequently developed in Manchester and in Melbourne. A number of comparative research studies have established a significant evidence base for the model, which by now in the UK was described as Psychodynamic Interpersonal Therapy (I shall discuss these in a later section). PIT has been demonstrated as beneficial across a range of presenting difficulties and in both brief and longer-term formats. Meares' work in Melbourne has developed the Conversational Model, particularly for people who have experienced early trauma and been given a diagnosis of Borderline Personality Disorder.

CORE VALUES AND ASSUMPTIONS OF PIT

We now accept that the therapeutic relationship is a significant factor in positive therapeutic outcome, and indeed there is a body of psychotherapy research to support this (Horvath and Luborsky, 1993; Martin et al., 2000), but this was not the case at the time Hobson placed the relationship as central to the therapeutic task. The term 'Conversational Model' refers to a particular form of relatedness that Hobson called 'aloneness-togetherness', through which there could be a generation of self, a process emerging in conversation, a corrective to early destructive ways of relating but also understood as a dynamism between people. 'Conversation' in this context has a specific definition: 'the action of living or having one's being *in* or *among*' (Shorter Oxford English Dictionary, 1933), indicating that conversation 'both constitutes and manifests a form of personal being' (Meares, 2004: 52). Personal being and the sense of self are key aspects of PIT, which I shall consider further in this section.

At its most fundamental, the core assumption of PIT is that the creation of, and attention to, a personal relationship between the therapist and client is the key task of the therapy through which new learning emerges, enabling change. Rather than the relationship being seen as between therapist and client, however, it is between 'persons'. The therapeutic relationship takes on a subtly different aspect under this emphasis. Hobson identified six qualities of a personal relationship that he saw as the foundation of psychotherapy:

> [S]ix qualities of a personal relationship which are at the heart of conversational therapy: it happens between experiencing subjects, it can only be known from 'within', it is mutual, it involves aloneness-togetherness, its language is a disclosure of private 'information', and it is shared here and now. (Hobson, 1985: 25)

This paragraph encapsulates the essence of the form of relatedness integral to PIT; acknowledging the need to respect the autonomy of the other while engaging with them in maintaining an evolving relationship. The centrality of relatedness and the individual's sense of self within a relationship reflects Buber and his concept of *I–Thou*: 'The one primary word is the combination *I–Thou*' (Buber, 1958: 3). In this statement Buber refers to the essential relatedness of being human. We exist in relation to others. Buber goes on to distinguish the difference between relating to a person, from relating to an object, when he makes the statement: 'For the *I* of the primary word *I–Thou* is a different *I* from that of *I–It*.' In this second statement Buber is referring to the difference for the subject of the *I*, as well as object, when we relate in this depersonalised way. *How* the therapist is in the therapy, rather than the content of her words, impacts upon her as well as on the client.

Persons not things: We may be horrified at the idea of treating another person as a thing, a dehumanised object, but to some extent we all do this on a daily basis. When, for example, we relate to someone as their role, our manager, the estate agent, the man who sells the newspapers, we may know something *about* them, that they support Manchester United, or were born in Italy. We do not, however, really know *them*, as a person; we are relating in an instrumental context rather than one of true connection. We can know a great deal about our clients, and care about their welfare, but it is hard work to really know them and to connect with them.

The development of 'self': A crucial assumption of PIT is that the becoming and being a person are essentially relational tasks and happen between people. Much in the way Winnicott insisted that the infant needs relatedness with the mother in order to establish a sense of an autonomous self, similarly, as adults we need relatedness in order to maintain our sense of ourselves and tolerate separation. The concept of self in PIT is much as it is described by William James in his identification of the duplex self, implicit in the words 'I' and 'me' (James, 1892), and our recognition that both words reflect aspects of ourselves that are not the same and yet not divisible from each other. Meares (2000) suggests a third term: 'myself'. We refer easily to 'not feeling myself today' or 'that wasn't the real me', recognising that we have more than one 'self', and that these might be in conflict.

Rather than conceiving of the self as forged through the achievement of developmental tasks and maintained by fundamental instinctual drives as in Freudian theory, PIT reflects a development of the self which is closer to that described in attachment theory. That is, infants consolidate a sense of self through empathic responsiveness and careful mirroring from their primary caregiver: 'When I look I am seen, and so I exist' (Winnicott, 1971: 134). Stern (1985) provides a fascinating insight into the subjective world of infants and the emergence of a structuralisation of the self through the relationship with the primary caregiver, thereby emphasising the interpersonal aspects of the sense of self. This process is, however, disrupted if the interaction with the caregiver lacks what Stern refers to as attunement, the empathic response to the infant's feeling states. Stern describes the significance of this: 'Through the selective use of attunement, the parents' corresponding intersubjective responsivity acts as a template to shape and create intrapsychic experiences in the child' (Stern, 1985: 208). In this way, humour, delight, but also disapproval and disgust may be communicated in response to aspects of the child's behaviour, eroding their sense of value. Crucially, the claim here is that our sense and experience of self is shaped and structured in relationships. This is similar to Kohut's view that the 'self' develops from interpersonal experiences and that psychological difficulties can be attributed to faulty relationships with parental figures; similarly, he suggests that chronic lapses in parental empathy can lead to a damaged sense of self and a loss of self-esteem.

Pearmain (2003) uses a musical metaphor to describe the shaping of the caregiver's affective response to the infant and the term 'dance' is frequently used in this context, referring to the delicate sequencing of interaction. It is not always so harmonious, however. As Meares (2004) observes, behind the profound distress of those seeking therapy is a 'specific disturbance of the ordinary ongoing sense of personal existence, an experience we might call "self"'. This disturbance may originate in the apparently trivial, such as the implicit but repeated communication of disappointment, or the experience of more significant trauma, such as neglect or abusive behaviour on the part of the caregivers. The consequence of misattunement may be a sense of loss of agency, or a more destructive disavowal of personal value and a sense of alienation.

Disruption of self: Meares describes how trauma impacts upon our experience of self and the 'self system', our sense of personal coherence, identity and, most especially, 'the central *feeling* of self' (Meares, 2004: 60) so that our ability to experience intimacy, and our sense of personal worth are compromised. He draws on the investigations into memory by Tulving (1972) and Nelson (1992) to describe different types of memory, and at what stage of an infant's development they occur. For example, early semantic memory, recalling to mind something that may not be present, generally develops in the last part of the baby's first year, before words are first used. In noting these stages we can more easily understand the impact of trauma both on memory and on the development of the sense of self. In his earlier work, *Intimacy and Alienation* (2000), Meares refers to the memory system recording early trauma in a perceptual representation as a physical memory. Traumatic memory is described as 'anxiety-ridden and underpinned by an alienated form of relationship' (2012: 29) stored 'beyond reflective awareness' and not therefore easily accessed.

Language and symbolisation: Most of us are only too familiar with the devastation resulting from the experience of trauma for our clients. We have also encountered the difficulty many people face in translating their pain into words. Partly, this reflects their reluctance to revisit the experience, but more fundamentally, powerful feelings often elude our attempts to describe them. We often turn to music, art or poetry to express our pain, joy or bewilderment. Through the elliptical language of poetry, or non-verbal images we are sometimes able to convey, or tolerate, complexity, things that said more directly may be unbearable, even unsay-able. Crucially, however, traumatic memories may be stored as semantic memory, as facts detached from the sense of self, rather than as autobiographical memory. Meares (2012) suggests that such memories are in the form of attacks on the self, stored as what might be seen as 'scripts', for example, 'I am stupid/ugly/worthless'. He emphasises the importance of achieving a sense of value as of greater importance than establishing meaning. Some experiences may have been so severe that the memory is stored not as a memory but as a perceptual representation. Lenore Terr (1988) describes traumatised young children repeating with specific accuracy the physical sensation of the original trauma. As therapists, therefore, we need to find a language through which we can safely facilitate the recovery and integration of such memories, a language that can symbolically represent the experience. Metaphor is a way of representing our inner world as visual images and enables us to put our feelings into words. Feelings are also, as demonstrated by Terr's work, rooted in the body. We often use imagery to describe our physical sensations: 'gnawing pain' or 'thumping headache'. The requirement is therefore for the therapist to adopt an attitude that views all communication as potentially metaphorical and a means of 'visualising the inner world' (Meares, 2000: 125). Staying with the experience in the therapy room, following the client's feelings rather than asking questions about events, allows the therapist to remain open to whatever may unfold and facilitates the integration of disowned aspects of the self.

THE ESSENTIALS OF PIT IN PRACTICE

As is so often the case with over-familiar phrases, the term 'being with', rightly beloved by counselling psychologists, now slips rather too easily into our descriptions of our work without us paying full attention to the enormity of the task that the phrase requires of us. Being with and attending with care to the other person in the therapy room is at the heart of PIT. My aim in this section is not to offer a menu of skills to be picked up and tried, but to indicate the reality of the therapy in practice.

We have seen that a central assumption of PIT is that disruption to early significant relationships threatens an individual's personal sense of existence and damages their self-esteem; a key aim is therefore to re-create self-esteem, restoring the person's hope and ability to be at ease with 'myself'. PIT is a sequential model in which the therapist tentatively tests her understanding of the client's feelings, inviting correction or agreement. The aim is to generate a genuinely shared understanding of the client's experience in a safe environment that facilitates acknowledgement of the underlying interpersonal traumas that contributed to the difficulties brought to therapy. More fundamentally, therapy is seen as a true meeting of two persons who join to shape the conversation. In itself, this might sound aspirational but vague. Like all therapies, PIT requires that the therapist establishes a safe, uninterrupted environment in which to meet, that she is clear about the time and other boundaries, and clarifies the purpose of the meeting.

- *Establishing the interpersonal basis for change*: From the outset the therapist introduces the therapy as a personal but shared enterprise, providing a clear rationale for the therapy. At the same time, the therapist makes explicit the embryonic relationship between therapist and client. This might be through acknowledging the client's discomfort, anxiety or hope at finding themselves facing a therapist. For example, she might say 'I guess it feels a bit strange, coming to talk to someone like me'.

- *Using statements not questions*: Rather than asking questions which can restrict responses, in PIT tentative statements are seen as the starting point from which the conversation and greater understanding can develop. The therapist might start with an open-ended invitation to the client to talk about their difficulties. As the conversation progresses, the statements more explicitly invite expression of feelings along the lines of: 'Perhaps you are feeling rather worried about that' or 'I wonder if you felt rather cross with your sister....'. It is important these statements are offered in a tentative way, inviting correction or elaboration so that we might well then be saying: 'It sounds like I haven't got that quite right'.

- *Language of mutuality*: The use of 'I' and 'we' indicates a shared involvement in the exploration and the centrality of the relationship between therapist and client, reflecting the concept of I–Thou. It also establishes a direct way of communicating, for example, 'I'd like to understand more about that'.

- *Language of negotiation*: This is to convey that the therapist is seeking collaboration with the client. The therapist tests her understanding through tentative statements indicating the possibility of being wrong, implicitly inviting the client to modify her statement, for example, 'I'm not sure I've got this right, but I think you might be saying you are pretty fed up about....'.

- *Staying with feelings in the here and now*: Rather than talking about feelings in the abstract or belonging only to the past, the therapist facilitates expression of them in the immediacy of the session, for example, 'There's something of that crossness now...here'.

- *Focus on difficult feelings*: These are often 'hidden feelings', when a client is expressing something, perhaps through body language or metaphor, but is not aware of the feeling. The therapist might suggest something like, 'I notice when you talk about X (client's partner), you look quite upset', or 'Maybe we could look at that ... I wonder what the feeling would be'.

- *Use of metaphor and living symbols*: Metaphor brings a greater vividness to the client's description of their experience. It can also be a way to gain a more profound understanding of their feelings and to deepen the emotional exchange between client and therapist, acting as a bridge between the client's internal world and the external world. We all use metaphor on a daily basis, sometimes in much used phrases, such as 'butterflies in my tummy', 'over the moon' or 'hitting a brick wall', and it can be easy to miss their significance. Clients may also offer metaphor in a more subtle way, perhaps referring to physical complaints, for example 'my back's seized up', or an observation about the weather 'it's really bleak out there'. Both these statements reflect facts, but the exact language used can provide an additional insight into the client's world. The therapist's task is to be alert to the images offered by the client, to use them in further exploration and amplification of feelings.

- *Use of hypotheses*: In PIT the therapist does not interpret in the way a more traditional psychodynamic therapist might. Rather, she offers guesses or tentative expressions of understanding which are then explored with the client. These are statements in which the therapist refers to how she imagines the client is feeling, based on non-verbal cues or responding to spoken cues and to facilitate greater insight. There are three kinds of hypotheses, reflecting increasing insight, and also greater trust, in the therapeutic relationship to sustain the client in the face of painful feelings. *Understanding hypotheses* might be seen as both establishing a connection with the client, as well as testing out the therapist's understanding of the client's experience. They are expressions of empathy or imaginative statements of what the therapist guesses the client is experiencing now in the therapy, for example 'I wonder if you feel a bit lost'. *Linking hypotheses* are statements that link feelings that have emerged in the therapy to other feelings both within the therapy and in other circumstances. They draw links between important relationships in the client's life, past or present. For example, 'Perhaps it's rather like this at work when…' or 'I'm wondering if these feelings of being left behind are rather like when your sisters went off…'. *Explanatory hypotheses* are more complex and are only offered once a good relationship has been established and the therapist has gained an understanding of the client's history. These introduce the possibility of underlying reasons for the client's difficulties. The therapist offers a link between the client's relationship problems to some earlier, but often unacknowledged, conflict or difficulty. Explanatory hypotheses are much like Malan's triangle of conflict. (Malan, 1979)

While a list of competences indicates something of what occurs in the therapy room, it cannot of course capture the experience. PIT is a therapy that emphasises the need for the therapist to respond to the precise indications of communication from the client and to the minute-by-minute shifts in the interaction between therapist and client. We can see that the 'how' of the therapist's talk is crucial. It is not, of course, possible to convey the true flavour of a therapy encounter but the following brief vignette may illustrate the nature of PIT.

Maggie

Maggie is in her late forties. She lives on her own and is not in an intimate relationship. She has come to therapy concerned that her angry feelings towards her boss keep erupting at work. She realises she is in danger of losing her job.

She talks at length about her fury with her manager and is contemptuous about her colleagues' abilities. She refers to former colleagues whom she respected having left or retired. She tells me she feels 'out of synch'.

Maggie is the oldest of four siblings with twin brothers and a much younger sister. Her father, a merchant seaman, was away for her birth and until she was four. She lived with her mother and doting grandfather. When her father returned the family moved, leaving her grandparents' house; subsequently, Maggie's two brothers and sister were born. She talks of her mother's preoccupation with 'the babies' and being left to her own devices, playing in the wonderful, but dangerous docks. She mentions that had she fallen, it was unlikely that she would have been found: 'I'd have vanished without trace.' She laughs but looks bereft.

(Continued)

(Continued)

Maggie fills the sessions with amusing anecdotes and the room with her flamboyant clothes. I wonder if she feels she needs to entertain me. She agrees that she feels reassured if people laugh at her stories. Later she takes a few days' holiday from work. 'No one noticed. No one missed me.' I feel a great sadness and suggest that perhaps she feels forgotten about. She acknowledges that she feels left behind. She talks of not wanting an intimate relationship but makes frequent references to her previous partner, whom she misses, and to a man she knew some time ago. After a brief holiday Maggie brings me a witty postcard. Perhaps she wondered if she might have vanished without trace from my mind in the break? Maggie responds saying she knows I must see many people and that her problems do not amount to 'a hill of beans'.

As the therapy progresses we continue to notice what is happening between us, in particular her anxiety whether I can hold her in mind. Parallels in her relationships outside therapy become clear; we are able to talk about her anticipation of rejection and how anger can mask this fear, protecting her from overwhelming feelings. Her language is rich in metaphor and I build on this to deepen my understanding of her more hidden feelings – her terror of being passed over for the 'next baby' – to test out this understanding with Maggie. As she gradually makes sense of her anger, a profound sadness emerges; the sharp witticisms continue but there is more space for connection and feeling. Later in the therapy Maggie risks contacting her friend, suggesting they meet up and is delighted that he takes up her invitation. At the end of therapy both she and I are able to acknowledge our sadness at the ending and to recognise that we have both valued the connection.

THE RESEARCH BASE OF PIT: VALUING PRACTICE-BASED EVIDENCE ALONGSIDE EVIDENCE-BASED PRACTICE

Discussion continues, within counselling psychology and beyond, concerning what constitutes evidence and the relevance of research to clinical practice. It is not in the scope of this chapter to discuss such a complex topic, but as practitioners we cannot afford to avoid the discussion. Readers may like to consult Corrie (2010) for a thoughtful review and Marzillier (2014) for a passionate argument against the prevailing political privileging of outcome research. Barkham and Barker (2003: 113) make a strong case for us to engage in the evaluation of our practice, placing practice-based evaluation as a 'natural complement to the current focus on evidence based practice', arguing that both have a place in extending our knowledge base of what constitutes good therapeutic practice. It is in this context that I approach a brief review of the 'scientific attitude' adopted by PIT and suggest that PIT's requirement of the therapist to adopt a 'scientific attitude' fits with counselling psychology's principle of the scientist-practitioner role as well as its contribution to the development of evidence-based practice.

Until recently, few psychodynamic therapists have taken a scientific stance towards their clinical work, preferring to present this as case studies to colleagues rather than engaging in quantitative research studies, such as randomised control trials (RCTs). While we might sympathise with the argument that much research conducted under controlled conditions does not reflect the messier reality of clinical work, or allow the nuances of therapy to be presented, this has led to the unfortunate consequence of keeping from the harsh world of political assessment much impressive clinical work. From its inception, PIT has included scientific enquiry as a fundamental plank of its development, with both Hobson and Meares requiring that the model should be evaluated, researched and evidence-based (Guthrie, 2013, unpublished). As a result, there has been scientific study into the model for over 30 years, covering, in addition to outcome research, studies on the process of therapy and how the model is practised. PIT's emphasis on practice-based evidence demands micro-analysis of clinical material in order to identify what enables change, what promotes and what hinders the benefit to the client within the therapeutic setting, mirroring the concept of 'minute particulars'. This is a fundamental aspect of the research which requires detailed scrutiny of clinical material captured on audio-recording equipment.

Research studies using PIT in a range of clinical presentations have been conducted in the UK, Australia and Germany. These include the 'gold standard' RCT as well as a benchmarking study (Paley et al., 2008) evaluating the model in routine clinical settings. Early evaluations of the model were conducted as a series of randomised comparative studies (e.g. Shapiro and Firth, 1987; Shapiro et al., 1994), comparing PIT with CBT and showing broadly equivalent benefits in the treatment of depression. A similar comparison was found in a later study with those with less severe depression in a more typical service setting (Barkham and Hobson, 1989). Subsequent studies have shown efficacy across a range of difficulties, including deliberate self-harm (Guthrie et al., 2001). Guthrie et al.'s study became the basis for a key service within Manchester Mental Health and Social Care NHS Trust that continues to be offered to people who deliberately self-harm. I am, however, particularly underlining the research into the use of PIT with patients' medically unexplained symptoms (MUS). Previously known as somatisation, this refers to physical symptoms from which people suffer but for which no obvious explanation can be found through structural pathology. These symptoms can often be experienced as debilitating and distressing, leaving people feeling let down by the apparent lack of medical explanation. There have been five randomised controlled trials evaluating the effectiveness of PIT for patients with MUS (Hamilton et al., 2000; Sattel, 2012). Several of these trials focused on unexplained bowel symptoms with patients with severe and persistent symptoms. The research team included a consultant gastroenterologist who was 'blind' to which groups the patients were assigned. The outcome of early studies demonstrated that PIT offered greater benefit than the supportive condition; subsequent trials resulted in significantly improved outcomes as well as reduced subsequent use of health care, with consequent cost savings. It is perhaps important to remind ourselves how many people presenting with MUS will see a referral to psychology or psychotherapy as proof that no one believes that their symptoms are real and we might well start the session by some acknowledgement of this. PIT adopts the stance of real interest in the symptoms experienced by the particular person sitting with us, picking up and amplifying their language, noting the 'minute particulars', especially the particular language they use to describe their physical symptoms. The therapist remains with the physical symptoms in some detail, finding out about the impact on relationships and other aspects of the person's life, all the time listening for emotional cues, until the person moves into feelings. As in all PIT sessions, we are attending to how the person shares details of their experience in an interpersonal context. PIT is now being developed as the IAPT model for this client group.

Colleagues in Australia have focused on developing the model for those who meet the criteria for a diagnosis of Borderline Personality Disorder (BPD) (Meares, 2012). Whether or not we use such diagnostic terms, we are likely to be familiar with the extreme distress and often frightening states of mind associated with BPD. The work undertaken by Meares and his colleagues continues and extends the focus on the representation of feeling, both how this is stored in our memory system and how we communicate feeling. There have been two major evaluations of PIT for those with BPD (Stevenson and Meares, 1999; Korner et al., 2006) as well as a study in a clinical setting which demonstrated significant benefit for the treatment group (Korner et al., 2006).

CONCLUSION

Reading about research studies can be a dusty activity, but it is important to know, and to be able to show, that we offer our clients something of value. In addition to citing some of the evidence supporting PIT, I hope I have conveyed here something of its richness.

You may ask – why this approach rather than one of the many others? I have sought to demonstrate in this chapter the particular relevance of PIT to the intersubjective philosophy which underlies counselling psychology. PIT's profound humanistic stance, integrated with its theoretical grounding in a number of psychological and therapeutic traditions, allows it to be seen as a distinct model of therapy (Guthrie, 1999). The range of inspiration, drawing from the works and insights of thinkers from Freud to Bowlby, Winnicott to Kohut, Wordsworth to Buber, allows, perhaps demands, a creativity within a clear framework. The professional curiosity and rigour established from its inception have enabled PIT to develop in a number of settings both in the UK and Australia across client groups and across a range of presenting psychological problems.

For those wishing to explore the model further, there is a lively Special Interest Group based in Manchester which organises workshops, seminars and conferences. Details about the SIG and associated training courses can be found on the website: www.pit-sig.uk.

 Visit the companion website to listen to Psychodynamic Interpersonal Therapy.

REFERENCES

Barkham, M. and Barker, C. (2003) 'Establishing practice-based evidence', in R. Woolfe, W. Dryden and S. Strawbridge (eds), *Handbook of Counselling Psychology* (2nd edn). London: Sage.

Barkham, M. and Hobson, R. F. (1989) 'Exploratory therapy in two-plus-one sessions: 11 – a single case study'. *British Journal of Psychotherapy*, 6: 89–100.

Bowlby, J. (1980) *Attachment and Loss, Vol. 3. Loss: Sadness and Depression*. London: Hogarth and Institute of Psychoanalysis.

Buber, M. (1958) *I and Thou*. Edinburgh: T. & T. Clark.

Corrie, S. (2010) 'What is evidence?', in R. Woolfe, S. Strawbridge, B. Douglas and W. Dryden (eds), *Handbook of Counselling Psychology* (3rd edn). London: Sage. pp. 44–61.

Gomez, L. (1997) *An Introduction to Object Relations*. London: Free Association Press.

Guthrie, E. (1999) 'Psychodynamic Interpersonal Therapy'. *Advances in Psychiatric Treatment*, 5: 135–145.

Guthrie, E. (2013) The Evidence Base. Paper given at conference in Manchester: Foundations of Conversational Model Therapy (15 March 2013).

Guthrie, E., Kapur, N., Mackway-Jones, K., Chew-Graham, C., Moorey, J., Mendel, E., Marino-Francis, F., Sanderson, S., Turpin, C., Boddy, G. and Tomenson, B. (2001) 'Randomised controlled trial of brief psychological intervention after deliberate self- poisoning'. *British Medical Journal*, 323: 1–4.

Hamilton, J., Guthrie, G., Creed, F., Thompson, D., Tomenson, B., Bennett, R., Moriarty, K., Stephens, W. and Liston, R. (2000) 'A randomised controlled trial of psychotherapy in patients with chronic functional dyspepsia'. *Gastronenterology*, 119: 661–669.

Hobson, R. (1985) *Forms of Feeling: The Heart of Psychotherapy*. London: Tavistock.

Holmes, J. (2000) 'Object relations, attachment theory, self-psychology and interpersonal psychoanalysis', in M. G. Gelder, Juan J. Lopez-Ibor and Nancy C. Andreasen (eds), *Oxford Textbook of Psychiatry*. Oxford: Oxford University Press.

Holmes, J. (2003) 'Borderline personality disorder and the search for meaning: An attachment perspective'. *Australian and New Zealand Journal of Psychiatry*, 37: 524–532.

Horvath, A. O. and Luborsky, L. (1993) 'The role of the therapeutic alliance in psychotherapy'. *Journal of Consulting and Clinical Psychology*, 61: 561–573.

James, W. (1892) *Psychology: Briefer Course*. London: Macmillan.

Kohut, H. (1971) *The Analysis of the Self*. London: Hogarth Press.

Korner, A., Gerull, F., Meares, R. and Stevenson, J. (2006) 'Borderline personality disorder treated with the conversational model: A replication study'. *Comprehensive Psychiatry*, 47 (5): 406–411.

Malan, D. (1979) *Individual Psychotherapy and the Science of Psychodynamics*. London: Butterworths.

Margison, F. (2002) 'Psychodynamic interpersonal therapy', in J. Holmes and A. Bateman (eds), *Integration in Psychotherapy: Models and Methods*. Oxford: Oxford University Press.

Martin, D. J., Garske, J. P. and Davis, M. K. (2000) 'Relation of the therapeutic alliance with outcome and other variables: A meta-analytic review'. *Journal of Consulting and Clinical Psychology*, 68: 438–540.

Marzillier, J. (2014) 'The flawed nature of evidence-based psychotherapy'. *BPS Psychotherapy Section Review*, 51 (Spring): 25–33.

Meares, R. (2000) *Intimacy and Alienation: Memory, Trauma and Personal Being*. London: Routledge.

Meares, R. (2004) 'The Conversational Model: An outline'. *American Journal of Psychotherapy*, 58 (1): 51–66.

Meares, R. (2012) *Borderline Personality Disorder and the Conversational Model: A Clinician's Manual*. New York: W. W. Norton.

Moorey, J. and Guthrie, E. (2003) 'Persons and experience: Essential aspects of psychodynamic interpersonal therapy'. *Psychodynamic Practice*, 9 (4 November): 547–564.

Nelson, K. (1992) 'Emergence of autobiographical memory at four'. *Human Development*, 35: 172–177.

Oxford University Press (1933) *The Shorter Oxford English Dictionary*. Oxford: Oxford University Press.

Paley, G., Cahill, J., Barkham, M., Shapiro, D., Jones, J., Patrick, S. and Reid, E. (2008) 'The effectiveness of psychodynamic-interpersonal psychotherapy in routine clinical practice: A benchmarking comparison'. *Psychology and Psychotherapy: Theory, Research and Practice*, 81: 157–175.

Parker, I., Georgaca, E., Harper, D., McLaughlin, T. and Stowell-Smith, M. (1995) *Deconstructing Psychopathology*. London: Sage.

Pearmain, R. (2003) 'Psychotherapy: The art of relating'. *BPS Psychotherapy Section Newsletter*, 35 (December): 36–46.

Pilgrim, D. (1997) *Psychotherapy and Society*. London. Sage.

Ryle, A. (1990) *Cognitive-Analytic Therapy: Active Participation in Change*. Chichester: Wiley.

Sattell, H., Lahman, C., Gundel, H., Guthrie, E., Kruse, J., Noll-Hussong, M., Ohmann, C., Ronel, J., Sack, M., Sauer, N., Schneider, G. and Henningsen, P. (2012) 'Brief psychodynamic interpersonal therapy for patients with multisomatoform disorder: Randomised control trial'. *British Journal of Psychiatry*, 200 (1): 60–67.

Shapiro, D. and Firth, J. (1987) 'Prescriptive vs exploratory psychotherapy: Outcomes of the Sheffield Psychotherapy Project'. *British Journal of Psychiatry*, 151: 790–799.

Shapiro, D., Barkham, M., Rees, A., Hardy, G., Reynolds, S. and Startup, M. (1994) 'Effects of treatment duration and severity of depression on the effectiveness of cognitive-behavioural and psychodynamic-interpersonal psychotherapy'. *Journal of Consulting and Clinical Psychology*, 62: 522–534.

Stern, D. (1985) *The Interpersonal World of the Infant*. New York: Basic Books.

Stevenson, J. and Meares, R. (1999) 'Psychotherapy with borderline patients, Part 11: A preliminary cost benefit analysis'. *Australian and New Zealand Journal of Psychiatry*, 33 (3): 473–477.

Terr, L. (1988) 'What happens to early memories of trauma?' *Journal of the American Academy of Child and Adolescent Psychiatry*, 1: 96–104.

Tulving, E. (1972) 'Episodic and semantic memory', in E.Tulving and W. Donaldson (eds), *Organisation of Memory*. New York: Academic Press.

Winnicott, D. (1971) *Playing and Reality*. London: Tavistock.

20

THE PRACTICE OF THERAPEUTIC LETTER WRITING IN NARRATIVE THERAPY

ANJA BJORØY, STEPHEN MADIGAN AND DAVID NYLUND

The use of letter writing in psychotherapy has a long and varied history (Riordan and Soet, 2000). This chapter describes the application of therapeutic letters from a *narrative therapy* perspective. Therapeutic documents from a narrative therapy framework are informed by different theoretical traditions from those of counselling psychology, psychiatry, family therapy and social work – namely post-structuralism and anti-individualism.

After a brief overview of narrative therapy, the theoretical justification for narrative letters, guidelines for the practice and various categories of narrative letters are discussed. Examples of our most prevalent and more recent types of narrative therapy letter are illustrated (with actual letters that were written to clients we work alongside). The categories of letters included in this chapter are: letters as narrative, letters of prediction, therapeutic letter writing campaigns, therapeutic letters as 'case notes' for institutions and group consultations, unique developments in couple relationship letters, relational letters written to the couple's relationship, and counter-documents. Other types of letter – letters of invitation, brief letters and counter-referral documents – are briefly described without examples. The reader is referred to White and Epston (1990) for more detailed illustrations of those kinds of written documents.

Narrative therapy is viewed as a collaborative and non-pathologising approach to counselling and community work that centres people as the expert of their own lives. Narrative therapy, developed by Michael White and David Epston (1990), is based on the premise that persons make meaning of their lives through stories. Stories from a narrative therapy perspective are viewed as a sequence of events, linked by a theme, occurring over time and according to particular plots. A story emerges as certain events are privileged and selected out over other events that become neglected and 'un-storied'. The stories people live by are not a mirror of a person's life but are actually shaping of people's lived experiences. Narrative therapy suggests that stories and the lives of the persons we see in therapy do not exist in a vacuum; they are instead viewed as under the influence of a powerfully shaping broader context – particularly in the various dimensions of class, race, gender, sexual orientation and ability. The discursive contexts of a person's life and relationships are viewed as primary to the shaping of lives and relationships. Placing a primary emphasis on person and problem making on the discursive contexts is one example of how narrative therapy is viewed as different from other forms of counselling in the authors' home countries of Canada, Norway and America.

By the time a person has decided to come to therapy they have often developed a dominant story about who they are as persons. The person's deficit story, as told to the therapist, has often recruited the person into a 'thin' identity conclusion of themselves – and one that is considered problem saturated. Such negative identity conclusions can invite a powerfully negative influence in the way people see their lives, values, skills, capabilities and futures. For example, a person may come to therapy and describe themselves as 'depressed', concluding that these descriptions are predetermined and biologically innate to who they are as persons (leading to a sense of hopelessness). These thinly described problem descriptions are informed within structuralist, scientific and individualist theoretical paradigms that suggest that identity is fixed, ahistorical and de-contextualised.

Narrative therapy takes up an anti-individualist approach to therapy that is informed by the post-structuralist idea that identity is fluid, dynamic and contextual (Madigan, 1992, 2011; Madigan and Goldner, 1998). Hence, within a narrative perspective, people's lives, identities and relationships are viewed as multi-storied versus single-storied. By conceptualising a post-structuralist view of identity, narrative practices are able to linguistically separate persons from 'fixed' and deficit conclusions/descriptions about their identity. When this point of view is practised in therapy it is known as the process of externalising the problem (White and Epston, 1990). Externalising problems allows people to consider that the problem is not located and privatised solely inside their bodies. Problems are viewed as contextually influenced, situational, discursive and communally learned and agreed upon (Madigan, 2011). Hence the rather simple narrative practice motto is: 'The person is not the problem, the problem is the problem.' For example, when a person in therapy states that 'I am depressed', the narrative therapist might ask a question such as, 'when did you notice that depression first entered into your life?', or 'are there times when you feel depression gets the better of you as opposed to other times when you get the better of it?'

Separating the problem from the person allows the narrative therapist to listen for contradictions or exceptions to the discourse of the dominant problem story being told, otherwise known as 'unique outcomes'. These unique outcomes can serve as entry points into alternative stories that assist persons to redefine their relationship with the problem. From there, preferred stories that highlight a person's skills, abilities and competencies are drawn out and amplified. With curiosity and exploration through the careful crafting of questions, these preferred stories and accounts of people's lives can become 'thickened', richly described and eventually performed. Common lines of therapeutic inquiry include curiosities concerning the person's values, commitments, intentions, treasured memories, influential relationships and how these areas connect with each other and live outside and beyond the person's relationship with the problem.

There are many practices in narrative therapy that help enrich and expand the person's preferred stories. One key aspect of narrative practice is the use of therapeutic documents or letter writing. Using letters fits nicely with the text analogy (Madigan and Epston, 1995; Madigan and Goldner, 1998) and is a sensible extension of doing therapy from a narrative perspective. Stories take on an added meaning and permanence when they are written down. David Epston (1994: 31), who has been instrumental in the practice of narrative letter writing, writes:

> Conversation is, by its very nature, ephemeral. After a particularly meaningful session, a client walks away aglow with provocative new thoughts, but a few blocks away, the exact words that had struck home as so profound may already be hard to recall. ... But the words in a letter don't fade and disappear the way conversation does; they endure through time and space, bearing witness to the work of therapy and immortalizing it.

Narrative therapy letters can provide a very powerful tool for consolidating the alternative story and for rendering it less likely to be taken over by the problem story. Below are detailed examples of various types of narrative therapy letter.

LETTERS AS UNIQUE DEVELOPMENT NARRATIVES AND COUNTER-STORIES

Unique development narratives and counter-stories letters are the most commonly used in narrative practice. They are used to depict the linear nature of the client's story with a particular focus on documenting the new stories that are developing (Nylund, 2002). Letters as narrative typically record and summarise the session and are used for the following purposes:

1. To assure the client that the therapist has heard the client's story accurately. The letter positions the client as the final editor of their story.
2. To reflect and think about the meeting and the newly available and emerging counter-stories they have re-called and re-told outside the therapy session and thereby take up these ideas without waiting for the next session.
3. To provide an opportunity to document (counter-filing), support and re-tell their own emerging and preferred story to the client. Through the session's lettering of their experience the client is positioned to be a witness to their own life and forgotten abilities and values.
4. To extend the conversation between meetings so that this supports and maintains the relevance and, more particularly, the endurance of the ideas comprising the new story.
5. To enhance the therapist–client relationship, building trust and mutual respect in future sessions.

Freeman et al. (1997) and Nylund and Thomas (1994) provide some useful tips for letter writing. Some of the things they suggest that could be included in the letter are:

1. An introductory paragraph reconnecting the client to the previous therapy session.
2. Verbatim quotes of the clients.
3. Statements describing the relative influence of the problem on the client. This section usually includes a variety of comments that reinforce the separation of the problem from the person and what the person has lost/suffered during their relationship with the problem.
4. Questions rather than direct statements regarding areas that were under-explored in the session.
5. Questions that punctuate unique outcomes and imply a grammar of agency.
6. The use of reflexive verbs and/or evaluative questions: For instance, 'John, does this mean that you have been more in charge of your anger rather than it being in charge of you?' versus 'John, you have been controlling your anger.'
7. The use of humour and puns.

Below is an example of a letter written to a client, Kyle, who has struggled with anxiety.

Dear Kyle,

This letter, as promised, summarizes our meeting the other day. You shared how Anxiety has influenced your life; it has a long history. Anxiety had many allies, kids who teased you a lot, and a culture that ostracizes difference. These allies recruited you into a negative story about yourself.

Yet in spite of the power of Anxiety and its friends, you never completely surrendered to it. In looking back, can you remember moments of you standing up for yourself? I asked you who most appreciated you as a young person. You movingly shared about your physics teacher. When I asked you what your teachers saw in you, you said, 'he believed in my … he knew I was smart and a strong person.'

Kyle, What did your teacher see in you that the kids who teased you were blind to? What might happen if you kept your teacher's version of you close to you? How might it help to undermine the power of Anxiety?

Anxiety definitely took a back seat when you found the bravery to approach and meet your girlfriend, Susan, in San Francisco. I enjoyed hearing about the story of how you met Susan and what she values about you. When I asked you about what Susan appreciates about you, you shared how you haven't been asked that question before. Have you given that question any more thought? How might thinking more about this question help you to further embrace a 'modest bravery'? Perhaps you can share this with me next session. Yours against Anxiety,

David Nylund

Letters written to a young person often have a playful quality to them. Here is an example of a letter written to an eight-year-old boy, who was experiencing night fears, and his mother:

Dear John and Mom,

Thanks for our talk the other day. I got a sense that fear took a back seat to our conversation. Do you agree Mom? John, I really like how you, your mom, and I came up with the Rules of Fear:

1. Fear grows the more you don't confront it;
2. Fear can lurk around the corner;
3. It tricks kids into thinking they are not brave;
4. It grows smaller by taking small steps.

So, we were thinking about what can help you to find your bravery. Your mom brought up Popeye and how he got stronger after eating spinach. BTW, Mom have you shown John an episode of Popeye yet?

Yes, I know you don't like spinach. But you're in luck because your Mom is Greek! And she makes a great Spinach Pie (Spanakopita). And just your luck – you love Spinach Pie! So, Mom you agreed to make Spanakopita and John will eat a slice around bed time. Then his Popeye will come out to fight Fear!

I can't wait to find out how it went!!! Mom, could you bring me a piece of the Spinach Pie to our next meeting? I love it too; you see, my Dad grew up near Greektown Detroit and he introduced Spinach Pie to me when I was kid. I think if I eat some, the team of us three – the Spanakopita Fear Busting Trio – can tackle any Fear.

Yours against Fear,

David the Sailor Man.

LETTERS OF INVITATION

Given that narrative therapy looks at the wider relational social context, it is advantageous to involve multiple members of a family and/or the other important members of the person's community. There are often times when a member of the family is not present at a therapy session although their presence can be useful. With the consent of the attending family member, these confidential letters are sent to both people. They recognise an understanding of the person not being ready to attend the counselling and/or encourage the person to attend a session by sharing some of the new narratives of the attending people with the absent person(s).

LETTERS OF PREDICTION

In these letters the therapist writes a new narrative which encompasses the visions and hopes of the client. These documents have a future temporal dimension. The idea is that the client will consider the future story and the conviction in the new story will result in the forecast coming true. These letters of prediction provide an opportunity to envision a future where the problem story is in the background or the past. Here is an illustration of a prediction letter written to Steve, a 12-year-old who was caught up in conflict and bickering with his mother. The letter was written and given to Steve in January 2004 and sealed, stating 'Do not open till December 25'. The document predicts a future of Steve stepping more into responsibility, less conflict and more appreciation of his mother. Of course, Steve could not wait till Christmas as he opened it up two days after he received the letter (February 2004)! And, to be sure, he followed through with most of the developments suggested in the letter.

Don't open till Dec 25, 2004!!!!!!!!!!

Hi Steve,

Growing up has been hard, huh? You can't blame others (especially your mom) for your problems anymore. And there are more responsibilities which can kind of suck! So this has made your move towards growing up even that much more remarkable. I remember the turning point, though. Do you recall? Was it when your mom asked you to clean your room and you went ahead and did it without arguing or complaining? Or was it when you did your homework without your mom having to remind you?

Now that you are becoming a teenager, there are advantages however, eh? – more freedoms for sure. Do you like it so far? What's it like for your mom to stop commenting on your homework and other things and just turn it over to you trusting that you will complete it on your own (or you won't complete it)? That she has actually come to trust that you can make the right decision for yourself.

What's it like to no longer bicker with your mom? What's it like for you to be the supervisor of your own life rather than your mom supervising your life for you? Are you impressed more with yourself or more with your mom and the two of you breaking the 'never ending teenager/mom bickering pattern'? What is it about your recent mother–son relationship that has led it to be so bicker-free? Have you asked David how surprised he is? Is he proud of you? Why do you think I knew you could do this?

BTW, I was blown away when you actually complimented your mom on several occasions throughout early 2004, even asking her how her day was. And you definitely shocked your mom when you planned and threw your mom a mother appreciation party!!!

Yours sincerely,

David

COUNTER-REFERRAL LETTERS

In these letters the new narrative is sent to the person who referred the client or family to the therapist, such as a child welfare worker, teacher or probation officer (Nylund, 2000). This letter is a means of spreading the new narrative and offering a follow-up with the referral source.

BRIEF LETTERS

There is a vast array of content that might be included in brief letters, and there seems to be one consistent theme. The theme is to let the client know that the therapist is thinking about the conversation after the meeting. These letters offer a brief summary of the newly emerging preferred narratives of the previous session. Brief letters can also be sent to a former isolated client simply to let them know that you are thinking about them. The act of receiving mail can help the client to feel valuable, connected and less alone in the world.

THERAPEUTIC LETTER WRITING CAMPAIGNS

The purpose of our designing therapeutic letter writing campaigns was a response to help people/clients re-remember preferred aspects of themselves that had been forgotten within the limitations and restrains of a dominant problem story. We initially developed the therapeutic letter writing campaign from within specific *contexts of fear*. More specifically, the relationship to fear that we experienced as therapists was a response to construct new methods of practice when problems posed a serious threat to the very lives of the people we were working with.

The therapeutic context(s) we found ourselves in involved consulting families whose loved ones had ended up staying for long periods of time on psychiatric wards, living terribly frightening and limited lives involved with massive regimes of psychiatric drugs, long durations of ECT, forced feeding tubes, isolation, etc. We were working alongside people who had given up on hope when confronted with retirement, the death of a young child, anorexia, bullying, despair, financial loss and an assortment of other contextualised tragedies that they themselves had not invented on their own but had somehow blamed themselves for. Many of the persons we were working with had been convinced by the problem that death was a far better option than living.

The initial letter campaigns were designed to assist persons to be re-membered back towards membership systems of love and support from which the problem had dis-membered them. Creating letter writing campaigns through communities of concern was a therapeutic means to counterbalance the problem-saturated story and dominant memory of despair and failure (Madigan and Epston, 1995).

These therapeutic situations felt desperate and many (if not most) of our clients' bodies had been inscribed with a diagnosis of 'chronic', meaning that, according to the psychiatric teams they were encountering, the problems our clients were experiencing were viewed as a life sentence. Our clients were viewed by the institution as persons who could not be helped.

Letter-writing campaigns were invented as a response to these life-threatening problems and our disbelief in chronic identities. The campaigns recruited the client or the person's community of concern (Madigan and Epston, 1995) as re-membering, loving others who held onto different, competing and preferred stories of the client, while the client's idea of themselves remained restrained by the problem and expert discourse. The community of concern's written stories were solicited and offered quite a different version of the person (a counter-version). The community counter-stories, written and told, lived outside the professional and cultural inscriptions of failed personhood. The communities' letter campaign told stories of hope, revised histories and offered a preferred imagination and future possibilities. The client's community stood in support of the person and on the firm belief that change for their loved one was possible.

What stood out early on was the dramatic way problems, and the professional discourse supporting the problems, had convinced persons to remember to forget anything worthy, trustworthy or valued in themselves. We viewed the story clients told and the problem story they were living through as severely restrained by negative imagination and the public discourse of a less than worthy/not measured up lifestyle.

Over the last 18 years, the authors' therapeutic letter-writing campaigns have been designed for persons as young as six and as old as 76. We found that persons receiving letters began to rediscover a discourse of the 'self' that assisted them to re-member back into healthy living situations from which the problem has most often dis-membered them (Madigan, 2008, 2011). These include claiming back former membership associations with intimate relationships, school, sports, careers, health and family members, and re-acquainting themselves with aspects of themselves once restrained by the problem identity.

LETTERS FOR COUPLE RELATIONSHIP FUTURES: RE-REMEMBERING HEALTH IN THE FACE OF ANXIETY, LOST HOPE AND DEPRESSION

Travels with Oscar

A psychiatrist colleague referred 70-year-old Oscar and his wife Maxine. In our first session, Oscar informed us that he had been struck down by a truck at a crosswalk a year before. He was not supposed to live but he did; he was not supposed to come out of his three-month-long coma but he did; and it was predicted that he would never walk again but he did, and so on. As you might imagine, it didn't take long to realise we were sitting before quite a remarkable man. However, it seemed that Oscar had paid dearly for his comeback because somewhere along the way he had lost all 'confidence' in himself. He also told us he would panic if Maxine (his partner) was not by his side '24 hours a day'. Maxine had spent the year before organising the complicated task of Oscar's medical care, and stated at our first visit that she was 'absolutely exhausted', and 'looking forward to getting back to her own business pursuits'. Unfortunately, her interests were being pushed aside and taken over by what they both called 'anxiety'.

The conversational experience of his relationship to anxiety, which had been the 'legacy' of Oscar's accident, had him believing that 'I am only half a man', and further more 'Maxine will leave me for another man – and I believe she is planning to put me in an old-age home'. There was also a seemingly odd twist in that anxiety had him believing that 'I did not deserve a good life' and, furthermore, 'I should kill myself'. The relationship with anxiety was allowing him to *remember to forget* 'the lovely sweet life' Maxine explained he had lived prior to the accident. Oscar also let us know that he was becoming more and more 'isolated and depressed'.

Oscar and Maxine had let us know that they had moved from England to Canada ten years earlier and that their life together had been 'blissful' prior to the accident. In the first session we all agreed the anxiety was gaining on Oscar and that the situation was – as Oscar stated – 'desperate'. During the next session we decided to design an international anti-anxiety letter-writing campaign. Below is the letter we co-authored in five minutes near the end of the second session (it can be viewed as a 'standard' letter-writing campaign letter). As Oscar was concerned that his friends might consider the letter 'a crazy idea', he insisted that we include my professional credentials to give the letter 'credence'. Oscar's words from our sessions are directly included and written within quotation marks.

Dear Friends of Oscar and Maxine:

My name is Stephen Madigan and I have an MSW as well an MSc and PhD in family therapy. Your friends Oscar and Maxine have asked me to write to you so that we might solicit your support. As you are probably aware, Oscar suffered a terrible accident 14 months ago, and since then has instituted a remarkable comeback. What you may not know is the after-effects of the accident have left Oscar a captive of anxiety, and this anxiety is currently bossing him around. You may not believe this but some of the messages anxiety gives to Oscar is that 'he is a good for nothing,' that 'he is a useless human being,' and that 'sooner than later all of his friends will come to know him the way anxiety knows him.' Through anxiety's influence, Oscar is beginning to 'give up on himself', and we ask your support in bringing Oscar back from anxiety's grip. We think you can help Oscar win back his life from this terrible anxiety. Could you please send Oscar a brief letter expressing (1) how you remember your history with him, (2) your thoughts and feelings about his physical comeback and his person in the present, and (3) how you believe you would like to see your relationship with Oscar and Maxine grow into the future.

We hope that your letters of support are not too much to ask, and we want you to know that they will be greatly appreciated. Oscar would also like all of you to know that he will respond to all of your replies.
Warm regards,

Stephen Madigan PhD, Oscar's anti-anxiety consultant

The structure of the therapeutic letter-writing campaign letters are usually the same. Together with the client(s), I write a letter to selected members of the family/community (whom the client and/or family member selects), and ask them to assist in a temporal re-remembering and witnessing process through lettered written accounts outlining (a) their memories of their relationship with the client, (b) their current hopes for the client, and (c) how they anticipate their relationship growing with the client in the future.

The letters' written accounts are directed towards countering the problems' attempt to re-write a person's past as entirely 'negative' while predicting a future filled with the hopelessness of worst-case scenarios. The community letters also begin to re-write any negative profes-sionalised stories found to be unhelpful to the person and helpful to the problem. Community letters are *always* diametrically different from what had been written previously in the client's professional mental health file. Campaign letters written by the person's community of concern re-present a *counter file*.

A few months later, Oscar wrote to me from his long-awaited 'anti-anxiety' trip to France with Maxine. He once stated his trip to France would mark 'my arrival back to health'. He told me through the postcard that he was sitting alone, drinking espresso, while Maxine had gone sightseeing for the day. He wrote, 'I am thanking my lucky stars that I am no longer a prisoner of anxiety'. His said the only problem now was 'keeping up with all of his return correspond-ence!' He stated that the return correspondence was a problem he could manage and was willing to take full responsibility for.

Without the recruitment of a community of concern, Oscar might never have rebounded to re-remember all his personal abilities/qualities/values and the contributions he had made during his lifetime – the problem from which he had dis-remembered.

Letter-writing campaign structure

Letter-writing efforts can take on a variety of shapes and forms, but the most standard cam-paigns involve the following (Madigan, 2008, 2011; Madigan and Epston, 1995; Madigan and Goldner, 1998):

1. The campaign emerges from a narrative interview when alternative accounts of who the person might be are questioned, revived and re-remembered. The person is asked to consider wheth-er there are other people in his/her life who may regard the person differently from how the problem describes them. These different accounts are then spoken of. I might ask the follow-ing questions: 'If I were to interview _____ about you, what do you think they might tell me about yourself that the problem that you would not dare to tell me?' Or 'Do you think your friend's telling of you to me about you would be an accurate telling, even if it contradicted the problem's telling of you?' Or 'Whose description of you do you prefer, and why?'
2. Together, the client and myself (along with the client's family/partner, friend, therapist, insiders, etc., if any of these persons are in attendance) begin a conversation regarding all the possible other descriptions of the client as a persons that she/he might be, but has forgotten to remember

because of the problem's hold over her/him. We dialogue on who the client might be, who the client would like to be, and who the client used to be well before the problem took over her/his life. We recall their forgotten alternative lived experiences of herself/himself that the client may have forgotten through the problem's restraining context.

3. We then begin to make a list of all the persons in the client's life who would be in support of these alternative descriptions. Once the list is complete, we construct a letter of support and invitation.
4. If finances are a problem, my office supplies the envelopes and stamps for the ensuing campaign.
5. If privacy is an issue, we use the office as the return address.
6. If the person comes to the next session (with letters) alone, I will offer to read the letters back to them as a textual re-telling. However, my preference is to invite as many of the community of concern letter writers to attend the sessions. The therapist can never predict how many letter-writers may come to the session, although planning the session at day's end and for more than one hour can easily accommodate the number of people attending. Three other letter-writer support persons is generally the average, although upwards of seven to ten is not unheard of.
7. The client is asked to go through the collection of letters as a way of conducting a 're-search' on herself/himself.

The 'general' structure for reading and witnessing the letters in therapy is as follows:

1. All campaign writers are invited to the session (if this is geographically possible) and in turn are asked to read aloud the letter they have penned about the person. In attendance is usually the client, myself, the other writers of their community and sometimes a therapy team that may include insiders.
2. After each writer reads aloud, the client is asked to read the letter back to the writer, so both writer and client can attend to what is being said/written from the different positions of speaking and listening.
3. After each letter is read by the writer and discussed with the client, the community of others in the session (who are sitting and listening) offer a brief reflection of what the letter evoked in their own personal lives.
4. This process continues until all letters are *read, reread, responded to and reflected upon.*
5. Each response team member (usually but not always made up of professionals[1]) then writes and reads a short letter to the client and his community. They reflect on the counter-view of the client offered up by the person and their community, the hope that was shared and aspects of the letters that moved them personally.
6. Copies are made of each letter and given to everyone in attendance.
7. We then follow up the session with a therapeutic letter addressed to everyone who attended the session, including the client, the community of concern and reflecting team.

---

1 In some campaigns I have asked former client insiders on the problem or members of the Anti-anorexia/bulimia League to sit in on the session as 'insiders'.

Letter-writing campaign contributors

Our experience has shown that once community of concern support persons have received a letter inviting them to contribute to a campaign, they will often feel compelled to write more than once (three and four letters are not uncommon). Contributors often state that they have had the experience of feeling 'left out' of the helping process. Contributors to the campaign have reported feeling 'blamed' and 'guilty' for the role they believe they have played in the problem's dominance over the person's life. They suggest that many of these awkward feelings about themselves have been helped along by various professional discourses they have encountered as well as self-help literature. Being left out can often leave them with the opinion that they are 'impotent' and 'useless'. As one older man who committed himself to an anti-depression campaign for his 22-year-old nephew explained: 'The letter campaign helped me to come off the bench and score big points against the problem so my nephew could pull off a win. In helping him I helped myself.'

THERAPEUTIC LETTERS USED AS 'CASE NOTES' FOR INSTITUTIONS AND GROUP CONSULTATIONS

We have found that when used creatively and explained rationally, therapeutic letters can be used within even the most conservative and scientific psychology supporting institutions and hospitals. For example, the usual protocol for writing up notes on patients in hospitals is an individualised procedure. This means that each patient performance in the group is separately written up and shared with other members of the professional team. It is rare that the patient themselves receives a copy of these professional notes written about their lives and relationships. We find this practice of withholding information from the person about the person by the professional, keeping secrets in a landscape supporting of trust, holding private privileged/professional information/conversations away from clients, etc., is quite an odd 'therapeutic' practice.

I had the wonderful opportunity to consult two days a week in a psychiatric in-patient eating disorder ward in Vancouver, Canada, for a few years. My job was to run in-patient groups as well as facilitate multiple family groups. A narrative therapy-supporting psychiatrist, who gave me free rein to run my part of the group therapy programme through a narrative therapy practice, ran the ward. This included the way the groups were structured, who would be involved and how, recruiting an ongoing response team from the other mental health departments of the hospital (representatives from social work, psychiatry, nursing, psychology, nutrition, etc. would sit in on all the groups and respond from a narrative practice point of view that I'd taught them), and the writing of patient files/charts/reports.

The practice of the psychiatric eating disorder wards of having separate discussions about person/patients when they were not physically present and writing private professional notes about patients and not sharing these notes with them never fit well with me. As an alternative, the hospital allowed me to write one letter after each group to all parties involved. This meant I would write one therapeutic letter to the group after each group and this letter to the group members was shared with the entire professional staff. The therapeutic letter was the only professional correspondence/conversation I took part in. I was also afforded the grace to not be asked to consult on patients if they were not present. Below is an example of a therapeutic letter to the group that was shared within the institution and documented professionally as a 'case note/file'.

Dear Anti-anorexic group and response team members:

I want to write and thank you for quite an inspiring anti-anorexic filled two hours. As always, your conversations with one another inspired questions in me after you left. I thought I'd share a few of them with you for you.

Sheri, when you supported Gwen's story of standing up to anorexia's habit of predicting 'nothing but a negative future' you said – 'yes and if we all agree with anorexia's future for us as Gwen's says, then everybody here will all end up dead'. When you and Gwen tutored me on this anorexic tactic, Sheri, I wondered how it was that anorexia gets away with always predicting a negative future for women. How it was that anorexia tricked this group of women's minds into thinking the future was only futile? If all of you as a group stood against this anorexic tactic what kinds of futures do you predict for one another and for your selves?

The other comment that stood out was when Julie said to Akeiko that she 'totally recognised' her stepping up and 'defying anorexia by stepping backwards on the weigh scale' during her doctor's check-up (so as to not see the weight registered). I wondered what other group members felt about Akeiko's defiance and Julie's noticing of this defiance? Do you notice any other acts of anti-anorexia rebellion? Does it ever feel fun to rebel against anorexia's rules and regulations? As a group I wondered what anorexia would do if you all protested what Megan called anorexia's 'terrible lifestyle'? Do you believe there is strength in numbers and if so what effect do you think your group strength might have on anorexia?

Thanks again for tutoring me and including me in your insider's view of anorexia.

Yours anti-anorexically

Stephen Madigan

RELATIONSHIP LETTERS TO COUPLES EXPERIENCING CONFLICT

The authors write many different kinds of letters to couples. We will outline the letters we tend to send most often. Anja and Stephen were seeing couples at her clinic in Oslo, Norway. Written below are two common forms of letter writing specific to couples in conflict.

Letters outlining unique developments

Dear Pier and Anita,

We are writing as a follow up to our last session. Anita, in conversing together after you left, we were both struck with your comments regarding how you both had abilities in other relationships you have in your lives to be 'patient', 'service minded', 'to say nice things' and 'to understand' other people. We enjoyed how both you and Pier contemplated how you might bring these relation-ships skills you already have to your own relationship with one another. If you were to transport your skills of relationship to your own relationship what do you imagine the result would be? Do you feel your relationship abilities would flourish with these abilities? And if so, in what ways? What difference would your own relationship to one another notice? How would it feel?

And Pier when you said that you were beginning to notice how you wanted to choose your conversations with Anita 'at the right time and in the right place', we wondered how you managed to come up with this plan and what you thought Anita might experience if you were to do this? We were also quite touched with your 'hidden plan' to make Anita a CD of songs. We wondered if these songs had a particular meaning and history that were once meaningful at one time to you both.

We also wondered what it meant when Anja noticed you were both looking into each other's eyes during the session – something that we'd never witness you doing before. What were you seeing and how did this feel to look at each other?

And finally, when Pier mentioned that he wanted to 'hold you up high' above all other relationships, and Anita you laughed and stated to Pier 'I'd like this!' we were curious about what specifically you like about this elevated position in his life the most? And Pier what would it be like to raise Anita up and hold her up high? What would be most likely to happen to the relationship if you were to hold her in this position in your life?

Looking forward to discussing these new developments further,

Anja Bjorøy and Stephen Madigan

Relational letters written to the couple's relationship

Another form of therapeutic letter writing is to write directly to the couple's relationship when we are working with couples experiencing conflict. From a post-structural perspective, we theoretically view couple relationships as relational. At times, dominant psychological and self-help ideas about couples, along with the neo-liberal individualising contexts influencing of couple relationships, can act to wrongly inform the couple relationship that it is an indi-vidualised relationship/enterprise. To counter these individualising ideas about couples and to assist in the acknowledgement that 'the whole of the relationship is greater than the sum of the parts', we write to the relationship of the couple – 'directly'. From this narrative therapy practice position we begin the letter with a simple 'Dear X and Y's relationship'. As part of the letter-writing practice, we ask each member of the couple to write a letter back from the relationship to the couple – and *from the relationship's point of view*. For example:

To Jon and Monica's relationship; we are couple therapists working with Jon and Monica and we wondered if you might write a letter to them to express your relationship's view of them as a couple. We were hoping you might write a few thoughts on: (a) how they first formed you as a relationship, (b) comment on what their growing love felt like, (c) what you believe currently gets in the way of them being able to continue to nourish and feed you, (d) what would it mean to you if the arguing and complaining stopped and trust was renewed, and (e) what hopes do you have for them being able to bring you back towards a renewed loving relationship like they once had with you.

Thanks a lot relationship!

Anja Bjorøy and Stephen Madigan

COUNTER-DOCUMENT LETTERS

These are awards or diplomas for the successful completion of a goal in therapy. They are a visual reminder of success. For example, a 12-year-old male, Sam, who had a history of bullying his peers in school and had earned a reputation as a 'bully', 'trouble-maker' and 'defiant' was awarded a certificate of accomplishment for 'Reputation Re-Working' due to his anti-bully behaviour, improved grades and holding others responsible for harassing other students. The certificate read:

Reputation Re-worker Certificate

This diploma recognizes Sam's efforts to change his reputation from a 'Trouble-maker' and 'Bully' to 'Kind' and 'Accountable'. Since earning a new reputation is no small task, it is important that we recognize this achievement. Congratulations Sam! You have helped change the school climate.

David, President of the Reputation Re-worker's Club

At the present time, there is not much evidence for the effectiveness of therapeutic letters in narrative therapy. However, both David Epston and Michael White (Freeman et al., 1997) have conducted informal clinical research, asking clients questions such as these:

1. In your opinion, how many sessions do you consider a letter such as the ones that you have received is worth?
2. If you assigned 100 per cent to whatever positive outcomes resulted from our conversations together, what percentage of that would you contribute to the letters you have received?

The average response to Question 1 was that the letter had the equivalent value of 4.5 sessions. In response to Question 2, letters were rated in the range of 40 per cent to 90 per cent for total positive outcome of therapy.

Such findings were replicated in a small-scale study performed at a large medical facility in California. Nylund and Thomas (1994) reported that their respondents rated the average worth of a letter to be 3.2 face-to-face interviews (the range was 2.5–10) and 52.8 per cent of positive outcome of therapy was attributed to the letters alone. As supported by this research, the amount of time it takes to write letters seems worth the effort.

CONCLUSION

The narrative therapist's primary purpose within the written tasks in all the many forms of therapeutic letter writing is to work with and acknowledge the complexity of the person's story being told so that contradictions can be opened up and used to bring forth something different (by sustained reflection), moving towards a sparkling alternative undergrowth needing attention. It is through letter writing that dominant problem stories missing relational context and contradictions are exposed, and this allows for the elaboration of alternative and competing perspectives as the person's story unravels. These different competing perspectives seem to lay side-by-side and fit together, but for the client there is now an undeniable proposed tension between them. Therapeutic letters help to try to make us see the world in different ways at one and the same time with the hope that preferred change occurs.

REFERENCES

Epston, D. (1994) 'Extending the conversation'. *Family Therapy Networker*, 18(6), 31–37, 62–63.
Freeman, J., Epston, D. and Lobovits, D. (1997) *Playful Approaches to Serious Problems: Narrative Therapy with Children and their Families*. New York: W.W. Norton.
Madigan, S. (1992) 'The application of Michel Foucault's philosophy in the problem externalizing discourse of Michael White. Additional commentary by Deborah Anne Leupenitz, Re-joiner by S. Madigan'. *British Journal of Family Therapy*, Summer Edition.
Madigan, S. (2008) 'Anticipating hope within conversational domains of despair', in I. McCarthy and J. Sheehan (eds), *Hope and Despair*. London: Bruner-Mazel.
Madigan, S. (2011) *Narrative Therapy: Theory and Practice*. Chicago: The American Psychological Association.

Madigan, S. and Epston, D. (1995) 'From "spychiatric gaze" to communities of concern: From professional monologue to dialogue', in S. Friedman (ed.), *The Reflecting Team in Action: Innovations in Clinical Practice*. New York and London: Guilford Press.

Madigan, S. and Goldner, E. (1998) 'A narrative approach to anorexia: Reflexivity, discourse and questions', in M. Hoyt (ed.), *Constructive Therapies*. San Francisco, CA: Jossey-Bass.

Nylund, D. (2000) *Treating Huckleberry Finn: A New Narrative Approach with Kids Diagnosed ADD/ADHD*. San Francisco, CA: Jossey-Bass.

Nylund, D. (2002) 'Poetic means to anti-anorexic ends'. *Journal of Systemic Therapies*, 21(4): 18–34.

Nylund, D. and Thomas, J. (1994) 'The economics of narrative'. *Family Therapy Networker*, 18(6): 38–39.

Riordan, R.J. and Soet, J.E. (2000) 'Scriptotherapy: Therapeutic writing for couples and families', in R.E. Watts (ed.), *Techniques in Marriage and Family Counseling* (Vol. 1, pp. 103–110). Alexandria, VA: American Counseling Association.

White, M. and Epston, D. (1990) *Narrative Means to Therapeutic Ends*. New York: W.W. Norton.

21
NEUROPSYCHOLOGY AND COUNSELLING PSYCHOLOGY
HAMILTON FAIRFAX

INTRODUCTION

Neuropsychology and the application of neuropsychological theory to psychotherapeutic practice is an expanding and exciting area. Developments in neurocognitive research, particularly the technological advances in brain scanning (e.g. Functional Magnetic Resonance Imaging, fMRI), have shown the workings of neurological processes in the greatest detail we have known. With this has come a much fuller understanding of the interrelatedness between physical and psychological disciplines (Karmiloff-Smith et al., 2014). Counselling psychology, which historically has been cautious of medical or seemingly reductionist theories, has also become more interested in how neuropsychology can enhance clinical practice. However, there still remains an uncertainty about what a neuropsychological perspective may be, how it is relevant and what applying this from a counselling psychology perspective might look like.

Many counselling psychologists and psychotherapists feel ambivalent towards neuropsychology. In part, it has been imposed by the British Psychological Society's (BPS) restriction of neuropsychological training predominately to clinical and educational psychologists, which will be addressed later. However, there has also arguably been an attitude from some counselling psychologists that neuropsychology represents a medicalisation of therapeutic practice or is somehow a separate activity from a 'proper' therapeutic intervention.

This chapter is intended to identify what neuropsychology is, what it looks like, how it is highly compatible with counselling psychology and, finally, ways in which counselling psychologists can start to apply it to their practice. The difficulties with training will also be explored, together with a consideration of why the profession needs to campaign for equal parity across the applied psychologies. Much like the increasing understanding that moves from discrete brain regions to interconnectedness of neural networks, the psychological professions need to embrace the contributions of psychological trainings to establish a more meaningful and integrated understanding of what it means to be human and how to help more effectively when needed.

In preparing this chapter I asked three clinical neuropsychologists and a clinical psychologist working with older adults for their perspective and am grateful to Dr Claire Bazen-Peters, Dr Jo Cheffey, Dr Isobel Ewart and Dr Ann Turner for their contribution and permission to use their accounts. I am also grateful to David Goss, Trainee Counselling Psychologist, University of Manchester Doctorate in Counselling Psychology, who also generously contributed his experiences of completing a neuropsychological placement. Quotes from these accounts will be used throughout the chapter and with the exception of David they will be anonymous.

THE IMPORTANCE OF NEUROPSYCHOLOGY TO COUNSELLING PSYCHOLOGY

I have previously described this in more detail (Fairfax, 2007), but it feels relevant to briefly identify why I became interested in neuropsychology, largely to provide a context. I was fortunate to meet with a neuropsychologist more than 15 years ago when I was an assistant psychologist. I had completed an MSc in Counselling Psychology a few years before and had been working in a variety of voluntary counselling organisations. It was my first experience of NHS employment in a deprived area of the country. At that time I avoided psychometric measures of any form, in part due to a concern that human experiences could not be quantified and a fear that, once they were, the richness of the person could be lost within a number. This was also based on my poor mathematical abilities, negative exposure to quantitative measures and statistics in my psychology degree plus a lack of appropriate training in the use of psychometrics and neuropsychology. Legitimate concern about these issues notwithstanding, I was also insecure and ill-prepared and responded to these inadequacies by dismissing and attacking, as opposed to being open to, gaps in knowledge and abilities. I am dyslexic and dyscalulic, but these do not prevent applying neuropsychological perspectives. In fact I feel that this has helped me relate better to this area. I was lucky to meet with a patient and skilled neuropsychologist who very quickly helped me to understand and develop a specialist interest in cognitive testing and neuropsychological theory from a therapeutic perspective. Over time I have also been surprised by how many clinical psychologists I have met who have avoided neuropsychology since they qualified. Later I discovered that this often reflected their training experiences, the lack of investment in developing these skills, and neuropsychology being seen as a specialism in itself. I was therefore delighted by David's description of his experience:

> I feel neuroscience can be used by counselling psychologists with any client group and in any practice or research setting. Neuropsychology generally relates to working with clients who have a (usually) diagnosed neurological impairment, condition, deficit etc. One of the ways we can develop our understanding of the healthy functioning human brain and nervous system is by understanding what happens when things goes wrong. ... I foresee my learning can not only benefit my future neurological clients, but also every other client I see, as well as inform my research career.

This reflects counselling psychology as I see it: fresh and eager, unafraid to use theories such as neuroscience in order to formulate from a holistic and integrated understanding of the client. This, I feel, is the foremost reason why neuropsychology is important. We are all, client and therapist alike, embodied beings: minds, feelings, sensations, synapses, dreams, all interactions within ourselves, and between each other, leave emotional and neurological traces as we go forward in the process of being who we are. To ignore any one part of the fabric of one's being is to miss an important component of who we are, and, from a counselling psychology perspective, neuropsychology can only ever be part of the wider understanding of the individuals we meet. Interestingly, as will be argued, current neuropsychologists are more than happy to welcome this position.

HISTORY OF NEUROPSYCHOLOGY

Sterling (2002: 2) defines neuropsychology as: 'to understand the operation of human psychological processes in relation to brain structures and systems'. Although a relatively new discipline, neuropsychology can claim to have extensive historical origins. Interest in the brain as a coordinator of human behaviour dates from more than five thousand years ago in ancient Middle Eastern and ancient Greek cultures and evidence of trepanning in prehistorical societies may also indicate a belief in the importance of brain processes in human behaviour (Sterling, 2002). Despite developments based on surgical observation by the likes of Hippocrates and Galen, early neurological interest fell out of favour as academic theories became motivated by attempts to locate the soul, although brain structures such as the pineal gland were posited as possible locations for the soul. The Renaissance in the fifteenth century, which involved revisiting ancient wisdom and the development of modern scientific epistemologies, started the process of what would eventually be recognised as medical and neurological theories. In bringing together what were then the interrelated disciplines of philosophy, medicine, theology and alchemy, the theory of localisation developed. This expounded the belief that different parts of the brain were responsible for particular psychological actions. Subsequently, the theories of Gall (1785–1828) initiated the modern era of brain–behaviour research. Replacing the traditional Aristotelian view that the heart was the centre of control for mental activity, this posited that the brain was the locus for mental activity. This resulted in the popularity of phrenology which, despite erroneous claims based on size and shape of cerebral anatomy, began to link qualities such as personality and spirituality to the workings of the brain.

By the early to mid-nineteenth century research into aphasia (the loss of language following head injury or cerebral event) used behavioural observation and post mortem studies to locate function with brain region in precise detail (Krestel, 2013). This led to the identification of specific forms of aphasia and their subsequent cortical location. At the same time, physiologists, influenced by observations in which focal damage did not result in loss of function, were interested in philosophical theories of 'mass location' and 'equipotentiality'.

The former argued that the entire cortex was involved in all functions, the latter that cortical regions could develop to assume control of behaviours (Finger, 2001). However, these positions became more adversarial and, concomitant with the development of psychoanalysis and then behaviourism in the early twentieth century, interest in neuropsychology dwindled. By 1960, with the application of more sophisticated medical testing, connectionist models emerged which both accepted the role of localisation but also highlighted the interrelated nature and collaboration of neural networks between brain regions (Houghton, 2005).

NEUROPSYCHOLOGICAL ASSESSMENT

The common image of a neuropsychologist is often one of a serious-minded individual administering a series of complex-looking tests that results in a pronouncements of impressive-sounding medicalised terms. This can leave the impression that neuropsychology is a process of 'doing to' as opposed to the therapeutic process of 'being alongside'. It can also, certainly for me, seem intimidating and too 'specialised' to understand. Although neuropsychological assessments are used, they are often only a small part of the intervention, as the quotes below from neuropsychologists describe:

> I think the first thing would be to say that assessment and diagnostics is just a tiny bit of the role. Yes it requires some specialist knowledge and training to do it properly but the vast amount of my work is therapeutic (and assessments can be therapeutic in their own right). I find a lot of the time I have referrals from neurologists who have only been able to spend 15 minutes with someone but worked out enough that things aren't ok. I am then in the privileged position to be able to spend hours with someone to pick that apart with them and come up with a bit of a plan of action.

> Not just psychometrics but a full history in the same way as a clinical psychology assessment. This would include family relationships, values, etc. We also undertake capacity assessments often related to decisions about accommodation.

David reflected:

> I have had the chance to liaise with neuropsychologists, though often it is in relation to a client referral. I have also had the opportunity to discuss and explore neuropsychological testing. However, for me, testing is only one piece of the puzzle. From my short-lived experience, neuropsychology is currently associated more with assessment, testing (memory, intelligence, etc.) and medical/pharmacological intervention, as opposed to counselling therapy.

In this description, the process of 'being with' the client to develop a collaborative, person-centred, phenomenological understanding of their current difficulties in the system context for that individual is seen as not only the purpose of the role, but is also described as 'privileged'.

Already, this is in contrast to the stereotypical view previously outlined and is one much more compatible with how counselling psychologists and psychotherapists understand their position. What, then, is the purpose of cognitive assessments?

Neuropsychological assessments can be used to indicate either localised or diffuse problems. They can provide a cognitive profile of an individual, identifying strengths and weakness. Repeated testing can provide a measure of change from initial baseline performance. This can include a battery of tests but is tailored to the difficulties of the individual being tested. Poor results on one test may indicate specific issues while a consistent range of poor scores can indicate generalised brain damage. Like any psychometric measures, or indeed therapeutic formulation, it is not simply a matter of producing a set of numbers or opinion about the client. The skill and responsibility lies in their interpretation of application in a meaningful way for the individual. The quote below explores this further:

> Part of the role of the neuropsychologist is in determining the nature and level of an individual's cognitive functioning. This has implications for the nature of therapy; for example, work which requires the ability to comprehend and work with abstract concepts would be inappropriate for someone whose neurological impairment means that they are only able to work at a concrete level. Working with emotional dysregulation may involve an understanding of the neurobiology of trauma but may also involve work about shame or attachment.

Neuropsychological assessment can also be a way to bring a psychological understanding to clients with severe brain injuries or organic difficulties (e.g. dementia), ensuring that their voice is represented even in circumstances where they can't speak:

> So this morning (to give you a flavour) I have spent my time visiting a gentleman at home who has a degenerative disorder (can't move or speak) and have conducted a cognitive assessment to form part of a mental capacity act in order for decisions to be made about his care.

Neurocognitive assessment measures, therefore, are only one component in the practice of neuropsychology. They do require training and skill, not just in the technical process of how to administer, score and interpret, but also in their individual meaningfulness and application. This is something that all psychologists can do but it does require an understanding of basic physiology and organic pathologies to a level where the clinician can include theories of cognitive functioning as part of a holistic formulation. We don't all have to be neuropsychologists, nor do we have to feel that we should be able to deliver a comprehensive neuropsychological assessment. It can be enough to raise the question. However, to do this, counselling psychology in particular must engage on this level and embrace the need for neuropsychology training as a component in all postgraduate training. This is beginning to happen in the UK and will be explored in more detail later.

In summarising this brief section, the most important message is that the 'technicalities' of neuropsychology are less important than the conception and application in discovering how a condition may enhance the individual to understand themselves and how they interact in the world. Developing a neuropsychology perspective, similar to training in a therapeutic model, is another way of developing the comprehensive skills of the counselling psychologist, and in so doing provides the best resource for our clients. We are embodied and physical creatures and as such thinking about this alongside learning ways of helping with psychological changes complements this perfectly.

NEUROPSYCHOLOGY IN THERAPEUTIC PRACTICE

The author has suggested that the view of neuropsychologists as 'bashing through tests' is at best archaic. Rather, they are actually concerned with formulations based on integrating brain–behaviour relationships with knowledge of psychological models. The examples below give an indication of what this looks like in practice:

> [I work] … with clients and often in ABI [Acquired Brain Injury] with carers, family members to help cope with problems. … This can cover a range of psychological difficulties including loss, grief, trauma, adjustment to diagnosis, and psychological problems arising from the neurological problem. Rehabilitation covers cognitive and behavioural rehabilitation. This is also often undertaken in conjunction with an MDT [Multidisciplinary Team].

This was also suggested in the reflections of another neuropsychologist:

> The work is sometimes about working with people in a rehab capacity where they expect to have some recovery and for others it's about gaining acceptance around a diagnosis (possibly a progressive condition) and working with the family around that. A lot of my work is enabling people to engage with their community and take part in activities they enjoy. This involves a lot of liaison and consultation with other professions e.g. OT [Occupational Therapist], physio, etc. Additionally, we work very closely with mental health colleagues as there is often overlap. There is also quite often a lot of trauma work, i.e. car accidents, assaults, etc.

Commenting on therapeutic considerations, one neuropsychologist identified the following:

> It is quite hard to encapsulate the role of therapy in neuropsychology in an email, but some thoughts about this: much of what happens in neuropsychology involves working with issues such as trauma, loss, or adjustment. This needs to be considered in the context of individual, couples, and family experiences. So clearly, there is an important role for therapy here.

An example of this is provided by another neuropsychologist:

> I also spent some time with a lady with MS who has become very fearful about going out (at all and especially alone). I have worked with her gradually in accepting her new physical limitations and ways of communicating with her family about what her new needs are.

She has now got a mobility scooter and is accessing her local area more independently and we're working on her being able to go to Tesco on her own.

These responses remind me of my introduction to neuropsychology. Far from horrors of reductionist number crunching, I experienced deeply thoughtful, systemic, client-centred and highly compassionate clinicians. They were passionate about the need to make sure that individuals who may be unable to communicate their distress, or who had baffled and sometimes been dismissed by medics and psychologists as 'malingering' or 'medically unexplained', were properly understood and represented. When you have been shown how to use a cognitive test from a neuropsychological perspective it becomes a much richer and enjoyable experience for both the client and clinician. When I first used the WAIS-R (Wechsler Adult Intelligence Scale Revised), I learnt how the IQ score was perhaps the least interesting outcome of the test. I began to understand the true value of these assessments and, with it, the importance of them being used appropriately. The WAIS is now in its fourth version, its ongoing development is heavily influenced by neuropsychological research, and it is one of many readily available tests through which to start learning about a neuropsychological perspective. This highlights a further part of the neuropsychologist's role – supervision and consultation.

Supervision and consultation

The desire to 'test everyone' with a huge battery of tests is not one shared by the clinical neuropsychologists I have met. Far from it, a principal skill is knowing what parts of tests are useful to minimise any distress or pressure on the client. Taking the WAIS-IV as an example, it can take between an hour and half to two hours to administer in entirety, more so if the person has specific difficulties. Under guidance and supervision from a neuropsychologist, using only subtests that are useful for that particular client can significantly reduce the time involved and demand on the client.

In terms of a consultation with neuropsychologists, they are often reluctant to insist that cognitive assessments are automatically undertaken. This is not due to a privileging of knowledge, but shows the importance of formulation and desire to limit intrusive assessments. Often it has been enough to take a full history with a more accurate understanding of current problems for the client to be helped in other ways (such as referral for medical assessments or occupational therapy). When assessments are indicated, they can help to advise on the most helpful tests or subtests to limit the demand on the client.

Given their relationship with medical and physical health services, neuropsychologists often consult and offer advice in different settings:

Supervision of the neuropsychological aspects of care for other professionals is a key part of the role. The emphasis is on helping people understand brain–behaviour relationships. We also offer advice to ward staff, social services and other agencies in the management of challenging behaviour.

Sometimes there is great pressure in these situations for psychologists to come up with quick solutions or a diagnosis. This can be an expectation in all applied psychology settings and, managing expectation, particularly in physical health contexts which have clearer treatment outcomes than mental health, is a significant challenge. For example:

> My approach has flavours of CBT, lots of systemic, narrative, community psychology and some psychodynamic. The most important thing I think I have learnt and what my trainees find the most challenging is learning when NOT to do something and not to pathologise a normal reaction to a difficult event, e.g. having a stroke or being diagnosed with Parkinson's disease. Sometimes my work is about just being alongside someone as they go through a natural process of coming to terms with this and there isn't a specific 'therapy' that 'fixes' that, as there is nothing to 'fix'.

HOW TO DEVELOP NEUROPSYCHOLOGY WITHIN COUNSELLING PSYCHOLOGY

There is of course inequality within the psychology profession, whereby currently only a clinical and educational psychologist can apply for further neuropsychological training and this therefore disadvantages all other divisions. This is not acceptable. However, it is incumbent on those of us who are prevented from this training to understand why. It is based in part on history and in part on assumptions about professions, some of which are inaccurate and old-fashioned; others, however, are appropriate. We therefore need to ensure that we understand these objections, engage with the Division of Neuropsychology, clarifying and correcting views where necessary, but also acknowledging the legitimate deficits in our professions. I feel there are two main ways that we can respond, structurally and clinically.

Structural responses

The structural concerns are centred on the main objection to counselling psychology (and other divisions wanting to undertake training), that unlike clinical psychology there is no consistent neuropsychology training programme within any course, and most counselling psychologists have no experience of neuropsychology. Therefore, counselling psychologists are unable to demonstrate any level of accredited training and lack the basic knowledge to undertake further training. This is an accurate criticism and, as previously suggested, our historical response to neuropsychology and cognitive testing has, at best, been suspicious. In this respect, and the lack of its presence in our training courses, it is fair to say that we haven't done ourselves any favours. The Division of Counselling Psychology and Training Institutions have recognised this and are developing neuropsychology modules in collaboration with the Division of Neuropsychology (DoN). This is reflected in the recent *Standards for the Accreditation of Doctoral Programmes in Counselling Psychology* (British Psychology Society, 2014), particularly standards 2.6 and 2.7. We must ensure, however, that it is equitable to clinical psychology.

All clinical psychology doctorate courses have a module on neuropsychology and an expectation that trainees will undertake assessments under supervision, although, given their scarcity, it is unlikely to be with a neuropsychologist. Some courses offer several different modules throughout the training and have established placement providers or tutors with a strong neuropsychological interest. Others offer the minimum. The latter is still vastly superior to the present situation in counselling psychology, but the existence of intensive postgraduate neuropsychology training courses indicates that neither provision is sufficient for accredited DoN chartership. If we are going to push at the door, we need to ensure we have enough strength, through updating our skills and profile. In this, our neuropsychology colleagues can be of invaluable help:

> Regarding knowledge – this is an interesting one! ... Clearly counselling psychologists are well acquainted with the usual assessment and therapy skills required for working with any condition. Thinking back over what I went through for the QiCN [Qualification in Clinical Neuropsychology], I would say the things that are important are: gross neuroanatomy, functional neuroanatomy, main neuro pathologies (e.g. TBI, Stroke, MS, Epilepsy, Dementia); test validity and reliability (seems obvious, but I was forced to be much more informed as part of the training) and biological and cognitive rehabilitation. Neuropsychology is a bottomless pit of info, but these are the areas I felt have made a difference to my practice.

As a professional group, counselling psychologists need to pressurise course providers, including the BPS independent route, to ensure they provide accredited basic neuropsychology training. With the new *Standards of Accreditation* (British Psychology Society, 2014), this process has already begun. We also need to ensure that similarly accredited neuropsychology workshops are delivered on an ongoing basis. In correcting this deficit we could also embrace it as an exciting way to show the application and clinical utility of a phenomenological and process-based discipline. This is something highly compatible with the accounts of the neuropsychologists. We feel that our approach is of value in clinical settings and therefore have to take the opportunity to be alongside our colleagues and not develop tension with them. There is evidence that neuropsychologists would welcome it:

> I think (hope) that neuropsychology has moved on from individual test bashing to encompassing a wider viewpoint and I am sure that there is significant overlap between our respective training and skills. The key is going to be how we recognise our relative contributions to this area rather than feeling threatened or competitive.

Clinical responses

One way is to declare an interest from the outset of a training course or request a placement or secondment as part of continuing professional development. In both cases it is important to argue for the benefits to the service, yourself and the profession. Nationally, neuropsychology is a small provision with a huge demand. It is being applied to a variety of clinical settings, including national priorities such as cancer, cardiac care, dementia and medically unexplained symptoms. The latter two in particular overlap with mental health services and more so given that demand already stretches psychological service resources. Models such as skills escalators and apprentice-ship models that cascade knowledge through consultation are increasingly indicated. For counselling psychologists, support in developing these skills has obvious benefit to the service. In the case of counselling psychology training courses, there is already an acceptance of the need to include a neuropsychology training that is comparable to clinical psychology programmes. In the meantime, it is important for trainees to include it as part of their placements. There are of course difficulties with some services, and a history of exclusion from the Division of Neuropsychology and Clinical Psychology. David's experiences illustrate a way of pursuing it:

> Through a mixture of luck, chance and perseverance, I came across a local charity which sup-ports people with neurological conditions. They had a counselling department and to cut a long story short, I began a placement there. So far, I have worked with a range of clients who have conditions ranging from epilepsy, ME, MS, Parkinson's, Huntington's, haemorrhage, cer-ebral palsy, acquired brain injury (ABI), stroke and tumour, to name a few. … Not only can I learn about developing as a counselling psychologist, but I can also simultaneously develop my understanding on my particular interest, the human brain (and mind – I am humanistic after all). I foresee my learning can not only benefit my future neurological clients, but also every other client I see, as well as inform my research career.

There is much you can learn neuropsychologically without resorting to testing. Simple observa-tion of some of the immediate behaviours, for example handedness, gait, balance problems, language and speech production, can be noticed and enquired about. You can learn much from questions about using everyday objects and performing daily activities, for example changes in handwriting, difficulties using a telephone, remembering dates and numbers, holding a pen, telling the time, dropping objects. There are many standardised questionnaires to help guide this, such as the Neuropsychological Checklist (NSC). While this may feel intrusive, in keeping with any assessment process, it is important to develop the relationship and explain the purpose.

In my experience, clients have been interested, and often relieved, that they can talk about these difficulties. They have reported feeling they were being taken seriously, and described a sense of being more holistically cared for. Like us, our clients can often separate the mind from the body and, not until they are asked about their physicality, do you learn of something that is significant diagnostically or developmentally. The process is also the opportunity to be openly collaborative with the client, involving them in developing understanding and formulation, modelling uncertainty and interest, and sharing the therapeutic process in the moment with them. They can see why you might consider certain responses or referrals and be part of it as opposed, for example, suddenly finding they have been sent an appointment for a scan. It is also an opportunity to involve wider systems, such as partners, who are often neglected in traditional mental health services. With the client's consent, their observations can be crucial in understanding everyday issues that can reveal important details that otherwise may not have been revealed, particularly if the person is, for example, reporting memory problems.

I believe that any psychologist can develop these skills and in so doing include a neuropsychological perspective without the need to feel they have detailed knowledge of tests. However, this needs to be done in a consistent way, in collaboration with neuropsychology, which calls for a far less divided professional identity and one that respects difference while working together. David's experience reflects a similar view:

> One thing I would say is that even though a lot of neuro-based client work does not necessarily require formal knowledge of neurological conditions, a solid understanding does help. It is important we begin developing our neuroscientific knowledge so that we can increase our ability and value when working in a neuropsychological counselling setting, and in truth, in any other setting.

The next stage for interested psychologists would be to develop familiarly with tests and when to use them. Again, doing this from a neuropsychologically informed perspective is crucial and best done under guidance from a neuropsychologist or experienced clinical psychologist. This does not have to be an exhaustive range, but can include a few well-known tests. Particular services, such as Older Adults or Learning Disabilities, will have standard tests. Practitioners often have their favourite tests but a well-known assessment used by both Adult and Older Adult services is the Repeatable Battery of Neuropsychological Status (RBANS), which provides a global measure of cognitive functioning (immediate memory, attention, language, visuo-spatial delayed memory). It is a relatively unobtrusive test that takes about 45 minutes to administer and is a good place to start learning. Most psychology departments in NHS services will have the RBANS and many private providers also use it.

Administering any psychometric test, particularly neuropsychological assessments, is as much qualitative as quantitative. Most record forms will have space for you to record any observations about how the individual undertakes subtests and how they present during the appointment. These may be discussed at a later time, keeping in mind the need to find out whether these are new behaviours or something they have always done. Difficulties listing a number of fruit and vegetables in a minute, for example, could be suggestive of a particular organic problem, but may also relate to educational difficulties or hearing problems. It is surprisingly difficult to administer a test, observe and record, particularly if the subtests are timed, and it is therefore important to be familiar with the test before you administer it. Practising on yourself, family or friends also helps develop an understanding of how people generally perform, making you aware of any differences with clients. However, it is important to be cautious, as performance on a test, or specific subtests, does not automatically suggest cognitive problems and needs to be understood in the wider context. Supervision is vital, particularly when starting to use measures, and the temptation to make a prognosis based on results has to be resisted. It is possible to be lost within a neurological understanding and forget the psychological. A significant number of memory problems reported to GPs, for example, are the result of depression, which will also affect performance on cognitive tests. Antidepressants and psychotropic mediation commonly affect cognitive abilities, as does stress and anxiety (Kasper and Resinger, 2003). Research into difficulties such as Post Traumatic Stress Disorder (PTSD) and Personality Disorder has highlighted specific cognitive issues related to these conditions (Silk, 1994). This again highlights the importance of appropriate supervision, and a further skill of neuropsychologists in being able to help understand comorbidity and cognitive performance.

The earlier comments indicate that clinically neuropsychologists often see comorbid presentations. I have previously argued that counselling psychologists are best placed to respond to this level of complexity, particularly as our training does not invite us to see a person as blocks of disease but to try to understand their difficulties in the context of their individual reality. David's experiences highlight this further:

> I feel one thing I have to stress is that so far in my experience, working with neurological clients is very similar to working with any other clients. Very often, the presenting issue of the condition is not the focus of our therapy. I work in a private practice and there are huge parallels with the work and subjects I experience with clients in that setting as I do in my neuro placement. For sure, there are times when my neuro work is focused primarily on the difficulties of living and/or having been diagnosed with a condition; this work is often similar to grief/bereavement work in that there is a process of the client experiencing a trauma, onset of condition or diagnosis, leading to a feeling of loss, which then requires a process of acceptance and often major life adjustment. However, many of my clients have comorbid issues, including depression (mild to major), anxiety, PTSD, bipolar, psychosis, OCD, etc. These can either be as a result, separate or a precursor to their neurological condition. So my approach is always one of trying to hear the client's full world and what it is that they would like to work on.

For example, in the case of a head injury, dysfunction of a brain region may cause depression, but so may the circumstances and reality of the dysfunction. A previously undisclosed traumatic experience could have been managed until the injury occurred and the person may now be left with trying to understand this while others see only organic damage. All this could be relevant and without attempting to discover the experience of the client, they are likely to be let down. In this central intention, the motives of the neuropsychologist and counselling psychologist are identical. I feel David shares this perspective:

> I feel counselling psychologists are perfectly placed for this type of work. A primary reason is that we are integrative. In truth, I believe an integrative stance should be adopted for pretty much every client group in the world, however, never more so, in a context where clients have a range of communication abilities and presenting issues, is an integrative stance

required to help achieve a truly collaborative and beneficial therapeutic relationship with each person. I am fortunate that the service doesn't dictate my way of working, therefore it is a decision between each client and I on how we work.

CONCLUSION

I was extremely fortunate to encounter neuropsychologists when I did, and delighted to hear of the interest of many counselling psychologists which are encapsulated by David's reflections. The aims of this chapter have been to present a wider understanding of neuropsychologists in practice, demonstrate how there are many overlaps with the profession, and hopefully to generate interest and excitement that this new and fascinating area is one in which counselling psychology should be involved. It is a huge field of exploration, and one to which this chapter cannot do sufficient justice. Neuropsychology has a current value in the theoretical and promotion of therapies. The neurobiology of conditions such as PTSD, Personality Disorder and OCD, along with qualities such as compassion and practices such as mindfulness, has never had a higher political capital. While it represents a greater integration of the body with the psychological, there is also a caution as to how greater neurobiological insights are being identified as a mechanism in the change process to justify a given theory. Some of the greatest concerns come from neuropsychologists. This identifies once again the importance of maintaining a united psychological front in the desire to provide the best interventions to our clients.

Finally, neuropsychology is an example of an active and clinically driven discipline. It is continually testing the limits of assessments, ensuring they are regularly updated and that findings are actively disseminated. The impact on therapy, research and practice from such a small professional group is significant and impressive. It can be argued that as a model of practice-based evidence neuropsychologists set a standard for the rest of us.

REFERENCES

British Psychology Society (BPS) (2014) *Standards for the Accreditation of Doctoral Programmes in Counselling Psychology*. Leicester: BPS. Retrieved on 28/2/2015 from www.bps.org.uk/system/files/Public%20files/PaCT/counselling_accreditation_2014_web.pdf

Fairfax, H. (2007) 'Testing times: Counselling psychology and the neuropsychological perspective: A personal view'. *Counselling Psychology Review*, 4, 44–48.

Finger, S. (2001) *Origins of Neuroscience: A History of Explorations into Brain Function*. Oxford: Oxford University Press.

Houghton, G. (2005) *Connectionist Models in Cognitive Psychology*. New York: Psychology Press.

Karmiloff-Smith, A., Casey, B. J., Mass, E. and Premyslaw, T. (2014) 'Environmental and genetic influences on neurocognitive development: The importance of multiple methodologies and time-dependent intervention'. *Clinical Psychological Science*, 2, 628–637.

Kasper, S. and Resinger, E. (2003) 'Cognitive effects and antipsychotic treatment'. *Psychoneuroendocrinology*, 28, 27–38.

Krestel, H. (2013) 'Language and brain: Historical introduction to models of language and aphasia'. *Swiss Archives of Neurology and Psychiatry*, 164, 262–265.

Silk, K. R. (1994) *Biological and Neurobehavioral Studies of Borderline Personality Disorder.* Washington, DC: American Psychiatric Association Press.

Sterling, J. D. (2002) *Introducing Neuropsychology.* New York: Psychology Press.

22
COMMUNITY PSYCHOLOGY AND THE COUNSELLING PSYCHOLOGIST
PAUL MOLONEY

I've been told that I'm now being cared for in the community ... the only problem's that I wish someone would tell me what 'the community' is ... (British mental health services user, BBC Radio 4, 2009)

This chapter attempts a critical overview of some of the key similarities and differences between the disciplines of community and counselling psychology. While it suggests that the former has much to teach the counselling psychologist about the limits of talking therapy, it also confronts some of the problems and contradictions that beset the field of community psychology itself: arguing that practitioners are sometimes as blind to the shortcomings of their field as are the psychological therapists whom they so ably criticise. The chapter concludes with tentative suggestions for a workable, integrated counselling-community psychology practice, built upon careful thinking and realism.

INTRODUCTION: THE MANY FOUNDATIONS OF COMMUNITY PSYCHOLOGY

In the early twentieth century European and British researchers such as Marie Jahoda had shown how neighbourhood deprivation and mass unemployment could lead to personal demoralisation and declining physical health: a finding that would not have surprised Victorian writers like Engels or Dickens, in their accounts of the lives of British working-class people. However, the idea of a distinct profession of applied psychologists, building their work upon the insight that private troubles might have public causes was the creation of the Swampcott conference, which took place in 1965 in the USA, in Boulder, Colorado.

A reflection of the growing power of the community mental health-care movement and of the rising acceptability of talking treatment, the conference was also a response to the accumulating clinical experience and research evidence that suggested that ordinary people could be driven into misery or madness not by their faulty thinking or lack of insight – but by their having to struggle with a harsh world (Ira, 1974; Tyrer, 1973). On this basis, social and clinical psychologists came together for the first time, to pool their ideas towards the goal of tackling personal ills. In coining the term 'community psychology', they concluded that, in the long run, psychologists might be at their most therapeutic when focusing upon communities rather than upon individual clients, and thus becoming agents of social change (Albee and Joffe, 1977; Orford, 2008).

Community psychology is multidisciplinary in nature. It draws upon the same kind of clinical and epidemiological research literature that, in the decades since 1965, has continued to uphold the observations discussed in the Swampcott meeting. To paraphrase the words of one British mental health service user, people who suffer from psychological problems are not so much ill, as hurt – by what others have done to, or withheld from them (Adam, 2003). For those of us who live in the 'developed' world, our propensity to inflict psychological harm upon one another is worsened by rising social and economic inequalities; and it is usually the poor who suffer most (Clark and Heath, 2014; Wilkinson and Pickett, 2013).

> [M]adness, distress, alienation is not simply located in individual heads. It is a social phenomenon through and through, and as such requires a social response ... poverty, racism, unemployment, loneliness, relationship difficulties, spiritual conflicts, sexual abuse and domestic violence are at the heart of mental health crises. (Bracken and Thomas, 2004: 13)

The main approach of community psychology, therefore, is an ecological one. Rather than seeking to mend individuals via talking and behavioural treatment – or 'technologies of personal change' – practitioners meet with groups of local people – who may or may not be using mental health services – working alongside to help them diagnose and ameliorate the psychologically noxious aspects of their world. To the extent that these specialists are sometimes involved in local or national health-care research, consultation and planning – then they can also claim to better the lives of their fellow citizens through the improvement of preventative health services.

The wide scope of community psychology allows its practitioners to look to any of the social and environmental sciences that illuminate the relationship between individuals and the families, neighbourhoods, nations and international political and economic spheres that encapsulate their lives. Social power – sometimes defined as the ability to secure and maintain advantage – is a central concept. Practitioners espouse a commitment to social justice, to working in partnership with non-psychologists, especially with members of downtrodden groups, and to strengthening communal connections, political representation, and perhaps economic and material resources (Harrison, 2013; Kagan et al., 2011).

In this field, the use of experimental methods, including randomisation, double blind measurements and the use of control groups is next to impossible. Therefore, community practitioners often use an action research framework to collect knowledge about the community and its strengths and weaknesses, in order to identify useful themes and ideas for achieving community goals, which are put into practice and then tested and modified in the field. Community psychologists have borrowed concepts such as 'empowerment' and 'social capital' from the disciplines of community work and political science, respectively (Kagan et al., 2011; Orford, 2008).

Besides the familiar rating scales and tick-box questionnaires that purport to measure attitudes, beliefs, feelings, or mental health, community psychologists, in common with their counselling psychology colleagues, have looked to qualitative data collection methods, some of which are almost indistinguishable from journalism: in-depth interviews, narrative accounts written with or by local people, or perhaps film and the creation of works of art. There is an emphasis upon collaborating with neighbourhood representatives to ensure that the usefulness of the work is judged from their standpoint. For example, if the intervention is deemed to have diluted or stopped the social causes of distress; combated racial, gender or ethnic inequality; fostered community strength and resilience; and promoted environmental change – such as an improvement in public housing stock, the creation of allotment gardens, or more efficient rubbish collection by the council (see Cox et al., 2013). In principle, the scope of community psychology projects can run from mental health service user groups to neighbourhoods; or even to nations, in the case of advice on health and social policy, for example. In practice, most such projects are at the smaller end of this range (Kagan et al., 2011; Orford, 2008).

Community practitioners openly recognise what most of their colleagues do not: that, implicitly, all psychologists are trying to define what it means to be human, and that this is inevitably a political endeavour. Indeed community psychology takes slightly different political hues across the world. In the USA, as in Britain, it is a minority pursuit. Membership of the Division of Community Psychology within the American Psychological Association – the professional body for US community psychology – reached its peak in the late 1970s and early 1980s, and is currently about half of that modest maximum (APA, 2015). North American community psychology has been sustained mainly by several large universities, which have provided shelter for non-mainstream left-wing thinkers. Over the last thirty years, the discipline has cross-pollinated with the work of Latin American community psychologists, some of them having emerged from indigenous political and religious liberation movements (Nelson and Prilleltensky, 2005). While the overall political tone of US community psychology is left of centre, there is an even smaller minority of right-wing practitioners. These writers promote the idea that communities can be renewed from street level upwards, as it were, by socially minded entrepreneurs: using psychological techniques to promote businesses and services that benefit the community as well as their own pockets (Lillis et al., 2005).

British community psychology – originating from the fields of educational psychology, learning disabilities, and child and family therapy – has managed to survive in several academic university departments as well as within a handful of university-based clinical psychology training courses, and in the practice of small groups of clinicians working within the NHS (Burton et al., 2007). However, because of its political orientation and accent upon prevention, rather than treatment, it has often struggled to survive in hostile academic and clinical worlds. It is doubtful that the British variant could have persisted without the National Health Service. The kinds of insights into personal distress that are garnered from clinical settings, free at the point of delivery, could not have come from the treatment of fee-paying clients, rich enough to afford private therapy. The openness of the NHS towards health prevention (fickle though it has sometimes been) and the opportunity to work with some of the most disadvantaged individuals in society have led these practitioners to take the operation of social power in people's lives seriously (Bostock and Diamond, 2005; Orford, 2008).

By contrast, community psychology in New Zealand and Australia has a firmer tradition of official acceptance. In New Zealand, particularly, its practitioners are widely consulted by government and community representatives as an established aid to achieving and measuring collective change, often with a focus on the status and plight of indigenous peoples (Fisher et al., 2008). In South Africa, the discipline has strong historical links with the anti-apartheid movement and, as in Latin America, with post-colonial theory. The approach is also expanding into other regions of Sub-Saharan Africa, allied with local environmental, women's and peasant's movements (Painter et al., 2006).

SOME AFFINITIES BETWEEN COUNSELLING AND COMMUNITY PSYCHOLOGY

There is obvious overlap between the concerns of the community and counselling psychologist. If the latter discipline started out in the US with a focus upon the guidance and support of people who were deemed to be 'well' or 'normal' (rather than distressed), it has over the last fifty years steadily expanded the range of its operations in most countries, to become one of the broadest of the psychology specialisms, its practitioners to be found, for instance, in private practice, schools, prisons and vocational guidance facilities, adult learning disability services, acute psychiatric units, hospices, college and university pastoral care, and community mental health teams. While offering guidance and treatments, counselling psychologists have also focused, like their community-oriented colleagues, upon the prevention of mental health problems and upon helping people to flourish – albeit largely through the application of individual therapeutic techniques.

There are other parallels with community psychology. The counselling psychologist, in their role as adviser, often has to build up their knowledge of community resources and how to obtain and make the best use of them. They are trained to think about how their clients' personal insecurities and struggles reflect the interplay of their unique biography on the one hand, and of the social and cultural context that nourished or distorted it, on the other (Strawbridge and Woolfe, 2010; Tyrer, 1973). Therapeutic conversations might sometimes touch upon each client's cultural values and outlook, and upon their experience of abusive power – in the form of prejudice, discrimination and marginalisation. Indeed, the intellectual roots of counselling psychology lie not only with clinicians like Carl

Rogers, and his desire to maximise personal authenticity and freedom via talk therapy, but with critical theorists, like George Mead and Irving Goffman, who showed the extent to which our 'selves' are also, in large part, the gift (and sometimes the victim) of communities – including those 'mental health' institutions that disguise control as care. Because of the discipline's link with the academic and political movements of the postwar period (especially in the USA) that questioned the alliance between capitalism and the military-industrial state, some practitioners trace their professional ancestry to the 'unrest and resistance of 20th century street protests' (Steffen and Hanley, 2012: 4) – a pedigree similar to that claimed by many community psychologists (see, for example, Tindall et al., 2010; Parker, 2007).

Some of the specific therapeutic approaches likely to be used by the counselling psychologist also make a good fit with the outlook of community psychology. For example, narrative therapists argue that traditional talking treatments, in locating psychological problems largely inside each client's head, have sought to adjust them to a harmful world, rather than help them to try to change it. Narrative therapists are similar to community psychologists in that they will work with clients, their families and their communities with the aim of helping everyone to develop a respectful account of personal and social problems, which seeks to shift the 'blame' from the alleged pathology of the individual to the circumstances with which they have been struggling (Davy, 2010; White and Epston, 1990). Feminist and multiculturalist approaches to talking therapy can likewise make use of therapeutic groups, intended to raise awareness of the personal effects of widespread sexism and racism, respectively, and to help the disempowered individuals to recognise and challenge the political roots of what they may have taken to be their own, exclusively personal, ills (Tindall et al., 2010). Besides this emphasis on social harm and resistance, therapists in these traditions are likely to share their community colleagues' willingness to question the primacy and relevance of western views of what it means to be a person – as a supposedly self-contained and self-motivating universe (Throop, 2011). We all have some individual agency but, as counselling psychologists increasingly perceive, this condition of our being is not seen or valued in the same way by people in all cultural groups and is constrained, as well as enabled, by our circumstances (Eleftheriadou, 2010; Harrison, 2013).

Some counselling practitioners have allied themselves with politically radical causes, such as the feminist and mental health service user movements, and with disempowered groups such as the homeless, the elderly, and people with severe mental health problems or with learning disabilities. Some of them have officially practised and published as community psychologists. In some quarters the profession continues to debate the issue of social justice – conceived usually in terms of equable access to respect, opportunities and services – and of how counselling psychologists might better incorporate a commitment to these principles into their work. Some practitioners have focused on the issue of power differences between therapist and client, and of the need to be honest about them and about what they imply for the client's ability to benefit (or not) from their therapy (see, for example, Edwards, 2013; Harrison 2013). Once again, all of these themes are familiar to the community specialist.

WHAT CAN THE COMMUNITY PERSPECTIVE ADD TO THE PRACTICE OF THE COUNSELLING PSYCHOLOGIST?

If most counselling psychologists already see their discipline as an outward looking, politically aware and thoughtful one, which seeks to give people greater control over their own lives, then why bother with a discussion of its community counterpart? The answer to this question depends upon one's view of the science, philosophy and practice of psychological therapy in general and of counselling psychology in particular. The profession – fixated upon therapeutic humanism – is not as open to new ideas as it likes to think (Moller, 2011); and not all counselling psychologists display thoughtfulness and caution about the scope and potency of their work, which, in part perhaps, reflects their status as members of an (arguably) still insecure and self-conscious late arrival on the mental health treatment scene (Feltham, 2014; Howard, 1998; Konzelman et al., 2007; Moloney, 2000). Of late, some counselling psychologists have begun to talk about power – as already noted. One advantage of community psychology is that it offers a set of theories and ideas by which the practitioner can grasp this topic as a concrete factor in the client's life, and their own. Most community psychologists would recognise that social power is not just about our thoughts, attitudes or speech, but has material and economic dimensions that resist easy change. Community psychologists thereby appeal to theorists like the developmental psychologist Ulrich Bronfrenbrenner and the late David Smail, clinical psychologist, both of whom conceptualised environmental and social influence as a series of nested zones, extending from our immediate realm – family and friends, for example – to the intermediate reaches of our neighbourhood and its institutions, and then outward, to regional government and thence to the national and geopolitical systems that set the scope of our lives and that help to determine, in the end, who and what we become (Bronfrenbrenner, 1980; Smail, 2005). Their work underlines the critical realist outlook that animates much of community psychology. Our mental health is shaped most of all, not by the way we choose to see or talk about things, but by the weight of a pre-existing and (often) non-negotiable external reality, which can nonetheless be described and understood in diverse ways. Critical realists acknowledge that science, as a human enterprise, is seldom free of sectional interests or of political influences which must be acknowledged, scrutinised – and sometimes resisted – if we are to approach the truth (Bhaskar, 1998).

Indeed, even the most socially concerned counselling psychologists often appear to be squeamish about naming the issue of power for what it is (Steffen and Hanley, 2013), and when they do, then it usually becomes little more than a form of discourse, to be unravelled and rewoven in the consulting room, or in the work of an 'empowerment group'. It is assumed that clients can be encouraged or inspired to change once their subjugated condition – as a woman or as a gay person, for example – has been openly explored, and once the therapist has made an effort to reduce the power differences between themselves and their client by acts of transparency and collaboration within the consulting room (see, for example, Davy, 2010; and Edwards, 2013). For most community psychologists, however, this outlook is blinkered and naïve, since power has multiple dimensions, of which discourse is but one. Our degree of social strength is also about the amount of safety, security, privacy and prestige afforded by our home, school, locality and mode of transport; it is about our physical embodiment – the deep-seated emotional and personal dispositions that we have acquired through our exposure to social influence; and it is about our access to money – to the advantages and security that it can buy when we have enough (or too much), versus the insecurity and turmoil that we suffer when we are lacking. For the poorest and the hardest pressed, the experience of power is intimately intertwined with coercion and brutalisation. When it comes to the alleviation or prevention of distress, or even to achieving 'personal growth', words are no substitute for substance (Midlands Psychology Group, 2012; Smail, 2005; Wilkinson and Pickett, 2013).

Community psychologists are also more aware of how the mental health professions are as likely to be moulded by the interests of their members (their need to earn a living and to achieve professional status), as by any conception of truth. Counselling psychologists – rooted in a tradition of private practice and faced with having to pay for their own training in British universities – may sometimes find it harder to stomach such possibilities (Feltham, 2014; Moloney, 2000). Perhaps it should be no surprise, then, that community practitioners have been among the first to acknowledge the questionable scientific and clinical evidence adduced for the effectiveness of the talking treatments (see Epstein, 2006, 2013; Howard, 1998; and Moloney, 2013). They have also been the main group to accept that these therapies can become a form of victim blaming: to the extent that practitioners ignore or downplay the toxic social situations in which many of their clients have to live, and then seek to locate the causes of (and responsibility for) the resulting distress within each client's supposed personal failings – whether of insight, motivation, or learning (Ryan, 1976; Smail, 2005).

So far, this discussion has sketched some of the ideas and perspectives that, from a critical realist standpoint, community psychology can offer the counselling psychologist. However, it is important to realise that community psychology might itself turn out to be more limited in what it can realistically achieve than some of its practitioners have been prepared to realise. This is an important issue. Before counselling psychologists can find common cause with their community brethren, they need to identify which aspects of their discipline are worth embracing: moreover, consideration of these issues might shine a clearer light upon the nature and limitations of counselling psychology itself. These are worthy goals for a profession that claims to encourage critical self-scrutiny (Strawbridge and Woolfe, 2010).

SOME OF THE CONTRADICTIONS OF COMMUNITY PSYCHOLOGY

Reliance upon exceptionally dedicated and charismatic individuals?

Common sense suggests that any attempt to achieve significant community change is likely to be difficult, protracted and not for the fainthearted, and this raises the question of to what extent community transformation can ever be professionalised. Some of the most successful community psychology schemes – the few that are remembered and widely cited and that have managed to become institutionalised within the communities that hosted them – have depended upon unusually dedicated and perhaps charismatic individuals. The best example perhaps being the White City Project: established by the clinical psychologist, Sue Holland (see Holland, 1988, 1995), in an impoverished inner-city housing estate in West London, where many of the tenants were marginalised and socially isolated black women. Most had come to believe that their misery was not the inevitable consequence of their hard lives, but the meaningless symptoms of a biological imbalance, requiring corrective treatment with 'anti-depressant' drugs. These women had been well taught by their doctors, and by the state institutions that had sought to manage them.

Holland set out to help the women understand and articulate the roots of their malaise as a predicament widely shared, and one that might be changed through an attempt to tackle some of its more obvious local causes. She worked with these residents and with health and social care services to set up a three-tier mental health project on the estate, directed towards prevention more than cure. In its final form, the Women's Action for Mental Health, or the WAMH initiative, as it came to be known, comprised a substantial network of support and care, running from individual counselling to group work and then to community action – aimed at improving facilities and security on the estate, entailing the foundation of a crèche and a respite house for anyone suffering an acute mental health crisis. Over time, many of these tenants found themselves giving and receiving emotional and practical support and friendship, as the distinction between expert and lay knowledge began to dissolve – a key signature of community psychology. With some justice, this project is widely cited in the literature as a high watermark of theory and practice.

In the years that marked the growth of WAMH, Sue Holland worked intensively: as well as providing therapy and attending community development meetings, she made herself available as a trainer in mental health techniques and as a key support for the estate's crisis unit. Holland discusses neither her own feelings, nor her general health. Still, her many roles and responsibilities must have exerted a considerable personal and professional demand.

If community psychologists need to be unusually devoted to their work, then a closely related problem concerns the question of just how politically radical and confrontational they can afford to be? Like their clinical counterparts, community psychologists are educated and funded by the state and (occasionally) by voluntary agencies. In these circumstances, how easy can it ever be to argue with the king who pays the shilling?

The Men's Advice Network was set up in West Nottingham, an area comprising several housing estates with great social need and high rates of male unemployment, by Steve Melluish, a clinical and community psychologist, and Don Bulmer, a council development worker (Melluish and Bulmer, 1999). Inspired by Sue Holland's achievement, the intention was to help working-class unemployed men suffering from depression and physical health problems to come together for mutual support. The initial aims were straightforward: to help the men to share their personal experiences and ways of coping, and to gradually regain some of the beneficial attributes of the employment that they had lost, including a valued identity, a time structure, a sense of purpose, meaningful activity and the opportunity to form social contacts.

Like the women helped by Sue Holland, these men started to shift their preoccupations from self-blame and psychiatric symptoms outwards, into the wider world. They established a successful drop-in centre, which expanded to include a local resource and benefits advice library, a hot meal or 'grub club' for visitors, and regular open sessions in welfare rights and in arts and crafts. The scheme took on a contract for the delivery and then publication of a community newspaper, followed by responsibility for a neglected allotment site, restoring it to grow vegetables in supply of a local café.

MAN helped its constituents and local residents to defend their welfare rights and to question and sometimes challenge the longstanding neglect of the estate by local government. It became a site of low-key political activism, moving sharply into a higher register, when it came to be linked with opposition to council housing policies. One participant, dissatisfied with what he felt to be the shoddy manner of his re-housing by the council, gained the support of some of his comrades in MAN to promote the idea of an estate-wide rent strike, intended to force the council to mend its ways. As well as his own home, he used the MAN premises to publicise this proposed action, which divided the group, since not everyone felt that it should have a political role. However, this situation squarely compromised both of the facilitators. Don Bulmer, as a council worker, found himself in the unenviable position of backing a project that was attacking both his employer and his managers. For Steve Melluish as an NHS psychologist, the conflict was not quite so acute, but he reports that his involvement in this successful project placed him in an uncomfortable and almost untenable position, in which he started to cross the boundary between paid professional and community activist.[1]

Does community psychology 'work' as an applied science?

There are difficulties in regard to the coherence and value of the ideas and methods that underpin many community psychology projects, and the ability to demonstrate the effectiveness of those projects themselves.

Social capital

Social capital refers to those features of social life – informal networks, norms of conduct and the kinds of mutual faith that help people to pursue shared objectives (Putnam, 2000). Many community psychologists look to the literature on this subject, which argues that it is possible

---

1 Parts of this account, especially the final four paragraphs, are based upon a personal communication from Steve Melluish.

to boost the happiness and health of a community by enhancing the strength and number of connections between people.

Like the works of Dickens, social capital has unique ability to appeal equally to both sides of the political spectrum. The concept fits rather well with calls from politicians and psychologists in Britain and the United States – especially in this era of official 'austerity' (see Bergland, 2013; BPS, 2009; Stuckler and Basu, 2013) – for community renewal and volunteering as the best ways of tackling everything from personal distress to crime. But social capital is hard to measure, because it encompasses a confusing range of connections amongst individuals, as well as within and between families, friendship networks, businesses, and communities. Too often, there is an assumption that social capital is a psychological property of individuals. Communities can be supposedly rebuilt or strengthened, largely by appeal to people's capacity for 'rational choice' – via persuasion, inspiration and bargaining, usually with the help of local leaders, or of appropriately trained psychologists. Such interpretations of social capital and civic engagement are flawed, because they ignore the influence of context, habit, tradition and history (Chaiklin, 2011; Epstein, 2010). Community psychologists have failed to appreciate the forces in the economy and the polity that cause civic indifference and that can blight a community. Recent decades have witnessed many aspects of life – from work and education to retirement and leisure – losing some of what they once offered in the way of stability, amity and solidarity; in part, because of the growth of global trade and corporate power and, in the last few years, because of official 'austerity' policies, which have shrunk the space and personal energy available for public participation (Clark and Heath, 2014; Stuckler and Basu, 2013). In these circumstances, the attraction of social capital for government often seems to lie more with the money than with the metaphysics (Midlands Psychology Group, 2008; Moloney, 2013). It is cheaper to boost a vague notion like 'inclusion' or the level of contact between people, than it is to raise their income or their material conditions.

Questions of effectiveness

If we adopt a reasonable standard of evidence – of the kind that would be required in the field of epidemiology, for instance – then the vast majority of studies in support of community psychology appear far less conclusive than we might hope. This is because of the credulous and poorly planned research that is often adduced in support of them, and which, ironically, mirrors the situation for the talking therapies (see, for instance, Epstein, 2006; Moloney, 2013; Newnes, 2014). For instance, few community projects have been rated for helpfulness by people who are independent and without a large personal, political, financial or professional stake in the outcome. Appraisal has focused upon what people *say* about changes in their community, instead of upon any alterations in what they are actually doing on a day-to-day basis. In general, the community psychology research literature ignores the large gap – well demonstrated by researchers over the last sixty years – between the views that people express, versus their conduct in 'real life' situations (Chaiklin, 2011; Khaneman, 2011; Schwitzgebel, 2011).

WHAT THEN CAN WE DO?

Community psychology is a lively discipline that 'is attended by a number of challenges, controversies and contradictions' (Orford, 2008: 382) as it grapples with questions of science, power and politics as they relate to distress and well-being. It has avoided the blinkered individualism that, for many critics, afflicts the fields of therapeutic and academic psychology. However, the field remains awkwardly balanced between a taste for political activism on behalf of the underdog and for improved professional status as a respectable, applied and (perhaps) scientific discipline. These aims are hard to reconcile.

Should we then conclude that the discipline is too unwieldy to offer much to the counselling psychologist? Not quite. For the critically minded practitioner, it is impossible to overstate the value of community psychology's questioning attitude towards the goals of mainstream psychology; of its focus upon the importance of world, body and power interactions in the sowing (and amelioration) of distress; and finally, of its unique potential for fostering modesty, on ethical and scientific grounds, about what we can hope to achieve via any form of direct psychological work.

Might it be possible, then, to indicate some of the features of a more coherent and defensible community psychology practice? Some clinicians have argued that community psychology ideas, when used carefully, can inform health service development and the practice and evaluation of individual therapy (see Diamond, 2013). In the latter case, for instance, the integrative method of 'power-mapping' can inform a better understanding of the client's unhappiness, as the result of the interplay of social and material influence. Therapy becomes the provision of comfort, of clarification and of the encouragement required to obtain those external resources that might help the client to reduce their unhappiness – where of course such assets can be found in the first place (Hagan and Smail, 1997; Orford, 2008; Smail, 2005). See Figure 22.1.

What, then, of direct community work itself? Given the open-ended and unpredictable nature of this kind of endeavour, there can be no single recipe for creating useful or sustainable community psychology projects. However, if we leave aside any requirement for unusually determined and charismatic founders, then it is possible, drawing upon some examples from the literature, to suggest forms of community psychology practice that perhaps minimise the trenchant scientific and political problems mentioned earlier.

Such attempts are likely to be relatively small-scale, and founded by psychologists who have lived or worked in a given geographical area or service, respectively, for many years, and who know thereof of what they speak. The instigators of such programmes, whilst advocating changes to the services in which they work, might also recognise that they are a part of those services and that the changes that are sought are likely to be minor in relation to the extant way of doing things (Bostock and Diamond, 2005).

Created within existing public health care services, such as the British NHS, where they appear to satisfy government and managerial directives for 'healthcare consumer participation', community psychology-inspired projects of this kind have extended, for example,

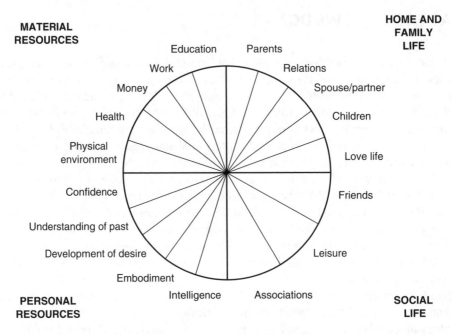

Figure 22.1 Power map (from Hagan and Smail, 1997: 261)

from a news-gathering project focusing upon developments within the mental health care system and service user movements, to a creative writing group dealing with mental health issues, to groups for men and women with learning disabilities – intended to help them gain more solidarity with their colleagues and to evaluate and perhaps influence the care systems that affect their well-being (Cox et al., 2013). Other practitioners have supported mental health service users to challenge the medical labels that have been forced upon them and to develop their own informal support as a complement to that provided by professionals (see Diamond, 2013). By contrast, practitioners like the clinical psychologist Guy Holmes have brought people together around a common interest rather than a shared diagnosis or personal problem. Advertised locally, and open to the general public as well as to mental health service users, the participants in these countryside 'Walk and Talk' groups have been encouraged to share their own experiences when discussing the social causes and prevention of unhappiness and distress, and have sometimes made new friends along the way. Within a more conventional indoor seminar format, Holmes' 'Psychology in the Real World' courses, open to all, have invited people to explore some of the key themes of community psychology, how they might relate to local problems, and the possible implications for campaigning or other community action (Holmes, 2010). Other practitioners have helped local health and social care services to improve their assistance to the straitened and to the poor (Bostock and Diamond, 2005; Orford, 2008). Some community psychologists, drawing upon their own clinical experience, have continued to publish work that highlights the personally and communally damaging consequences of government 'austerity' policies (Harris, 2014; Midlands Psychology Group, 2012). All of these areas are ones in which counselling psychologists are well placed to contribute, owing to their training in research methods, writing, teaching and group work.

In future, however, even modest efforts such as these may face additional obstacles. Across the globe, neoliberal health-care policies cast the patient as consumer rather than citizen, bearing most of the responsibility for their own health and well-being (Friedli, 2014; Kennedy, 2012). In many countries, including the UK, mental health care and 'treatment' is premised upon dubious psychiatric diagnoses and official treatment guidelines that emphasise individually delivered therapies and computerised 'advice packages' (Moloney, 2013). The British NHS, a nominally public institution, is in the throes of its own market revolution. The resulting focus upon the competitive achievement of managerially defined targets is not always friendly towards the creative and longer-term preventative work of the community psychologist (see Davis and Tallis, 2013; Pollock, 2011).

But there are ways to resist these pressures. One of the most important being the maintenance of solidarity with like-minded colleagues and service users; and community practitioners have found ways of meeting and supporting one another to sustain their ideas and their work, sometimes instigating or assisting public campaigns around social and political issues such as child poverty or militarism (see Burton et al., 2007). Solidarity is often the only form of significant social power available to ordinary people – including counselling psychologists interested in community practice – and it is the one of which they might need to make increasing use, in the years ahead.

Visit the companion website for links to further resources on community and critical psychology.

REFERENCES

Adam, D. (2003) 'I'm a cliché'. *Variant*, 2(18): 25–26.

Albee, W. and Joffe, J. M. (eds) (1977) *The Issues: An Overview of Primary Prevention.* Hanover, NH: University Press of New England.

APA (American Psychological Association) (2015) *Division 27: Society for Community Research and Action: Division of Community Psychology.* www.apa.org/about/division/div27.aspx (retrieved 20 February 2015).

Bergland, C. (2013) 'Positive action builds social capital and resilience'. *Psychology Today.* www.psychologytoday.com/blog/the-athletes-way/201306/positive-actions-build-social-capital-and-resilience (retrieved 12 March 2014).

Bhaskar, R. (1998) *The Possibility of Naturalism: A Philosophical Critique of the Contemporary Human Sciences* (3rd edn). London: Routledge.

Bostock, J. and Diamond, B. (2005) 'The value of community psychology: Critical reflections from the NHS'. *Clinical Psychology Forum*, 153: 22–25.

BPS (British Psychological Society) (2009) *Psychological Health and Wellbeing: A New Ethos for Mental Health. A Report of the Working Group on Mental Health and Wellbeing.* Leicester: BPS.

Bracken, P. and Thomas, P. (2004) 'Out of the clinic and into the community'. *Openmind*, 126: 13.

Bronfrenbrenner, U. (1980) *The Ecology of Human Development: Experiments by Nature and Design.* New Haven, CT and London: Harvard University Press.

Burton, M., Boyle, S., Harris, C. and Kagan, C. M. (2007) 'Community psychology in Britain', in S. M. Reich, M. Riemer, I. Prilleltensky and M. Montero (eds), *International Community Psychology: History and Theories.* New York: Springer-Verlag.

Chaiklin, H. (2011) 'Attitudes, behavior and social practice'. *Journal of Sociology and Social Welfare*, 38(1): 31–54.

Clark, T. and Heath, A. (2014) *Hard Times: The Divisive Toll of the Economic Slump.* New Haven, CT and London: Yale University Press.

Cox, R., Holmes, G., Moloney, P., Priest, P. and Ridley-Dash, M. (2013) 'Community psychology', in J. Cromby, D. Harper and P. Reavy (eds), *Psychology, Mental Health and Distress.* London: Palgrave Macmillan.

Davis, J. and Tallis, R. (2013) *NHS SOS: How The NHS Was Betrayed – And How We Can Save It.* London: Oneworld Publications.

Davy, J. (2010) 'A narrative approach to counselling psychology', in R. Woolfe, S. Strawbridge, B. Douglas and W. Dryden (eds), *Handbook of Counselling Psychology* (3rd edn). London: Sage.

Diamond, B. (2013) 'Rebuilding the house of mental health services with home truths', in S. Coles, S. Keenan and B. Diamond (eds), *Madness Contested: Power and Practice.* Ross-on-Wye: PCCS Books.

Edwards, W. (2013) 'Collaboration in cognitive behavioural therapy: In the shadow or in the light of power dynamics?' *Counselling Psychology Review*, 28(2): 118–124.

Eleftheriadou, Z. (2010) 'Cross-cultural counselling psychology', in R. Woolfe, R., S. Strawbridge, B. Douglas and W. Dryden (eds), *Handbook of Counselling Psychology* (3rd edn). London: Sage.

Epstein, W. (2006) *The Civil Divine: Psychotherapy as Religion in America.* Reno, NV: University of Nevada Press.

Epstein, W. (2010) *Democracy without Decency.* New Brunswick, NJ: Transaction.

Epstein, W. (2013) *Empowerment as Ceremony.* New Brunswick, NJ: Transaction.

Feltham, C. (2014) *Counselling and Counselling Psychology: A Critical Examination.* London: Palgrave Macmillan.

Fisher, A.T., Gridley, H. and Thomas, D.R. (2008) 'Community psychology in Australia and Aotearoa/New Zealand', *Journal of Community Psychology*, 36(5): 649–660.

Freidli, L. (2014) 'A response: The ethics of psycho-policy – reflections on the role of psychology in public health and workfare'. *Clinical Psychology Forum*, 256(April): 11–16.

Hagan, T. and Smail, D. (1997) 'Power-mapping – I: Background and basic methodology'. *Journal of Community and Applied Social Psychology*, 7(4): 257–267.

Harris, C. (2014) 'The impact of austerity on a British council estate'. *The Psychologist*, 27(4): 250–253.

Harrison, K. (2013) 'Counselling psychology and power: Considering therapy and beyond'. *Counselling Psychology Review*, 28(2): 107–117.

Holland, S. (1988) 'Defining and experimenting with prevention', in R. Ramon and M. Giannichedda (eds), *Psychiatry in Transition: The British and Italian Experiences*. London: Pluto Press.

Holland, S. (1995) 'Interaction in women's mental health and neigbourhood development', in S. Fernando (ed.), *Mental Health in a Multi-Ethnic Society: A Multi-Disciplinary Handbook*. London: Routledge.

Holmes, G. (2010) *Psychology in the Real World: Using Community Groups to Help People*. Ross-on-Wye: PCCS Books.

Howard, A. (1998) *Challenges to Psychotherapy and Counselling*. London. Palgrave Macmillan.

Ira, I. (1974) 'Community psychology and the competent community'. *American Psychologist*, 29(8): 607–613.

Kagan, C., Burton, M., Duckett, P., Lawthom, R. and Siddiquee, A. (2011) *Critical Community Psychology*. London and New York: John Wiley and Sons.

Kahneman, D. (2011) *Thinking, Fast and Slow*. London: Macmillan.

Kennedy, A. (2012) *Authors of Our Own Misfortune? The Problems of Psychogenic Explanations for Physical Illnesses*. Market Rasen: The Village Digital Press.

Konzelman, S. J., Wilkinson, F. and Mankelow, R. (2007) *Work Intensification and Employment Insecurity in Professional Work*. Working Paper No. 345. Centre for Business Research, University of Cambridge, Cambridge.

Lillis, J., O'Donahue, W.T., Cucciari, M. and Lillis, E. (2005) 'Social Justice in Community Psychology'. in, R. H. Wright, and N. A. Cummings, (eds) *Destructive Trends in Mental Health: The Well Intentioned Path to Harm*. New York: Routledge.

Melluish, S. and Bulmer, D. (1999) 'Rebuilding solidarity: An account of a men's health action project'. *Journal of Community and Applied Social Psychology*, 9: 93–100.

Midlands Psychology Group (2008) 'Blissed out Britain is back in business', *Clinical Psychology Forum*, 184: 52–55.

Midlands Psychology Group (2012) 'Manifesto for a social-materialist psychology of distress'. *The Journal of Critical Psychology, Counselling and Psychotherapy*, 12(2) (June): 93–107.

Moller, N. (2011) 'The identity of counselling psychology in Britain is parochial, rigid and irrelevant, but diversity offers a solution'. *Counselling Psychology Review*, 26(2): 8–16.

Moloney, P. (2000) 'Counselling psychology: Are we allowed to disagree?' *The Journal of Critical Psychology, Counselling and Psychotherapy*, 1(4) (Winter): 209–216.

Moloney, P. (2013) *The Therapy Industry: The Irresistible Rise of the Talking Cure, and Why It Doesn't Work*. London: Pluto Press.

Nelson, G. and Prilleltensky, I. (eds) (2005) *Community Psychology: In Pursuit of Liberation and Well-being*. London: Palgrave Macmillan.

Newnes, C. (2014) *Clinical Psychology: A Critical Examination*. Ross-on-Wye: PCCS Books.

Painter, D., Terre Blanche, M. and Henderson, J. (2006) 'Critical psychology in South Africa: Histories, themes and prospects'. *Annual Review of Critical Psychology*, 5: 212– 235.

Parker, I. (2007) *Revolution in Psychology*. London: Pluto Press.

Pollock, S. (2011) *NHS, Plc*. London: Verso.

Putnam, Robert D. (2000) *Bowling Alone: The Collapse and Revival of American Community*. New York: Simon & Schuster.

Ryan, C. (1976) *Blaming the Victim*. New York: Plenum.

Sayer, A. (2015) *Why We Can't Afford the Rich*. London: Polity Press.

Schwitzgebel, E. (2011) *Perplexities of Consciousness*. Cambridge, MA: MIT Press.

Smail, D. (2005) *Power, Interest and Psychology: Elements of a Social Materialist Understanding of Distress*. Ross-on-Wye: PCCS Books.

Steffen, E. and Hanley, T. (2013) 'The power of counselling psychology in an age of powerlessness: A call to action'. *Counselling Psychology Review*, 28(2): 3–7.

Strawbridge, S. and Woolfe, R. (2010) 'Counselling psychology: Origins, developments and challenges', in R. Woolfe, S. Strawbridge, B. Douglas and W. Dryden (eds), *Handbook of Counselling Psychology* (3rd edn). London: Sage.

Stuckler, D. and Basu, S. (2013) *The Body Economic: Why Austerity Kills*. London: Allen Lane.

Throop, E. (2011) *Psychotherapy, American Culture, and Social Policy: Immoral Individualism*. London: Palgrave Macmillan.

Tindall, C., Robinson, J. and Kagan, C. (2010) 'Feminist perspectives', in R. Woolfe, S. Strawbridge, B. Douglas and W. Dryden (eds), *Handbook of Counselling Psychology* (3rd edn). London: Sage.

Tyrer, E. (1973) 'A counselling psychologist looks at community psychology'. *American Journal of Community Psychology*, 1(1): 1–7.

White, M. and Epston, D. (1990) *Narrative Means to Therapeutic Ends*. New York: W.W. Norton.

Wilkinson, R. and Pickett, K. (2013) *The Spirit Level: Why Equality Hurts* (2nd edn). London: Penguin.

23
PSYCHOLOGICAL PRACTICE IN A TIME OF ENVIRONMENTAL CRISIS: COUNSELLING PSYCHOLOGY AND ECOPSYCHOLOGY

MARTIN MILTON

This chapter considers ecopsychology and its relationship to our profession; it invites readers to consider the way in which ecopsychology's and counselling psychology's fundamental assumptions overlap; how an ecopsychological perspective contributes to our understanding of people; and the contribution it can make to our work in the clinic and the wider world. The chapter also considers the way ecopsychology can inform our deliberations as to how our profession might evolve – whether we slide into an uncritical mainstream, bystanders to problematic social and other practices, or whether we might adopt other stances. But first, our contemporary contexts.

THE WORLD WE INHABIT

The world has changed enormously over time and we are constantly made aware of the benefits of such progress, advantages that affect all areas of our existence – physical, psychological and environmental (Milton, 2010). Such change also brings significant risks. The most pertinent to this chapter are the environmental challenges that have become clear.

Nickee Higley and I noted that:

> The environment is no longer the discourse of physical scientists or activist eco-warriors. It has become one of the major social issues of our time (Mayer and Frantz, 2004). The scientific evidence from most quarters (e.g. Intergovernmental Panel on Climate Change, 2001, 2014) now supports the view that we are facing significant and unprecedented environmental

problems on a scale that will have powerful repercussions for our current ways of life (Gore, 2006) and psychological well-being. As the originators and potential agents of change of these problems, humanity's largely unhealthy and unsustainable relationship with the planet is being called into question. It is becoming clearer that, as Evernden puts it, 'we are not *in* an environmental crisis, but *are* the environmental crisis' (1985: 125). One might expect a field such as psychology to be playing an essential part in helping to understand and change these detrimental patterns, however, some argue that so far, its impact has been limited (e.g. Kidner, 1994). (Higley and Milton, 2008: 10)

There is significant evidence that humanity is damaging the environment, e.g. through monocultures and pesticides (Monbiot, 2013), ever-growing populations (United Nations, 1991), food crises (United Nations, 1991), habitat destruction and extinction crises of animals, traditional peoples and their cultures (Griffiths, 2006; Macfarlane, 2007). Alongside other scientists, counselling psychologists are warning us that unless we act now, we might soon realise that we have done 'too little, too late' (Seligman, 1993: 627). Rust notes that while the 'awareness of this crisis is far greater than it was a decade ago, there is still little sign of a serious shift in public attitudes' (2012a, Kindle edition: 4%).

There is a range of evidence noting that we are suffering – physically, sociologically and psychologically. While it may not be clear as to why, the rise in urbanisation brings with it an increase in physical disease such as asthma (Woodcock and Peat, 2007) and psychological distress such as eating disorders (James, 2007). While counselling psychologists may not see their role as one of parliamentary policy making, we are involved in working with the recipients of such damage – those with addictions, eating problems, rampant anxiety and depression.

COUNSELLING PSYCHOLOGY

Counselling psychology emerged as a challenge to a static, limited approach to psychological understanding that was predominant in the 1980s and 1990s. At that point, political culture and, within it, health service policy were conservative in outlook, prioritising the streamlining of the mental health services (Parry, 1996), the manualisation of 'treatment' and seeming not to be attuned to (or actively resist) what many different sciences were recognising, that people are not self-contained individuals and much of our behaviour is social and sociological in nature (Billington et al., 1998; Strawbridge, 1996).

Counselling psychology espoused a different view – a relational one, recognising that we live in *relationship* as well as in *relationships*. It is not possible for people to be uninfluenced by people and the world around them, whether they are formally in a relationship or not. While counselling psychology recognises personal distress can be linked to obvious and traceable manifestations of biological illness or interpersonal abuse, it recognises that socio-political dimensions have a strong impact on experience (Billington et al., 1998) and that poverty, discrimination, racism (Lofthouse, 2010) and sexism (Kagan and Tindall, 2003) lead to difficulty – on a personal and discursive level (Burr, 2003). Counselling psychology recognises the importance of research that shows how good relationships are at the heart of psychological well-being and promotes approaches to practice that draw on relational strengths. In good relationships we can heal distress or even thrive (Woodward and Joseph, 2003)!

Counselling psychology's contribution has been significant and has contributed to the evolution of health-care policy, career structures and status. Unfortunately, once they are established, professions risk losing their original, challenging mission through absorption into the mainstream (Macdonald, 1995). We now see counselling psychologists embracing manualisation of therapy while others voice concern over the 'commodification' of disorders and therapy (Shillito-Clarke, 2008a). Indeed, our sociological critique seemed to get 'lost' and only recently did Moller challenge us to return to this, using the advent of state regulation to highlight that we are legally required to consider context and its impact on clients (Moller, 2011).

SO WHAT?

Like modern culture, counselling psychology faces a tension: how do we engage with the difficulties that face us individually and collectively, courageously, directly and creatively, while, like others, we may want to do so while retaining the advantages of the current situation? The impact of the environmental crises, mass extinction, pollution and climate change demonstrates that we, other people, animals, plants and the wider planet suffer when we insist on positioning the individual above the collective (Chatalos, 2012). 'Climate change shows us our human-sized powerlessness and vulnerability, and faces us with death – not least the extinction of so many species as well as our own' (Sampson, 2012, Kindle edition: 8%). Yet we struggle to cut back on our excesses, waiting till we 'really have to', and we try to do so without experiencing loss (Randall, 2009).

In the meantime, we revert to the illusion that we are separate from the rest of nature, and in doing so ignore the damage we are doing at an ever-increasing rate (Adams, 2006). Paying too much attention on the rights of the individual (often meaning the *powerful* individual) limits our ability to see the wider system (Adams, 2005, 2006). Or is it less a case of apathy, and more a manifestation of our paralysis (Lertzmann, 2008) in the face of such enormous pain and anxiety.

Unfortunately, the psychological professions have been complicit in developing a picture of the world where humans are separate from everything else – separate from our surroundings, and nature and the planet become simply the backdrop on which human life exists (Higley and Milton, 2008), or, as Bodnar puts it, 'the earth as scenery' (2012: 20). This allows us to treat difficulties as exclusively individual; we use CBT to suggest that it is just an individual's faulty set of assumptions that create problems. Psychoanalysis only recently moved to a 'two person' psychology (Bateman, 2000) and Searles (1972) noted that it relegates the world to being a mere backdrop. And much humanistic theory and practice limits itself to equally narrow lines, privileging human–human relationships. Existential therapy, alone on the psychotherapeutic landscape, has at its core people's inevitable embeddedness in a biopsycho-socially diverse web of life. But even *its* potential is not fully utilised. Existentialists, as members of our society, also struggle to fully enunciate the challenge of non-dichotomous, relational and environmental understandings.

While recognising challenges, it is useful to note that there are attempts to explore the relationship between psychotherapeutic approaches and the natural world (see existential-phenomenology (Adams, 2005), person-centred theory (Blair, 2011) and analytical psychology (Rust, 2008a; Samuels, 1993) and this gives rise to an increasing body of work available to counselling psychologists.

So the scene is ripe for a psychology that draws upon non-dichotomous, relational and environmental understandings.

INTRODUCING ECOPSYCHOLOGY

Ecopsychology was born out of a range of intellectual, theoretical and philosophical fields, including deep ecology, feminism and shamanism (Roszak, 1995), and has links with environmental psychology, conservation psychology, climate science and analytical psychology. Ecopsychology literature and practices are being used by clinical and counselling psychologists, and psychotherapists and by organisations such as Mind (2007) and the National Trust (Moss, 2012). It may be that because it is a discipline in its youth, ecopsychology is able to draw on this wide variety of traditions and so be freer than mainstream psychology to break away from its normalising preoccupations.

Ecopsychology focuses on the relationship between humanity, the environment and nature, not just in a uni-directional manner but more widely relational – including how we affect the world and how there are loops of influence, i.e. X affects Y, which affects X again. Nickee Higley and I noted that:

> It is in the discipline of ecopsychology that we can find some deeper thinking about the problems arising from our current relationship with nature. Inherent within its position on the fringe come potential problems in academic rigour and scientific credibility. However, when dealing with big shifts in consciousness it is often essential to look to the less mainstream fields for inspiration and fresh perspectives albeit to do so with a critical eye. (Higley and Milton, 2008: 15)

Ecopsychology offers insights into the ways in which a disconnect from nature is bad for humanity (Louv, 2006). For example, ecological discontent/damage can lead to such difficulties as eating problems (Rust, 2008b), depression (Eko, 2012), grief and loss (Adams, 2006; Randall, 2009), trauma (Corbett and Milton, 2011) and problematic gender relations (Anapol, 2012; Bloodheart and Swim, 2010; Higley, 2008).

Ecopsychology also helps us consider the notion of healthy relationships with nature, and considers the forms that might lead to transformative relationships (Macgregor, 2013) and enhanced psychological benefits (Gatersleben, 2008).

THE LANDSCAPE

With such a wide intellectual heritage, it is apparent that ecopsychology is not, and cannot, be based on one singular set of underlying assumptions. However, some common assumptions stand out.

Ecopsychology 'commits itself to understanding people as actors on a planetary stage who shape and are shaped by the biospheric system' (Roszak, 1995: 14). It recognises the psycho/cultural pathology in our relationship with nature and models are being extended and applied in new and innovative ways. We see 'many authors draw from psychodynamic models of pathology in their explanations. At its extreme, our destructive and dysfunctional behaviour and our modern industrialised living are seen as a kind of "collective madness" (Shepard, 1982)' (Higley and Milton, 2008: 15). The engagement with psychoanalytic thought is not simply an adoption of a problematic paradigm of self-contained intrapsychic problems being overlaid onto society (Higley and Milton, 2008). Rather, psychoanalytic insights are developed further (see Lertzmann, 2008; Mishan, 1996; Randall, 2005, 2009; Rust, 2008a; Weintrobe, 2010).

Ecopsychology theorising is often characterised by non-dichotomous thinking, challenging discourses that focus on 'us and them'. This is not that 'us and them' has always to be doubted, as differences are of course factual. But ecopsychology recognises that reducing understandings down to dichotomies, or ultimate 'causes' of an event, is a human act rather than an ecological reality (Chatalos, 2012; Ulstrand, 2002).

Like many counselling psychologists, a number of ecopsychologists are recognising that the world constructs us as much as we construct it. Indeed, 'our minds are shaped by the bodily experience of being in the world' (Macfarlane, 2007: 203) and in humanity's destruction of the environment 'it is not only unique species and habitats that disappear, but also unique memories, unique forms of thought. Woods, like other wild places, can kindle new ways of being or cognition in people, can urge their minds differently' (Macfarlane, 2007: 98).

A key concept in ecopsychology is that of the *web* of relations in which we exist. To ignore this is, firstly, to ignore reality and, secondly, to overlook the limits/problems associated with our view of ourselves as 'self-contained' entities (Strawbridge, 1996). Like social geography, ecopychology is beginning to illuminate a range of factors that are important for psychological well-being within and beyond human–human relationships and so we see studies noting human engagement with space (Sustainable Development Commission, 2008), place (Mest, 2008; Samuels, 1993; Ward and Styles, 2006), economics (Hamilton, 2004; James, 2007), forests (Rolston, 1998), oceans (Nichols, 2014; Wheeler et al., 2012), relationships with animals (Hicks, 2008; Sacks, 2008), and with horses specifically (Favali and Milton, 2010; Scheiner, 2012, 2013).

IMPLICATIONS FOR THEORY AND PRACTICE

In line with counselling psychology's commitment to understanding the wider psychological landscape, challenging discrimination (British Psychological Society, 2005) and social justice (Cutts, 2013; Ersahin, 2013; Hore, 2013; Moller, 2011), ecopsychology offers us ways to think about the ways in which humanity is damaging the environment.

View of people

Ecopsychology and counselling psychology both recognise that people are conscious and meaning-making beings who exist within a wider web of relationships. Ecopsychology draws on the idea of biophilia, which helps us to understand the evolutionary, conscious and unconscious, and embodied reliance on our environment (Wilson, 1984) and notes that people evolved with strong connections with animals and the environment as a way of survival (Wilson, 1984); as an ontological rather than as an ontic aspect of Being (Gillies and Milton, 2007).

Ecopsychological work is also extending the concept of the 'Self'. Over time, psychology moved from a 'Self' which is 'self-contained' (Strawbridge, 1996) and separate to its context to one that is understood to be mediated through the relationships with key care-givers, as illustrated by Winnicott's (1960) view that there is no baby without a mother. Psychology has broadened its view to consider socially constructed Selves created through discourse (Burr, 2003) and ecopsychology is helping to consider the 'ecological Self' (Higley, 2009; Jordan, 2012) or 'borderland Self' (Bernstein, 2012).

Understanding our distress

Ecopsychology does not reject what we know about human relationships being important, nor does it question that distress is often linked to abusive or demeaning relationships or those characterised by violence or deprivation. What ecopsychology does challenge is the idea that human relationships satisfactorily accounts for *all* that leads to human distress. Ecopsychology recognises that our relationships to the wider environment can equally be at the root of distress – and on a significant scale. Large-scale studies have drawn our attention to the fact that despite not being at the forefront of people's minds, urban, technologised living gives rise to depression, eating disorders and trauma (Hamilton, 2004; James, 2007). We have other studies that note how anxiety and depression manifest in relation to ecological events (see Adams, 2006). We have long understood that eating difficulties have a cultural dimension (Orbach, 2009), and we have seen that eating problems also have a link to the natural world (Rust, 2008b).

Depression has been conceptualised from different perspectives and these have been extended as depression is often intensified in urban contexts and relieved with access to time outdoors, in the woods and the wilds (Eko, 2012). There is also a degree of depression that comes from recognising that the world is being damaged, e.g. by mountain-top coal mining (Cordial et al., 2013; Hendryx and Innes-Wimsatt, 2013). As well as suffering when we lose people, studies illuminate the pain, loss and trauma experienced in the face of environmental loss and species extinction (see Griffiths, 2006; Randall, 2009).

As in the spirituality literature where the distinction between madness and unusual yet meaningful experiences has been outlined, Bernstein (2012) notes that some people have experiences that others might want to pathologise, but that, on closer examination, are not pathology but 'Borderland' states – with deep and primary connections to nature.

Ecopsychology also helps consider more hopeful findings too – insights that show the ways in which healthy relationships with nature afford transformative relationships (Macgregor, 2013), enhanced psychological benefits (Gatersleben, 2008; Greenwood, 2014a) and a way to alleviate the impact of trauma (Corbett and Milton, 2011).

Thriving in nature

Gaterslaben (2008) notes that living near nature has beneficial effects on physical and psychological well-being (see Kaplan, 2001; Kaplan and Kaplan, 1989) and how these benefits can be understood in specific subsets, including:

1. contact with animals (see Frumkin, 2001; Katcher et al., 1983);
2. exposure to nature and its positive effect on cognitive functioning (see Greenwood, 2014a; Hartig, Mang and Evans, 1991; Kaplan and Kaplan, 1989);
3. people preferring natural scenes over man-made environments (see Hagerhall, 2000) and this leading to an increased sense of well-being;
4. people preferring half-open park-like environments (see Orians and Heerwagen, 1992; Wilson, 1984);
5. favourite places being dominated by natural elements (see Korpela et al., 2001);
6. spectacular nature being awe-inspiring and promoting confidence and well-being (see Frederickson and Anderson, 1999; Hartig et al., 1991).

This suggests that we require a degree of 'ecological intimacy' (Rust, 2012b).

Understanding our environmentally damaging behaviour

Ecopsychology is interested in such questions as: What makes humanity treat its life-giving resources so badly? Why do we poison our water? Why do we deplete our oxygen supply? Why do we increase our radiation levels? It allows us to consider why we appear unable to stop such self-defeating and self-damaging behaviours despite such clear evidence? These are questions similar to those we explore with clients in the consulting room, whether it is in relation to damaging relationships, engagement in addictive behaviours or self-harm.

One possibility is, as Freud noted, that 'the principle task of civilization, its actual *raison d'être*, is to defend us against nature' (1961: 15–16). It is, after all, scary, demanding, risky and downright dangerous (Jordan, 2012; Milton, 2003). Equally, one of the main religions, Christianity, encourages us in this path. Bernstein notes 'that dominion by Man, as mandated in the Bible, is how we arrived at the point of looming self-annihilation' (2012, Kindle edition: 63%). This 'dominion' fosters an 'anthropocentric superiority towards other species' (Robertson, 2012, Kindle edition: 83%).

Humanity's environmentally damaging behaviours mirrors the destructive stance we take to many people and objects. We pathologise and oppress people on the basis of gender, sexuality, religion and more, and we see our dominance and intent to objectify and 'use' other animals and plants (Robertson, 2012; Rust, 2012b). Rust addresses these parallels noting that:

> [I]t is clear from the history of apartheid, women's rights and slavery that untangling cultural projections is very complex. For those in positions of 'power over' this involves unbearable guilt for the damage inflicted, as well as humiliation. This psychological work takes generations, and it sheds some light on the difficulties involved in recovering ecological intimacy, for humans are in a position of 'power over' the nonhuman world. (Rust, 2012b, Kindle edition: 53%)

Some ecopsychologists conceptualise our exploitative and destructive stance as addictions, arguing that the 'hallmark of this process is the out-of-control, often aimless compulsion to fill a lost sense of meaning and connectedness' (Glendinning, 1995: 46). It seems that:

> [A] number of symptoms of the addictive process … can be related to our current condition. First, a society-wide denial that the problems are real and that our lives will change, which, despite more awareness, still seems deeply rooted. Next, the addict's obsession with control characterises our ways of being with the world, our desire to gain ever-increasing domination over nature. Finally, Glendinning argues that we as a society have 'undergone an untenable violation: a collective trauma … the systemic and systematic removal of our lives from the natural world' (1995: 51). (Higley and Milton, 2008: 15)

This area has also been explored from an *eco-psychoanalytic* perspective (Dodds, 2011, 2012; Lertzmann, 2008), hypothesising that destructive behaviour can be seen as paralysis in the face of, maybe unconscious, recognition of the scale of the damage and pain. Lertzmann (2008) argues that we should not consider humanity as apathetic, but as stuck in a paralysis.

PRACTICE

When thinking about practice, there is overlap with issues that the other chapters in this section are concerned with. People within the person-centred (Blair, 2011), psychodynamic (Mishan, 1996; Searles, 1972), Jungian (Rust, 2005; Samuels, 1993), existential (Adams, 2005; Macgregor, 2013) and counselling psychology (Jordan, 2012; Jordan and Marshall, 2010;

Milton, 2009; Owen, 2008; Shillito-Clarke, 2008a, 2008b) traditions have commented on the contributions of ecopsychology.

Assessment and formulation

A core skill of counselling psychologists is the ability to assess and formulate psychologically (Health and Care Professions Council, 2012). It is the basis of decision making for practice. On occasions, aspects of a client's presentation are directly related to their relationship with the natural world, e.g. anxiety and depression after the Deepwater Horizon disaster (Koger, 2010). The counselling psychologist will consider these issues as both objective (ontological) reality as well as personal, ontic, meanings.

However, quite frequently, clients may not be clear on the nature of their distress, and it is here that a wider ecopsychological perspective is helpful – it allows us to 'consider all contexts that might affect a client's experience' (British Psychological Society, 2005: 7). Counselling psychologists will balance traditional approaches to assessment with those that emerge from understanding the client in the wider ecological domain. This is because there are 'similarities between humans and animals that a knowledge of the natural world, and especially the instinctive behaviour which seems so much more raw in nature, ... help one to understand the often suppressed instinctive behaviour of mankind' (Steyn, 2008: 60).

In practical terms, this means that in:

> the same way that a counselling psychologist may ponder a client's presentation with a number of important topics in mind (nature of the distress, severity and longevity, origins, triggers and protective factors, etc.) and a variety of models in mind (e.g. what are the cognitive aspects of this presentation? what is going on consciously and unconsciously? how will the client respond to different styles of therapeutic response?), an ecopsychological mindset will help us also consider the nature of the client's embodied experience, their relationship to the wider political and natural aspects of their lives. (Milton, 2010: 299)

To do this, I have suggested that:

> in addition to the traditional question of 'Tell me about your Mom and Dad' we might also ask 'Tell me about your politics/faith/relationship to the natural world'. At its basis, an ecopsychological awareness is simply an invitation to broaden our thinking. It is to truly think in a pluralistic and scientific manner. It is 'to bring the entire human history into the consulting room'. (Milton, 2010: 300)

This is a strategy that Robertson (2012) also discusses, leading to an ecopsychologically enriched formulation, helping the psychologist to recommend potentially useful interventions. This may mean that traditional forms of psychological therapy are recommended or that other, more innovative approaches to therapy are considered.

Environmentally aware therapy

Environmentally aware therapy need not be a different 'brand' of therapy; it simply requires the natural world to be taken seriously (Milton, 2010; Shillito-Clarke, 2008a). It attends to geographical, environmental and evolutionary factors (Maiteny, 2012) and in doing so the significance that people give (or do not give) to their encounters with the natural world. Kerr and Key (2012) suggest that 'the most complete setting for us to encounter and heal our psychological wounds combines an accepting, holding, human presence with wild nature' (2012, Kindle edition: 26%), something evident in adolescents' relationship with nature (Greenwood, 2014b). McCallum suggests that 'the patient needs a guide (someone who knows the terrain, the animals, the weather patterns and when it is appropriate to proceed or withdraw)' (McCallum and Milton, 2008: 65). It may be that this form of practice is easiest for psychologists to engage with as it can assist us without any need to change our consulting rooms or other material. Having said this, the ecopsychology literature does question why we often limit ourselves to the rigid times, frequencies and separations from nature (Milton, 2010). There is a great deal to learn from those running therapeutic walking groups (see Priest, 2007) or out in nature (Jordan, 2005; Jordan and Marshall, 2010; Wright, 2009).

Diverse and evolving therapeutic frames

The growing body of research opens up discussion of the frame. Some recognise that our relationship to the natural world is an embodied one and we benefit from capitalising on this by changing from seated, indoor work to moving, outdoor work. We see therapists acknowledging the contribution that non-human creatures have for therapy, and moving to work with non-human co-therapists with the use of pets in practice (Sacks, 2008), the use of horses for both disabled riding and as part of a psychological therapy programme (see Scheiner, 2012, 2013) as we know that equine-assisted therapy addresses 'a variety of mental health, human development and behavioural issues, such as ADHD, depression, substance abuse, eating disorders and abuse' (Favali and Milton, 2010: 252).

Ecotherapy

Ecotherapy is a term that describes approaches to therapy undertaken outdoors, in nature and in relation to nature. McCallum suggests it requires us to 'Stand still. Listen. Be patient. Try and make sure that the space between you and the other is safe and containing for you both. As practiced in analytical therapy, "begin by giving a free-floating attention to the encounter"' (2007: 188).

There are divergent practices, from traditional sessions held outside (Jordan, 2014) to conservation work (Wright, 2009), horticultural therapy (Wise, 2015), therapeutic walking groups (Priest, 2007), and wilderness retreats/Visionquests (Jordan, 2005).

Ecotherapy is 'a clinically valid treatment option for mental distress and a core component of an adequate public health strategy for Mental Health' (Mind, 2007: 4). It is recommended for people who have suffered violence and torture as 'people who are so very badly hurt by other humans, as well as being dislocated from their homes and country, often find it easier to connect to nature first, before daring to risk human relationships again' (Rust, 2004: 1). This is a feature of the Natural Growth project in London (Corbett and Milton, 2011). It is hoped that a healing encounter with nature can also 'lead to pro-environmental behaviour by activating an "environmental identity"' (Crompton, 2012, Kindle edition: 65%).

CONCLUSION

If counselling psychology is to regain its original challenging stance and to help in reconsidering our responses to urgent social and psychological issues, ecopsychology has as important a contribution to make as other theories. It may help us reconnect – with our original ethos and values, our evolutionary and environmental heritage and also with a sense of well-being. It is also the only way in which we can hope to fully utilise the core skills and talents of the profession in moderating the distress of our environmental crises and, even more importantly, help people find ways in which to live more relationally and ecological healthy lives so as not to continue to damage the web of life in which we exist.

The human–environment issues are increasingly urgent. They are the same ones that underpin our brutalising of humans and non-humans alike, whether through racism, sexism and homophobia, the rape of our rain forests, the extinction crisis we fuel for hardwood floors and the climate change that is already driving people away from the homes of their forefathers. It is all based on 'assumptions of superiority built into our relationships with other species '(Rust, 2012a, Kindle edition: 5%) and our environment. This and our consumerist mindset combine to create a constant appetite for things that requires re-orienting (Maiteny, 2012: 59). And urgent it is, if we want to contribute efficiently and successfully, now is the time to widen our thinking. If we don't, we will risk offering what Seligman (1993: 627) warned us about: 'Too little, too late.'

Visit the companion website to watch Ecopsychology.

REFERENCES

Adams, A. A. (2005) 'Ecopsychology and phenomenology: Toward a collective engagement'. *Existential Analysis*, 16(2): 260–283.

Adams, W. W. (2006) 'The Ivory-Billed Woodpecker, ecopsychology, and the crisis of extinction: On annihilating and nurturing other beings, relationships and ourselves'. *The Humanistic Psychologist*, 34(2): 111–133.

Anapol, D. (2012) 'Gender queering Mother Earth'. *European Journal of Ecopsychology*, 3: 104–108.

Bateman, A. (2000) 'Integration in psychotherapy: An evolving reality in personality disorder'. *British Journal of Psychotherapy*, 17(2): 147–156.

Bernstein, J. (2012) 'What if it were true …'. In M. J. Rust and N. Totton (eds), *Vital Signs: Psychological Responses to Ecological Crises*. London: Karnac.

Billington, R., Hockey, J. and Strawbridge, S. (1998) *Exploring Self and Society*. Basingstoke: Palgrave Macmillan.

Blair, L. (2011) 'Ecopsychology and the person-centred approach: Exploring the relationship'. *Counselling Psychology Review*, 26(1): 43–52.

Bloodheart, B. and Swim, J. (2010) 'Equality, harmony and the environment: An ecofeminist approach to understanding the role of cultural values on the treatment of women and nature'. *Ecopsychology*, 2(3): 187–194. DOI: 10.1089/eco.2010.0057.

Bodnar, S. (2012) '"It's snowing less": Narratives of a transformed relationship between humans and their environments'. In M. J. Rust and N. Totton (eds), *Vital Signs: Psychological Responses to Ecological Crises*. London: Karnac.

British Psychological Society (BPS) (2005, February 14) *Professional Practice Guidelines for Counselling Psychologists*. Leicester: BPS. Retrieved 20 January 2007, from: www.bps.org.uk/dcop/publications/publications_home.cfm

Burr, V. (2003) *Social Constructionism* (2nd edn). London: Routledge.

Chatalos, P. (2012) 'Gaia living with AIDS: Towards reconnecting humanity with ecosystem autopoiesis using metaphors of the immune system', in M.J. Rust and N. Totton (eds), *Vital Signs: Psychological Responses to Ecological Crises*. London: Karnac Books.

Corbett, L. and Milton, M. (2011) 'Ecopsychology: A perspective on trauma'. *European Journal of Ecopsychology*, 2: 28–48.

Cordial, P., Riding-Malon, R. and Lips, H. (2013) 'The effects of mountaintop coal mining on mental health, well-being and community health in Central Appalachia'. *Ecopsychology*, 4(3): 201–208. DOI: 10.1089/eco.2012.0032.

Crompton, T. (2012) 'Back to nature, then back to the office'. In M. J. Rust and N. Totton (eds), *Vital Signs: Psychological Responses to Ecological Crises*. London: Karnac.

Cutts, L. A. (2013) 'Considering a social justice agenda for counselling psychology in the UK'. *Counselling Psychology Review*, 28(2): 8–16.

Dodds, J. (2011) *Psychoanalysis and Ecology at the Edge of Chaos: Complexity Theory, Deleuze|Guattari, and Psychoanalysis for a Climate in Crisis*. London: Routledge.

Dodds, J. (2012) 'The ecology of phantasy: Ecopsychoanalysis and the three ecologies'. In M. J. Rust and N. Totton (eds), *Vital Signs: Psychological Responses to Ecological Crises*. London: Karnac.

Eko, M. (2012) 'Depressed individuals' relationship with nature: An interpretative phenomenological analysis account'. Unpublished doctoral thesis, University of Surrey.

Ersahin, Z. (2013) 'The elephant in the room: Implications of the ongoing conflict between religion and science and what pluralism offers working with the (in)visible'. *Counselling Psychology Review*, 28(2): 39–54.

Evernden, N. (1985) *The Natural Alien: Humankind and Environment*. Toronto: Toronto University Press.

Favali, V. and Milton, M. (2010) 'Disabled horseriders' experience of horse-riding: Exploring the therapeutic benefits of contact with animals'. *Existential Analysis*, 21(2): 251–262.

Fredrickson, L. and Anderson, D. (1999) 'A qualitative exploration of the wilderness experience as a source of spiritual inspiration'. *Journal of Environmental Psychology*, 19(1): 21–39.

Freud, S. (1961) *The Future of an Illusion*. New York: Hogarth Press.

Frumkin, H. (2001) 'Beyond toxicity: Human health and the natural environment'. *American Journal of Preventive Medicine*, 20(3): 234–238.

Gatersleben, B. (2008) 'Humans and nature: 10 useful findings from environmental psychology research'. *Counselling Psychology Review*, 23(2): 24–34.

Gillies, F. and Milton, M. (2007) 'From biology to being'. *Journal of the Society for Existential Analysis*, 18(2): 247–260.

Glendinning, C. (1995) 'Technology, trauma and the wild'. In T. Roszak, M. E. Gomes and A. D. Kanner (eds), *Ecopsychology: Restoring the Earth, Healing the Mind*. San Francisco, CA: Sierra Club Books.

Gore, A. (2006) *An Inconvenient Truth: The Planetary Emergency of Global Warming and What We Can Do about It*. New York: Rodale.

Greenwood, A. (2014a) 'Let's go outside! Restoration amongst adolescents and the impact of friends and phones'. Unpublished doctoral paper, University of Surrey.

Greenwood, A. (2014b) 'Picturesque and peaceful or disagreeable and difficult? A grounded theory exploration of teenagers' experience of natural environments'. Unpublished doctoral paper, University of Surrey.

Griffiths, J. (2006) *Wild: An Elemental Journey*. New York: Jeremy P. Tarcher: Penguin.

Hagerhall, C. M. (2000) 'Clustering predictors of landscape preferences in the traditional Swedish cultural landscape: Prospect-refuge, mystery, age and management'. *Journal of Environmental Psychology*, 20(1): 83–90.

Hamilton, C. (2004) *Growth Fetish*. London: Pluto Press.

Hartig, T., Mang, M. and Evans, G. W. (1991) 'Restorative effects of natural-environment experiences'. *Environment and Behavior*, 23: 3–26.

Health and Care Professions Council (HCPC) (2012) *Standards of Proficiency: Practitioner Psychologists*. London: HCPC.

Hendryx, M. and Innes-Wimsatt, K. A. (2013) 'Increased risk of depression for people living in coal mining areas of Central Appalachia'. *Ecopsychology*, 5(3): 179–187.

Hicks, C. (2008) 'Vox-pop: Dr Colin Hicks'. *Counselling Psychology Review*, 23(2): 7–8.

Higley, N. (2008) 'Psychoanalysis and the current environmental crisis: Its part of the problem and its potential contribution to bettering our relationship with "mother" Earth'. Unpublished doctoral paper, University of Surrey.

Higley, N. (2009) 'Connectedness to nature explored: An IPA analysis of people's experiences of their ecological self'. Unpublished doctoral thesis, University of Surrey.

Higley, N. and Milton, M. (2008) 'Our connection to the Earth: A neglected relationship in counselling psychology'. *Counselling Psychology Review*, 23(2): 10–23.

Hore, B. (2013) 'Is homelessness a matter of social justice for counselling psychologists in the UK? A review of the literature'. *Counselling Psychology Review*, 28(2): 17–29.

Intergovernmental Panel on Climate Change (IPCC) (2001) *Climate Change 2001: The Scientific Basis Contribution of Working Group I to the Third Assessment Report of the IPCC*. Edited by J. T. Houghton, Y. Ding, D. J. Griggs, M. Noguer, P. J. van der Linden and D. Xiaosu. Cambridge: Cambridge University Press.

Intergovernmental Panel on Climate Change (IPCC) (2014) *Climate Change 2014: Mitigation of Climate Change, IPCC Working Group III Contribution to AR5*. Retrieved on 25 April 2014 from http://mitigation2014.org.

James, O. (2007) *Affluenza*. London: Vermillion.

Jordan, M. (2005) 'The process of the vision fast: A (trans)personal journey'. Paper presented at the Transpersonal Psychology Section of the British Psychological Society, 17 September. Retrieved on 2 April 2008 from www.ecotherapy.org.uk/files/ecotherapy/home/The_vision_fast_unmarked.doc on.

Jordan, M. (2012) 'Did Lacan go camping? Psychotherapy in search of an ecological self'. In M. J. Rust and N. Totton (eds), *Vital Signs: Psychological Responses to Ecological Crises*. London: Karnac.

Jordan, M. (2014) *Nature and Therapy: Understanding Counselling and Psychotherapy in Outdoor Spaces*. Hove: Routledge.

Jordan, M. and Marshall, H. (2010) 'Taking counselling and psychotherapy outside: Destruction or enrichment of the therapeutic frame?' *European Journal of Psychotherapy and Counselling*, 12(4): 345–359.

Kagan, C. and Tindall, C. (2003) 'Feminist approaches to counselling psychology'. In R. Woolfe, W. Dryden and S. Strawbridge (eds), *Handbook of Counselling Psychology* (2nd edn). London: Sage.

Kaplan, R. (2001) 'The nature of the view from home'. *Environment and Behavior*, 33(4): 507–542.

Kaplan, R. and Kaplan, S. (1989) *The Experience of Nature*. Cambridge: Cambridge University Press.

Katcher, A. H., Friedman, E., Beck, A. M. and Lynch, J. (1983) 'Looking talking and blood pressure: The physiological consequences of interacting with the living environment'. In A. Katcher and A. Beck (eds), *New Perspective on Our Lives with Companion Animals*. Philadelphia, PA: University of Pennsylvania Press.

Kerr, M. and Key, D. (2012) 'The ecology of the unconscious'. In M. J. Rust and N. Totton (eds), *Vital Signs: Psychological Responses to Ecological Crises*. London: Karnac.

Kidner, D. W. (1994) 'Why psychology is mute about the ecological crisis'. *Environmental Ethics*, 16: 359–378.

Koger, S. (2010) 'Coping with the Deepwater Horizon disaster: An *Ecopsychology* interview with Deborah Du Nann Winter'. *Ecopsychology*, 2(4): 205–209.

Korpela, K., Hartig, T., Kaiser, F. and Fuhrer, U. (2001) 'Restorative experience and self-regulation in favorite places'. *Journal of Environmental Psychology*, 33: 572–589.

Lertzmann, R. (2008) 'The myth of apathy'. *The Ecologist*, June: 16–17.

Lofthouse, J. (2010) 'The R word'. In M. Milton (ed.), *Therapy and Beyond: Counselling Psychology Contributions to Therapeutic and Social Issues*. Chichester: Wiley-Blackwell.

Louv, R. (2006) *Last Child in the Woods: Saving Our Children from Nature-deficit Disorder*. Chapel Hill, NC: Algonquin Books.

Macdonald, K. (1995) *The Sociology of the Professions*. London: Sage.

Macfarlane, R. (2007) *The Wild Places*. London: Granta Books.

Macgregor, C. (2013) 'An existential formulation of transformative experiences in nature: Thematic findings'. Unpublished doctoral thesis, New School of Psychotherapy and Counselling, Middlesex University.

Maiteny, P. (2012) 'Longing to be human: Evolving ourselves in healing the earth'. In M. J. Rust and N. Totton (eds), *Vital Signs: Psychological Responses to Ecological Crises*. London: Karnac.

Mayer, F. S. and Frantz, C. P. (2004) 'The connectedness to nature scale: A measure of individuals' feeling in community with nature'. *Journal of Environmental Psychology*, 24: 503–515.

McCallum, I. (2007) *Ecological Intelligence: Rediscovering Ourselves in Nature*. Cape Town, SA: Africa Geographic.

McCallum, I. and Milton, M. (2008) 'In conversation: Ian McCallum'. *Counselling Psychology Review*, 23(2): 62–67.

Mest, R. (2008) 'Ecopsychology: The transformative power of home'. *The Humanistic Psychologist*, 36: 52–71.

Milton, M. (2003) 'The call of the wild: Lessons from natural history', *Counselling Psychology Review*, 18(1): 3–11.

Milton, M. (2009) 'Waking up to nature: Exploring a new direction for psychological practice'. *Ecopsychology*, 1(1): 8–13. DOI: 10.1089/eco.2008.0004.

Milton, M. (2010) 'Coming home to roost: Counselling psychology and the natural world'. In M. Milton (ed.), *Therapy and Beyond: Counselling Psychology Contributions to Therapeutic and Social Issues*. Chichester: Wiley-Blackwell.

Mind (2007) *Ecotherapy: The Green Agenda for Mental Health: Executive Summary*. London: Mind.

Mishan, J. (1996) 'Psychoanalysis and environmentalism: First thoughts'. *Psychoanalytic Psychotherapy*, 10(1): 59–70.

Moller, N. (2011) 'The identity of counselling psychology in Britain is parochial, rigid and irrelevant but diversity offers a solution'. *Counselling Psychology Review*, 26(2): 8–16.

Monbiot, G. (2013) *Feral: Searching for Enchantment on the Frontiers of Rewilding*. London: Penguin.

Moss, S. (2012) *Natural Childhood*. London: National Trust.

Nichols, W. (2014) *Blue Mind: The Surprising Science that Shows How Being near, in, on, or under Water Can Make You Happier, Healthier, More Connected, and Better at What You Do*. Boston, MA: Little, Brown & Co.

Orbach, S. (2009) *Bodies*. London: Picador.

Orians, G. H. and Heerwagen, J. H. (1992) 'Evolved responses to landscapes'. In J. H. Barkow, L. Cosmides and J. Tooby (eds), *The Adapted Mind: Evolutionary Psychology and the Generation of Culture*. New York: Oxford University Press, pp. 555–579.

Owen, J. (2008) 'A blue tit got me thinking …: Reflections on the therapeutic aspects of human–animal relationships'. *Counselling Psychology Review*, 23(2): 47–52.

Parry, G. (1996) *NHS Psychotherapy Services in England: Review of Strategic Policy*. London: NHS Executive.

Priest, P. (2007) 'The healing balm effect: Using a walking group to feel better'. *Journal of Health Psychology*, 12(1): 36–52.

Randall, R. (2005) 'A new climate for psychotherapy?' *Psychotherapy and Politics International*, 3(3): 165–179. DOI: 10.1002/ppi.7.

Randall, R. (2009) 'Loss and climate change: The cost of parallel narratives'. *Ecopsychology*, 1(3): 118–129. DOI: 10.1089/eco.20090034.

Robertson, C. (2012) 'Dangerous margins: Recovering the stem cells of the psyche'. In M. J. Rust and N. Totton (eds), *Vital Signs: Psychological Responses to Ecological Crises*. London: Karnac.

Rolston, H. (1998) 'Aesthetic experiences in forests'. *The Journal of Aesthetics and Art Criticism*, 56(2): 54–64.

Roszak, T. (1995) 'Where psyche meets Gaia'. In T. Roszak, M. E. Gomes and A. D. Kanner (eds), *Ecopsychology: Restoring the Earth, Healing the Mind*. San Francisco, CA: Sierra Club Books.

Rust, M. J. (2004) 'Ecopsychology: Seeking health in an ailing world'. *Resurgence Magazine*, February.

Rust, M. J. (2005) 'Psychotherapy for a change: From inertia to inspiration for action'. Schumacher Lecture, Totnes, October.

Rust, M. J. (2008a) 'Climate on the couch: Unconscious processes in relation to our environmental crisis'. *Psychotherapy and Politics International*, 6(3): 157–170.

Rust, M. J. (2008b) 'Nature hunger: Eating problems and consuming the earth'. *Counselling Psychology Review*, 23(2): 70–78.

Rust, M. J. (2012a) 'Introduction'. In M. J. Rust and N. Totton (eds), *Vital Signs: Psychological Responses to Ecological Crises*. London: Karnac.

Rust, M. J. (2012b) 'Ecological intimacy'. In M. J. Rust and N. Totton (eds), *Vital Signs: Psychological Responses to Ecological Crises*. London: Karnac.

Sacks, A. (2008) 'The therapeutic use of pets in private practice'. *British Journal of Psychotherapy*, 24(4): 501–521.

Sampson, V. (2012) 'The darkening quarter: An embodied exploration of a changing global climate'. In M. J. Rust and N. Totton (eds), *Vital Signs: Psychological Responses to Ecological Crises*. London: Karnac.

Samuels, A. (1993) '"I am a place": Depth psychology and environmentalism'. *British Journal of Psychotherapy*, 10(2): 211–219.

Scheiner, J. (2012) 'Spirite equus: Therapists experience of the perceived benefits of equine-assisted psychotherapy'. Doctoral portfolio, Regents University, London.

Scheiner, J. (2013) 'Spirite equus: Therapists experience of the perceived benefits of equine assisted psychotherapy'. Paper given to the International Conference on Psychology, Autism and Alzheimer's Disease, San Antonio, TX, September.

Searles, H. (1972) 'Unconscious processes in relation to the environmental crisis'. *The Psychoanalytic Review*, 59(3): 361–374.

Seligman, C. (1993) 'Ecocounselling psychology: Too little, too late?' *The Counselling Psychologist*, 21(4): 624–627.

Shepard, P. (1982) *Nature and Madness*. San Francisco, CA: Sierra Club Books.

Shillito-Clarke, C. (2008a) 'Vox-pop: Carol Shillito-Clarke'. *Counselling Psychology Review*, 23(2): 5–6.

Shillito-Clarke, C. (2008b) 'Journey into the natural world of the counselling psychologist'. *Counselling Psychology Review*, 23(2): 81–90.

Steyn, V. (2008) 'Interview: Villiers Steyn'. *Counselling Psychology Review*, 23(2): 60–61.

Strawbridge, S. (1996) 'Myth of the self-contained individual in counselling psychology'. Paper presented at the third annual conference of the BPS Division of Counselling Psychology, York.

Sustainable Development Commission (2008) *Health, Place and Nature: How Outdoor Environments Influence Health and Wellbeing: A Knowledge Base*. St Andrews: Sustainable Development Commission, University of St Andrews.

Ulstrand, S. (2002) *Savannah Lives: Animal Life and Human Evolution in Africa*. Oxford: Oxford University Press.

United Nations (1991) *Consequences of Rapid Population Growth in Developing Countries*. New York: Taylor & Francis.

Ward, C. and Styles, I. (2006) 'Evidence for the ecological self: English-speaking migrants residual link to their homeland'. *International Journal of Applied Psychoanalytic Studies*, 4: 319–332. DOI: 10.1002/aps.

Weintrobe, S. (2010) 'Engaging with climate change means engaging with our human nature'. *Ecopsychology*, 2(2): 119–120. DOI: 10.1089/ECO.2010.0041.

Wheeler, B., White, M., Stahl-Timmins, W. and Depledge, M. (2012) 'Does living by the coast improve health and wellbeing?' *Health and Place*, 18(5): 1198–1201.

Wilson, E. O. (1984) *Biophilia*. Cambridge, MA: Harvard University Press.

Winnicott, D.W. (1960) 'The theory of the parent–infant relationship'. *International Journal of Psychoanalysis*, 41: 585–595.

Wise, J. (2015) *Digging for Victory: Horticultural Therapy with Veterans for Post-traumatic Growth*. London: Karnac.

Woodcock, A. J. and Peat, J. K. (2007) *Evidence for the Increase in Asthma Worldwide*. Ciba Foundation Symposium 2006: The rising trends in asthma. Retrieved 25 April 2014 from http://onlinelibrary.wiley.com/doi/10.1002/9780470515334.ch8/summary. DOI: 10.1002/9780470515334.ch8.

Woodward, C. and Joseph, S. (2003) 'Positive change processes and post-traumatic growth in people who have experienced childhood abuse: Understanding vehicles of change'. *Psychology and Psychotherapy: Theory, Research and Practice*, 76(3): 267–283.

Wright, R. (2009) 'Conservation work: A therapeutic intervention'. *The Psychologist*, 22(2): 118–119.

SECTION V

DIFFERENT TERRITORIES

CONTENTS

The first chapter of this book introduced the idea of mapping the world of helping. A large-scale map, such as an atlas of the world, covers a lot of territory and individual countries may appear only as relatively small items. The United Kingdom, for example, will be represented by a tiny space on such a map. However, if for example we want to go walking or sightseeing in the Lake District, an atlas of the world is not of much use. A different scale of map is required. This section of the book responds to that need by highlighting the specific territories in which counselling psychologists operate.

If we pursue the idea of scale a little further, there is a limit to the detail that can be encapsulated in 7,000 words. Hence what each chapter offers is something more detailed than a map of the world but inevitably less than could be included in a whole book on its subject.

In a sense, each chapter offers a framework of its respective field; a kind of guide towards further exploration. If you like the analogy of mapping, stay with the Lake District (for most people a pleasant experience) and think of each chapter as being equivalent to describing a different area of the National Park but not as a detailed guide to footpaths for walking up or climbing Helvellyn, which is the third highest mountain in England.

As a reader you may relate to the respective territories in a variety of ways and may gain particular types of benefit. For example, for the individual in training, each chapter offers a flavour of what involvement in that field is like. This might impact upon decisions about career choice. Others may be familiar with or have experience of a particular territory and for them the chapter may have more of an updating or continuing professional development function. Yet others may find it helpful and interesting to find out more about the work of colleagues in cognate fields.

Taken overall, what the section reveals is the breadth of activity in which counselling psychologists have an interest. Added to the previous section, which focuses on newer developments, it would be difficult to identify a psychological field of activity in which counselling psychologists are not involved.

The section contains nine chapters and twelve authors. Each author brings their own particular slant to their subject matter. Some write primarily as practitioners while for others their perspective is rooted in their academic and research experience. This raises the question of whether there is anything that links these chapters together. Does each stand in isolation or can we identify common issues which transcend more than one field? Arguably, the one factor that does emerge is the importance of inter-professional collaboration with colleagues from a wide variety of professions. This reflects the spirit of the age in which we live and the reality of professional practice as it exists at the present time.

24

COUNSELLING PSYCHOLOGY AND ITS INTERNATIONAL DIMENSIONS

PAMELA JAMES

INTRODUCTION

The title of this chapter began a period of reflection for me, initially about two related concepts: firstly, the discipline of counselling psychology itself and, secondly, its relationship with the perspective of internationalism. It's almost as though this reflection is facilitated by imagining a world view and seeing if there are counselling psychology 'hot spots' across the globe. Why should this discipline occur in different countries, and why might counselling psychologists be interested in this concept, either for their practice and research, or for their own professional development?

A consideration of these questions, when trained and working in England, suggests that this chapter author needs to be vigilant regarding 'decentring', aiming to avoid possible criticisms of only viewing an issue through one's own culture and country. This chapter aims to provoke thought about the emergence of the discipline in other countries across the world. For example, did this come about as a result of the interaction between socio-political and academic factors in that country itself, or did one country influence another by learning about research, practice and application? These musings are perhaps of academic interest, and those of you who take a pragmatic view might be frustrated and wish to move forward with the application of the discipline, so that people who need psychological help might receive it.

The concept of internationalism and the discipline of counselling psychology suggest the proposal of two hypotheses. Firstly, the emergence hypothesis: why and how did the discipline emerge? For the United Kingdom (UK) the answer to these questions is well furnished by Woolfe and Strawbridge (2010). In addition, I am noting that in the UK the discipline emerged in the context of:

the Western perspective on the development of the self, acknowledging how learnt experience can affect responses to perceived distress;

the need to examine both old and current relationships between philosophy and psychology;

revisiting the philosophy that states that knowing about a person involves talking to them and hearing their perspective located in context;

seeing the person in the context of their relationships in their family and community groups;

seeing the person in the context of the historical perspectives of their current presenting issue, rather than accepting psychopathology. (Douglas and James, 2013)

When these factors are considered, the following question can arise: Did counselling psychology emerge in other parts of the world, influenced by the same factors, or was there a copying or emulating process of one country by another (the influence hypothesis) whereby another applied psychology (counselling psychology) was born? Alternatively, were both these processes simultaneously occurring in interaction? Later in the chapter we look at other countries and try to furnish some answers. Furthermore, the advantages of a country taking an active stance in pursuing an 'international strategy' will be considered.

THE RATIONALE FOR INTERNATIONALISM: WHY AND FOR WHAT PURPOSE?

Perhaps another question that might be asked is why a discipline should look to its international perspectives. Interestingly, counselling psychology is represented in many other countries outside the UK, each having its origins, histories, developmental differences and philosophical variants. Looking beyond the shoreline of one country to learn about other countries' research, application to practice, contextual and cultural settings must surely enlarge the knowledge base.

Yet it's almost as though interest in international perspectives on this discipline is currently growing. Reasons to explain this upsurge perhaps lie in the expansion of electronic communications which enable the spread of research papers and developments in practice. Telecommunications now permit instant conversations across the globe. From a world peace perspective, there is a need to learn as much as possible about the way in which other nations lead their lives and manage their resulting pain and distress, and the facilitation of living in a manageable way. Is this sufficient for an interest in international perspectives? In the writing of this chapter I would suggest that an emerging answer is perhaps more complex.

Orlans and Van Scoyoc's text in 2009 gave a wide and encompassing discussion of different countries where counselling psychology either exists as a regulated profession (UK, Ireland, USA, Canada, Australia, New Zealand, Hong Kong, Korea and South Africa), or non-regulated as in Japan, Israel, India, China, Portugal, France and Greece. They also draw attention to counselling psychology being awarded division status in the International Association of Applied Psychologists (IAAP) in 2002.

The countries approached by the author, as discussed in the initial part of this chapter, were those with which I had experienced some professional contact. However, I was mindful of this orientation towards the West (with the exception of Australia). Later in the chapter, when I began to reflect on the concept of globalisation, I was aware that maybe counselling psychology in its 'Western form' was perhaps not a directly transferable discipline.

FIVE COUNTRIES

The five countries approached have had associations with current colleagues in UK counselling psychology in recent years. It was hoped that some arising themes and issues might have universal applicability in the profession's research and practice.

1. When did counselling psychology emerge as a discipline in your country? That is, how long ago? What was the reason for its development? Was there influence from other countries? How many counselling psychologists are there now?
2. Now that counselling psychology exists as a discipline in your country, what is its philosophy and training programme? Which psychological theories underpin the practice? Are there state regulators to observe?
3. Are there any current focal areas of interest for research?
4. Where do counselling psychologists practise?
5. What would you describe as the current challenges for the discipline in your country?
6. From your perspective, what do you think are the advantages of international connections?

From Denmark

In Denmark, counselling psychology is in an embryonic form. In 2011, four counselling psychologists from the UK were invited by Syddansk University, Odense, to introduce Counselling Psychology into their university system. In 2011 and 2012, a series of lectures were given over a three-week period; since 2013, one counselling psychologist now remains as the consultant to this Danish University. The following has been contributed with acknowledgements to Mogens Horder, Kaya Roessler (from Syddansk University) and Ray Woolfe.

> Counselling Psychology in Denmark is still in its infancy and there is as yet no profession as such. However, there is interest in the discipline and the major centre for this development is at the Institute of Psychology at the University of Southern Denmark (Syddansk University) based at Odense. The subject is now an established module within the undergraduate psychology programme (Bachelormodule 06). This is located within the Faculty of Health Sciences.

The origins of this development lay in the Institute's desire to widen the philosophical base of its psychology degree beyond narrow definitions of scientific method and to this end decided to introduce a more humanistic element into its psychology programme. It invited a number of counselling psychologists from the United Kingdom to teach and thus to assist in this process. The programme has now run for three years and has become a well-established part of the psychology course. While still a small part of the whole degree, the intention is to build upon this development by introducing more humanistic elements into other modules within the programme. With its emphasis on integration and pluralism, counselling psychology fits well with the broadly based emphasis of the psychology programme. Such a move, with its humanistic emphasis, would parallel the position within the counselling (as opposed to psychology) sector in Denmark which, as Dixon and Holland Hanson (2010) point out, is 'historically focussed on phenomenological … approaches' (p. 38).

After five years' study, students receive a masters (doctoral) degree and the Institute intends that the fourth year and upwards will be based upon an internship (placement) in an appropriate setting within the community. This is likely to be within the area of health, including psychiatry, somatic medicine and psychotherapy. In addition, a variety of school and work settings will also be involved.

The Faculty has a strong research base, particularly in the fields of trauma research and pain management, and is thus well placed to assist students with their dissertations and to build upon the expertise in qualitative methods which already exists within the Institute of Psychology. The focus of research projects is likely to reside within the area of health.

In the longer run, there is the possibility of moving beyond the present stage of development in which counselling psychology is seen as a vehicle for bringing a philosophically informed humanistic and existential approach to the psychology programme. This would involve using the internship as a framework for developing the discipline into a more formal programme of advanced and possibly accredited training. Either way, it would seem important to expand the teaching of counselling psychology beyond its present geographical base into other institutions. The Universities of Copenhagen and Aarhus are particularly important. Were a more formal training programme to emerge, it could potentially result in a situation not unlike that in the United Kingdom, in which counselling psychology finds a recognised place, not as a competitor, but existing alongside the well-established profession of clinical psychology. Whereas the latter is largely based within the psychiatric sector in Denmark, the opportunity for counselling psychology, as in the UK, lies in demonstrating its relevance across fields such as the workplace, schools, prisons and the wider community sector in addition to health. Professional status for counselling psychology is still some way away but the seeds of a profession are being sown at the University of Southern Denmark.

From Ireland

Connolly et al. (2014) provide much detail about counselling psychology in Ireland. From the sources considered, it seems that there is evidence to suggest that both the emergence and influence hypotheses are occurring. It would seem that there is less focus on the underlying philosophy and epistemology as a driver for discipline development.

Currently, there are two professional bodies, the Psychology Society of Ireland (PSI) (accredits courses in the south of Ireland). There are no training courses in Northern Ireland, and counselling psychologists train entirely or partially in Great Britain to become BPS accredited.

In replying to my questions posed above, Ladislav Timulak (from Trinity College Dublin, TCD) described some milestones in its development and its current position in the Psychology Society of Ireland (PSI):

1987: Formation of the 'Counselling and Therapy Interest Group' (CTIG) within PSI.

1989: First Postgraduate Training Programme in Counselling Psychology commenced at TCD. There are now Programmes in University College Dublin and in University College Cork.

1994: Special Interest Group established in PSI; in 1995 renamed *Counselling Psychology SIG*.

1997: PSI Division Status received; there was a strong influence from the UK, informed by counselling psychology, counselling and psychotherapy. Currently, TCD's Programme has more than 300 graduates.

Timulak goes on to say that there is state regulation, similar to the Health and Care Professions Council (HCPC) in the UK. The register of psychologists, however, is not open yet. Practice areas are similar to the UK's National Health Service (NHS); its Irish equivalent is the Health Service Executive (HSE), i.e. hospitals, clinics, primary care services. Other areas include: HSE's National Counselling Service, student counselling services, prison services, schools (in limited numbers as it is mainly the domain of educational psychology) and private practice.

Areas of research include: the development of emotion-focused therapy for a variety of presenting problems, online interventions, outcome assessment in routine practice, lesbian, gay, bisexual and transpersonal (LGBT) and other diversity issues, supervision, therapists' development and self-care, and childhood abuse.

Timulak comments on some of the political aspects that are deemed to affect the recruitment of counselling psychologists, in that the recruitment in the national health provider HSE, as on the advice of a small number of clinical psychologists in senior positions, does not allow counselling psychologists to apply for the majority of HSE psychology posts, limiting these to clinical psychologists. PSI condemned such practices and tries to actively address this situation; it is in communication with the HSE about the issue, which was brought to the Commission for Public Service Appointment. However, the practice remains unchanged (although at the time of writing this chapter, HSE committed to review its recruitment criteria). The issue is perhaps more complicated given that clinical psychology training is currently funded by the HSE, while counselling psychology training is not.

The biggest advantage of international dialogue comes from the countries where counselling psychology is firmly established and has a long history (currently, perhaps only the USA meets fully this criterion, although recent developments in the UK are welcomed), as they can be inspiring, particularly if we also want to firmly place counselling psychology in the public health service provision.

Apart from political reasons, the main area is the development of the discipline by treating counselling psychologists as one community of professionals. Clear benefit is in the publication of research, as seen in the international journal *Counselling Psychology Quarterly*, co-edited by Timulak.

From Greece

Malikiosi-Loizos and Giovazolias (2013) explain that the discipline of counselling psychology is young and developing. In 1984, the first psychology department in higher education was formed; in 1992–1993, separate disciplines of counselling and counselling psychology were recognised. The Hellenic Psychological Society was established in 1991 and by 1999 the first of ten divisions were formed, namely the Division of Counselling Psychology. The authors give the probable explanation for the discipline's slow growth as that Greece is a collective society, where the extended family has strong family loyalties. As Western counselling psychology holds the facilitation of the individual at its centre, there may be some cultural incongruence.

Notwithstanding, there is now a Masters in Counselling Psychology associated with the Universities of Athens and Thrace. Those Greek students who seek a doctorate study in the UK and the USA. Within the British Psychology Society Division of Counselling Psychology (as from 2013) there is now an Interest Network Group of Greek Counselling Psychologists, some of whom are UK qualified and some are trainees. In the past few years, UK counselling psychologists have been invited to Greece to give lectures and workshops to Kapodistrian University, Athens, and a keynote address at Aristotle University, Thessaloniki, in 2012.

From Australia

Michael Di Mattia, Chair of the Australian Psychological Society's (APS), College of Counselling Psychologists (2011–2015), writes that the term 'counselling psychology' was first officially used in discussion at the APS in 1970. The Rose Committee report (Rose, 1971) was the first attempt to define the training and roles of counselling psychologists. The early definition of counselling psychology came about through a need to establish something different from clinical psychology. Grant et al. (2008) note that the Rose Committee discussed the need to reach all sectors of the population, requiring specialist training in psychological assessment, diagnosis and therapy. The distinctiveness of counselling psychology was presented as being to assist all people in society, not only those in a clinical setting, but also those living in the community requiring psychological therapy. A few years later, in 1976, the Division of Counselling Psychologists of the APS was formally established. In 1983 the Division became the Board of

Counselling Psychologists, with the current title of College of Counselling Psychologists introduced in 1993 (currently 1,119 members).

The College's competencies document provides a thorough overview of the skills and competencies covered in postgraduate counselling psychology programmes in Australia (they are available at: https://groups.psychology.org.au/Assets/Files/Counselling%20Psychologists%20Competencies%20-%20December%202012.pdf).

All psychology programmes (undergraduate and postgraduate) are regulated and accredited by the Australian Psychology Accreditation Council (APAC) (more information on APAC can be found at: www.psychologycouncil.org.au/).

Reported research in counselling psychology is broad, reflecting the diverse nature in which counselling psychologists practise. A common feature is a focus on process and outcome variables in counselling and psychotherapy.

Over 50 per cent of counselling psychologists work in private practice. Other common areas of employment include community health centres, community counselling agencies, non-government organisations (NGOs), government departments, tertiary education (often in university counselling services), schools (primary and secondary), hospitals and employee assistance programmes (EAPs).

The current challenge for counselling psychology is the ongoing survival of training programmes. In recent years, since the introduction of rebated psychological services in Medicare (Australia's health system) in 2006, which created a two-tier model – one rebate for clinical psychologists and all other psychologists classed as general psychologists on a lower rebate – there has been an increase of students choosing to study clinical psychology, as this is more financially lucrative. While clinical psychology programmes have expanded, counselling psychology programmes and other applied areas of psychology are seeing programmes close. At the beginning of 2014, there were five postgraduate programmes; this year two have closed, leaving only three counselling psychology programmes in the country, with subsequent reduced opportunities for training.

The advantages of international connections for the individual counselling psychologist include a sharing of research and practice-based issues. It is important for the discipline to develop an identity of counselling psychology that is universally consistent.

From America

Orlans and van Scoyoc (2009) describe the origins of counselling psychology in the USA, which involves antecedents before the confirmation of the name Counseling Psychology, Division 17 in the American Psychological Association (APA) 1956. Societal changes in the USA at this time included the civil rights movement, the Vietnam War, the rise of feminism and the demands of a variety of cultural and social groups who were not or were underrepresented.

In 2003, Division 17 Counseling Psychology was renamed as the Society for Counseling Psychology, although it is frequently referred to as Division 17, and the main thrust of their issues has been the emphasis of promoting the needs of underrepresented social groups and to facilitate counselling psychologists as leaders who are learning partners/learning leaders. There is an expressed need to work with, while remaining distinct from, clinical psychology.

Forrest (2010) wrote in her presidential address (APA: Division 17 President 2008–2009) that she wanted to push ahead to internationalise counseling psychology and promote a movement to identify and codify standards of professional competence. She writes (Forrest, 2010: 97) that Douce's APA, Division 17 Presidential Project in 2004 'focussed on a paradigm shift in counseling psychology, challenged [the] Eurocentric knowledge base, questioned its applicability to clients and psychologists in other parts of the world, and raised concerns about the domination of English as the language of psychology'.

In the last two years, following the BPS Division of Counselling Psychology Conference at Leicester where Dr Barry Chung, APA Division 17 President between 2012 and 2013, gave an invited keynote address ('Counselling Psychology: The Natural Home for the Celebration of Minorities'), there has been an interchange between the APA Division 17 and BPS UK Counselling Psychology. In August 2013, the BPS Vice-Chair of Counselling Psychology attended the APA Conference in Honolulu, where he gave a presentation on cultural aspects of supervision. In 2014, the Chair-Elect BPS Counselling Psychology met with the Chair of the APA Division 17, Sharon L. Bowman, where they discussed her presidential theme 'counseling psychology in action: conversations, collaborations and commitments to change' and how DCoP and Division 17 could move forward in a collaborative manner. The Chair-Elect outlined her plans for the year and hopes for the future of the Division. A further meeting was held with the newly elected APA Division 17 Chair, Michael Mobley, whose presidential themes include engagement, empowering youth and integrative behavioural mental health. It is expected that the relationship between DCoP and Division 17 will continue to develop and grow with future collaborative projects already underway.

SOCIAL JUSTICE AND SOCIAL INCLUSION

The concept of social justice describes the realisation of people's potential in the society in which they live. This transferable concept has meaning for all minority groups (whether described by gender, ethnicity, sexuality, religion or other defining identities) in all countries. Consequently, in my view, social justice is one of the dimensions of internationalism. From the USA, Toporek et al. (2006) includes chapters wherein counselling psychologists focus on being active participants in changing systems that constrain clients' ability to function. This emphasis on social justice is depicted in Dr Barry Chung's keynote speech in Leicester BPS Counselling Psychology Conference in 2012, where he articulated the promotion of facilitating minority and underrepresented groups both within and without the USA. On reflection, did Dr Chung's keynote invite UK counselling psychologists to consider in what way these themes were represented in their own policies and practices? Non-discrimination is intrinsic to the beliefs and values of counselling psychology, yet perhaps the introduction of more proactivity is currently occurring, with resulting political resonance.

For example, in response to UK Black and Asian counselling psychologists, an interest group of this name was formed in 2012. Objectives of the Black and Asian Counselling Psychology Group (BACPG) include increasing the number of Black and Asian counselling psychologists and thus to the diversity of The Society (BPS). The concept of social inclusion is further depicted by the BPS Division of Counselling Psychology's recent strategy document, *Towards a Culture and Diversity Strategy within and across Ethnic Minorities* (British Psychological Society, 2013). In this document, social justice and social inclusion principles are translated into action with regards to practice, research, supervision, continuing professional development, and to be intrinsic to the Division's work.

Conference organisation further evidences an active stance. A BPS Cross-divisional conference on 'Therapeutic Interventions: Action not Words' was held in October 2013 at the BPS offices in London. A follow-up conference will be held on the topic 'Negotiating Multiple Identities' in October 2014. In the same month, the North West Branch of DCoP is organising a conference entitled: 'Social Justice: Towards a Model of Personal and Collective Empowerment'.

Cutts (2013) considers what a 'social justice agenda' might mean for counselling psychology in the UK. Social justice generally focuses on equity or equality for individuals in society in terms of:

> access to a number of different resources and opportunities, the right to self-determination; or autonomy and participation in decision-making, freedom from oppression, and a balancing of power across society. (Cutts, 2013: 8)

Cutts introduces the literature in the area of social justice within counselling psychology which comes from the USA. Finally, she considers more explicitly what a consistent adoption of a social justice perspective would look like for UK counselling psychology by reviewing three areas of potential consideration: training issues; involvement in private practice; and involvement in the NHS.

GLOBALISATION: STRATEGIES AND POLICIES

Globalisation as a concept is not synonymous with internationalism, although the two are related. Conceptually, for example, an ideology, a belief or a product can begin in one country and then be spread across the globe. Yet there is a naïvety perhaps in that this 'export' will have the same meaning and use that it had in its place of origin. The reader is asked to bear this in mind while considering the globalisation of counselling psychology.

The Globalization Special Task Group (GSTG) is Professor Barry Chung's initiative. It aims to examine the impact that globalisation is having on psychology through the creation of world-wide cooperation networks and the development of new international knowledge.

Kannellakis and Wood (2013) write about the GSTG. Kannellakis attended the APA Convention on behalf of BPS UK Counselling Psychology in 2012. They say that globalisation could affect the activities of the BPS UK Counselling Psychology Division in the following ways:

- memoranda of understanding with the counselling psychology divisions/sections of other psychological societies, along the lines that the BPS has already done at corporate level;
- updating their webpage, noting in conferences, in their journal (CPR), in research awards and grant applications;
- noting in training curricula and CPD and setting up projects, secondments, visits and joint conferences.

In summary, almost in the same way that cultural awareness should become an integral stand of the discipline, so should globalisation and internationalism. Furthermore, increased globalisation creates the need to make it possible for psychologists to work across countries, so transferable qualifications and common standards are sought.

In the BPS President's column, Mallows (2013) draws attention to the International Union of Psychological Science (IUPsyS), which meets quadrennially. He stated that there needs to be a presidential level of attendance. He noted that the President of IUPsyS, Saths Cooper, was elected a BPS Honorary Fellow at this year's AGM, thus strengthening links with international psychology and also with South Africa. In this letter, Mallows (2013) also noted the need for the BPS to have an international policy.

Linked with this, the BPS is considering its international strategy. At the Professional Practice Board in October 2013 it was recommended that a small task force be convened to address some of the complex issues arising in the creation of an international strategy with five overarching aims which are designed to begin to shape up the international initiative. These include the signing of memoranda of understanding between countries and promoting psychology through existing organisations, such as the World Health Organization and the European Federation of Psychologists' Associations. The focal points of action turn around research through collaborative activity, practice through knowledge exchange and the application to assist psychologically in areas of international concern, such as disasters and environmental change.

Mallows' letter (as above) triggered a response from Martin (2013), who noted the advantages of bringing together psychologists from different divisions and groupings, as experienced in the APA's Convention. Here, input focused on research and clinical input around such issues as 'sexual trauma in military personnel, treating children and spouses of the military in addition to the welfare of veterans, as well as asking bigger questions about the origins of conflict' (Martin, 2013: 707). The point is that although there is a Division of Military Psychology, the approach was asking the much more inclusive question: What can the whole of psychology's output say about this enduring phenomenon in human affairs?

Hence the shift occurs from a particular perspective, i.e. counselling psychology, to a multi-psychological perspective, and if other related professionals are included, then even wider. There are conflating strands here:

- focusing on the issue itself and taking a multi-professional stance;
- further enhancing a knowledge base for the issue, by taking an international perspective. If there was a three-dimensional image, where the issue was the focus, then a 360-degree global view would occur.

However, Gilbert (2006) writes that there needs to be a critical awareness regarding the globalisation of mental health. In her article, she refers to the generic term 'counselling' as meaning one-to-one talking therapies. She invites the reader to beware of the export of counselling from North American/European cultures to those where individualism and the concept of the self are not so described, i.e. there is a collective sense of people in 'community'. For example, Omonzejele (2004) speaks of the self in interrelationship, as expressed in an African perspective which would embody the importance of community links, i.e. 'we' in the location of 'I', where perceptions of I (self) are always viewed as connected to 'we' (self in community). This interplay between self and community is further embellished by the movement of people across countries and cultures, whereby someone who is born into a family may be brought up in a country where the predominant culture differs from that of the family of origin.

EMERGENCE, INFLUENCE, GLOBALISATION AND OFFERING AID

On looking at the countries where counselling psychology is established, it would appear that there is some evidence to support an emergence hypothesis, which is commonly described as a wish to work from a humanistic-valuing base. America and Australia describe the need for distinctiveness from clinical psychology, while the latter explains that it is struggling to maintain the discipline in the face of competition with clinical psychology. America, on the other hand, is vigorous in its promotion of social justice. Where the discipline is more developed, this will no doubt have an influence on less developed systems.

In Greece it is suggested that the network of the extended family may restrain individual freedoms, while in Africa the emphasis of the community collective is of focal importance. Leach et al. (2003) write that the 40-year history of counselling psychology in South Africa is associated with the context in which it has emerged, namely racial struggles and HIV/Aids. They urge connection with community needs. More recently, Pretorius (2012) makes a plea for the work of the psychologist to be more focused on community-based applications and less on one-to-one contexts (see also Chapters 20 and 22 in this volume).

Silove (2013) focuses on working with the 'collective' as the response by mental health workers to distress in countries where the sense of the self is expressed more in terms of links with community others rather than as an individual. He puts forward the Adapt model, which describes five pillars underpinning human communities, namely safety and security, bonds and networks, justice, roles and identities and existential meaning. When these are disrupted by mass conflict and displacement, as for example in the last decade in Iraq and Syria, then the model provides a framework that considers both collective and individual responses to a disruption of each of these pillars.

Offering aid is an essential inclusion in the international dimension. Here counselling psychologists have entered Eastern countries, often after there have been wars and natural disasters. Professor Rachel Tribe's contribution has been extensive in this area, and her published articles depict her work as:

- offering support and therapy to aid workers in Sierra Leone, Afghanistan, Iraq and Sri Lanka;
- working with people post-conflict and post-tsunami in Sri Lanka – see, for example, Tribe (2007), where she comments on the appropriateness of Western psychology in this context, as the relationship between culture and its healing rituals is complex;
- working with the mental health needs of asylum seekers and refugees – Tribe and Patel (2007) not only consider the application of psychological work to help people who have been persecuted and tortured, but the further dimension of psychologists' own stance on human rights is raised;
- working with interpreters in Culture and Mental Health – Tribe and Lane (2009) provide guidelines to assist this task, including being aware of the possible effects on the interpreter, and being aware that so much is communicated not only by the language itself but also by the particular cultural and contextual information.

 Visit the companion website to watch two videos on Counselling Psychology and its International Dimensions.

REFLECTIONS ARISING FROM INTERNATIONAL DIMENSIONS

On the discipline itself

This chapter has considered the *emergence* hypothesis within each country, the effect of *influence* of one country on another regarding training and application, and the *bringing* of the discipline into a country when there is a perceived need from conflict and disaster. There is a difference between countries in the emphasis of the inclusion of philosophy, as depicted by epistemology. Is the discipline stronger when depicted in this way, when compared with a description that is based on psychology together with theories of therapy in application? I would argue yes, the rationale being that this results in the entwining of psychology, philosophy and psychotherapy, and makes it distinctive. Counselling psychology needs to be distinctive as it has disciplines that press on its boundaries and blur its identity. Without a firm understanding of the roots of the discipline, it would only be a subject in application, whereby its actions (i.e. workings of the named professional) were so similar to those of another discipline that they are imperceptible.

Furthermore, perhaps one of the developmental aspects of America's Division 17's influence of social justice may be an enlargement of the role of counselling psychology.

While retaining its place as a profession that strives to enhance well-being, in the celebration of minority groups and their facilitation, is counselling psychology now taking on a political role as an agent of change in whichever social milieu it is located?

Has an exploration of international dimensions of the discipline illustrated its transferability and adaptability to work in cultures and countries where the *collective response* (e.g. to disaster) is embedded? This could be seen as developmental in terms of adapting and responding to people across context, cultures and countries. I acknowledge countries that have *not* been explored in this chapter, for example, India, Russia and China; also the inclusion of ways of working *coming from* the East, namely mindfulness.

On the counselling psychologist

Training courses across countries show similarity and difference. The differences lie mainly in emphasis on epistemology, range of included theories of therapy and cultural emphasis. These differences are part of the difficulties with accrediting a person from one country by another. There are strong efforts being made to see how a counselling psychologist trained in one country can work in another. For example, counselling psychologists who were trained in Australia or America were able to become HCPC-registered during the grand-parenting phase, which finished in June 2013, allowing them to work in the UK. There are procedures that are necessary for those going from the UK to work outside this country. The European Federation of Psychologists Association is working to gain transferability across European countries. Its website describes the EuroPsy qualification and Training Standards for psychologists specialising in psychotherapy. The British Psychological Society is currently working to see how it can accredit training in other countries. Currently, there are no universal standards for the profession, and this is similar in many other professions (e.g. nursing and medicine).

The regulation of the profession within its own country marks its acknowledgment in formal systems where the discipline has been longer established. Common training standards and syllabi across countries would assist passage and movement of the professionals concerned. However, without such structures counselling psychologists adapt their training to work with people from different cultures. Yet Wilk (2014) points out that there is little or no research to provide evidence to support how and with what outcomes this process entails. The article also brings to attention that as ethnic groups migrate across the globe, a counselling psychologist could have a multi-ethnic case load, while working in a Western country.

On the clients and their presenting issues

How can the client be helped to return to well-being? It is almost as though clients' presenting issues are now seen in terms of individuality, universality and cultural variation. The sharing of research and practice takes on a real meaning. Consider working with life-experience issues such as loss and bereavement in a Western culture as compared with working in the East or in Africa. Gilbert (2006) focuses on the socialisation of the individual as having different perspectives: where the former sees the self as predominantly individual; the other two cultures associate well-being as prioritising connection with others. For example, Von Peter (2009) writes that in working with trauma post-tsunami, the Eastern emphasis is on collective mourning, and the self is seen through the action of rebuilding towns and villages. Balanced against this is the range of cross-over when travelling between cultures, creating an overlay between the socialisation effect of growing up in the East and then living in the West. An international dimension now throws open many such questions. The extent of research studies is now almost infinite, in terms of seeking how practice might be enhanced.

Internationally focused research opens the door to the concept of universality regarding how people in different countries experience well-being and psychological distress. Marsella (2009) has written about this concept, showing its complexity. He asks the reader to celebrate life's diversity. Forrest (personal communication, 2014) wonders if the cultural variation in human response to distress may be one of the most emerging aspects of future study arising from the international sharing of research. Furthermore, decisions made by academic boards regarding the status of a journal consider its international connections as paramount. Several journals exist to furnish such input, for example the *European Journal of Counselling Psychology* and *Counselling Psychology Quarterly*, while other journals have International Issues, for example *Counselling Psychology Review*.

On matters of ongoing questioning and reflection

While globalisation shows advantages for the discipline in terms of establishing working relationships, care and caution is necessary in transferring one particular way of working to another country.

Watters (2010) writes about the influence on mental health by North American perspectives. He puts forward examples of the ways in which this has occurred in Hong Kong, Zanzibar, Japan and Sri Lanka. In Sri Lanka, Watters writes on the basis of evidence from those working there after the tsunami in 2004, when approximately 30,000 people were described (using the concept of psychopathology) as having post-traumatic stress disorder (PTSD). Western mental health workers noticed a lack of the wish to engage in Western one-to-one therapy. On closer examination, Watters writes that 'those who continued to suffer long after a horrible experience were those who had become isolated from social networks or who were not fulfilling their role in kinship groups' (Watters, 2010: 100). He also describes how meaning-making involves religious systems which are often not given consideration by Western mental health workers. These themes have been expressed by Moodley and West (2005), who consider healing in many non-Western countries, where there is often a long history involving spirituality, divinity, the supernatural and religion. These concepts are also individually relevant in Western cultures, but not so predominantly as in the country *itself* (see, for example, Aboriginal or Chinese healing practices). The subjective experience of the other will allow for communication and understanding, yet the concept of working towards healing through the talking process may need to be accommodated to see this as, at best, a genuine encounter.

The underlying valuing system of counselling psychology facilitates practice with diversity. With the increased spread of the discipline across the globe, the question arises of whether that value system is challenged when working in a culture that purports, for example, arranged marriage, religious intolerance or lack of opportunity for education for both genders.

Sparked by experiences of working with people with different ethnic backgrounds, questions can be posed about the universality of the human condition in distress. For example, is belongingness central to being human, but the response to rejection and alienation different, depending on individual differences of which ethnicity and its cultural connection plays a major part? Transferability of practice in the framework of the discipline's philosophy means counselling psychology is well placed to research and contribute to its knowledge base, which comprises study from other applied psychologists and related professionals.

REFERENCES

British Psychological Society (BPS) (2013) *Towards a Cultural and Diversity Strategy within and across Ethnic Minorities*. Leicester: BPS Publications.

Connolly, A., O'Callaghan, D., O'Brien, O., Broderick, J., Long, C. and O'Grady, I. (2014) The development of counselling psychology in Ireland. *The Irish Psychologist*, 35(1): 16–24.

Cutts, L.A. (2013) Considering a social justice agenda for counselling psychology in the UK. *Counselling Psychology Review*, 28(2): 8–16.

Dixon, A.L. and Holland Hansen, N. (2010) Fortid, nutid, fremtid (past, present, future): Professional counseling in Denmark. *Journal of Counseling and Development*, 88: 38–42.

Douglas, B. and James, P.E. (2013) *Common Presenting Issues in Psychotherapeutic Practice*. London: Sage.

Forrest, L. (2010) Linking international psychology, professional competence, and leadership: Counseling psychologists as learning partners. *The Counseling Psychologist*, 38(1): 96–120.

Gilbert, J. (2006) Cultural imperialism revisited: Counselling and globalisation. *International Journal of Critical Psychology*, Special issue: Critical Psychology in Africa, 17: 10–28.

Grant, J., Mullings, B. and Denham, G. (2008) Counselling psychology in Australia: Past, present and future – part one. *Australian Journal of Counselling Psychology*, 9(2): 3–14.

Kanellakis, P. and Wood, K. (2013) The Globalisation Special Task Group at the 2012 American Psychological Association Annual Convention: Recommendations for action. *Counselling Psychology Review*, 28(1): 93–94.

Leach, M.M., Akhurst, J. and Basson, C. (2003) Counseling psychology in South Africa: Current political and professional challenges and future promise. *The Counseling Psychologist*, 31: 619–640.

Malikiosi-Loizos, M. and Giovazolias, T. (2013) Counseling in Greece: Current status and future directions. In T. Hohenshil, N. Amundson and S. Niles (eds), *Counseling around the World: An International Handbook* (pp. 215–223). Alexandria, VA: American Counseling Association.

Mallows, R. (2013) Presidents column. *The Psychologist*, 26(8): 586.

Marsella, A.J. (2009) Diversity in a global era: The context and consequences of differences. *Counselling Psychology Quarterly*, 22(1): 119–135.

Martin, P. (2013) Making the most of divisions. *The Psychologist*, 26(10): 707.

Moodley, R. and West, W. (eds) (2005) *Integrating Traditional Healing Practices into Counselling and Psychotherapy*. Thousand Oaks, CA, London, New Delhi: Sage.

Omonzejele, P.F. (2004). Mental health care in African traditional medicine and society: A philosophical appraisal. *Eubios Journal of Asian and International Bioethics*, 14: 165–169.

Orlans, V. and van Scoyoc, S. (2009) *A Short Introduction to Counselling Psychology*. London: Sage.

Pretorious, G. (2012) Reflections on the scope of practice in the South Africa profession of psychology: A moral plea for relevance and a future vision. *South Africa Journal of Psychology*, 42(4): 509–521.

Rose, D.E. (1971) *The Professional Training of Counselling Psychologists*. Report of Standing Committee on Training. Melbourne: Australian Psychological Society.

Silove, D. (2013) The ADAPT model: A conceptual framework for mental health and psychosocial programming in post conflict settings. *Intervention*, 11(3): 237–248.

Toporek, R.L., Gerstein, L.H., Fouad, N.A., Roysircar, G.S. and Israel, T. (eds) (2006) *Handbook for Social Justice in Counseling Psychology: Leadership, Vision, & Action*. Thousand Oaks, CA: Sage.

Tribe R. (2007) Health pluralism: A more appropriate alternative to western models of therapy in the context of the conflict and natural disaster in Sri Lanka? *Journal of Refugee Studies*, 20(1): 21–36.

Tribe, R. and Lane, P. (2009) Working with interpreters across language and culture in mental health. *Journal of Mental Health*, 18(3): 233–241.

Tribe R. and Patel, N. (2007) Refugees and asylum seekers. *The Psychologist*, 20(3): 149–151.

Von Peter, S. (2009) The concept of mental trauma and its transcultural application. *Anthropology and Medicine*, 16(1): 13–25.

Watters, E. (2010) *Crazy Like Us: The Globalisation of the American Psyche*. New York: Free Press (a division of Simon & Schuster Inc.).

New York Wilk, K. (2014) Using a pluralistic approach in counselling psychology and psychotherapy practice with diverse clients: Explorations into cultural and religious responsiveness within a western paradigm. *Counselling Psychology Review*, 291(1): 16–28.

Woolfe, R. and Strawbridge, S. (2010) Counselling psychology: Origins, developments and challenges. In R. Woolfe, S. Strawbridge, B. Douglas and W. Dryden (eds), *Handbook of Counselling Psychology* (3rd edn). London: Sage.

25
THERAPEUTIC WORK WITH CHILDREN
GAIL SINITSKY

INTRODUCTION

Counselling psychology's position in the field of child and family work is evolving dynamically and historical discourses about the absence of a role of counselling psychology within child and family work have gradually began to 'seep into the practice-related experiences of trainees' and qualified counselling psychologists (Sinitsky, 2010: 55). These discourses have been evident in the challenges that trainees have experienced in obtaining child and family placements, and in the inconsistencies in the extent to which this field is promoted within training courses. Eager to establish a career having qualified, counselling psychologists have faced further disappointment as they experience the lack of jobs open to them within child and adolescent mental health services. However, in the words of Bob Dylan, the times they are a-changing. In 2011, Young Work, a Division of Counselling Psychology networking group, was formed, with the aim of challenging these discourses and promoting the profession's presence in this area. Training institutions are demonstrating a greater focus on children, young people and families in their courses; counselling psychologists are increasingly obtaining work in child and adolescent services; and a specialist Young Work learning event celebrated the significant contribution that counselling psychologists make in this field.

Counselling psychologists engage with children and families experiencing an array of complex and adverse bio-psycho-social issues: trauma, abuse, domestic violence, poverty, loss, substance misuse, physical illness and mental health problems. We offer humanistic and constructivist lenses through which children and their families can make sense of their experiences and rediscover stories that are helpful and empowering. In practice, this translates to therapeutic relationships in which children and their families feel safe and valued, a focus in the work on subjective and socially constructed meaning, and recognition of strengths and resources. Moreover, counselling psychologists offer theoretically grounded, child-centred and creative therapies to harness positive emotions and promote children's capacity to deal with and recover from adversity (Hutchinson and Pretelt, 2010).

In writing this chapter, I have aimed to offer an insight into this contribution and to illustrate some of the many opportunities and complexities involved in therapeutic work with children and adolescents. In doing so, I hope that readers will be encouraged and inspired to contribute to this growing field.

CONTEXT

To contextualise this chapter, it may be helpful for readers to have an overview of the structure of mental health services for children, adolescents and families. Child and adolescent mental health services (CAMHS) are predominantly provided by the NHS, although there are also an increasing number of community-based services provided by not-for-profit organisations. A common framework for conceptualising and organising these services is known as the 'tier' system. Accordingly, services are organised within a structure of four tiers in order to account for and respond to the range of difficulties that children and adolescents experience.

Tier 1 offers 'universal' services, provided by non-mental health specialists, that is professionals including GPs, health visitors and school nurses. Tier 1 services focus on mental health promotion and early identification, and offer onward referrals where necessary. Tier 2 professionals (for example, psychologists, and speech and language therapists) often work within community and primary care settings. These services are often accessed by children, young people and families who are experiencing complex mental health difficulties, often co-existing with social difficulties. Tier 3 services provide specialist, multi-disciplinary input to children and young people with more severe and persistent needs. These services are traditionally underpinned by a medicalised view of mental health difficulties. Tier 4 specialist services include intensive community services and inpatient units for children and young people who are at greatest risk of harm (for example, significant self-harm or suicide).

Despite this seemingly unambiguous structure, the boundaries and thresholds of services are nuanced. Often children and young people do not fall neatly into this structure; they may, for example, require simultaneous input from different services. Moreover, many tier 2 and tier 3 services in England are currently transforming their delivery of care, through the adoption of the Children and Young People's Improving Access to Psychological Therapies programme (CYP IAPT), leading to further changes in referral thresholds and the types of treatment provided across different services.

Counselling psychologists may be employed in various services within this structure, and my own experiences may reflect those of many other counselling psychologists specialising in work with children and young people. My experiences have included: offering integrative psychological therapies to children, young people, parents and families at a child and family therapy charity; facilitating school-based therapeutic groups for children; providing specialist psychological input to children and adolescents with complex needs in a Tier 3 NHS service; and providing teaching and training to professionals working with children and families. As such, this chapter presents my reflections of the work of counselling psychologists through a collection of 'snapshots' of my own experiences of working therapeutically with children and adolescents.

CHAPTER OVERVIEW

The chapter is structured into five 'themes' that represent pertinent and at times challenging clinical issues experienced by counselling psychologists working with children and young people. For the purpose of concision, the terms 'child' and 'children' will be used throughout the chapter to represent any person aged 0 to 18 years. Further, readers are asked to interpret the term 'parent' in this chapter as any adult who holds responsibilities as parent/carer/guardian for a child. The first theme, *conceptualising 'the child'*, considers the meaning of the term 'children', with reference to varying socio-cultural ideas. The second theme, *negotiating ethics*, covers some challenges in clinical decision-making. The third theme, *child-centred communication*, emphasises the importance of going beyond verbal language as a therapeutic tool. Working to *safeguard children* constitutes the fourth theme and the complexities involved are discussed. The final theme focuses on counselling psychologists' *professional identity*.

THEME 1: CONCEPTUALISING 'THE CHILD'

Take a few moments and consider the concept of 'the child'. What images, words, phrases, or ideas spring to your mind? Perhaps words such as these: innocent, cute, naughty, cheeky, dependent, obedient, vulnerable, strong, commercialised, protected, independent. Perhaps you are drawn to well-known phrases such as 'better seen and not heard'. Or you may be struck by the proliferation of media images depicting children living in contrasting worlds: consumerism and technological sophistication at one end and famine and deprivation at another.

Our notions of childhood and children are varied and nuanced, and are largely culture-bound. The way in which we make sense of childhood is influenced by personal, social, economic, political and cultural factors (Das Gupta, 2004; Hendrick, 1990). The varying ways in which children have been regarded and treated in the UK over the last few centuries is reflective of this social construction of childhood. Children of the Victorian era were widely regarded as physically capable and as economic assets – a stark contrast to the contemporary notion that children are in fact very expensive to raise. Significant economic hardship and extreme poverty were the reality for many families in the nineteenth century, and children were expected to contribute financially by working in factories and mines, often for very long hours and in dangerous conditions.

In contrast, children of today are regarded as vulnerable and worthy of protection. Childhood labour is no longer an acceptable phenomenon. In its place, social campaigns and legal frameworks have been established to protect children from the very same conditions that were once socially accepted and expected. This movement towards protecting children can be mapped across changes to the law that have occurred over the past century or so (such as the Children Act 1989/2004) and the establishment of organisations promoting the safety of children, such as NSPCC and Barnados. In fact, children of today hold an especially valued place in society, as they are regarded as society's most precious resource. The following quote, taken from The National Service Framework for Children, Young People and Maternity Services, depicts children as 'the future':

> Children and young people are important. They are the living message we send to a time we will not see; nothing matters more to families than the health, welfare and future success of their children. They deserve the best care because they are the life-blood of the nation and are vital for our future economic survival and prosperity. (Department of Health, 2004: 4)

This ideal pervades our culture. For example, the 2012 Olympic motto was 'inspire a generation' and involved seven young aspiring athletes lighting the Olympic cauldron, symbolising the value that children hold as future ambassadors of society. Moreover, the last few decades have been marked by a growing ideology of a child-centred society in which children are empowered, their autonomy is valued, and their rights are treated as paramount (United Nations Convention on the Rights of the Child, 1989). Nonetheless, implicit within this commitment to cherish and protect children is an assumption that children are not fully capable of looking after their own interests and safety. This is a legally supported position: children must reach the age of at least 16 years before they are entitled to make decisions that impact on their lives, decisions such as starting a family, enlisting in the Army and political voting. Before this, children are expected to live, be educated and flourish in an adult-centred world in which their own best interests are in fact promoted by others. The concepts of 'autonomy' and 'independence' are thus underpinned by a sense of ambivalence and confusion regarding the rights of children.

Conceptions of children and childhood in the UK are ever changing. The boundaries between these different conceptions blur and competing definitions of what it means to be a child may exist simultaneously. The increasingly ethnically diverse population in the UK (Office for National Statistics, 2011) leads to further cultural nuances and variations in the ways in which children are regarded in the twenty-first century. Communities that emphasise the collectivist value of interdependence may struggle with the current drive to promote children's autonomy and independence. Communities experiencing poverty may greatly value their children's economic contributions despite the mainstream ideal of further and higher education. In addition, differences in parenting ideologies – such as the extent to which parents maintain physical closeness with their child or set strict boundaries – are underpinned by cultural beliefs about children and the processes by which they develop and flourish. Graham Music highlights the 'extraordinary richness of cultural diversity' (Music, 2010: 81) in the ways in which children are reared, represented and conceptualised around the world.

For counselling psychologists working with children and adolescents, the clinical implications of these culture-bound constructions of children and childhood are vast. The ideas and values held about children and young people impact on how we engage and work with them. A socio-political ideal of children as 'the future' may, for example, have implications for how therapy effectiveness is measured, with service objectives linked to future-orientated outcomes associated with children's social adjustment and academic achievement.

In the following example, a parent adopts a view of her daughter as subordinate, which leads to a prescriptive approach demanding that the child thinks and acts in particular ways, as defined by the adult.

Joyce and her 12-year-old daughter Grace came to see me because they had been arguing a lot. Joyce thought Grace was becoming increasingly defiant, and Grace felt sad as she felt her mum criticised her a lot. We agreed to do some work with the goal of improving their relationship. Joyce would begin each session by saying, 'Grace, tell Gail what you did this week so she can tell you what you've done wrong'. She would also spend much of the session recounting to Grace the kinds of behaviour she expected of her and often say, 'Isn't that right, Gail?'

I felt I was being pulled into being an arbiter of rules and I felt uncomfortable with this. In addition, Grace told me she felt her mum constantly lectured and criticised her, and I was mindful that I could replicate this. Values of autonomy and independence are central in my work with children and I would usually approach these kinds of parent/child tensions by attending to all perspectives and providing space for both the child and parent to reflect on and negotiate behaviours. The arbiter role I felt Joyce wanted me to fulfil was at odds with my approach, but it was clear that it was very important to her. In exploring this dilemma with both Joyce and Grace, we considered the family's cultural belief system that adults hold great responsibilities to guide children down the right path and that children prosper and flourish through strict guidance. This helped us to reach a shared understanding of Joyce's compassion and concern for her daughter's future, as well as Grace's growing independence, and helped to strengthen the bond between them.

Being aware of our own and our clients' ideas about the relationship between adults and children helps to make sense of therapy impasses in which therapists and clients hold somewhat conflicting beliefs and ideals. We can be reminded of the importance of being transparent about our roles and our work with families. Remaining reflective on our own perspectives enables us to remain client-centred, to be open to difference and to hold varying competing ideas in mind. This enables us to work effectively by working alongside our clients.

Consider your responses to the question posed at the start of this section. What assumptions do you make about children and their families? Neimeyer (1998) suggested that 'socially constructed practice will enhance our reflexivity and creativity as helping professionals' (Neimeyer, 1998: 147). A social constructionist approach challenges the idea that there is an objective, true definition of 'children', and places such definitions in the context of human exchange. That is, people's ideas of what it means to be a child will be influenced by cultural, political, social and economic ideas. This may be a particularly valuable approach when working with children and families. Taking a position of reflexivity encourages us to be curious about our own and our clients' constructions of childhood and how they may be shaping clients' experiences. Moreover, this approach helps us to negotiate with our clients the construction of additional and alternative narratives about children and their families, narratives that may be empowering and may take into account their experience in the social world (White, 1995). Readers are invited to keep in mind this approach when reading the following sections.

THEME 2: NEGOTIATING ETHICS

Negotiating ethics is an inevitable part of working therapeutically with children. There are clear guiding codes of conduct (e.g. British Psychological Society, 2009) but it is a complex area and, in practice, counselling psychologists regularly face dilemmas relating to aspects such as autonomy, confidentiality, discrimination, and harm (Daniels and Jenkins, 2010). This section reflects on children's entitlement to make decisions about their therapy – whether they attend, who is involved, what it involves, and so on.

As the previous section highlighted, there exists in contemporary UK society an assumption about the vulnerability and dependency of children, and many child mental health services operate to a greater or lesser extent in accordance with this idea. There is a tendency, for example, to invite adults to take the lead in the referral process. Marketing materials about counselling and therapy is largely targeted at the adult population, and access to child psychologists often requires transport to centres (or money, in the case of private services) for which younger children rely on parents. There are certainly realistic reasons for this: parents have a responsibility to ensure the well-being of their children, and children (particularly those of a young age) are physically dependent on their parents. Of course, some services do provide child-friendly materials and resources, and there are a number of child-accessible psychological services, for example, in schools or online. Yet, children most often arrive at the doors of counselling psychologists having been referred by adults in their lives, and they may have a number of requests:

- 'Can I have therapy even if my mum and dad decide they don't want me to?'
- 'I don't want to come to therapy – do I have to?'
- 'Will you promise not to tell my parents what I say in sessions?'
- 'Can I see you alone? I don't want my parents/brothers/sisters to be there.'

Offering inclusive, sensitive, and ethically sound responses to these requests involves a thoughtful consideration of several complex factors. A child's developmental stage is one such factor. 'Gillick competency' refers to a commonly applied set of principles used to determine a child's developmental capacity for making informed decisions about treatment (Department of Health, 2008). In order to be judged sufficiently competent, children must demonstrate intellectual and emotional maturity as well as an ability to understand the difficulties they are experiencing, the risks and benefits associated with the proposed treatment, and any future implications of their decision. 'Gillick competency' is often related to children's developmental stage rather than their chronological age. However, children under 12 are usually judged not to demonstrate such competency, and parents (or those with parental responsibility) would be authorised to make decisions about therapy. Yet, what makes sense from a 'Gillick competency' perspective may not necessarily make therapeutic sense.

Nine-year-old Kevin had been the victim of severe bullying at school. His mother had been concerned about the effects it might have on his confidence and referred him for therapy. After a consultation with Kevin and his mother, we agreed to six sessions of individual therapy applying a narrative approach. The sessions involved a variety of play and arts interventions aimed at: developing Kevin's recognition of his strengths and resources through the identification of 'unique outcomes'; enhancing his feelings of competency and worthiness through externalisation of his 'inner critic'; and providing strategies to help him deal with future instances of bullying.

After a few sessions, I noticed that Kevin did not seem to engage meaningfully in the activities and I had an overwhelming sense that he was acquiescing to the tasks in order to please me. When I gently reflected this to him, Kevin was able to let me know that he did not want to come to these therapy sessions. I invited Kevin's mother to join us for the next session in order to explore this issue. It transpired that the bullying had involved Kevin being ordered by his peers to do things he felt extremely uncomfortable with, but did not feel able to say no to. It seemed this had been replicated during the consultation process: his mother and I had made big decisions about Kevin without offering him enough space to understand what therapy would involve and to communicate his feeling about it. Although Kevin was not 'Gillick competent', it made little therapeutic sense to make therapy compulsory. In fact, it was more therapeutic to end our sessions in order to provide him with an experience in which his views were listened to and respected.

Determining children's rights to make decisions about the boundaries of therapeutic work also involves a consideration of the legal framework. Daniels and Jenkins (2010) offer an overview of the legal context for decision-making for children receiving psychiatric care, highlighting that the law 'provides an uneasy mix of respecting children's autonomy ... and more coercive elements, where parental consent or a court order can override the child's refusal of necessary treatment' (Daniels and Jenkins, 2010: 144). This may be particularly relevant when working with children at significant risk, but counselling psychologists working at varying stages of interventions may face dilemmas relating to children's rights to make autonomous decisions. Children are promised a fundamental human right to express their wishes in decisions made about them and to have these wishes listened to (e.g. United Nations Convention of the Rights of the Child, 1989). Yet parents too have rights, duties, powers, responsibilities and the authority to make decisions about their children's welfare, including the treatments they receive (Children Act, 1989/2004). Decisions about therapy involve a sensitive and thoughtful negotiation with and between children and their parents. Exploration of parents' own wishes and feelings about the therapy, and an understanding of their commitment to the work, aids this negotiation. Counselling psychologists may also need to attend to tensions that arise when family members hold conflicting ideas about the nature of problems and where they are located. Further, providing therapy to a child may not be ethical (or even safe) if problems are best formulated within a systemic framework. For example, a seven-year-old child experiencing heightened levels of anxiety and school refusal may be sent for therapy to help with 'their' problem. Yet an assessment of the child's needs may draw attention to domestic abuse and the child's fear of leaving their mother alone each day. In such cases, safeguarding processes and/or parental work may precede therapy for a child.

It is not uncommon for counselling psychologists to be drawn into identifying with one member of the family over another, which can lead to prioritising one person's rights and wishes. Being aware of and reflecting on these dynamics are integral to what it means to be an ethical practitioner, and can help to facilitate a more collective approach in which all family members' rights are heard. To use a sporting analogy: it may be helpful to approach competing tensions between family members in the same way that a premiership manager may negotiate the team's formation for their next game. Team members hold varying positions, roles and responsibilities, but each forms part of the same team. With thoughtful facilitation and transparency, the family team can feel empowered to work towards their aligned goals, each member feeling that their position is valued. As in the frequent adaptation to team formations, the boundaries of work with children change frequently, and so decision-making about therapy becomes an ongoing process.

THEME 3: CHILD-CENTRED COMMUNICATION

Spoken language is a greatly valued tool within traditional adult therapy, which places an emphasis on the therapeutic benefits of verbalising one's feelings, thoughts and experiences in order to process pain and move forward. However, it has a lower profile in therapeutic work with children. Although adolescents may engage effectively in 'talking' therapies, for many children, verbal expression may be too challenging cognitively, or too intimidating, or simply too foreign. Moving beyond the verbal to incorporate, even *prioritise*, more arts- and play-based mediums of communication in therapy is important.

Freeing up children and young people to express themselves, this helps to ensure formulations and interventions are congruent with children's subjective experiences and understandings.

In practice this means many things. Expressive modes of therapy such as play (West, 1992), sand-tray (Homeyer and Sweeney, 2011) and arts (Rubin, 2005) can be applied during assessment and therapy sessions, as well as creative tools and exercises (e.g. Selekman, 2010). These all offer children a means of communicating with us their distress, their experiences and their hopes. For younger children, outcome measures could incorporate symbolic and pictorial images, as well as space for children to express their experiences of therapy using drawing, colours, stickers, and so on.

Above all, the challenge for the therapist is to let go of the expectation that children must engage in adult forms of communication. Emphasising child-centred communication in the therapy opens up avenues for work with children to be fun, playful and raw. It also offers children and young people the therapeutic medium that best suits them, and 'matching the medium with the client serves to establish the therapeutic relationship' (Homeyer and Sweeney, 2011: 2). The following case study offers a reflection on the value of play-based therapy for one child and her mother.

Child-centred communication: A case example

Seven-year-old Aysha was referred by her school to a child and family counselling and therapy service. Aysha was an only child and lived with her mother. Aysha had a complex history of early childhood trauma, which included witnessing her father abuse her mother and being placed in care for one year. Aysha had a heightened fear of abandonment. She experienced frequent nightmares, became emotionally distressed when leaving her mother for school, and had low confidence, evidenced through a great deal of negative self-talk.

Contracting the work had been a tricky process. Unsurprisingly, Aysha said very little in our consultation sessions. Her mother joined us, and while we spoke, Aysha spent the sessions drawing and using the sand-tray. I found it difficult to discern what she understood of why she was being asked to have therapy and whether she was happy to try a few sessions with me. What was evident, though, was her low self-esteem: 'I am rubbish', she shouted, throwing away a picture of a roaring lion she had drawn during the session. Following another two consultation sessions all together, Aysha felt able to see me alone and we agreed that we would do some work together, with a view to including her mother at a later date. We hoped that the therapy would provide a safe and contained space for Aysha and an opportunity to develop a non-rejecting relationship with an adult in which she experienced herself as worthy.

(Continued)

(Continued)

Aysha attended weekly sessions with me for 10 months. The sessions drew on a non-directive play therapy framework, which was underpinned by the principle that 'toys are the child's words and play is the child's language' (Homeyer and Sweeney, 2011: 19). The therapy room was child-focused, containing a variety of toys, art supplies, a doll's house and sand-tray and miniatures. Each session, Aysha was invited to choose what she wanted to do, and she frequently chose the sand-tray.

Aysha consistently selected a group of animal miniatures: a lion, a snake, cows, sheep and horses. To begin with, she buried the animals in the sand. Sometimes she simply buried them and then would move on to another toy in the room. Other times, she buried the animals and then invited me into a game of hide-and-seek. As the sessions progressed, Aysha's focus changed. She stopped burying the animals and started to act out interactions between them. There would often be an aggressor (usually the lion) that hit the other animals and threw them out of the sand-tray. Once thrown out, they would not be allowed to return. After several sessions, I noticed increasingly more gentle interaction between the animals. Occasionally, the lion returned and threw the animals out, but the animals would always return to the sand-tray and reconcile.

The sand-tray offered a vehicle for Aysha to express her feelings, experiences and relationships metaphorically and symbolically. In doing so, the sand-tray process offered me information about Aysha's possible feelings and hopes and dreams, information which I could tentatively use to consider how our relationship could help her to overcome the pain she had been feeling. Aysha once told me 'I wish I was an animal'. I wondered whether she had been trying to 'bury' her feelings, or if the aggressor and other animals signified her family and the destructive relationship she had witnessed which had preceded her being placed into care. I wondered too if the aggressor represented her own feelings of anger towards her parents for the rejection she had felt. I recognised the importance of being consistent and accepting, so that Aysha could feel able to express her feelings without the fear of being rejected. Most importantly, I realised the importance of being able to offer her a 'respite from the captivity of pain and chaos' (Homeyer and Sweeney, 2011: 3) and a non-judgemental space that moved the focus away from the verbal to the symbolic.

At the end of therapy, Aysha and her mother reported that she no longer experienced frequent nightmares and that she felt more confident to do things without her mother. Indeed, this was demonstrated in her capacity to build a trusting and warm relationship with me. Most striking to me, though, was Aysha's shift in the way she felt about herself. In our last few sessions together, Aysha spent less time using the sand-tray and increasingly more time with arts materials – making cards, collages, drawings. At the end of each session, she would hold her creation close to her heart, a sense of pride emanating. This was a wonderful change to see in a girl who had destroyed her work several months previously.

THEME 4: SAFEGUARDING

'Safeguarding children – the action we take to promote the welfare of children and protect them from harm – is everyone's responsibility. Everyone who comes into contact with children and families has a role to play' (Department for Education, 2013: 7). Indeed, counselling psychologists are an integral part of this system that works towards assuring children's human right to be protected from harm and abuse (United Nations Convention on the Rights of the Child, 1989). Yet, safeguarding children (see Boxes 25.1 and 25.2) is a complex process, often fraught with anxiety and an often seemingly endless list of 'what ifs'. Working with child abuse challenges some of our basic beliefs about the world and forces us to confront our own experiences of being parented and of parenting, as well as our values and beliefs about abuse and abusive practices. Indeed, there are varying (and often competing) cultural norms relating to the ways in which children are talked to, treated and disciplined. Negotiating our way through this cultural diversity, while maintaining children's safety, can be difficult. Moreover, the media spotlight on children who have tragically slipped through the child protection net – children like Victoria Climbié and Peter Connelly – can instil in us a heightened sense of anxiety and fear, making us suspicious and overly cautious in our work.

Deciding what to do in the face of a safeguarding concern – who to talk to, what information to obtain, whether to make a referral to social services – is a complex process. Breaking client confidentiality to share information with a family member or another professional can create ripples in an otherwise strong therapeutic alliance. Clients for whom trust is an already fragile act may experience this particularly painfully. Yet maintaining confidentiality can leave a child at risk of harm. Counselling psychologists are well placed to negotiate these safeguarding dilemmas and processes, not least because of their primary focus on the therapeutic relationship. There can be no greater guidance for finding our way through the safeguarding maze than the child itself. Sadly, the failure to listen to the voice of the child has been highlighted as a recurrent theme in the analysis of serious case reviews into children who have been seriously harmed or who have died at the hands of an abusive parent (Ofsted, 2011). Importantly, with our humanistic philosophies and skills, we are able to develop relationships with children and young people in which they feel safe, listened to, and taken seriously. At times, this must involve acting on our duty to ensure children are safe, as well as conveying to them through such actions that their well-being is paramount.

Safeguarding children is not straightforward and can involve a multitude of tasks, from direct assessment, formulation and intervention work, to conducting research into child abuse, and evaluating policies and procedures (British Psychological Society, 2007). There exist various avenues of support for counselling psychologists, including supervision and training. Readers are also encouraged to refer to the various policy and legal frameworks for further insight into the complexities and processes involved in safeguarding children. These include the Children Act (1989/2004), which emphasises children's welfare as paramount, and the government policy *Working Together to Safeguard Children* (Department for Education, 2013), which offers guidance about what constitutes abuse as well as procedures and best practice.

Box 25.1   Safeguarding: A definition

1. Protecting children from maltreatment;
2. Preventing impairment of children's health or development;
3. Ensuring that children grow up in circumstances consistent with the provision of safe and effective care; and
4. Taking action to enable all children to have the best outcomes.

(Department of Education, 2013)

Box 25.2   Safeguarding: Some statistics

- 1 in 5 children today in the UK have experienced serious physical abuse, sexual abuse or severe physical or emotional neglect at some point in their lifetime.
- 12% of under 11s, 18% of 11–17s and 24% of 18–24s have been exposed to domestic abuse between adults in their homes during childhood.
- Children with disabilities are at greater risk of abuse and neglect.
- For every 1 child subject to a child protection plan, another 8 children are estimated to have suffered maltreatment.

(Harker et al., 2013; Radford et al., 2011)

Before moving on to the final section, readers are invited to consider the following safeguarding examples.

Box 25.3   Safeguarding: An exercise

The following statements represent examples of safeguarding issues faced by counselling psychologists. Imagine you are working with the child/family and consider:

- How concerned would you be for the child/children?
- What information would you need to inform your response?
- What challenges might you experience in working with this case?

1. A 12-year-old boy tells you his father has threatened to punch him and he often hears him swearing at his mother.
2. A single mother of two children under 5 discloses that she has been drinking 'a few glasses of wine' every night after the children are in bed.

3. A 14-year-old girl arrives at her next session distraught because her parents punished her for smoking by cutting her much-loved long hair.
4. A mother battling with PTSD tells you she hits her 18-month son's hand whenever he 'throws a tantrum'.

THEME 5: PROFESSIONAL IDENTITY

Counselling psychologists' work with children exists in the context of a larger picture, myriad colours and contrasts denoting various professionals in their lives, among them: teachers, health visitors, social workers, support workers, psychiatrists, speech and language therapists, pediatricians. Multi-agency working is integral to practising ethically and safely, and it offers a holistic approach to promoting well-being as well as more streamlined services (Department for Education, 2013). To return to our sporting metaphor, working with children and families requires us to 'assemble a squad and use the bench' in order to ensure a better outcome and greater support (Gaffney, 2010: 8).

Counselling psychologists' dual heritage – with roots in both the behavioural science and phenomenological paradigms – translates to a capacity to contribute in varied and multiple ways to this multi-professional and multi-agency network. With our 'scientist practitioner' heritage, we are committed to drawing upon and contributing to the wider knowledge base. We offer in-depth, multi-faceted psychological formulations that take into account a range of bio-psycho-social factors. We are also in a position to enhance professionals' understandings of the experiences of children through teaching and training, offering consultation and conducting child-centred, scientifically grounded research (e.g. Karlsen et al., 2014). Significantly, counselling psychologists often apply such psychological knowledge and theory in ways that reflect a shift from a focus on pathology and objectivity towards a focus on strength and subjectivity. Indeed, we often work in services underpinned by the 'medical model' of distress and change, and so, drawing on our phenomenological and constructionist philosophies, we can offer our colleagues – as well as the children, young people and families with whom we work – alternative discourses to reflect and draw upon.

Undoubtedly, counselling psychologists hold a valuable and unique position within the multi-professional network. However, it has been argued that counselling psychology as a profession faces a crisis of identity (Corrie and Callahan, 2000). Counselling psychologists hold a variety of roles and responsibilities within this field of work, which are held together by the philosophies underpinning the profession: the emphasis on clients' values, beliefs and experiences; the search for subjective understanding and meaning; and the positioning of the therapeutic relationship as central to the therapeutic task (Strawbridge and Woolfe, 2003).

Yet, it can be challenging at times to hold on to these values and maintain a sense of professional identity. For example, in the current cost-effective and payment-by-results culture, counselling psychologists are being driven to apply objective criteria as a means of demonstrating effectiveness. The capacity to work with the psycho-social-economic complexities that children and families bring to therapy is increasingly being limited by the changing scope of services, with many services adapting to funders' expectations for particular service delivery models, such as CYP IAPT. These changes place pressure on counselling psychologists who may struggle with the incongruency between their values and their work. Nonetheless, counselling psychologists are harnessing their passion, skills and professional values and are increasingly getting involved in the field of child and family work.

CONCLUSION

This chapter highlighted five key clinical issues that counselling psychologists may experience in their work with children and young people. These themes remind us of the importance of reflecting on the conceptions we hold about children, as well as thinking carefully about our responsibilities and the ethics that are integral to therapeutic work with children and young people. This work is as rewarding as it is challenging. It offers meaningful opportunities to make long-term difference to people's lives, facilitating the development of resilience so that children can feel empowered to face the challenges they may experience in life. Constructing alternative narratives and strengthening family relationships are among the many ways counselling psychologists help children and those closest to them. With this comes various challenges, not least the challenge of bearing the pain, risk and adversity that many children face. It is important to look after ourselves, to recognise these challenges as they occur and to draw on the experience and support of our colleagues and supervisors. Above all, it is a privilege to work with children and families, to be offered an insight into their rich and diverse worlds and to be part of their journeys towards health and well-being.

 Visit the companion website to watch Working in a Child and Adolescent Setting.

REFERENCES

Acts of Parliament (1989). *Children Act 1989* (c. 41). London: The Stationery Office.
Acts of Parliament (2004). *Children Act 2004* (c. 41). London: The Stationery Office.
British Psychological Society (2007). *Child Protection: Position Paper*. Leicester: BPS.
British Psychological Society (2009). *Code of Ethics and Conduct: Guidance Published by the Ethics Committee of the British Psychological Society*. Leicester: BPS.

Corrie, S. and Callahan, M. M. (2000). A review of the scientist-practitioner model: Reflections on its potential contribution to counselling psychology within the context of current health care trends. *British Journal of Medical Psychology*, 73, 413–427.

Daniels, D. and Jenkins, P. (2010). *Therapy with Children: Children's Rights, Confidentiality and the Law* (2nd edn). London: Sage.

Das Gupta, P. (2004). Images of childhood and theories of development. In J. Oates (ed.), *The Foundations of Child Development*. Oxford: Blackwell Publishing.

Department of Health (2004). *Core Document: National Service Framework for Children, Young People and Maternity Services*. London: The Stationery Office.

Department of Health (2008). *Mental Health Act 1983: Code of Practice*. London: The Stationery Office.

Department for Education (2013). *Working Together to Safeguard Children: A Guide to Inter-agency Working to Safeguard and Promote the Welfare of Children*. London: The Stationery Office.

Gaffney, P. (2010). The teenage psychotherapy first XI: On learning from the beautiful game. *Counselling Psychology Review*, 25, 6–12.

Harker, L., Jütte, S., Murphy, T., Bentley, H., Miller, P. and Fitch, K. (2013). *How Safe are Our Children?* London: NSPCC.

Hendrick, H. (1990). Constructions and reconstructions of British childhood: An interpretative survey, 1800 to present. In A. James and A. Prout (eds), *Constructing and Reconstructing Childhood: Contemporary Issues in the Sociological Study of Childhood*. London: Falmer Press.

Homeyer, L. E. and Sweeney, D. S. (2011). *Sandtray Therapy: A Practical Manual* (2nd edn). London: Routledge.

Hutchinson, J. and Pretelt, V. (2010). Building resources and resilience: Why we should think about positive emotions when working with children, their families and their schools. *Counselling Psychology Review*, 25, 20–27.

Karlsen, M. L., Coyle, A. and Williams, E. (2014). 'They never listen': Towards a grounded theory of the role played by trusted adults in the spiritual lives of children. *Mental Health, Religion and Culture*, 17(3), 297–312.

Music, G. (2010). *Nurturing Natures: Attachment and Children's Emotional, Social and Brain Development*. London: Taylor & Francis.

Neimeyer, R. A. (1998). Social constructionism in the counselling context. *Counselling Psychology Quarterly*, 11, 135–149.

Office for National Statistics (2011). *Census: Aggregate Data (England and Wales)* [computer file]. UK Data Service Census Support. Retrieved on 28 April 2014 from http://infuse.mimas.ac.uk.

Ofsted (2011). *The Voice of the Child: Learning Lessons from Serious Case Reviews. A Thematic Report of Ofsted's Evaluation of Serious Case Reviews from 1 April to 30 September 2010*. Manchester: Ofsted.

Radford, L., Corral, S., Bradley, C., Fisher, H., Bassett, C., Howat, N. and Collishaw, S. (2011). *Child Abuse and Neglect in the UK Today*. London: NSPCC.

Rubin, J. A. (2005). *Child Art Therapy*. Hoboken, NJ: John Wiley & Sons.

Selekman, M. D. (2010). *Collaborative Brief Therapy with Children*. New York: Guilford Press.

Sinitsky, G. (2010). A trainee's experiences of counselling psychology's contribution to therapeutic work with children and adolescents. *Counselling Psychology Review*, 25, 52–56.

Strawbridge, S. and Woolfe, R. (2003). Counselling psychology in context. In R. Woolfe, W. Dryden and S. Strawbridge (eds), *Handbook of Counselling Psychology* (2nd edn) (pp. 3–21). London: Sage.

United Nations (1989). United Nations Convention on the Rights of the Child. Available at: www.unicef.org/crc/ (accessed 28 April 2014).

West, J. (1992). *Child-centred Play Therapy*. London: Edward Arnold.

White, M. (1995). *Re-authoring Lives*. Adelaide, South Australia: Dulwich Centre Publications.

26
COUNSELLING PSYCHOLOGY IN EDUCATIONAL SETTINGS
DEE DANCHEV

INTRODUCTION

This chapter aims to familiarise counselling psychologists with the practice of counselling psychology in education. It will give a sense of what such work involves and will provide the basic information that counselling psychologists would need to prepare for an interview for a placement or job in this setting.

Counselling psychologists (CPs) will be very aware that many of the issues that underlie adult mental health problems have their origins in childhood experiences. The mental health of children and young people is a matter of national concern (Cole, 2006; Doward, 2014) and there are currently calls for a more consistent well-funded mental health provision for this age group. A parliamentary select committee is enquiring into these matters and will publish its findings when it has concluded its investigations.

Gosline (2008) observes that early intervention with children at risk of mental health disorders can make a lasting difference to their lives. Yet child mental health services have not been well-funded and there has been a paucity of expertise in this field. There has also understandably been a reluctance to refer children to the NHS mental health system because of concerns about labelling and possible stigmatisation. I would like to argue that the best and most natural place to provide psychological support to children and young people is in their educational setting. In this environment, where they are seen by teachers and lecturers on a daily basis, depressed, anxious or troubled children and young people may be more readily identified. The increasing understanding of the importance of early intervention (Allen 2011a, 2011b; Walter et al., 2011) adds to the argument that this is an ideal setting for the location of counselling and psychological services. Bor et al. (2002) emphasise the need to move away from viewing dysfunction in individual terms and to work systemically with the family, school and social context of the child. The educational setting provides opportunities to work with all these dimensions.

CPs have an excellent range of skills that make them well suited to working in schools, further education (FE) colleges and universities. With their doctoral level training and psychological understanding, CPs can provide additional breadth and depth. Being trained in more than one theoretical orientation gives practitioners a flexible and critical approach to their work that is ideally suited to short-term settings. They are also adept at thinking systemically and understanding organisational dynamics. CPs based in educational settings can provide support and interventions at an early stage before issues become chronic. This setting also has the advantage of not being within the medical system. Problems do not have to be serious for a referral to be made and students are not subjected to diagnostic labels. Moreover, CPs can engage in preventative work with students and staff to achieve a more psychologically aware and healthy environment within the educational institution. Schools, FE colleges and universities are ideal settings to provide preventative and timely therapeutic work for children, young people and adults. This is a field that counselling psychologists should consider.

At present there are not many CPs working in this setting. However, there is increasing interest by CPs in work with children and young people and an active, engaged Division of Counselling Psychology (DCoP) interest group called Young Work has been formed (www. bps.org.uk/networks-and-communities/member-networks/division-counselling-psychology/young-work-london). Most people providing therapeutic work in education are counsellors rather than psychologists. Jobs are usually advertised on the universities' website (www.jobs.ac.uk) and may also be found on the British Psychological Society (BPS) and British Association for Counselling and Psychotherapy (BACP) websites (www.bps.org.uk; www.bacp.co.uk/jobs). The range of skills needed by CPs include competence in: therapeutic work with children and young people; time-limited therapeutic work; groupwork; and referral and liaison. While there is good job satisfaction in working in schools, there is not much in terms of career progression. In FE colleges and universities there are opportunities to progress to senior counsellor, head of service and director of student services. A CV that includes placements or jobs with mental health experience, counselling in an organisation and counselling in an educational setting is likely to increase the probability of securing an interview for paid employment.

THE DEVELOPMENT OF COUNSELLING IN EDUCATION

Counselling in education is comparatively new. The first endeavours in the field of school counselling occurred in the 1970s and were pioneered by Tony Bolger, a counselling psychologist who had had a previous career as an educational psychologist in Tasmania. On his return to the UK he started a DASE (Diploma in the Advanced Study of Education) course in counselling at Keele University and students on this course had placements in local Staffordshire schools (Bolger, 1985). This venture contributed to a brief expansion of counselling provision in these schools but this unfortunately dwindled by the 1980s.

Undeterred, Bolger pursued the establishment of postgraduate counselling courses at Keele and a similar development occurred at the University of Reading. Slowly from the late 1980s postgraduate counselling trainings became established in many universities. Some students taking these courses were teachers who were seeking to understand more about their pupils' problems and to provide effective support. Other counselling students obtained placements in schools and, having established their usefulness, were employed as counsellors in their schools after qualification.

In recent years there has been a resurgence in school counselling. Baginsky (2004), Collishaw (2009), Jenkins and Polat (2005), and Leach (2008) cite several factors for this expansion, which are: an increase in administrative duties for teachers with an allied reduction in time for pastoral care; a decline in the mental health of young children; an increase in behavioural difficulties; and a recognition that professional support is needed. It is estimated that almost three-quarters of secondary schools in England and Wales are providing therapeutic individual counselling (Jenkins and Polat, 2005). However, recent reductions in mental health funding, resulting in cuts to child and adolescent mental health services (CAMHS), have raised concerns about the provision of counselling in schools (O'Hara, 2014). Young Minds (a charity committed to improving the emotional well-being and mental health of children and young people) reports that many local authorities have reduced their CAMHS budget (Young Minds, 2014). This has resulted in reduced support available to schools and a greater focus on severe mental illness. At present, school counselling is organised on a local basis. Counselling sessions are likely to be less than 50 minutes as 30 minutes has been found to work well with the attention span of children and young people (Baginsky, 2004). For a comprehensive account of the range of interventions and brief forms of work that are effective with school children see Bor et al. (2002) and Lines (2006).

Three patterns of provision predominate in schools:

- Teachers who have had some counselling training provide counselling/pastoral care.
- The school employs a counsellor. This is often on a short-term contract basis and the role can also embrace welfare as well as counselling.
- Counselling is provided by the voluntary sector. Lee et al. (2009) note that the Place2Be (a children's charity) is a significant provider. It currently offers school-based therapeutic interventions to 230 schools across the UK (Place2Be, 2014). Relate is a major contributor providing counselling support in 625 schools in the UK. (Hanley et al., 2011)

FE colleges and universities have a separate development trajectory. There has been a more steady growth (Bell, 1996), beginning in the mid-twentieth century and gradually expanding to replace pastoral care provided by academics that has been eroded by increased administration and research demands. There are further factors that have led to the development and expansion of counselling services. Although previous assessments of student mental health placed them at a lower risk than the general population, the move in recent decades to widen participation means that the student population includes increasing numbers of students who may be more vulnerable to the pressures inherent in further and higher education (Connell et al., 2007). In addition to this, student debt and the reduced opportunities for employment due to the current economic situation add to the feelings of pressure. The nature of academic courses has also changed. Modularisation provides increased choice for students but also regularly disrupts the composition of established peer groups. A study of 4,699 first-year university students who completed GP-Clinical Outcome Routine Evaluation (CORE) on four occasions showed that there is a rise in anxiety during the first year and that although levels of strain rise and fall during the first year, they do not return to pre-university entry levels (Cooke et al., 2006). There are also greater numbers of international students who may face difficulties in adapting to new linguistic and cultural circumstances, and the repositioning of the student from a more passive recipient of education to an active consumer with entitlement to support services all add to the need for professional counselling services.

IS COUNSELLING IN EDUCATION EFFECTIVE?

The first question that CPs will ask is: 'Is counselling in education effective?' Research in this new field is limited but there are encouraging signs that it produces good results (Cooper, 2009; Cooper et al., 2013; Lee et al., 2009; McArthur et al., 2013). Research conducted by counselling psychologist Mick Cooper and his team at Strathclyde University has provided sound evidence and information about counselling in schools. In terms of severity, they have found that students attending school counselling services have similar levels of distress to those presenting at CAMHS (Cooper, 2009). A systematic literature search involving 30 studies of the effectiveness of counselling provided in secondary schools found that counselling was associated with large improvements in mental health and 50 per cent of clinically distressed clients showed clinical improvement. Just over 80 per cent rated counselling as moderately or very helpful. The most helpful factor identified was 'talking to someone and being listened to' (Cooper, 2009). Fox and Butler (2009), utilising Teen-CORE scores, not only showed that scores were significantly lower after counselling, but also found that the improvement was sustained in a group that was followed up at three months. There is also evidence that counselling in schools is viewed positively by the students themselves (Fox and Butler, 2007; Lynass et al., 2012).

In the UK, the most solid evidence for research in university settings comes from the CORE team. Connell et al. (2008) examined data from seven UK student counselling services that used the CORE system. Seventy per cent of students showed reliable improvement. Their study showed that students who complete counselling show a significantly greater improvement than clients who have an unplanned ending or who drop out of therapy. Students who drop out of therapy before the third session were found to be the most vulnerable on the CORE measure. Another of their studies showed that students attending university counselling services show severity levels only slightly lower than young people presenting at primary care and with a similar level of risk to self (Connell et al., 2007).

DOES COUNSELLING IN EDUCATION DIFFER FROM OTHER SETTINGS?

How does work in education differ from other forms of counselling psychology? Firstly, as already mentioned, the setting is non-medical and the lack of a clinical diagnosis aids the normalisation of attending for counselling and avoids stigmatisation. The downside to this is that the practitioner is practising without clinical back-up and needs to make good links with local mental health services so that they can refer serious cases and summon appropriate support promptly should the need arise. As the practitioner is working without the support of a medical team, a thorough knowledge of mental health problems and experience in assessing and working with suicidal young people is required. There are also many opportunities for proactive and very early interventions. Workshops and discussion groups can increase understanding, disseminate self-help knowledge, and encourage peer support.

Secondly, there is a need to balance therapeutic work with educational factors such as academic achievement and the rhythms and demands of the academic year. This means that therapeutic work has to be carefully paced with academic demands in mind. For example, in-depth work may not advisable in the weeks leading up to exams.

Thirdly, there are time constraints in that work has to be tailored to fit within terms and semesters and to take account of holidays and the long summer breaks. The progress of therapy sometimes faces what can feel to be an untimely ending when, for example, the student leaves the school, FE college or university. Preparation for such endings and careful referral to other forms of support are part of the work. Interruptions of therapy occur when students study abroad for a semester or year, or participate in field trips. Therefore, forethought about the pacing of therapeutic work is especially important.

Fourthly, most of the therapeutic work is short term and it is often completed within a matter of weeks, with 4–5 weeks being the average length of contact. Skill in short-term and time-limited work is essential. However, some long-term work is necessary. This usually involves work with people who have serious mental or physical health problems or who are enduring difficult continuing circumstances.

Fifthly, as with any work within an organisation, the CP needs to be sensitive to the dynamics of the organisation. The skills of managing organisational tensions are not unique to education, although three areas present particular challenges:

- CPs in education work within organisations that have educational success rather than mental health as their primary objective. At times the emphasis on academic achievement can be at odds with the promotion of positive mental health. All organisations have their flaws and may have practices that work against good mental health (Andrews and Wilding, 2004; Sinclair et al., 2005). Part of the CP's role is to highlight the organisational practices that are harmful. Good statistical recording can help to identify parts of the organisation that are not working well. For example, on reviewing the annual statistics, there may be a significantly raised number of students from a particular class or department presenting with clinical levels of anxiety. This may indicate that some aspect of this part of the institution is detrimental to mental health and tactful discussions with managers to remedy the situation may be needed.

- A deeper layer of complexity for practitioners is that educational settings can differ from other organisations in that there is a stronger sense of community. Community activities and celebrations, including social and academic events, are common and the CP is often expected to take part and be involved. The art is to engage with the community to such a degree so as to understand and feel the pushes and pulls of the organisational dynamics but to keep enough distance to facilitate reflection. Boundary-keeping is likely to be the most complex task that counsellors in education face. It is necessary to maintain an open, warm and approachable persona without compromising confidentiality or being recruited into internal disputes.

- Successful therapeutic work can often be invisible to the rest of the organisation. Everything runs smoothly and credit may not be adequately assigned to the counselling practitioners. One of the challenges is to find ways of making the work visible to ensure the maintenance of funding and staffing levels. It is, of course, important that client confidentiality is not compromised and this can be done by using anonymised data to communicate successful outcomes. The routine use of a reliable measure of mental health, such as CORE, provides solid evidence that clinical improvements are achieved. It has also been found to be effective in assessing suicide risk when used alongside therapeutic discourse (Reeves and Coldridge, 2007). The *Inform* system for collecting demographic data developed by Mark Phippen at the University of Cambridge is a particularly useful statistical tool. Also details of allied activities including groupwork, proactive work and external liaison presented as part of an annual report are really important. Active engagement on university committees helps to maintain the visibility of CPs and awareness that they are making a valuable contribution to the success of the institution.

Obtaining adequate room space is often difficult and a factor that constrains the development of counselling services and the possibilities for diverse kinds of provision. As well as counselling rooms, space for groups, workshops and training sessions is needed. The location of the service needs to be in a place that is both discreet, soundproof and readily accessible. Arguing for appropriate, adequate and accessible accommodation is a priority for CPs. In FE colleges and universities the counselling service is frequently located within student services, which provides a degree of anonymity for clients entering the building. It also enables ease of referral to other support services. The compromise is that booking and waiting areas are more public and this can present difficulties for distressed students.

Of the three educational sectors, the most developed is university counselling with counselling in FE colleges a close second. Less consistent provision is found in the school sector but this is developing rapidly and presents the greatest opportunities for interventions at an early age to explore any problem areas and to promote good mental health.

WHAT IS THE DAY-TO-DAY WORK LIKE?

In order to give an idea of the work, the experiences of several counsellors and CPs are described in the following pages. The work is specific to their individual workplaces and there will be variation from institution to institution, but it is hoped that this will help counselling psychologists to decide whether this setting is for them.

Lane (2014), an experienced school counsellor, describes her day and highlights the kinds of issues that she encounters in her work at a state comprehensive school. She also discusses the most challenging aspects of the work.

Lane's school employs two part-time counsellors; there are also two fully trained volunteer counsellors and two trainees. The all-encompassing nature of their work is impressive. Over the course of a year they provide approximately 1,000 counselling sessions. They encounter a wide range of presenting issues, including self-harm, suicidal ideation and attempts, eating disorders, low self-esteem, bereavement, anxiety, sleep problems, anger, depression, drug use, alcohol, friendship issues, relationships, family separation, adoption and academic stress. Counselling sessions last for 50 minutes and short-term work predominates. Longer-term work is more likely to occur when there are gender, sexuality or transgender issues, self-harm, anorexia, bulimia, or a bereavement involving close relatives and friends. Records are kept to a minimum of essential information.

In addition to individual work, the counsellors run groups for immediate issues such as for those affected by the death of a pupil. They also provide proactive workshops on mindfulness, and issues such as drug awareness and mental health. Weekly information and discussion sessions called 'Chat' are open to all pupils in years 10/11/12 and focus on topical issues such as drug use, eating problems, etc. Chat is staffed by a school counsellor, an early intervention worker, and a drug and alcohol support worker. Lane (2014) emphasises the usefulness of Chat in enabling students to familiarise themselves with counsellors, which makes approaching them for an individual session easier. It also brings complicated issues and the stresses and strains of school life out into the open. A recent session explored sexual health and involved sexual health specialists. Lane is keen on involving the expertise of external agencies and ensures that the students are aware of the range of local sources of help and support should they prefer to use these alternatives. Chat also contributes to the counsellors' endeavour to reduce any stigma that may be attached to mental health issues and promote counselling as a normal part of everyday life.

A further aspect of the work is consultation and advice given to the school staff and to parents. Parents often consult on issues such as family breakdown, bereavements, and students' behavioural and psychological problems. Explaining the role and functioning of the counselling service, including the bounds of confidentiality, to parents and staff members is an integral part of the work.

Given the age of their clients, confidentiality in schools is a complex issue and requires very sensitive handling. Counsellors aim to contribute to general discussions about the welfare of individual students with school staff without compromising the trust and confidentiality they have established. However, they do provide the names of students they have seen to the exclusion officer, year head and senior management; and identified risks are discussed with the students' year head. The counsellors attend multi-agency meetings every half-term with social workers, year heads, the senior managers, the police and early intervention workers. High-priority cases are discussed at these meetings. The well-being and safety of the individual child is prioritised and information is shared when this is clearly in the interests of safety and the well-being of the child concerned.

The main referral routes are through deputy year leaders, staff and self-referral. Self-referral is through email contact or via a designated post box. The services offered by the counsellors are advertised through leaflets and announcements in assemblies. They have fortnightly supervision and attend departmental meetings and regular meetings with deputy year heads. The teaching staff are appreciative of the counselling service as long-term support is difficult to achieve from the NHS and voluntary sectors.

Lane (2014) starts her day at 7.30am by texting appointment reminders to her clients. A further use of technology is the use of *survey monkey* in obtaining feedback. Satisfaction rates are very high, with appreciation expressed for help in understanding problems, enabling students to cope better with their schoolwork, and improving behaviour and relationships.

Reflecting on organisational dynamics, Lane and Turner (2014) are aware that at times a sense of rivalry between counsellors and also with staff can cloud relationships. A further dynamic is the filtering of pressure from the government, to the heads, and down the staff chain, that can threaten the therapeutic purpose. Unrealistic academic targets within a school may create pressures that contaminate expectations of the counselling service. It may be tempting to take on extra volunteers to cope with extra demands, with the danger of risking quality. Lane and Turner (2014) highlight the need to be aware of a reactive compulsion within counsellors to solve and soothe with immediate effect, which can distort decision-making.

Barnard (2014) works in a private school in a team of three psychodynamically trained counsellors. Much of his work has similarities with the state sector, as described above, but there is a greater provision of support services within the school. The therapeutic team includes a clinical psychologist who can provide specialist services. In addition there is a medical centre with medical and nursing staff available on-site, each residential house has a matron providing care, and there are chaplains who also provide support. A support team that meets regularly is drawn from these additional support services and individuals felt to be at risk are discussed. During these discussions the counsellors take care to ensure that confidentiality is maintained for their clients.

In contrast to the state sector, external agencies are involved to a lesser extent but referrals are made to CAMHS and to counselling and clinical psychologists. However, the overall level of support provided to individual students is greater. The school population tends to be more international and widely drawn than the state sector. This means that some students are boarders and homesickness is a frequently encountered presenting problem. Students generally self-refer and the presenting issues are similar to those encountered in state schools with anxiety, depression, friendship, relationship and family issues predominating. Evening sessions are provided to enable ease of access for residential students. One of the counsellors facilitates peer listening groups.

An important preventative factor in Barnard's work is that the counsellors have small group meetings with all new pupils. This enables them to explain how they work and to identify any vulnerable students at an early stage. The counsellors also give a short talk at the first assembly for new students and for new sixth formers. In contrast to the state sector, the school staff also have access to counselling service.

In 2009 Pattison et al. published a set of ten recommendations for good practice for school counselling in Wales. A summary of their recommendations is listed in Box 26.1 and is a useful aide-memoire for anyone who may be involved in setting up a school counselling service.

Box 26.1   School counselling in Wales: Recommendations for good practice

1. School counselling services should have sustainable funding.
2. Services should employ professionally qualified counsellors who have experience of working with young people, who access appropriate clinical supervision with experienced supervisors, and who take part in regular, relevant continuing professional development.
3. Deliver accessible counselling in an appropriately private but safe setting within the school vicinity.
4. Be seen as non-stigmatising by the school community and a normal part of school provision, which is integrated into the school community.
5. The service is evaluated and monitored by individuals or an agency (in or out of school) with experience in this specialised area of work.
6. Pay due regard to current legislation and guidance, and offer confidentiality within usual ethical and safeguarding limits.
7. Respond flexibly to local needs in respect of diversity (e.g. language) and practicality (e.g. availability during holidays).
8. Work with and alongside other services and agencies in a collegial manner, while maintaining appropriate levels of confidentiality.
9. Counsellors should be members of a professional body and as such have an established ethical framework and complaints procedure.
10. Employ counsellors whose personal qualities will mean that they are approachable, have good listening skills and a manner that encourages a climate for safe and trusting relationships.

Pattison et al. (2009)

Provision in FE colleges tends to be more pressured than in other settings. Leach (2008) describes a working day that involves seeing nine students for individual work, several consultations with members of staff, two journeys to different campuses and administration work. It is not unusual for sessions in FE colleges to be restricted to 30 minutes to meet the demand. Leach (2008) estimates that she sees 56 students a week and has long working days. However, despite the pressures, Leach underlines that she finds working to improve and maintain the mental health of young people immensely rewarding.

The university sector has more generous provision. Almost all UK universities have counselling services and provide 50-minute individual sessions that are available for all students. Some university services also provide counselling for academic and university staff. Individual work is usually limited to five sessions a day for each counsellor. A wide range of group sessions, preventative workshops, staff consultation, trauma interventions, committee work, administration and evaluation are regular additional features of the work. The university sector attracts students from all over the world and counselling people from very different cultures who may have English as their second or third language is a daily experience.

A typical day for a university counsellor can involve four individual sessions, attendance at a welfare committee meeting, liaising with a local mental health team about available support for a particular student, facilitating a mindfulness group session, managing appointments, answering emails, writing up notes and recording statistics on the service system. The rhythms of the academic year create particular service pressures with examinations and February/March being times of heightened demand. Mindfulness is being found to be increasingly useful. It aids the development of a reflective space and enables students to become aware of how their mind wanders, and how to draw it back to the task in hand. This assists the development of focus and concentration. Increasing numbers of practitioners working in educational settings are taking mindfulness training courses and facilitating mindfulness groups. In a study of 522 young people aged 12–16 it has been shown to be associated with a reduction in stress and better well-being (Kuyken et al., 2013).

A factor that is impacting on student counselling is that students are currently more dependent on parental contributions and support and there are concerns that the span of childhood is extending, resulting in a delay in maturation and the ability to be self-supporting. Percy (2014), who has substantial experience in the university sector, notes a change in the nature of the child–parent relationship and is concerned that parents are prioritising friendship with their children over boundary-keeping and discipline. He suggests that this can result in students experiencing difficulty in self-containment. It may also contribute to a reduced ability to delay gratification and tolerate frustration. This is manifest in the academic world in demands for immediate responses to communications; demands for a greater degree of help from staff with academic work; and difficulty in assimilating feedback. These concerns about the changing nature of childhood and young adulthood are speculative but it is a subject much discussed among practitioners and is an area ripe for research (see also Chapter 31 in this volume).

PEER SUPPORT

Students' attitudes towards counselling in education are changing. It is becoming more accepted as a part of normal life. Whereas students used to be very concerned about their attendance for counselling being noticed by others, this is now much less apparent. It is not unusual for clients to say that they are openly discussing counselling attendance with their peers and recommending it to them for support when the need arises. Some counselling services develop peer support systems that provide an extra layer of support and choice for students. There is persuasive evidence that these systems are valuable (Cowie and Wallace, 2000; Greenland et al., 2003; Smalley et al., 2005). Mentoring and peer support systems can aid a reduction in bullying and its effects (Cowie and Hutson, 2005; McGowan, 2002). These schemes range from helplines to the identification of students who are then trained as peer supporters. In a university setting, Ford (2004a) selects and trains peer supporters in active listening, assertiveness and referral skills. Supporters are given 30 hours of training in ten three-hour sessions. Peer interventions range from befriending/counselling support to mediation and conflict resolution. Peer tutoring, information giving and advocacy are also offered. Peer supporters make themselves known to fellow students and then wait to be contacted. Supporters are carefully selected and schooled in confidentiality and how and when to refer. Supervision is provided on a regular basis and emergency consultation and advice is available. Such schemes provide a valuable addition to existing services. Cooper and Dagupta (2008) found that in one university scheme 9 per cent of students contacted peer supporters. Ford (2004b) provides useful information and advice for those involved in setting up peer-support schemes for the 15–18 age group.

THE USEFULNESS AND IMPACT OF MODERN TECHNOLOGY AND MEDIA

An ever-expanding variety of technology and media suffuses all aspects of modern life and children and young people are especially adept at using the latest methods. Maintaining awareness of developments and using popular methods aids communication with students. As we have seen, text messages can be used by school counsellors to reduce the instance of DNAs by reminding people of their appointments. User-friendly counselling service websites with links to useful mental health sites can provide students with information and a variety of means of self-help. Websites can also be used to advertise and make visible the range of work provided by the counselling service. Texts and emails are now the main mode of communication to request appointments and seek advice. While it is rarely a substitute for face-to-face counselling, e-counselling can be a useful means of maintaining contact with vulnerable clients during vacations and while studying abroad (Evans, 2007). It can also be useful in helping to build a relationship with a potential client who has initial reservations about face-to-face counselling.

An area relating to media that is causing much concern in the education field is the upsurge in cyberbullying. Cowie (2013) asserts that the increase in cyberbullying is a frequent cause of emotional disturbance in children and young people. Cyberbullying is complicated by the fact that it is generated by the victim's peer group and its 'hidden' nature makes it hard for adults to control. Cowie (2013) outlines the nature of cyberbullying, discusses its emotional impact and reviews strategies for prevention.

CONCLUSION

University counselling is now well embedded in the educational sector but both FE and school counselling are fields that are clearly in need of further development and funding. In view of the concerns about the lack of provision and mental health support for children and young people, it is a matter of urgency that new ways of supporting the healthy psychological development of school, FE college and university students is found. In this chapter I have suggested that the first line of mental health support for students should be provided within their educational setting. This would enable the effective promotion of positive mental health, other forms of targeted preventative work, and the provision of speedy therapeutic intervention before problems become chronic. Counselling psychologists have the training and skills to excel at these tasks. I hope you will feel sufficiently enthused to take up the challenge.

Visit the companion website for the following:

- Counselling Psychology in Education Settings.
- Links to resources on helplines for drug abuse, counselling and suicide.

REFERENCES

Allen, G. (2011a) *Early Intervention: Smart Investment, Massive Savings – The Second Report to Her Majesty's Government.* London: HM Government.

Allen, G. (2011b) *Early Intervention: The Next Steps.* London: HM Government.

Andrews, B. and Wilding, J. M. (2004) The relation of depression and anxiety to life-stress and achievements in students. *British Journal of Psychology*, 95: 509–521.

Baginsky, W. (2004) *School Counselling in England, Wales and Northern Ireland: A Review.* London: NSPCC.

Barnard, M. (2014) Interviewed by D. Danchev, February.

Bell, E. (1996) *Counselling in Further and Higher Education.* Buckingham: Open University Press.

Bolger, A. W. (1985) Training and research in counselling. *British Journal of Guidance and Counselling*, 13(1): 112–124.

Bor, R., Ebner-Landy, J., Gill, S. and Brace, C. (2002) *Counselling in Schools.* London: Sage.

Cole, A. (2006) Inquiry opens into the state of childhood in the UK. *British Medical Journal*, 333: 619.

Collishaw, S. (2009) *Trends in Adolescent Depression: A Review of Evidence. Depression in Childhood and Adolescence.* ACAMH Occasional Papers, 28. London: Association for Child and Adolescent Mental Health (UK).

Connell, J., Barkham, M. and Mellor-Clark, J. (2007) CORE-OM mental health norms of students attending university counselling services benchmarked against an age-matched primary care sample. *British Journal of Guidance and Counselling*, 35(1): 41–57.

Connell, J., Barkham, M. and Mellor-Clark, J. (2008) The effectiveness of UK student counselling services: An analysis using the CORE system. *British Journal of Guidance and Counselling*, 36(1): 1–18.

Cooke, R., Bewick, B. M., Barkham, M., Bradley, M. and Audin, K. (2006) Measuring, monitoring and managing the psychological well-being of first year university students. *Journal of Guidance and Counselling*, 34(4): 505–517.

Cooper, J. and Das Gupta, C. (2008) From bystanding to standing by. *AUCC Journal*, March.

Cooper, M. (2009) Counselling in UK secondary schools: A comprehensive review of audit and evaluation data. *Counselling and Psychotherapy Research: Linking Research with Practice*, 9(3): 137–150.

Cooper, M., Stewart, D., Sparks, J. and Bunting, L. (2013) School-based counselling using systematic feedback: A cohort study evaluating outcomes and predictors of change. *Psychotherapy Research*, 23(4): 474–488.

Cowie, H. (2013) Cyberbullying and its impact on young people's emotional health and well-being. *The Psychiatrist On-line*, 37: 167–170.

Cowie, H. and Hutson, N. (2005) Peer support: A strategy to help bystanders challenge school bullying. *Pastoral Care in Education*, 23(2): 40–44.

Cowie, H. and Wallace, P. (2000) *Peer Support in Action*. London: Sage.

Doward, J. (2014) Child mental health care in meltdown – NHS study. *Observer*, 18 May.

Evans, J. (2007) A pull-out guide to online counselling and psychotherapy in universities and colleges. *AUCC Journal*, December.

Ford, A. (2004a) *Peer Support in Colleges and Universities: A Training Manual* (2nd edn). Rugby: Pettifer Publishing Services.

Ford, A. (2004b) *Peer Supervision in Teenagers Aged 15 to 18 Years Old*. Rugby: Pettifer Publishing Services.

Fox, C. L. and Butler, I. (2007) 'If you don't want to tell anyone else you can tell her': Young people's views on school counselling. *British Journal of Guidance and Counselling*, 35(1): 97–114.

Fox, C. L. and Butler, I. (2009) Evaluating the effectiveness of a school-based counselling service in the UK. *British Journal of Guidance and Counselling*, 37(2): 95–106.

Gosline, A. (2008) When kids go bad. *New Scientist*, 39: 38–41.

Greenland, K., Scourfield, J., Smalley, N., Prior, L. and Scourfield, J. (2003) *Young People, Gender and Suicide Prevention: Helpseeking in 17–18 Year Old Men and Women*. Draft Report for the Wales Office of Research and Development in Health and Social Care. Cardiff: Wales Office of Research and Development in Health and Social Care.

Hanley, T., Sefi, A. and Lennie, C. (2011) Practice-based evidence in school-based counselling. *Counselling and Psychotherapy Research: Linking Research with Practice*, 11(4): 300–309.

Jenkins, P. and Polat, F. (2005) *The Current Provision of Counselling Services in Secondary Schools in England and Wales*. Manchester: University of Manchester.

Kuyken, W., Weare, K., Ukoumunne, O. C., Vicary, R., Motton, N., Burnett, R., Cullen, C., Hennelly, S. and Huppert, F. (2013) Effectiveness of the mindfulness in schools programme: Non-randomised controlled feasibility study. *The British Journal of Psychiatry*, 203(2): 126–131.

Lane, L. (2014) Interviewed by D. Danchev, February.

Lane, L. and Turner, S. (2014) What does it mean to be (and to employ) a volunteer school counsellor? Unpublished paper.

Leach, G. (2008). Helping students achieve. *AUCC Journal*, March: 15–19.

Lee, R. C., Tiley, C. E. and White, J. E. (2009) The Place2Be: Measuring the effectiveness of a primary school-based therapeutic intervention in England and Scotland. *Counselling and Psychotherapy Research: Linking Research with Practice*, 9(3): 151–159.

Lines, D. (2006) *Brief Counselling in Schools: Working with Young People 11–18*. London: Sage.

Lynass, R., Pykhtina, O. and Cooper, M. (2012) A thematic analysis of young people's experience of counselling in five secondary schools in the UK. *Counselling and Psychotherapy Research: Linking Research with Practice*, 12(1): 53–62.

McArthur, K., Cooper, M. and Berdondini, L. (2013) School-based humanistic counselling for psychological distress in young people: Pilot randomised controlled trial. *Psychotherapy Research*, 23(3): 355–365.

McGowan, M. (2002) *Young People and Peer Support: How to Set Up Peer Support Programmes*. Brighton: Trust for the Study of Adolescence.

O'Hara, M. (2014) Teachers left to pick up pieces from cuts to youth mental health services. *Guardian*, 15 April.

Pattison, S., Rowland, N., Richards, K., Cromarty, K., Jenkins, P. and Polat, F. (2009) School counselling in Wales: Recommendations for good practice. *Counselling and Psychotherapy Research: Linking Research with Practice*, 9(3): 169–173.

Percy, A. (2014) Personal communication, March.

Place2Be (2014) *Supporting Schools*. www.place2be.org.uk (accessed 27 September 2014).

Reeves, A. and Coldridge, E. (2007) A question of balance: Using CORE-OM when assessing suicide risk. *AUCC Journal*, March.

Sinclair, A., Barkham, M., Evans, C., Connell, J. and Audin, K. (2005) Rationale and development of a general population well-being measure: Psychometric status of the GP-CORE in a student population. *British Journal of Guidance and Counselling*, 33(2): 153–174.

Smalley, N., Scourfield, J. and Greenland, K. (2005) Young people, gender and suicide: A review of the social context. *Journal of Social Work*, 5(2): 133–154.

Walter, H. J., Gouze, K., Ciccetti, C., Arend, R., Mehta, T., Schmidt, J. and Skvarla, M. (2011) A pilot demonstration of comprehensive mental health services in inner-city public schools. *Journal of School Health*, 81(4): 185–193.

Young Minds (2014) Briefing on cuts to children and young people's mental health services. www.youngminds.org.uk (accessed on 27 September 2014).

USEFUL WEBSITES

www.student.counselling.co.uk: This website was set up by the Heads of Student Counselling Services in UK Universities. It provides information and has links to counselling services and other sources of help.

www.studentdepression.org: This website was set up by the Charlie Waller Memorial Trust in consultation with the Association for University and College Counselling. It is a user-friendly site with clearly presented information and students' own accounts of recognising and coping with depression.

27
COUNSELLING PSYCHOLOGY IN ORGANISATIONS: FROM PROBLEM FIXING TO EMERGENCE AND GROWTH

DAVID A. LANE

INTRODUCTION

As counselling psychology emerged in the UK, organisational applications were among the primary areas of practice (Woolfe, 1990). Initially, this included one-to-one counselling to fix problems. In a sense this worked for organisations adopting a problem-solving approach to management. Philosophically, in drawing on humanistic values and the Human Potential Movement counselling psychologists were able to influence organisations to adopt a more positive view of behaviour. Increasingly, managers were trained in counselling skills as a way to change the nature of the conversations taking place and hence organisational relationships. As coaching in recent years became a popular intervention in organisations, a similar pattern developed from an initial problem fixing to a more humanistic value base. These patterns of convergence from problem fixing to a more developmental basis have appeared across the clinical, counselling, psychotherapy and coaching arenas as well as significant divergence around the role of evidence-based practice and individualised interventions. This chapter explores the role of counselling psychologists in organisations and in particular focuses on the potential to create cultures supportive of growth. This includes increasing emphasis on the ability to work with complexity and uncertainty. The challenge to our field is to adopt a broader theoretical base to our work yet remain true to the values that have served us and our clients.

THE JOURNEY OF COUNSELLING PSYCHOLOGY IN AN ORGANISATIONAL CONTEXT

In both the UK and USA, counselling psychology was born out of the interests of psychologists who saw the importance of the field of counselling to a wide range of issues. In both examples, the birth was not without difficulty as the field sought both to find a place within psychology yet differentiate itself from sister fields such as clinical and occupational psychology. Barkham (1990) referred to our search for an identity. Nelson-Jones (1999) has traced this development for the UK and Meara and Myers (1999) for the USA. Through an analysis of the discourse on the field within the *Counselling Psychology Review*, Pugh and Coyle (2010) have looked at the concern in the early 1990s to construct our identity and obtain legitimation through this process of representing our similarity and difference from the related fields at a broad level. By the later 1990s our confidence increased and we see a more fine-grained analysis. It is also the case that areas of practice have changed in our sister fields. Thus, whereas clinical psychology saw itself as based within a scientist practitioner and empirical model, and the emphasis within counselling psychology was on subjective experience and reflective practice, these approaches have found their way into the clinical field (Lane and Corrie, 2006a). In part, we are less different because we have all adopted frameworks from our sister fields.

Woolfe (1990) identified the rise of counselling psychology as deriving from six major sources:

1. A growing awareness among many psychologists (and certainly not just counselling psychologists) of the importance of the helping relationship as itself a key variable in working with people.
2. A growing emphasis in the work of helpers on well-being as opposed to sickness.
3. A growing realisation of the value of counselling as a tool in organisational development and stress management.
4. A growing recognition of the need for a more articulated scientific basis for counselling.
5. A growing appreciation that counselling offers an appropriate form of employment for psychology graduates.
6. A growing acceptance of the humanistic value system underlying counselling psychology.

It is this combination of the humanistic value system and recognition that counselling psychology offers more than an individualised model of intervention that has marked the discipline ever since. This is particularly the case in the organisational field; work on the characteristics of organisations that are flourishing or languishing has given rise to an understanding of the impacts on mental health resulting from the way they function (Fredrickson and Losada, 2005).

COUNSELLING AS AN APPROACH IN ORGANISATIONS: FROM EMERGENCE TO DECLINE AND GROWTH?

By the 1990s, as Woolfe (1990) illustrated, counselling had become increasingly familiar to managers in a wide variety of organisations. Woolfe was able to draw on many examples. Management development programmes increasingly focused on the importance of active listening and related skills (Orlans, 1989). Principles of counselling were employed in the development of person-centred and facilitative organisational structures. Reddy (1994) drew attention to the growth of counselling at work through the provision of trained counsellors. The use of external counsellors, in particular in 'Employee Assistance Programmes' (EAPs), beyond just individual support influenced approaches to dealing with the emotional and physical well-being of employees. This was achieved by providing feedback about how organisational structures affected individual well-being and engagement.

This change from an historical emphasis on individual problem fixing to a broader focus on promotion of health and productivity in the workforce has led some authors to suggest we have moved towards a more systemic model of 'organisational counselling' for understanding the challenges faced (Ginsbery et al., 1999). In this way counsellors can be seen to have an important preventative and developmental role which functions to facilitate organisational change and development. However, they will still have to pay attention to the goals of the business unit that may have to fund the activity (Dickens, 1999) and recognise that organisations may see individual change as valuable to the extent it enhances profit (Kahn, 2014).

Thus, although change is often seen as a prerequisite for survival, and counselling helps to support staff during this process, funding pressures result in more manualised approaches being sought. Organisations say they want to address complexity but to do so with a set package of skills training. Lane (1990) drew attention to this in the early days of our field and Strawbridge (2010) has done so more recently.

Applications in community and organisational contexts were an established part of the field from the early days. Thus while many counselling psychologists operated within therapeutic contexts, others saw their role within the community or working within organisational settings. However, the identity of counselling psychology found an ambiguous space between established practice and evolving fields. Thus while many have found a home within the provision of therapy services in the health sector, somehow there is a continuing sense of being outsiders. A similar ambiguity exists between counselling, occupational and coaching psychology. Moore and Rae (2009), looking at a small group of practitioners, identify how they see themselves as occupying a 'maverick' repertoire. This places them in a position outside established schools of psychological therapy.

One response from counselling psychology has been to adopt the frameworks of the medical model from our clinical peers. Thus, we see an emphasis on diagnosis and narrower forms of case formulation. As counselling psychologists working therapeutically get absorbed into medical contexts, it is understandable that they are impacted by local, national as well as international trends in health care (Lane and Corrie, 2006a). However, it is important to recognise our origins and the broader basis of our understanding, including engagement with the subjective nature of experience. The narrowness of many approaches to formulation was recognised in the British Psychological Society's (BPS) guidelines on good practice in case formulation (2013), which sees an emphasis on diagnosis or single theoretical frames. As the guidelines noted, there were few examples of approaches built around the full complexity of the client's narrative. (They quoted Corrie and Lane, 2010, and Strawbridge, 2010, as exceptions to this.)

However, the same narrowing is evident in occupational practice. As Kwiatkowski and Winter (2006) argue, the pressure to conform to organisational constraints is part of the negotiation in which we have to engage.

An ambiguous identity appears more problematic as coaching psychology has emerged to engage in much the same space as counselling psychology in organisations. While coaching went through the same journey from problem fixing to transformation, for some having a coach was less ambiguous than having a counsellor/therapist/psychologist. Coaches, while starting as problem fixers, seem to have been able to throw off that perception and be seen as a trophy for the high performer rather than a remedial support for the underperformer (Jarvis et al., 2006). Having a counsellor is not likely to be a trophy to be displayed.

As the world of organisations becomes more uncertain in response to complexity, the importance of the relationship as central to effectiveness has begun to re-emerge. In the public sector disillusionment with New Public Management (NPM) is noted in a number of countries. Both the European Commission and the National Council for Voluntary Organisations have launched initiatives to move away from the transactional basis of NPM to more cooperative arrangements. Hence relational 'compacts' replace transactional targets. (See Phillips and Smith, 2011, for examples.) Organisations have increasingly looked to approaches such as appreciative enquiry to understand themselves and build more collaborative relationships. (See http://appreciativeinquiry.case.edu and http://collaborative-practices.com#sthash.g7SvmXRU. dpuf for examples of projects.) Hence the mood is now towards a humanistic collaborative value base that welcomes varied contributions. Hence, models and approaches in organisations, such as appreciative enquiry, open space and deep democracy, which are more suited to our values, are emerging (Lane and Down, 2010). We are now moving in a growth direction. Issues raised originally by the Human Potential Movement are re-emerging.

AREAS OF APPLICATION IN WORKPLACE

Briefly, I will explore a number of areas of application to indicate the breadth of engagement, and then go on to look at some of the issues we face and the directions in which counselling psychology has contributions to make to organisations.

One area that has received a lot of attention is the responsibility of the organisation for the welfare of their employees and the possible role of line managers. Lane (1993) reported on a bank employee's view of counselling proposals to respond to stress generated by armed raids. A number of initiatives to enable competitor organisations to work together to develop shared understandings of how to respond to the impacts were reported. The way line managers can help was outlined. Nixon and Carroll (1994), noting that line managers are the group most concerned with success in their role, considered the use of counselling skills and the extent to which line managers could act in that role. They concluded that they cannot be counsellors but should build their counselling skills. (Similar comments have appeared in relation to managers as coaches (e.g. Jarvis et al., 2006).) Upton (1997) considered the managerial mechanisms that might facilitate the development of workplace counsellors. More recently, Singh (2007) has taken up this theme, pointing to the impact of an increasingly competitive environment on employees' physical and mental health. The need for proper and timely counselling skills is identified.

Tehrani (2004) has pointed to the concern in organisations for the welfare of the staff having a long history, of which provision of counselling services is but one example. Furthermore, she examines assessment, counselling and support within the Post Office (as was) (Tehrani, 2004, 2011). The point is made that effective services require a comprehensive process of assessment to look at needs so that the type and level of help required can be defined. Bullying in the workplace is another area where counselling psychologists have been prominent in making a contribution. Tattum and Lane (1988) produced the first book to look at this issue in schools and other workplaces and discussed various organisational level interventions as well as counselling. Askew (1988), in the same volume, looked at the extent to which the culture of an organisation generated bullying behaviours. This issue was further explored by Roland and Munthe (1989). Tehrani (2006), from the perspective of a counselling psychologist, looked at emotional abuse in the workplace and considered the role of counselling but also broader organisational issues that could be addressed. She also considered the impacts of harassment and made the point that it is not just about having policies which define inappropriate behaviours; it is about creating a culture that promotes positive ones (Birkeland Nielsen et al., 2015). Thus, dealing with bullying was not just a matter of providing individual counselling, but included our role in developing wider systems more conducive to well-being.

A major area of involvement for counselling psychology in organisations was in the provision of employee assistance programmes (EAPs) (Bull, 1992; Carroll, 1995; Deverall, 1997). These came in various forms and, while EAPs maintained a degree of confidentially in terms of the content of individual sessions, they increasingly found that they had a role in feeding back general conclusions to organisations that might help develop effective policies. As Deverall (1997) concluded, it is not simply a case of providing a service; there is a need to develop a consultancy-based relationship so that the appropriate forms of support are provided.

There are multiple areas where counselling has found a place, including in disaster situations (Lane, 1991), working with organisations to develop counselling services for people with cancer (Gallagher and Meehan, 1996), and in global development programmes (Lee, 1998). Across a range of interventions we have increasingly journeyed from providing individual sessions to engagement with systemic processes to develop organisational-level responses.

FUNDAMENTAL ISSUES FOR OUR PLACE AS COUNSELLING PSYCHOLOGISTS IN ORGANISATIONS

The first fundamental issue is our identity.

1. Our identity

What type of practitioner are we and what is our relationship to psychological research? The role of the scientist practitioner model in counselling psychology has always been contentious (Strawbridge and Woolfe, 1996; Woolfe, 1996; Corrie and Callanan, 2000; Bury and Strauss, 2006; Lane and Corrie, 2006b). Yes, we adopt science as the basis of our work. Without it we could not claim to be psychologists. Woolfe (1996) made the point early on in arguing that what distinguishes counselling from counselling psychology is the latter's base in psychological research. We also, as Bury and Strauss (2006) and Larsson et al. (2012) point out, privilege the personal subjective experience of the client over diagnosis and assessment. McLeod (2003) makes the point strongly in arguing for an approach to our research base that honours the values and practices of counselling psychology. Integrating our professional identities in our work is a matter for personal struggle. Vespia (2006) has explored this struggle from the point of view of a counselling psychologist working as an educator.

Bury and Strauss (2006) have explored this from the perspective of counselling psychologists influenced by very different theoretical stances. They draw upon Wilkinson's (personal communication, 2004) idea that we have to develop a psychological mindedness to enable clients to arrive at meaningful narratives rather than fitting them to a particular diagnostic or theoretical tale. They contend that we must enlarge our definition of what constitutes the scientific aspects of our identity. Thus we enlarge but do not abandon a scientific practitioner stance. In particular, they warn against the move to a medical model that could threaten the attributes that make counselling psychology distinctive. Kahn (2014), in looking at organisations (as a coaching psychologist), makes the point that at an organisational level things change all the time and are therefore unpredictable. Thus goals are points of direction not destinations and are under continual review.

These twin themes of our own individual identity and that of counselling psychology are an ongoing refrain. The interest in the concept of identity in the social (or organisational) world has occupied not just psychology but also sociology and pedagogy. Identity and self have emerged as key issues in understanding the social and the process of change – from sociology (Giddens, 1991; Rose, 1996), from critical psychology (Henriques et al., 1984), and from education (Yates and McCloud, 2000). Work on the formation of identities in work contexts, and its implications for lifelong learning (Yates et al., 2003), has particular relevance for our role. One of the challenges to traditional ways of seeing identity as anchored in universal and normative frames of reference comes from the post-structuralist critique. As Lo (2005) argued, identity arises in sites of action; thus, in organisations it is shaped by the engagement with the client in the context of the work. Negotiating that moving agenda is part of the task we increasingly face.

One way to approach this is to look at identity as a narrative. Chappel et al. (2003) refer to reflexive and relational narrative identification (Gergen and Gergen, 1988; Somers and Gibson, 1994). In reflexive identification, a person can construct their own identity through a process of self-narration. I can take a view on my identity as a counselling psychologist. There will be a series of events from which I can plot the narrative of my identity. I can enter an organisation with that pre-existing narrative. However, the engagement results in a re-negotiation as there will be organisational definitions of possible identities that I and others might inhabit. A narrative will be constructed between us so that the characters in the story evolve as the plot of the story emerges (see Corrie and Lane, 2010). What it is to be a counselling psychologist in an organisation is co-constructed (as a process of relational narrative identity) in specific sites of action as the work unfolds. Hence our purpose in an organisation has to be defined, engagement by engagement.

A case example: Negotiating the purpose of an engagement

I was invited to create a performance management system for a telecoms company undergoing major change. The CEO had in mind a traditional model based on targets, measures and key performance indicators. The role, as initially defined, could have been undertaken by a management consultant or occupational psychologist. What could I contribute from a background in counselling psychology? Given that the organisation was undergoing rapid change, with staff being asked to undertake new roles, it certainly occurred to me that there were potential challenges to existing identities. I wondered in a dialogue with the CEO if a series of conversations with staff might precede any decision so that we could understand what they felt about the changing demands. My purpose had moved from implementer of a management system to conduit for the various narratives. The story as it emerged indicated that a performance management system as envisaged would not be well-received and alternative tales to support change were manifest in the staff group.

Eventually, a series of focus groups identified what staff felt were:

1. the key values that would drive the probability of change,
2. the factors that would help or hinder the change, and
3. the competencies they felt would be necessary to enable the change.

The final outcome was a flexible performance system designed by the staff group and built around commitment to core values, measurement against competencies seen as relevant by the staff groups and support through feedback and coaching to implement the changes. It showed respect for the subjective experience of the people involved and used a collaborative process.

Could this same approach have been adopted by others (not a counselling psychologist) – of course it could have been. However, as counselling psychologists we are alert to issues of identity and impacts of change, which seemed relevant to the engagement. The way we sought to define the purpose of the work was informed by that understanding – a personal reflexive narrative (identity) is shaped by the engagement itself, which is the relational narrative (identity).

Defining our purpose as counselling psychologists in organisations

Purpose (where we are going and why?)

As Corrie and Lane (2010) argue, as you undertake any psychological enquiry, it is vital to be clear about its fundamental purpose. The conversation to create the engagement starts from there. In any work in an organisational setting the shared journey begins as you define the Purpose of your work together. We ask:

'What is the Purpose in working with the stakeholders? Where are you going with this client group? What do they want to achieve? Where do they want to go in their overall journey with you as their guide?'

Defining the Purpose of the work comprises four essential elements:

1. Understanding the question you jointly wish to explore.
2. Understanding the expectations of key stakeholders.
3. Clarifying the role that each party wishes to play.
4. Appreciating the wider context that gives meaning to the Purpose and the way in which it has come to be defined.

To explore these elements we need to ask ourselves the following questions:

- What does the client(s) need to make it possible for them to tell their story and feel heard? Can you meet that need?
- What type of client Purpose is best served by your narrative of yourself as counselling psychologist? Do you have a match or mismatch in this particular case?
- What boundaries do you place on the Purpose of the work that would require you to refer the client elsewhere? Should the client be referred?
- With whom would you not work and where is the margin of that boundary?
- Have you been able to define a shared concern (a relational narrative) that fits within the identified boundaries and is best served by working with you rather than another professional or profession?
- Have you identified and understood the position of other key stakeholders who might be beneficiaries (or victims; Checkland, 1989) of the intervention?

2. Our values

For some of us, we started our journey into counselling psychology through the Human Potential Movement. It had many attractions in its positive view of humankind. It was based on the premise that we could develop our potential and, through this, be capable of happiness, creativity and fulfilment. It predates by a long way the positive psychology movement and the science of happiness. However, it was not about just individual change but directed us to consider the development of others and positive change within society. It was a social, not simply a personal, movement. (See Grogan (2012) for an exploration and critique of the movement.)

Thus the movement was about journeys. It was about growth not problem fixing. Bury and Strauss (2006) point us to the same assumptions and remind us of Strawbridge and Woolfe's (2004) contention that the critical task for counselling psychology is one of problem setting, not fixing. This sits at the centre of our role in organisations. The challenge is to move outside the diagnostic assessment-led models that feature in much of the organisational response to issues (problem solving) to redefine the questions so that they better enable potential (problem setting). The movement seemed to disappear for a while (in the market-driven 1990s) but we can see in the rediscovery of the importance of collaborative relationships and the quality of the conversations happening in organisations that we are rediscovering some of the core values. A Taylorist 'scientific management' has held sway in one form or another for many decades. The humanist view of the likes of Meyer and Mayo (see Kwaitkowski and Winter, 2006) has re-emerged. These perspectives carry with them different ways of seeing and valuing those with whom we work and the activities on which we engage. The values inherent in different perspectives are part of what we bring.

There is an increasing understanding of the relationship between patterns of behaviour in organisations and the impact on performance and well-being. Losada and colleagues (Losada, 1999; Losada and Heaphy, 2004; Fredrickson and Losada, 2005) have pointed to the relationship between positivity in organisations, broader behavioural repertoires, greater flexibility and resilience to adversity, more social resources and optimal functioning. Cavanagh and Lane (2012), drawing on research into leadership in high stress environments, point also to the role of positivity, mindfulness and a clear purpose. Using complexity theory (applied to coaching), they identify how organisations are increasingly unpredictable and that non-linear relationships predominate. Many of the theories we have relied upon in counselling (and coaching) psychology are based on the idea of linear relationships – cause–effect. They are, therefore, unsuitable to enable understanding of situations in constant flux or to explore messy problems. If we are going to live the values of counselling psychology in our work in organisations, we will need to look increasingly to different perspectives to inform our work. There are many to which we can turn, including complexity theory, social constructionism, critical realism, narrative theory, appreciative enquiry, deep democracy and, increasingly, to fields such as socio-drama topography (Sillett and Jimenez, 2014). These provide ways to honour the experience of our clients yet work with challenging perspectives. It enables us to change the way we think about problems (problem setting).

As Kahane (2007) points out, problems are complex in three ways:

Dynamically – because cause and effect are far apart in time and space.

Generatively – because they unfold in unpredictable and unfamiliar ways.

Socially – because of the varied, sometimes conflicting, ways participants see things.

This goes to the heart of the perspectives we bring to our work as counselling psychologists in organisations. Thus, in an organisational context, our data are derived from multiple sources and individuals, each of whom may favour a particular *tale* but out of which we generate a *story* that provides a basis for creating a shared meaning.

A case example: Defining the perspectives in an engagement – taking multiple tales and co-narrating a shared story

The changing nature of the employment relationship across the UK in both public and private sectors gave rise to the concept of an employability relationship. That is, no longer could jobs for life be promised; instead a compact was encouraged whereby organisations helped employees develop their skills to become more employable and, in return, they delivered better productivity. This was much talked about but little was known about how it worked in practice. Bringing together employer and employee representative bodies, private and public sector organisations and government departments, a study was undertaken to look at how the concept worked in practice (see Rajan and Lane, 2000). Initially, a team of 23 organisations came together for three days to design a research framework to explore this area. Hence, rather than academic researchers devising the study and inviting others to participate, the group themselves undertook the design. This involved initially a process of problem setting, which defined the purpose of the enquiry and the question we thought we should explore.

In order to ensure participants' perspectives were used to explore this question individuals listed the factors they felt were relevant (producing more than 400 topics). Participants grouped the topics where they felt they had features in common and, following this, the groupings were named in discussion around a common theme. Using the common themes in groups, stories were recounted to examine the themes in depth and, out of this, shared themes across the stories were clustered to produce a final set of overarching themes to form the basis for a further research phase. The individual tales gradually became a shared story and a research process was created.

Engaging with these Perspectives (using Corrie and Lane, 2010) in an organisational context gives rise to questions such as:

- What Perspectives ('tales') are informing your approach to the enquiry? Do you prefer a tale- or story-based approach to formulation?
- What Perspectives ('tales') are informing the client's approach to the enquiry?
- What are the beliefs (and prejudices) that you each bring to the encounter?
- Some journeys prescribe and proscribe certain routes of investigation and intervention (Perspectives and methodologies). How do you ensure coherence between your journey and the journey of the client?
- What do you do to ensure that the client(s) is able to explore their beliefs, knowledge and competencies within the encounter?

3. Our ways of working – Process

The final fundamental issue is our ways of working, or Process. To be coherent, our ways of working, the Process we use in our engagements with client, need to be informed by our values and reflect our identity. However, in organisational contexts those values and our identity are part of a landscape of competing narratives. The challenge from social constructionist (and other) theory is to recognise those narratives as a co-constructed process and, from complexity theory, that there is no linear relationship that can be discovered to explain the unfolding events. We have to look to adopting a broader perspective in which we can see change as a personal, interpersonal and systemic process.

This could have been a very difficult challenge and certainly would be if we relied solely on models from counselling psychology predicated on personal change. However, recent years have seen the advance of methods for exploring the subjective in our experience. We are able to draw on tools in which large groups come together to create narratives of change. Techniques such as Deep Democracy (Mindell, 1996), Appreciative Enquiry (Cooperrider and Whitney, 1998), Participant Directed Facilitation (Rajan and Lane, 2000), World Café (Brown and Issacs, 2005), Socio-drama Topography (Sillett and Jimenz, 2014), and many others provide a way to work with complexity and enable groups to come together to make changes in their own lives and in the society they inhabit. These approaches are consistent with the value base of counselling psychology and provide a new set of processes that enable us to work in organisations undergoing change. These may not have originated in our field but we can embrace them. Our sister fields, such as coaching and organisational psychology, are increasingly looking to methods that deal with complex change. In the early days of counselling psychology in the UK, dealing with messy problems (Lane 1990; Stern et al., 1994) was part of the uniqueness we offered. The subjective, the nebulous, the conflictual and the collaborative were part of what we brought to the table. We looked beyond linear approaches to understanding. We must do so even more as the world gets less predictable and embrace wider decision-making tools in counselling psychology and psychotherapy (Lane and Corrie, 2012).

Our relationships with sister disciplines have sometimes been contentious but we have also actively learnt from each other. For some in our field, we have grown closer to psychotherapy and we may even define ourselves as part of that field. Where we do so, we face dangers from the self-medication of our identity – to be enslaved by the grip of the medical model of diagnosis and treatment options (an issue raised by Larsson et al., 2012). For others, we have found ourselves in the field of coaching and perhaps defining ourselves as such. The danger is to adopt too closely a goal-orientated approach to our work, which does not fully address the client journey and the multiple meanderings it might take before it reaches a destination. Our work can also overlap with others. For example, in dealing with trauma, psychologists with a background in counselling, trauma and coaching all have a role to play (Tehrani et al., 2014). Various narratives can unfold in our journey with clients, as long as we do not stifle them.

We construct, deconstruct and reconstruct the narrative as we proceed and our clients do the same. We, just like our clients, may retrace our steps, stop, start, restart, give up, re-commit and arrive somewhere, before starting all over again. (Lane and Corrie, 2006a: 54)

A case example: Ensuring a process that is consistent with our values and identity

The Global Convention on Coaching as a complex system. In a study for the Chartered Institute of Personnel and Development, Jarvis et al. (2006) explored the rapidly burgeoning field of coaching. While leading companies were making use of coaches, many HR professionals found it difficult to make sense of this area. As a field, coaching offered no agreement on purpose, an unpredictable context and competing stories about what was the best form of practice.

Out of this fairly chaotic situation conversations started to emerge. The idea that a convention be held to bring together different parties across the globe gradually took hold. The traditional linear process for such a convention would be to find a group of experts to present papers, and attendees would be able to listen and engage in conversations. However, in recognising both the turbulent state of this market and the possibilities of working with the framework of complexity, an alternative idea was proposed that rather than adopt that approach we would meet together for five days of dialogue, with no presenters, no hierarchy of experts and no predefined outcomes. We would see what emerged from a self-organising space. The process of dialogue was adapted from Brown and Isaacs' 'World Café' process (Brown and Isaacs, 2005) and Kahane's work on 'Solving tough problems' (Kahane, 2007) and Appreciative Enquiry (Cooperrider and Whitney, 1998).

Prior to the event, more than 200 people contributed ideas for scenarios across ten core areas. Once these scenarios were available, 61 people agreed to commit five days to meet in Dublin (July 2008) to engage in dialogue about these scenarios. No agenda was set, no outcome was agreed for the dialogue; rather all present agreed to take part and see what emerged. What did emerge was a Declaration. It was jointly crafted, read out and participants signed up to it and agreed to take it back to their respective organisations to take the tasks forward. Within three months over 15,000 signed up to the Declaration, which has since become a catalyst for collaborative dialogue between a diversity of different and sometimes competing professional disciplines and cultures across the world. (The output of the meeting is available to download at: http://gccweb.ning.com/forum/topics/2328492:Topic:47.)

Subsequent meetings have taken place and further work undertaken, but the key is not that this group did the work but rather that the conversations generated multiple activities in other groups which each form self-generating constellations who take forward their own stories.

Think about yourself as a counselling psychologist. Based on your sense of identity (your Purpose) and the values you hold dear (your Perspectives) and what you actually 'do' with the client in organisational settings (your Process), you may wish to consider the following questions:

- What Process (including any method or tool) do you use to ensure that the Purpose is met within the constraints of the Perspectives available to you and your client?
- How do you structure the Process for the work?
- How is this Process similar or different from your initial assumptions as the relational narrative of the work unfolds? What factors mediated your choices?

Consider, if you were present in Dublin (having read the Declaration), what would you bring to that encounter?

A BRIEF NOTE ON TRAINING IN COUNSELLING PSYCHOLOGY

As a counselling psychologist working in organisations, I worry that the exposure of those in training is largely to work in therapeutic contexts. While important, this should not exclude placements in community and organisational settings. Seeking to place students in community contexts does expose them to much of the complexity that a contemporary approach to counselling psychology demands. The opportunities in private-sector organisations are more limited, although coaching placements are sometime available and this at least provides some flavour of the field. Counselling psychology incorporates psychotherapeutic work but traditionally was not defined by it. As a field, it encompassed the dispossessed, the radical and the marginalised in our communities as well as celebrating human potential (Stern et al., 1994). We need to ensure future trainees have the experience of working in settings that draw upon the full range of our discipline and its complex decision-making frameworks (Lane and Corrie, 2012). We cannot assume that the technical knowledge acquired in training will fit our trainees for the challenges of tomorrow but we can encourage them to commit to the lifelong discipline of critical thinking.

CONCLUSION: FROM LINEAR THINKING TO THE MESSY WORLD OF COMPLEXITY – THE FUTURE OF COUNSELLING PSYCHOLOGY IN ORGANISATIONS

Much of our traditional theoretical base has been predicated on the idea of change as a personal and often linear process. This is perhaps most marked in cognitive approaches (Antecedents lead to Beliefs which result in Consequences), where it is assumed that if we change the way we view (think about) situations we can alter our behaviour. The challenge from social constructionist (and other) theory is to recognise change as a co-constructed process and, from complexity theory, that there is no linear relationship that can be discovered. By adopting a broader perspective we can see change as a personal, interpersonal and systemic process (Lane, 1990; Lane and Down, 2010; Lane and Corrie, 2012). This gives us perspectives where working towards linear goals can be replaced by embracing emergence in conversations. This enhances the potential for more creativity. This chapter argues that the work of counselling (and coaching psychology) can address an organisational world of increasing uncertainty and ambiguity. Counselling psychologists will continue to be asked to work with individuals requiring more input than is typical of coaching interventions. However, embracing our ability to work with the messy world of complexity is both our biggest challenge and opportunity.

REFERENCES

Askew, A. (1988) Aggressive Behaviour in Boys: To What Extent Is It Institutionalised. In D.P. Tattum and D.A. Lane (eds), *Bullying in Schools*. Stoke-on-Trent: Trentham.

Barkham, M. (1990) Counselling Psychology in Search of an Identity. *The Psychologist: Bulletin of the British Psychological Society*, 12: 536–539.

Birkeland Nielsen, M., Tangen, T., Idsoe, T., Berge Matthiesen, S. and Magerøy, N. (2015) Post-traumatic Stress Disorder as a Consequence of Bullying at Work and at School: A Literature Review and Meta-analysis. *Aggression and Violent Behavior*, 21: 17–24.

British Psychological Society (2013) *Good Practice Guidelines on the Use of Psychological Formulation*. Leicester: BPS. http://shop.bps.org.uk/good-practice-guidelines-on-the-use-of-psychological-formulation.html (accessed 18 September 2015).

Brown, J. and Issacs, D. (2005) *The World Cafe Book: Shaping Our Futures through Conversations that Matter*. San Francisco, CA: Berrett-Koehler.

Bull, A.D. (1992) Confidential Counselling Service: A New Breed of EAP? *Employee Counselling Today*, 4(2): 25–28.

Bury, D. and Strauss, S.M. (2006) The Scientist Practitioner in a Counselling Psychology Setting. In D.A. Lane and S. Corrie (eds), *The Modern Scientist-Practitioner: A Guide to Practice in Psychology* (pp. 119–129). Hove: Routledge.

Carroll, M. (1995) The Counsellor in Organizational Settings some Reflections. *Employee Counselling Today*, 7(1): 23–29.

Cavanagh, M. and Lane, D. (2012) Coaching Psychology Coming of Age: The Challenges We Face in the Messy World of Complexity. *International Coaching Psychology Review*, 7(1): 75–90.

Checkland, P. (1989) Soft Systems Methodology. In J. Rosenhead (ed.), *Rational Analysis for a Problematic World: Problem Structuring Methods for Complexity, Uncertainty and Conflict* (pp. 71–100). Chichester: Wiley.

Cooperrider, D.L. and Whitney, D. (1998) Appreciative Inquiry: A Positive Revolution in Change. In P. Holman and T. Devane (eds), *The Change Handbook* (pp. 245–263). San Francisco, CA: Berrett-Koehler.

Cooperrider, D. and Whitney, D. (2005) *Appreciative Inquiry: A Positive Revolution in Change.* San Francisco, CA: Berrett-Koehler.

Corrie, S. and Callanan, M.M. (2000) A Review of the Scientist Practitioner Model: Reflections on its Potential Contribution to Counseling Psychology within the Context of Current Health Care Trends. *British Journal of Medical Psychology*, 73: 413–427.

Corrie, S. and Lane, D.A. (2010) *Constructing Stories, Telling Tales: A Guide to Formulation in Applied Psychology.* London: Karnac.

Deverall, M. (1997) The Counselling Consultant's Role in Assessing Organizations for Counselling. In M. Carroll and M. Walton (eds), *Handbook of Counselling in Organizations* (pp. 111–129). London: Sage.

Dickens, R.S. (1999) The Alignment of EAP and Business Unit Goals. In J.M. Oher (ed.), *The Employee Assistance Handbook* (pp. 421–438). Hoboken, NJ: John Wiley & Sons.

Fredrickson, B.L. and Losada, M.F. (2005) Positive Affect and the Complex Dynamics of Human Flourishing. *American Psychologist*, 60(7): 678–686.

Gallagher, M.S. and Meehan, K. (1996) Training Counsellors to Work with People who Live with Cancer: A Needs-led Approach to Planning. *Journal of Community & Applied Social Psychology*, 6(4): 281–285.

Gergen, K.J. and Gergen, M.M. (1988) Narrative and the Self as Relationship. In L. Berkowitz (ed.), *Advances in Experimental Social Psychology* (Vol. 21, pp. 17–56). New York: Academic Press.

Giddens, A. (1991) *Modernity and Self-identity: Self and Society in the Late Modern Age.* Stanford, CA: Stanford University Press.

Ginsberg, M.R., Kilburg, R.R. and Gomes, P.G. (1999) Organizational Counseling and the Delivery of Integrated Human Services in the Workplace: An Evolving Model for Employee Assistance Theory and Practice. In J.M. Oher (ed.), *The Employee Assistance Handbook* (pp. 439–456). Hoboken, NJ: Wiley.

Grogan, J. (2012) *Encountering America: Humanistic Psychology, Sixties Culture, and the Shaping of the Modern Self.* New York: Harper.

Henriques, J., Hollway, W., Urwin, C., Venn, C. and Walkerdine, V. (1984) *Changing the Subject: Psychology, Social Regulation and Subjectivity.* London: Methuen.

Jarvis, J., Lane, D.A. and Fillery-Travis, A. (2006) *The Case for Coaching: Making Evidence Based Decisions.* London: Chartered Institute of Personnel and Development.

Kahane, A. (2007) *Solving Tough Problems: An Open Way of Listening and Creating New Realities.* San Francisco, CA: Berrett-Koehler.

Kahn, M.S. (2014) *Coaching on the Axis: Working with Complexity in Business and Executive Coaching.* London: Karnac.

Kwiatkowski, R. and Winter, D. (2006) Roots, Relativity and Realism: The Occupational Psychologist as Scientist-Practitioner. In D.A. Lane and S. Corrie (eds), *The Modern Scientist-Practitioner: A Guide to Practice in Psychology* (pp. 158–172). Hove: Routledge.

Lane, D.A. (1990) *The Impossible Child*. Trentham: Trentham Books.

Lane, D.A. (1991) Psychological Aspects of Disaster: Issues for the 1990s. *British Journal of Guidance and Counselling*, 19(1): 31–43.

Lane, D.A. (1993) Counselling Psychology in Organisations. *Review of Applied Psychology/ Revue Européenne*, 43(1): 41–46.

Lane, D. A. and Corrie, S. (2006a) *The Modern Scientist-Practitioner: A Guide to Practice in Psychology*. Hove: Routledge.

Lane, D.A. and Corrie, S. (2006b) Counselling Psychology: Its Influences and Future. *Counselling Psychology Review*, 21(1): 12–24.

Lane, D.A. and Corrie, S. (2012) *Making Successful Decisions in Counselling and Psychotherapy: A Practical Guide*. Maidenhead: Open University Press.

Lane, D.A. and Down, M. (2010) The Art of Managing for the Future: Leadership of Turbulence. *Management Decision*, 48(4): 512–527.

Larsson, P., Brooks, O. and Loewenthal, D. (2012) Counselling Psychology and Diagnostic Categories: A Critical Literature Review. *Counselling Psychology Review*, 27(3): 55–67.

Lee, C.C. (1998) Professional Counseling in a Global Context: Collaboration for International Social Action. In C.C. Lee and G.R. Walz (eds), *Social Action: A Mandate for Counselors* (pp. 293–304). Alexandria, VA: American Counseling Association.

Lo, M.-C.M. (2005) Professions: Prodigal Daughter of Modernity. In J. Adams, E.S. Clemens and A.S. Orloff (eds), *Remaking Modernity: Politics, Processes and History in Sociology* (pp. 381–406). Durham, NC: Duke University Press.

Losada, M. (1999) The Complex Dynamics of High Performance Teams. *Mathematical and Computer Modelling*, 30(9–10): 179–192.

Losada, M. and Heaphy, E. (2004) The Role of Positivity and Connectivity in the Performance of Business Teams: A Nonlinear Dynamics Model. *American Behavioral Scientist*, 47(6): 740–765.

McLeod, J. (2001) Developing a Research Tradition Consistent with the Practices and Values of Counselling and Psychotherapy: Why Counselling and Psychotherapy Research is Necessary. *Counselling and Psychotherapy Research*, 1(1): 3–11.

McLeod, J. (2003) *An Introduction to Counselling* (3rd edn). Milton Keynes: Open University Press.

Meara, N.M. and Myers, R.A. (1999) A History of Division 17 (Counseling Psychology): Establishing Stability amid Change. In D.A. Dewsbury (ed.), *Unification through Division: Histories of the Divisions of the American Psychological Association* (Vol. 3, pp. 9–41). Washington, DC: American Psychological Association.

Mindell, A. (1996) Discovering the World in the Individual: The World Channel in Psychotherapy. *Journal of Humanistic Psychology*, 36(3): 67–84.

Moore, T. and Rae, J. (2009) Outsiders: How Some Counselling Psychologists Construct Themselves. *Counselling Psychology Quarterly*, 22(4): 381–392.

Nelson-Jones, R. (1999) On Becoming Counselling Psychology in the Society: Establishing the Counselling Psychology Section. *Counselling Psychology Review*, 14(3): 30–37.

Nixon, J. and Carroll, M. (1994) Can a Line Manager also be a Counsellor? *Employee Counselling Today*, 6(1): 10–15.

Orlans, V. (1989) Counselling in the Workplace: A Review and Thoughts for the Future. *Employee Counselling Today*, 1(1): 3–6.

Phillips, L. and Smith, R. (2011) *Developing School Counselling Services for Children and Young People in Wales*. Slough: NFER.

Rajan, A. and Lane, D.A. (2000) *Summary of the National Employability Study*. London: Chartered Institute of Personnel and Development.

Pugh, D. and Coyle, A. (2010) The Construction of Counselling Psychology in Britain: A Discourse Analysis of Counselling Psychology Texts. *Counselling Psychology Quarterly*, 13(1): 85–98.

Reddy, M. (1994) EAPs and Their Future in the UK: History Repeating Itself? *Personnel Review*, 23(7): 60–78.

Roland, E. and Munthe, E. (eds) (1989) *Bullying: An International* Perspective. London: Fulton Press.

Rose, N. (1996) The Death of the Social? Re-figuring the Territory of Government. *Economy and Society*, 25(3): 327–356.

Sillett, S. and Jimenez, J. (2014) Looking beyond Needs: Capacity Focused Development through the Socio-Drama Topography Processs. In S. Locke and L. Allibone (eds), *Knowledges and Publics: Beyond Engagement and Transfer* (pp. 119–147). Newcastle-on-Tyne: Cambridge Scholars Publishing.

Singh, K. (2007) *Counselling Skills for Managers*. New Delhi: PHI.

Somers, M.R. and Gibson, G.D. (1994) Reclaiming the Epistemological 'Other': Narrative and the Social Constitution of Identity. In C. Calhoun (ed.), *Social Theory and the Politics of Identity* (pp. 37–99). Oxford: Blackwell Publishing.

Strawbridge, S. (2010) Prologue: Telling Tales. In S. Corrie and D.A. Lane (eds), *Constructing Stories, Telling Tales: A Guide to Formulation in Applied Psychology*. London: Karnac.

Strawbridge, S. and Woolfe, R. (1996) Counselling Psychology: A Sociological Perspective. In R. Woolfe and W. Dryden (eds), *Handbook of Counselling Psychology*. London: Sage.

Strawbridge, S. and Woolfe, R. (2004) Counselling Psychology in Context. In R. Woolfe, W. Dryden and S. Strawbridge (eds), *Handbook of Counselling Psychology* (2nd edn). London: Sage.

Stern, E., Lane, D.A. and McDevitt, C. (1994) *Europe in Change: The Contribution of Counselling*. Rugby: European Association for Counselling.

Tattum, D. and Lane, D.A. (1988) *Bullying in Schools*. Stoke-on-Trent: Trentham.

Tehrani, N. (1996) Counselling in the Post Office: Facing up to the Legal and Ethical Dilemmas. *British Journal of Guidance and Counselling*, 24(2): 265–275.

Tehrani, N. (2006) Counselling in the Workplace: The Organizational Counsellor. *Counselling Psychology Quarterly*, 11(1): 23–32.

Tehrani, N. (2004) Bullying: A source of chronic post-traumatic stress? *British Journal of Guidance & Counselling*, 32(3): 357–366.

Tehrani, N. (2011) *Managing Trauma in the Workplace*. Hove: Routledge.

Tehrani, N., Osborne, D. and Lane, D.A. (2012) Restoring Meaning and Wholeness: The Role for Coaching after a Trauma. *International Coaching Psychology Review*, 7(2): 239–246.

Upton, D. (1997) Developing Employee Counselling. Research thesis, Cranfield University. Available at http://dspace.lib.cranfield.ac.uk/handle/1826/3628

Vespia, K.M. (2006) Integrating Professional Identities: Counselling Psychologist, Scientist-Practitioner and Undergraduate Educator. *Counselling Psychology Quarterly*, 19(3): 265–280.

Woolfe, R. (1990) Counselling Psychology in Britain: An Idea Whose Time Has Come. *The Psychologist: Bulletin of the British Psychological Society*, 12: 531–535.

Woolfe, R. (1996) The Nature of Counselling Psychology. In R. Woolfe and W. Dryden (eds), *Handbook of Counselling Psychology*. London: Sage.

Yates, L. and McCloud, J. (2000) Social Justice and the Middle. *Australian Educational Researcher*, 27(3): 59–78.

Yates, L., Tennant, M., Solomon, N., Rhodes, C. and Chappell, C. (2003) *Reconstructing the Lifelong Learner: Pedagogy and Identity in Individual, Organisational and Social Change*. Hove: Routledge.

28
WORKING AS A COUNSELLING PSYCHOLOGIST IN FORENSIC CONTEXTS
CLIVE SIMS

INTRODUCTION

The purpose of this chapter is to introduce some of the varied forensic contexts in which counselling psychologists work. These range from the obvious, such as forensic mental health units, through secure children's homes to court work as a professional or expert witness. The one thing that won't be included is how to be a criminal! Those who have ambitions to become another 'Cracker' will also be disappointed as fiction and fact do not match and, unlike the Mounties, we do not always get our man.

Before proceeding further, a brief definition of 'forensic' is required. Previously, in 'Counselling Psychology in Forensic Settings' (Sims, 2010), I went into some detail about the popular misconceptions associated with the word. Counselling psychology has since moved on and there are now many more practitioners working in those settings and most trainees will have some idea about what is meant by the term, but may not know the detail, or the broad range of 'forensic' settings. I propose to divide the chapter into two main sections, the first being work in statutory, private and third sector settings, which is directly 'forensic', and, secondly, private practice, specifically the practice of the expert witness. Before addressing these, the philosophical dilemmas for counselling psychologists working with offenders are briefly examined. Psychology continues to grow in its influence and the importance of psychological input at the assessment, the administration of justice and at the treatment stages is increasingly valued across the agencies associated with the legal systems in the United Kingdom. Counselling psychology, with its humanistic philosophical background, is able to offer an important challenge to the prevailing positivistic models in medicine and in the law.

Currently, three groups of applied psychologists, in addition to counselling psychologists, provide forensic services: (a) forensic psychologists, (b) clinical psychologists, including forensic clinical psychologists, and (c) educational psychologists. Academic psychologists may, on occasion, be called on as experts or to make comment to the media on forensic matters but this is not common. All the applied groups have defined training pathways at postgraduate level and defined career pathways although there may be considerable overlap in professional practice, both in activities and settings, and more than one professional grouping may be working together in the same setting. Examples of this are educational and clinical psychologists working in secure units for young people, and forensic and clinical psychologists working in specialist units for older adults within the prison estate (Sims, 2008). Each has a specific role but together aim to provide a comprehensive psychological service to the particular client group. It may appear that there is little space or opportunity for counselling psychologists, but that is far from the case. Counselling psychologists are able to bring a unique perspective to the field of criminological psychology, but the very nature of this unique perspective can cause difficulties.

PHILOSOPHICAL DILEMMAS

Counselling psychologists, particularly those who espouse a broadly humanistic approach based on the works of Carl Rogers' Client Centered Therapy (CCT) (Rogers, 1961) or Albert Ellis's Rational Emotive Behaviour Therapy (REBT) (Ellis, 1962), heavily influenced by Adlerian psychotherapy but which many do not consider as humanistic, although Ellis himself did (Ellis, 1957, and 1996, personal communication), may find that they are forced into a position where they may feel that they have to compromise the basic principle of 'unconditional positive regard' with the requirements of criminological rehabilitation. This is particularly relevant as REBT has introduced a general embargo on the use of 'demanding language', which conflicts with the need to use prescriptive words in the moral discourse required by forensic rehabilitation. However, a modified Hegelian approach (Hegel, 1977) may overcome this problem. If the 'unconditional positive regard' refers to the client as an individual and not to the client's criminal activities, then so-called 'demanding language' can reasonably be used to address the offending behaviour. To do otherwise would do a major disservice to the client as it would leave unaddressed the very behaviours that have brought them into conflict with the law.

Whatever developmental model the psychological therapist uses, all would agree that moral behaviour is acquired through learning. The vast majority is learned in early childhood and adolescence, but moral growth continues through the life-span as the adult encounters new challenges and has to make new decisions. If the internalised moral code derived from childhood is 'skewed', then adult moral decisions are also necessarily skewed unless new moral learning has taken place. The child is born with a set of genetically innate predispositions. However, by about the age of five, a child's heredity has gone as far as it can, and innate predispositions are moderated by the social environment. It is the development of what Alfred Adler calls 'social interest' that predetermines the psychological and moral health of the individual (Ansbacher and Ansbacher, 1956). There is a balance between 'social interest' and 'self-interest'; the greater the weight on the self-interest side the less psychologically and morally healthy is the individual. Therapy within the criminal justice system is aimed, in the long term, at helping the client develop a greater sense of 'social interest'. For the individual client, of course, there may well be a shorter-term self-interested goal as it will keep them away from the courts and punishment.

In summary, therapy for clients who have offended requires them to explore their offending behaviour with the ultimate aim that they choose not to re-offend. To do this without exploring the individual's moral perceptions and internalised moral code is difficult, if not impossible, and to do this the therapist has to use moral language. This is not inconsistent with either the humanistic or phenomenological background of counselling psychology. A person is more than simply the sum of their individual behaviours.

CAREER PATHWAYS

Within the overall forensic psychology environment there are two major subdivisions, criminological psychology and legal psychology. These, in their turn, reflect two of the major subdivisions of the law and legal practice, criminal law and civil law. The third major area of the law, constitutional law, need not detain us as it is unlikely that counselling psychologists will be professionally involved. Anyone aspiring to become a counselling psychologist working in a forensic setting has to achieve a good first degree in psychology from a course accredited by the British Psychological Society (BPS), followed by postgraduate training on a doctoral-level course that is accredited both by the BPS and by the Health and Care Professions Council (HCPC), or take the 'Independent Route', which leads to the doctoral-level 'Qualification in Counselling Psychology' of the BPS and which is also accredited by the HCPC.

Whichever route is taken, supervised practical placements are a key part of the learning experience. It is at this point that the aspiring counselling psychologist may be able to get a forensic placement. Direct criminological forensic placements can, for example, be in forensic mental health services, with the Probation Service or with youth offending teams. It may also be possible to obtain placements in other secure facilities, including those for people with learning disability or Autistic Spectrum Disorder (ASD). Indirect forensic placements, i.e. placements where there is a strong forensic element but where the main purpose of the service is otherwise defined, may be sought in Psychiatric Intensive Care Units (PICU) and Challenging Behaviour Units (CBU) in local NHS Mental Health Trusts, or in secure units for children and adolescents run by local authorities. Drug and Alcohol Services may also offer the opportunity to gain some forensic experience. A number of privately run forensic facilities also offer training placements. By whatever means, the only way to get a valid insight into forensic criminological work is to gain the supported experience that comes from a training placement. Working in a secure setting is not everyone's cup of tea so and it is better to find out sooner rather than later.

It is essential that overall placement supervision is the responsibility of a qualified counselling psychologist who is, ideally, registered on the BPS Register of Applied Psychology Practice Supervisors (RAPPS). On university-based placements this will normally be a member of staff, but on the Independent Route it will be a Co-ordinating Supervisor who is an experienced counselling psychologist who has undergone training by the BPS. For anyone aspiring to take the Independent Route, it is essential that all the BPS guidelines and regulations for that route, available on the BPS website, are consulted, and that anyone who is approached to be Co-ordinating Supervisor is registered specifically as such on RAPPS. Also, for the QCoP, the Co-ordinating Supervisor should not be one of the candidate's Placement Supervisors, nor should they be the candidate's line manager, to avoid conflict of interest. While ideally the day-to-day supervision in any placement should be with a counselling psychologist, this is less likely to occur in a forensic setting than elsewhere, such as in an NHS acute mental health unit. Often practice supervision will be provided by the employer as part of their governance programme. If the supervisor is not a counselling psychologist, then they must be approved by the Co-ordinating Supervisor or by the university. Ideally, the practice supervisor in university-approved placements should not be the line manager of the supervisee but this is often not possible, particularly in small NHS departments. If, as a trainee, you are lucky enough to get a forensic placement, it is important to take full advantage of it in order to experience as wide a range of settings as possible. The trainee should try to arrange visits to magistrate's courts and crown courts to see justice being administered. They should also engage in visits to prisons, hostels and other settings where they may not be working, e.g. NHS Regional Secure Units (RSUs). These visits will add breadth to the trainee's experience and allow them to make an insightful choice should they decide to work in a forensic setting once they have qualified.

WORKING IN FORENSIC CRIMINOLOGICAL SETTINGS

Once qualified, the next choice is where to work. In the forensic criminological field there are usually two broad areas worth investigating: (a) working with 'mentally disordered offenders', usually in a healthcare setting, either the NHS or private; or (b) working in what might be broadly termed an administration of justice setting. This may be closed secure, such as a prison, open secure, such as a probation hostel, or may be within the community. Specific settings and the types of job that might be available are outlined below. In this period of major change, driven both by government initiatives and by financial constraints, only broad-brush guidance can be offered, but it is hoped that this will give a flavour of the opportunities that are there.

HEALTHCARE SETTINGS

Secure facilities that are specifically forensic are tiered in three levels in the NHS. High, sometimes described as maximum, security are represented in England by the Special Hospitals, Broadmoor, Rampton and Ashworth hospitals and by Carstairs in Scotland. In these facilities patients present an immediate and severe risk of danger to others and require a significant period of treatment, usually lasting several years, before they can be considered for step-down to a lower level of security. Below these are the medium secure units, of which there is usually at least one in each NHS region. Below these are the low secure forensic units found in most NHS Mental Health Trusts. Parallel to the NHS facilities are privately run medium and low secure units, some of which are specifically forensic while others are Challenging Behaviour Units which take both difficult-to-manage patients and ones referred from the courts. Secure, in this context, relates to the range of physical, relational and procedural measures taken to ensure the provision of a safe and secure environment. All security measures are in place to ensure the safety of patients, staff and the general public, to prevent escape, absconding and to ensure patients return from periods of leave into the community. All patients, whether in NHS or in private facilities, are detained under sections of the Mental Health Act 1983 (revised 2007) (Department of Health, 2008), and are subject to all the safeguards contained in the Act. Convicted prisoners who are transferred from prison are also detained under the Act until such time as they are returned to prison. It should be noted that compulsory treatment under the Mental Health Act can only take place in a hospital context, not in prison, thus there is frequently a waiting list for the most seriously ill patients, given the limited number of beds available. According to the Prison Reform Trust (2014), 72 per cent of male and 70 per cent of female sentenced prisoners have two or more mental health disorders, 20 per cent of prisoners have four of the five major mental health disorders, and 10 per cent of men and 30 per cent of women have had a previous psychiatric admission before coming into prison. Neurotic and personality disorders are particularly prevalent – 40 per cent of male and 63 per cent of female sentenced prisoners have a neurotic disorder, over three times the level in the general population. Sixty-two per cent of male and 57 per cent of female sentenced prisoners have a personality disorder. For a prisoner to be transferred, their illness has to be such as to be unmanageable in prison, the most common reasons being severe psychosis, severe self-harm and attempted suicide. We will look at the management of mental illness in prison when we look at Prison In-reach Services, where counselling psychologists have a very important role to play.

In addition to the issue of mental illness, a large proportion of prisoners have a recognised learning disability or a neuro-developmental disorder such as autism. As a result of financial constraints, the government has delayed extending the trial court liaison and diversion sites, and so the inappropriate placements continue. While the main aim of diversion is social care where a significant crime has been committed and where there is a co-existing mental illness or personality disorder, a hospital order under the Mental Health Act may be substituted. In such cases, detention may be either in a specialist NHS or a private sector unit or in a general forensic mental health unit.

The foregoing background is necessary for the counselling psychologist to understand the environment that they will be entering should they wish to work in secure mental health services. The philosophy of counselling psychology is essentially libertarian, with the patient/client being the focus. In the secure services the approach is quite different. Firstly, all patients are detained under the Mental Health Act 1983 (Department of Health, 2008) and thus are subject to limitations to their freedom of action and, where necessary, to compulsory treatment. Secondly, the main focus is public safety and all therapeutic processes are subsumed to this overarching requirement. This may seem draconian, but it must be remembered that any patient detained in a secure mental health facility will have committed a crime, usually of a violent or sexual nature, which would lead to a substantial prison sentence. Within these constraints, however, there is much scope for psychological work. Traditionally, this has been carried out by clinical psychologists, whose treatment model is largely medically based. However, increasingly counselling psychologists are making inroads, bringing with them the humanistic philosophy of the discipline which is a valuable addition to the multidisciplinary team (MDT). The core team usually consists of psychiatrists, psychologists, nurses and occupational therapists. There may also be arts therapists and physiotherapists attached to the team. All treatment is co-ordinated by the MDT and all feedback is to the MDT. Because of potentially dangerous and disruptive behaviour by the patients, confidentiality is maintained within the team, rather than with the individual, and all notes and records are shared. Working in such an environment may seem to compromise the very essence of counselling psychology but it is absolutely necessary for the safety of staff and for security. Much of what the counselling psychologist does in the unit will be similar to the work carried out by clinical psychologists. Assessments are an important feature of this work. Therefore, any counselling psychologist aspiring to work in forensic mental health will need a sound background in basic psychological assessments, including neuropsychological assessment, as the incidence of neurological damage, particularly among those patients with a history of interpersonal violence, is over 70 per cent. Additionally, psychologists usually carry out risk assessments using standardised actuarial tools, such as the Historical, Clinical Risk Management 20 (HCR-20, Version 3) (Douglas et al., 2013; Guy et al., 2013), a comprehensive set of professional guidelines for risk assessment and management. Typically, these are done for prediction in order to identify future criminal acts and then to identify the risk factors associated with them and for risk management purposes. The latter might be considered to be the 'bread and butter' of the psychologist's work as it aims to identify what interventions are required to reduce the risk of re-offending, what therapy is needed to reduce the client's level of risk or what conditions need to be implemented to manage any future risk. There is considerable literature on risk assessment and its uses and limitations, which is beyond the scope of this chapter. It is therefore recommended that counselling psychologists should access it and form their own conclusions as it its value, particularly the ethical element (Arrigo and Shipley, 2005: Chapter 1; Guy et al., 2013).

Therapy in forensic mental health settings always consists of interlocking multidisciplinary elements. Besides psychological therapy, there will be medication and occupational therapy as well as the specialised nursing care provided by the forensic psychiatric nurses.

Psychological therapy will, in many ways, be similar to that found in non-forensic settings but with the additional elements of helping the client to address the offending behaviour and of risk management. For many clients this will involve specific therapy aimed at the use of illicit substances. Therefore, the counselling psychologist will need to be aware of the interaction between such substances and mental illness (Dual Diagnosis) and specific interventions for clients with substance use issues, such as Motivational Interviewing (Miller and Rollnick, 2002). Few clients will have experienced any psychological therapy previous to their referral to the forensic unit and those that have are likely to have had Cognitive Behaviour Therapy (CBT) or possibly Dialectical Behaviour Therapy (DBT). Because of the interlocking nature of the therapies provided by other professions, a holistic approach is necessary in order to avoid psychological therapy being marginalised. This is where the broad-based training of the counselling psychologist comes into its own, in that a person-centred humanistic approach, valuing the clients as human beings while addressing their criminal behaviour, is, in the author's experience, the most effective approach and provides a balance to the medical model being used elsewhere. In addition to the in-patient facilities, all low-security services will have both day services and community services. In both, the therapeutic programme is continued until such time as the client is stepped down to the general psychiatric services or is discharged. As can be seen, the psychologist's involvement is usually very long term, thus enabling long-term engagement in long-term therapy to enable the clients to address the issues that have brought them into forensic services in depth and to rebuild their lives.

SOCIAL SERVICES SETTINGS

Secure services for children and adolescents are the responsibility of the Social Services. At present it is unlikely that counselling psychologists will be working directly within them as most psychologists employed are educational psychologists and child psychotherapists. If a counselling psychologist was also a qualified child psychotherapist, then they would be employed specifically in that role. The local Child and Adolescent Mental Health Services (CAMHS) may be involved but would not be providing a specifically forensic service.

CRIMINAL JUSTICE SERVICES (CJS)

For the purposes of this chapter, the term 'Criminal Justice Services' (CJS) is being used very broadly but excluding forensic mental health services, discussed above, and expert witness services and the courts, which will be discussed below. In some ways the services provided by the CJS parallels that of the health services in that there are secure services with varying levels of security and community services provided by the Probation Service. Some services are directly provided by central government while others, including prisons, have private provision.

PRISON PSYCHOLOGICAL SERVICES

Much of the work carried out by psychologists in the prison estate is focused on clinical risk assessment and clinical interventions designed to reduce the possibility of reconviction. The majority of this work is carried out by 'prison psychologists' who are qualified and HCPC-registered forensic psychologists. Currently, unless dual qualified, both as a forensic psychologist and as a counselling psychologist, it is unlikely that a counselling psychologist would be directly employed within the Prison Service. However, there are occasionally opportunities for counselling psychologists in training to obtain placements, usually in Young Offenders' Institutions, so in future we may see such employment opportunities develop. In the meantime, that experience would be particularly useful should the counselling psychologist seek employment in forensic mental health services, NHS Prison In-Reach services (see below) or with the Probation Service.

The most likely area in which counselling psychologists would be working directly in prisons would be as members of 'Prison In-Reach Teams', who provide care and treatment for inmates' mental and emotional ill-health. Research in the latter part of the last century, showing a high prevalence of mental disorder in prisons (Gunn et al., 1991), played a key role in identifying the need for comprehensive mental health services throughout the prison estate. *Patient or Prisoner?* (HM Inspectorate of Prisons for England and Wales, 1996) made it clear that prisoners were not getting the same standard of care as was expected in the NHS, and recommended that the NHS should on take responsibility for all prison health care. This included mental health care. Comprehensive needs assessments were carried out and it was clearly demonstrated that prisoners with mental disorders differed significantly from general adult patients in having more complex needs relating to mental health and more unmet needs (Harty et al., 2003). Unmet needs were in the management of symptoms of psychosis, general psychological distress, daytime activities, company, welfare benefits, money and food. A major problem that was identified was the lack of prompt transfer to in-patient facilities when required, resulting in very distressed individuals having to be managed for long periods in the prison hospital wing or in segregation (McKenzie and Sales, 2008). This continues to be a problem due to the shortage of beds in secure hospital facilities.

As a result, 'Prison In-Reach Teams' were commissioned from local NHS mental health trusts. These parallel Community Mental Health Teams (CMHTs) and are usually made up of a psychiatrist, a clinical or counselling psychologist and community psychiatric nurses. Here it must be emphasised that, although operating within a secure forensic setting, with all that that implies, this is not a forensic mental health team but rather a community mental health service operating within a specific community, and it is usually managed by the local NHS trust's Adult Mental Health Services (AMHS) rather than from the Forensic Mental Health

Service, except in exceptional circumstances. In-Reach services should offer comprehensive mental health care for vulnerable prisoners with the active co-operation of discipline and other prison staff so that the regime does not undermine care. In a local prison, with remand facilities, comprehensive multidisciplinary assessment is carried out followed by community care, day care or care within the estate's health centre. The latter would normally be prisoners with severe mental health problems awaiting transfer, under the Mental Health Act 1983 (Department of Health, 2008) to secure NHS facilities for specialist in-patient treatment. On return, these prisoners would, once again, become the responsibility of the In-Reach Team. Another important function of the team is that of liaising with the courts and the various criminal justice agencies and providing reports to the courts, to disciplinary panels, to the Probation Service and to parole boards.

Within the In-Reach Team, the counselling psychologist will play the same important role that they would play in any CMHT. In addition to being part of the multidisciplinary team, they will assess and treat clients individually, they will actively encourage psychological mind-edness within the team, they will provide leadership and clinical supervision to other team members, and they will provide training in psychological techniques both to team members and to prison staff. A further important function for the counselling psychologist is to liaise and, ideally, work with prison forensic psychologists. This is particularly important where specific manualised programmes, usually based on CBT models, for sex offenders, for anger management, and for prisoners with challenging behaviour are being carried out under the supervision of prison psychologists. Here the counselling psychologist can bring their humanistic/person-centred philosophy to bear on what is essentially a mechanistic approach. However, such approaches are deeply ingrained within the prison regime, so the counselling psychologist will need to bring to bear all their diplomatic skills.

Finally, a new development related to Prison In-Reach is the extension of Improved Access to Psychological Therapies (IAPT) to prisons. This is a relatively new approach and reflects the extension of IAPT from working-age adults to other groups with mental health issues in England. The approach is CBT and there are two levels. Currently, it is being tested for effectiveness in selected prisons but will eventually be rolled out to all local prisons. It will probably be linked to the Prison GP Service rather than to the Prison In-Reach service, which will continue to work with prisoners with more severe and enduring mental health problems.

THE PROBATION SERVICE

We have looked at the input that counselling psychologists can give to the criminal justice system in hospitals and in prisons. They can also contribute to the work of the Probation Service, either directly through training as Probation Officers, or indirectly in the treatment of offenders, offering specialist therapeutic input. Currently, most of this work is done by forensic psychologists but certainly openings are available. With government-driven changes in the Probation Service, in particular with a number of its functions being taken over by private firms or the third sector, it is likely that more openings will be available in such areas as substance misuse programmes, anger management and sex offender treatment programmes.

THE COURTS

Counselling psychologists may contribute to the functioning of the courts and the administration of justice in three ways: (a) as a witness of fact, (b) as a professional witness, and (c) as an expert witness. In the first case, the psychologist is simply a witness to an incident like any other witness; no professional judgement or opinion is required. As a professional witness, the counselling psychologist may be required to give evidence concerning a client with whom they are working. This will largely be factual but they may be required to give an opinion to the court. Professional witnesses are not independent and this will be taken into account in the judge's summing up and directions. Finally, there is the expert witness, who is independent and who is instructed by the solicitors for one side or the other, except in the case of the 'Single Joint Expert' (SJE) who is instructed by both sides. This is increasingly common in civil proceedings, e.g. personal injury, and in the Family Courts. Experts have been giving advice to the courts since at least the Middle Ages: 'ale tasters' were a common feature of manorial court rolls, although how 'expert' they were is lost in the mists of time. The position was also very unpopular probably due to the dreadful quality of much of the ale (Sims, 2012).

THE MODERN EXPERT

Expert witnessing in its modern form dates from the eighteenth century and the case of *Folkes v Chadd* (1782), in which Lord Mansfield, in his judgment, defined the role of the expert witness: 'The opinion of scientific men on proven facts may be given by men of science within their own science.' There has been no better definition since, although refinements, such as the requirement that the expert witness should be a 'skilled person, who has by dint of training and practice, acquired a good knowledge of the science or art concerning which his opinion is sought...' (*R v Bunnis*, 1964), have been added (Sims, 2012).Of considerable practical importance is the requirement that the evidence, given by the expert, should be 'outside the experience of a judge or a jury' (*R v Turner*, 1975). Thus, for example, a psychologist cannot give expert testimony on so-called 'normal' behaviour which can have unfortunate consequences as what is generally believed and considered normal may actually not be true. Nowhere is this more clearly demonstrated than in the field of memory, where the average person regards memory as a simple replay of events in the mind, whereas the reality is far more complex and has led to the Research Board of the British Psychological Society (BPS) producing a guidance document for the Courts and the police, *Guidance on Memory and the Law: Recommendations from the Scientific Study of Human Memory* (British Psychological Society, 2008).

SELECTION OF EXPERTS

In the light of the above, the first dilemma facing the solicitor is the selection of a suitable 'expert', but how is this suitability to be judged? Is it by eminence in the field? Is it by excellence in report writing? Or is it by ability to give expert testimony in court? In an ideal world it would be all three, but sadly that ideal world rarely exists. Help appears to be at hand in the various directories of expert witnesses that are available, some of which are published by professional bodies, for example the BPS's *Directory of Expert Witnesses*, others by expert witness societies, and still others that are simply advertising media. However, none provides a guarantee of quality, although some, such as the Association of Personal Injury Lawyers (APIL) Approved Expert scheme, require recommendation from instructing solicitors before an expert can be included in the listing. Research by Professor Jane Ireland on Psychological Reports to Family Courts found ten areas of concern about the content of reports, ranging from evidence being presented as fact when it is conjecture, e.g. recovered memories, through to the use of emotive terms that could prejudice the outcome. Perhaps more worrying, it was found that a fifth of the instructed psychologists were not qualified to provide a psychological opinion and that the majority of the expert witnesses were not maintaining a clinical practice but were, in effect, professional expert witnesses who may not be able to comment upon current clinical practice and the availability of required treatments (Ireland, 2012).

For an expert report to be disallowed by the Court for any reason is expensive, not just in monetary terms but in terms of both the reputation of the instructing firm of solicitors and that of the expert. There are several ways that instructing solicitors minimise that risk. The first is by ensuring that the opinion being offered is outside the normal range of experience expected of the Court. In most cases this is straightforward but, as indicated above with reference to memory, 'common sense' does not necessarily concur with scientific evidence. Secondly, the 'expert' must be capable of having his expertise qualified by the court. To do this the expert needs to preface all reports with a 'Personal Statement' laying out the grounds for his/her expertise. In the case of members of professions, such as counselling psychologists who are registered with the HCPC, this is straightforward as an account of education, qualifications, career history and publications is all that is usually required. The only challenge may be if the court does not consider the expert to be sufficiently experienced. Unfortunately there is no hard-and-fast rule as to how much relevant professional experience is sufficient. Since, by definition, experts have direct, personal knowledge or direct experience of their areas of expertise it is essential in reports and in evidence to the court that they restrict their statements to those areas. Failure to do so will lead to the inevitable challenge and the possibility that the whole report will be discredited. Further to this, it is vital that the expert's opinion, as presented to the court, is balanced and based upon evidence that falls within the boundaries of professional competence. Bias must be avoided as the expert is advising the court, irrespective of who is paying the fee. Experts are not 'hired-guns', despite the frequent contention of the 'red top' press.

EXPERT REPORTS

It should go without saying that all reports, and the evidence based upon them, must be accurate and must include all relevant information, including that which may be contradictory, as it is for the court, not the expert, to make the final judgment. The expert must not attempt to usurp this function of the court, whether in the body of the report or in the opinion, otherwise the evidence will be disallowed and the expert is likely to be heavily criticised in open court to the detriment of the expert's professional reputation. The court is also likely to refer them for misconduct to the HCPC. It is important for the instructing solicitor to appraise the report and to return it to the expert for amendment if this is happening. While 'sins of commission' should be reasonably easy to spot, 'sins of omission', where evidence has been omitted, thus giving an unjustified bias to the report, will be more difficult and may be impossible to spot by the lay-person. Here it is important that the solicitor's instructions make it clear to the expert that all relevant information, including references, must be included. Failure to take this simple precaution may lay the solicitor and the expert open to criticism in Court and may lead to the report being disallowed, with consequent pecuniary disadvantage.

What should a 'good' report look like? After the title page and, in the case of a long report, the index, there should be the 'Personal Statement' enabling the court to 'qualify' the expert. Next, either a copy or a summary of the instructions should be given, including the initial instructions and any subsequent additions and amendments, including spoken instructions. This allows the court to place the report within its context and misunderstandings can be avoided. Following this, and depending on the purpose of the report, there should be a detailed account of the accident, crime or, in the case of the Family Courts, the reasons that the case is being brought before the court, with detailed references to the documentary evidence and other sources of information. This must be a balanced account without commentary or opinion. Then, where relevant, there should be an account of the client's personal and family history, e.g. birthplace, education, jobs or career path. Relevant medical and psychological history, including substance misuse, can be included here, which may be obtained directly from the client and from medical records. Where possible information provided by the client should be validated from independent sources. The above are the essential basics required before the detailed account of the client is presented. While many different tests and assessments may be carried out, a basic format for a psychological report which follows a logical progression is set out below. A similar progression should characterise the reports provided by other expert professionals, e.g. psychiatrists and social workers.

1. Mental state examination.
2. Formulation of the problem based upon the instructions and the supplied documentation.
3. Hypothesis testing. This will usually involve psychological testing, full details of which, including validity and reliability, must be given.
4. Test results and interpretation. Where several tests are given, the results may be in an appendix which should be referred to in the detailed interpretation and consequent discussion.

The final major stage of the report is the expert's opinion. Without this the report is valueless. The instructions and the nature of the case will determine the psychologist's opinion, which must be based upon the facts as presented and must be within their personal knowledge and expertise. It is important that the opinion is balanced and that the expert does not omit to consider material facts that may detract from it. At this stage the instructing solicitor needs to determine whether the expert is trespassing on the court's prerogative and prejudging the verdict as opposed to presenting an opinion that can be accepted or rejected in the course of a verdict being given. If this happens, the solicitor must point this out to the expert so that appropriate amendments can be made. Finally, there should be a brief summary listing, in bullet points, the report's content and the expert's opinion.

Following the body of the report, the expert is obliged, under practice and procedural rules, to make a statement of veracity. There is a standard format for this which changes from time to time so occasionally an expert will use an outdated formula. This can cause problems and lead to judicial criticism. The instructing solicitor needs to be aware of the current formula. Finally, the expert must provide a list of references and an appendix of test results, if appropriate. It would be very unusual in a psychologist's expert report if no references were made, especially if psychometric tests have been used. Therefore, the instructing solicitor should ensure that a full list appears. To prepare for this specialised role it is essential that continuous professional development (CPD) is undertaken.

There has been concern for some time about the cost of using experts, which has led to the recently introduced restrictions where the public purse is involved. This is particularly so in the Family Courts system. Solicitors are also being encouraged to use Single Joint Experts (SJE) wherever possible. Finally, the rules by which judges may exclude expert evidence have been tightened so it is essential that the counselling psychologist, embarking on expert witness work, obtains a contract from the referring solicitor so that payment will be made even if the report is subsequently excluded through no fault of their own. Expert Witness work is normally part-time private practice, so any counselling psychologist entering the field needs to consider whether they have adequate time to do it justice. Strict deadlines have to be met, which often implies a swift turn-around of work. They also need adequate professional-indemnity insurance as a large proportion of complaints to the HCPC come from this area, particularly from the Family Courts. A sound knowledge of court functions and legal procedures is also essential. On the positive side, it is very challenging and satisfying work, to which counselling psychologists can bring their unique humanitarian philosophical perspective.

CONCLUSIONS

This chapter has examined the main areas where counselling psychology interfaces with the legal system and shows some of the many career pathways that are potentially available. Working in forensic contexts does not suit everyone, but it is an area that I have found very satisfying over the years.

Visit the companion website for the following:

- Working in a Forensic Setting.
- Links to resources on working in forensic settings.

REFERENCES

Ansbacher, Heinz L. and Ansbacher, Rowena R. (eds). (1956). *The Individual Psychology of Alfred Adler*. New York: Basic Books.

Arrigo, Bruce A. and Shipley, Stacey L. (2005). *Introduction to Forensic Psychology: Issues and Controversies in Law, Law Enforcement and Corrections*. London: Elsevier.

British Psychological Society. (2008). *Guidance on Memory and the Law: Recommendations from the Scientific Study of Human Memory*. London. BPS.

Department of Health. (2008). *Mental Health Act 1983*. London: The Stationery Office.

Douglas, K. S., Hart, S. D., Webster, C. D. and Belfrage, H. (2013). *HCR-20V3: Assessing Risk of Violence: User Guide*. Burnaby, Canada: Mental Health, Law, and Policy Institute, Simon Fraser University.

Ellis, Albert. (1957). Rational Psychotherapy and Individual Psychology. *Journal of Individual Psychology*, 13: 38–44.

Ellis, Albert. (1962). *Reason and Emotion in Psychotherapy*. New York: Stuart.

Gunn, J., Maden, A. and Swinton, M. (1991). Treatment Needs of Prisoners with Psychiatric Disorders. *British Medical Journal*, 303: 338–341.

Guy, L. S., Wilson, C. M., Douglas, K. S., Hart, S. D., Webster, C. D. and Belfrage, H. (2013). *HCR-20 Version 3: Item-by-item Summary of Violence Literature. HCR-20 Violence Risk Assessment White Paper Series, #3*. Burnaby, Canada: Mental Health, Law, and Policy Institute, Simon Fraser University.

Harty, M., Tighe, J., Leese, M., Parrott, J. and Thornicroft, G. (2003). Inverse Care for Mentally Ill Prisoners: Unmet Needs for Forensic Mental Health Services. *Journal of Forensic Psychiatry & Psychology*, 14(3): 600–614.

Hegel, G. W. F. (1977). *The Phenomenology of Spirit*. Oxford: Clarendon Press.

HM Inspectorate of Prisons for England and Wales (1996). *Patient or Prisoner? A New Strategy for Health Care in Prisons*. London: Home Office.

Ireland, J. (2012). *Evaluating Expert Witness Psychological Reports: Exploring Quality*. Burnley: University of Central Lancashire.

McKenzie, N. and Sales, B. (2008). New Procedures to Cut Delays in the Transfer of Mentally Ill Prisoners to Hospital. *Psychiatric Bulletin*, 32: 20–23.

Miller, W. R. and Rollnick, S. (2002). *Motivational Interviewing: Preparing People to Change*. New York: Guilford Press.

Prison Reform Trust (2014). *In Depth – Mental Health and Social Care*. London. Prison Reform Trust.

Rogers, Carl R. (1961). *On Becoming a Person: A Therapist's View of Psychotherapy*. Boston, MA: Houghton Mifflin.

Sims, C. A. (2008). Elderly Mentally Disordered Offenders: What Next? *PSIGE Newsletter*, 102: 76–78.

Sims, C. A. (2010). Counselling Psychology in Forensic Settings. In R.Woolfe, S. Strawbridge, B. Douglas and W. Dryden (eds), *Handbook of Counselling Psychology* (3rd edn). London: Sage.

Sims, C. A. (2012). Inside the Mind of an Expert Witness. *Private Client Advisor*, 13: 42–43.

29
JOURNEYING THROUGH PHYSICAL HEALTH
RACHEL DAVIES

This chapter will take a journey through physical health using a systemic and relational lens to view some of the territory for counselling psychologists, including:

- How people make sense of illness
- Psychological challenges in chronic and acute illness
- The impact of illness on families
- Life after illness and end of life work

The content is not only relevant to counselling psychologists who work in physical health settings, or aspire to, but to anyone who works with clients in any context as physical health problems can affect us all. Many of the ideas covered in this chapter can be applied to different health conditions and so can inform our work whenever a client has a physical health problem.

WHAT IS THE TERRAIN?

Physical health has a significant impact on our psychological well-being. It follows that psychologists can have an impact through working with people who are experiencing diverse physical health problems. Currently, the specialities where psychologists are most likely to be found are cancer, diabetes, stroke, lung and heart disease (Chwalisz, 2008; Kneebone and Dunmore, 2000). Many of these psychologists will be clinical or health psychologists and it is difficult to get an accurate picture of how many counselling psychologists are employed in physical health. The last survey of employment of counselling psychologists in the UK undertaken by the British Psychological Society's Division of Counselling Psychology (DCoP) in 2011 found that 58 per cent of respondents were working in the NHS or were NHS-funded, but this is likely to include a substantial majority working in mental health (Division of

Counselling Psychology, 2011). The situation is further complicated by some counselling psychologists working in the voluntary sector or in private practice specialising in working with particular health conditions.

It has been my experience that many counselling psychologists in physical health work in isolation, often not connected to others who work with the same physical problems but in another location. Becoming aware of each other and creating opportunities to cross-fertilise ideas is a challenge and one that is starting to be addressed. For example, in 2012 the Division of Counselling Psychology set up a Special Interest Group for those working in Cancer and Palliative Care. In summarising the role of counselling psychologists in this field, this chapter will adopt the following definition:

> Counselling psychologists apply psychological knowledge to enable people with physical health problems to improve their well-being and maximise their potential while minimising the impact of illness on their mental health.

Our broad repertoire of skills allows us to achieve this aim through a range of activities:

- assessment and psychological therapy for patients and their carers
- group interventions for people with particular conditions (facilitated or supporting self-help)
- education workshops for clients, families, health professionals (for example, coping with fatigue)
- psychological consultation to multi-disciplinary teams (MDT)
- the conduct of one's own research or the provision of the psychological angle to health research
- training for health professionals on psychological aspects of physical health conditions
- clinical supervision for health professionals
- roles on medical/research ethics committees

The multi-modal training of counselling psychologists equips us well as a tailoring of interventions is recommended by relevant national guidance (for example, the National Institute for Health and Care Excellence's guidance on *Improving Supportive and Palliative Care for Adults with Cancer* (NICE, 2004). However, there is a gap between need and the provision of psychological support in physical health. For example, a recent report by The Stroke Association (2013) found that over half of stroke units in England, Wales and Northern Ireland have no access to psychology services. In the same report, a UK-wide survey found that over two-thirds of stroke survivors reported feeling depressed or anxious as a result of their stroke, and yet 79 per cent said they had received no information or practical advice to help them with the emotional impact of their condition.

It is problematic that in some healthcare contexts psychologists are seen as desirable assets rather than an essential part of the MDT. The healthcare community can at times question our relevance and the psychological aspects of illness can be poorly understood (Tucker et al., 2007). A further challenge is how to co-exist within the diagnosis-driven culture of physical healthcare. To meet only the diagnosis is to fail to meet the whole person and it is through applying a holistic approach to work in physical health that counselling psychologists can have most impact.

In this chapter journeying through physical health, we will meet various clients en route, including Jeffrey and Margaret, who we will revisit at several points. All case material used in this chapter has been anonymised.

Jeffrey (74) has diabetes and bowel cancer and his wife Margret (66) is in good health. They have been married for 45 years and have three grown-up children. Margaret had been an art teacher and had retired somewhat reluctantly at 60. Prior to his retirement Jeffrey had travelled around Europe as a sales manager and the couple were heavily involved in work-related social functions. When Jeffrey retired he became involved in charity fundraising and sat on various committees.

SETTING OUT

Does anyone have a map?

It sounds relatively straightforward; you get symptoms, are diagnosed, receive treatment and are cured as a result. However, the journey through illness is rarely a neat sequential process. While two people will experience the same biological disease, it will be experienced through a unique amalgamation of individual, social, cultural and environmental filters. This results in a personalised experience of illness. As counselling psychologists, we work with this individualised subjective experience and are therefore interested in the patterns of impact of these filters.

The subjective experience can begin with the first appointment with a doctor. Healthcare professionals can have a significant impact on how people make sense of their illness. For example, where a power hierarchy is experienced by the person, it may work helpfully, 'I must pay attention as I need to remember all the doctor said', or unhelpfully, 'I get so nervous everything I want to say goes right out of my mind'. There is a multiplicity of factors that can influence people's behaviour in a consultation, how it is experienced and what is carried forward from the experience.

Ahmed (72) did not like to make too much of being hard of hearing. He refused his daughter's offer to come to see the stroke consultant with him as he preferred to be 'do things his way'. He did not ask any questions of the doctor and was unable to tell his family anything that happened in the consultation and they were left with many questions about his treatment and prognosis.

(Continued)

(Continued)

Ian (36) went through a divorce around the same time as he was diagnosed with Motor Neurone Disease and feels very negative. His doctor often talks about other men he knows who are still playing sport and working. He thinks that his doctor does this to make him 'buck up'. He believes that the doctor thinks he is not as determined as his other patients and that this will make him deteriorate more quickly. Ian now keeps his fears to himself in the consultations and his doctor has said he seems more positive.

Both Ahmed and Ian brought their own personalities, previous experiences and beliefs into their medical consultations and these contributed to how the consultations were experienced. These experiences in turn can be influential in the beliefs and expectations they carry forward on their illness journey (Walsh and McGoldrick, 1995).

One of my roles involves taking referrals for counselling from a multi-disciplinary team within a cancer speciality. Initially, when I meet clients I ask them to tell me their illness story. Some clients do not expect this and assume that the 'truth' of their illness is in the medical files. They are surprised that I take a position of curiosity in their stories. There are three reasons why valuing clients' subjective experience is important:

1. It gives permission for their experience to be their truth – many clients are plagued by 'shoulds' and 'oughts' about how they should think, feel and behave when ill.
2. It starts a rebalancing of the relationship, moving from expert and patient to co-collaborators.
3. As co-collaborators we can look together at their current experiencing to determine the course of the work.

Jeffrey and Margaret had responded to the bowel cancer diagnosis in different ways and avoided talking to each other about it at home. The therapy sessions became a place that they could explore what they felt, the differences in their beliefs and experiences. Jeffrey had a generally optimistic outlook and saw the news as a mere setback that could easily be overcome. He backed up this belief by citing his many friends who had beaten cancer. Margaret saw herself as a realist and believed that the diagnosis would radically change their lives and was emotional when they were given the news.

Speaking the language

Language has a vital role in shaping the construct of illness and I always try to be acutely tuned in to the words clients use to describe their illness. Overt exploration of words and the meanings ascribed to words can help clients to access deep-seated beliefs that shape their illness experience. For example, George lives in a small, close-knit community but reported feeling lonely since he had become ill. He spoke about how his neighbours talked in hushed terms about his illness as 'Big C' and his wife used the phrase 'the unmentionable'. Sometimes ways of describing the illness have been consciously adopted as a palatable way of sitting with it. At other times cultural or family scripts influence these constructions. In George's case, he found this language shut down the possibility of talking openly about his illness and this left him frustrated and isolated.

During exploration in therapy the individual can identify how language helps or hinders their ability to cope. Through awareness there is potential for a new language that better allows the client's needs to emerge. For example, where the language of 'fighting, being strong, not giving up' has become a burden, new language can be developed with the client, such as 'coping, getting by, looking after myself', and this can become integrated into their self-narrative. For some clients, they need to go further and change the illness narratives they have with their families.

George wanted his family to 'call a spade a spade' and believed he had the right to be able to discuss his treatment with his family. A joint session with his wife was helpful here as he was able to explain how difficult it was to keep his feelings to himself and to avoid saying words that might upset people. In addition, his wife shared her own fears and how her mother's death from cancer had resulted in her avoidance of the word and what that meant for her. The couple were able to talk more at home about George's illness and treatment, and reported a strengthening of their relationship as a result.

What helped the outcome of therapy was that George was determined to take steps to reduce his sense of loneliness. People vary widely in the extent to which they believe they have agency over illness or whether they are passive passengers on the ride. When clients ascribe firmly to ideas, such as 'doctor is expert', they attribute to the medical profession control over their illness experience. Encouraging clients to find and value their voice around their illness experience can be an important therapeutic outcome and sometimes this voice finds expression through non-verbal means. For example, Carole used poems to explore her feelings at different stages of her cancer journey and to share these with her family as a method of communicating her experience. Creative expression lacks a 'right' and 'wrong' and this can free up mental space for honest emotional expression. It also allows individuals to gain ownership of their illness experience.

Being a navigator

Since the early 2000s there has been an increase in the availability of self-management group programmes, including the Expert Patient Programme, run through the NHS. These programmes have the potential of building self-efficacy through improved knowledge, sense of control, normalising of experience and providing informed social support. A growth area is the online expert patient who uses forums and other web-based resources to gain healthcare information. There is huge variability in the extent to which people perceive them to be active participants in their own healthcare. Here again, research suggests that patients vary in their levels of empowerment and engagement (see Table 29.1).

Table 29.1 Attitudes to healthcare and involvement in healthcare (adapted from Keeling et al., 2007)

Engagement category	Descriptor	Vignette
Active sceptic	Moves within and between conventional and alternative medicine and gathers information from both.	Lilia is fully engaged in the post-stroke rehabilitation programme but is also seeing a healer, eats a vegan diet and practises mindfulness.
Active convinced	Accepts conventional medicine but is interested in locating the best practitioner.	Wayne spends a lot of time on the internet looking into who the lead consultant was for his condition and asked his GP to refer him to this 'expert'.
Compliant convinced	Still expect to be directed by their doctor because of the professional's superior knowledge and experience.	Laya takes careful notes of all the doctor says as she wants to get it right. She regularly quotes her doctors when talking to her family.
Compliant sceptic	Is doubtful of authority but sees little alternative to consulting a doctor.	Mo believes little can be done to improve his condition and tends to moan about his doctor but always attends his appointments.

Understanding the attitudes of our clients and the extent to which they take ownership or defer to professionals can help us to ensure our interventions are client-led. For example, compliant convinced clients are most likely to benefit from psycho-education and strategies that they can adopt between sessions.

NEGOTIATING THE TERRITORY

Marathon or sprint

There are different approaches to illnesses and how they are categorised. One approach is to consider illness adjustment as a stage model, from a crisis phase to an embedded phase and, possibly, to a terminal phase. Classically, a distinction can be made between the psychological challenges presented by acute versus chronic conditions. The actual picture is often more complex than a simple two-way split as there are different sub-categories of acute and chronic conditions. Table 29.2 expands on these different sub-categories, providing examples of the challenges individuals may face, and considers the sorts of interventions that may help. However, people's subjective experience will steer how psychological challenges play out for the individual and therefore should shape our response.

Table 29.2 Examples of challenges faced with different types of illness

Nature of illness	Examples of psychological challenges	What may help
Acute – one-off	• Shock • Anxiety • Rapid adjustment	Short-term interventions for anxiety, panic, needle phobia or pain management.
Acute – episodic	• Uncertainty/unpredictability • Life becomes split (well life and unwell life) • Confusion for loved ones due to unpredictability	Managing variable expectations of self and others, developing affirmative self-talk and strategies for communicating about illness.
Chronic – degenerative (or progressive)	• Longer period of adjustment but toll of cumulative losses over time • Incremental loss of person • Hopelessness/depression	Exploring existential issues regarding 'who am I' and redefining of self-identity. Grief work may be useful as well as psycho-education on incremental loss. Mindfulness exercises and relaxation strategies.
Chronic stable/constant	• Illness gets reframed into a 'new normal' • Identity reformation • Permanent role changes	Adaptive functioning and goal setting as part of redefining identity.
Chronic/fluctuating (or relapsing)	• Uncertainty/confusion • Disengagement from normal life due to lack of reliability • Health anxiety	Develop long-term anxiety management strategies. Becoming an expert patient (knowing triggers, managing symptoms, self-care).

Another approach is to consider loss of the healthy self as a form of grief. Processes of adjustment can be understood though mapping them on to the different emotional stages a grieving person goes through. Perhaps the most well-known of these stage models of grief defines five stages – denial, anger, bargaining, depression and acceptance (Kübler-Ross, 1969). When people lose their health they can experience all of these stages and far from being fixed, movement can occur over a period of days, weeks, months or even years. For example, initial reactions may be 'they must have made a mistake as I feel totally fine' (denial) and this may shift into 'it's working in that factory that did it, someone is going to have to pay for this' (anger) but may end up with 'I just have to get on with it and do all I can to keep healthy' (acceptance).

Finding our way or getting lost

Learning helpful ways of living with illness can stave off the depression that can result from a physical health problem (Lane et al., 2000). Popular culture about coping with illness is littered with advice about maintaining positivity, holding on to hope and fighting off your condition. For some people these 'scripts' about how to live with illness can give them a blueprint for living. For others they can become an additional pressure. They are not only ill, but also not coping the way society promotes is 'right'. This can lead to clients experiencing shame. By meeting the client within a humanistic frame we can create therapeutic spaces where the reality of their coping and not coping can be shared without fear of judgement.

As Yalom (2005: 277) said: 'Every person must choose how much truth he can stand.' To return to the journey metaphor, if the sun is in your eyes you may be unable to move forwards, you may stumble, or lose your way entirely.

By valuing individual difference we are open to exploring the functions of different ways of coping and not judging them to be 'maladaptive' (Tallman, 2013). Sullivan et al. (2000) found that catastrophising can be a useful adaptive strategy, especially if it prompts the person to seek help or adhere to advice. For example, Kay had a belief that 'pain is a sign something serious is wrong'. This meant that she did not delay going to the doctor when she noticed both the location of her pain and its intensity had changed. Her swift diagnosis led to less radical treatment than if she had minimised her symptoms and delayed seeking help.

In Kay's case, her belief encouraged her to engage with healthcare, but for Jo his beliefs made him resistant.

Jo is a 73-year-old retired solicitor. He has chronic obstructive pulmonary disease (COPD) but has never accepted that he has this condition and instead refers to his problem as 'a bit of asthma'. Exploring his family story it became apparent that Jo's father had died of COPD at 75. It appeared that Jo was so scared of dying in the same way as his father that he had denied the reality of his condition and accepted the more palatable narrative of 'a bit of asthma'. That Jo was approaching the age his father was when he died further exacerbated his fears, his need to reject the label of COPD and his resistance to treatment.

Coming to terms with being ill can involve a grief for the healthy self and what being healthy meant to self-identity. For example, Erin was well known locally as a charity marathon runner and that she was being held in such high regard was central to her identity. For Erin, being sick meant grieving her self as a runner, her physically strong body and also the affirmation from her community.

Like Erin, many clients report that it is not the physical health problem itself that is hardest to cope with but the associated limits to normal functioning, or the rigours of treatment and its associated side-effects. For example, when undergoing cancer treatment, 'chemo brain' (impeded cognitive functioning) and radiotherapy-related fatigue (exhaustion not relieved by sleep) are problematic. Both can impact on daily activities, sense of self and relationships with others. Because of this, psychological work in the treatment period may focus on strategies to cope while also maintaining a sense of self.

With growing recognition of the concept of 'total pain' (physical, social, spiritual and psychological elements), psychologists are sometimes now involved in a multi-disciplinary approach to pain management. When clients are able to recognise that aspects of pain are within their control it can be immensely reassuring. Once the possibility of mastery has been acknowledged there is the potential to work with the client to find tailor-made approaches to living with pain that minimises its impact. For example, clients can devise strategies based on the 3Ps approach to managing pain – prioritise, plan, pace (Kralik et al., 2004). There is often a complex relationship between pain and depression for many clients, and this was true for Myra.

Myra is a 66-year-old woman with severe rheumatoid arthritis and thyroid disease. She has always loved her garden and walking with her children. Both of these activities have become impossible as her pain increased. She has become depressed and sees the future as only holding increased degeneration and restriction in her activities. Exploration of alternative pleasures in life only appeared to reinforce how much gardening and her walks with her family had defined her. We channelled this resolve into developing a tailor-made pain-management strategy. For example, she would prioritise one physically demanding activity each day, such as weeding her pots. She would plan in advance what she needed to complete the job, for example collecting her tools and her stool before she started to prevent wasted journeys. She would work in five-minute chunks and then sit back on her stool and use a mindfulness technique. Being mindful helped her to experience pleasure in the moment and to appreciate that she was still engaging with something important to her. Her favourite technique is focusing on the sensation of the air on her bare arms, especially when it's sunny. Re-integrating her reasons for living into her life in this way significantly improved Myra's depression.

Maps can help

Research into what clients find helpful in therapeutic work suggests a dual function. They value the more humanistic aspects of therapy, for example a space to tell their story, a supportive therapeutic relationship and gaining a sense of control. They also value more specific aspects that fall under the umbrella of psycho-education, for example for clients to have information about treatments or side-effects and to work on strategies that can help to live with all of these (Omylinska-Thurston and Cooper, 2014; Ramsay et al., 2007). Psycho-education also appears to raise the potential of choice to think or behave differently through considering how others have negotiated their illness. New strategies can be explored, practised, revised and become integrated into a way of living with illness.

But clients will vary in the degree to which they need a humanistic or educative space, or indeed another approach entirely. Tuning in to the subjective experience of each client will help the counselling psychologist to know how to intervene at each given point and sometimes some mindful reflection can help us to meet clients' needs. Palmer (2003), considering what Gestalt-informed ideas can bring to client work with chronic health conditions, revisits the Paradoxical Theory of Change (Beisser, 1970, cited in Palmer, 2003), where the aim is not to remove the symptom but to support movement through the process:

> The more you try to change the more you stay the same. On the other hand, if you just collapse into your condition and remain stuck in it then no change is possible. It is only when you let go of the aim of changing, but remain present in your process that transformation occurs. Essentially this means that change happens when you are working in the present. Having a future aim like balance or health can take you away from the present and so block change. (Palmer, 2003: 32)

This is similar to the acceptance element within Acceptance and Commitment Therapy that appears to show positive results even with advanced cancer (Angiola and Bowen, 2013). The benefits of finding calm through acceptance can be seen to be in conflict with working towards hopeful mastery of the illness experience. However, the reality is that both hope and acceptance often co-exist, can serve different functions at different times and can be worked with rather than fought against (O'Hara, 2011).

Many people find a sense of mastery by engaging with approaches influenced by the positive psychology movement and, more recently, positive psychotherapy (Frude, 2014). Shifting the focus from avoiding negative consequences of illness (for example, depression and anxiety) and on to maximising positive coping, resilience and resource building has particular relevance in physical health. Psychological consultations can therefore be a highlight of the healthcare package. They are the one aspect of medical intervention that will be focused on nurturing of positive potential as opposed to being problem-focused.

FELLOW TRAVELLERS

Our relationships impact on our health and there are correlations between good levels of psychosocial support, good health status and the ability to adapt well after a period of illness (Kidd and Sheffield, 2005; Tedeschi and Calhoun 2004). Patterns of interactions between our relationships and health are complex and not one-directional. Health and ill-health impacts not only on the individual, but on their family and the relationships between family members. For example, a couple's relationship may suffer while they focus on caring for their sick child. Frequently, family members walk different paths, some lag behind, some rush ahead. For some families there can even be crashes and competitive races.

When Andrew's heart disease became very serious it appeared to reunite a dispersed family. His five children returned to the UK for the first time since four of them moved over ten years ago with only sporadic communication during this time. But thrown together through serious illness, families are forced to face many of their difficulties that may have been lying dormant. Old problems do not disappear in the face of illness and some may even be exacerbated. For Andrew's children being reunited brought a revisiting of:

- decisions made about the care of their mother who had died twelve years ago
- sibling rivalry between the two boys now played out through who could best care for their father
- the eldest daughter's role as the sensible and practical one versus the younger daughter's high level of expressed emotion

In the same way as people who are ill make sense of their own illness, how family members respond to illness will be influenced by multiple factors, such as personality, and the ability to be flexible and adapt. Other factors of influence are illustrated with reference to Margaret (see Table 29.3).

Table 29.3   Understanding Margaret's response to Jeffrey's illness

Factors that influence family responses to illness	
Current developmental stages of family members	Although in their 70s, the couple is used to having an active life. The sons who live close have young children and work stress and Margaret does not want to bother them for support.
Family scripts about health and illness	Born in the 1940s she has a traditional view that her role is to support her husband but, paradoxically, watching her mother nurse her father at the end of his life has made her want to rebel against this destiny.
Wider social support	Margaret is outgoing and talkative and has found counselling and talking to others at a carers' group helps her cope.
Resources and resilience	Margaret's self-image was as a resilient person but she resented how Jeffrey's illness depleted her of the life outside the home that had been a source of distraction and had energised her.
Relationship dynamics pre- and post-illness	In therapy Margaret became aware of how she had always been the crutch that allowed Jeffrey to succeed in his business. Jeffrey tended to make the major decisions and Margaret had to adjust to him now deferring to her.

Sometimes it may be appropriate for the counselling psychologist to work with other family members and not the ill person themselves. In some cases it may be more viable to work with the family, for example when people are in intensive care. At other times, working together with the ill person and their family can facilitate communication about the illness. Altschuler et al. (1997) suggests the following tasks when counselling families affected by illness:

- Sharing the story of the illness
- Normalising the impact of illness
- Respecting the family's authority
- Reframing illness narratives
- Addressing communication issues
- Recognising resources

- Addressing loss and gain
- Addressing previous family functioning
- Preparing for the future

An additional benefit of involving the family in the therapy is that it can help reduce some of the isolation that individuals or nuclear families can experience around illness. There are many psychological and practical factors that interact to contribute to this.

For example, limited energy means hard choices need to be made about what the family can and cannot do. This may mean limiting participation or levels of social interaction. This in turn can mean that the ill person, or family, feel less emotionally connected and less able to let others see the reality of their world, furthering the disconnection. This isolation can also be driven by psychological factors, for example the individual, or family, worry about burdening the extended family and friends and fear that they will not understand. They become insular, which results in a self-imposed isolation. For their part, friends and acquaintances may find it uncomfortable talking about illness, witnessing its impact or worry about saying the wrong thing and so withdraw. Many people report significant changes in their social interactions, in effect a shrinking of their social world as a result of illness.

Darren (24) had originally coped well with his cancer diagnosis but since it came back he is feeling depressed, suffers fatigue and has lost confidence talking to people. His girlfriend Emma wants them to make the most of the time they have together and to go out more, have a holiday and socialise. He doesn't want people to know how ill he is and tends to stay behind when Emma goes out. Emma prefers to go out dancing with a large group of friends rather than having a heart to heart with her close girlfriends. She knows she is keeping them at a distance because she finds it upsetting to talk about what is going on with her and Darren. She only came to one therapy session as she felt that Darren was the one who needed to 'get over it'. While he had wanted them to attend together, he was able to use his therapy for his depression and self-esteem issues. He found it helpful to have a space that was just for him and to accept that, while they had gone through something difficult together, it was OK for them to be coping differently now. Darren now feels ready to book that holiday.

JOURNEY'S END

Sometimes the destination is not always clear at the start of the journey. It may be that a chronic or acute illness enters a terminal phase, or that a cure may lead to rehabilitation and total recovery. Alternatively, the journey may not have an actual end, where a condition is chronic but not life-threatening or it is in remission but not necessarily gone for good. All of these different paths present psychological challenges.

Arriving in port

When someone is discharged from medical care they may not feel that they are at journey's end in that their illness will have left a legacy. Illness will have become a chapter in that person's life story and many people describe that they have been changed by either a chronic illness or a period of serious, acute ill health. Psychological services may therefore have a role even after active medical treatment has been completed, for example psychological therapy for depression post-stroke (Kneebone and Dunmore, 2000).

For some people, even if the risk of getting ill again is low or non-existent, they can experience anxiety that can impede them moving forward with life. This post-illness reaction may result in family members, once again, walking a different path. Individuals may feel changed, isolated and not understood (Knowles, 2010).

After illness people may need to adjust to a new definition of themselves, especially if the illness has left a longer-term disability that impacts on quality of life. One consequence of improvements in cancer treatment is that more people are 'living with cancer' and this phrase, as well as 'survivorship', has entered the illness lexicon. But knowing how to cope psychologically with survivorship in the longer term is largely an unexplored area and is ripe for research that can inform therapeutic work.

Sometimes people recover well and are able to rehabilitate from their illness. One of the ways psychological knowledge can help is through the application of positive psychology approaches, for example Post Traumatic Growth (PTG). There is potential for people to emerge from a traumatic illness with an enhanced appreciation of life, a greater sense of meaning, stronger relationships and a realisation of their own potential (Tedeschi and Calhoun, 2004). Interestingly, research into PTG for cancer patients suggests that those people who anticipated they would experience positive growth as a result of their illness appeared to have higher post-illness ratings of positive growth (Tallman, 2013). It appeared that positivity can sometimes act as a self-fulfilling prophecy.

The final journey

Not all illness journeys end with recovery and counselling psychologists can have an important role in working with people at the end of their life. Ultimately, preparing to lose and then losing a family member is the biggest transition a family must confront (Walsh and McGoldrick, 1995). Perhaps the key challenge is negotiating the feelings of hope and despair mentioned earlier. As O'Hara states:

> It is important how we as therapists conceptualise the nature of hope and despair. If they only remain as polarised opposites within our own understanding, the tendency is to aid the client in being rid of despair. Despair, in this context, is constrained from doing its work. It is seen as an evil to be expelled. Of course, despair unchallenged may wreak havoc, but despair coexisting in a mutual dance with genuine hope, may serve a vital purpose. (2011: 327)

There may be times when as counselling psychologists we are called on to wade into the havoc, to share that part of the journey, and when we shy away from it we do a disservice to our clients. In an article where therapists reflect on their work in this field, one of the contributors recalls her work with a woman mourning the death of a baby and acknowledged that in the face of intense sadness and pain the role of 'being with' is an ethical stance that overrides technique (Shochet et al., 1998). This is demanding work as it requires us to give of ourselves. Worthington (2009) notes that this sort of work requires us to be with the unbearable parts of another's experience and this can feel unbearable for us.

When working with people at the end of their life, there should be some negotiation of the territory, especially around pacing and language use. Clients with terminal illnesses and their families can find metaphor useful. Worthington (2009) suggests that intangibles can be given shape as 'objects' that are easier to relate to than 'ordeals'. This was true for Julie's ordeal of letting go of Brian.

Julie and Brian had been married for twenty years and had two teenagers. Brian had an aggressive brain tumour and a short prognosis. Julie would sit with him in the hospice every evening and, although Brian could no longer speak, he seemed to understand what Julie said.

The white balloons were an idea she came up with one night when she wanted to find a way to calm his agitation, which she interpreted as distress about his situation. As she held his hand, she described to him a bunch of white balloons that she visualised above his bed. Initially, the strings of the balloons were entwined around Brian's fingers. One by one, she suggested a label they could give to each balloon – choosing things that she felt Brian was finding it hard to let go of. For example, there were balloons for 'worrying about me and the kids', 'pains in your head', 'how the boys are coping in the factory', 'feeling that you've let us down'. As each balloon got labelled she talked Brian through untying each string from his fingers and watching each individual balloon float away, unfurling his fingers as she spoke.

She was very emotional recounting this episode and I sensed that this was as much her process of letting go as Brian's. It seemed to me that this metaphor could be used as a bridge between his experience and her own. I asked her about how she had decided on the labels for each balloon. She was able to identify certain balloons that were perhaps her own and some that were more her attempt to see his situation through his eyes. This led to Julie re-naming her own bunch of balloons.

The session where we explored this metaphor also led to a new language being created – 'holding on', 'tethering to earth', 'release', 'floating', 'tangles'. This new language increased her ability to talk about losing Brian.

In working in the context of end of life there can at times be conflict between the ethical principles of autonomy and beneficence. There is often an implied judgement that to optimise health is to assent to medical intervention. Counselling psychologists co-construct their work with clients and do not stand in an expert position, and this can ameliorate this value judgement. In fact, we can make a substantial contribution to helping the client find and express their voice about the care they want at the end of their life. In the UK in 2015 the Assisted Dying Bill is being considered by the House of Commons. If it progresses, the role for counselling psychologists will increase in helping clients, families and professionals to navigate this new and challenging territory (Golijani-Moghaddam, 2014).

CONCLUSIONS

People with physical health problems face many psychological challenges. Counselling psychologists work in varied settings and their role encompasses providing psychological therapy, supervision, consultancy, training and research. Because counselling psychologists value the subjective experience of clients, unique journeys through physical health can be validated. Being constantly curious about individual differences means psychological support can be led by and tailored to the client.

Some people benefit from specific support with the anxiety or depression that can accompany illness, or help with coping with pain or the rigours of treatment. For other clients counselling psychologists can be of most use in providing a broad therapeutic space for them to make sense of their experience. People also value psycho-education and it is helpful for counselling psychologists to be knowledgeable about the psychological challenges commonly experienced with particular diagnoses or prognoses. Illness not only effects individuals but is a challenge for the whole family. How families adapt to illness can in turn influence the ill person's journey through illness

Working in physical health provides diverse experiences for the counselling psychologist that span the entire life course. The physical health journey is often not a linear one and the work can involve negotiating setbacks, detours, rocky terrain and there are times when the therapeutic path is not clear. However, accompanying people on their physical health journeys can be a rich experience where we can make a tangible contribution to this journey.

Visit the companion website to watch Palliative Care.

REFERENCES

Altschuler, J., Dale, B. and Byng-Hall, J. (1997) *Working with Chronic Illness: A Family Approach*. Basingstoke: Macmillan.

Angiola, J.E. and Bowen, A.M. (2013) Quality of Life in Advanced Cancer: An Acceptance and Commitment Therapy View. *The Counseling Psychologist*, 41: 313–335.

Chwalisz, K. (2008) The Future of Counseling Psychology Improving Quality of Life for Persons with Chronic Health Issues. *The Counseling Psychologist*, 36: 98–107.

Division of Counselling Psychology (2011) *DCoP Questionnaire (Questback)*. London: British Psychological Society.

Frude, N. (2014) Positive Therapy. In R. Nelson-Jones (ed.), *Theory and Practice of Counselling and Therapy* (6th edn). London: Sage. pp. 383–406.

Golijani-Moghaddam, N. (2014) Practitioner Psychologists in Palliative Care: Past, Present and Future Directions. *Counselling Psychology Review*, 29(1): 29–37.

Keeling, D.I., Shiu, E., Newholm, T., Laing, A. and Hogg, G. (2007) A Conceptual Framework for Understanding Use of the Internet for Health Related Information. In P. Cunningham and M. Cunningham (eds), *Expanding the Knowledge Economy: Issues, Applications, Case Studies. Part 1*. Amsterdam: IOS Press. pp. 495–504.

Kidd, T. and Sheffield, D. (2005) Attachment Style and Symptom Reporting: Examining the Mediating Effects of Anger and Social Support. *British Journal of Health Psychology*, 10(4): 531–541.

Kneebone, I.I. and Dunmore, E. (2000) Psychological Management of Post-Stroke Depression. *British Journal of Clinical Psychology*, 39(1): 53–65.

Knowles, C. (2010) Recalled to Life. *Therapy Today*, 21(5): 24–7.

Kralik, D., Koch, T., Price, K. and Howard, N. (2004) Chronic Illness Self-management: Taking Action to Create Order. *Journal of Clinical Nursing*, 13(2): 259–267.

Kübler-Ross, E. (1969) *On Death and Dying*. New York: Macmillan.

Lane, D., Carroll, D., Ring, C., Beevers, D.G. and Lip, G.Y.J. (2000) Effects of Depression and Anxiety on Mortality and Quality of Life Four Months after Myocardial Infarction. *Journal of Psychosomatic Research*, 49: 229–238.

National Institute for Health and Care Excellence (NICE) (2004). *Improving Supportive and Palliative Care for Adults with Cancer: The Manual*. London: NICE.

O'Hara, D.J. (2011) Counselling and Psychotherapy in Action: Psychotherapy and the Dialectics of Hope and Despair. *Counselling Psychology Quarterly*, 24(4): 323–329.

Omylinska-Thurston, J. and Cooper, M. (2014) Helpful Processes in Psychological Therapy for Patients with Primary Cancers: A Qualitative Interview Study. *Counselling and Psychotherapy Research: Linking Research with Practice*, 14(2): 84–92.

Palmer, B. (2003) Developmental Processes in Clients with Chronic Health Conditions. *British Gestalt Journal*, 12(1): 31–39.

Ramsay, K., Ramsay, J. and Main, D. (2007) Both Group Peer Counselling and Individual Counselling Reduce Anxiety and Depression, and Increase Self-esteem and Overall Life Satisfaction in Palliative Cancer Care. *Counselling Psychology Quarterly*, 20(2): 157–167.

Shochet, I., Roth, R., Jones, S. and Lohyn, M. (1998) Family Therapy with the Dying. *Australian & New Zealand Journal of Family Therapy*, 19(1): 40–47.

Sullivan, M.J.L., Tripp, D.A. and Santor, D. (2000) Gender Differences in Pain and Pain Behaviour: The Role of Catastrophizing. *Cognitive Therapy and Research*, 24: 121–134.

Tallman, B.A. (2013) Anticipated Posttraumatic Growth from Cancer: The Roles of Adaptive and Maladaptive Coping Strategies. *Counselling Psychology Quarterly*, 26(1): 72–88.

Tedeschi, R.G. and Calhoun, L.G. (2004) *Posttraumatic Growth: Conceptual Foundation and Empirical Evidence*. Philadelphia, PA: Lawrence Erlbaum Associates.

The Stroke Association (2013) *Feeling Overwhelmed: The Emotional Impact of Stroke*. London: Stroke Association.

Tucker, C.M., Ferdinand, L.A., Mirsu-Paun, A., Herman, K.C., Delgado-Romero, E., van den Berg, J.J. and Jones, J.D. (2007) The Roles of Counseling Psychologists in Reducing Health Disparities. *The Counseling Psychologist*, 35: 650–678.

Walsh, F. and McGoldrick, M. (eds) (1995) *Living beyond Loss: Death in the Family* (6th edn). New York: W.W. Norton.

Worthington, R. (2009) Losses and New Positions. *Context: Family Therapy and Systemic Practice in the UK*, 101: 36–39.

Yalom, I.D. (2005) *When Nietzsche Wept: A Novel of Obsession*. New York: HarperCollins.

30
WORKING AS A COUNSELLING PSYCHOLOGIST IN PRIMARY CARE

GARRETT KENNEDY AND
YESIM ARIKUT-TREECE

INTRODUCTION

The purpose of this chapter is to provide a practical guide to a career but also to be of relevance to trainees in placement in primary care. This chapter documents the core features of a primary care service, the role of the counselling psychologist within it and the experience of the client seeking help. It is not possible to capture every aspect of primary care in a single chapter due to innumerable regional and local adaptations, hence broad consistencies, strategies and common issues will be the focus here. This chapter examines two broad strands to be woven into a functioning professional framework. The first documents the structure and function of primary care as a part of the overall health system, moving from the international agenda to UK-specific adaptations. The second examines the journeys of people, both client and professional working within a system, and adapting to challenge and change. By the end of this chapter it is hoped readers will understand the landscape of this arena.

The authors chose to collaborate on this project due to shared experiences of working in primary care and other settings. Our experience includes being part of a local strategy to establish a new primary care Improving Access to Psychological Therapies (IAPT) service, supervision of trainees seeing this world from a fresh perspective and legal settings with those whom services have been unable to help. We write this chapter aware of the most challenging issues for those entering this field, with the hope of critiquing current practices while identifying areas where our profession has something to offer.

STRAND 1: THE SYSTEM – HISTORY AND STRUCTURAL DEVELOPMENTS

The 'system' has its roots deeper than current NHS strategy, and it is valuable to consider the purpose and role of primary care from a wider international perspective. Current primary care practices stem in part from international efforts to develop higher quality healthcare across areas where it may be neglected. The now famous Alma-Ata Declaration (World Health Organization, 1978) called for action by all governments to view health as a socio-economic issue and a human right. This expressed the view that primary care should encompass: 'Essential care; based on practical, scientifically sound and socially acceptable method and technology; universally accessible to all in the community through their full participation; at affordable cost and geared towards self-reliance and self-determination' (World Health Organization, 1978). The step towards self-reliance can only come by affording individuals greater access to usable resources, offered in terms that are meaningful to the client and indicate a reliable evidence base.

The Alma-Ata conference was a key force in creating a 'Primary Care Movement' aimed towards tackling 'politically, socially and economically unacceptable' health inequalities (World Health Organization, 1978, p. 2), and had the specific aim of calling on governments, institutions, researchers, professionals and grassroots organisations to tackle gaps in healthcare across the globe. The relevance here is to view current primary care efforts as part of a historical movement and as a stepping stone on the path to an ideal, where the responsibility lies with the broader community of professionals to engage in 'bottom up' initiatives rather than await change from above. Taking part is not optional. Commemorating the Alma-Ata Declaration in 2008, the World Health Organization acknowledged the challenges of a world subject to the pressures of globalisation. It focused on complexities arising out of economic demands as 'putting the social cohesion of many countries under stress' (World Health Organization, 2008). Professionals in primary care are keenly aware of the power economic forces have in shaping the structure and function of regional and local services.

The purpose and function of primary care

The first task of a professional entering primary care is to understand key structures, agendas, policies and practices. Although specific areas of the day-to-day job will likely change over time, the broader structures under which we carry out our work should remain recognisable. We live in a world continually struggling under economic and social pressures, where a typical NHS workplace brings a plurality of professions, perspectives and roles in the pursuit of the common goal of distress reduction. Although professional perspectives will differ in how human pain is conceptualised, and the road to resolution will take different paths, end goals remain the same, namely distress alleviation using evidence-based approaches and in a context of efficiency and purpose.

Box 30.1   Primary care

Primary care:

1. Co-ordinates the care of the many people with multiple, complex health needs.
2. Delivers care closer to people, increasing convenience, especially in areas remote from hospitals.
3. Is a first point of contact for patients to facilitate the early detection of illness, and thereby improves outcomes.
4. Provides a long-term perspective to support disease prevention and healthy lifestyles.
5. Provides more cost-effective treatment for minor illnesses and injuries than hospitals. (Department of Health, 2014)

The first task in primary care is to position the service to meet the needs of the local community, providing care close to the point of need. Usually the first point of contact, services are positioned to address mental health issues at early stages as well as at more pressing points of crisis in settings familiar to the patient, such as the patient's local GP practice, where helping relationships have already been established.

UK developments

On a bedrock of international efforts, UK-specific efforts have been layered over time through a series of reforms and developments. The Beveridge Report (1942) recommended that 'medical treatment covering all requirements will be provided for all citizens by a national health service' (The Nuffield Trust, 2012), and over the following decades acts of policy, research and reporting slowly crafted the context and activities seen in primary care today. Core features have been part of the NHS since inception (Roland et al., 2012) in that care is usually provided in local GP practices and free at the point of contact.

To understand the function of a primary care service it is necessary to understand some of the more recent driving forces and agendas behind decision making. In England since March 2013 the coordination of primary care projects has been under the charge of clinical commissioning groups, as the Health and Social Care Act 2012 led to the abolishment of primary care trusts in an effort to invest resources more strategically. Outside England, NHS systems hold the same broad set of governing principles but with differing structures, such as the more integrated approach in Scotland where primary and secondary care strategies have not been separated.

Visit the companion website to read The NHS in Scotland.

The implications are for colleagues to recognise the wider economic forces governing which particular service structures and therapeutic models are chosen to offer to the patient. We may hold a particular model of working, and be expected to adapt to a commissioned model. We may encounter moments where client need does not fit within inclusion criteria, and be required to carefully plot the line at which the most suitable option is referral to specialist services or different 'steps'.

Stepped care: Mapping provision

Services function in the context of the larger NHS regulatory structures and are subject to forces governing commissioning, care quality assessment and efficacy monitoring. Current NHS strategy is structured according to a 'stepped care' model, a resource management approach originating in the United States (Norman and Ryrie, 2013, p. 547). Ekers (2013, p. 171) states stepped care 'is one system used to organize delivery of psychological therapy that stratifies interventions across several levels of symptom severity', suggesting that the most effective yet least resource-intensive treatment option be employed first. It may be argued this approach is economically prudent and has practical benefits in allowing responsibility for public spending and addresses 'issues of cost and the efficient use of limited psychological therapy resources' (Bower, 2005, p. 11).

As part of a larger approach, the rationale for stepped care is to reserve more specialist intensive treatments for those who derive little or no benefit from simpler approaches, or those who can be accurately predicted to require more complex intervention (Newman, 2000). Although the research in stepped care is largely directed to medical procedures where the line between 'moderate' and 'severe' may be more easily drawn, the principle remains relevant for psychological problems, even when the borders of complexity are less clear. Despite criticisms in practice, this approach asks us to make best use of available resources, with responsibility to the greater society in mind.

An outline of the current NHS stepped care stratified approach can be seen in Figure 30.1.

Referral to a primary care service is not exclusively made through a GP, as the stratified approach of the stepped care model encourages collaboration between services. Coordinated efforts with secondary care teams offers the potential for several clinicians to assist with different aspects of client need, thereby freeing up the psychological therapist to focus on mental health rather than more fundamental issues that may be faced at steps one and two, such as the impact of mobility issues or social difficulties. An example of multi-disciplinary

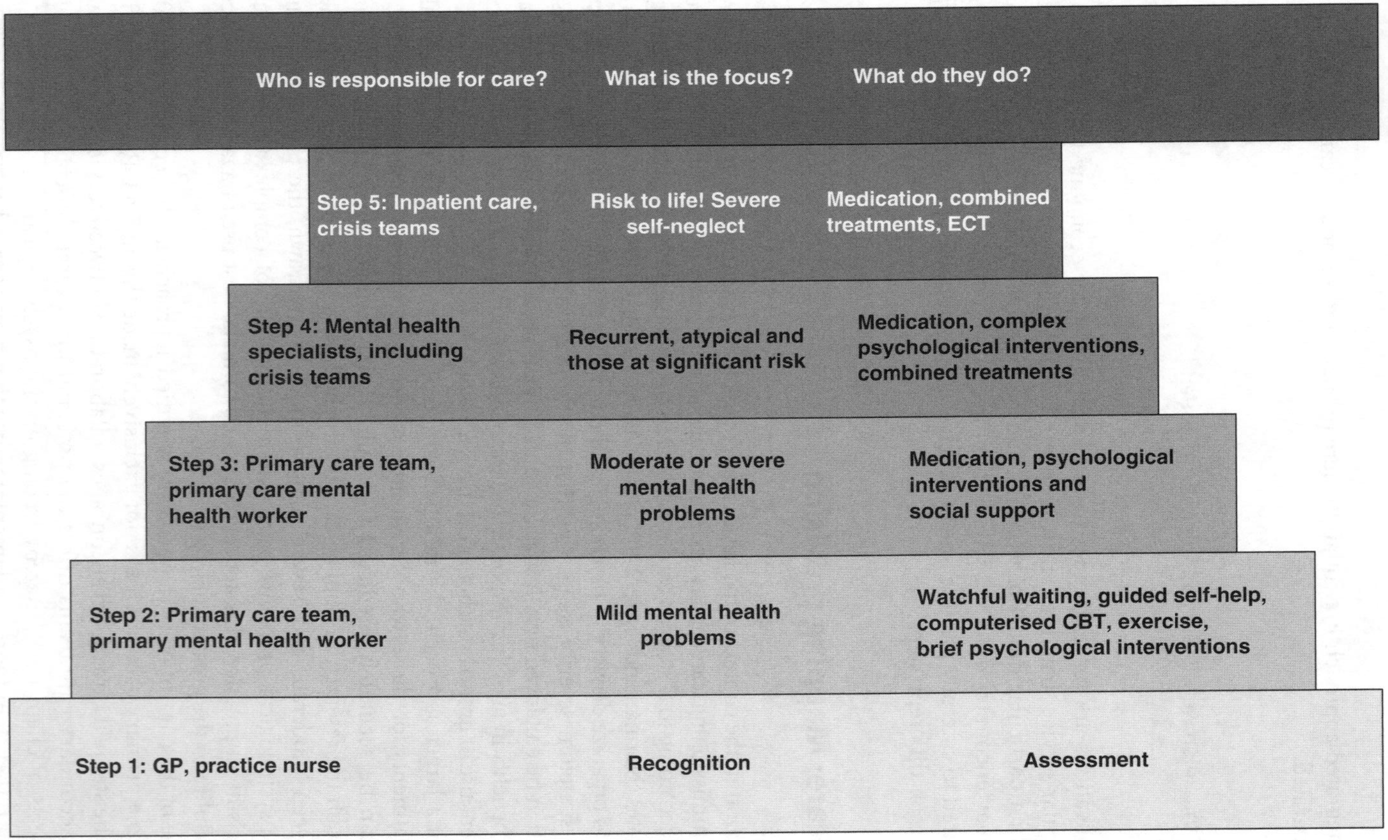

Figure 30.1 NHS stepped care stratified approach in England

Who is responsible for care?	What is the focus?	What do they do?
Step 5: Inpatient care, crisis teams	Risk to life! Severe self-neglect	Medication, combined treatments, ECT
Step 4: Mental health specialists, including crisis teams	Recurrent, atypical and those at significant risk	Medication, complex psychological interventions, combined treatments
Step 3: Primary care team, primary care mental health worker	Moderate or severe mental health problems	Medication, psychological interventions and social support
Step 2: Primary care team, primary mental health worker	Mild mental health problems	Watchful waiting, guided self-help, computerised CBT, exercise, brief psychological interventions
Step 1: GP, practice nurse	Recognition	Assessment

working may be seen where a patient steps out of specialist care and easily accessible support from a primary care team provides a cushion. Typically, a client seeking help may present at Step 1 to a GP or practice nurse. This step includes recognition, assessment and 'active monitoring' (Cohen, 2008). National Institute for Health and Care Excellence (NICE) guidelines for depression argue a proportion of individuals recover spontaneously from a depressive episode, and active monitoring without immediate intervention is recommended as the most appropriate course of action. 'Active monitoring' is a more recent term introduced as the successor to 'watchful waiting', which may have been received as somewhat passive by those who did not understand a stepped care approach is in use.

Should the patient continue to experience distress, a referral to 'Step 2' services may be made for further assessment and psychological intervention. At Step 2, initial screening may be carried out by a practitioner who is an NHS staff member from any profession trained to postgraduate certificate level in brief psychological interventions, in England currently termed a Psychological Wellbeing Practitioner (PWP). In the spirit of the primary care movement's key principles, mentioned earlier, clients may be offered a range of low-intensity interventions, which include guided self-help, computerised CBT, psycho-education groups or classes and one-to-one interventions. The differentiation marker here is that while these interventions are not yet what we might call 'therapy', they are intended to be therapeutic, practical and purposeful. At Step 3, High Intensity Psychological Therapists offer NICE recommended therapies such as Cognitive Behavioural Therapy, Eye Movement Desensitisation and Reprocessing (EMDR), Interpersonal Therapy (IPT) and/or Counselling (National Institute for Health and Care Excellence, 2011). Referral to specialist provision may be made where the client is deemed to require more complex care (see Chapter 31).

The counselling psychologist working in primary care is likely to be employed under the remit of a 'High Intensity Psychological Therapist' (HIPT), working with clients at Step 3, offering psychological assessment and therapy. At this step we work alongside other professional groups, such as colleagues from Counselling, Nursing, Mental Health Nursing and Social Work. The drive for efficient and appropriate use of resources shifts the core purpose of a typical primary care service towards brief therapies, where services tended to offer between eight and ten sessions of high-intensity work (Improving Access to Psychological Therapies, 2011), although many services are reported to have used different upper session limits, in line with NICE recommendations to offer sessions 'up to the number of sessions provided in the Randomized Control Trials (RCTs) that generated the relevant guidance' (IAPT, 2011, p. 2).

Economic costs and forces

The Department of Health presents the health service in an economic context, with challenges arising from a range of sources, chief among them the need to tackle 'the rising burden ...

[against] a backdrop of both growing and ageing populations as well as greater expectations of health services' (Department of Health, 2013, p. 3). It is undeniable that for the health service to function, resources must be carefully and efficiently managed. Resources are not unlimited for if they were we would undoubtedly 'do' primary care differently. We would enable greater access to longer-term treatments and make even greater use of multi-disciplinary approaches. If resources were even more restricted we would structure healthcare differently again, and it is important to recognise the current situation as the result of a large community working towards a greater goal under a pragmatic need for efficiency.

The 2006 Layard Report crystallised the economic cost of mental health difficulties and prompted more resources to be directed towards the alleviation of depression and anxiety. The report was seminal in highlighting both the need and potential benefit of investing in mental health, and spurred a flurry of activity in setting up integrated services that operated according to evidence-based, stepped-care models. The core rationale in this report was that investment in mental healthcare made financial sense, as it would 'lift at least a half of those affected out of their depression or their chronic fear' (Layard et al., 2006, p. 4) and return those in receipt of sickness benefits to the active workforce.

Recent attempts to quantify the economic cost of mental health problems cite figures of £100 billion (Department of Health, 2011). It has been estimated that 44 per cent of health problems have a mental health connection (Centre for Economic Performance, 2012). A 2012 report suggested that of the six million adults for whom labels of 'mental ill health' may apply, only one-quarter receive an appropriate level of care (CEP, 2012). This is attributed to a lack of available services in remote or impoverished areas, and too high a demand in centralised locations. Numbers of this magnitude cannot be left to fester, and the policy research reveals a landscape more uneven than localised strategies may be fit to address. The inevitable economic pressure places health services under more challenging demands than may be ideal as drives for efficiency and accountability take centre stage.

More recent political agendas have placed pressure across the NHS to make significant efficiency savings. Despite the light shed on the importance of early intervention by the Department of Health, continuing cuts raise concern for the welfare of those seeking help where services at many steps are being squeezed for resources. A 2013 report by the UK Council for Psychotherapy (UKCP) and British Psychoanalytic Council (BCP) (McDonnell and Stelmaszczyk, 2013) suggest that budget cuts have caused services to shrink and some to close, leading to displacement of some of the more specialist psychotherapy services. The UKCP and BCP report negative outcomes for clients, such as longer waiting lists, premature ending of treatment and reduced choices around therapy types (McDonnell and Stelmaszczyk, 2013).

Opportunities for social justice

Regardless of the political and economic agenda shaping the NHS, current services were initially set up with a clear label: to deliver psychological therapy free at the point of access to patients who otherwise may receive little support or a medication-only approach. Mental health and inequality are interrelated, where '[s]ocial inequality of all kinds contributes to mental ill health, and, in turn, mental ill health can result in further inequality. ... Mental health strategy is both a public mental health strategy and a strategy for social justice' (Department of Health, 2011, p. 3). The opportunity to bolster the well-being of the most vulnerable is presented here, especially in consideration of the roots of counselling psychology arising from a position of 'concern with developing a person's potential, not in relation to curing sickness and disease' (James and Bellamy, 2010, p. 399).

The constituent structures of the NHS and the overall organisation form the foundation on which professional practice is built, providing policies and guidance on the overall direction services take. James and Bellamy (2010) highlighted the issues of differing professional perspectives, such as the use of psychometric tools and diagnostic criteria, and suggested the best course of action was to work within the NHS arena, challenging and influencing the system in more meaningful ways. The challenge is to shape the service while working within it.

STRAND 2: CLIENTS, PROFESSIONALS AND MOVEMENT

Occasionally labelled 'the doorstep' of mental health services, primary care both teaches and tests competencies in working quickly, formulating thoroughly and rapidly adapting to challenges. The following vignettes illustrate the journeys of two clients moving through the system and seeking help from the perspective of service user. Services may have different steps and procedures suited to local need than those illustrated here, such as whether an individual may refer themselves directly or need to be referred through a gateway, but the overall process will be similar. (Case material has been anonymised for confidentiality.)

Vignette 1: Anxiety

The first vignette is an example of a system making efficient use of resources, building one level of provision on top of another.

Paul has been experiencing anxiety in social situations. He had been reluctant to take anxiolytic medication out of concern for possible side effects, and requested referral to the primary care team. He underwent telephone assessment with a Psychological Wellbeing Practitioner (PWP) and was offered three options. He first used a computerised CBT programme, some self-help books and had regular contact with his PWP. Psycho-education

(Continued)

(Continued)

seminars offered opportunities for contact with others suffering similar issues, and he later requested to be 'stepped-up' for therapy. He felt that the earlier resources provided a bed-rock on which to work, and meant he could engage with the therapy more directly without initial learning stages. A detailed longitudinal formulation was developed collaboratively in addition to situation-specific formulation exercises, which he felt allowed him to tell his story and develop 'maps' of the factors fuelling his nervousness. At the end of therapy Paul had completed a series of reflective and behavioural activities as well as a completed well-being plan.

Vignette 2: Complicated care

The following case study represents an account of work with a client involving a number of disclosures that required response to needs that were outside the service remit. It focuses on the impact of some unexpected events on the therapeutic relationship within the context of a primary care service.

Denise presented to her GP experiencing low mood. She lived in an impoverished area of the UK and was unemployed. She had recently had a confrontation with a neighbour and found herself becoming more isolated due to a loss of social support. The GP discussed available options and recommended a psychologist working within the practice. The client felt comfortable with the familiar environment of the GP practice. A psychologist working within the practice under an IAPT initiative arranged to meet the client for an assessment, after which therapy was offered. The service offered therapy based on a CBT approach, with practitioners often employing behavioural approaches and exploratory written exercises to research the factors leading to mental health issues. The client outlined how she tended to withdraw from relationships so the therapist suggested that sessions begin by plotting patterns of attachment and withdrawal.

She was given some homework exercises to complete but these were often not completed, with the client saying 'I do not really do books' and that she had a literacy issue. She felt ashamed of this and worried she would not be suitable for therapy since she could not complete the homework. The therapist acknowledged the difficulty and reassured her that therapy was not isolated to a set of specific techniques. The aim would be to find a way of working that was helpful to her. As a result, it was possible for trust to develop and for more complex issues to be disclosed.

In the early stages therapy was largely procedural, with the application of specific techniques aimed towards understanding the client's current problems. Due to the reassuring response offered at the disclosure of her literacy issue, the client felt a degree of safety in disclosing a history of self-harm and domestic violence. The client had suffered many years of domestic violence, humiliation and verbal torment. She said her experience of therapy had presented challenges to her fear in trusting males she perceived as authority figures. Despite assurance that the therapeutic space was offered from a position of respect, the client's historical scars presented a barrier to accepting such statements as entirely true. At a core level the client believed that men were innately predatory, unpredictable and any relationship would eventually lead to her being abused.

The client felt that although the more immediate issues of low mood and social isolation needed to be dealt with, they were the result of her longer-term experiences in a relationship of powerlessness and vulnerability. The therapist offered choices about how to continue, acknowledging difficulty with working with the longer-term issues in a brief therapy setting. Choices offered included referral to a secondary service, completion of brief therapy with later re-referral, and assistance sourcing therapy elsewhere. The client indicated she was not willing to be referred to an external service because she had unexpectedly found herself beginning to trust and wished to examine the deeper relational issues in depth.

From a service-level perspective, the client no longer met inclusion criteria as the case history presented an added layer of complexity that would ordinarily be reserved for longer-term therapy. Although work with the immediate social and mood issues could continue, the client felt this would be a temporary resolution to the underlying vulnerability issues. The therapist discussed the case with supervisors, and the assessment team in the attached secondary-care service. Despite the evident need for longer-term therapy, it was suggested that she would 'fall between the gaps' in service criteria. Symptom severity could be considered 'too severe' for primary care yet 'not severe enough' for the specialist care available. It was decided through supervision that the client's best interests would be best served by continuing therapy in a primary care context, with adaptations to the therapeutic approach to examine the relational issues, and the option of rapid re-referral at a later stage.

Principles in practice

The increasing complexity of the current economic and mental health climates provoke an array of ethical, social and political debates relevant to our profession. Our core challenge as counselling psychologists is to maintain a principle-driven ethical practice in a rule-driven world, where alignment between core professional values and the demands of one's daily work is under regular threat. Workload demands may mean feeling buried under administrative processes with little time or space for reflection and critique. Under pressures to formulate quickly, we may risk squeezing the client's narrative into a pre-determined model, minimising important nuances and overlooking valuable therapeutic signals. A culture based on economic drives and limited resources may also permit a particular style of rhetoric to evolve that encourages clinicians to downplay complexity.

Practice decisions founded on a thorough understanding of the professional principles of respect, autonomy, integrity and responsibility are fundamental in ensuring each clinical decision receives careful thought using supervision, collegial wisdom and intimate knowledge of one's own gaps. It is important that we maintain our commitment to a client-centred form of working that enables us to shape primary care services from within.

In vignette 3, John, a psychologist working in a primary care psychology service, offers the experience of how he managed some of the encountered pressures successfully.

Vignette 3: Managing pressures

I previously worked in a family therapy service with a systemic underpinning and used transactional analysis in my client work. For personal reasons I needed to move to a different part of the country and took a job in primary care that offered CBT training. It had been a few years since I had worked in an exclusively CBT framework, so I embraced the chance to expand my skill set a little in a situation involving the need for immediate solutions. The caseload I was expected to see in a typical day was higher than in my previous role, and I had much less time in which to write notes or reflect. A dilemma came when I was using one of the service assessment documents and realised I was slipping into the trap of letting the form direct my assessment and into ticking boxes. Without time to make detailed notes and reflect afterwards, I felt pressure to complete paperwork quickly and reach a more superficial formulation by the end of the first session. My worry was that I was missing something, potentially something important, and doing the client a disservice. I suggested a redesign of the form we were using, so that it was less prescriptive and followed a more open model of formulation.

Facing economics: Measurement and funding

There is sometimes a tension between our purpose as professionals and the reality of the working landscape. With increasing resource accountability and measurement comes a variety of potential challenges for individual therapists. Needing to navigate through a regulated system, with treatment targets and outcome measurement requirements, presents the potential to nudge the clinician away from activities based on professional values and perspectives. The danger is we may face workload pressures that lead us to neglect the slower and more methodical practices of introspection and reflective supervision.

Many primary care service processes function on a detailed reporting of quantifiable data, enabling audit and service improvement to take place. In physical health services quantifiable data might reflect the quality of the service, such as patient volumes, waiting times, treatment outcomes and patient experience. As primary care services operate as a layer within a medicalised system, similar expectations apply to the delivery of psychological therapies. The IAPT programme places weight on the use of routine measurement as:

Central to improving service-quality and accountability. It ensures the person having therapy and the clinician offering it have up-to-date information on an individual's progress. ... At an overview level, where individual patients are anonymised, service providers and commissioners can see a performance pattern for the service. (IAPT, 2014)

The rationale for data collection is not without criticism. Rizq (2012) raises the possibility that clients may be impacted through potentially unethical practice:

data collection is sponsored by the continual pressure to meet clinical and activity targets, to which end there is an injunction to ensure that: 'Patient distress or objection should be minimized wherever possible in order to meet at least 90% complete patient outcomes data' (IAPT Data Handbook, Version 2.0, March 2011). (Rizq, 2012, p. 319)

It could be argued that certain types of complexity, such as trauma, require time and a carefully containing relationship for the extent of injury to be fully recognised. In reality, a psychological practitioner cannot assume reduced symptoms or 'lower scores' equates to alleviation of causes. A therapist under pressure may offer a client a multitude of 'coping strategies', neglecting to check how many merely become new avoidance skills. We can see that the risk of downplaying complexity emerges once again under the pressure to achieve.

Funding and outcome measurement are closely linked. Continued commissioning of IAPT primary care services is dependent on evidencing the meeting of targets. Recently published documents indicate the potential for increasing pressure on practitioners needing to meet new target thresholds: 'By March 2015, access to high quality evidence-based psychological therapies, capable of delivering recovery rates of 50% or more, is expected to be available for at least 15% of the adult population' (Department of Health, 2012, p. 3). Practitioners working in this environment have expressed to the authors an awareness that further commissioning services are dependent on successful outcomes.

Language: Psychotherapeutic and medical discourses

Much has been written on the utility of the medical model in the field of mental health issues, with critique striking the core issues of whether diagnostic criteria accurately capture the diversity of human experience, and the inherent power inequality raised by the disorder-treatment model. Patil and Giordano (2010) highlight the core assumption of the medical model as a 'differentiation between what counts as normality (i.e. order) and what counts as abnormality (i.e. disorder). The distinction(s) between normality and pathology entail assumptions that are often deeply presupposed' (Patil and Giordano, 2010, p. 1). In a 'therapist–client' scenario, discovery of 'disorder' nudges the professional into a role of expert, provider of treatment, and provides an accessible rationale for methods of classification and measurement.

We live in a world where therapeutic help for complex social and personal issues is, in some areas, reduced to a package of protocols. In addition to historical undulations between medical and psychological discourses, professionals increasingly work within settings where the line between professional autonomy and compliance with a system is becoming more difficult to spot. Beckett and Maynard (2005) highlight the potential for 'therapy' in medical settings to become a didactic application of technique in which critical reflection and scrutiny of the process become lost, leaving the human being behind a wall of 'diagnosis' instead of more individually meaningful terminology. Contemporary approaches in psychotherapy hold the view that each individual perspective is inherently valuable, a thread in the tapestry of shared social construction (Gergen, 2009).

The use of any paradigm not only carries a set of linguistic constructs, but also dictates how these concepts are used in relation to one another. Bond (2010) uses the concept of linguistic communities and suggests that the experience of distress is to some extent socially constructed. Within psychology, we may communicate using a range of theoretical models and creative metaphor, recognising that our language is often indeed metaphor. Psychotherapy is accustomed to working to the client's pace, using language and metaphor unique to each person; it embraces process-oriented traditions, abstract psychological concepts and philosophies that are not always easily defined. Yet in primary care we may find ourselves in terrain where the need for rapid solutions fosters a diagnostic terminology that is sometimes accepted as fact rather than more broadly as metaphor, while the medicalised language of such a framework arguably provides a 'lingua franca' and some consistency across professional groups. However, exposure to medical terminology has implications for the loss of a descriptive, process-oriented edge that bridges abstract theory and terms individually meaningful to the client. The task is one of holding the tension between different linguistic frameworks used to conceptualise a client or client issue, and it may be argued that the proliferation of cognitive behavioural approaches and third-wave therapies stem from a need for multi-disciplinary practitioners to conceptualise therapy coherently and consistently.

CONCLUSION: WEAVING A FRAMEWORK

This chapter presents an account of the factors and forces that are encountered when working in primary care settings. As counselling psychologists, like every other health professional, we endeavour to work in ways that ensure our professional work remains aligned with our ethical principles, seeking collegial and supervisory support to remain securely rooted in a critical thinking perspective. The reality of the workplace often conjures unexpected problems and urgent calls for action, with the potential to become too busy to invest adequate time to reflect on the impact of these outward environments on our own internal worlds.

Through engagement with the larger NHS systems, we have the potential to place ourselves in positions where we may shape services to emphasise the importance of qualitative measurement, in which tools measure wellness rather than just pathology. More recent expansions in the NICE guidelines acknowledge interpersonal subjective approaches in greater detail, and this may signify a mental health system with growing awareness of person-centred values and the centrality of the therapeutic relationship. A framework for success in primary care settings begins with an awareness of one's own strengths and limitations, recognising that there may sometimes be a tension between principle and protocol which may not be immediately apparent.

Visit the companion website to read A Day in the Life of .... A Chartered Counselling Psychologist Working in a Primary Care IAPT Service.

REFERENCES

Beckett, C. and Maynard, A. (2005). *Values and Ethics in Social Work*. London: Sage.

Beveridge, W. (1942). Beveridge Report: Social Insurance and Allied Services. Retrieved 10 March 2014 from www.sochealth.co.uk/national-health-service/public-health-and-well-being/beveridge-report/.

Bond, T. (2000). *Standards and Ethics for Counselling in Action* (2nd edn). London: Sage.

Bower, P. (2005). Stepped care in psychological therapies: Access, effectiveness and efficiency. *The British Journal of Psychiatry*, 186, 11–17.

Centre for Economic Performance (CEP) (2012). *How Mental Illness Loses Out in the NHS*. London: London School of Economics and Political Science.

Cohen, A. (2008). The primary care management of anxiety and depression: A GP's perspective. *Advances in Psychiatric Treatment*, 14, 98–105.

Department of Health (2011). *No Health without Mental Health* [Web Resource]. London: Department of Health. Retrieved 30 January 2014 from www.gov.uk/government/publications/mental-health-priorities-for-change.

Department of Health (2012). *Improving Access to Psychological Therapies (IAPT): 'Supporting No Health without Mental Health'*. London: Department of Health. Retrieved 3 March 2014 from www.iapt.nhs.uk/silo/files/iapt-3-year-summary-leaflet.pdf.

Department of Health (2013). *Primary Care: Working in Partnership*. London: Department of Health.

Department of Health (2014). *Closing the Gap: Priorities for Essential Change in Mental Health* [Web Resource]. London: Department of Health. Retrieved 30 January 2014 from www.gov.uk/government/publications/mental-health-priorities-for-change.

Ekers, D. (2013). An overview of the effectiveness of psychological therapy for depression and stepped care service delivery models. *Journal of Research in Nursing*, 18(2), 171–184.

Gergen, K. (2009). *An Invitation to Social Construction* (2nd edn). London: Sage.

Health and Social Care Act (2012). Retrieved 14 March 2013 from www.legislation.gov.uk/ukpga/2012/7/contents/enacted.

Improving Access to Psychological Therapies (2011). *Enhancing Recovery Rates in IAPT Services: Lessons from Year One*. London: IAPT National Team.

Improving Access to Psychological Therapies (2014). *Measuring Outcomes*. Retrieved 15 March 2014 from http://iapt.nhs.uk/iapt/data/.

James, P. and Bellamy, A. (2010). Counselling psychology in the NHS. In R. Woolfe, S. Strawbridge, B. Douglas and W. Dryden (ed.), *Handbook of Counselling Psychology* (3rd edn). London: Sage. pp. 397–415.

Layard, R., Clark, D., Bell, S., Knapp, M., Meacher, B., Priebe, S., Turnberg, L., Thornicroft, G. and Wright, B. (2006). *THE DEPRESSION REPORT: A New Deal for Depression and Anxiety Disorders*. London: Centre for Economic Performance's Mental Health Policy Group, London School of Economics.

McDonnell, L. and Stelmaszczyk, L. (2013). *Quality Psychotherapy Services in the NHS*. London: UKCP & BCP.

National Institute for Health and Care Excellence (2011). *Commissioning Stepped Care for People with Common Mental Health Disorders* [Web Resource]. Retrieved 3 February 2014 from http://publications.nice.org.uk/commissioning-stepped-care-for-people-with-common-mental-health-disorders-cmg41/3-a-stepped-care-approach-to-commissioning-high-quality-integrated-care-for-people-with-common.

Newman, M. (2000). Recommendations for a cost-offset model of psychotherapy allocation using generalized anxiety disorder as an example. *Journal of Consulting and Clinical Psychology*, 68, 549–555.

Norman, I. and Ryrie, I. (2013). *The Art and Science of Mental Health Nursing: A Textbook of Principles and Practice* (3rd edn). Maidenhead: Open University Press. p. 547.

Patil, T. and Giordano, J. (2010). On the ontological assumptions of the medical model of psychiatry: Philosophical considerations and pragmatic tasks. *Philosophy, Ethics, and Humanities in Medicine*, 5(3), 1–7.

Rizq, R. (2012). The Ghost in the Machine: IAPT and organizational melancholia. *British Journal of Psychotherapy*, 28(3), 319–335.

Roland, M., Guthrie, B. and Thome, D. C. (2012). Primary medical care in the United Kingdom. *The Journal of the American Board of Family Medicine*, 25(Suppl. 1), S6–S11.

The Nuffield Trust (2012). *The History of NHS Reform: Evidence for Better Healthcare* [Website]. Retrieved 3 August 2014 from http://nhstimeline.nuffieldtrust.org.uk.

World Health Organization (1978). *Primary Health Care: Report on the International Conference on Primary Health Care*. Alma-Ata: WHO.

World Health Organization (2008). *The World Health Report 2008 – Primary Health Care (Now More Than Ever)* [Website]. Geneva: WHO. Retrieved 12 August 2014 from www.who.int/whr/2008/en/.

31
THE ROLE OF COUNSELLING PSYCHOLOGY IN SECONDARY ADULT MENTAL HEALTH CARE
HAMILTON FAIRFAX

INTRODUCTION

The aim of this chapter is to provide an overview of counselling psychology practice in secondary care health services. It is an exciting and dynamic area of practice and one within which counselling psychology can become a leading profession. While it would be impossible to cover all this encompasses, the chapter attempts to give basic grounding for those considering a career in secondary care services, and perhaps points of debate for colleagues already in practice. In the former aspiration, I am grateful to the counselling psychology trainees on the doctoral course at the University of the West of England, who responded to a request to find out what they wanted to know about secondary care services. The chapter will explore the following:

- What is meant by 'secondary care'
- Current mental health policy, in particular Payment by Results (PbR) and implications for practice
- Client presentations and client need at this level
- The role of the counselling psychologist as part of a multidisciplinary team, understanding the perspectives and roles of other professionals
- A discussion of the practical differences between clinical and counselling psychologists
- The remit of the role in secondary care, including consultation, supervision, leadership, research and training, in addition to therapeutic provision.
- The conclusion will consider the influence of a counselling psychology perspective, how this works alongside the medical model, it's compatibility with service-user outcomes, and how counselling psychologists may be in the ideal position to influence psychological practice for complex conditions.

I work within the English NHS and an outline of the different structures and processes of Scottish and Welsh mental health services can be found in the chapter's associated web features.

Visit the companion website for the following:

- The NHS in Scotland.
- Two Days in the Life of Counselling Psychologists Working in Secondary Care.

Discussing health-care organisations and mental health policies inevitably involves use of abbreviations, and although these are explained within the chapter, a brief guide for frequently used terms is provided at the end of the chapter (see Table 31.2).

SECONDARY CARE

The basic division between primary and secondary care is premised on notions of complexity and severity. Recent initiatives in England, in particular Improving Access to Psychology Therapy (IAPT), have helped to add greater clarity by identifying the expectations of services at the primary care level and highlighting the more nebulous territory of secondary care. Complexity and severity can be determined diagnostically (e.g. psychosis), by duration, past history (such as several discrete episodes of eating disorder), risk (the likelihood of there being significant harm to self or other), co-morbidity (describing multiple diagnostic difficulties) and assessments of impact which involves considering the wider systemic effect on issues such as family, occupation and housing. While no means definitive, one could expect a person described as having secondary care needs to present with a longstanding set of mental health difficulties resulting in inability to secure or maintain employment, compromised financial situation and impoverished relationships. They may also be prescribed psychiatric medication, have a mental health history that could involve multiple diagnosis, psychiatric ward admission and suicide attempts. They are likely to be subject to continuous assessment of social benefits and, as a result of these issues, may feel a level of pessimism about change or no longer be certain what this actually means to them.

A key issue, therefore, in being able to articulate that 'change' in this context is not simply an absence of symptoms but necessitates more psychosocial and phenomenological determined outcomes. Given the more robust and demonstrable framework of IAPT, which includes clearly defined outcomes based on evidence-based research, there is an implicit challenge for secondary care to be as similarly transparent. It will be argued that such an intention is far easier to design than to implement in practice.

The previous chapter in this book has described how primary care and IAPT has introduced a more clearly defined 'stepped care' system based on National Institute for Health and Care Excellence (NICE) guidelines that identifies 'evidenced-based practise' (EBP). Stepped care (1 to 5) increases proportionally with assessments of complexity, Step 5 indicating specialist therapeutic communities or inpatient services. Although there is considerable debate concerning the validity and clinical application of EBP (Hammersley, 2005; Michie et al., 2005), IAPT services are estimated to reduce just under 50 per cent of referrals to sub-clinical levels (Clark et al., 2009). Further discussion of this exceeds the remit of this chapter.

Regardless of criticisms, however, IAPT provides a helpful illustration of the current environment of mental health services and the place of psychotherapeutic practice within it. Although this chapter will discuss specific instances of secondary care practice, the underlying theme will be how counselling psychology can be an effective and influential force in the design and commissioning of services. While considering these issues, attention should also be paid to how these may develop and how the profession can contribute and offer leadership. The new commissioning structure implied by Payment by Results (PbR) has the potential to fundamentally redefine secondary care provision and counselling psychology is well placed to establish new models of service delivery (Fairfax, 2013; Vermes, 2014).

SECONDARY CARE PSYCHOLOGICAL SERVICES

Secondary care is largely identified with 'Step 4' and 'Step 5' provision. A very basic description of how mental health services have been commissioned is provided below. However, for more detailed accounts see McCulloch and Lawton-Smith (2012) and Webster (2002). Traditionally, secondary care provision has been dominated by National Health Service (NHS) services as part of 'block contracts' negotiated by regional commissioning groups such as Strategic Health Authorities (SHAs). This involved the SHA passing money awarded to the region by the national government to local Mental Health Trusts (the 'block') with agreement that the Trust will provide the services required by primary care stakeholders, such as GPs. While this allowed a level of autonomy, it was also beset by difficulties in attempting to create entirely comprehensive and high-quality services. The most obvious failing is demonstrated by long waiting lists. Over time the organisational need for more clearly defined contracts was more apparent, particularly as the commissioning bodies became increasingly clinically directed. The current commissioning model requires GPs to identify and create services based on their local needs. However, although structurally intelligible in practice, it is at odds with the staff and public perception of the NHS founded, as it was, on socialist principles to provide equality in free health care for all at the point of need.

During the 65 years of the NHS's existence it has become one of the largest employers in the world, admired and respected globally, but often the main agenda of policy change for new and established governments. Arguably, therefore, the NHS has become an institution to which huge expectations are attached (the public expect the best care, without cost, for all conditions) and one that is in a continuous process of change as successive governments seek to appeal to the electorate through reorganisations which attempt to meet these expectations. It is, of course, an impossible situation, but like the Emperor's new clothes, one that no one is allowed to directly expose for risk of public outcry. Arguably, this demand has led to the establishment of target-based cultures that attempt to describe the effectiveness of the organisation but in practice demoralise and alienate the staff, resulting in increasing bureaucracy and instances of bad practice, for example the Mid Staffordshire scandal (Francis, 2013).

In tandem, and encouraged to varying degrees by governments across the political spectrum, private organisations have developed and grown to provide physical and mental health-care services. As private enterprises are far more suited to the market force economy, they are used to delivering specific contracting protocols enabling commissioning bodies to have a level of clarity previously unknown under the block contracts. This includes clear, costed aims detailing the number and types of clients seen, the treatment received, and outcomes to be expected over the period of the contract. As opposed to having 'to make do' with local Trusts, GP commissioners can now begin to select from a range of providers, some of which are cheaper and seemingly more efficient. (A wider discussion of this topic is outside the scope of this chapter, but for more see Player and Leys (2011) and Pollock (2005).) Counselling psychology is a profession that has eschewed the division between private and public health care, and the new commissioning climate therefore provides an environment where this kind of experience can be an enormous advantage.

MULTIDISCIPLINARY TEAMS: WORKING WITH OTHER PROFESSIONS

The effect of PbR on the organisation of services remains to be seen, but it is likely they will develop along the lines of super-clusters, Non-Psychosis and Psychosis (see later section).

Following the closure of asylums, secondary mental health care evolved to be community-based teams (Community Mental Health teams, or CMHTs) comprising core professional groups: Community Psychiatric Nurses (CPNs), Occupational Therapists (OTs), Social Workers, Community Support Workers and Consultant Psychiatrists (see Table 31.1). Psychological services were usually embedded into the teams, although sometimes a separate department contracted services into the CMHTs. Psychological services could include psychotherapists and creative therapists, although these professional groups could also set up separate departments.

An initial challenge, therefore, was (and is) for psychological professionals to be able to communicate their role and contribution to the wider professional network. As a small professional group, psychologists, psychotherapists and creative therapists behaved differently from other professionals, were managed differently and were better paid. These differences, particularly the latter, became more apparent through payment negotiations, the most recent of which, Agenda for Change (AfC), for example, resulted in clinical psychology trainees being placed on the same banding as senior CPNs.

Table 31.1 Core professional groups in community mental health services

Profession	Description
Community Psychiatric Nurse (CPN)	The largest professional staff group, requiring three years' psychiatric training, CPNs have several years' experience working in psychiatric wards and the community. They can administer and advise on medication. They may have additional training as nurse prescribers, and in therapeutic interventions and management.
Social Worker Mental Health (SW)	In a statutory role, Social Workers uphold laws that protect the vulnerable clients with whom they work. SWs have a duty to abide by the legislation and a power to enforce it. SWs often have additional training in Mental Health Act legislation, and most are often involved in sectioning (see AMP below) and may have therapeutic training. The training involves a three-year undergraduate degree and a two-year Master's postgraduate degree.
Occupational Therapist (OT)	OTs create individual treatment programmes, develop rehabilitation programmes, can advise on home and workplace environmental alterations, anxiety management, and assist in returning to work, help with social skills and everyday activities. Training is a three-year undergraduate degree or two-year accelerated programme.
Approved Mental Health Practitioner (AMP)	Formally known as Approved Social Workers (ASWs), AMPs are practitioners who have specialist training in Mental Health Act legalisation and are qualified to be involved in sectioning. Although any mental health professional, including psychologists, can train to be AMPs, it is still largely Social Workers who form this group.
Community Support Worker (CSW)	CSWs can be generic or specialised. The role involves developing new resources in dialogue within existing programmes, building links with other groups and agencies, raising public awareness on issues relevant to the community, preparing reports and policies, liaising with interest groups, managing conflict, planning, attending and coordinating meetings and events, challenging behaviour, and general administrative duties. Qualifications include a minimum QCF qualification at level 2 or 3, but CSWs often have a range of qualifications and experience.
Consultant Psychiatrist	Consultant Psychiatrists are medically trained practitioners whose responsibilities include the management of complex, severe clients, who are often at risk, within a team. Their role includes teaching, training, undertaking research, and providing clinical leadership. Psychiatrists are responsible for prescribing medication, undertaking medical investigations and procedures such as ECT. They are involved in sectioning clients and are often the main professional group that decides on care plans if there is uncertainty. Psychiatrists often have an organisational leadership role. Training involves a five-year **medical degree**, two years foundation training and six years speciality training.

The questions of identity, difference and 'added value' of psychological therapists were also raised as a result of CMHT professionals undertaking extensive therapeutic training and delivering high-quality accredited interventions in models such as Cognitive Behavioural Therapy (CBT). It could be argued that the psychological professions have a history of tribal factionalism which can be hostile and dismissive and bewildering to other professionals and the wider public (Vermes, 2014). At its worst, this can influence interactions and communication with CMHT professionals, confusing others and resulting in feelings of 'specialness' and 'superiority'. The profession of Psychology has arguably never grasped the problem of identity positively, tending to define itself in contrast to others, e.g. 'not medical model' or 'more scientific'. There is a danger we can come across as elitist and privileged. In laying sole claim to a role of 'therapist', for example, we can also be too defensive, referring to 'proper' training or therapy.

Personal experience is that this misses the point of true multidisciplinary practice and is antithetical to examples of good practice. Experience suggests that where the different professions sit comfortably alongside each other, this working culture persists beyond changes in personnel. It should not be a threat if other professionals may have trained in a therapy. For example, a CPN may be a much better CBT therapist than some psychologists, but that diminishes neither person and only serves to enhance the provision of the whole service. Far from detracting from the role of a psychologist, this highlights and defines the real issue, which is: What is needed from a psychological practitioner in secondary care?

Even the most hostile team, with a proliferation of skilled therapists, will refer clients to a psychologist, which perhaps recognises that the requirements of a psychologist at Step 4 is to offer a more holistic approach to client need. In outcome studies, when clients are asked what is most helpful, their responses can be surprising but incredibly helpful (Hubble et al., 1999; Ward and Boag, 2009). Similarly, if you ask other professionals, particularly those with therapeutic training, what they want when referring to a psychologist, they can be just as clear. These include: 'I'm not able to offer what they need', 'I've gone as far as I can, they just need the next stage', 'could you just give me an opinion?', 'what's going on here?' It seems that what is being requested and recognised is the importance of the dissolution of psychological knowledge and experience applied to a given individual at a particular time. They do not want a therapy by numbers, a 'how to' guide, nor do they want a different person offering a similar version of what the client has already received. In these requests, they perhaps draw a line between a more proscribed encounter and one that requires a new collaborative agreement informed by in-depth psychologically informed intimacy. This is the heart of integrative and phenomenologically informed practice, which by no means is the preserve of counselling psychologists but is core to our identity.

If one considers the essence of multidisciplinary principles, it is the amalgam of a psychosocial perspective from individual professionals with a specific, but not exclusive, training. The role of the psychologists can often be not just to present the psychological perspective, but also to look at ways to harmonise each view collaboratively (and, from personal experiences, often to be so 'harmonised' by others). It calls for sensitivity, diplomacy, respect, humility, willingness to abandon previously held formulation for the agreed good of a client. However, it is also a role in which the psychologist can be expected to offer leadership and be prepared to be assertive to advocate their position. With its emphasis on understanding the individual in context, and not just through the lens of a particular viewpoint, counselling psychology offers a natural fit whether embedded in a team or consulting to one.

WORKING ALONGSIDE THE MEDICAL MODEL

Counselling psychologists are not the only professionals who have issues with a purely medicalised way of understanding mental health distress. Social workers, for example, are a professional group closely allied with more constructionist and systemic interpretations

(Turner, 2007). With the growth and proliferation of psychotherapeutic practice in secondary care, psychological formulations are recognised as a vital part of an individual's care plan. Consultant psychiatrists, GPs and other interested medical professionals commonly attend training courses for therapies such as Cognitive Analytic Therapy (CAT), CBT or Mentalisation Based Therapy (MBT). Although far less than the absolutist viewpoint of the 1950s, the medical model is still the most dominant voice, particularly in NHS services, but like any powerful narrative it is one that needs to be engaged with.

Adopting a purely anti-psychiatrist stance is as unhelpful as advocating a solely reductionist position, more so clinically, as both often deny the reality of the client. As argued earlier, Psychology is not served by identifying with oppositional positions. This does little for the status and influence of the profession and has the potential to reinforce negative stigma. It is without contention, for example, that psychiatric medication can be of great help to some, but certainly not all, individuals (Moncrieff, 2009). To deprive a person of anything that could improve their quality of life based on personal opinion is in conflict with the ethics of counselling psychology practice (British Psychological Society, 2009). Moreover, secondary care services in operation are the best advocate for the need of psychological presence. If one simply considers that the vast majority of clients will be prescribed a range of medication yet still experience distress, it is the best evidence for the importance of a psychologically integrated approach to care.

The relative helpfulness of medication identifies a further role for psychotherapeutic practitioners. If a client continues to struggle, despite various and repeated pharmacological regimes, the team needs to be helped to consider their response. For example, is medication being used to help professionals or carers limit their exposure to distressing feelings? Is the client avoiding confronting difficulties through their use of medication? Have the team become stuck in repeating a historical care plan? Discussing these issues and facilitating the different professional perspectives during a case meeting can be as effective as arranging a series of assessment appointments. However, to be of use in this capacity it is also incumbent on counselling psychologists to be better informed about psychiatric medication, and the role of medical practitioners (Hammersley, 2005).

The next few paragraphs draw on the author's personal clinical experience and, therefore, are written in the first person. Many service clients have a diagnosis of Personality Disorder, usually at least two, and with a level of symptomatic, social and interpersonal problems perhaps expected in someone with high levels of distress. These complex clients need and deserve an equally comprehensive response from different professionals who operate from a shared understanding of the individual's need. Clients with these diagnoses can often be experienced as challenging and demanding due to the nature of how they have perhaps learned to communicate their difficulties. It is, therefore, a vital consideration that a psychological perspective helps unify a team response and it is incumbent on the psychologist to advocate without dividing or alienating other professionals.

We need to be able to engage and work with our colleagues collaboratively without abandoning our core professional and individual beliefs. For example, despite my personal difficulties with the conceptual diagnosis of Personality Disorder, it helps no one, least of all the client, to

518   V: DIFFERENT TERRITORIES

choose to use their involvement in the team as an opportunity to attack the perspectives of others, or refuse to cooperate with those who find the diagnosis more helpful. Instead, we need to use our psychological trainings to help find ways to work alongside different perspectives while exposing others to our viewpoint and, just as vitally, being exposed to theirs. CPNs, for example, spend much of their time responding to crisis, visiting clients in their homes and communities, and therefore have greater real-life understanding of the individual's wider realities than of that purely experienced in a therapy room. Both perspectives can inform each other, particularly when there is tension. Spending time listening to the experiences of keyworkers not only helps to develop a more holistic formulation, but provides opportunities for developing a team-based ethos and creative individualised care.

I have worked alongside a number of consultant psychiatrists, some of whom would be described as 'old-fashioned' or 'reductionist', although many are far more aware and supportive of multi-perspective interventions. In relating to psychiatrists, it is important to understand their roles, pressures and accountability. For example, it is often the consultant psychiatrist who carries responsibility for complex care plans and has ultimate responsibility. This includes questions on whether someone is 'at risk' or not, whether they should be admitted, sectioned, when they may be discharged or whether they should have increases in medication or be allowed to reduce or stop it completely. These decisions need to be made quickly, with references to available clinical evidence and under significant pressure from organisations.

Most psychiatrists, similar to us, want to help the clients in the best way they can and are happy to be engaged with. However, it is important to communicate an understanding of their needs and demands and use the language that is most likely to help a wider debate. For example, when confronted by what I described earlier as a old-fashioned reductionist view, while I may know it is more helpful to confront this, it is very tempting to 'work secretly' and hope it is not noticed. If we are feeling uncomfortable by a dominant view, it is likely that other members of the team are as well, and it is important to draw support form this without being mutinous. As psychologists, we can draw on a range of theoretical understandings and can support this with appropriate psychometrics and clinical informed formulations. I have found that presenting this kind of evidence with an understanding of the particular pressures on the psychiatrist, together with either potential solutions or a willingness to engage in them, can help make entrenched positions flexible. Alongside this we need to be to be aware of the reference points relevant to Trust organisations and managers, for example, knowing that medication is not a recommended treatment by NICE in the treatment of Borderline Personality Disorder and nor is therapeutic intervention shorter than six months.

INPATIENT TEAMS

It is likely that working in secondary care will involve contact with psychiatric inpatient units either through liaison if a client is admitted, attending ward rounds or case meetings, or being employed in a ward-based post. (For a more detailed description of psychological role on inpatients wards, see Kerfoot et al., 2012; Royal College of Psychiatrists, 2011; British Psychological Society, 2014).

The role of inpatient wards in mental health care can be confusing and, with an increasing emphasis on short admissions, they more often become places of containment during crises which can result in stressful working environments for staff and other clients. While some wards retain an emphasis on treatment during the admission, many others are only able to provide essential nursing required to keep an individual safe or see them through crises such as suicidal attempts, psychotic episodes, or extreme and dangerous weight loss. They are environments where the medical model pervades the culture, sometimes necessarily given the physical health of clients, e.g. in the prevention of self-harm, in refeeding and by the introduction, or change, of medication (Alexander and Bowers, 2004).

Over the last twenty years more psychological principles have been incorporated into inpatient care with the popularity of Wellness Action Recovery Plans (WRAP) and the Recovery Model, both placing the client at the heart of determining their care (Copeland, 2012). The Recovery Model in particular emphasises the increasing responsibility of the clients in identifying the ingredients they need for a personalised response from services (Roberts et al., 2006). The Recovery Model understands mental illness as a lifelong process of well-being as opposed to a fixed point of 'cure', and has been adopted by the Royal College of Psychiatrists as the recognised model of service design for community and inpatient services (Royal College of Psychiatrists, 2010). In this design and aspiration, there are clear overlaps with the phenomenological, empowering and holistic ethos of counselling psychology. Entering onto a ward environment with a 'Recovery perspective' is therefore more compatible with therapeutic practice and allows the psychological practitioner not only to offer a psychological 'treatment', but also the flexibility to be alongside clients in helping to shape and identify the meaning of change for them.

Similarly to increasing understanding of medication, it is important for the counselling psychologist to have a working knowledge of practices relevant to the ward, for example the differences between types of Mental Health Act 2007 section, what they involve and the implications for the client. Furthermore, a good awareness of the Mental Health Care Act 2014 and issues of 'apacity' are important, not only as they inform a relationship with services but issues of liberty and personal choice are core considerations of psychotherapeutic practice.

SPECIALIST TEAMS

In addition to community teams, the psychologist may liaise or be part of specialist services, the most common of which are described below.

Early Intervention in psychosis (EI)

Early Intervention (EI) teams developed following significant research, predominately in Australia and Scandinavia, which suggested that if a dedicated multidisciplinary team intervenes at the first signs of psychosis, they could prevent a more severe or lifelong problem (Singh, 2010). Given that psychosis often occurs in teenage years and early adulthood, EI teams often relate to both Adult and Child Services and can be involved for up to three years, with team members contributing specific episodes of care as appropriate throughout that period. The outcomes of EI teams are mixed, but they are a much used form of intervention and recommended in NICE Guidelines for Schizophrenia (Marshall and Rathbone, 2011).

Assertive Outreach

These teams were developed to support individuals who, despite significant difficulties, find it hard, or are reluctant, to engage in mental health services (Bond et al., 1995). Clients often have a diagnosis of psychosis and are described as 'treatment resistant'. Members of the team are involved in supporting clients in community accommodation and can be involved in administering depot medication, resolving community difficulties and increasing socialisation. Some clients are involved with the team as a result of criminal justice proceedings and Community Treatment Orders and Assertive Outreach teams often liaise with Probation Services.

Crisis and Home Treatment

Crisis teams are multidisciplinary and offer 24-hour support to clients at risk of harming themselves or others. They offer telephone support but also in many Trusts they have evolved to provide a gate-keeping role for referrals to the ward offering assessment and brief treatment. Teams have also developed a period of home treatment to prevent admission or support post-discharge. This usually lasts up to three weeks and involves stabilising and crisis management.

Specialist Therapeutic Teams

In the NHS and private companies there are also specialist units created to deliver treatment for specific client groups and diagnoses such as Borderline Personality Disorder, Obsessive

Compulsive Disorder and Eating Disorder. These services usually consist of multidisciplinary teams, often with inpatient facilities, and accept national referrals. Units often have dedicated psychologists and psychotherapeutic practitioners as part of the team.

WHAT ARE THE DIFFERENCES BETWEEN COUNSELLING AND CLINICAL PSYCHOLOGISTS IN PRACTICE?

This has been a significant issue for counselling psychologists for sometime, initially very legitimately but increasingly less helpfully as the profession developed an identity of its own. There are perhaps two main ways to respond to this question: theoretically and practically. This chapter is concerned with the realities of clinical practice in secondary care and therefore predominantly refers to the latter response. Why are clinical psychologists more likely to be appointed over counselling psychologists? A simple answer is that there are more of them and they answer interview questions better, mostly because they are trained from within the NHS culture and their placements are all within the NHS. There is not usually any greater conspiracy. However, this presents a challenge for training providers, the Division of Counselling Psychology and those of us employed in such organisations to encourage counselling psychology trainees and promote our services.

A straightforward answer to what is different between the two could be: 'very little but the subtle differences are important'. In stating this I am not rejecting discrimination; it does happen and now there are much better systems in place to address it. It is something I have experienced in the past but I have fortunately also experienced rewarding and enriching working relationships with other professionals, particularly clinical psychologists. I have also been informed of a marginal but no less disappointing antagonistic trend between trainees in each profession. In the most cases, however, historical vilifications and the scramble for identity remain in the past. NHS job adverts now have to state 'Clinical or Counselling Psychologist' and many Trusts now use the term 'Applied Psychologist'.

The threat the psychological professions in all their various tribes need to grapple with is not from within but from much larger external systems. While we continue to negatively identify and demark from each other instead of enjoying the vast mix of colours contained by the term 'therapeutic professions', the outside world is increasingly losing interest and moving ahead without us. Once regulation was removed from professional organisations such as the British Psychological Society (BPS) and given to the Health and Care Professions Council (HCPC), there is no need for the extra effort and expense previously required. Why not appoint someone to be an 'HCPC accredited psychological therapist' as opposed to wrestling with seemingly aloof professional bodies? Unlike the British Medical Association (BMA), the BPS has never had the same level of authority within the NHS. In part this is because the NHS is a medically dominated organisation in design, but it also reflects the lack of communication between psychologists and other professional groups, which I feel has been typified by the repeated assertion of negative identity (e.g. 'proper therapists', 'formal psychological practice' alluded to earlier). We are different but we don't have to be so insecure about it.

I am not advocating the development of a single amorphous profession; far from it, there is great strength in difference. It is how we describe and relate to difference that is critical. Acting as a 'family' of psychological professions that values each member as distinct but 'part of', advocating the merits of one 'sibling' in a particular situation, for example, does not mean devaluing the other. This conception of a rainbow nation for psychological professions may seem naïve but acceptance and promotion of diversity is core to all our ethical standards. Without a more unified and positive collegial agreement, we risk being marginalised and voiceless, leaving behind territory that was so hard fought for (Woolfe, 2012).

In the final resort, the difference therefore between clinical and counselling psychology at secondary care is mainly one of perspective and how this affects the therapeutic process. Both share the same common values: quality of care for clients, psychosocial and contextual understandings, scepticism of diagnoses or purely 'illness-led' interventions, the importance of individually based treatment, even in the context of specific therapy models, representing client needs. Counselling psychologists are perhaps more comfortable with the existential stance of 'not knowing' when meeting with a client and can find it easier to use the relationships as a therapeutic technique. They are more likely to integrate from a wider range of therapeutic approaches and more familiar with the dynamics and tensions of integrative practice. While from one perspective these seem quite minor differences, in practice they highlight a fundamental need at Step 4 that has become obscured by evidence-based practice (EBP). The need is for a skilled multi-model trained practitioner who can provide interventions based on an assessment of the client as a whole rather than their suitability for a particular model.

Clinical psychologists are skilled at distilling and applying the wider 'science of psychology'. They provide clear and precise assessments and formulations that reflect a good knowledge of theory and systems. Clinical psychologists have been well trained in the use of psychometric assessment and a level of neuropsychological assessment and skilled at drawing on these to inform formulations. As such, they are more likely to reference 'what is known' as opposed to 'what is felt'. Neither positions are exclusive or superior, both have the potential to complement and inform high-quality practice. However, if looking for a very basic difference, it could be suggested that in orientation clinical psychology is more 'rigour based' and counselling psychology more 'process based'.

As argued elsewhere (Fairfax, 2013), Stepped Care helps to identify what should be offered, and, as importantly, what is not. Increases in 'steps' (complexity of client difficulties) necessarily implies increases in therapeutic skill and knowledge; clients cannot simply be offered the same intervention but just 'slightly longer'. While Step 1 and 2 from an IAPT perspective can draw on very clear findings from NICE, as complexity increases the surety of the guidelines does not. In part this reflects the lack of the kind of available research evidence prioritised by NICE, e.g. Randomised Control Trials (RCTs), but in turn highlights the problem of applying these standards of research to secondary care. Psychology is concerned with the activity of making areas of confusion more intelligible and the difficulties of describing Step 4 is best met by clinical and counselling psychologists using their different but complementary perspectives to work together.

PAYMENT BY RESULTS (PBR)

The increasing need for governments to make the NHS accountable and affordable resulted in the development of Payment by Results (PbR). Initially developed in physical health care, whereby a clear costing could be established for routine operations, it is currently in the process of being applied to mental health care in the NHS. Such a significant reform is also of interest to an Any Qualified Provider (AQP), who will need to be aware of the commissioning guidelines to design competing services. The development of PbR is confined to England, and NHS services for Scotland are outlined in the companion website resources for this chapter detailed above.

Payment by Results divides mental health care into three 'super-clusters': Non Psychosis, Psychosis and Organic. Each cluster is in turn divided into sub-clusters, Non Psychosis 1 to 8, Psychosis 10–15, and Organic 16–21. A client is ascribed to a cluster and sub-cluster following an initial assessment and completion of Health of the Nation Outcome Scales (HoNOS). HoNOS is a general measure of functioning, the answer to each of the questions is graded on a Likert scale of severity. Professionals then apply the details of the assessment and HoNOS to the PbR criteria contained within the 'Clustering Booklet' (Department of Health, 2012). Each sub-cluster is described, providing a range of expected diagnosis, indication of need and risk, and a matrix which delineates essential criteria for that cluster (e.g. sub-cluster 8 history of self-harm).

Although the introducing of PbR has been delayed due to lack of agreement on national tariffs for sub-clusters, services across England have begun to redesign services in anticipation of changes (Department of Health, 2013). For example, some CMHTs have become to split into teams that represent each super-cluster. Currently, there is no firm national guidance on how this should be achieved and at the discretion of each local commissioning group.

The advantage of PbR is that it provides structure to what commissioners, and thereby public funding, can expect from their local service. Each sub-cluster is costed not only for psychotherapeutic needs but also for what can be expected from medical and social care. Clusters also indicate the length of the treatment period, duration of treatments within sub-clusters, what outcomes can be expected and when the person should be reviewed. From a client perceptive, therefore, what level of care they are entitled to is more clearly detailed. If properly applied, PbR would end regional differences in service provision, being more faithful to the founding principles of the NHS to provide fair access to all regardless of economic background. PbR also allows NHS services to state what they can and cannot provide, allowing private or voluntary organisation either to form partnerships with statutory organisations or to offer a service for an entire sub-cluster.

PbR has the potential to have a radical and long-term effect on the future of the NHS, which in itself may 'be no bad thing', and calls for one to consider their wider political views regarding health care. Such a debate is beyond the remit of this chapter. However, to briefly elaborate this assertion it has been argued that PbR in physical health has resulted in many minor operations being commissioned by private organisations, which has attracted senior and highly trained practitioners away from NHS roles either part-time or in their entirety. This has resulted in what some have feared in a gradual process of the NHS existing for only the most severe and complex conditions which require a commensurate level of care and resources (Player and Leys, 2011). Concerns have been raised that workloads consisting of only the most challenging and often more terminal cases are likely to lead to a demoralisation and eventual disintegration of existing staff. One also has to consider whether the 'mixed' economy of private and statutory services is positive. While there is the opportunity for clarity and mutual skills sharing, there is also the possibility of division and lack of communication, both of which were highlighted in the Francis Report into the Mid Staffordshire scandal (Francis, 2013).

The design of PbR also raises questions for service implementation. It places a great deal of responsibility on the initial assessor. This is usually a CPN, who tends to be less well paid and have less organisational authority than a psychologist or consultant psychiatrist. They usually have approximately an hour to assess clients, which includes other routine and essential requirements (e.g. safeguarding). While they can consult with the team, lack of time and volume of referrals usual prevents a full discussion. Given that PbR could guide a client's care for up to 12 months, sometimes longer, it is a high burden to place on the hour assessment. Although clusters are not as limited as simple diagnosis, they still operate within this framework and still call for a categorisation of experience along presubscribed definitions. It is open, therefore, to the same criticisms of the medical model, and debates on topics such as whether someone is 'more psychotic than personality disordered' can have radical implications for the quality and appropriateness of their care.

It seems fair to conclude that despite uncertainties in delivery and structure in some form, the principles of PbR are here to stay. However, once again this provides ground for counselling psychologists to help lead other psychotherapeutic professionals to make sure PbR does not just become a remote accounting mechanism. Counselling psychologists are used to working within and outside organisations such as the NHS. They have operated privately and developed organisations that are AQP (Vermes, 2014). We have a perspective informed from both environments, which, if harnessed properly, can be a powerful voice, and one that continues to represent the need for a personalised understanding of client need.

BEYOND THE 'THERAPY ROOM', CONSULTATION, SUPERVISION, TRAINING AND RESEARCH

Traditional secondary care practice has mainly been providing therapy to respond to long and ever increasing waiting lists. While I agree that therapy remains a core role of psychotherapeutic professions, in the NHS the lack of practitioners and the restructuring caused by Agenda for Change (AfC) and Stepped Care have highlighted the need for a much wider role. It is not that consultation, training, research and assessment did not happen previously, more that they could be less visible, not prioritised or offered on an 'ad hoc' basis.

The aim of consultation and supervision, similar to that of the therapeutic process, is to increase the psychological awareness and flexibility with the individual or group to create a more informed and empowered decision-making process. Multidisciplinary teams were designed to allow this contribution but the psychological perspective could often be squashed under a need to respond swiftly to crisis or dominated by a medical culture. In response, some psychotherapeutic practitioners became more removed by providing strict referral criteria, offering heavily theoretically laden opinions or separating themselves from general team activity sometimes through establishing different departments. Not all of this was unhelpful but perpetuated a general feeling of 'superiority and specialness' discussed earlier, decreasing the sphere of influence reflected by the lack of psychologists at senior organisational levels. Despite this, a psychological perspective is valued and, as other professionals recognise the need for a different way of responding to an issue, it is up to us to not only be available but also to advertise the ways we can be helpful.

Psychological consultation does not have to be restricted to clinical needs, but we can help within an organisation, including team structures and the higher level decision-making of Trusts. Managers need to be reminded that applied psychologists are a resource that can be deployed in various capacities throughout an organisation, ultimately both saving cost in efficiency and avoiding employing external consultants who do not have a vested interest in the local Trust.

Although most job descriptions include reference to providing training to others, it is often a neglected role. Developing psychological thinking, however, has a demonstrative effect on client care and, when formalised, has been associated with examples of best practice (Mental Health Foundation, 2013). It is not just restricted to training in a specific model or client group, but in the whole activity of applying psychological principles, such as formulation, transference and countertransference. With appropriate organisational support, training can help promote and instil an effective culture, whereby all staff can feel part of inclusive principles, increasing both clients and their own well-being. Training from a psychological 'expert' in this sense does not have to be a purely hierarchal, but more a process of sharing and encouraging others to create a healthy working environment that includes the opportunity for personal development.

Research is a core part of all psychological qualifications and most practitioners in secondary care have been trained to a doctoral level of research. Yet in practice very few have the time, thinking space or organisational support to plan or undertake research. Instead, it can often be seen, with some envy, as an 'activity of universities'. Under pressure of waiting lists and demands of the organisation, Trusts often do not encourage research or, if they do, service-based audits are prioritised over clinical research. As a consequence, a highly trained skill is not being utilised and a vital contribution to developing the profession is lost.

There is a mismatch between EBP, favoured by NICE, and the growing influence of Practice-Based Evidence (PBE), which takes a 'bottom-up' position, applying high-quality research principles to 'real-life' clinical realities (Margison et al., 2000). While qualitative research and service user-led research has championed PBE, it is does not have a competing narrative to rival NICE and the greatest disparity between these two positions can be seen in secondary care.

As previously argued, NICE guidelines effectively 'run out' at Step 4, where the needs of comorbidity and contextual understanding of individual experience are more visible. It is not good enough simply to complain about EBP or bicker about it in our small tribes. We have to present and promote our feelings by actively participating in the debate, undertaking research and distributing the findings as widely as possible. In the short term this will mean negotiating with managers, insisting that job descriptions which usually refer to 'research activities' are enforced and, where possible, developing research partnerships with other professionals, universities and organisations. The British Psychological Society needs to support this and in so doing may show its value to colleagues deciding whether to renew their membership or not. Secondary care provides access to a vast range of research activities, from reflection on the results of routine data collection to specific research initiatives. Importantly, it also provides a powerful arena to justify the value of psychological practice in an increasingly sceptical environment.

CONCLUSION

It is impossible for a single chapter to cover the breadth of working in secondary care, but it is hoped that it has given a small insight into an exciting, dynamic, creative and rewarding area of psychological practice. Secondary care can be challenging both in working with complex clients in significant distress and taking account of the wider political issues. However, it is precisely these challenges that can attract the counselling psychologist, as sometimes we can make the greatest difference when situations seem at their worst. It is hoped that this chapter has not only helped to give a flavour of secondary care but also identified significant areas for counselling psychologists to offer their knowledge, interest and enthusiasm. There has never been such an opportunity, but there has never been such a need for it. The NHS is in crisis and historically at these times the less publically attractive services, like mental health, have suffered in the fight for survival. Ironically, it is the most distressed and most complex clients that increasingly receive less attention but are those that require the greatest support. Whether one feels this is accomplished through the NHS, establishing a new organisation or being part of both is a matter for personal feeling. What is clear, however, is that there is a marginalised client group that needs to be a priority and in the process of doing so enables the profession to demonstrate its value.

Table 31.2 Description of frequently used abbreviations

AfC	Agenda for Change
AMP	Approved Mental Health Professional
AQP	Any Qualified Provider
BPS	British Psychological Society
CHMT	Community Mental Health Team
CPN	Community Psychiatric Nurse
EBP	Evidence-Based Practice
EI	Early Intervention teams, mostly for psychosis
HCPC	Health and Care Professions Council
HoNOS	Health of the Nation Outcome Scales
IAPT	Improving Access to Psychological Therapies
NICE	National Institute for Health and Clinical Excellence
PBE	Practice-Based Evidence
PbR	Payment by Results
SHA	Strategic Health Authority

REFERENCES

Alexander, J. and Bowers, L. (2004). Acute psychiatric ward rules: A review of the literature. *Journal of Psychiatric and Mental Health Nursing*, 11, 623–631.

Bond, G.R., McGrew, J.H. and Fekete, B.M. (1995). Assertive outreach for frequent users of psychiatric hospitals: A meta analysis. *Journal of Mental Health Admission*, 22, 4–16.

British Psychological Society (2009). *Code of Ethics and Conduct*. Leicester: BPS. Retrieved on 26 March 2014 from www.bps.org.uk/system/files/documents/code_of_ethics_and_conduct.pdf.

British Psychological Society (2014). *Impatient Psychological Practitioner Network (IPPN)*. Leicester: BPS. Retrieved on 29 May 2014 from www.bps/facultynetworks.

Clark, D.M., Layard, R., Smithies, R., Richards, D.A., Suckling, R. and Wright, B. (2009). IAPT: Initial evaluation of two UK demonstration sites. *Behaviour and Research Therapy*, 47, 910–920.

Copeland, M.E. (2012). *Wellness Recovery Action Plan*. Retrieved on 27 April 2014 from www.mentalhealthrecovery.com.

Department of Health (2012). Mental Health Clustering Booklet. London: Department of Health. Retrieved on 13 April 2014 from www.gov.uk/government/uploads/mentalhealth clsuteringbooklet.

Department of Health (2013). Mental Health Payment by Results Guidance for 2013–2014. London: Department of Health. Retrieved on 20 April 2014 from www.gov/government/uploads/system/paymentbyresults.

Fairfax, H. (2013). Where will counselling psychology be in the next 30 years? From a conference to the premiership. *Counselling Psychology Review*, 28, 81–87.

Francis, R. (2013). *Mid Staffordshire NHS Foundation Trust Public Enquiry*. Retrieved on 30 March 2014 from www.midstaffspublicinquiry.com.

Hammerlsey, M. (2005). Is the evidence-based practice movement doing more good than harm? Reflections on Iain Chalmer's case for research based policy making and practice. *Evidence and Policy*, 1, 95–100.

Hubble, M.A., Duncan, B.L. and Miller, S.P. (1999). *The Heart and Soul of Change: What Works in Therapy*. Washington, DC: American Psychological Association.

Hubble, M.A., Duncan, B.L. and Miller, S.P. (2011). *The Heart and Soul of Change: What Works in Therapy* (2nd edn). Washington, DC: American Psychological Association.

Kerfoot, G., Bamford, Z. and Jones, S.A. (2012). Evaluation of psychological provision into an acute inpatient unit. *Mental Health Review Journal*, 17, 26–38.

Margison, F.R., McGrath, G., Markham, M., Mellor Clark, J., Audin, K., Cornnell, J. and Evans, C. (2000). Measurement and psychotherapy evidence based practice and practice based evidence. *British Journal of Psychiatry*, 177, 123–130.

Marshall, M. and Rathbone, J. (2011). Early intervention for psychosis. *Schizophrenia Bulletin*, 37, 1111–1114.

McCulloch, A. and Lawton-Smith, S. (2012). Mental health policy. In T. Sandford (ed.), *Working in Mental Health Practice and Policy in a Changing Environme*nt. London: Routledge.

Mental Health Act (2007). www.legislation.gov.uk/ukpga/2007/12/contents

Mental Health Care Act (2014). www.legislation.gov.uk/ukpga/2014/23/contents/enacted/data.htm

Mental Health Foundation (2013). *Crossing Boundaries*. Retrieved on 4 March 2015 from www.mentalhealth.org.uk/pdf/publication/crossing-boundaries.

Michie, S., Johnson, M., Abraham, C., Lawton, R., Parker, P. and Walker, A. (2005). Making psychological theory useful for implementing evidence based practice: A consensus approach. *Quality and Safety Health Care*, 14, 26–33.

Moncrieff, J. (2009). How do psychiatric drugs work? *British Medical Journal*, 338, b1963.

Player, S. and Leys, C. (2011). *The Plot against the NHS*. Powys: Merlin Press.

Pollock, A.M. (2005). *The NHS Plc: The Privatisation of Our Healthcare*. London: Verso.

Roberts, G., Davenport, S. and Holloway, F. (2006). *Enabling Recovery: The Principles and Practice of Rehabilitation Psychiatry*. London: Gaskell.

Royal College of Psychiatrists (2010). *Recovery is for All*. London: Royal College of Psychiatry. Retrieved on 16 May 2014 from www.rcpsych.ac.uk/pdf/recovery.

Royal College of Psychiatrists (2011). *Do the Right Thing: How to Judge a Good Ward*. London: Royal College of Psychiatrists. Retrieved on 24 March 2014 from www.rcpsych.ac.uk/pdf/OP79_forweb.pdf.

Singh, S.P. (2010). Early intervention in psychosis. *British Journal of Psychiatry*, 169, 343–345.

Turner, B.S. (2007). *Medical Power and Social Knowledge*. London: Sage.

Vermes, C. (2014). Revisioning counselling psychology: The need for bigger thinking. *Counselling Psychology Review*, 29, 62–65.

Ward, S. and Boag, S. (2009). 'Do you hear what I hear?' Client voice in the evaluation of counselling. *The Australian Journal of Counselling Psychology*, 10, 12–21.

Webster, C. (2002). *The NHS: A Political History*. Oxford: Oxford University Press.

Woolfe, R. (2012). Risorgimento: A history of counselling psychology in Britain. *Counselling Psychology Review*, 27(4), 72–77.

32
RESEARCH: FROM CONSUMER TO PRODUCER

TERRY HANLEY, EDITH STEFFEN AND DENIS O'HARA

INTRODUCTION

The journey from trainee to fully-fledged professional is a mixture of excitement, struggle, enjoyable challenge, relief at graduation and then the surprise that comes from embracing the profession's identity and practice. The question of 'Who am I as a counselling psychologist?' will be one that may never be fully answered. This is partly because our professional contexts keep changing, the profession keeps redefining itself and we keep changing as individuals. As we continue the journey of personal/professional growth, we accumulate extensive experience of other people and their struggles, we experience new dimensions of ourselves, and we gain more and more knowledge of how best to help others. In effect, we have become a healing and growth resource for others to draw on, both in our personal and professional lives. The curious thing is that our own growth process is often so incremental that we do not appreciate the significance of our own development. If we stop and reflect on all that has gone into developing our accumulating expertise, we realise that there is much that we could share with other helping professionals. It is in this moment that we might move from prioritising knowledge consumption to knowledge production. Production here refers not to a crass capitalist mechanistic package but an organic offering of substance. We all have something to share, the question is how best to do this.

A MAP OF THE CHAPTER

With the above in mind, the aim of this chapter is to present an overview of the different avenues that counselling psychologists might find themselves in when disseminating their own knowledge and understanding to others. In doing so, we cover a wide territory with the hope of reflecting the many formal and informal ways that may be possible. These include: (1) the consideration of publishing research (whether course work, doctoral theses or independently conducted studies), (2) presenting at research conferences, (3) delivering professional training seminars, (4) engaging with different stakeholders, and (5) engaging in less formal dialogues and debates about counselling psychology and beyond (book reviews, blogging and bar-based discussions). To end, we then wrap up by considering an issue that pervades each of the areas above. This is the issue of going global. Whether writing for a research journal or blogging for fun, it will be important to tailor the work to your audience. As a profession that is increasingly playing a role on the global stage, we have to be increasingly mindful of the broader currency of our work.

Throughout the chapter we provide brief case examples of the dissemination strategies mentioned above. So as not to distance ourselves from the discussions noted throughout, we have included reflections on our own experiences in the case studies where possible. Additionally, we direct the reader to the companion website for additional material.

PUBLISHING RESEARCH

When considering how counselling psychologists move from being a consumer to becoming a producer of research we start with the most obvious way, notably publishing research in its written form. Such an output can take a multitude of forms and includes writing published papers in academic journals, writing a doctoral thesis or piece of course work, writing a textbook/monograph and producing reports for interested stakeholders. As some of these areas cross over with sections that follow, the focus here will be on getting research published in journals and considering authoring a textbook.

Writing for public consumption can often be a daunting task and many people choose not to once they have completed their dissertation or thesis. This is clearly evident when reflecting upon the limited number of counselling psychologists in the United Kingdom who presently publish their work (Gordon and Hanley, 2013). We would anticipate that some of this echoes the common sentiment that therapists do not always see the direct relevance of research to their own practice (e.g. Orlinsky et al., 2001). In particular, we would imagine that priorities change at the end of a project (course of study or commissioned) and publishing an article based upon this work becomes less of a priority for many. Despite this, we would challenge the ethical stance both of the individual researchers and academic institutions that let this work, in which individuals/participants have invested so much, sit on an academic's shelf gathering dust.

In considering the above, we would argue that counselling psychologists should be publishing their work more often. There are numerous opportunities for counselling psychologists to disseminate their ideas to interested others, with common places being research journals, professional journals and textbooks (such as this). Such work provides the profession with an opportunity to grow and develop and for psychological practice to be appropriately research-informed (Hanley et al., 2013). Conducting research can also be a means of counselling psychologists stopping and reflecting upon their own work (Corrie and Callahan, 2000). If people do not do it, however, the system stalls and the opportunity for the profession to grow follows suit.

When aiming to publish in any of the above directions it is vitally important to read the guidance prior to any submission. When proposing a book or submitting a journal article it is expected that authors create products that fit within the overarching theme of those investing money into them. Journals and publishers therefore have specific guidance to support people in getting it right, but it is expected that you do your homework, and if a journal expects a paper to follow a structure, comply to a word count or to utilise a particular referencing style, you do it. If you do not, it is likely that you will receive a very swift response asking you to do so, or an immediate rejection based upon these grounds. In the instance that you want to stray from this standard format, then expect to have to put forward a very strong case, most likely prior to submission.

Once you make it past the threshold of a particular journal or have a book chapter completed, it is then important to be mindful that, like any worthwhile enterprise, there will be obstacles and setbacks. Papers or book contributions are commonly subjected to peer reviews. These are often conducted by colleagues in the field who are invited to comment on the quality of the work that you put forward. More often than not they are offered confidentially, and as a consequence they are not always framed in the most sensitive of ways. With this in mind, and given the cut and thrust of the peer-review process, it is often helpful in the first instance to align your work to someone familiar with such a process (e.g. a supervising academic). Such people can then help navigate the turbulent waters that you may encounter and explain and support you through the process.

Case example: Terry Hanley

As a Programme Director of a Counselling Psychology Doctorate, publishing research is now an incredibly important part of my role. My hope to publish was not, however, forced upon me and grew during my own studies. My doctoral thesis focused upon the therapeutic alliance in online youth counselling and below I outline some of my decision-making process related to publishing this work.

Articles directed at professionals

This seemed an important area for me to target as I felt that some of my work had clear implications for therapeutic practice. I was also mindful that many of the people I hoped to reach might not read some of the research journals I was also looking to publish in. In the end I published three professional papers. In the short term these are some of the papers that I have received the most correspondence about. They have also provided me with the opportunity to share my work at a variety of professional practice seminars/conferences nationally and led to the development of the textbook, *Adolescent Counselling Psychology*, that I jointly edited (Hanley et al., 2013).

Targeting research journals

I also wanted my research to reach beyond national professional audiences and so I aimed to publish work in a number of research journals. From a thesis, I estimated that three papers would be a relatively good crop (two based upon the findings and one methodological paper) and I was successful in publishing my work in three different journals. Getting these into print proved a challenge and I had to respond to a variety of opinions expressed in the peer review processes (some of which I agreed with and others that I definitely did not). Ultimately, it has been worth the effort and I can slowly see the work being used/cited by national and international colleagues.

PRESENTING RESEARCH

The next area we move on to consider is the realm of the research conference. These events can provide a useful test-bed for trialling ideas that have yet to become fully baked. The format of such presentations can vary greatly, with some people presenting research papers, others taking part in symposia and others presenting posters of their work. Each of these formats has differing expectations and we hope to provide a useful insight into such activities below.

Probably the most common form of presentation at a research conference is the act of presenting a paper. More often than not this takes the form of giving a 15 to 20 minute overview of your work before allowing for 10 to 15 minutes of questions. Usually, presentations are accompanied by slides and the speaker goes through a research piece in a relatively conventional order, covering topics such as the background and research questions posed, the methodology adopted, the findings of the work and any conclusions/key discussion points. At times presentations vary, but not often. The question-and-answer component requires some thinking on your feet but is often an opportunity for interested others (from national or international backgrounds) to find out more, and for you to consider issues that you may not have considered before (for all those readers working towards a thesis, this can be great viva practice).

Symposia are very similar forums to the research presentations noted above. They differ, however, as they often involve bringing together researchers who have similar interests into a series of presentations. Typically, there may be three or four back-to-back presentations about a particular topic or large research project (once again, these are usually 15 to 20 minutes in length), and then a discussion follows. Commonly, an individual nominated as the symposium discussant leads this final discussion and it is their role to provide reflections upon the work and to pull out some salient threads that link together the presentations. Once this individual has commented, presenters are then provided with the opportunity to respond to the discussant if they wish or for the audience to ask any questions they may want answering.

A very different type of presentation is the research poster. A research poster is a brief communication about a research project that is presented visually as a poster (usually A1 or A0 in size). They often cover similar territory to an oral presentation, but do so in a relatively brief written format. Such a format can often mean that it proves a nice way of easing into the research conference world, with the less formal presentation style proving attractive to some. It can also provide a forum for discussing projects that have yet to be completed. In contrast to the presentations noted above, research posters are not commonly presented to a stationary audience and often rely on interested others seeking them out within an allocated space at a conference during a break period. It can be a real challenge creating a poster that balances content and design in a way that becomes palatable to a passing audience, but increasingly there are professional-looking frames that can be adapted online very easily and support people in doing so. The end result can often be very rewarding and some would argue that such a style provides a neat way of narrowing the research–practice gap.

Case example: Laura Winter

Laura graduated from a doctorate programme in Counselling Psychology in 2013 and is now a Lecturer at the University of Manchester. During her studies, her thesis work focused upon social justice in UK counselling psychology. This is a topic that led to the writing of several research articles and also the delivery of a number of presentations. Each of the presentations related to this topic is noted below.

The first outing for Laura's research was a poster presentation at the British Psychological Society's (BPS) Division of Counselling Psychology's annual conference. This was based upon a programme research assignment and was entitled 'Exploring the social justice interest and commitment of UK-based counselling psychologists'. As Laura was a trainee at the time, a bursary was provided from the Division of Counselling Psychology for accommodation and attendance, and travel expenses were paid by the institution of study. Laura had to print off an A1 poster, stick it to a board in the plenary room and then be available for any questions during break periods at the conference.

In the following year Laura moved on to present at the International Society for Psychotherapy Research annual conference. This 20-minute presentation was called 'Social justice in counseling psychology: An international perspective'. Laura presented collaboratively with her colleague and fielded questions from interested colleagues from all corners of the globe.

Finally, Laura presented her research at the Division of Counselling Psychology conference once again ('Counselling Psychology and Social Justice: Is there a rhetoric–action gap?'). This time it took the form of a workshop, a type of presentation that takes us directly into the next section for this chapter.

DELIVERING PROFESSIONAL TRAINING SEMINARS

Professional training seminars and workshops are not unlike presenting papers at annual conferences with the exception that you are usually paid to conduct a seminar and you have greater responsibility to facilitate the participants' learning. Counselling psychologists have a lot to contribute to professional training across a wide range of topics and audiences. It is easy not to attend to the possibility of offering professional training because we are usually focused on providing individual and group mental health support and recovery. While as counselling psychologists we share a core base of professional knowledge and skills, many also have specialist knowledge that can be shared with colleagues, other health professionals and the wider community. Maybe the first challenge we face before we are ready to present professional seminars is to consider the relative uniqueness of the knowledge we hold. Your training and experience as a counselling psychologist affords you deep insight into human social and psychological functioning and such knowledge is worth sharing beyond the counselling room. We often do not realise how much we have to give beyond our everyday work.

After reflecting on your own professional strengths you might deem it worthwhile to present a professional seminar or workshop. Presentations of any ilk have much in common but also some unique features. You have already presented to peers on many occasions – peer seminars, vivas, to work colleagues, and conferences. The context of the professional seminar is similar with one important difference – you are more responsible for the participants' learning. You now have an audience who, in some form or other, expects you to provide a learning environment that will facilitate their learning on a particular topic. There now is a pedagogical element to your task.

How we structure learning and convey information is very important. We know from learning theory that learning is really a process of constructing meaning (Ramsden, 1988). It is much less a process of simply receiving information. Learning is enhanced when there is a clear stimulus and motivation to learn. One of the great stimuli in the learning process is the teacher/presenter themselves. As one champion of teaching and learning, Palmer (2007) has said, 'we teach who we are'. One of the ways we can motivate is to tell our own professional story. This may be a story about therapeutic encounters, research endeavours, managerial struggles, learning discoveries and stories about one's own successes and failures, but these stories are full of rich illustrations and are fundamentally real. Another quality that is highly motivational for others is your own passion. What professional area, topic or activity do you feel most passionate about? Passion provides energy and this energy is contagious.

Good pedagogy allows for the strengths of the teacher/presenter and the strengths of the learners/participants to come to the fore. It provides space for both and does so in a way which scaffolds learning – progressively linking concepts and skills. Adult learning theory holds that the adult learner already has a wealth of knowledge on which to draw and, as such, learning occurs best when we move from what is known to the unknown (Lipscomb et al., 2004). It is therefore highly beneficial to identify the participants' knowledge base from which you can scaffold your presentation of new ideas and skills.

A practical issue worth considering is your knowledge theme. A marketing executive might speak of your 'brand' but maybe a term such as 'theme', which is less linked to profit margins, is appropriate. Whether you present seminars and workshop on your research, theories and therapeutic interventions, or war stories, it is likely that over time you will become expert in a particular topic and may well become known for this expertise. Speaking about topics of personal interest and strength can only be an advantage. The more we, as counselling psychologists, are prepared to present in the public arena, the more we will promote the profession and benefit society.

Case example: Denis O'Hara

To illustrate how one may begin to offer professional training seminars it is easiest to outline some of my own experiences. As mentioned above, paying attention to one's passions is always a good starting point. One of my early professional passions was exploring the theories and applications of couples therapy. I found in my counselling practice that it was couples who formed a substantial percentage of my client group. I was fortunate that I had a colleague who had similar interests and so we decided to pool our resources and see if anyone would be interested in coming to weekend workshops on couples therapy. To our surprise, these workshops were very successful. We knew our material was theoretically sound and also reflected our professional experience, but we didn't know if others would be interested. Our main concern in starting off was our limited public platform – we weren't particularly well known. The two main platforms we had were our professional roles: we were both university lecturers and therapists. With this relatively small springboard, we did our own advertising and were off the starting blocks – couples came to our seminars.

Another personal and professional passion of mine is the topic of *hope*. My interest here gathered ground as I began to conduct research on the topic, eventually leading to several articles and even a book entitled *Hope in Counselling and Psychotherapy* (O'Hara, 2013). The more I spoke of *hope studies* the more I had students wanting to collaborate in research on *hope* as well. I also found myself providing professional development seminars and even internet interviews. In my experience, presenting professional seminars and training always works best when the topic has moved beyond an academic curiosity into an area of some passion. I believe that this is a key for anyone wishing to offer their professional expertise to a wider audience – engage your passion and risk a little.

ENGAGING WITH DIFFERENT STAKEHOLDERS

Imagine you have chosen a doctoral research topic that really interests you, say the plight of an underrepresented group. You have conducted your research, you have interviewed 'experts by experience' and you have presented your findings at a national conference, allowing the voices of your participants to be heard clearly and resonantly for the first time. You now come home and find that you 'have been inundated with emails, suggestions and requests; requests for more information about [the topic]; to write articles, suggestions for collaborative research – even an invitation to make representation to a national government'. This may sound like a dream, but it is a dream that came true for trainee counselling psychologist Sue Whitcombe (2014, p. 34), who later wrote in *The Psychologist* about her research on parental alienation and the interest it has sparked. This may be an exceptional story but we would like to argue that greater engagement with colleagues, client groups, organisations, policy makers, the public in general and other stakeholders is essential if we want to produce and disseminate research that is relevant to its context and has true impact.

As 'scientist-practitioners' we conduct research with an applied purpose: it is to inform professional practice (see also Hanley et al., 2013), however broadly we define professional practice (Kasket, 2013), which may include contributions to wider political and social contexts (Milton, 2010). All research, whether 'pure' or applied, has to address the 'So what?' question and clarifying the usefulness of our research forms part of our ethical commitment and accountability. In the UK, the value and impact of practice-relevant research has tended to be evaluated against the 'hierarchy of evidence' criteria adopted by the National Institute for Health and Care Excellence (NICE). This favours randomised controlled trials (RCTs) as the 'gold standard' for outcome research while service-user views tend to rank at the bottom of that hierarchy (Harper et al., 2013). For example, the full NICE guideline for a particular condition often includes such viewpoints, but by the time the guideline has been subbed down to a 'quick reference guide', user perspectives have been edited out and thus become 'silenced voices' (McLeod, 2011, p. 244).

Counselling psychology research often attempts to give voice to those who have been silenced, especially through qualitative research, which is not to diminish the value of quantitative research per se, but to redress the balance. As McLeod (2011) argues, qualitative research is much better at capturing what matters to service users than the kinds of measures used in RCTs. The question whether such research can stand up to the scrutiny of commissioning bodies and policy makers therefore needs to be answered with greater confidence. The confidence to engage with policy makers, for example, is fed not only from an awareness of the methodological rigour and quality of the work, but also from an awareness of its (potential) impact, and this comes from working closely with key stakeholders in the relevant contexts (Brown et al., 2011). The point we are making here is that the value of a piece of applied research comes from its value for those who have a 'stake' in it, particularly those who have previously been underrepresented, and that this value is not necessarily captured in so-called gold-standard research.

'Stakeholder engagement' has become a buzzword in recent years. It is a term that developed in connection with the pressure on corporate organisations to involve those affected by its decisions in communication of information, consultation and decision making (Sillanpää, 2007), but it is increasingly applied in a research context. For example, under the banner of 'excellence with impact' the Economic and Social Research Council (ESRC, 2014, p. 20) provides the following guidelines for research grant applicants, asking them to:

- Demonstrate an awareness of the wider environment and context in which their research takes place
- Demonstrate an awareness of the social and ethical implications of their research, beyond usual research conduct considerations, and take account of public attitudes towards those issues
- Engage actively with the public at both the local and national levels about their research and its broader implications
- Identify potential benefits and beneficiaries from the outset, and through the full life cycle of the project(s)
- Maintain professional networks that extend beyond their own discipline and research community
- Publish results widely – considering the academic, user and public audiences for research outcomes
- Exploit results where appropriate, in order to secure social and economic return to the UK

We believe that there is much overlap between these guidelines and our ethical stance as counselling psychologists, and we would therefore encourage readers to confidently engage with stakeholders at all stages of their research.

Case example: Rachel Tribe

Professor Rachel Tribe is a counselling and organisational psychologist and a Fellow of the BPS. In 2014 she was the recipient of the BPS award for Challenging Social Inequalities in Psychology. While working as a psychologist in London, she became aware of the need for interpreters to ensure that all members of the community could access appropriate psychological services and she looked into this further. (Copies of the DVD Rachel made with Dr Lane for the Department of Health are available at www.youtube.com/watch?v=k0wzhakyjck.)

Her personal interest in multiculturalism and social justice led her to expand her work with survivors of trauma. These have included asylum seekers, refugees (many of whom had experienced torture and organised violence) and migrants. Furthermore, her work has not been solely concerned with clinical practice and research; it has also aimed to promote equality and justice through engaging with a range of stakeholders. Examples of these include: the Department of Health, the Department of Education, the British Psychological Society, the Foreign and Commonwealth Office, MIND, the Royal College of Psychiatrists, the World Psychiatric Association and the World Health Organization.

Following publication of her research, she was asked to give talks or run workshops for psychiatrists, GPs, psychologists, nurses, the Prison Service, various health trusts, education and social services in the UK, as well in over twenty other countries.

Rachel has contributed to policies on mental health and migration, working with interpreters, refugees and 'other vulnerable groups'. Engaging with stakeholders is vital if research is to have value over and above its academic significance. Engagement with policy makers took place as a result of Rachel continuously lobbying service providers, advocating at all levels, participating in meetings with a range of professional groups, making her publications available and accepting invitations to give talks or be involved in working parties. Rachel's latest book, edited with Jean Morrissey, is the second edition of the *Handbook of Professional and Ethical Practice* (Tribe and Morrissey, 2015).

ENGAGING IN LESS FORMAL DIALOGUES AND DEBATES ABOUT COUNSELLING PSYCHOLOGY AND BEYOND

What should be obvious by now is our view that being a research-active and publication-active counselling psychologist is very broadly defined in this chapter and extends beyond publishing and presenting research in academic fora. It can mean contributing anonymous peer reviews to academic journals, writing book reviews or even small opinion pieces. It can mean taking part in dialogues and debates, not only in conference halls but also through writing letters to editors, responding to consultation papers and engaging with stakeholders and the wider public in as many ways as our imagination and initiative allow us to consider. It can even mean taking our research to the pub as some groups in the British Psychological Society do.

Furthermore, a broad dissemination approach can involve a range of public media, including popular/mass media such as radio, television, magazines and newspapers (e.g. Atcheson, 2010). Beyond these forms of media, the internet offers a vast array of non-traditional and increasingly popular opportunities for publication and communication. Academic journals have been making progressively more use of electronic channels for disseminating research, and there is now a growing number of 'online-only' journals. 'Open access' has become a particularly useful way for making research publications more easily available. At the time of writing, the Directory of Open Access Journals is listing 9,834 peer-reviewed journals (DOAJ, 2014).

Not only academic journals but also researchers themselves now seek to have an online presence, witness the growth of dedicated research sites such as academia.edu or researchgate. Members can set up their own page, publish their research interests and activities and upload papers or abstracts. Additionally, these sites allow researchers to communicate with other researchers who may share their interests, broadcast open questions, seek research participants or collaborators, read what other people do and also monitor traffic to their own page and see which of the uploaded papers attract the most views and downloads.

It may go without saying that for counselling psychologists with an interest in networking, participation in social media seems crucial. Many counselling psychologists are active members of designated Facebook groups and networking groups on LinkedIn and beyond, and there is also an increasing number of counselling psychology Twitterati. Their output may concern research or practice, politics and societal issues as well as the personal and the quotidian. One of the outstanding features of social media tends to be the mixing of the professional and the personal. This may make social media particularly attractive to counselling psychologists, creating spaces to position ourselves as 'real selves' and bringing something individual and authentic to our public persona.

There is, however, also a danger in engaging too closely with the electronic media world, especially when we consider writing blogs as they originally evolved, namely as private journals and diaries. For example, Hanley (2011) described how he started a research blog, similar to keeping a reflexive journal, only for it to be closed down once it became 'too' public. Even if our main intention is to blog about research only, the personal cannot be completely taken out of the equation. This raises questions about our ethical responsibilities, as we are not only researchers but also practitioners, meaning that our clients can read our professional-cum-personal musings. In one of his blogs, Balick (2013) asks 'Should shrinks tweet?' Balick argues that practitioners need to think carefully about how they use social media, and he utilises psychodynamic theory to make sense of the phenomenon (Balick, 2014). Guidance for therapists is beginning to trickle in. For example, one practitioner has drawn up a 'private practice social media policy' (Kolmes, 2010), which is handed to clients at the start of therapy.

Here we would suggest that the following questions could be a starting point for counselling psychologists who would like to engage in social media:

- What is the main purpose of your account/blog?
- Who is your audience? Who do you want to connect with?
- What kinds of topics do you want to write/tweet about?
- How do you want to position yourself? As a professional? Anonymously?
- How do you manage 'the personal'? Where are the boundaries?

Before posting a new blog or tweet, you might want to consider:

- How might my clients (past, present and future) feel if they read this?
- What would my (future) employer think if they read this?
- How might my colleagues understand this?
- Am I prepared to receive criticism for this?
- Am I happy to put my name to this?

Case example: Edith Steffen

After qualifying, I was keen to remain connected to the world of research and academia. Having published some of my doctoral research, I was asked to conduct *peer reviews* of manuscripts dealing with similar topics for a number of academic journals. This made me realise that I had actually gained some kind of expertise that was considered useful, allowing me to make a contribution to the field in a different way.

The next step was to start writing *book reviews* on subjects I was interested in, for example qualitative research. I found that writing a book review is a good way of using any existing knowledge of a particular topic and applying it in response to a novel text. It also enabled me to continue practising to write for publication in a relatively brief and manageable way.

Setting up a page on the *research websites* academia.edu and researchgate then was an exciting as well as daunting step, given that I had no time to conduct new research at that time. However, I reckoned that this could be a way of putting at least some 'output' out there, hoping that interested people might find it and get some use from it. Having a presence within the wider research community also helped me maintain my identity as a researcher, which can sometimes be difficult for counselling psychologists going straight into practice after qualifying.

Apart from the research-focused sites, I have also used more general *social networking sites* such as Facebook, LinkedIn and Twitter as well as a blogging site. It's nice to hear what your colleagues think and get up to, to share interesting links or discuss relevant issues in counselling psychology and beyond. It all contributes to a vibrant discipline and professional/ research community which I feel privileged to be part of.

THE INTERNATIONALISATION OF COUNSELLING PSYCHOLOGY

To end, we wrap up by considering an issue that pervades each of the areas above. This is the issue of going global (also see Chapter 24 in this volume, 'Counselling psychology and its international dimensions').

The last ten to fifteen years has seen an enormous movement towards globalisation. The world is interconnected in myriad ways, making borders between countries and cultures much more permeable. The ease of access to the internet, Facebook, Skype, and various other media means that we can communicate across the global village within seconds. Societies and cultures are much less protected from external influences because social trends and shifting values move quickly from one country to another. In this environment it is imperative that psychology become internationalised. This is particularly true in the case of counselling psychology, which has largely been a Western phenomenon, and even more specifically a phenomenon of the English-speaking world. While a number of non-English-speaking countries have counselling psychology programmes, and these are growing, the development of the specialisation sprang from the United States and later in Britain with healthy representation from Canada, South Africa, Australia and New Zealand (Orlans and Van Scoyac, 2009). Counselling and counselling psychology has also grown in other countries, such as Singapore, India, Taiwan, and in the special jurisdiction of Hong Kong.

Given the growing internationalisation of psychology, it is in some respects a curious fact that the vast majority of journal articles published in prominent counselling psychology and in counselling journals come from the United States (Pieterse et al., 2011). As counselling psychology first emerged in the United States, and given the size and strength of the field there, it is not surprising that it accounts for a large percentage of the published literature. While the United States has no doubt contributed much to strengthen the field, the relative volume of literature coming from this source does impact on the international character and identity of the profession. Counselling psychology represents many values that are shared by all national counselling psychology bodies. However, just as the field was originally shaped by the culture from which it first emerged, so too, other cultures can, and do, add important colour and tone to the discipline.

The British contribution to counselling psychology is a good example of how different societies influence the nature and character of professions. Counselling psychology is a little over thirty years old in Britain and in that time has firmly established the fundamental place that humanistic-existential schools of thought have within the British form of the discipline. More recently in British counselling psychology, there is a growing awareness of the role that counselling psychologists have in engaging in and promoting social action. British psychology has also made a significant contribution to the development and expansion of qualitative research methodologies (e.g. McLeod, 2011). It is important that the theoretical, methodological and social reforms that have developed in Britain be accessible to an international audience.

Another example of home-grown differences within counselling psychology is found in more collectivist cultures, such as India, Taiwan, Singapore and Hong Kong. Psychology is an emerging force in these countries and there is a growing sense of professional identity that represents a much less Western view of human relations and social structures. The influence of an Eastern cultural mindset brings to the table, for example, different perspectives on therapeutic strategies and interventions (Jeong, 2014).

As someone who has lived and taught psychology in a number of different countries, I (Denis) can attest to the fact that each cultural expression of psychology adds something unique to the discipline. This brings me to an important point about the importance of promoting research and publication on the world stage. Counselling psychology can only grow as an international force when it is strengthened by diversity (Marsella, 2009). We have come to a time in history where counselling psychology has grown sufficiently to be an influence internationally. However, for this influence to expand we need to encourage counselling psychologists to publish and present their ideas and research findings in international fora. There are a wide range of important topics for debate and scientific research which need to occur. One important issue for examination is how different countries and jurisdictions accredit and organise counselling psychology. There are significant differences, for example, in the nature and extent of qualifications, the psychology curriculum, and in the relative status of the profession. Other topics for research and dialogue include: indigenous approaches to mental health and psychological interventions, emerging research methodologies, research into specific health concerns, development of international policies on mental health and training, obstacles to internationalisation of the profession, and the establishment international exchanges.

We encourage students, new and experienced counselling psychologists to think about publishing their ideas and research findings so that there is a much greater representation of the profession cross-culturally in the variety of media noted above. Our experience is that what may appear relatively 'everyday thinking and practice' in one cultural setting is not necessarily so in another. Your ideas and findings may be more interesting and important than you realise. You will have to be prepared for peer-reviewed feedback and lots of personal reflection but the profession can only benefit from your contribution.

CONCLUSION

Within this chapter we have provided the reader with a whistle-stop overview of some of the ways in which counselling psychologists might engage in dissemination activities around their research. In this move, from being a consumer of research to becoming a producer of it, we have outlined the ethical importance of informing interested others about the work that we do and outlined a number of ways that this might be achieved. Specifically, we describe and discuss the realm of publishing research in a variety of ways, presenting at conferences and developing professional workshops. We also explore the need to engage with the different stakeholders of our research and the importance that less formal conversations and social media can play in contemporary dissemination strategies. In pulling things together, we then reflect upon the importance of being outward-facing and considering how what we do does not act in isolation. Counselling psychology is a growing international community and research can provide a useful thread for professionals from all around the world to engage in meaningful conversation.

Visit the companion website for examples of dissemination strategies.

REFERENCES

Atcheson, L. (2010). Counselling psychology and the media. In M. Milton (ed.), *Therapy and beyond: Counselling psychology contributions to therapeutic and social issues* (pp. 277–291). Chichester: Wiley-Blackwell.

Balick, A. (2013). Should shrinks tweet? Public personae in the private context of work. Retrieved on 15.06.2014 from www.mindswork.co.uk/wpblog/should-shrinks-tweet-public-personas-in-the-context-of-private-work/.

Balick, A. (2014). *The psychodynamics of social networking: Connected-up instantaneous culture and the self.* London: Karnac Books.

Brown, D., Coyle, A. and Coyne, P. (2011). QMiP workshop: Maximising the impact of qualitative psychological research on health. *Qualitative Methods in Psychology Bulletin, 1* (May), 23–25.

Corrie S. and Callahan M.M. (2000) A review of the scientist-practitioner model: Reflections on its potential contribution to counselling psychology within the context of current health care trends. *British Journal of Medical Psychology, 73*(3), 413–427.

Directory of Open Access Journals (2014). Accessed on 14.06.2014 at http://doaj.org/.

Economic and Social Research Council (2014, February). *ESRC research funding guide.* Retrieved on 01.05.2014 from www.esrc.ac.uk/_images/Research-Funding-Guide_tcm8-2323.pdf.

Gordon, R. and Hanley, T. (2013). Where do counselling psychologists based in the UK publish their work? A systematic review. *Counselling Psychology Review, 28*(4), 7–17.

Hanley, T. (2011). Virtual data generation: Qualitative research, computers and counselling psychology. *Counselling Psychology Review, 26*(4), 59–67.

Hanley, T., Cutts, L., Gordon, R. and Scott, A. (2013). A research informed approach to counselling psychology. In G. Davey (ed.), *Applied psychology*. London: British Psychological Society/Wiley Blackwell.

Hanley, T., Humphrey, N. and Lennie, C. (eds) (2013). *Adolescent counselling psychology: Theory, research and practice*. London: Routledge.

Hanley, T., Lennie, C. and West, W. (2013). *Introducing counselling and psychotherapy research*. Los Angeles, CA: Sage.

Harper, D.J., Gannon, K. and Robinson, M. (2013). Beyond evidence-based practice: Rethinking the relationship between research, theory and practice. In R. Bayne and G. Jinks (eds), *Applied psychology: Research, training and practice* (2nd edn, pp. 32–46). Los Angeles, CA: Sage.

Jeong, H. (2014). Consideration of indigenous ethos in psychotherapeutic practices: Pungryu and Korean psychotherapy. *Asia Pacific Journal of Counselling and Psychotherapy, 5*(1), 10–20.

Kasket, E. (2013). The counselling psychologist researcher. Supplementary material to accompany G. Davey (ed.) (2011). *Applied psychology*. London: British Psychological Society/Wiley Blackwell. Retrieved on 19.05.2013 from http://bcs.wiley.com/he-bcs/Books?action=resource&bcsId=6466&itemId=1444331213&resourceId=29315.

Kolmes, K. (2010). My private practice social media policy. Retrieved on 18.06.2014 from www.drkkolmes.com/docs/socmed.pdf.

Lipscomb, L., Swanson, J. and West, A. (2004). Scaffolding. In M. Orey (ed.), *Emerging perspectives on learning, teaching, and technology*. Retrieved on 11.06.2014 from http://projects.coe.uga.edu/epltt/.

Marsella, A.J. (2009). Diversity in a global era: The context and consequences of differences, *Counselling Psychology Quarterly, 22*(1), 119–135.

McLeod, J. (2011). *Qualitative research in counselling and psychotherapy* (2nd edn). London: Sage.

Milton, M. (ed.) (2010). *Therapy and beyond: Counselling psychology contributions to therapeutic and social issues*. Chichester: John Wiley & Sons Ltd.

O'Hara, D. (2013). *Hope in counselling and psychotherapy*. London: Sage.

Orlans, V. and Van Scoyoc, S. (2009). *A short introduction to counselling psychology*. London: Sage.

Orlinsky, D.E., Botermans, J. and Rønnestad, M.H. (2001). Towards an empirically grounded model of psychotherapy training: Four thousand therapists rate influences on their development. *Australian Psychologist, 36*(2), 139–148.

Palmer, P. (2007). *The courage to teach: Exploring the inner landscape of a teacher's life*. San Francisco, CA: Jossey-Bass.

Pieterse, A., Fang, K. and Evans, S. (2011). Examining the internationalization of counseling psychology scholarship: A content analysis of two US journals. *International Journal for the Advancement of Counselling, 33*, 280–292.

Ramsden, P. (ed.) (1988). *Improving learning: New perspectives.* San Francisco, CA: Jossey-Bass.

Sillanpää, M. (2007). Stakeholder engagement. In *The A to Z of corporate social responsibility.* Retrieved on 01.06.2014 from http://libezproxy.open.ac.uk/login?qurl=http%3A%2F%2Fsearch.credoreference.com.libezproxy.open.ac.uk%2Fcontent%2Fentry%2Fwileyazcsr%2Fstakeholder_engagement%2F0.

Tribe, R. and Morrissey, J. (eds) (2015). *The handbook for professional and ethical practice for psychologists, psychotherapists and counsellors* (2nd edn). London: Brunner-Routledge.

Whitcombe, S. (2014). Parental alienation – time to notice, time to intervene. *The Psychologist, 27*(1), 32–34.

SECTION VI

BECOMING A GUIDE

CONTENTS

Congratulations – it's been a long road but at last you've qualified! The exciting and possibly frightening result is that you are now expected to act as a guide to your fellows who are still in training. Using the mapping metaphor introduced in the Introduction to Section V, you are, in the eyes of the professional world, now equipped to lead parties up Helvellyn and in time Scafell Pike, Snowdon or even Ben Nevis. On this journey, more detailed route maps listing easy and hard paths, obstacles and dangers are required. This section offers detail about some of the paths you might wish or are sometimes required to take.

Any guide has to perform a number of functions, as spelled out in the chapters within this section. These include training others, supervising them, leading and managing people and organisations, and carrying out research. It is necessary for those who would be guides to develop the skills and competencies associated with these functions. They are common both to the therapeutic situation and to the task of guiding people safely across Striding Edge (a rather scary but exhilarating knife-edged ridge on Helvellyn).

The chapter on training explores the kind of issues faced in such work. It involves teaching skills but also instilling confidence in people to confront uncertainty and possible danger. A key aspect of that confidence comes from supervising trainees and accompanying them on their journey. Standing alongside and ensuring everyone's safety is as important within the world of therapy as it is on Striding Edge on a rainy day. The chapter on supervision addresses these and related issues.

In time your career will, we hope, prosper and you will be invited to take on positions of even greater responsibility in which skills of leadership and management become prominent. You have now moved beyond an easy route up Helvellyn, such as via Grisedale Tarn, and are confronted with the challenge of Striding Edge and maybe even Ben Nevis if you are very successful in your career. The challenges involved are outlined in a chapter entitled 'Leading and managing'. They include issues like resourcing (such as staffing levels in the one context and ensuring there are sufficient walking poles in the other); time management (avoiding work overload or ensuring you get back before dark); and risk management (effective governance or adequate safety equipment). Of course as the chapter on research suggests, a good guide always monitors, evaluates and generally researches their work.

At the present time, organisations are reducing their staffing establishments and increasingly many psychologists are setting up in independent practice. Indeed, you may eventually feel sufficiently confident in your own skills that you have a positive desire to go it alone or with associates. This choice is assessed in the chapter on becoming an entrepreneur-practitioner. Another chapter examines the transition to becoming a guide at a more personal level.

Becoming a guide opens up a range of options and possibilities and, like the journey on Striding Edge, can be exciting if scary, but the sky's the limit – let's meet up next year on 19 June on the summit of Mont Blanc.

33
THE TRANSITION FROM TRAINEE TO QUALIFIED COUNSELLING PSYCHOLOGIST

LEWIS J. BLAIR

INTRODUCTION

The transition from trainee to professional counselling psychologist is an exciting, distinctive and important phase of professional life. It can bring a great sense of accomplishment, relief and confirmation. It can involve a significant alteration of one's personal and professional sense of self. It is also marked by external changes, such as the end of a training course, no more assignments, beginning a new job or combination of jobs, and (hopefully) being paid as a counselling psychologist. As with all transitions, it can involve a significant sense of ending, and a period of upheaval and disorientation before a new beginning emerges. The transition is characterised by a number of distinctive features and presents a variety of developmental tasks to be navigated. There are good reasons, then, to consider that the transition to qualified status and practice for counselling psychologists and the first two to three years post-qualification is a unique and important stage of development that deserves further study.

This chapter is therefore intended to contribute to our collective knowledge of this transition period by describing some of these features and tasks, as well as discussing how these can best be navigated. Although aimed particularly at newly qualified practitioners and those soon to qualify, the chapter also aims to inform the work of course staff, employers, supervisors and the profession as a whole, in guiding and accompanying newly qualified counselling psychologists through this transition period. The chapter reviews some of the existing literature on professional development in counselling psychology and related fields, and literature on career development more broadly. It draws on interviews conducted with counselling psychologists at various stages of their careers and in various roles, to help identify the factors most relevant to navigating this transition. It also draws on a small pilot questionnaire study of qualified counselling psychologists carried out by the author and a focus group conducted with final-year counselling psychology trainees regarding their hopes, fears, expectations and perceived developmental needs as they approach this transition. In addition, I draw on my own recent experience of this transition, having faced some of these transitional tasks since qualifying in 2010. The chapter, therefore, offers a synthesis of the existing literature with the lived experience of practitioners. As such, the chapter seeks to embody the scientist-practitioner philosophy.

There has been only a little written outside the US about the career transitions of counselling psychologists (e.g. Martin, 2009; Palmer and Bor, 2008; Strawbridge, 2006). However, further literature exists regarding the professional development of therapists more generally (e.g. Orlinsky and Rønnestad, 2005; Rønnestad and Skovholt, 2012). Within psychology in the NHS there exists a notion of preceptorship in the early career period, which applies to newly and recently qualified psychologists. Preceptorship assumes that the initial banding for psychologists (band 7) is a *transitional* grade, and that the newly qualified psychologist requires a period of consolidating and further developing their skills with a view to moving up to band 8a (BPS/Unite, 2010).

The lack of detailed literature on this transition almost suggests an unspoken assumption that once qualified, counselling psychologists develop in predictable ways with no significant difficulty. Most of us would agree, however, that qualification does not mean everything falls easily into place and that the self-doubt and questions of the pre-qualification period disappear. Indeed, only a small percentage of survey respondents felt that the transition had been very easy (visit the companion website for survey results).

As psychologists, we ought surely to be especially interested in this transition and its effect on practitioners, colleagues and clients. It behoves us, then, to explore whether we can assist each other to navigate this transition more effectively. In this vein, the chapter may help to 'normalise' some of the concerns and questions that can affect us during this transition period. The chapter discusses the existing literature on transitions, career development and the development of therapists; key personal and professional aspects of this transition; finding suitable employment; and suggests some implications for training courses, supervisors and mentors.

LIFE TRANSITIONS

There are a number of models of transition that can help people make sense of the varied and sometimes confusing and distressing experiences of change (Sugarman, 2001). One of the models most relevant to this transition is the seven-stage model of Adams et al. (1976). They highlight a sequence of immobilisation, minimisation, depression, acceptance of reality and letting go, testing, the search for meaning and internalisation. This model has been applied to changes both planned and unplanned, desirable and undesirable (Sugarman, 2009). It illustrates that transitions are dynamic, likely to contain both positive and negative experiences, and that regression as well as progression is possible. In such processes, it is common for us to experience disorientation and anxiety about change, and perhaps cling all the more to solid ground, the 'old' things of which we feel more sure, as illustrated by the case study below.

Case study: Lindsay

When I started in this post I was only qualified six months and I felt pretty anxious for a while, working with presenting issues that I really didn't have much experience of. The NHS context also felt a bit new and there was a different culture to get used to. I think I compensated for this by going back to my solid ground of knowing how to build a therapeutic relationship with clients. That was a foundation for everything else.

CAREER DEVELOPMENT AND TRANSITIONS

As well as considering the literature on transitions in general, it is beneficial here to bear in mind the various models of career development and career transition. Rønnestad and Skovholt (2012) provide a good overview of such models. Their research is reviewed below but for now it is worth highlighting the evolving, dynamic nature of development in professional life. For example, Donald Super developed a model of career development that suggests that we develop a vocational self, and actualise our self-concepts partly through work (Super et al., 1995). He postulates that we cycle and recycle through five stages of growth, exploration, establishment, maintenance, and decline. These can occur sequentially through the life cycle but can also be experienced at different life stages, e.g. decline can occur in teenage years just as growth can occur in older adulthood. This transition period overlaps with the growth and exploration stages of Super's model. These models of transition and development may help illuminate our experience as we move through the transition to being a professional counselling psychologist.

ASPECTS OF THE TRANSITION FROM TRAINEE TO QUALIFIED COUNSELLING PSYCHOLOGIST

Tasks and stages of the transition

There are many aspects of this transition that could be discussed, and a comprehensive treatment of them all is not possible here. In deciding which to focus on, I have taken into account the existing literature, as well as the opinions expressed by counselling psychologists through the interviews, survey and focus group. Many of these aspects are very much intertwined, but will be separated for the sake of clarity.

When asked about important tasks of this transition, survey respondents rated the following tasks as the most important:

- Growth in confidence in my abilities as a counselling psychologist
- Finding paid counselling psychology work of any type
- Finding a preferred/ideal post
- Finding my preferred way of working therapeutically
- Finding my place in the profession
- Discovering what I am most interested in
- Becoming more autonomous
- Making significant choices about career direction
- Managing a heavier and more complex workload

When asked which factors were most helpful in managing these tasks, respondents cited:

- Supervision appropriate to my stage of development
- Growing confidence in my abilities
- Informal contact with other counselling psychologists/therapists
- Good self-care

When final-year trainees were asked about their expectations and feelings regarding this transition, some of their comments were:

- 'It feels scary, because I'm expected to have more autonomy and be competent.'
- 'It seems hard to shift to believing in ourselves, especially when training requires and encourages so much self-questioning and self-criticism.'
- 'I want to be still able to ask the stupid questions but feel I won't be able to once I'm qualified.'
- 'I'm really hoping to come to a recognition that it's okay to be my type of counselling psychologist.'
- 'Some of us will be transitioning to working in other countries and maybe settings where counselling psychology may not be widely known or understood. So I feel like I'll have to explain our value and identity all over again!'
- 'It feels a bit like being thrown into the lion's den. I'm expecting challenge, expecting to have to fight for recognition and respect.'

These findings give a flavour of some of the tasks and aspects of this transition that are considered pertinent by those who have gone through it as well as those approaching it. Many of these points will be discussed in greater depth throughout the chapter. Although there is little literature on this transition for counselling psychologists, there is much more literature on the development of therapists more generally.

The large-scale studies of Rønnestad and Skovholt (2012) and Orlinsky and Rønnestad (2005) offer some of the most in-depth exploration of therapists' career development and career phases. It is therefore worth introducing their methodologies and some of their findings and theory regarding key aspects of the post-qualification phase.

Rønnestad and Skovholt (2012) interviewed 100 therapists across different career levels and specialisms, and interviewed a subsection of senior therapists ten years on from the original study. They define four developmental tasks in the 'novice professional phase', which are quoted in full:

- To develop an identification with the profession and commitment to the professional sector to which the person belongs (e.g. counseling, psychology, psychiatry, etc.).
- To succeed in the transformation from the dependency of graduate school to the independence that is expected, both from oneself and from others, after having completed professional training.
- To master any disillusionment with training, self, and the profession that may emerge some time after graduation.
- To keep exploring and defining one's work role. (Rønnestad and Skovholt, 2012, p. 83)

These authors also postulate three sub-phases that may occur within the novice professional phase, which are confirmation, disillusionment and exploration. More broadly, Rønnestad and Skovholt suggest that this post-qualification phase is also characterised by a dependency–autonomy conflict, previously articulated by Hogan as 'growing pains', during which the practitioner vacillates between feeling overwhelmed and feeling confident (Hogan, 1964, p. 10). Each of these tasks and phases resonate with my own experience and that of others whose experience was researched for this chapter.

Case study: James

At times I felt like I was getting somewhere, getting the hang of this work. Then I might encounter a new challenge or make a mistake or miss something important, and all of a sudden I would feel like I really didn't know very much. I used to think that confidence always grew steadily but it actually varies quite a lot and I've had to get accustomed to that.

The other major study of therapist development is Orlinsky and Rønnestad (2005). Through the Collaborative Research Network of the Society for Psychotherapy Research, nearly 5,000 therapists from across the world completed an extensive questionnaire on numerous aspects of their work, personal characteristics and processes of professional development. Among other analyses, the authors compare the work practice patterns of different cohorts of therapists. This analysis demonstrates, for example, that compared to highly experienced therapists, newly qualified therapists are likely to have a lower sense of both retrospected (overall) career development and of felt therapeutic mastery, and to be somewhat more reserved in their interpersonal style. Their analysis also identifies significant variation within cohorts, with some newly qualified therapists being very confident in their abilities and some very experienced therapists feeling quite unsure of their abilities and distressed in their professional work. Both Orlinsky and Rønnestad (2005) and Rønnestad and Skovholt (2012) are key resources in understanding not just the early career period but how we develop as therapists across the career span.

In trying to summarise the existing literature and the findings from the research for this chapter, it is tempting to postulate a series of distinctive stages or phases in the early career period, such as those suggested by Rønnestad and Skovholt (2012). However, there is a danger of over-operationalising the process. We should acknowledge that there are a number of important tasks or features that may (or may not) be faced in the post-qualification period, and that are more likely to be encountered concurrently rather than sequentially. It is to these tasks and features that we now turn.

Parallel developmental processes: Person, professional and the profession

As we consider the counselling psychologist in transition, we can do so in the context of parallel developmental changes occurring across three domains of the personal self, the professional self and the wider profession. We can illustrate this with reference to Erikson's model of development (Erikson, 1959), though other models could no doubt also be fruitfully applied.

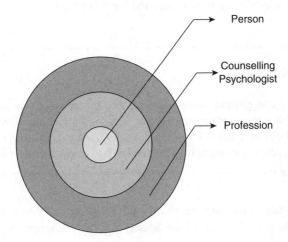

Figure 33.1   Nested developmental processes: Person, professional and the profession

Development may be at similar or different stages across these linked domains (see Figure 33.1). For example, a 45-year-old woman may, in her personal life, be at a point within Erikson's seventh stage – *generativity versus despair*. However, as a newly qualified counselling psychologist, she may be much more concerned with professional *identity versus role confusion*, the fifth stage in Erikson's taxonomy. She may be keen to differentiate herself as a counselling psychologist from other similar professions, focusing on what is *distinctive* about counselling psychology (du Plock, 2006). At the same time, she is entering a profession which is arguably at a particular developmental stage. The current developmental stage of the profession in the UK is a matter of opinion. However, a case could be made that the profession is in Erikson's sixth stage, *intimacy versus isolation*. Arguably, we are trying to learn how to create mature 'intimate' relationships with other psychology and therapy professions.

Therefore, there may or may not be synchronicity across development in each of these three domains. Becoming qualified may fit quite congruently with the developmental stage of one's personal life. In this case, we may feel that the qualified identity 'fits', and has come at the right time. In other cases, these processes may be somewhat out of step, and this may account for some of the adjustment difficulties experienced by newly qualified counselling psychologists. Normal personal developmental milestones may have been delayed because of training and the post-qualification period can therefore require a re-balancing between these domains (Green and Hawley, 2009).

Increased autonomy and responsibility

In the pilot survey conducted for this chapter, 86 per cent of the survey respondents cited becoming more autonomous as a moderately or very important task of this transition. Interviewees and other colleagues have described the surprise they felt at how much more autonomy and responsibility they had once qualified. Although a great deal of independent work is required as a trainee, traineeship is still quite a protected and slightly artificial reality. Increased autonomy and responsibility are key aspects of the qualified identity and the expectations associated with it. Learning to manage this increased autonomy goes hand in hand with increased confidence, and requires some trust in ourselves and our training.

The training institution can temporarily provide externally imposed direction and boundaries, occupying a quasi-parental position and protecting us from fuller autonomy. We project onto the training institution our desire for affirmation, for security, guidance and certainty, and the hope that our struggles and insecurities will somehow be resolved for us. These desires will have been only partially met, as neither the training course nor the British Psycological Society (BPS) can wholly meet those needs, or be as responsive to our individual desires and preferences as we would like. With the training course no longer fulfilling that role (albeit imperfectly), the qualified counselling psychologist has to 'own' these needs more explicitly, take responsibility for their own development, and find other networks or organisations that assist in the managing of greater autonomy. At the same time, we may welcome and be eager for this greater independence and responsibility. It can be a validation of the progress we have made and the level of professional maturity we have developed.

Case study: Hannah

I was never made to feel like a beginner. In fact if anything, I was having to be reminded of my status, like, 'you're one of the more highly qualified people in the department'. That took time to get used to and time to get comfortable with. I realised there was leadership required. Sometimes, in the absence of others, it's your call.

However, although increased autonomy is to be expected, there is a danger that we take this too far, especially in the early years of our careers. Various studies have found that younger therapists and those with fewer years in practice tend to have higher rates of emotional exhaustion and burnout (Ackerley et al., 1988; Vredenburgh et al., 1999). The Therapist Belief Scale (McLean et al., 2003) measures therapist beliefs relating to a sense of responsibility, fear of making mistakes, and high and rigid expectations of self. Endorsement of items on the Therapist Belief Scale is slightly higher for early career therapists, suggesting a greater risk at this stage of feeling excessively responsible in therapy and having very high and rigid expectations of oneself (Emery et al., 2009). Indeed Baron et al. (1984) suggest that avoiding over-commitment is a key task of the early career period. Good self-care (including maintaining/rebuilding a life outside counselling psychology) and honest exploration of this domain in supervision and in other professional contact can help us 'catch' this tendency towards autonomy and responsibility before it becomes excessive.

Becoming a more competent scientist-practitioner

Counselling psychology training is especially challenging because it proceeds on a number of parallel streams (theoretical learning, producing research, therapeutic practice, personal development and personal therapy). Furthermore, these strands interweave substantially and perhaps the ideal is to interweave them in a way that is dynamic and enriching. Alternatively, it can feel like being pulled in four or more different directions, without a clear sense of how not to get ripped apart! Nonetheless, this 'enforced' combination of these modes of development helps teach us to reflect pre-action, in-action and on-action (Schön, 1983). This learning experience also prompts us to consider and evidence the scientific approach behind our therapeutic practice, as well as to thoughtfully weave personal experience and insight into our studying and practising (Blair, 2010; Stricker, 2003). Once we are qualified, this creative learning process and reflective cycle is no longer prompted by assignments or tutors, and thus can becomes less formalised or even neglected.

My own experience during the early career period is that broader and more complex experiences of therapeutic work in this period led to greater critical reflection on the effectiveness and values of my preferred models of therapy as well as numerous other aspects of therapeutic work. I also found that a small amount of 'extra-curricular' activities (e.g. writing for publication, teaching) helped me in my efforts to be a 'scientist-practitioner', to reflect on my own developing practice, and to feel connected to the wider profession. Some of the scientist-practitioner literature advocates a fairly equal weighting of science and practice (Vespia and Sauer, 2006), and no doubt some posts or portfolio careers can enable this type of balance. However, I am probably not alone in finding that in the context of a full-time NHS post and life outside counselling psychology, such endeavours are best treated as an added bonus during the early career, rather than my 'core business'.

Evolving expertise

In the context of wishing to keep growing and developing, I also began to look more closely at the broader literature on expertise (Ericsson et al., 2006; Ericsson et al., 1993). Ericsson and colleagues have studied the most effective performers across different domains of expertise, and find remarkably similar patterns across diverse domains, including music, athletics, chess, and so on. Attaining expertise seems to depend on at least 10,000 hours, or ten years, of deliberate practice. This does not mean simply practising the same skills repeatedly. Deliberate practice involves knowing your current baseline effectiveness, setting goals just beyond your current level of ability, deliberately and repeatedly practising particular skills to try to meet the new target, getting accurate feedback on progress, finding out where you went wrong and re-adjusting.

It is perhaps understandable that after the intense scrutiny of our practice during training, we enjoy the relative freedom to practise with less evaluation when we are qualified, unless working in a setting with close monitoring of outcomes (e.g. research trials, research clinics). However, there seems to be a danger within counselling psychology as well as other therapy professions that we plateau at a level where we feel comfortable and confident (Nyman et al., 2010). Feedback-informed treatment seems to offer one way of actively working towards ever-greater therapeutic skill (Miller et al., 2007). The act of seeking formal feedback from clients about outcome and alliance *by itself* improves engagement and outcome (Miller et al., 2007). More broadly, it can be useful to re-visit the scientist-practitioner literature, which offers a rich variety of ways to apply scientific principles to our practice and ongoing development (e.g. Vespia and Sauer, 2006; Corrie and Callahan, 2000; Spengler et al., 1995). Lastly, the 'ten-year rule' discovered by Ericsson and colleagues reminds us that the journey towards expertise is a marathon rather than a sprint, and that training is a good start rather than the whole race.

Supervision and developmental stage

Supervision as a qualified counselling psychologist can and should be different from that experienced as a trainee, although this difference is likely to be less dramatic for those who have already been working as therapists prior to counselling psychology training. The Integrated Developmental Model of Supervision (Stoltenberg et al., 1998) affirms this shift, positing that the needs of the practitioner in supervision (as well as other contexts) will change depending on their developmental stage. Therefore the supervisor of the newly qualified practitioner (and others involved in supporting practitioners) should recognise the personal and professional developmental stage of the practitioner and adapt their engagement accordingly, illustrated by the case study below.

Case study: Kate

Supervision was the first thing I recognised was different from the training period. Being more responsible for my own client work and my supervisor not holding overall clinical responsibility was a significant change. I was given more autonomy generally, and wasn't used to that. I notice less teaching in supervision now and the priorities for supervision are more self-directed. I still find myself wanting formal feedback from supervisors, and have to get used to not having that kind of feedback.

On the other side of the coin, the practitioner's challenge is to recognise their own vulnerabilities, defences and limitations in the context of the work they are doing and sometimes this involves re-visiting basic skills, such as empathic listening. Therefore, developmental supervision models are heuristics and need to be applied flexibly.

This change in the nature of supervision means moving from trainee supervisee identity (looking for didactic advice and evaluation, being afraid to discuss weaknesses or being overly focused on weaknesses, idolising the supervisor) to professional supervisee identity (more collaborative supervision, becoming more autonomous, assessing one's own competence voluntarily and reflectively, trusting one's training, choosing therapeutic style more deliberately and freely). This transition in supervisee identity can be slightly harder if continuing with the same supervisor as during training, as an idealised or novice–expert relationship may have developed. See Chapters 7 and 35 in this book for further discussion of supervision.

Discovering and developing a personal therapeutic style

Although there are many aspects to counselling psychology practice, for most of us, direct therapeutic work is likely to be a core part of our work. While training, our choice of which approach(es) to use at any given time may be strongly guided by the training course and our stage of training. Some trainees will have already been working as psychotherapists or counsellors prior to becoming counselling psychologists and may, therefore, already have a strong allegiance to a particular therapeutic model, though this is likely to be changed by counselling psychology training, particularly in the direction of pluralism.

After qualifying, some counselling psychologists may choose to work in settings such as Improved Access to Psychological Therapies (IAPT) in England or in equivalent services elsewhere in the UK, or in research clinics or trials, where strict adherence to a manualised therapeutic model may be required. In such cases, the individual practitioner is relatively constrained and thus not yet able to fully discover and work out their own preferred model or integration of models. However, there may be for many of us the opportunity to make more autonomous decisions about which models and interventions to use in our therapeutic practice.

Where there is some choice over therapeutic style, this represents a very important aspect of the transition to qualified practice and identity and is profoundly influenced by a number of factors, including the employment context and the individual's personality (see the case study below).

Case study: Kate

As a trainee, I tended to take excessive responsibility for clients, but didn't realise it at the time. At first, going into an NHS post with quite strict structures (maximum number of sessions, no time for home visits, etc.) was something I rebelled against (at least internally). However, I gradually concluded that this was a better way of working for me because looser boundaries might have resulted in overwork, emotional over-involvement, and possible burnout, and that the boundaries actually helped focus my therapeutic work.

Ward et al. (2011) found that for many trainees, the integration of therapeutic models and ideas is challenging, and that training courses do not necessarily provide a systematic and explicit way of achieving this integration. Therefore, we are likely to engage in an idiosyncratic process to develop our own particular therapeutic style, though it is to be hoped that this is guided by the scientist-practitioner model of research-informed practice (Blair, 2010; Corrie and Callahan, 2000). It is likely that the early post-qualification phase of a counselling psychologist's career constitutes as much a 'trial and error' discovery of what one does and prefers, as much as constituting deliberate, mindful choice. The specific combination of therapeutic models used by an individual counselling psychologist is likely to relate at least as much to their own personal experience and working model of reality (Bilgrave and Deluty, 2002) as it is to the models and examples of integration offered by training, or in specific integrative therapy models, such as the pluralistic framework (Cooper and McLeod, 2010).

Therapeutic practice post-qualification may also become more outward-looking and generative, to use again Erikson's language (Erikson, 1959). As trainees, while we no doubt have the client's interests at heart, we are also by necessity much concerned with our own performance and our own grasp of theory and practice. As qualified practitioners working under less scrutiny and less pressure of fidelity to models, we may be freed up to focus more on the client's needs rather than on our own.

Therapeutic practice is also likely to develop and change as a result of the wider and broader range of clients and presenting issues that we may encounter post-qualification. We will be more likely to experience longer-term therapy relationships (longer than that possible within a ten-month placement, for example). We may well experience more complex clients, including those with higher associated risks (from which we are likely to have been 'protected' as trainees). For these reasons and simply by the accumulation of more experience, we are likely to experience more cases where therapy seems to be ineffective. As we face these challenges, which may be fairly unfamiliar, we will ideally be aided by further and more targeted reading and training, developmentally appropriate supervision and informal discussion with other psychologists and therapists, particularly those with more experience of such challenges.

Finding appropriate mentoring and professional support

Mentoring is a partnership, usually between two people, where the less experienced person is encouraged to develop through learning and breadth of experience, to fulfil their potential, and is helped to navigate challenges in their professional life. The more experienced person functions as a coach and role model, assisting the less experienced person with their professional performance as well as their general work–life balance (American Psychological Association, 2014). Mentoring can provide many things: a source of encouragement, advice, sharing of frustrations and challenges, reduces isolation, assists new developments in career and provides perspective. Mentors can also 'protect' the mentee to a degree (the word 'protégé' comes from the Latin *prōtegere*, meaning 'to protect'). Mentoring should be distinct from line management and from clinical supervision, offering a place for reflection and action on broader professional development and well-being. Mentors can help normalise, based on their own experience, and can be a sounding board for the less experienced professional (Green and Hawley, 2009). Wanberg et al. (2003) found that individuals who had been mentored were more satisfied and committed to their profession than those who had not been mentored. Mentoring was also highlighted as highly desirable by interviewees and respondents to the survey for this chapter.

Case study: James

Throughout my training and into my first few years qualified, I realise, more with hindsight, that I have benefited from various informal mentors. The affirmation and advice of certain older males in the profession in particular, has enabled me to trust that I can do this kind of work, and they have also pushed me to develop in particular directions. Even one-off encounters can do that, although it's also great to have ongoing contact with people whose experience and wisdom I can call on.

In addition to mentoring, broader professional support and connection can of course be established and maintained through friendships, supervision groups, reflective practice groups, BPS events (conferences, regional networks, training events), special interest groups and research networks, to name but a few. Professional networks (e.g. the Division of

Counselling Psychology) and events (e.g. conferences) can also be good ways to meet potential mentors. Further resources regarding mentoring can be found on the companion website resources that accompany this chapter.

Professional registration

Newly qualified counselling psychologists will already be aware of the need to be registered with the appropriate regulatory body, which in the UK is the Health and Care Professions Council (HCPC). This registration aims to protect our clients. To use the protected title of counselling psychologist requires such registration, based on completion of a HCPC-approved training course or route. For counselling psychologists working in other countries, equivalent registration will be required. The process of registration should be undertaken as early as possible.

Although practitioner psychologists are now regulated by the HCPC, the BPS Division of Counselling Psychology continues to promote the interests of counselling psychologists and support them to develop and thrive throughout their careers. In the context of the variety of career choices available and the prevalence of portfolio careers, the BPS can serve as an anchor for professional identity and a focus for the production and consumption of research through journals and conferences (Strawbridge, 2013).

In order to protect oneself further as a professional, joining a union is also strongly advised. Membership of a union can offer protection, advice and legal support in the event of employment-related difficulties.

Finding suitable employment

A variety of aspects relating to transition have now been discussed but as we look for suitable work in the post-qualification period it may be helpful to ask a number of questions about proposed work settings. Questions to consider in this process may include:

- Does the organisation recognise the nature of this transition and the value of 'preceptorship'? (see introduction)
- Will I be given time and space to grow into the role and build up a caseload gradually?
- Will I be specialising too much before my general skills are adequately consolidated?
- Does the work match my current level of competence and confidence and does it match my interests?

Decisions about type of employment should not be taken lightly. For example, working for a well-established and highly structured organisation like the NHS may be particularly suitable if one prefers more external structure, reliable and consistent salary, established terms and conditions, and working closely with colleagues. Alternatively, fully independent practice may be best suited to people who can relish rather than fear the lack of external structure. This might involve living with variations in busyness and income and an ability and willingness to develop their own policies and business practices from scratch, and for whom practising with great freedom in therapeutic models is very important (Buckner, 1992; Wilding, McMahon, & Palmer, 2008). In this context, where externally imposed structures are, to a larger extent, absent, it is very important to set clear boundaries and good practices to protect both clients and oneself.

Some of those interviewed for this chapter exited their training with a very clear idea of where they wanted to work and what kind of work they wanted to do. Others were less sure and required a period of trying things out, and tussling with the direction in which to go. If life circumstances allow, it can therefore be helpful to give oneself permission to try things out and even let the dust settle on training before making a decision about what kind of work to pursue. Furthermore, it is important to bear in mind that one's first post does not rule out other types of work in future. The 'portfolio' career is common among counselling psychologists and offers a significant choice of different types of work and in quite different contexts (see Chapter 38 in this volume).

RECOMMENDATIONS FOR THE BROADER PROFESSION

Although it is hoped that the foregoing material offers some ideas for how the wider profession can support newly qualified counselling psychologists, some brief, specific recommendations are given below.

Recommendations for training institutions

Although this transition occurs as trainees leave their training course or the independent route, it may be that training institutions could focus some teaching or tutorial time on specifically preparing trainees for this transition. This was certainly appreciated by the final-year trainees who attended the focus group for this chapter, and some survey respondents suggested training courses should acknowledge the realities of this transition more explicitly to trainees. A draft presentation is available on the companion website.

Recommendations for supervisors

Supervision should recognise the greater level of responsibility and competence in the qualified practitioner, but should also bear in mind the disorientation that the newly qualified supervisee may be experiencing. The supervisee may also be accustomed to more didactic input and clear guidance in supervision, and may look for this either explicitly or indirectly. From the supervisee's point of view, the desire for advice-giving may have to be resisted in order to develop an internal supervisor (Casement, 1985), to build the confidence that is appropriate to qualified work, and to test out their competence. From the supervisor's point of view, the supervisee needs so far as possible to be allowed to make mistakes yet to be guided in a manner which helps to facilitate the supervisee's own learning and reflective process. This in turn enables the supervisee to notice changes in their practice and self-concept since qualifying, in order to highlight progress and recognise the realities of this transition.

Recommendations for mentors

Interviewees and survey respondents expressed a strong appreciation for mentors and the desire for more mentoring to be available. As discussed earlier, a mentor can, in small ways, protect the mentee (from over-extending themselves, from excess disillusionment, from isolation, etc.). Mentors can also bring a different and perhaps broader perspective of this transition, helping to normalise and perhaps explain why the transition brings so many internal and external changes. Drawing again on Erikson's developmental stages (Erikson, 1959), mentors can therefore assist mentees with establishing identity in the context of possible role confusion. For mentors themselves, mentoring can thus be an act of generativity, which reduces the risk of stagnation. There is also further guidance on mentoring on the companion website.

CONCLUSION

This chapter has identified and discussed many of the pertinent tasks and aspects of transitioning to fully qualified status as a counselling psychologist. The breadth and complexity of these areas demonstrate that this transition is a distinctive and important stage of career development. Although it involves challenges to navigate, counselling psychology training can prepare us well for this process. Achieving the doctorate in counselling psychology is no mean feat and those who do so should feel some confidence in their ability to make the transition to qualified status. In addition, the wider profession has an important role to play in accompanying and supporting counselling psychologists through this early career period. It is well worth remembering that professional development as a counselling psychologist is a career-long process, but a 'good enough' start to our professional careers can set us on the right track for the further aspects of development discussed in the following chapters.

Visit the companion website for the following:

- Links to further resources.
- A PowerPoint presentation on Navigating the Transition to Professional Life.
- Study guide/Self-reflection questions.
- Survey results.

ACKNOWLEDGEMENT

I am extremely grateful to all those who contributed richly to the development of this chapter through the trainee focus group, the online survey and the interviews.

REFERENCES

Ackerley, G. D., Burnell, J., Holder, D. C. and Kurdek, L. A. (1988). Burnout among licensed psychologists. *Professional Psychology: Research and Practice, 19*(6), 624–631.

Adams, J., Hayes, J. and Hopson, B. (1976). *Transition: Understanding and managing personal change*. London: Martin Robertson.

American Psychological Association (2014). *Centering on mentoring*. Retrieved on 6 November 2014 from www.apa.org/education/grad/mentor-task-force.aspx.

Baron, A., Sekel, A. C. and Stott, F. W. (1984). Early career issues for counseling center psychologists: The first six years. *The Counseling Psychologist, 12*(1), 121–125.

Bilgrave, D. and Deluty, R. (2002). Religious beliefs and political ideologies as predictors of psychotherapeutic orientations of clinical and counseling psychologists. *Psychotherapy Theory, Research, Practice, Training, 39*, 245–260.

Blair, L. (2010). A critical review of the scientist-practitioner model for counselling psychology. *Counselling Psychology Review, 25*(4), 19–30.

BPS/Unite. (2010). *Joint Unite/BPS statement regarding preceptorship 2010*. Leicester: British Psychological Society.

Buckner, M. O. (1992). New professionals in private practice. *The Counseling Psychologist, 20*(1), 10–16.

Casement, P. (1985). *On learning from the patient*. London: Routledge.

Cooper, M. and McLeod, J. (2010). *Pluralistic counselling and psychotherapy*. London: Sage.

Corrie, S. and Callahan, M. M. (2000). A review of the scientist-practitioner model: Reflections on its potential contribution to counselling psychology within the context of current health care trends. *British Journal of Medical Psychology, 73*(3), 413–427.

du Plock, S. (2006). Just what is it that makes contemporary counselling psychology so different, so appealing? *Counselling Psychology Review*, *21*(3), 22–32.

Emery, S., Wade, T. D. and McLean, S. (2009). Associations among therapist beliefs, personal resources and burnout in clinical psychologists. *Behaviour Change*, *26*(2), 83–96.

Ericsson, K. A., Charness, N., Feltovich, P. J. and Hoffman, R. R. (eds). (2006). *The Cambridge handbook of expertise and expert performance*. Cambridge: Cambridge University Press.

Ericsson, K. A., Krampe, R. T. and Tesch-Romer, C. (1993). The role of deliberate practice in the acquisition of expert performance. *Psychological Review*, *100*(3), 363–406.

Erikson, E. H. (1959). *Identity and the life cycle*. New York: International Universities Press.

Green, A. G. and Hawley, G. C. (2009). Early career psychologists: Understanding, engaging and mentoring tomorrow's leaders. *Professional Psychology: Research and Practice*, *40*(2), 206–212.

Hogan, R. A. (1964). Issues and approaches in supervision. *Psychotherapy: Theory, Research and Practice*, *1*(139), 141.

Martin, P. (2009). Training and professional development. In R. Woolfe, S. Strawbridge, B. Douglas and W. Dryden (Eds.), *Handbook of counselling psychology* (3rd edn, pp. 547–568). London: Sage.

McLean, S., Wade, T. D. and Encel, J. (2003). The contribution of therapist beliefs to psychological distress in therapists: An investigation of vicarious traumatisation, burnout and symptoms of avoidance and intrusion. *Behavioural and Cognitive Psychotherapies*, *31*, 417–428.

Miller, S. D., Hubble, M. and Duncan, B. (2007). Supershrinks: What's the secret of their success. *Psychotherapy Networker*, *31*, 26–35.

Nyman, S. J., Nafziger, M. A. and Smith, T. B. (2010). Client outcomes across counselor training level within a multitiered supervision model. *Journal of Counseling and Development*, *88*, 204–209.

Orlinsky, D. E. and Rønnestad, M. H. (2005). *How psychotherapists develop: A study of therapeutic work and professional growth*. Washington, DC: American Psychiatric Association.

Palmer, S. and Bor, R. (eds). (2008). *The practitioner's handbook: A guide for counsellors, psychotherapists and counselling psychologists*. London: Sage.

Rønnestad, M. H. and Skovholt, T. (2012). *The developing practitioner: Growth and stagnation of therapists and counselors*. New York: Routledge.

Schön, D. A. (1983). *The reflective practitioner: How professionals think in action*. London: Basic Books.

Spengler, P. M., Strohmer, D. C., Dixon, D. N. and Shivy, V. A. (1995). A scientist-practitioner model of psychological assessment: Implications for training, practice and research. *The Counseling Psychologist*, *23*(3), 506–534.

Stoltenberg, C. D., McNeill, B. and Delworth, U. (1998). *IDM supervision: An integrated developmental model for supervising counselors and therapists*. San Francisco, CA: Jossey-Bass.

Strawbridge, S. (2006). Thoughts on becoming, being and developing as a counselling psychologist. *Counselling Psychology Review*, *21*(1), 27–30.

Strawbridge, S. (2013). Personal communication.

Stricker, G. (2003). Evidence-based practice: The wave of the past. *The Counseling Psychologist*, *31*(5), 546–554.

Sugarman, L. (2001). *Life-span development: Frameworks, accounts and strategies: Theories, concepts and interventions.* Hove: Psychology Press.

Sugarman, L. (2009). The life course: A framework for the practice of counselling psychology. In R. Woolfe, S. Strawbridge, B. Douglas and W. Dryden (eds), *Handbook of counselling psychology* (3rd edn, pp. 547–568). London: Sage.

Super, D. E., Sverko, B. and Super, C. M. (1995). *Life roles, values, and careers: International findings of the work importance study.* San Francisco, CA: Jossey-Bass.

Vespia, K. M. and Sauer, E. M. (2006). Defining characteristic or unrealistic ideal: Historical and contemporary perspectives on scientist-practitioner training in counselling psychology. *Counselling Psychology Quarterly, 19*(3), 229–251.

Vredenburgh, L. D., Carlozzi, A. F. and Stein, L. B. (1999). Burnout in counseling psychologists: Type of practice setting and pertinent demographics. *Counselling Psychology Quarterly, 12*(3), 293–302.

Wanberg, C. R., Welsh, E. T. and Hezle, S. A. (2003). Mentoring research: A review and dynamic process model. *Research in Personnel and Human Resources Management, 22*, 39–124.

Ward, T., Hogan, K. and Menns, R. (2011). Perceptions of integration in counselling psychology training: A pilot study. *Counselling Psychology Review, 26*(3), 8–19.

Wilding, C., McMahon, G. and Palmer, S. (2008). How to set up and develop your private practice. In S. Palmer and R. Bor (eds), *The practitioner's handbook: A guide for counsellors, psychotherapists and counselling psychologists* (pp. 142–155). London: Sage.

34
LEADING AND MANAGING
NICOLA GALE

INTRODUCTION

The chapter is designed to encourage you as an early career counselling psychologist to start thinking about what leading will involve for you, and also offer a practical guide to some of the key tasks of management. It has been written with a practical focus (as a 'handbook') to explore some of the facets of leadership in healthcare contexts, and to demystify some of the practical know-how of management, which is rarely part of core training, and which clinicians are often somehow expected to absorb by osmosis.

LEADERSHIP

Leadership encompasses personal qualities, competences, styles and interpersonal engagement; political and contextual knowledge and skill; and role modelling professional expertise and capability (clinical leadership). Being a psychologist and a leader or manager presents some particular opportunities as well as challenges and dilemmas. Management and clinical skill sets can be quite different: the latter have been honed during training and first posts in a variety of settings; the former are often not taught and many of the tasks of management require an understanding of and competence in a wide range of organisational functions from processes to resourcing to management of people.

There is a vast array of competence frameworks, lists of characteristics, styles of leadership and measurement tools. Leadership competences are now taught in counselling psychology training. Trainees develop competences to influence teams and organisations, their interpersonal skills and collaborative team working. They also need to understand relevant organisational policies and contextual and legal frameworks, management, audit, how to recognise and respond to unethical practice, and about contributing to development of the profession (British Psychological Society, 2014a).

Leaders need to keep current and be in the know. Understanding the bigger context is important. Gopee and Galloway (2014) provide a useful overview of the current context in national healthcare, with Sullivan and Garland (2013) helpfully outlining the differences across the four nations in the UK. Leaders may have the opportunity to set the agenda and influence policy, for example by participating in the development of guidelines, working parties on policy documents, research and publishing, being part of professional alliances. Day to day, it is about being familiar with changing government priorities, initiatives, documents, and how they affect your area of work. Barr and Dowding (2012) describe various levels of health policy making and influence. Being influential requires strategic vision to bring about change. It also, as Sullivan and Garland (2013) point out, requires political skills, but political skills based on integrity, including persuasion, patience, open-mindedness and compassion.

A key unit of function for the leader is the team. There is the immediate team which delivers the service. There are also often wider organisational groupings, often linked to type of service provided or service-user population, e.g. acute services, or children and young people. Beyond that there are (often short-life) groups brought together to undertake specific tasks (e.g. a goal of quality improvement such as record-keeping); to deal with a particular presenting issue across services (e.g. focus on domestic abuse); to address a problem (e.g. sickness absence management). The leader will therefore have multiple loyalties and need to build relationships in different settings and across disciplines, often quickly. Barr and Dowding (2012) give a helpful account of team life. This covers the history of the research on groups in organisations, including the power of groups to work contrary to the desired goals of management despite the usual incentives, roles in groups, group processes and factors in the effectiveness of groups. In this context, psychological training comes in very handy, although it is important not to forget that the psychologist leader/manager is also a group member and so expertise on group functioning needs to be worn lightly and used sensitively.

Interprofessional working is a reality of managing in health settings. Barr and Dowding (2012) cite some of the challenges (including differing philosophies; professional backgrounds, value systems and trainings; agendas; and structural barriers) that need to be addressed to make multidisciplinary team working effective.

Debates about whether there are differences between leadership and management, and if so what those are, are longstanding. Barr and Dowding (2012: 8) make the point that a manager will have 'formal authority to direct the work of a given set of employees; they are formally responsible for the quality of that work and what it costs to achieve it'. This is not, however, necessary to be a leader, which can be a broader role driven more by influence. Schedlitzki and Edwards (2014) comment that leadership is seen more favourably than management but that discounting management in this way may well be an error, both because management is necessary, and also as dichotomising people in this way is a distortion of what happens in practice. They cite work indicating that transactional leadership may be seen as management, with transformational leadership being seen as leadership. Gill (2011) suggests we need in the same person leaders who are managers and managers who are leaders. Sullivan and Garland (2013) note that a number of writers now believe the terms are virtually interchangeable. They do, however, go on to differentiate the actions of leading and managing, with managing being more about planning and organising to achieve organisational goals, and leading being about influencing for change. With some small inconsistencies where the felt sense in the context of the other term appeared right, this is the approach adopted in this chapter.

Leadership is a much researched area. Gopee and Galloway (2014) overview styles of leadership. Traditional views of styles include authoritarian – power and authority; democratic – consultative; permissive – autonomous working with few rules; bureaucratic – fixed rules and norms. More modern styles include connective – collaboration; servant – altruism; transactional – achievement of organisational goals; transformational – visionary inspiration for change. How the styles are used and in what combinations will depend on the context, the times, the relationships between and within organisations, and the task in hand. Contexts are changing as the boundaries between public and independent and third-sector working become more fluid, and services respond to times of resource constraint.

What are the qualities needed for leadership? Gopee and Galloway (2014) address this subject in the context of nursing but the qualities cited are widely generalisable. They refer, among other things, to characteristics of service orientation, positive energy, leading balanced lives, (interestingly) a sense of professional adventure; core personal skills of communication, motivation, influencing, adaptability, responding positively to change; and qualities such as being emotional resilient, self-aware, knowledgeable, forward thinking, articulate, adaptable, energetic, analytical but decisive, sensitive. What underlies them is a sense in which the leader role models, is available to the team, the team can have confidence that the leader will do the right thing and do it well.

THE TASKS OF MANAGING

There are many components to the managerial role. Gopee and Galloway (2014: 29) provide a useful table of the many functions and roles of the manager, in terms of human resource activities, managing staffing levels, problem solving, quality, policy, training, and also their role in clinical care. The sections below outline what is involved in some of these core areas.

RESOURCING TEAMS

Someone leaving can be destabilising for the team, whether they are popular and always reliable, or indeed perhaps were at odds with the manager much of the time. What are the main steps to take?

Firstly, how are you going to manage their departure? It is important for morale to acknowledge the loss that you and other team members will be feeling honestly, but also to show there is a plan, and you are able to contain the situation. Agree with the staff member how and when their leaving will be announced, but do it quickly. However careful people are, a chance remark somewhere will already have spread the news. Think about how different constituencies in the organisation will perceive it, what will different factions think, what might people seek to make happen or capitalise on as a result? How you are seen to manage all this, and it needs to be done with generosity of spirit, will set the tone for how things are going forward.

In thinking about replacement, the purpose and functions of the role need to be considered. It is tempting, in filling a position, to dust down the job description and person specification and get an advertisement out, to avoid a gap, and to be seen to be doing something. The first step, however, is to look at what the service needs. Is this an opportunity to reshape this role, perhaps to deliver some aspect of the service in a different way? What about the aspirations and development needs of other team members? Can and should roles be reconfigured? Organisations generally have recruitment procedures to be followed. In a larger organisation there may well be a fully-fledged recruitment department that can guide a manager though the process of developing/revising a job description (what the role is), and the person specification (the knowledge, skills, attributes and experience of the person required to fill the role).

The primary goal of the recruitment process is to find the candidate who is most likely to add value to the service. To achieve this, it needs to meet equality of opportunity requirements, with the recruitment net drawn widely. For this reason, the British Psychological Society (2011) endorses the principle of recruitment for psychologists by competence, not adjectival title. Thought needs to be given to the opportunity for an informal visit for the candidate. Recruitment is a two-way process and you want to attract a high-quality and motivated candidate who is also well informed as to the nature of the post and service and team they will be working in. What is to be the composition of the interview panel? Who are the stakeholders in this post? Would setting job-related scenarios be appropriate? Is it possible/ appropriate to involve service users? Newer forms of recruitment include values-based recruitment (NHS Employers, 2014).

Once you have chosen your preferred candidate, you can start pre-employment checks. These are important to get right and employment should not be confirmed until these procedures are complete. Sullivan and Garland (2013) give a helpful account. Usually included are an enhanced Disclosure and Barring Service check; occupational health clearance; checking of registration, qualifications and identity documents, including right to work; and references. Occupational health is usually now limited to ensuring the candidate has the opportunity to request 'reasonable adjustments' for any health condition, so as not to disadvantage disabled candidates.

The big picture in recruitment is workforce planning. For the individual manager, workforce planning is generally about building flexibility and transferable skills in a team, and succession planning. There is also the longer-range planning to ensure that the right staff are available to employers in sufficient numbers to meet the demand of services. Workforce planning takes account of demographics, especially time to qualification and losses (e.g. due to retirements), and the numbers of different professionals with the skill mix and values needed to deliver services. The inclusion of values is a focus that has particular salience given recent history of failures of care at Mid Staffordshire NHS Foundation Trust, reported on by Sir Robert Francis QC (Francis, 2013), Winterbourne View (Department of Health, 2012), and Abertawe Bro Morgannwg University Health Board (Andrews and Butler, 2014). This is a role generally carried out in organisations by Human Resources, who often produce data 'bottom up' to feed into national workforce plans (for information on workforce planning in healthcare across the nations see the useful websites at the end of the chapter).

MANAGING TEAMS

The team is the unit of delivery and leading and managing teams demands knowledge and skill, requires training and benefits in the main from experience, as does any other aspect of job performance.

One of the first questions that often confronts a new team manager is how are they going to 'be' in the new team. All staff in teams, irrespective of role, bring with them their own past, relationship history, schemas, beliefs and assumptions about self, people and the world, attachment patterns, needs, fears, interpersonal abilities, and so on. In the workplace, the team-mates are by and large not chosen by the individual. Individuals will manage themselves in the workplace in different ways: some will seek greater intimacy, others be more distant; some will be hugely invested in relationships in the team, others much less so; some staff will complement each other, others will clash in terms of personality, beliefs, personal style, value base, and on dimensions related to, for example, gender, age, culture and belief system. The team manager needs to be aware of these things both in relation to team members and their own positioning within the team. It is the manager's role to ensure the team remains effective and these personal and interpersonal aspects are not allowed to derail the team's performance. Often when things go awry in team relationships it is when a personal friendship or intimacy has developed and then broken down. The working relationship is then extremely difficult to sustain.

What options are open to managers to deal with difficulties in teams? A general rule of thumb is to address things quickly and informally wherever possible, at the same time as setting clear expectations for the future. If there are difficulties, they need to be talked about before people become hurt; poor behaviour needs to be stopped in its tracks before it escalates or becomes entrenched. The most useful interventions are often the simplest: an open culture, regular team discussions so things do not fester, staff having access to supervision, a shared understanding of what constitutes a respectful climate.

Where a particular matter needs to be attended to, a facilitated discussion led by the manager can be helpful. Here, your clinical skills will come in handy, such as careful attention and listening, communication skills, problem definition and analysis. However, they do also need keeping in check so as not to overstep the boundary in relation to the managerial role, as you are not there to make a clinical judgement! Use of a mediation model can be helpful in keeping on track. This gives everyone a chance to step back from the heat of the immediate issue and resolve things in a calmer frame of mind. Crawley and Graham (2002) have written a straightforward guide for managers with case examples.

Sometimes working relationship difficulties can lead to a formal employee-led complaint (alternatively known as a grievance). Faced with one of these, a manager needs to access the relevant organisational policy. Polices will vary by organisation but all have common features. The Code of Practice of the Arbitration and Conciliation Service (ACAS) (2009) gives the main points. It is also essential to take advice from the Human Resources department, which will have experience of managing such matters. As a manager, though, it is important to stay engaged with the issue and ensure it is resolved in a way that works for the service concerned.

Sometimes as a last resort a staff member's conduct or job performance is lacking either consistently or to such a degree that there is a need to progress to formal employment action, either disciplinary in the case of conduct, or capability in the case of job performance. An important management skill is spotting this developing as early as possible and ensuring you have started to take appropriate steps, such as giving clear feedback and documenting it, and ensuring the annual appraisal appropriately reflects the concerns, for example. Sullivan and Garland (2013) provide useful coaching on these matters. Again, carefully following the correct procedures in the policies and taking HR advice is essential. It is also important as a manager to try to do such things while maintaining a respectful and caring relationship with the staff member concerned. The staff member is likely to need both practical support at work, such as from their union representative, and emotional support, for example from staff psychological services.

Neither grievance nor disciplinary processes are straightforward. Often they are protracted and, frequently in the case of grievance, reach no clear conclusion. They are therefore to be approached with some humility and from a mindset of compassion.

In developing processes at work and especially when managing performance, one of the main legal frameworks is the Equality Act 2010, which makes discrimination on the basis of protected characteristics (age, disability, gender reassignment, marriage and civil partnership, pregnancy and maternity, race, religion or belief, sex and sexual orientation) unlawful both at work and in society. In selecting staff for promotion, roles, opportunities, or in performance appraisal, for example, managers need to be careful that they do not either directly discriminate against someone on the grounds of a protected characteristic, or indirectly discriminate against them by putting in place a requirement that is harder for someone with a protected characteristic to meet. Following good practice in relation to appraisals is important. Organisations usually offer training which is sometimes mandatory; trade unions also offer guidance, for example Unite the Union (2013).

The Equality Act 2010 also deals with harassment and victimisation on the grounds of a protected characteristic. Allegations of harassment on the grounds of a protected characteristic or bullying (ACAS, 2014a) are common at work and acts may be perpetrated by service users or their relatives, between colleagues, from manager to staff member, or so-called upwards bullying from staff/teams to the manager. Organisations usually have a dignity at work or similar policy on these matters. The issues can be complex and need to be addressed sensitively using the various means described above.

There are other practical aspects of people management with which a manager must become familiar. Management of sickness absence, especially in public services, is high profile due to the cost to the organisation, and the cost to the individual and to society where there is not a successful return to work. Early intervention, which takes account not only of the health condition, but also any personal or work-related factors, is key to a successful return. Managers should not be afraid to keep in touch with the staff member to demonstrate personal and organisational concern, although it is good practice to agree with them how that is to happen so it is not misconstrued as bullying. It is also important to consider the need for workplace adjustments to facilitate return. These may be short or longer term, and usually Occupational Health advice is sought on making adjustments. Organisational polices will cover the various aspects of sickness absence management. The Health and Safety Executive (HSE) (2004) provides an overview of the legal requirements and good practice in the area.

Bereavement is an area where similar considerations apply. ACAS (2014b) have produced guidance for managers, and good employers will have policies in place.

Employers have many responsibilities for health and safety in the workplace under Health and Safety at Work legislation (HSE, 2014a). Managers are required to undertake regular risk assessments and put in place procedures to mitigate risk. It is advisable to seek training in this complex area. A key area in psychological services is to identify and manage the risk of work-related stress. The HSE *Management Standards for Work Related Stress* framework (HSE, 2007a), comprising consideration of the demands of work, the staff member's degree of control over their work, the support they experience, work relationships, role clarity and impact of change, is widely used, and teams can be surveyed using the HSE indicator tool (HSE, 2007b). Stress is a big issue. Statistics (the most recent are from 2013/2014) suggest 39 per cent of all work-related illnesses are from stress, anxiety and depression, and health is one of the top industries and professions reporting stress cases (HSE, 2014b).

When a staff member reports stress, managers should undertake a stress risk assessment with the individual and consider what can be adjusted in the workplace using the framework. Again, it is likely to be helpful to draw on staff support services. Whole teams can benefit from interventions designed to identify and reduce/eliminate specific stressors, and to build individual and team resilience. Interventions can be aimed at the work environment, lifestyle, time management, assertiveness, relaxation and mindfulness, and personal meaning of work. Bamber (2011) offers useful content.

It is inevitable that in today's workplace, managers and their teams will be faced with change, challenges, excess demands, complexity, difficult relationships and sometimes limited support. It is important to be able to build personal resilience in order not just to cope without going under, but to be able to thrive and flourish in the work environment. Neenan (2009) takes a strengths-based approach which has much relevance in the workplace. This draws on past track record, such as how have you managed before, and how can you draw on those resources in the present. It also includes visualising handling things resiliently, dealing with adverse changes as they happen in the present moment, not becoming unnecessarily distressed by what-if thinking, and exposure to things outside the personal comfort zone. Price and Scowcroft (2011) take a practical approach: have team time-out; get a work–life balance; sort out the demands of diary and desk and make them work for you; where there is a need for change, model it yourself first. All this is part of your own self-care as a manager, which is the foundation for your role.

An innate sense of fairness and being seen to be fair will carry a manager a long way. So will consistency and boundaries, and, on the other side, knowing when to cut some slack, to make an exception, to turn a blind eye.

SUPERVISION

What is the role of the manager in supervision? Looking at the functions of supervision from an organisational perspective is likely to assist here. Supervision is generally considered to have educational, restorative and quality assurance functions. Hawkins and Shohet (2006) give a helpful overview of the three main functions of supervision from different professional heritages. The manager is responsible for ensuring safe systems of work. Particular responsibilities that are likely to interface with supervision are staff performance and development, health and safety at work in particular management of stress, and clinical governance. The manager therefore needs to consider what the supervision needs of the team are, and how they can be met.

What sort of supervision is needed? Given the different functions of supervision, this decision requires the consideration and balancing of the perspectives of both staff and manager. Provision of supervision for the team in a group will have advantages in sharing of experiences, addressing the difficulties of the team as a team, building bonds between team members, and growing mutual understanding and capacity for mutual support. The group is unlikely to address adequately specific individual performance or support needs. The goals, accountabilities, level of confidentiality, keeping of records and priority given to supervision need to be considered by the manager and agreed in a way that is safe for the service.

CLINICAL GOVERNANCE

Running a safe and clinically effective service that gives service users a positive experience requires a good knowledge of the legal and ethical underpinnings that keep service users, staff and the organisation safe. The job of the leader is to develop a culture where these things are valued, are seen as important, where the attitude is one of 'how can we do this better' rather than 'how can we get around this'. The manager ensures that policies and procedures are up to date, promulgated, and that staff are trained and confident in their use. Staff also need to know when to refer upwards to management. Clinical governance has been described by the Department of Health (2000: 1) as 'a framework through which NHS organisations are accountable for continuously improving the quality of their services and safeguarding high standards of care by creating an environment in which excellence in clinical care will flourish'. The need for a solid framework of clinical governance is regularly in the public gaze. Gottwald and Lansdown (2014) set the scene in relation to the history of high-profile failings in care, criminal acts and the regular adverse occurrences that cause (sometimes fatal) harm.

Ethical competences are taught in training. Common approaches develop ethical sensitivity, ethical reasoning, motivation and implementation (British Psychological Society, 2014b). In a busy and pressurised clinical service, staff need to remain alert (sensitised) to ethical issues that may lie just under the surface in their day-to-day interactions with service users and colleagues. An environment with sufficient reflective time, for example staff meetings, supervision and one-to-one, is important for issues to emerge and be thought about. Often it is motivation and implementation that present the main organisational challenges. Poor practice can become the norm where there are staff shortages, cuts in services, and corners are habitually cut. The corner-cutting 'works' for a bit, so the underlying problems are not addressed until there is an incident. Staff can, for example, become desensitised to risk where the service user population is complex and high in need. Measures and targets can focus staff on one area of practice at the expense of another, leading the organisation to, as Berwick, who leads the National Advisory Group on the Safety of Patients in England, has said, 'hit the target but miss the point' (National Advisory Group on the Safety of Patients in England, 2013: 8) or through 'the gaming of data and goals ... aim ... above all to *look* better, even when truth is the casualty' (2013: 9, emphasis in original). Implementation of ethical practice can be lacking due to lack of time, lack of resources, fear of the consequences, and experiences of stress.

Information governance is an important area of a manager's responsibility. Larger organisations will have clear policies and procedures, generally an Information Governance Manager/Data Protection Officer to provide guidance, and IT systems that provide a high degree of physical security. Managers need to understand data protection legislation. The core (there are eight) principles of data protection are the starting point, in particular those concerning processing information only for agreed purposes and keeping data for no longer than is necessary. A grasp of what sensitive personal data is under the law is needed. Working in mental health, it is probably safest to assume that all service-user information falls under this category. Of practical importance is to know what rights service users have under the legislation to ask to have copies of their information, and how to manage such 'subject access' requests, and to ask for their data not to be processed. Regular update training in these matters is advisable. A useful overview is given by the Information Commissioner (2014a).

The keeping of notes and records is an area where, in part due to the rights of service users to access their information, and in part due to the rise in complaints and clinical negligence cases, increasing management oversight is desirable. As a manager, what is in place for you to monitor that notes and records are being kept up to date by the team, that records are appropriate, that good practice in relation to the content and style of notes is being adhered to (British Psychological Society, 2008)? Are the financial and outcome measures that may be required being recorded? If staff are under pressure to see more service users, for example, these things may not be being done to the required standard.

Freedom of Information (Information Commissioner, 2014b) is sometimes confused with data protection rights. This deals with the right of the public to obtain broader information (not personal data), such as performance data or waiting-list times, from organisations. The individual manager's need to know in this area is more limited as usually once a request is received decisions about it will be made elsewhere in the organisation.

A further area of managerial accountability is dealing with compliance with clinical guidelines and protocols. For NHS services in particular this will mean having regard to National Institute for Health and Clinical Excellence (NICE) and Scottish Intercollegiate Guidelines Network (SIGN) guidelines. As a manager, you may be asked to make a return demonstrating compliance and to audit compliance. When new guidelines are issued changes to procedures can be required. There may be differing views to reconcile about the appropriateness of a particular guideline. Service users may use guidelines to ask, for example, for a particular number of sessions and there may be pressure on services both from the users and from the existence of the standard when resourcing makes full provision difficult. As the manager with accountability for the quality of the service, for the husbandry of resources, for the staff, and the service user's safety, experience and outcomes, this requires some careful thinking, consultation and discussions within the organisation.

SERVICE QUALITY

Quality is also a facet of clinical governance, and comprises many different aspects of the service from design to the various components of delivery. This includes the people, their recruitment, training, motivation, how they are led and managed and supported, the clinical resources, the systems, the physical infrastructure, the safety of the environment, to name a few. This part of the chapter deals with some aspects of how quality is typically measured and monitored.

Service-user experience is increasingly seen as central to the provision of care. A simple measure in the NHS is the Friends and Family Test (NHS England, 2013). This asks people if they would recommend the services they have used. Services frequently measure service user satisfaction at various points during the care pathway with their own satisfaction surveys, and staff meetings can be used to review the consolidated results and generate ideas for improvement.

Understanding staff experience is also important both for meeting management's duty of care to the staff themselves, and also because of the proven links between well-led and motivated staff and patient outcomes (West, 2012). In the NHS, the NHS staff survey has been running since 2003 and measures areas such as views on patient care, job satisfaction, training and development, health and safety, engagement and involvement, equalities and raising concerns.

Service audit is a must in clinical settings and organisations require staff to participate. NICE (edited by Scrivener) describe clinical audit as 'a cycle or a spiral' (Scrivener, 2002: 2), considering what we are trying to achieve, asking why we are not achieving it, and doing something to make things better. Topics for audit will vary widely depending on setting and type of service, and may include outcomes, compliance with clinical guidelines, and the following of service procedures and protocols (e.g. related to notes, completion of reports, collection of service-user demographics, waiting times, equality of access and progress with specific initiatives). There may also be requirements imposed by service commissioners. Gottwald and Lansdown (2014: 170) firmly link audit back to clinical governance as 'a systematic method of reviewing the quality of care and the quality of services', and perhaps more pertinently for the manager, 'an incentive to improve the quality of care delivered'.

Inspections are a final piece of the quality jigsaw. The outcome of the inspection can be seen as a reflection of the whole culture and organisation of the service and the role the manager has played throughout in engaging staff and inspiring quality care. The inspection framework that will apply will depend on the type of service, and the bar is being raised. For example, it often now includes leadership, emphasising how the tone set from the top influences how services are likely to fulfil the other elements of the standards (Care Quality Commission, 2014). Overall, as Gopee and Galloway (2014) note, the aim is to create a culture of quality in each team/department and throughout the organisation as a whole.

Service development is a separate topic. However, it is often the various forms of service evaluation, as well as market forces changes (e.g. due to government policy drivers, public expectations and commercial opportunities) that drive the need for service change. A key role of leadership is to be both reading the bottom-up data and horizon-scanning so that such forces are met with a readiness to develop and change.

SERVICE USERS

Managers need to give consideration to how service users are engaged. There are formal mechanisms, for example NHS Foundation Trusts which have patient governors on the board. Service users may be part of recruitment interview or presentation panels. They may be part of inspection teams. Gottwald and Lansdown (2014) track the movement from service-user involvement to service-user engagement, and the benefits that it can bring in terms of how services are designed and delivered; it is another plank in the clinical governance framework.

How as a manager do you deal with something that goes wrong? This can be one of the most challenging aspects of the job, where loyalties, personal and professional values, the requirements of procedure, and potentially the processes of litigation and the law, can come into play.

When something goes wrong, organisations generally have a formal incident reporting process, which managers need to know. Staff should be encouraged or even required to record details of the incident before being unduly influenced by comments from others and the possible outcomes of the situation. Incidents are usually graded by severity, and this will determine who else from the organisation needs to be alerted to manage the situation. Appropriate support needs to be provided by the manager to staff affected, including considering if they are fit to remain at work (the Occupational Health department can advise here) and if staff either individually or collectively need psychological support (through the organisation's staff psychological service provision). Often, staff most of all want time to talk, their manager to be there for them, and time to support each other. Managers should not just assume this is better done by someone else.

For the most part, managers find themselves dealing with service-user dissatisfaction around poor service delivery. This necessitates developing skills in handling complaints. Like many things managers need to do, part of the success in handling complaints well is to know the procedure and ensure it is followed so as to provide a protective framework should events take an unexpected turn. This involves ensuring service users know what they are entitled to. A major difference, however, to how a complaint is handled is the personal and interpersonal skill of the manager. You don't leave your psychological knowledge and skill behind when dealing with a complaint. Have you really listened? Have you put yourself in their shoes? How did it feel, for example, to have that assessment appointment with all the hopes, fears and practical arrangements surrounding it (e.g. for childcare or work) rearranged four times by your service? Have you expressed empathy, acknowledged that it was not OK, clearly said that this is not the sort of service you want to provide? Have you asked what would make amends? Offered something more? An understanding of how the subject matter of the complaint might interact with or exacerbate the service user's mental history is also important; this should be without pathologising the service user for something that was your service's fault. At the same time, it is important to keep the clinical/managerial boundary, and in the complaint meeting you are not in a clinical role.

PERSONAL AND PROFESSIONAL DEVELOPMENT

Leaders and managers who grow and progress in their roles are those who are on the lookout for opportunities to develop. Immediate demands of the role can mean it is easier to stay at the desk. However, it is a mistake not to be seen at the monthly managers' forum meeting, to miss out on the update on the new process for managing referral to treatment targets or the clinical update session on using mindfulness approaches. Progressing in your career requires an element of strategic self-focus. Price and Scowcroft (2011) suggest doing five things to foster learning as a manager. These are: seeking feedback; getting a mentor; shadowing a role model; having a personal development plan; and reflective practice. All of these help you feel grounded and secure in the work you are doing.

Organisations also have more formal development opportunities. These may include a formal mentoring scheme, which is an opportunity to get regular time with a more senior manager and learn from them; it is also good networking. There are also formal routes to senior management, such as talent management programmes, and various leadership programmes, which usually comprise formal development inputs, often with national figures on key topics, an element of personal development, perhaps including psychometrics, 360 degree feedback and sessions on management style, and action learning set meetings to consolidate the learning in practice. The NHS Leadership Academy is a good source of information here. Entry to these can be competitive so doing a good-quality application, getting the right references, and building senior relationships to get support are all important. Part of development is taking on new tasks, so take care not to be so bogged down in the day-to-day of management that you do not have time to take on the strategic project that gets you noticed and builds new skills and contacts.

In some organisations, it may be necessary to choose between a more clinical leadership role and a more purely management one. If this is the case, longer-term consideration needs to be given to your career goal so as not to lose skills that will be needed if you change role.

People have different approaches to how they manage their careers. Some plan carefully and tactically, making regular moves towards the desired goal. Others have a more general sense of a valued direction and are able to spot and seize a congruent opportunity when they see one. Still others operate on the serendipity model and take different opportunities as they present themselves. For most, career needs to give space to personal interests and family life, and the balance of that can shift over time. Careers are usually most satisfying when they are consistent with an individual's values.

IN CONCLUSION

Gill (2011), in considering how leadership can be developed and how leaders are chosen, cites the importance of different assignments and experiences, the influences of other people, the learning from adverse events, and also the importance of addressing the potential derailing characteristics of the individual as much as developing the desirable ones. This chapter aimed to provoke thinking about leadership and management, the roles, qualities required, and to provide a handbook to some of the main tasks. In developing as a leader and manager, you will find your own unique way.

Visit the companion website to read Leadership and Management.

USEFUL NATIONAL WEBSITES

Department of Health, Social Services and Public Safety Northern Ireland: www.dhsspsni.gov.
uk/sqsd-guidance-nice-guidance
Health Education England: http://hee.nhs.uk/work-programmes/workforce-planning/
Information Commissioner: http://ico.org.uk/
NHS Leadership Academy: www.leadershipacademy.nhs.uk/
NHS Wales: www.wales.nhs.uk/governance-emanual/home
NHS Scotland Workforce Planning: www.knowledge.scot.nhs.uk/workforceplanning.aspx
NICE: www.nice.org.uk/
SIGN: www.sign.ac.uk/index.html

REFERENCES

Andrews, J. and Butler, M. (2014) *Trusted to Care. An Independent Review of the Princess of Wales Hospital and Neath Port Talbot Hospital at Abertawe Bro Morgannwg University Health Board.* Available at: www.wales.nhs.uk/sitesplus/863/opendoc/240096 (accessed on 23 November 2014).

ACAS (Advisory, Conciliation and Arbitration Service) (2009) *Code of Practice 1 – Disciplinary and Grievance Procedures.* Available at: www.acas.org.uk/index.aspx?articleid= 2174 (accessed on 12 October 2014).

ACAS (2014a) *Bullying and Harassment.* Available at: www.acas.org.uk/index.aspx?articleid= 1864 (accessed on 12 October 2014).

ACAS (2014b) *Bereavement in the Workplace.* Available at: www.acas.org.uk/index.aspx?articleid= 4977 (accessed on 12 October 2014).

Bamber, M.R. (2011) *Overcoming Your Workplace Stress.* Hove: Routledge.

Barr, J. and Dowding, L. (2012) *Leadership in Health Care.* London: Sage.

British Psychological Society (2008) *Generic Professional Practice Guidelines.* Leicester: BPS.

British Psychological Society (2011) *Advertising of Psychology Posts.* Leicester: BPS. Available at: www.bps.org.uk/networks-and-communities/member-networks/division-counselling-psychology/employment (accessed on 23 November 2014).

British Psychological Society (2014a) *Standards for the Accreditation of Doctoral Programmes in Counselling Psychology.* Leicester: BPS. Available at: www.bps.org.uk/careers-education-training/accredited-courses-training-programmes/useful-accreditation-documents/counselling-psychology/counsell (accessed on 18 October 2014).

British Psychological Society (2014b) *Guidance on Teaching and Assessment of Ethical Competence in Psychology Education.* Leicester: BPS.

Care Quality Commission (2014) *A Fresh Start for the Regulation and Inspection of Mental Health Services. Working Together to Change How We Regulate, Inspect, and Monitor*

Socialist Mental Health Services. London: CQC. Available at: www.cqc.org.uk/content/mental-health (accessed on 23 November 2014).

Crawley, J. and Graham, K. (2002) *Mediation for Managers: Resolving Conflict and Rebuilding Relationships at Work*. London: Nicholas Brealey.

Department of Health (2000) *An Organisation with a Memory. Report of an Expert Group on Learning from Adverse Events in the NHS*. London: The Stationery Office. Available at: http://webarchive.nationalarchives.gov.uk/20130107105354/www.dh.gov.uk/prod_consum_dh/groups/dh_digitalassets/@dh/@en/documents/digitalasset/dh_4065086.pdf (accessed on 23 November 2014).

Department of Health (2012) *Transforming Care: A National Response to Winterbourne View Hospital. Department of Health Review: Final Report*. Available at: https://www.gov.uk/government/uploads/system/uploads/attachment_data/file/213215/final-report.pdf (accessed on 12 October 2014).

Equality Act 2010. Available at: www.gov.uk/equality-act-2010-guidance (accessed on 12 October 2014).

Francis, R. (2013) *Mid Staffordshire NHS Foundation Trust Public Inquiry Chaired by Robert Francis QC*. London: The Stationery Office. Available at: www.midstaffspublicinquiry.com/sites/default/files/report/Executive%20summary.pdf (accessed on 23 November 2014).

Gill, R. (2011) *Theory and Practice of Leadership*. London: Sage.

Gopee, N. and Galloway, J. (2014) *Leadership & Management in Healthcare*. London: Sage.

Gottwald, M. and Lansdown, G.E. (2014) *Clinical Governance: Improving the Quality of Healthcare for Patients and Service Users*. Maidenhead: Open University Press.

Hawkins, P. and Shohet, R. (2006) *Supervision in the Helping Professions* (3rd edn). Maidenhead: Open University Press.

HSE (Health and Safety Executive) (2004) *Sickness Absence: Introduction to Guidance for Employers*. London: Health and Safety Executive. Available at: www.hse.gov.uk/sicknessabsence/guidancehome.htm (accessed on 23 November 2014).

HSE (2007a) *Management Standards for Work Related Stress*. London: Health and Safety Executive. Available at: www.hse.gov.uk/stress/standards/index.htm (accessed on 12 October 2014).

HSE (2007b) *Management Standards Indicator Tool*. London: Health and Safety Executive. Available from: www.hse.gov.uk/stress/standards/downloads.htm (accessed on 12 October 2014).

HSE (2014a) *The Health and Safety Toolbox: How to Control Risks at Work*. London: Health and Safety Executive. Available at: www.hse.gov.uk/legislation/hswa.htm (accessed on 23 November 2014).

HSE (2014b) *Stress-related and Psychological Disorders in Great Britain 2014*. London: Health and Safety Executive. Available at: www.hse.gov.uk/statistics/causdis/stress/index.htm (accessed on 12 October 2014).

Information Commissioner (2014a). *Guide to Data Protection*. Available at: http://ico.org.uk/for_organisations/data_protection (accessed on 12 October 2014).

Information Commissioner (2014b) *Freedom of Information Act*. Available at: http://ico.org. uk/for_organisations/freedom_of_information (accessed on 12 October 2014).

National Advisory Group on the Safety of Patients in England (2013) *A Promise to Learn: A Commitment to Act. Improving the Safety of Patients in England*. London: Department of Health.

Neenan, M. (2009) *Developing Resilience: A Cognitive-Behavioural Approach*. Hove: Routledge.

NHS Employers (2014) *What Is Values Based Recruitment?* Available at: www.nhsemployers. org/your-workforce/recruit/employer-led-recruitment/recruiting-for-values/what-is-values-based-recruitment (accessed on 12 October 2014).

NHS England (2013) *Introduction to the Friends and Family Test*. Available at: www.england. nhs.uk/ourwork/pe/fft/ (accessed on 12 October 2014).

Price, A. and Scowcroft, A. (2011) *Essential Skills for Managing in Healthcare*. Oxford: Radcliffe Publishing.

Schedlitzki, D. and Edwards, G. (2014) *Studying Leadership: Traditional and Critical Approaches*. London: Sage.

Scrivener, R., National Institute for Clinical Excellence, Royal College of Nursing, and University of Leicester (2002) *Principles for Best Practice in Clinical Audit*. Abingdon: Radcliffe Medical Press.

Sullivan, E.J. and Garland, G. (2013) *Practical Leadership and Management in Healthcare for Nurses and Allied Health Professionals*. Harlow: Pearson.

West, M.A. (2012) *Effective Teamwork: Practical Lessons from Organizational Research*. Chichester: BPS Blackwell.

Unite the Union (2013) *Good Appraisals*. London: Unite.

35
BECOMING A SUPERVISOR
RAY WOOLFE

INTRODUCTION

This chapter is concerned with becoming a supervisor. This involves the development of a certain skill set but it also involves a process which is common to both supervisor and supervisee. To that extent, much of what is said here also applies to the discussion in Chapter 7 about becoming a supervisee. One might say that the same phenomenon can be examined through two different lenses. For example, both parties will have much to say about the importance of establishing a working relationship, but they will be examining the subject from different vantage points.

The chapter does not attempt to offer a list of the 'how to do it' variety. The emphasis will be on highlighting some of the key issues and dilemmas you might face and offering a framework for thinking about them. These include such items as whether there is a difference between supervision with trainees and more experienced practitioners; whether there must be a direct match between the theoretical model employed by the supervisee and the supervisor; and the thorny issue of supervision within complex organisations. Of course, psychologists are involved in supervising research as well as clinical practice, but the focus of this chapter is on the latter. I hope that the chapter will hold much that is of value not just for new supervisors but also for people more experienced in this role.

It is as well to remember that until relatively recently the mark of a qualified psychologist was seen as the ability to practise without supervision. This position is still widely held in many states within the USA. Conversely, one of the characteristics of counselling psychology in this country has been its historic commitment to supervision throughout a career. While this view is now generally supported within psychology, including clinical psychology, it remains a subject of debate in newer fields such as coaching psychology. The traditional use of the term 'independent practitioner' to describe the qualified psychologist rather lends itself to ambiguity. Hence it is worthwhile spending a moment or two thinking about why supervision is regarded as a mandatory requirement in counselling psychology. To do so allows us to emphasise that which is obvious but can easily be overlooked, namely the immensely private and interpersonal nature of the therapeutic relationship. Supervision offers a framework both for self-care and the care of the client and supervisee who operates in a situation that is emotionally complex and has the potential for isolation and abuse. Supervision offers a sounding board which protects and assists all parties and stakeholders.

WHAT IS SUPERVISION?

Guidelines laid down by the British Psychological Society Division of Counselling Psychology (BPS, DCoP, 2006) define supervision as an activity, a process, a relationship and a practice:

- An activity that involves a practitioner discussing their work with a professional colleague so that it can be reflected upon. The space should be clearly bounded and conducted in an ethical manner that extends support to all parties. It is distinct from therapy and line-management.
- A process described as one of 'ongoing, collaborative, experiential and transformative learning' (2006: 4). It uses evidence from both research and practice.
- A relationship described as one of 'mutual trust, respect and integrity which models best practice and sensitivity to the learning needs of the supervisee' (2006: 4).
- A practice based upon 'shared and explicit models of supervision' (2006: 4) bounded by a mutually negotiated contract defining roles and responsibilities and the limits of confidentiality.

More generally, the *Guidelines* identify the aim of supervision as being to promote best practice in the interests of the client. The focus on the client is emphasised as it is in the more behavioural list of objectives which is provided. However, this potentially neglects the fact that the interests of the client are best served by also taking account of the personal and professional development of the supervisee. Lane and Corrie (2006: 19) adopt this more universal view when they summarise the benefits of supervision as 'offering protection to clients, allowing practitioners a reflective space in which to identify their strengths and weaknesses, to facilitate learning from peers and to keep up to date with professional developments'.

These aims have come to be codified in the literature as functions of supervision. Kadushin (1968, 1992) refers to these as 'educative, supportive and managerial'. Proctor (1986), in a much-used formulation, refers to 'formative, restorative and normative functions'. While the former model focuses on the role of the supervisor the latter places emphasis on the benefit to the supervisee.

TYPES OF SUPERVISION

Given that we can define the functions of supervision in this manner, we can then examine the balance of these functions according to types of supervision. In what is arguably the most influential British text on supervision, Hawkins and Shohet (2012) identify four main categories: tutorial, training, managerial and consultancy. I propose to use these categories in this chapter and to unpack these terms systematically as they speak directly to the different circumstances in which supervisors find themselves, and they open up a range of issues for discussion.

The majority of trainees qualify via the accredited course route. However, it is important to note there also exists the independent route towards qualification. This involves each trainee having a Co-ordinating Supervisor, formally known as Co-ordinator of Training. The role incorporates aspects of each type of supervision, including general training, clinical development, quality control and monitoring progress. The role therefore demands the flexibility to perform a variety of functions and to be able to switch between them, as appropriate.

Common to each of the categories, however, is the requirement to create a learning environment and to monitor ethical and professional issues. Carroll and Shaw (2012) emphasise the need for ethical practice to come from within the individual acting from a mature understanding rather than from a reliance on external codes of ethics or regulatory guidelines. They elaborate this position in Chapter 15 of this book.

Training supervision

This situation is characteristically found in a context where there is a relationship between the educational/training organisation and the placement agency. The former is frequently a university department. Here the placement agency and the university agree a contract for the former to offer a placement and to supervise the work appropriately. The supervisor works within this framework. An alternative model is found when the university has a direct contract with a self-employed psychologist. Many counselling psychologists work in this self-employed manner and this situation is thus quite common.

Izzard (2003) offers some observations about the need for a clear contract between supervisor and university. Universities traditionally evaluate students on the basis of written, academic work but this becomes problematic when clinical competence becomes an additional component. This dilemma is illustrated in case study 1.

Case study 1

The supervisor has concerns about his supervisee, Gideon, who is a trainee on a postgraduate course in counselling psychology. His academic work is good but in his clinical work he is highly directive, tends to foist his own perceptions upon clients and generally displays difficulty in being empathic. The supervisor is of the opinion that his future as a clinician is problematic. However, after reporting back to the university, the supervisor was contacted

(Continued)

(Continued)

by the course leader and informed that the trainee had passed all his academic work and it would be difficult to fail him on the basis of a supervision report alone. After some discussion the supervisor is asked to modify the report.

Exercise

What would you do in this situation?

The case exposes a number of underlying issues about the nature of the contract between the university department and the placement agency. If you are involved in this type of supervision, it is important to ensure that your contract with the university is up to date and adequate?

In this setting, the supervisee might be described as in an apprenticeship role, with an emphasis in supervision on the educative function. The supervisor has the ultimate responsibility for ensuring that the clinical work is of an adequate quality. At this stage of their development, particularly if they are still at an early point in their course, supervisees may be uncertain, lack confidence, be afraid of making mistakes and sensitive about acknowledging difficulties within supervision. In addition, the trainee's own emotional issues may be activated by the nature of the clinical work, with a temptation to cross the boundary between therapy and supervision. One might describe the role of the supervisor at this point as being engaged in a holding situation.

Consultancy supervision

This situation occurs when supervision takes place between qualified professionals without a third party being involved. The ultimate responsibility for client work remains with the supervisee. This type of relationship will be familiar to many readers of this chapter as it represents the reality of supervision for the independent practitioner. It is also found in NHS settings where non-managerial supervision is available from a colleague. The term 'consultant' is indicative of equality within the relationship, although in practice one party may have a lot more experience than the other.

Tutorial supervision

This situation would take place within the university or training agency and involves a course tutor helping trainees to link their practice in the placement setting with the academic theoretical aspects of the course. Control of the quality of the client's casework would remain, however, with the training supervisor. In the case of the trainee on the independent route, the equivalent of the course tutor would be the Co-ordinating Supervisor.

Managerial supervision

Here the supervisor is also the supervisee's line manager and has the ultimate responsibility for the clinical work of the supervisee. There is strong encouragement within counselling psychology for the two roles to be separated and for the consultancy supervisor to be a different person. Unfortunately reductions in staffing across both the public and private sectors result in this practice becoming increasingly common, not least in the NHS. The most basic difficulty with this form of supervision is the danger that the emphasis shifts away from the needs of the supervisee or the latter's clients towards protecting the interests of the organisation.

Gale and Alilovic (2008: 62) refer to the need in this situation for careful contracting and maintenance of transparency. They point out that while the BPS distinguishes between line management and supervision, there is limited discussion of the 'interface' between the two. They suggest that the supervision function that creates the most complexity is that of clinical governance, which means that the activity should be monitored so as to serve the best interests of the wider public. They suggest the need for 'unbundling' those aspects of supervision that might legitimately be seen as residing within the management domain and those that might be more appropriately dealt with outside this frame.

Managerial supervision takes place within an organisational context and raises a whole series of complexities in which an understanding of the culture and ethos of the particular organisation is important. Towler (2008: 38) refers to the organisation as 'the invisible client'. He talks about supervisors and supervisees needing to 'wrestle with organizational boundaries' (p. 39). Gonzalez-Doupez (2008: 50–51) explores the issues that arise in organisations concerned with crisis management, such as the police, fire service, prisons and hospices. She points to what she describes as 'tension points' between supervision work and crisis work. For example, supervision emphasises 'taking time' and reflection, while crisis work emphasises 'reducing time' and responding. Copeland (2000) refers to the need for supervisors to work with and not against the organisation. She refers to issues around dilemmas concerning responsibilities, confidentiality, boundaries, contracts and ethical practice. These issues can be particularly acute in cases involving Employee Assistance Programmes (EAPs), where there are likely to be multiple stakeholders, including the supervisee, the supervisee's client, the client's company and the agency acting for the company in providing supervision. In practice, there may be an inherent conflict between counselling agencies which tend to have a learning and development culture and an organisation or department within an organisation which may have much more of a bureaucratic culture, emphasising financial prudence, competition or even creating a culture of insecurity as a motivator. Hawkins and Shohet (2012) refer to the need for organisations to develop a learning culture.

MULTIPLE SUPERVISORS

An issue faced by supervisors is when one is confronted with a situation in which the supervisee may have or want to have an additional supervisor. The dilemmas this poses can be discussed under each type of supervision.

Consultancy supervision

In the case of *consultancy supervision*, I have experienced the case of supervisees who ask me how I would feel if they had a different supervisor for when they worked in a particular theoretical model. It is possible to take a rather purist view in this situation and reject the idea outright, referring to the possibility of splitting, in which one supervisor becomes the goody while the other becomes the baddy. I would err in this direction if the individual is seeking supervision from me for the first time. In the case that the supervisee and myself were already involved in a relationship, I would want to talk carefully with the supervisee about what was behind the request. In the process, I would take into account my own competence to supervise the specific model in question for which outsourcing is being requested.

Managerial supervision

Managerial supervision can take many forms but essentially involves the supervisor in having line management responsibilities for the supervisee. On the face of it, it is difficult to envisage how confidentiality can be guaranteed when the emphasis is on case management in the interests of the organisation. Some supervisees in this position might seek to draw their own line within the relationship and seek to contract with another supervisor for a more consultancy-type relationship. On the other side of the coin, a lot depends on the manager. One would hope that a counselling psychologist would be sensitive to these issues. Of course any situation involving two supervisors will involve the potential for splitting and perhaps more than most in this case.

Tutorial supervision

The nature of *tutorial supervision* is that two supervisors do exist and, given that the supervision is being received by a trainee, it seems critical that there should be a clear boundary between the two supervisors.

Training supervision

Training supervision may well involve the individual having more than one supervisor at any given time if the trainee has a placement with more than one organisation. The issue of splitting will always exist but perhaps is more easily manageable if the two agencies work with very different client issues or different types of client. Perhaps it is also worthwhile at this point saying that it is desirable for a supervisee in training to have the experience of working with more than one supervisor, though not ideally at the same period of time.

THE NATURE OF THE RELATIONSHIP

The nature of the relationship varies with context but it can be argued that overall supervision is inherently hierarchical and contains within it the seeds of what Cornforth and Claiborne (2008: 156) refer to as 'the contradiction between hierarchical expertise and collaborative reciprocity'. One would expect all therapists and supervisors as an ethical priority to exercise power in the best interests of the client. Clients frequently project authority onto the psychologist and the issue concerns not so much whether power exists but how it is exercised. This can generate dilemmas, as we saw in case study 1, which involved a conflict of loyalty between the supervisor's contract with the training organisation and a commitment to the welfare and professional development of the supervisee. What this also illustrates is the complexity of the supervisory role in which the individual is not just involved in a one-to-one relationship, but can be at the centre of a nexus consisting of at least three parties. Other examples of three or more stakeholders may include situations in which the supervisor has to report to a work organisation or to a solicitor or to an insurance company or to a court.

The term 'supervision' seems particularly apt in situations of managerial supervision in which the supervisor has line management responsibilities in relation to the client. This might even extend to involvement in carrying out formal appraisal processes with and about the supervisee. There is vast potential here for role conflict and it would be difficult to deny that one had a great deal of authority. This power imbalance is highlighted in a qualitative study carried out by Kaberry (2000). She quotes one case in which the supervisor, who was the manager, also offered counselling and invitations to socialise. The supervisee was also invited to assist the supervisor as a trainer in workshops run by the organisation (Kaberry, 2000: 45). Kaberry concludes that blurring of boundaries regularly characterised cases in which power was abused.

Of course there is an issue here about choice. If working in private practice, the new supervisor has a choice about which potential supervisee to accept. This is an important decision and experience suggests that one is advised to explore carefully with the applicant why he or she has chosen yourself and what expectations are held. However, an interesting situation arises if the new supervisor is working in an organisation and is instructed to supervise a particular person, i.e. not given a choice. It does happen and can place the individual in a difficult place.

Whether working privately or in an organisation, there is a possibility of being asked to supervise people perhaps with equal or even more therapeutic experience than one possesses oneself, and in this situation terms like consultancy or collegiate support can feel more comfortable. But whatever the nomenclature, the type and characteristics of supervision required by the supervisee might be heavily dependent upon the latter's experience and level of competence. A useful way of thinking about this subject may be to perceive supervision as a continuum ranging from a more closed didactic model to a more open collegiate approach.

While the latter has a more comfortable feel about it, which resonates with the philosophy of counselling psychology, we should perhaps be careful about perceiving it as more than an ideal. The structural examples above illustrate why this is not always simple or possible. In addition, the content of supervision may demand a different approach, even involving taking control of a situation as in the vignette below.

Vignette 1

David, an inexperienced supervisee of mine, contacted me in a state of agitation about a client with whom he had just started to work. It transpired that the client had a high risk of suicide but that David had not carried out a risk assessment, did not know what medication if any the client was taking or the name of the client's GP. I saw my role in this situation as to tell the supervisee what he needed to do, which was to seek the client's approval to contact the GP and to ensure that the contract he had with the client was amended to allow unilateral action should he feel this was necessary. I was certainly being didactic, but my view as supervisor was that the situation demanded a directive approach for everyone's protection, including my own.

DEVELOPMENTAL ISSUES

It is helpful to think about the needs of supervisees by adopting a developmental framework; that is to say adapting supervisory skills to suit the stage of professional development reached by the supervisee. Thomas (1997: 63) talks about the developmental process involved in the trainee supervisor clinical dyad as 'a meaningful reflection of the trainee–patient therapeutic relationship'.

One of the questions faced by beginning supervisors relates to the difference between supervision with qualified practitioners and trainees. Of course the term 'qualified practitioner' itself refers to a continuum from newly qualified to vastly experienced persons.

On the whole, one would expect a very experienced practitioner to select a well-experienced supervisor but this is not always the case, particularly if the selection of a supervisor is imposed on the individual by an organisation. However, the assumption is that stages of development are characterised by growing levels of competence (see Holloway, 1987; Stoltenberg et al., 1998).

Case study 2

Theresa was a counselling psychologist with about five years post-qualifying experience. She had qualified via a well-regarded university course. The supervisor's initial experience of her was as a pleasant, intelligent woman open to sharing her work. She told the supervisor that she wanted to be challenged.

However, as the work progressed it appeared that Theresa's pleasantness was being used as a defence with clients with whom she found it difficult to be anything other than nice. The effect was that her work lacked edge and when the supervisor challenged her about this, in accordance with her request, her response was to take notes and agree with the supervisor's understanding, yet nothing changed. The supervisor became more and more frustrated and Theresa became withdrawn.

The problem was taken by the supervisor to her own supervisor, who commented that perhaps Theresa needed to idealise the supervisor, and that this lay behind her niceness towards clients in her need for clients to like and admire her.

It then became possible for this to be talked about with Theresa and for her to acknowledge a more shadow, repressed side of her personality, and gradually to become more confident and assertive in her work with clients.

Eventually she was able to share with the supervisor a number of transference issues, issues that affected how she used supervision, and she acknowledged the need to address these issues in therapy or some other form of personal development activity.

Exercise

Have you ever been in a similar position where the initial presentation of self by the supervisee turned out in practice to be misleading? If so, how did you manage this situation?

This case study demonstrates that all is not necessarily as it first seems. As the supervisee gains experience, the emphasis of the work may change. Initially there may be a focus on micro skills, with questions such as 'what do we really mean by congruence?', or a request for a standard method for responding to a particular client issue, such as an eating disorder. There may also be an unconscious exploration of the relationship. In the initial stages, the trainee, according to Webb (2000), has to learn how to become a trainee. It follows that, in this aspect, the task of the supervisor in this endeavour is essentially that of teacher. Experience suggests that like any learner in the early stages of development the supervisee can feel highly dependent and insecure and require a lot of emotional holding and support, which hopefully will diminish with greater experience. Brightman (1984) suggests that within the psychodynamic tradition, training supervision is best understood as a holding environment during a time of narcissistic vulnerability when the supervisee's self-esteem may be very low.

As the supervisee gains experience, the flavour of the work is likely to change. There may be less anxiety about performing and a greater grasp of self and its impact on the client. There may be a greater ability to tolerate challenge. The supervisor may be more able to use ideas relating to parallel process. This refers to the idea that the supervisee is understood to be unconsciously playing out with the supervisor the relationship as experienced with the client. Thus what the supervisee experiences with the client is paralleled by what the supervisor herself or himself is experiencing in the present with the supervisee. An 'unconscious communication' has taken place. This term is now widely used in talking about the practice of supervision (see Mattinson, 1977; Morrisey and Tribe, 2001). In a slightly different vein, Casement (1985) uses the term 'internal supervisor' to refer to the supervisee's capacity to reflect within the session on the meaning of the client's communication to the therapist.

Gradually, there may be a shift in the nature of the relationship from dependency to idealisation before a more mature collegiate relationship begins to emerge in which expressions of disagreement or disappointment can be articulated. At this point the term 'consultancy' can begin to feel appropriate.

While the notion of development is a useful one, I think that we need to take the idea of stages with a pinch of salt. Individual supervisees will progress at their own pace and there can be periods of regression associated with the supervisee's life outside supervision or with issues that arise within casework that have particular resonance for the supervisee. Taken as a guide, the idea of stages can be helpful but as Carroll (1996: 16) points out in his research on the literature, 'there is no evidence to suggest that the stages outlined … [in the literature] … are fixed or sequential'.

FORMATS FOR SUPERVISION

As a beginning supervisor you are most likely to be involved in one-to-one situations, but other possibilities exist in the form of facilitated groups and peer supervision either in pairs or groups. Each of these formats presents its own challenges. While the one-to-one situation mirrors the structure of individual therapy and thus makes possible insights such as parallel process, the other formats also have their advantages. The group format, for example, allows for the presence of additional feedback perspectives, offers a more democratic environment and a reduction in supervisory power, and lessens the risk of a dependent or collusive relationship.

Facilitated group supervision has the benefit of being economical and is thus popular in many organisations, particularly smaller ones. Proctor (2008) suggests that there are three broad types of group-facilitated supervision. In the first, the supervisor supervises each member of the group as if in individual supervision. The role of the other group members is confined, unless invited to comment, to observation and listening. She describes this model as authoritarian. In a second model, which she describes as participative, all group members are encouraged to participate. She also describes a third pattern termed 'consultative', in which the supervisor mentors participants in supervising each other. This is more equivalent to a group-analysis process.

While there are benefits to group supervision, there are also disadvantages. There is less time for each individual member to bring case material. In addition, the group dynamic has to be skilfully handled in order to avoid individuals feeling lost, overwhelmed or scapegoated. In addition, there is potential for envy and competition.

Issues about collegiality also arise in peer and peer-group supervision. In particular, in these contexts the question of insecure boundaries and confidentiality rise to the surface. There are issues about unequal time and distribution of responsibilities.

Social intercourse can take over sessions and intrude into the work if there are not clear boundaries about informal contacts between sessions. An experienced counselling psychologist might be able to avail themself of a combination of these approaches. For example, we might envisage an individual who works in a primary care setting for two days a week and receives fortnightly supervision for this work from a senior psychologist also working in that organisation. However, the person also has a private practice working with EAP clients and for this work individual supervision is purchased from another psychologist. Finally, the person himself or herself offers supervision to a group in a counselling agency for which they attend a monthly supervision of supervision peer consultancy group.

These ways of working do not exhaust the possibilities for supervision. Cummings (2002) describes an example of text-based computer-mediated communication in counsellor supervision. In some circumstances, most likely in systemic family therapy, there may be opportunities for supervision based upon live observation of clients via a one-way mirror. Of increasing significance is Skype, which has significant advantages where geographical distance is a major issue. However, it also offers the possibility of remote live supervision where a supervisor is able to observe a live therapy session and to give feedback in real time. The supervisor is directly able to observe non-verbal and emotional communication. The possible implications of the use of Skype or other forms of remote communication with supervisees and clients do need some careful thought. Hence guidelines are being introduced by various professional bodies, for example see Scotland's Professional Body for Counselling and Psychotherapy guidelines: www.cosca.org.uk/docs/COSCA%20Guideline%20on%20the%20 use%20of%20technologies06-25-15.pdf.

THE QUESTION OF THEORETICAL MODEL

In the early days of psychoanalysis the boundary between roles of therapist and supervisor was less than clear. The trainee's analyst was regarded as the supervisor of the trainee's clinical work. Seen through the prism of contemporary insights, this position can be seen to clash with the ethical dislike of dual relationships. However, with the passage of time, supervision came to be seen as an important subject in its own right and as it developed the psychodynamic approach to practice began to be explicitly mirrored in its approach to supervision. In other words the process of supervision began to match the form of the therapeutic process. So, for example, the emphasis on a framework characterised by transference, countertransference and projective identification has come to be seen as reflected in the supervision, hence the term 'parallel process'.

The schools of counselling and therapy which developed in the USA from the 1950s onwards approached the challenges of supervision from a similar vantage point. This includes both humanistic and cognitive-behavioural traditions. Carroll (1996: 26) explains the logic of this philosophy as follows: 'digging out the often implicit "educational theory" underlying a particular counselling model reveals its understanding of the learning process. This process is then related to supervisees.' Thus, in the humanistic model, learning is seen to take place when the Rogerian core conditions are experienced in the relationship. Formal teaching becomes secondary to the learning relationship. The same model is applied in supervision. Similarly in the cognitive-behavioural tradition, learning is seen to take place through a more formalised teaching relationship which is then applied in supervision. The same practice is also prominent in contemporary approaches. For example, Woskett (2006) employs the term 'treasure hunting' in the context of solution focused therapy to describe the manner in which the supervisor engages in the same process as the therapist, whose task is to search for the client's strengths rather than deficiencies.

This perspective on matching has the benefit of offering congruence between the two types of practice and might be particularly relevant to the supervisee who is still in earlier stages of training and still trying to get to grips with a particular model. There is a danger of the trainee becoming confused if the supervisor operates within a different framework. Both parties are reading from the same script and it facilitates the development of competence in the model in question. However, there are also disadvantages. A critique of this approach concerns its narrowness and its inability to envisage and benefit from the cross-fertilisation of ideas. Thus person-centred practice tends, in the words of Carroll (1996: 26), 'to relegate formal teaching to the side lines', while the cognitive-behavioural tradition neglects emotional and unconscious learning processes, and for its part the psychodynamic tradition ignores the value of skills training.

Common to all these examples of congruence between therapeutic model and approach to supervision is a focus on the supervisor as essentially a teacher, with a corresponding neglect of educational method concerning how trainees learn. As a response to this there has been a development of supervision-specific models of practice, in which supervisors are seen as facilitators with supervision-specific skills, and a commensurate shift in focus from teaching (an apprenticeship model) to how supervisees learn. Carroll emphasises the need for supervisors to become competent educators. In the process, he develops Kolb's well-known model of the experiential learning cycle through the use of the term 'transformational learning' (Carroll, 2008; Kolb, 1984).

Supervision-specific models engage with this question though a variety of approaches. Among the best known are those that direct attention to the level of development of the supervisee (Holloway, 1987; Stoltenberg et al., 1998); those that point to systems (Holloway, 1995); those that elaborate the process in detail (Hawkins and Shohet, 2012); and some that use the idea of cyclical stages (Page and Wosket, 1994).

So where does this discussion place the new supervisor? I think a lot depends here upon the stage of learning reached by the supervisee in the context of their training programme and whether it is based upon a core theoretical model. However, the nature of training in counselling psychology is essentially integrative in that the trainee must develop skills and competence in more than one model and working with different client groups. This suggests the need for a more broadly based educational view of supervision and the need for the supervisor to have the competence to move beyond strict model boundaries. This seems most likely to assist the trainee towards integration.

There may well be situational imperatives pushing in this direction, with a requirement for pragmatism in many situations in which supervisors now find themselves. For example, the advent of multi-disciplinary teams within the NHS means that the counselling psychologist will be confronted both as supervisor and supervisee with professionals from other disciplines and possibly working from different codes of ethics. The use of new approaches, such as acceptance and commitment therapy (ACT), eye movement desensitisation and reprocessing (EMDR) and solution focused therapy, can on occasions make it difficult to find people operating from within the same model. Each individual has preferred ways of working and in the case of supervisor and supervisee these may not always coincide. I can think of a number of newly qualified supervisees who selected me to offer supervision on the basis that my preferred model was psychodynamic and that they wished to develop their skills in this way of working. In practice, what occasionally happened in some cases was that they found it difficult to let go of more familiar ways of thinking and this created tension in the relationship. It emphasises yet again the need for clarity in the contract about what the supervisee requires, what the supervisor is able or willing to offer and the challenges this might pose.

CONFLICTS AND TENSIONS

I have sought in this chapter to sensitise new supervisors to some of the issues and dilemmas that exist within the practice. I would now like to take this discussion further by asking whether the view of supervision as an arena in which the needs of all parties can be met without friction is perhaps a little simplistic. Davy (2002: 30) refers to supervision as 'a contested locus in which several potential opposing beliefs and interests are at play'. We have seen, for example, that the goal of ensuring the client's best interests and well-being remains a primary concern. However, in the case of the new trainee the supervisor must expect and indeed allow the learner to make mistakes. All well and good, but what if this places the organisation in a difficult position?

In some contexts supervisors and supervision formats are assigned rather than chosen. This may result in personality clashes that interfere with the work and the supervisee's learning as the latter may feel neither safe nor supported. Supervision opens up the possibility of shame and humiliation for the supervisee as their work is exposed to the gaze of another person. This may have been reflected in a qualitative piece of research carried out by Valence (2004) of counsellor perceptions and experiences in supervision. She found that there was 'counsellor censorship of clients and the total absence of some clients in supervision' (Valence, 2004: 571). Milton (2008) refers to his own less positive experiences of supervision. He talks about envious attacks from one supervisor and being bored by another. Stafford (2008: 39) refers to 'working with seven different supervisors, I encountered negative power imbalances, untold difficulties with family transferences, plus corollary gender issues about working with men'. Henderson (2008) suggests that perhaps there are gender differences in the way in which male and female supervisors think about supervision and the way in which cross-gender relationships influence the process.

Peyton (2004) offers a number of examples of bullying within supervision. These included downright sarcasm as well as telling a supervisee that he would just have to get used to the way she worked even if he found it difficult. She makes the point that the essential characteristic of bullying is not the intention of the supervisor but the impact on the supervisee. In case study 2 in this chapter, the supervisor was concerned that attempts to challenge Theresa ran the risk of her beginning to feel threatened, even though she always denied that this was the case. More prosaically, Karter (2002: 86), describing his own training, says that 'what I and some of my fellow students found difficult was to retain one's individuality and thought processes in the face of intense pressure to go along with the supervisor's approach as the only way'.

Bullying is a form of abuse and Kaberry (2000: 55–57) developed a typology of abuse within supervision based upon her research. This consisted of the following profile. I have selected just a few of the abusive practices identified in her research.

- The context … where there is no choice of supervisor and no mechanism for considering possible difficulties faced by the supervisee in previous supervisions … where there is no consideration of other networks in which the two might be involved.
- Attitude … lack of respect as exemplified in over-familiarity … devaluing of previous experience … or personal criticism such as having time off to have a baby.
- Gratification of supervisor's needs … defensiveness if unresolved personal issues arise … needing to be admired … wanting friendship.
- Lack of awareness … of what constitutes persecutory behaviour … lack of understanding of group dynamics or parallel process.
- The role of the supervisee … even gentle criticism can be perceived as persecutory anxiety.
- Kaberry concludes by stating that it is the responsibility of the supervisor not to abuse the power vested in the role.

Pilgrim (1997) refers to supervision as a form of 'surveillance' and Davy (2002) points out that the emphasis on dyadic and triadic interactions has diverted attention away from or ignored the socio-cultural, political and organisational contexts in which these interactions take place. In a similar fashion, Goldstein (2008) suggests that the requirements for supervision are driven as much by political as professional considerations.

CONCLUDING COMMENT

Spinelli (1994) suggests that the therapy profession has a propensity to create escalating in-house demands for its own services. This is reflected in the growing requirement for supervision of supervision, an issue raised by Wheeler and King (2000). In the final resort, the question is does supervision work? Davy (2002: 21) offers a view on this question in a neat turn of phrase when he says that 'there is curiously little evidence, but much emotional rhetoric supporting the value of supervision'. The most rigorous British research on this subject commissioned by the British Association for Counselling and Psychotherapy (BACP) is that of Wheeler and Richards (2007). They conclude that supervision 'does seem to offer opportunities for supervisees to improve practice and gain in confidence and raises the likelihood that client outcome is improved as an indirect result of supervision. However, the link to improved outcome is tentative' (Wheeler and Richards, 2007: 35).

The evidence is still waiting to be gathered. In a study of counsellor perceptions of the impact of supervision on clients, Valence (2004) found examples of impacts that were both helpful and unhelpful. West (2003) notes that when supervisees are asked about their experience of supervision, a third describe it as excellent, another third as good enough, while the remaining third describe it as problematic. These doubts and uncertainties point to the necessity for supervisors to commit to evaluating their work and to engage so far as is possible in evidence-based practice. The challenge for the beginning supervisor is to be both a scientist and a reflective practitioner; perhaps exactly the same challenge that faces the counselling psychologist engaging in the practice of therapy.

Visit the companion website to watch a conversation on Supervision.

REFERENCES

Brightman, B. (1984) 'Narcissistic issues in the training experience of the psychotherapist'. *International Journal of Psychoanalytic Psychotherapy*, 10: 293–317.

BPS, DCoP (British Psychological Society, Division of Counselling Psychology). (2006) *Guidelines for Supervision*. Leicester: BPS, Division of Counselling Psychology.

Carroll, M. (1996) *Counselling Supervision: Theory, skills and practice*. London: Cassell.

Carroll, M. (2008) 'Supervision, creativity and transformational learning'. *Occasional Papers in Supervision*. Leicester: British Psychological Society.

Carroll, M. and Shaw, E. (2012) *Ethical Maturity in the Helping Professions: Making difficult life and work decisions*. Melbourne: PsychOz Publications.

Casement, P. (1985) *On Learning from the Patient*. London: Tavistock.

Copeland, S. (2000) 'New challenges for supervision in organisational contexts', in B. Lawton and C. Feltham (eds), *Taking Supervision Forward: Enquiries and trends in counselling and psychotherapy*. London: Sage.

Cornforth, S. and Claiborne, L.B. (2008) 'When educational supervision meets clinical supervision; what can we learn from the discrepancies?'. *British Journal of Guidance and Counselling*, 36(2): 155–163.

Cummings, P. (2002) 'Cybervision: Virtual peer group counselling supervision – hindrance or help'. *Counselling and Psychotherapy Research*, 2(4): 223–229.

Davy, J. (2002) 'Discursive reflections on a research agenda for clinical supervision'. *Psychology and Psychotherapy, Theory, Research and Practice*, 75: 221–238.

Gale, N. and Alilovic, K. (2008) 'Relationships between supervision and management: Challenges and rewards in practice'. *Occasional Papers in Supervision*. Leicester: British Psychological Society.

Goldstein, R. (2008) 'Supervision: Who needs it and for what purposes?' [Occasional papers on supervision]. *Counselling Psychology Review*, 23: 3–12.

Gonzalez-Doupez, P. (2008) 'Group supervision in crisis management organisations'. *Occasional Papers in Supervision*. Leicester: British Psychological Society.

Hawkins, P. and Shohet, R. (2012) *Supervision in the Helping Professions* (4th edn). Buckingham: Open University Press.

Henderson, P. (2008) 'Untitled article'. *Therapy*, 19(9): 40.

Holloway, E.L. (1987) 'Developmental models of supervision: Is it development?' *Professional Psychology*, 18(3): 189–208.

Holloway, E.L. (1995) *Clinical Supervision: A systems approach*. Thousand Oaks, CA: Sage.

Izzard, S. (2003) 'Who is holding the baby?' *Counselling and Psychotherapy Journal*, 14(5): 38–39.

Kaberry, S. (2000) 'Abuse in supervision', in B. Lawton and C. Feltham (eds), *Taking Supervision Forward: Enquiries and trends in counselling and psychotherapy*. London: Sage.

Kadushin, A. (1968) 'Games people play in supervision'. *Social Work*, 13(July): 23–32.

Kadushin, A. (1992) *Supervision in Social Work* (3rd edn). New York: Columbia University Press.

Karter, J. (2002) *On Training to be a Therapist*. Buckingham: Open University Press.

Kolb, D.A. (1984) *Experiential Learning*. Englewood Cliffs, NJ: Prentice-Hall.

Lane, D. and Corrie, S. (2006) 'Counselling psychology: Its influence and future'. *Counselling Psychology Review*, 21(1): 12–24.

Mattinson, J. (1977) *The Reflection Process in Casework Supervision London: Institute of Marital Studies*. London: Tavistock Institute of Human Relations.

Milton, M. (2008) 'Expectations of supervision? Everything to everyone … or nothing to no one?' *Occasional Papers in Supervision*. Leicester: British Psychological Society.

Morrisey, J. and Tribe, R. (2001) 'Parallel process in supervision'. *Counselling Psychology Quarterly*, 14: 103–110.

Page, S. and Wosket, V. (1994) *Supervising the Counsellor: A systems approach*. London: Routledge.

Peyton, P.R. (2004) 'Bullying in supervision'. *Counselling and Psychotherapy Journal*, 15(6): 36–37.

Pilgrim, D. (1997) *Psychotherapy and Society*. London: Sage.

Proctor, B. (1986) 'Supervision: A co-operative exercise in accountability', in M. Marken and M. Payne (eds), *Enabling and Ensuring: Supervision in practice*. Leicester: National Youth Bureau.

Proctor, B. (2008) *Group Supervision: A guide to creative practice* (2nd edn). London: Sage.

Spinelli, E. (1994) *Demystifying Therapy*. London: Constable.

Stafford, D. (2008) 'Supervision: The grown-up relationship'. *Therapy*, 19(9): 38–39.

Stoltenberg, C., McNeill, B. and Delworth, U. (1998) *IDM Supervision: An integrated developmental model for supervising counsellors and therapists*. San Francisco, CA: Jossey-Bass.

Thomas, S. (1997) 'Supervision as a maturational process'. *Psychodynamic Counselling*, 3(1): 63–76.

Towler, J. (2008) 'The influence of the invisible client: A crucial perspective for understanding counselling supervision in organisational contexts'. *Occasional Papers in Supervision*. Leicester: British Psychological Society.

Valance, K. (2004) 'Exploring counsellor perceptions of the impact of counselling supervision on clients'. *British Journal of Guidance and Counselling*, 32(4): 559–574.

Webb, A. (2000) 'What makes it difficult for the supervisor to speak', in B. Lawton and C. Feltham (eds), *Taking Supervision Forward*. London: Sage.

West, W. (2003) 'The culture of psychotherapy supervision'. *Counselling and Psychotherapy Research*, 3(2): 123–127.

Wheeler, S. and King, D. (2000) 'Do counselling supervisors want or need to have their supervision supervised? An exploratory study'. *British Journal of Guidance and Counselling*, 28(2): 279–290.

Wheeler, S. and Richards, K. (2007) *The Impact of Clinical Supervision on Counsellors and Therapists, their Practice and their Clients: A systemic review of the literature*. Lutterworth: British Association for Counselling and Psychotherapy.

Woskett, C. (2006) 'The SF Journey: Solution focussed supervision is like being a taxi driver'. *Journal of the Faculty of Healthcare Counselling and Psychotherapy*, 6(1): 9–11.

36
BECOMING A TRAINER
STELIOS GKOUSKOS

INTRODUCTION

Once qualified, almost all counselling psychologists will take on the role of trainer at some point in their professional careers. Depending on their work context they may offer training to a variety of audiences and for different purposes. For example, they may offer training to other mental health professionals as a way of enhancing their learning of psychological theories and clinical skills; train teachers and/or parents about aspects of child development or behaviour management; train staff members of an organisation on how to manage more effectively their work and relationships (e.g. conflict, stress and work–life balance) and improve their skills in certain areas of their work (e.g. communication, providing feedback and leadership). Likewise, they may choose to offer continuous professional development (CPD) workshops in areas of their expertise or become co-ordinating supervisors for candidates on the Qualification in Counselling Psychology (QCoP) as a way of enhancing and diversifying their professional portfolio. Finally, another context where counselling psychologists may assume the role of the trainer is on therapeutic training programmes. In fact, the steady growth of counselling psychology programmes in the UK over the past ten years and the increase of counselling and psychotherapy training programmes that are accredited by the UK Council for Psychotherapy (UKCP) and the British Association of Counselling and Psychotherapy (BACP) create employment opportunities for counselling psychologists who all now qualify to a doctoral level. However, the growth of this employment area does not mean that making the transition from practitioner/researcher to trainer should be seen as an effortless and straightforward career move. As Clarkson and Gilbert (1991) argued, it is erroneous to expect that all qualified professionals can become trainers just because they have gone through the process of training themselves. Being an expert practitioner/researcher does not mean that one can automatically become a good trainer. For example, knowledge and practical experience of a subject area do not necessarily guarantee an ability to instruct trainees, facilitate their learning and assess their professional development according to the training and educational standards set by the various professional and accrediting bodies. Becoming a trainer in this context requires a substantial shift in role, where one takes the responsibility to train future generations of professionals and by doing so s/he becomes accountable to trainees for their professional development, to the trainees' clients for their safety and to the professional and statutory regulators for upholding their standards of training and education. Such a shift in role necessitates the development of different sets of skills and competencies that are not directly taught during postgraduate training. Developing an understanding of the nature of professional training and acquiring the competencies to perform this new role and facilitate the learning process of trainees is, therefore, a significant area of continuing professional development. It is an area where it is important to reach beyond the therapeutic literature into that of education and training, to engage in workshops that focus on teaching and assessment and perhaps, if it is intended to take on major training roles, to consider undertaking a Postgraduate Certificate in Higher Education (or Professional Graduate Certificate in Education), which mainly focuses on the development of teaching skills and is gradually becoming a standard professional qualification for new university lecturers.

This chapter aims to help aspiring and novice trainers reflect on how to better prepare for this demanding line of work and thus enter their new role with better insight of its requirements and more confidence about their ability to train others. Following a consideration of the principles and philosophy of professional training and the multiple roles and tasks of trainers, the chapter discusses some of the typical challenges that may be encountered by novice trainers and refers to conceptual frameworks that can help them develop a better understanding of how to create an environment that facilitates the learning process and manage some of the challenges that they may face at the beginning of their careers. The chapter concludes by offering some suggestions on how to better prepare for taking on the role of trainer.

UNDERSTANDING THE PRINCIPLES AND PHILOSOPHY OF PROFESSIONAL TRAINING

In the UK, professional training in counselling psychology is founded upon two major conceptual frameworks: the scientist-practitioner and the reflective-practitioner models. It is a training that requires the 'marrying' of theories, practice and personal development in an effort to develop rounded practitioners who have expertise in psychological theories and research and can apply these in their practice, can evaluate the applicability and usefulness of their theories by reflecting on their practice, and can use their ongoing clinical experience as a resource for further learning. Evidently, this necessitates that aspiring and beginner trainers possess not only sound knowledge of the theories and skills that they will be called upon to teach, but also a clear understanding of how to develop reflective practitioners and foster experiential learning. It is of course beyond the scope of this chapter to provide a thorough account of the variety of models on experiential learning for adult educators (e.g. Fenwick, 2003; Jarvis, 2006; Kolb, 1984) and on the different stances on what constitutes reflective practice (e.g. Brookfield, 2000; Dyke, 2009; Schön, 1983). It is essential, though, to emphasise that novice trainers will need to engage with the literature that can help them comprehend key elements of professional training, such as: how to promote in others reflection-in-action (i.e. reflecting on one's practice while they are engaged in it) and reflection-on-action (i.e. reflecting on one's practice after it has taken place) (Schön, 1987); what do experiential learning theories teach us about the different stages of the experiential learning process (e.g. Kolb, 1984; O'Bannon and McFadden, 2008)?; how can a trainer adapt his/her teaching style and methods to meet the needs of learners with different learning styles (Kolb and Yeganeh, 2012)?

BEING AWARE OF THE MULTIPLE ROLES OF TRAINERS

Having developed an understanding of the major principles and philosophy of professional training, beginner trainers will then need to take account of the contexts in which they work and the demands made by employing institutions. For example, trainers on counselling psychology programmes may be required to also teach on undergraduate psychology programmes. This can prove to be quite demanding and stressful as it might involve a significant amount of time and effort to update their knowledge on areas that they have not engaged with since their own undergraduate training. Moreover, it requires an ability to adapt one's teaching and assessment criteria to an undergraduate academic level and thus it also necessitates a familiarisation with the corresponding Quality Assurance Agency for Higher Education (QAA) descriptors for this academic level.

Trainers who hold permanent posts are also expected to perform a variety of other roles and tasks, some of which do not involve student contact. For example, as the Course Leader of one of the accredited (British Psychological Society – BPS) and approved (Health and Care Professions Council – HCPC) professional doctorates, my chief role is to help manage the operation of the training programme on a day-to-day basis. Over the course of an academic year, this includes a long list of tasks and responsibilities, some of which are as follows:

- Ensure effective timetabling and allocation of teaching by the reporting staff.
- Liaise with registry and the admission office in matters concerning student recruitment, registration, student record keeping, and preparations for meetings of examination and boards of study.
- Develop and implement effective communication systems between trainees and trainers.
- Prepare and update relevant handbooks as needed.
- Participate in all relevant faculty and university committees.
- In conjunction with the programme director, select the course team, ensure a response by the course team to the external examiner's comments, and prepare any necessary documents for

matters relating to accreditation, registration of students, and validation of the programme by relevant accrediting and validating institutions.

- Have annual reviews with trainees about their overall performance and development, and in some cases discussing with them difficult choices such as exiting the programme due to academic or clinical competence problems.

Visit the companion website to read Having Difficult Discussions with Trainees about Competence Problems.

The above list indicates that, depending on the degree of involvement with the training programme, trainers will also need to develop leadership, managerial and administrative skills so that they can better perform their roles. Equally, they will need to learn ways of managing the needs of different stakeholders as it is evident that there are several stakeholders involved in the training process. These essentially are: the trainees, the professional and regulatory bodies (e.g. BPS and HCPC), the academic institution and its various departments, and the QAA. At times, it can be quite stressful working with all these stakeholders as they may have different expectations about the training content and process. For example, the needs and desires for trainees to take more responsibility and control of the content of training in a way that suits their own needs may not be consistent with the training and education standards of the accrediting and regulatory bodies; or the needs of the programme may not be well understood by central services within the institution (e.g. high staff–student ratio in order to provide enough support to trainees for the complex demands of doctoral professional training). Thus, trainers need to familiarise themselves with the guidelines and regulations of all relevant organisational stakeholders and endeavour to work collaboratively with all of them in an effort to negotiate their demands.

Finally, if trainers aspire to progress in academia, on top of all the above tasks, they will need to demonstrate their academic scholarship by being actively involved in research, producing publications, obtaining research funding and engaging with the scholarly and professional communities (e.g. at conferences).

FACILITATING THE LEARNING PROCESS

Since the majority of the work of trainers involves direct contact with students, I would now like to turn to one of the most significant tasks and responsibilities of trainers, which from my experience also often proves to be quite challenging for novices. This is the creation of an environment that facilitates learning. To this end, I will discuss those elements that in my view are essential for all trainers to be aware of, so that they can purposefully employ them in order to enhance the learning process. These are: developing the qualities of a motivating instructor, adopting a teaching style that enhances trainees' autonomy, creating a safe space for reflection and exploration, accepting authority and managing the power differential between trainees and trainers, being aware of interpersonal dynamics between trainees and trainer, and managing group dynamics.

Developing the characteristics and skills of motivating instructors

Naturally, one of the principal tasks for all trainers is to instruct trainees. Therefore, aspiring and novice trainers alike need to develop an understanding of the qualities and skills that make instructors more effective. As, to my knowledge, there is no specific literature within the mental health fields that addresses the issue of what makes a good instructor, aspiring trainers can turn to the adult learning literature that has discussed the importance of developing an instructional style that motivates learners. In particular, adult educators have identified that one of the main characteristics of adult learners is that they are intrinsically motivated to learn (Knowles et al., 2005) and that good teachers are those that adopt an instructional style that can 'elicit the intrinsic motivation of all learners' (Wlodkowski, 2008: 45). These assertions are also supported by recent studies that have demonstrated that enhancing the motivation of learners can have positive effects on their performance (Wlodkowski et al., 2001; Wlodkowski and Stiller, 2005).

Wlodkowski emphasised that motivating instructors can positively influence the learning process by stimulating and sustaining the learners' interest and attention. Thus, he proposed that motivating instructors possess five main characteristics: expertise, enthusiasm, clarity, empathy and cultural responsiveness.

 Visit the companion website to read a summary of Wlodkowski's skills and characteristics.

According to Wlodkowski, these characteristics are not personality traits but skills that any trainer can learn and improve by practice. He also contends that all five of them are equally important to becoming a motivating instructor. Thus, a potentially helpful reflective exercise for beginner trainers would be to use Wlodkowski's model as a guiding template for helping them consider the skills that they need to develop in order to be more capable of 'responding effectively to the many complexities that can strain an instructional relationship with adults' (Wlodkowski, 2008: 50). Equally, experienced instructors can use the list to periodically review their mode and methods of delivery.

Fostering autonomy and self-directedness

A review of the QAA descriptors for doctoral holders and of the HCPC's professional standards for practitioner psychologists indicates that counselling psychologists are expected, by the end of their training, to be in a position to 'make informed judgements on complex issues in specialist fields, often in the absence of complete data' (Quality Assurance Agency for Higher Education, 2011: 32), to 'be able to practise as autonomous professionals, exercising their own professional judgement' (Health and Care Professions Council, 2012: 7) and to 'understand both the need to keep skills and knowledge up to date and the importance of career-long learning' (Health and Care Professions Council, 2012: 8). Equally, the BPS's standards for counselling psychology require from programmes 'to promote the development of autonomous learning' (British Psychological Society, 2012: 23). Such statements indicate that trainers of counselling psychology need to consider not only the content of training (e.g. theories, clinical and research skills) but also how to create a training environment that fosters autonomy, encourages reflection and critical thinking, and eventually develops professionals who will be self-directed, lifelong learners. However, creating such an environment may not be as easily achieved as one would expect. One reason for this is that often trainees come to postgraduate training after years of pedagogical experiences where they have been conditioned at school, and sometimes even during their undergraduate training, to be overly dependent on their teachers for learning. Thus, as trainers we should not assume that all trainees will be ready to take a significant degree of responsibility for their learning on entry to their programmes. However, as becoming autonomous and self-directed are essential characteristics that trainees need to develop by the end of their training, it is important that we consider how to best support them in this process.

I would like to propose here that trainers can be facilitated in their efforts to create such learning environments by familiarising themselves with models from the adult learning literature that advocate that the ability to be an autonomous learner relates to the degree of experience and knowledge that one has of the subject matter (Grow, 1991; Pratt, 1988). Therefore, Grow (1991) and Pratt (1988) conceptualise the instructional process as a continuum with varying degrees of support and guidance from the instructor in a way that matches the needs and capabilities of trainees and eventually assists them into progressing into higher degrees of autonomy and assuming ownership and control for their learning. Moreover, these theorists note that misalignment between the instructor's degree of support and guidance with the autonomy needs of learners may result in dissatisfaction, frustration and loss of confidence in learners (Candy, 1991; Hiemstra and Sisco, 1990). Based on these theories, trainers need to be able to monitor their trainees' learning needs and adapt their style and teaching methods accordingly.

Visit the companion website to read Adapting Instruction to the Level of Knowledge of Trainees.

The purposeful adjustment to trainees' level of expertise advocated by Grow (1991) provides trainees with sufficient support and guidance at the beginning stages to feel secure and confident enough to gradually move from a temporary state of 'teacher-dependence' (Pratt, 1988) to a position of personal autonomy for their learning. That is, they learn to self-monitor and evaluate their learning needs and take more responsibility and control for the instructional process. This gradual developmental progression from 'teacher-dependence' to 'learner-autonomy' will eventually better prepare trainees to self-manage their own further learning after qualification.

Creating a safe space for developing reflective-practitioners

One of the core characteristics of counselling psychology training is that, aside from learning psychological and psychotherapeutic theories, trainees are expected to actively and systematically engage in skills training, self-reflection and personal development via a number of in-class activities (e.g. role-plays, skills and experiential exercises, training supervision). This kind of training requires a significant degree of self-disclosure and self-reflection from trainees and an openness to receive feedback from others. It is reasonable to assume that in this learning process the relationship between trainer and trainee can play an important role as it can enhance or hinder trainees' readiness and willingness to engage in the required degree of self-exposure and exploration. In fact, two recent studies with counselling psychology and counselling trainees (Jones et al., 2008; Smith, 2011) have indicated that from the trainees' perspective the relationship between trainee and trainer plays an essential role on the quality of the learning experience. Specifically, they have shown that trainees value in their trainers characteristics such as empathic understanding, acceptance, genuineness, respect, appropriate level of support, consistency, predictability, self-disclosure, ability to manage difficult interpersonal exchanges and a sense of equality. Thus, trainers need to consider how they incorporate such qualities in their contact with trainees as they can be important in creating an environment of safety and trust, where trainees can feel more confident to fully participate and take the kind of interpersonal risks that are necessary in a training that contains a significant amount of experiential and personal development components and aims to develop reflective-practitioners.

Accepting authority and managing the power differential

Having referred to the importance of creating a safe learning environment, it is essential to discuss next an aspect of training that inevitably affects the development of such an environment. This is the asymmetrical nature of the relationship and its inherent power imbalance. This imbalance derives primarily from the trainer's role as evaluator for and gatekeeper of the training and education standards of the relevant regulatory bodies and the academic institution, but also from the trainer's knowledge, experience and expertise in the subject area. In my experience, the tensions created by the asymmetrical nature of the relationship are often difficult to manage by trainees and trainers alike. On the one hand, trainees can find the power imbalance quite frustrating as they are adults, some of them even with significant prior academic, research and clinical experience, and naturally want to be treated as equals. On the other hand, just as it has been identified for supervisors (Hawkins and Shohet, 2006; Ladany and Bradley, 2010), trainers frequently seem quite uncomfortable and hesitant with accepting and exercising the authority that is inherent in their role. Similarly to what Munson (2002) identified for supervisors in social work, it often seems to me that counselling psychology trainers experience an ideological uneasiness with exercising their power since it may feel that this runs counter to the core humanistic values that form the philosophical basis of our profession (e.g. autonomy, self-actualisation, self-determination, subjectivity). Thus, one of the most challenging aspects of working as a trainer can be to learn to feel comfortable with one's authority and to manage sensitively and judiciously the power that comes with his/her role.

I consider that to be in a position to exercise appropriately and without hesitation and defensiveness the power that comes with his/her authority, a trainer first needs to develop an understanding of its aims and potential benefits. In my view, these are primarily four:

1. To support trainees' professional development by raising their attention to areas that require further development.
2. To reward them with praise when they are moving towards meeting the expected professional standards.
3. To protect trainees' clients by ensuring that trainees practise in a safe, effective and ethical manner.
4. To safeguard the reputation and future of the profession by ensuring that the training and educational standards are met.

Once the trainer feels more confident about accepting and exercising his/her power, then the next step is to find ways of managing it in a manner that is more acceptable to trainees and supports the learning process rather than impedes it. The literature on clinical supervision can prove to be an invaluable guide in this process.

Hawkins and Shohet (2006) propose that supervisees are more likely to accept supervisors' authority if this stems from respect and admiration for their knowledge and competence rather than the power inherent in their position. Thus, before assuming their role, trainers need to feel confident that they have enough knowledge and experience to gain their trainees' trust and respect. Equally, though, it is important that they try to reduce the inherent power differential in the trainee–trainer relationship by using their authority in a minimal manner. As Kadushin (1992: 97) notes, 'persistent use of authority ... intensifies a sense of status difference ... and tends to inhibit free communication'. One potential way of minimising the existing power differential is to convey to trainees that authority will be used as a means of supporting their development and caring for them and their clients rather than controlling them (Kadushin, 1992), and that it will be employed in an impartial, consistent and predictable manner. Furthermore, although accepting that 'equality is never completely possible due to the power differential' (Smith, 2011: 240), trainers need to adopt a collaborative stance that demonstrates to trainees that they are seen as equals in the learning process, whose contributions and opinions are welcomed, valued and respected. By adopting such a stance, trainers can facilitate the creation of a safe and supportive learning environment that is essential to helping trainees take interpersonal risks and engage fully in the personal and professional development that need to take place in counselling psychology training.

Finding a balance between emotional over-involvement and under-involvement

In recent years, we have seen attempts in the literature to provide a better understanding of the interpersonal dynamics that take place within the trainee–trainer relationship and how these may impact on the process of teaching. Rizq (2009) provided a psychodynamic perspective for understanding some of the intense reactions and projections of trainees and the role of trainer in tolerating and containing the 'attacks' of trainees in order to assist their journey towards developing a mature professional identity. Subsequently, Gil-Rodriguez and Butcher (2012) enriched this discussion by providing a reflective account of their own expectations, phantasies and projections as novice trainers and how these affected their teaching work. In an effort to contribute to this important area of the literature, I would like to focus here on an interpersonal process that, in my view, all trainers have to manage at one stage or other of their careers and one that is considered to be one of the major sources of stress for counselling trainers (McLeod, 1995). This is, finding a balance between emotional over-involvement and under-involvement with their trainees.

Skovholt (2001) has argued that effective therapists are in a position to regulate the cognitive and emotional overload from working with clients in ways that facilitate rather than hinder the therapeutic process. Adequate regulation ensures that therapists can remain empathic and emotionally attached towards their clients, while inability to regulate their emotional reactions may lead them to either defensively close down from the clients' experience due to an inability to handle their intense emotions or lose their own perspective and identity. In similar vein, I would like to propose that the same argument holds for effective trainers. As noted above, in order for trainers to develop relationships with trainees that are conducive to learning, they have to display relational characteristics that are akin to those of good therapists (e.g. empathic understanding, acceptance, genuineness, ability to manage interpersonal issues). This means that they have to be relationally invested in this process and be in a position to repeat this with different cohorts of trainees. This requires that they are able to regulate their level of emotional attachment to their trainees. Trainers need to be in a position to connect empathically with their trainees and understand their perspectives, worries and anxieties in order to respond appropriately to their learning needs. At the same time, though, they need to be in a position to retain their own sense of self and perspective so as not to get lost in the trainees' struggles.

Finding the balance between emotional over-involvement and under-involvement, between caring too much and not caring enough (Skovholt, 2005), is by no means an easy feat. However, I believe that it is an essential part of the work of trainers as prolonged periods on either end of this continuum can create obstacles to the learning process. If the trainer 'loses' himself/ herself by overly identifying with trainees, then s/he will not be in a position to help trainees manage their struggles and frustrations by offering a different perspective or by containing these anxieties and demonstrating to them that these can be sustained and managed. Furthermore, if this process is frequently repeated or prolonged, then the trainer may end up feeling emotionally depleted. This may eventually lead to 'caring burnout' (Skovholt, 2005) and the trainer may become emotionally unavailable to future trainees. On the other hand, if the trainer does not manage to empathically identify with the trainees' worries and anxieties, trainees may not feel safe enough to open up and engage in the reflective and self-exploratory work that is required in this type of training. This is a process that not only requires regular monitoring of the trainers' degree of involvement–detachment but also high levels of reflexivity and awareness of their expectations about their role and unconscious motivations for becoming a trainer. The following illustration briefly describes how my own unacknowledged expectations about my role as a novice trainer impacted on my relationship with trainees.

Personal illustration

When I made my first steps as a trainer, I quickly realised that when trainees became overly anxious and distressed about their performance or client work, I would feel quite disconnected from their anxiety and wanted to end meetings with them quite swiftly. As I was aware that this is not my typical reaction towards others when they are distressed, I took this to my supervision. Following several supervision sessions and a significant amount of personal reflection, I gradually realised that after several years of working almost exclusively as practitioner I had begun feeling the emotional pressures from clinical work and one of the mistaken implicit expectations in my decision to work as a lecturer was that working with trainees would not require me to manage such pressures. With this insight and by gradually including activities in my life that helped me replenish my energy, I became much more responsive to trainees anxieties and worries. I then noticed that this change in my attitude assisted trainees to feel more secure with me and able to self-disclose their worries or oversights relating to their clinical work.

Over the years, I have observed myself and my colleagues on numerous occasions working hard to find the balance on this continuum so that we stay close enough to the experience of trainees in order to support them adequately and make them feel safe enough to engage in the learning process but not too close so that we lose track of our own role and responsibilities in the process of learning. I believe that if one is to become an effective trainer, s/he needs to be mindful of his/her levels of emotional involvement with trainees and to be working towards what Skovholt and Jennings have called a position of 'boundaried generosity' (2004: 116). That is, a compassionate attitude of care towards trainees that is guided by a clear understanding of who is responsible for different aspects of the learning that needs to take place in order for trainees to develop their professional identity.

Working with groups

Much of the work that one does as a trainer in counselling psychology programmes takes place in the context of small groups. Therefore, it is important that trainers attain some understanding of the main processes that take place in groups and develop the skills to manage and facilitate these processes. This may extend from practical aspects of working with groups, such as finding ways to encourage participation or responding to typical participant behaviours (e.g. being very talkative and not giving space to others, rambling on and digressing from the topic under discussion, being silent and avoiding making any contributions), to more complex aspects, such as the handling of unconscious group dynamics and processes that interfere with the learning task. Since guidance on practical matters is something that is extensively addressed in the adult learning literature (e.g., Lakey, 2010; Lawson, 2006; McKeachie and Svinicki, 2006), I would like here to briefly focus on the role of group dynamics as it is an area of adult education that I consider to be of great significance to counselling psychology trainers. To achieve this, I would like to discuss an example that illustrates how the unacknowledged and powerful emotional undercurrents of a group can become an 'obstacle' to the learning process and how knowledge of group concepts and theory can help trainers bring back the focus to the task of learning.

Case illustration

Completing the postgraduate training in counselling psychology is an arduous and demanding process, since trainees are expected to demonstrate doctoral proficiency on a number of different areas (e.g. theory, research, personal development and clinical work). In my experience, this can prove taxing even to the most competent and experienced trainees. Unfortunately, this means that some trainees find this process too demanding and either choose to end their studies at an early stage or fail to successfully complete all the necessary requirements of training. I have noticed that when that happens, especially at the beginning of training, when a cohort is still at what is considered the 'forming stage' of a group (Tuckman and Jensen, 1977), one of the common reactions of trainee cohorts is to gradually become frustrated, and sometimes even angry, with their trainers. As a group, they gradually grow more and more demanding towards their trainers, whom they may regard as unsupportive and unwilling to provide enough support, guidelines and information about assignments and assessment criteria. At the same time, trainers may feel puzzled or frustrated by the group's reaction and they may even see trainees as 'too demanding', lacking in initiative and avoiding taking responsibility for their own learning.

If the above scenario is sustained for a prolonged period, then there is the likelihood that a discourse of 'us versus them' can develop between the two groups, which can affect the learning process, as the focus moves away from the task of learning and turns to the relationship between the groups. I believe that in such instances trainers need to help break the relational dynamic that is being developed by acting with reflexivity. That is, they need to reflect on what is happening so that they become attuned and respond to the underlying anxieties of trainees instead of their overt reactions. I have found that Bion's work on groups (1961) can be a useful conceptual framework in assisting trainers in this process. Based on Bion's group theory, it could be argued that the early withdrawals from the programme of some of their colleagues activate the most basic unconscious anxieties in the group, that of its survival. Under the fear that the group may not survive, its members are desperately looking for a leader, in this instance the trainers, to provide security and protect them. Thus, the group is operating primarily from a 'basic assumption of dependency'. Consequently, potential invitations to trainees by trainers to assume responsibility for their learning are not received as invitations but as resistance from the omniscient and omnipotent other, who, if s/he just desired, could ensure the 'survival' of the group by imparting his/her knowledge. I have observed that when my colleagues and I manage to provide trainees the space to express their fears and anxieties, indicate to them that we appreciate their fears and reassure them that, although we cannot offer them assurances that they will all complete the training, we are invested in supporting them through this process, the adversarial dynamic progressively diminishes. Trainees gradually take back responsibility for their role in the learning process and the group returns to operating as a 'working group' (Bion, 1961), where the focus again becomes the learning task rather than worrying about its survival.

The above illustration and analysis, which of course refers to just one of the numerous aspects of group dynamics that can evolve during the course of training, hopefully indicates that unconscious group processes can play a significant role in the learning process. Thus, knowledge of group theories can help trainers handle group processes in a manner that facilitates rather than hinders learning.

SUGGESTIONS FOR PREPARATION

In discussing some of the essential elements that trainers need to be mindful of in order to create a facilitating learning environment and some of the potential challenges that they may have to negotiate, I have referred to a number of conceptual frameworks that can support and guide them in their work. However, I would like here to also make a number of practical suggestions for beginner trainers, which might better equip them in their first stages of their development and in making the transition from practitioners to trainers.

Evidently, a useful exercise for all aspiring and novice trainers can be to reflect on what they found helpful and unhelpful in the training styles and techniques they have experienced as trainees. Moreover, for those who realise during their training that they are interested in working in academia, I would suggest that they enquire within their institutions about opportunities to teach undergraduates or even ask their tutors about any possibility to do some co-teaching on a topic that they feel knowledgeable and confident about. Furthermore, beginners might benefit from attending workshops within their institution that focus on the different aspects of the delivery of training. For example, in my university there are regular seminars/workshops on teaching, assessment, management and leadership skills. Equally, beginner trainers may find assistance in the form of discussing and consulting with more experienced colleagues about their experiences and how they manage aspects of the learning process. They can also ask them if they can observe them teaching. Personally, I consider any opportunities to observe colleagues in the role of trainer invaluable learning experiences. Although of course as students we all have attended numerous classes, the experience of attending a class of a colleague as an observer is entirely different, as the focus is less on the content and more on the colleague's mode and methods of instruction and how they manage the learning process. Furthermore, after the observation one has the opportunity to enquire about the colleague's reasoning behind some of their interventions in class. Finally, novice trainers may also benefit from reading some of the existing personal accounts of trainers who discuss their own experiences as trainers (e.g. Alilovic, 2007; Gil-Rodriguez and Butcher, 2012; Proctor, 1991).

CONCLUDING REMARKS

In an effort to assist aspiring and novice trainers manage more efficiently the gradual transformation process of incorporating into their pre-existing practitioner identity the newly acquired identity of trainer, I have indicated in this chapter the principal values of professional training and the multiplicity of roles and tasks that trainers may be called to fulfil. I have also discussed some of the typical challenges that they are likely to encounter in their work and pointed to conceptual frameworks that can help them navigate through these challenges. Finally, I have outlined some practical suggestions for better preparation, so that beginner trainers can enter their new roles with more insight into the requirements of this job and more confidence about their ability to train others. Of course, as adult learning theory is a widely diverse field, which is characterised by a lack of consensus between adult educators about the theories of learning (Merriam and Bierema, 2014), I had to be selective about the elements of the learning process that could realistically be explored in this chapter. Therefore, I would also encourage trainers to familiarise themselves with the current developments and wider debates addressed by adult educators. To this end, I would direct them to recent comprehensive reviews of adult learning theory, such those by Jarvis (2004), Knowles et al. (2005), and Merriam and Bierema (2014). Finally, I hope that more seasoned trainers have found the chapter stimulating and I would like to encourage them to contribute to this rather neglected area of research and literature within the mental health fields. Their experience and knowledge can prove to be an invaluable template for beginner trainers in their efforts to fulfil their tasks and responsibilities more effectively and provide solid training experiences to future generations of trainees.

Visit the companion website resources for Chapter 7 to listen to QCoP Co-ordinating Supervisor.

REFERENCES

Alilovic, K. (2007) 'Practice what you preach: A day in the life of an academic counselling psychologist', *Counselling Psychology Review*, 22(1): 5–7.

Bion, W.R. (1961) *Experiences in Groups and Other Papers*. London: Tavistock.

British Psychological Society (2012) *Accreditation through Partnership Handbook: Guidance for Counselling Psychology Programmes*. Leicester: BPS.

Brookfield, S.D. (2000) 'The concept of critically reflective practice', in A.L. Wilson and E.R. Hayes (eds), *Handbook of Adult and Continuing Education*. San Francisco, CA: Jossey-Bass. pp. 33–49.

Candy, P.C. (1991) *Self-direction for Lifelong Learning*. San Francisco, CA: Jossey-Bass.

Clarkson, P. and Gilbert, M. (1991) 'The training of counsellor trainers and supervisors', in W. Dryden and B. Thorne (eds), *Training and Supervision for Counselling in Action*. London: Sage. pp. 143–169.

Dyke, M. (2009) 'An enabling framework for reflexive learning: Experiential learning and reflexivity in contemporary modernity', *International Journal of Lifelong Education*, 28(3): 289–310.

Fenwick, T. (2003) *Learning through Experience: Troubling Orthodoxies and Interesting Questions*. Malabar, FL: Krieger.

Gil-Rodriguez, E. and Butcher, A. (2012) 'From trainee to trainer: Crossing over to the other side of the fence', *British Journal of Guidance & Counselling*, 40(4): 357–368.

Grow, G.O. (1991) 'Teaching learners to be self-directed', *Adult Education Quarterly*, 41: 125–149.

Hawkins, P. and Shohet, R. (2006) *Supervision in the Helping Professions* (3rd edn). Maidenhead: Open University Press.

Health and Care Professions Council (2012) *Standards of Proficiency: Practitioner Psychologists.* London: HCPC.

Hiemstra, R. and Sisco, B. (1990) *Individualizing Instruction: Making Learning Personal, Empowering, and Successful.* San Francisco, CA: Jossey-Bass.

Jarvis, P. (2004) *Adult Education and Lifelong Learning: Theory and Practice* (3rd edn). London: Routledge Falmer.

Jarvis, P. (2006) *Towards a Comprehensive Theory of Human Learning.* London: Routledge.

Jones, R., Mirsalimi, H., Conroy, J.S., Horne-Moyer, H.L. and Burrill, C. (2008) 'The Teaching Alliance Inventory: Evaluating the student–instructor relationship in clinical and counselling psychology training', *Counselling Psychology Quarterly*, 21(3): 223–235.

Kadushin, A. (1992) *Supervision in Social Work* (3rd edn). New York: Columbia University Press.

Knowles, M.S., Holton III, E.F. and Swanson, R.A. (2005) *The Adult Learner: The Definite Classic in Adult Education and Human Resource Development* (6th edn). New York: Elsevier.

Kolb, D.A. (1984) *Experiential Learning: Experience as the Source of Learning and Development.* Englewood Cliffs, NJ: Prentice-Hall.

Kolb, D.A. and Yeganeh, B. (2012) 'Deliberate experiential learning', in K. Elsbach, C.D. Kayes and A. Kayes (eds), *Contemporary Organizational Behaviour in Action.* Upper Saddle River, NJ: Pearson Education. pp. 1–10.

Ladany, L. and Bradley, L.J. (eds) (2010) *Counselor Supervision* (4th edn). New York: Taylor & Francis Group.

Lakey, G.M. (2010) *Facilitating Group Learning: Strategies for Success with Diverse Learners.* San Francisco, CA: Jossey-Bass.

Lawson, K. (2006) *The Trainer's Handbook* (2nd edn). San Francisco, CA: Pfeiffer.

Merriam, S.B. and Bierema, L.L. (2014) *Adult Learning Theory: Linking Theory with Practice.* San Francisco, CA: Jossey-Bass.

McKeachie, W.J. and Svinicki, M. (2006) *McKeachie's Teaching Tips: Strategies, Research, and Theory for College and University Lecturers* (12th edn). New York: Houghton Mifflin.

McLeod, J. (1995) 'The stresses of counsellor education', in W. Dryden (ed.), *The Stresses of Counselling in Action.* London: Sage. pp. 152–165.

Munson, C.E. (2002) *Handbook of Clinical Social Work Supervision* (3rd edn). New York: The Haworth Social Work Practice Press.

O'Bannon, T. and McFadden, C. (2008) 'Model of experiential andragogy: Development of a non-traditional experiential learning program model', *Journal of Unconventional Parks, Tourism & Recreation Research*, 1(1): 23–28.

Pratt, D.D. (1988) 'Andragogy as a relational construct', *Adult Education Quarterly*, 38: 160–181.

Proctor, B. (1991) 'On being a trainer', in W. Dryden and B. Thorne (eds), *Training and Supervision for Counselling in Action.* London: Sage. pp. 49–73.

Quality Assurance Agency for Higher Education (2011) *Doctoral Degree Characteristics.* Available at: www.qaa.ac.uk/Publications/InformationAndGuidance/Documents/Doctoral_Characteristics.pdf (accessed: 15 July 2014).

Rizq, R. (2009) 'Teaching and transformation: A psychoanalytic perspective on psychotherapeutic training', *British Journal of Psychotherapy*, 25: 363–380.

Schön, D.A. (1983) *The Reflective Practitioner: How Professionals Think in Action*. New York: Basic Books.

Schön, D.A. (1987) *Educating the Reflective Practitioner*. New York: Basic Books.

Skovholt, T.M. (2001) *The Resilient Practitioner: Burnout Prevention and Self-care Strategies for Counselors, Therapists, Teachers, and Health Professionals*. Boston, MA: Allyn & Bacon.

Skovholt, T.M. (2005) 'The cycle of caring: A model of expertise in the helping Professions', *Journal of Mental Health Counseling*, 27(1): 82–93.

Skovholt, T.M. and Jennings, L. (eds.) (2004) *Master Therapists: Exploring Expertise in Therapy and Counseling*. Boston, MA: Allyn & Bacon.

Smith, V.J. (2011) 'It's the relationship that matters: A qualitative analysis of the role of the student–tutor relationship in counselling training', *Counselling Psychology Quarterly*, 24(3): 233–246.

Tuckman, B.W. and Jensen, M.A. (1977) 'Stages of small-group development Revisited', *Group and Organization Studies*, 2(4): 419–427.

Wlodkowski, R.J. (2008) *Enhancing Adult Motivation to Learn: A Comprehensive Guide for Teaching Adults* (3rd edn). San Francisco, CA: Jossey-Bass.

Wlodkowski, R.J., Mauldin, J.E. and Gahn, S.W. (2001) *Learning in the Fast Lane: Adult Learners' Persistence and Success in Accelerated College Programs*. Indianapolis, IN: Lumina Foundation for Education.

Wlodkowski, R.J. and Stiller, J. (2005) *Accelerated Learning Online Research Project: Phase 1*. Denver, CO: Center for the Study of Accelerated Learning, Regis University.

37
BECOMING AN ENTREPRENEUR-PRACTITIONER
CAROLINE VERMES

INTRODUCTION

Counselling psychologists are employed in a wide range of corporate and academic settings, across the public and independent sectors, and, less commonly, the charity and voluntary sectors (DCoP, 2011). We also create successful careers beyond employment by setting up and managing our own practices and services. Independent practice is the focus of this chapter. Here we discuss why you might consider going into business for yourself, and how to create sustainable work for other psychologists.

First, we will consider why becoming an independent provider may be a route to protecting psychologist jobs in the next decade, particularly as UK public service economies will be increasingly allocated to outsourced service delivery. Then, we will look at unincorporated occupations, including sole traders, portfolio workers and group partnerships. Following this we will look at some of the essential business processes common to these jobs. Mastering these processes prepares you to create a registered company. We will touch on different forms of incorporation. We will also examine how your service can consolidate its trading identity and performance record in preparation to win and deliver service-level agreements and competitively tendered contracts. The chapter will conclude with a reflection on the skills and attitudes that are helpful for successful counselling psychology service leadership. Concepts in this chapter will be 'illustrated' by quotes from four fictional psychologists:

Dr Saoirse B qualified last year and works as Programme Development Lead for a youth services charity in Northern Ireland.

Mandy R has built a portfolio career. She lives in rural Wales.

Dr Sanjeet K manages an unincorporated group practice in a Scottish suburb.

Dr Alex A owns and manages a multi-contract NHS commercial partner organisation based in an English city.

WHY GO INDEPENDENT?

A recent members' employment survey by the British Psychological Society (BPS) Division of Counselling Psychology (DCoP, 2011) returned results suggesting that approximately half of the respondents were directly employed by the NHS. Another half worked in private practice; and just under a quarter also worked in independent (non-public sector) practices, demonstrating that a proportion of respondents had two or more part-time jobs in different sectors.

So, it can be inferred that many of us currently depend on NHS work for at least part of our income. However, the past decade has seen extensive reform in public sector commissioning processes and priorities, particularly in England and parts of Wales. In mental health care, the development of Improved Access to Psychological Therapies (IAPT) and other stepped care programmes are examples of such initiatives. More recently, with the inception of the Health and Social Care Act 2012 (Acts of Parliament, 2012a), the procurement of public health care has been further economically and clinically restructured. Under Section 75, *most new and re-commissioned services must be competitively tendered* to improve efficiency and cost-effectiveness. While it may be argued that the best way to preserve NHS values is to retain NHS direct provision, the NHS is inexorably transforming into a purchasing agent, while gradually giving up its provider arms. Current marketisation trends in the NHS foretell a year-on-year increase in the number and range of NHS services that will be outsourced over the next few decades (Kaffash and Sterling, 2013). We need to find ways to work with this.

The business of counselling psychology: A parallel universe

Saoirse: The commercial side of counselling psychology was not covered in my doctoral training, which focused on research and counselling skills development. The marketplace in which our real-world work is situated was uncharted territory as far as training was concerned. However, I became aware of this parallel universe in my first placement. I worked for a small agency serving vulnerable young people in their new NHS-commissioned sexual health advisory service. They had won this work via competitive tender, against two other well-known providers in the area. The funding was initially for only 12 months, which of course raised numerous pressures around budget management, clinical performance and data collection, all of which our manager was completely transparent about with the clinical team. My initiation to the tangible business environment in which all successful services must operate helped me realise there is much more to creating and sustaining employment for counselling psychologists, besides all the work it takes to earn the title, which is hard enough.

As these reforms have been progressing, some counselling psychologists have commented that their work in NHS employment has consequently been exposed to 'threat' (e.g. Benanti, 2006; James, 2009; Walsh and Frankland, 2009; Lewis, 2012; Parpottas, 2012).

But there is another side to this coin. Competitive procurement has ushered in exciting opportunities for independent organisations to take on delivery of services under the NHS brand. Historically, independent services enjoyed considerable freedom to conduct their work for the NHS as they saw fit. By comparison, these days newly commissioned services may be subject to close monitoring and ambitious outcomes-driven targets by their NHS commissioners. Ethically managed independent services thereby work to protect and preserve NHS values. They work nimbly and innovatively to meet targets *and* bring greater social capital to their communities. Furthermore, independent services can provide shelter against changing conditions for NHS psychologists, enabling some control over the work environment, and permitting therapeutic flexibility for clients.

The Public Services (Social Value) Act 2012 (Acts of Parliament, 2012b) requires public sector commissioning bodies, when designing, developing and commissioning any public service, to consider how it can bring added economic, environmental and social benefits, rather than simply representing the lowest-cost option. In theory, the Social Value Act lends some advantages to smaller, local providers who produce inventive social outcomes to benefit their communities, but who have previously been unable to compete with regional, national or international private or public sector oligopolies for tenders (Williams, 2012; HM Government, 2014). Moreover, NHS commissioners are encouraged to work in partnership with charity (not-for-profit) and social enterprise (profit-reinvestment) providers (Department of Health, 2008; National Audit Office, 2014).

So, for us to adapt to, and work well with, these powerful policy and procurement trends we need develop a new breed of psychologist: the 'entrepreneur-practitioner'. Using a combination of seasoned clinical experience, enterprising spirit and business acumen, we can work with the transforming NHS by becoming service providers ourselves. Moreover, we are not limited to working with the NHS. Purchasers abound in the UK mental health marketplace, such as local authorities, schools and universities, charities, government services such as prisons and courts, and private organisations, including insurance companies and employee assistance programmes (EAPs).

Entrepreneurial service provision can be described as falling along a continuum of business magnitude:

1. Unincorporated sole traders, portfolio workers and small partnerships whose work may derive largely from direct client sales or project-specific tariffs from a range of purchasers.
2. Micro-sized incorporated companies and charities that may deliver a limited number of relatively low-value agreements, grants or contracts. They have simple management hierarchies that are largely devoted to delivering existing obligations.
3. Growth-oriented companies and charities that manage an expanding portfolio of contracts. They may invest significantly in diversifying their management teams and knowledge bases to win new work and build staff capacity.
4. Mid-size, multidisciplinary health companies with complex management hierarchies, hundreds of employees and ambitious expansion strategies. They grow and mature by winning larger tenders. They may buy out or merge with smaller companies to acquire expertise in specific speciality areas, including psychology.

An entrepreneur-practitioner's career may over time traverse any or all of these stages, or may come to rest at a place on the service provision continuum that is favourable to a particular work disposition. Career progression requires the development of strong leadership skills, and the ability to navigate complex management relations and to foster multidisciplinary partnerships. The work of 'doing business' as a psychologist can sometimes seem formidable, not only when starting out, but at various junctures where big decisions, or big changes, have to be made. But these challenges are merely gift-wrapping around prospects for learning, development and the greater promotion of our values.

SOLE TRADERS, PORTFOLIO WORKERS AND GROUP PRACTICES

Individual workers and small group partnerships are generally 'unincorporated', meaning they are not a registered trading identity. They are generally differentiated from private practitioners by bearing a business title, rather than a person's name. Workers in unincorporated businesses must be registered with HMRC (Her Majesty's Revenue and Customs) as self-employed and file self-assessment tax returns. Unincorporated businesses do not need to file company accounts or directors' details, which protects owners' privacy, but conversely this can make it difficult for potential customers to find out how financially sound the business might be. Additionally, sole traders and partners are personally responsible for all debts, taxes, legal issues and other liabilities arising in the course of doing business. Unincorporated businesses are not allowed to bid for a wide range of publicly tendered opportunities, and may encounter difficulties borrowing capital to invest in growth activity (Bates et al., 2006). Additionally, income may be variable when it depends on individually funded referrals.

On the other hand, running an unincorporated business gives you considerable control over your work–life balance. You are free to distribute your time as you choose clinical work, teaching, writing, study or research, as well as family, recreation or volunteer activities. You can decide which clients and colleagues to work with, how to market your services and how much to charge for them.

Going it alone – or not!

The main difference between a sole trader and a portfolio worker is the variety of work taken on at any given time. One type of work is likely to dominate a sole trader's time and income stream, for instance counselling or consultancy. A portfolio worker generates a multi-source income stream by working for diverse customers or doing a range of different activities. Sole and portfolio workers may take on private work contracts, and can employ staff to help deliver their obligations, so being a sole trader does not necessarily spell a lonesome livelihood. It is vital, however, if taking on staff, that you have a good understanding of employment law, including the different rights of employed, self-employed and voluntary workers. For employees, you will need to create appropriate terms and conditions, contracts, handbooks, job descriptions and appraisal schemes. It is advisable to retain a reputable HR consultant to help you maintain compliance with legislation.

Becoming a portfolio worker

Mandy: Four years ago, my NHS post was cut to part-time when the MH Trust was restructured. My knee-jerk reaction was to worry about how I'd make enough money to live on and maintain my pension contributions. Initially, I made up the income by seeing clients at a private agency. But I was not comfortable with the high fees they charged clients. I soon left. This was when I did some serious 'career soul searching'. I identified that what I love about my work as a psychologist is harnessing the power of good training to transform people, systems, communities, futures, you name it. So I thought hard about how I could bring this passion for transformation into new projects that I could deliver on a self-employed basis. My business started tiny, while I was still employed part-time. I devised some team-development workshops for a friend who was a factory manager. These went on to become quite successful. I was soon going all around the country doing workshops for a range of industries. I developed my concepts into a team-coaching method which I trademarked. Now I have two employees who do most of the delivery for me. I quit the NHS job almost three years ago and have since expanded my portfolio. I work sometimes for the local education authority, on student assistance projects, devising and delivering stress management and confidence-building programmes for secondary schools. I am also a part-time college lecturer, and provide consultancy to our local CAMHS [Child and Adolescent Mental Health Services]. I love that I can be doing something different each day of the week. My work requires me to use the most creative side of my abilities as a psychologist. Best of all, my office is at home, where I enjoy the tranquillity of the countryside, and long thinking walks across the hills. And I look after my granddaughter every Wednesday. Becoming a portfolio worker taught me an important lesson: I don't have to worry about money if I follow my capabilities and interests, and just do what I am best at. The only drawback is that it's difficult to answer when I get asked that typical network event question, 'what do you do?'

Group practice

Unincorporated group practices are generally formed as 'hub and spoke' referral networks for affiliated therapists. In this model, the 'hub' is a referral reception and triage system and the 'spokes' are therapists who provide services for these clients, usually with requirements to report certain information about their activity back to the hub. Therapists generally work on a self-employed, fee-per-session basis. Hub and spoke services tend to be geared to sustain a stream of referrals and funding from a variety of sources, such as GP practices or insurance companies or via client private self-referral. Practices of this type can range in size from two therapists sharing a rented consulting room to large referral networks managing several regional hubs and retaining dozens of therapists who see clients in local settings. Practices may offer a wide range of therapies for a long list of issues, or may be specialised in specific psychological problem areas, methods and models of practitioner training and discipline.

Totten Psychology Group

Sanjeet: Three years ago I went into private practice, after leaving a CMHT where I had worked as a consultant psychologist for ten years. Due to my former post, I was well connected and received steady referrals from ex-colleagues, an EAP and a local faith community. I started Totten Psychology Group (TPG), a group practice, two years ago when I was receiving more referrals than I could see personally. Initially, two colleagues agreed to work with me and now we have a team of six psychologists and an occupational therapist (OT). They see TPG clients in their own practices located across the borough. TPG received over 100 referrals last year, so I took on a part-time administrator/book-keeper, as the insurance paperwork, accounting, client bookings and records management became more than I could handle myself. This also means client calls and enquiries can be dealt with immediately and professionally. I much prefer group practice to working solo, which I found isolating. I am very proud of the TPG team. Our meetings and peer-supervision groups are warm and mutually supportive. Everyone has a say in how the service is run and can be improved. The TPG business plan for this year is ambitious. I intend to create a board of trustees. Then I want to incorporate as a social enterprise as we want to be in a position to take advantage of new opportunities emerging in the public sector. Then I want to secure a business mortgage to purchase a consulting suite, as the two-room office TPG leases isn't fit for our growth.

DEVELOPING BUSINESS VALUES, SYSTEMS AND SKILLS

Now we will look at some of the business processes common to most forms of unincorporated practice: values and mission, premises, partnerships, business planning and marketing. These processes are also necessary, albeit in scaled-up form, for incorporated organisations, which will be the focus of the subsequent section of this chapter.

Values and mission

It is likely, if you are considering becoming an independent provider, that you have some deeply held ideas about why and how your work should be conducted. These feelings and beliefs are essential to your service's foundation and future. They can be summed up as 'values', and should lie authentically at the heart of your service culture. Your values form the basis of a foundational statement that explains 'why and how we work'. It stands to reason that the values of a counselling psychology service will centre on the welfare of the people and communities it serves, but the difference between a mediocre and excellent service lies in the way that values are lived out in everyday practice across an entire workforce and outwards to generate real social change. It takes significant effort, as a whole-service exercise, to define and distill company values. And it takes ongoing training to instill and reinforce these values into the thinking and behaviour of every worker (George, 2003).

TPG: mission and values

Sanjeet: TPG exists for the public benefit, to promote the advancement of psychological well-being for individuals, families and social groups, by carrying out counselling, psychotherapy, supervision, training and consultancy. This work is informed by our key values. We are dedicated to assisting people to explore meaning in life, to facilitate emotional growth and actualise potential, to improve interpersonal relationships and to achieve relief from distress and suffering. Our practitioners are committed to respecting human autonomy and dignity, to providing culturally competent outreach in a range of languages and to promoting social justice and community cohesion. TPG strives to make its services accessible to all, by providing a sliding fee scale for self-referring clients, free services for asylum seekers and refugees, and demonstrably cost-effective contractual arrangements for organisational customers.

Another foundational activity for your business is defining its central objectives and articulating these concisely in a mission statement that says 'what we do'. This statement explains the service to its stakeholders, or 'interested parties'. A mission statement should achieve several aims. First, it must be relevant to a specific and clearly identified social need, and state how the service will make a positive difference, and for whom. Next, it must be understandable and meaningful to disparate stakeholders with varying aims and terms of reference. Indeed, it may be a 'bridging' text that links the needs of clients and purchasers through the work of the practice. The mission statement also needs to provide direction and focus for the activities of the service's workers. While a mission statement may contain a variety of focal points shaped by its authors' priorities, it ought to wed the purpose and aspirations of the practice with the practical steps intended to bring them to life. A working mission statement will be reviewed and updated at least annually to ensure that it remains an accurate reflection of the activity and aims of the service, developed with fullest possible participation from owners, trustees, staff and clients.

Premises

Sole traders and portfolio workers may be able to do administrative work from home. You may also be able to see clients at home if you have consultation space sufficiently set apart from your personal space. Working from home can be more cost-effective than renting an office, and may therefore permit flexibility to offer lower fees to self-paying clients. If working at home is not possible, 'timeshare' room rentals are a common arrangement among otherwise unaffiliated colleagues. A suitable consulting room may be found in a variety of business settings or in an existing counselling practice.

The decision whether to rent or purchase a suitable property for your practice may be based on available capital and guaranteed income or the vicissitudes of the property market in your region. Consider your practice's growth plans when deciding on space. For instance, if the service were to double in size in the next five years, would the property still be suitable? Other important considerations include the reputation and safety of the location, and the image and condition of the property and its surroundings. A budget may be required for redecoration or reconstruction to create a professional yet comfortable setting, as well as to meet privacy, security, fire, health and safety protocols. You will need local conveniences such as post office, bank and shops, as well as integral amenities, including a kitchen, toilets, waiting area, disabled access and parking. Ideally, there will be public transport routes nearby. While 'non-perfect' rooms do not necessarily influence the quality of the work conducted within them, client experience may be significantly impacted by the look and feel of the counselling environment (McLeod and Machin, 1998).

Partnerships

Group practices are likely to require the creation of business partnerships, such as co-leaders or collaborations with other services. Successful partnerships comprise a number of essential elements. First, a complementary and strategic skills mix calls for partners with knowledge and experience of clinical leadership, marketing and public relations, financial and budget management, strategy and business planning, IT and data management and administrative systems. Next, detailed and legally binding partnership agreements detailing parties' contributions to the organisation protect against complicated divergences arising down the line. Additionally, there needs to be a clearly agreed balance of power among partners, with processes for decision-making and consultation in place. Finally, business partnerships may be close, deep and enduring, but they are not the same as friendships. Partners need to rigorously hold each other to objective standards, and be willing to challenge or even part from each other to protect the interests of the company.

A partnership learning curve

Alex: I set up Vesta Psychology Ltd as a company limited by shares, with two other psychologists in 1999. We took equal dividends. In those days our approach to business collaboration was naïve. Nothing by way of binding agreements was written up. For a few years we did very well together in medico-legal, injury, trauma and general clinical work. But there came a point in 2006 when we realised that between the three of us we did not possess enough knowledge of marketing, data analysis, or business strategy to realise our goals for the service. We were developmentally stuck, and had to make leadership changes if we were to grow. We needed a more business-oriented skills mix at director level, a more clinically diverse, medically led delivery team and an NHS-friendly business structure. Two of us wanted to bring in a GP. And I also wanted to bring in a former COO [chief operating officer] from the hospitality industry to lead operations. I was keen to convert to social enterprise and do away with shares. We disagreed about the proportionality of control we'd each be giving up. And one wanted to keep their dividends. Eventually, after much haggling and compromise, a reshuffle was agreed. We were then able to achieve the diversification we needed. But it was a protracted and painful process that could have been averted if we'd had future-proof partnership agreements in place from the outset.

Business planning

Your practice will have a range of current and potential stakeholders to whom you have many responsibilities. These include your clients and purchasers, employees and other retained workers, shareholders or trustees, your local community and society in general. Your strategic plans are blueprints for raising and organising resources, and allocating them to stakeholder interests according to the service's priorities, including the pre-eminent concerns of ensuring excellent client care and service sustainability. While the interests of key stakeholders may be at the heart of your practice's mission, it is not possible at any given time to meet all interests equally. Strategic plans will determine immediate and longer-term goals, and the organisational structure, staffing, systems, policies and procedures that will most effectively help your practice meet these goals. Another element of strategic planning is understanding your competitors, and securing commercial advantage by highlighting your practice's unique differences or by emulating and bettering your competitors' strengths. No matter what your practice's specialism or market sector, its goals almost inevitably will include delivering greater social and financial value to stakeholders than its competitors – which will protect the practice's prices and market share, while operating with maximum efficiency – which in turn controls the costs of providing services. These are all vital achievements for growth (Porter, 2003).

Strategic planning is an internally challenging yet vibrant, multi-area, ongoing process that helps you best position your practice to deliver its obligations and to deal competently with the unforeseen challenges that inevitably arise. Such planning is necessary whether you are a sole trader or director of a national organisation. It should cover all levels of operational hierarchy, including for the entire service, for specific contracts, customers, projects or localities, or for intra-project processes and systems. Planning processes are generally led by a senior management and/or trustee steering group, conducted with staff and client engagement; they are then converted into formal action plans with specific commitments adopted by key workers or teams, with regular review of progress and redefining of goals (Oliver and Memmott, 2006).

How I plan my work

Mandy: Initially I didn't do any formal work planning. I knew what I needed to do day by day, and I did it instinctively and without record. But once my coaching package took off, I was in a new league. I had to organise my time more efficiently and set higher goals. Really, we teach our clients to do this stuff so we need to practise what we preach. It's no good to just do it in your head. It has to be written down. I now create monthly plans and six-monthly overviews, using an app on my tablet. I back these up on a large dry-wipe, year-to-view calendar on my office wall, to help track projects over time. I update my five-year plan annually. That's always fascinating to see what I intended to achieve versus reality! These simple tools enable me to be more perceptive about the additional learning and activities I must embrace, to do more than I formerly believed I was capable of. Any time a new job looks really challenging, I find as soon as I get started it's nowhere near as tough as I thought it would be. Formal planning is a tremendous guiding force.

Marketing

A marketing and communications strategy is best embedded into your practice's business plan and budget at the outset of any new project. A growing service will benefit from taking on an experienced marketing lead. Targeted broadcasting of a new project's existence, remit, routes of access and intended outcomes takes considerable time, energy and resources, as does attracting sufficient numbers of suitable referrals, particularly in the first year or two. Information sessions for potential referrers and clients are helpful. Launch parties and other celebratory events can bring together diverse stakeholders, including clients, staff and commissioners in a sociable environment that generates goodwill and 'buzz' about your service.

Capable of either attracting or repelling potential customers at first glance, your website is the 'virtual doorway' to your practice. Professional design is worth the investment to keep your website fresh and attractive. As a primary vehicle for sharing your practice's story, your website will be more engaging if it includes video links, podcasts and interactive capabilities. You can also make it a direct sales portal where clients can book and pay for services.

Monitoring web traffic using search engine analytics enables you to understand the terms that led visitors to the site and the pages that are most and least visited, which then informs website modification and improvement.

Social media platforms dominate the business communications landscape. An active and strategic social media presence may be more influential in generating business leads than your website. New programmes, initiatives, awards, events, blogs and even job and consulting room vacancies are social media fodder. The immense popularity of video media enables you to showcase your work to a potentially vast international audience. Keeping up with social media posts is time-consuming, but admit it, you love doing it.

On top of the day-to-day demands of running a busy practice, the idea of producing research can seem onerous but it is fundamental to our scientist-practitioner identity. Publishing research on service outcomes and programme development creates a lasting legacy, not just for the reputation of the authors, but for the development of practice-based evidence for counselling psychology.

Above all these, the most valuable tool for service growth is face-to-face networking. If you have a new programme that could meet a demonstrable social need, and a team ready to provide it, a good first step in bringing this to market is requesting meetings with people with funding influence, such as NHS commissioners, public health and Clinical Commissioning Group (CCG) leads, psychological service leads, and education, insurance or charity directors. Procurement leaders can share information about their funding priorities and constraints, care pathway developments and criteria for purchasing. You might also attend networking meetings such as CCG annual general meetings, charity scoping exercises, local authority provider information days and Chamber of Commerce events. Effective networking requires you to be able to strike up engaging conversations with strangers, find common ground and 'tout your wares' without sounding like a salesperson. It also means leaving a favourably memorable impression and a way for interested parties to get in touch, so always carry business cards.

INCORPORATING, CONSOLIDATING AND EXPANDING

In this section we will explore the process of moving a practice to legal trading status, and some of the work associated with service expansion.

Incorporation

A first step in starting a company is deciding in which market sector to situate, as this will determine the legal framework surrounding business operations. If the service's aim is to generate profit for distribution to owners, shareholders or investors, a company limited by shares and located in the 'private' or 'independent' sector is the logical option. Alternatively, if the service's aims are primarily altruistic, then a company limited by guarantee, a charity, or a social enterprise, situated in the 'third' sector, may be more appropriate. No matter what the chosen business framework, it is sensible to obtain advice from an accountant or lawyer before finalising start-up plans, to ensure that all arrangements guard the business against potential future threats while maximising freedom to change and grow over time. The application process to set up a business in the UK with Companies House is relatively straightforward. Setting up a charity with the Charity Commission involves more steps but is not complicated.

It may be advisable at an early stage to appoint a board of non-executive directors or trustees, people with considerable business, research, clinical and service user expertise who serve in (generally non-stipendiary) advisory roles to provide objective governance for the organisation.

If needed, initial funds for premises, fittings and IT may be borrowed from someone within the business or a bank, secured by award or donated by a philanthropist. However, a start-up loan may burden a service with unnecessary debt. Beyond cash, new psychology services require considerable investment of time and knowledge, or 'intellectual capital', which may take several years to recoup financially. Founding members may initially pay themselves salaries that fall short of equivalent NHS or private sector pay bands, but the creativity and control permitted by building and running a service more than make up for this.

Another way of coming into a service is by taking a lead position in a going concern or by purchasing it outright. The advantage of taking over or buying an existing service is that some of the initial investment will have been made. Premises, equipment, administrative functions and staff are likely to be in place, and possibly existing contracts also. However, there may be considerable work needed to re-brand or re-position an existing business to make the most of its potential. Another possible downside is the risk of inheriting members of staff or trustees whose approach to work does not fit your values, or who are not keen on changing management. Employees have a range of legal rights under Transfer of Undertakings (Protection of Employment) (TUPE) legislation when their work with the new employer remains fundamentally the same (ACAS, 2014), so it is advisable to obtain legal advice when taking over an existing workforce.

Building a trading identity and performance record

There is no escaping the commercial imperative upon our work as practitioner psychologists. No matter where or how we work, basic rules of economics apply. These rules rest in the dynamic interplay between provision, or 'supply', and purchasing, or 'demand'. Becoming an entrepreneur-practitioner means working closely and knowledgeably with these economic forces. In the simplest terms, our work thrives when purchasers know, understand and need what we do, and are willing to pay the right price for it. One of the best forms of preparation for service growth is demonstrating and publicising a track record of excellent client care and cost-effectiveness (optimal use of resources). This leads to positive word of mouth between current and potential purchasers which in turn builds your 'brand', that is the feelings and values associated by customers with your service (Dearden-Phillips, 2012). A performance track record is built by regularly reporting service audit results. Outlets include your annual report, your website, conferences and social media. Reports ought to be organised around the interests of your target stakeholders. So, for instance, if you are seeking to become an NHS provider, show how your practice meets key commissioning priorities, including economy, efficiency, clinical effectiveness and equity of access (National Audit Office, 2014). Alternatively, your reported data may include descriptions of:

- service improvement initiatives based on learning from your outcomes;
- participation with your local Health and Wellbeing Board on a local Joint Strategic Needs Assessment (JSNA);
- project collaboration with local health and social care services or education;
- proof of ability to scale up a small initiative;
- grants awarded, new premises, staff qualification, areas of specialism or cultural competence, and achievements. (Robinson and Foster, 2014)

The process of professional growth

Saoirse: It takes years to build up the clinical expertise, performance record and professional relationships needed to successfully launch an independent service. I'm patiently heading in that direction, with the aim to eventually build a human rights and reconciliation charity. I worked for two charities while training in England. I shadowed my managers closely to understand how they conceptualised and organised their work. Now that I'm back home in Northern Ireland, I'm staying in the charity sector, currently learning loads as a programme manager for teenagers. We have a strong connection with the Youth Justice Agency. I get involved in local stakeholder surveys, finding out what clients and communities require, as well as what we can get funding for. We research all our pilot initiatives and I've used the results to show how our projects make a positive difference, whether funded or voluntary. Off the back of those results, we have been asked to scale up several projects, for bigger agreements. In the process, I have learned how to budget our services realistically. I've had to learn the language of cost-effectiveness. We psychologists need to balance our pride – that our particular skills add value to human services – against the risk that we price ourselves out of a job.

Forming provider consortia

Once your service is incorporated and has amassed a demonstrable track record, you may consider joining or forming a consortium in order to get involved with larger opportunities, or to bring an aspiring treatment or research programme to fruition. Wide-ranging relationship-building is the best way to meet prospective new business partners and colleagues. Scope the provider landscape in your region or your specialism, and directly approach possible collaborators with a carefully planned proposal – one that looks inviting without giving away too much of your commercially sensitive intentions.

Your service may join forces with one or more other organisations for specific projects or tenders to add diversity or capacity to the skills mix, to extend its geographical footprint or to reduce competition for work. Consortia can take a range of forms and it is worth obtaining legal advice before arranging a partnership. Conduct a background check on any organisation you are considering partnering with, for financial stability, ethical management and worthy reputation.

It is also helpful to explore whether values, mission and methods are compatible before agreeing to work with another organisation. If, for instance, one service's mission is primarily profit-driven (resource-retentive) and another's is focused on maximising the quality of client care and worker well-being (resource-liberal), mismatches in service cultures could become problematic. Likewise, if one organisation values strict worker management and another prefers a laissez-faire approach, mutual expectations may become frustrated. On the other hand, consortium working allows organisations to learn from each other and share knowledge, experience and resources.

Healthy consortium working is rooted in collaboratively established, closely monitored policies and procedures and strong relationships across all levels of the worker hierarchy. When distinct teams are co-delivering a project, it is vital to foster a sense of trusting interdependence and 'being in this together', and to actively work against the natural human tendency, when under stress, to form an 'us and them' mentality or, worse, a blame culture. It can be particularly helpful to provide a range of opportunities for staff from different teams to interact and give feedback directly and often, whether this is via co-delivery, multidisciplinary meetings or mutual training sessions.

Securing funding

Your service's trading structure will determine the range of funding sources you might pursue. When embarking on applying for foundational contracts or grants, it is worth obtaining advice from a tendering consultant. Also, good business sense will direct you to not rely on a single contract, especially in the public sector where services can be rapidly decommissioned or budget-stricken. Services broaden their income streams by diversifying delivery across different projects and programmes. So, as it grows, a service may form an in-house tender tracking and bidding team. Becoming listed on a 'provider framework', such as Any Qualified Provider (AQP), may also provide a source of income, although the amount of work offered may be unpredictable. More informal arrangements, such as service-level agreements and subcontracting affiliations, can be secured through professional networks.

Business schools, enterprise centres, charitable and governmental agencies provide timely, accurate and regionally specialised support for small businesses seeking to secure funding. Additionally, the BPS has published a guide for psychologists who want to become 'tender ready' (Vermes, 2013).

Financial management

Book-keeping, accounting and payroll can be done by internal staff or may be more economically outsourced to an accounting firm. Basic principles of financial management revolve around the primacy of cash flow and 'income in before expenses out'. Key functions include maintaining and adjusting budgets for current and future expenditure, tracking monthly and accumulated earnings on all projects, and forecasting year-end balances. Depending on the impact of any unbudgeted expenses, ensuring that targeted earnings are achieved by year end may require reducing expenditure and/or increasing earnings. Financial and clinical managers need to work together to track client capacity and therapist activity to ensure agreed performance indicators are met while staying within budget.

A criticism of the ongoing 'privatisation' of the UK public sector, including its mental health care, is that profit-driven organisations are snapping up contracts put out to tender by the NHS and local authorities (e.g. Fisher, 2013). There is currently no legal restriction on the profit organisations can achieve from public sector contracts, and NHS England does not (at the time of writing) collate information on commercial partners' budgets to ensure spending is in line with public interest (Cox, 2014). So, for psychologists, these are matters of conscience for self-policing. Can we, as NHS commercial partners, willingly and transparently show we retain the core values of the NHS, particularly principle six, *public funds for healthcare will be devoted solely to the benefit of the people that the NHS serves* (NHS Choices, 2014)? One way is to trade as an 'asset locked' social enterprise, which requires 100 per cent reinvestment of earnings into a social mission. Even companies that are not expressly not-for-profit can limit shareholding to workers directly involved in day-to-day operations and devote year-end savings to sustainably improving client care.

There are two keys to a service's long-term financial sustainability. The first is change management. A service thrives in so far as its mission remains commercially viable. The mission may evolve to meet social and economic pressures and prospects. People and processes may need to be replaced over time, to realise a service's potential. It may merge with another organisation or split up into trading divisions. The second key to sustainability is building a project portfolio with customers from diverse sectors, while retaining clinical focus. Diversification smooths financial risk. Maintaining a reputation for a broad but bordered specialism (such as clinical issues addressed, treatment modalities offered, social groups or treatment tiers served and so on) will inevitably form part of a service's identity, and ought not to be abandoned in a scramble to secure any and all available contracts.

Programme design and evaluation

Some purchasers detail in their tender and contract documents prescriptive evidence-based specifications of the service they want, including models and modalities, the professional disciplines that should deliver the services, even the outcome measures they want used. For instance, IAPT programmes require custom-trained therapists to deliver prescribed treatments. Other purchasers can be relatively vague about desired programme architecture, and are keen to work with their chosen provider (or leave it solely to the provider) to fill in a substantial amount of clinical and administrative detail to create and deliver a care package that is relevant, accessible and effective for clients within the remit of the tender.

New programme design is one of the most creative and exciting parts of a service's work. It builds on available literature, combined with the clinical and project management knowledge, experience and common sense of all staff. Pilot programmes generally require considerable reflection and revision in the first years of operation to hone them to optimum efficiency and effectiveness. The revision process includes making use of practice-based evidence, including feedback from clients and delivery staff, plus client attendance and retention rates, and analysis of outcome measures.

Outcomes, outcomes, outcomes

Outcome measure collection and analysis are central to successful service delivery. They chart the strengths and weaknesses of the service for internal clinical audits and associated programme revision, and they help translate the social and clinical value of the service's work into terms that are understandable to various stakeholders. Validated, benchmarked outcome measures need to be carefully selected to help answer key questions about client experiences of change over time. They need to be quick for clients to fill in on paper or tablet, and easy for staff to score and enter onto a database. Clients need to understand why the service collects this information, how it is used and stored, and must give consent for this. Staff training on routine outcome measures collection is an ongoing priority, as it can be therapist reluctance or disorganisation, rather than client objection, that causes detrimental gaps in outcome datasets (Bewick et al., 2006). Outcome data management forms a significant focal point for service activity, requiring appropriate security and information technology.

Information governance and management

All service clinical activities require accurate and timely record-keeping and analysis. No matter the size or sector of the organisation, if based in the UK it must be registered with the Information Commissioner and meet data protection obligations. Information governance

(IG) safeguards must be implemented, using appropriate policies and staff training to ensure data confidentiality and security. To ensure IG compliance, the Health and Social Care Information Centre (HSCIC) provides an Information Governance Toolkit which may be a mandatory process for services under contract to the NHS. It may also be useful for services in other sectors to undertake this process (HSCIC, 2014a).

Second to client work and associated care administration, the most resource-demanding aspect of service provision is data management. Without a close handle on service activity and outcomes data, managerial and clinical functions are operating 'in the dark' – a dangerous place to be. Data management is also essential for financial planning, for instance ensuring the service provides appropriate staff capacity, training and equipment to effectively meet clients' needs and contractual obligations, while minimising wasted resources. Data mastery is also required to quickly and cogently report on a wide range of service key performance indicators (KPIs) for contract management. Most purchasers require quarterly and annual reports, which aggregate large amounts of service activity data into digestible summaries. Additionally, more specialised statistical analysis may need to be performed, particularly on client outcomes, for research purposes. The creation of high-quality, practice-based research depends entirely on robust systems of in-service data collection and analysis.

Understand your numbers, understand your service

Alex: I admit I'm a data geek. It comes with the territory. Vesta is currently handling 3,500 referrals a year across seven contracts, including a high-intensity IAPT service, and a range of NHS health promotion projects. Our business manager and I are responsible for creating accurate models for capacity and budgeting, and maximising economies of scale by integrating our systems and knowledge sets across projects. We have a full-time administrator whose sole job is to maintain data quality and to produce comprehensive reports. Intensive data analysis with the latest academic-grade software enables me to spend about a quarter of my time creating and supervising client outcomes-focused research projects and service audits for continuous quality improvement.

Micro-sized services (e.g. up to 150 referrals a year) may securely manage client records on paper, backed up by password-protected electronic spreadsheets. However, as the number of referrals and funding sources increases, paper record-keeping becomes problematic. Storage uses physical space. File archiving and retrieval takes up staff time and is prone to data losses due to human error. It is exceedingly difficult to conduct financial and capacity planning, not to mention quantitative analysis, using paper records. Electronic data management is therefore an essential consideration for all developing services.

One solution for services wishing to retain basic service activity data on spreadsheets, while saving office space and staff time, is outsourcing scanning, cloud storage and paper shredding to a commercial document management service. A disadvantage to this approach is that reporting and analysis capabilities will be restricted to the functionality of the spreadsheets in which the data is stored.

Alternatively, electronic patient records and bookings systems (EPRs) are currently being adopted across the NHS and other sectors with the intention that most NHS services 'go paperless' by 2018 (Lansley, 2014). EPRs allow staff to enter activity data anywhere, any time they are working. They can facilitate engagement with service users, for instance by allowing clients to book their own appointments and sending appointment reminders by text or email. Additionally, EPR data can contribute to national statistics via relevant community or secondary care data omnibuses (HSCIC, 2014b). However, use of EPRs requires a sizeable budget allocation, first to acquire the software, and then to ensure staff have laptops, are trained on the system and have a sufficient proportion of their paid time allocated to data entry.

For services with routine responsibilities and commonplace outcome measures, buying into a commercial counsellors' database is a good solution. Although there are still relatively few well-developed options, those that are available offer a wide range of IG-compliant features, including: outcome measures analysis and benchmarking; the ability to manage therapist diaries, book appointments and send client e-reminders; manage correspondence, accept referrals directly into the system; and produce attractively presented reports. Such features streamline service administration and can improve client attendance rates (e.g. Stockwell et al., 2014). However, a potential problem with pre-defined databases can be their limited customisability to specific activities conducted by more complex services.

For services with specialised data management requirements, it may be preferable to build a custom database, which efficiently streamlines administrative and reporting functions and can be modified as the service changes, for instance as new projects or outcome measures come on-stream or a new report or piece of research is required. However, upfront capital is required to purchase a database, and it takes considerable staff time to work closely with the developers to ensure the database is well maintained and does exactly what the service needs.

Some purchasers (e.g. the Prison Service) or programmes (e.g. IAPT) require a commissioned service to use their database. While this can be easier in terms of not having to source an EPR, the service will still need its own system for tracking referrals, service activity and outcomes for financial and performance-related analysis.

THE COUNSELLING PSYCHOLOGIST IN SERVICE LEADERSHIP

In this section we will look at three areas related to becoming an entrepreneur-practitioner that require intuition and relational sensitivity: leadership, team development and self-care.

There is almost no research on counselling psychologists in service leadership. Therefore, the hallmarks of our work are anecdotal. They might be encapsulated in an idea adapted from the NHS England Nursing Directorate's *Compassion in Practice* initiative (2013), as 'Seven Cs':

1. **Can-do attitude**: Probably the key defining characteristic of the successful service leader, this generosity of spirit is manifested as wideness and optimism of vision; willingness and energy to get projects organised and funded; skill to bring new ideas to life; charisma to create, inspire and enable change; and perseverance to turn challenges into possibilities.
2. **Creative capacity-building**: Good service leaders have the knowledge, inspiration and ability to find the resources needed to improve existing services and to start new ones. They make the most of their colleagues' and volunteers' potential. They tap intellectual capital by translating innovative ideas into new ways of working.
3. **Collaboration**: We understand that our work in business and research is most powerful when we work synergistically with colleagues from other disciplines. Collaborative projects and multidisciplinary working require excellent communication.
4. **Communication**: Listening, clarifying, understanding, responding, sharing and initiating, in a timely, respectful and organised manner, are chief leadership qualities, as are being approachable, genuine and assertive. Communication style is a team-wide culture; it will make or break a service's reputation. Knowledge-sharing is wide-reaching and unstinting.
5. **Continual feedback**: As reflective practitioners, we not only provide advice and appraisal to staff, but invite regular and spontaneous feedback from team members across the workplace hierarchy to help understand and improve our own effectiveness. Non-defensive, proactive responses to feedback ensure a safe and nurturing environment for staff and clients. This culture fosters constructive conflict, openness, engagement and respect.
6. **Complexity**: Service provision requires the balancing of competing demands in complicated and ever-changing political and economic environments. Additionally, our work generally falls on the 'specialist' and 'severe' ends of mental health treatment pathways, for clients with multiple needs who may have exhausted other treatment options. We offer enduring hope, presence and engagement.
7. **Change management**: Finally, we competently facilitate and foster change: knowledge, practice and paradigm change, and social change. Indeed, it could be argued that the latter is our primary function, and that if we are not actively and demonstrably promoting social justice, then we are not doing our job.

Hiring and firing

Selecting, mentoring and retaining workers who are right for the organisation and its client groups requires finely tuned judgement and ongoing attention. Nurturing a mature, knowledgeable, creative and committed workforce is a top responsibility for the service leader and, third in line after client care and data management, requires the greatest investment of time.

Vesta Psychology recruitment

Alex: Effective recruitment at Vesta rests on four foundations: (1) accurate and thorough job descriptions and associated competencies; (2) advertising that's targeted to attract appropriate candidates; (3) evaluative job interviews that judge candidates against objective markers that are assessed by a committee of existing staff and clients; and (4) selecting people from the shortlist because they will fit well with our team, can meet the demands of the role and are likely to thrive in a changing environment. We have honed this process over the years and choose the right people about 90 per cent of the time.

Newly-recruited staff need full orientation to their work within the unique context of the service. Orientation also details the lines of accountability for standards of care, along with managerial and departmental responsibilities. Training on policies and procedures will be completed. A period of mentorship with a more senior colleague (who has performed a similar role) can help ease in a new worker. Regular line management meetings enable two-way feedback in the first six months of employment, which is a standard probationary period in which employee and employer can ascertain if they are a good match.

Annual reviews provide an opportunity for employee and line manager to formally and mutually appraise and document how the work has been going. Generally, feedback is given on specific markers such as job tasks and employment satisfaction. Areas for development and training can be agreed. Transparent and fair processes for promotion or salary increases can be applied. It may be necessary to remediate problematic practice via carefully documented redirection meetings, with clear and specific goals set. Regularly scheduled follow-up meetings should ensure appropriate changes are being made.

Even with carefully devised processes in place, an employer can occasionally make an error in hiring or promoting a worker. It is generally clear within the first year of appointment that a worker does not have the aptitude or attitude for their assigned role or does not fit well with the team. Client or co-worker complaints, unsatisfactory task completion, poor communications, insufficient contribution to the service's mission and expressions of unrealistic entitlement regarding pay or status are all danger signals to address promptly and head on. Dealing decisively with inadequate performance can represent a learning curve if we feel compelled by our counselling psychology training to be 'tentative and tender' towards everyone. For serious employee conduct issues it is essential to follow a disciplinary procedure, and to obtain employment consultancy to ensure compliance with legal requirements surrounding changing a person's role or terminating employment.

Team building

As the number of projects your service is involved with increases, specialised delivery teams will be built up for each. Although some team members may work on more than one project (e.g. administrators or directors), each team will have clearly defined objectives, client groups, and administrative and reporting methods. Members within each team will have job descriptions and evaluation markers specific to their project.

Teams are intended to work as 'performing units' (Onyett, 2007) that depend on trust and respect between members and managers, and a sense of mutuality in manifesting the project's goals and the service's mission. Teams also benefit from frequent performance reviews, using aggregated client comments and service activity data. As some team members may have little contact with each other in the normal course of their work, in-person team meetings are an essential ingredient in fostering team cohesion (even if this achieved 'virtually', for instance, with video conferencing).

Regular team meetings serve multiple aims. They provide time to understand and assess the team's work. They provide space for system planning and revision. They give opportunity for members to voice concerns and conflicts, and to propose ideas and solutions. Team meetings also provide opportunities for team member empowerment via task delegation. Importantly, training requirements emerge in discussions that bring to light individual worker differences in knowledge or approach. Promoting team-wide consistency in practice improves the fairness of client care and overall programme quality. Finally, team meetings engender a sense of the wholeness and wisdom of the team, and generate vital emotional safety and camaraderie.

Productive team meetings require dedicated preparation and follow-up on the team leader's part. Included on the agenda might be performance data reports, strategic planning and areas for development. Action plans and the people responsible for carrying them out will be documented in detailed minutes. These action plans will be followed up at (or before) the next meeting, with the expectation that most tasks will be complete or in progress unless serious barriers have arisen.

Self-care

In a service's developmental periods, work-time boundaries are stretched. Leaders may put in 60-plus hours a week, sometimes for months on end. A proportion of this time may go unremunerated. Those who have built up a successful business through years of dedicated effort may find their service and sense of identity become enmeshed. Maintaining work–life balance can be a challenge when your mind is constantly captivated by multiple (and sometimes stressful) demands. Remaining engaged in enjoyable non-work activity and rich personal relationships helps keep things in perspective. It is reassuring to be surrounded by highly committed colleagues who are willing to put in extra effort at times. It is also helpful to keep asking yourself when, and to whom, to give away tasks and responsibilities.

Delegation

Sanjeet: I am a 'Jack of all trades'. I enjoy contract sourcing, management and reporting, budgeting, seeing clients, hiring staff and providing colleague mentorship, and organising office procedures. It's tempting to hold on to tasks with which I am most familiar, but the service benefits each time we find a new team member to take a major area of responsibility off me. I am steadily departing from front-end management to focus on frontier management: strategy and development priorities.

As useful as supervision is for the clinician, so coaching is for the service leader. It is not important that your coach know anything about psychology provision; their job is to help you understand yourself within the leadership context, to hone and revise personal and business values and goals, and to overcome practical obstacles to improving overall functioning. It is also helpful to forge relationships with other service leaders, not just for the possibility of working together, but also for the assurance of being able to talk in-depth with someone who has similar experience of dealing with the problems of the day.

SUMMARY

Becoming an entrepreneur-practitioner requires considerable creativity and drive, and brings with it broad realms of responsibility. Key personal characteristics include the possession of a clearly defined social mission and the confidence to bring it to life. By necessity and by nature, an entrepreneur-practitioner is an excellent communicator, who builds professional relationships across disciplines, employment sectors, stakeholder parties and community health groups. Additionally, the entrepreneur-practitioner uses business management skills alongside extensive clinical knowledge and experience. So, a career path into your own practice may be aided by training in bidding for competitive tenders, employment law and human resources, team leadership, strategic and financial planning, and technology for data management and analysis. Future employment security for practitioner counselling psychologists depends heavily on the efforts of today's entrepreneur-practitioners to engage ethically with diverse opportunities in the ever-changing health and social care marketplace. Embedded in these opportunities are possibilities to create and publish influential practice-based research to help shape the ways health priorities are addressed now and in the future.

Visit the companion website to listen to Becoming an Entrepreneur.

REFERENCES

ACAS (Advisory, Conciliation and Arbitration Service) (2014). 2014 Changes to TUPE. London: ACAS. Downloaded from www.acas.org.uk/media/pdf/l/1/9908-2901767-TSO-ACAS-TUPE_is_changing-ACCESSIBLE.pdf on 08.03.2014.

Acts of Parliament (2012a). *The Health and Social Care Act.* London: The Stationery Office. Downloaded from www.legislation.gov.uk/ukpga/2012/7/contents/enacted on 23.08.2014.

Acts of Parliament (2012b). *The Public Services (Social Value) Act.* London: The Stationery Office. Downloaded from www.legislation.gov.uk/ukpga/2012/3/enacted on 20.05.2014.

Benanti, J. (2006). The bane identity. *Counselling Psychology Review*, 21(1): 44–46.

Bewick, B.M., Trusler, K., Mullin, T., Grant, S. and Mothersole, G. (2006). Routine outcome measurement completion rates of the CORE-OM in primary care psychological therapies and counselling. *Counselling and Psychotherapy Research*, 6(1): 33–40.

Cox, B. (2014). BBC Radio 4: *File on 4: The Accountant Kings.* Downloaded from www.bbc. co.uk/programmes/b03wpjjq on 09.03.2014.

Dearden-Phillips, C. (2012). *Start Your Social Enterprise.* London: Social Enterprise UK. Downloaded from www.socialenterprise.org.uk on 03.04.2014.

DCoP (Division of Counselling Psychology) (2011). *Questback Attitudes Survey.* Leicester: BPS. Downloaded from http://dcop.bps.org.uk/document-download-area/document-download$. cfm?file_uuid=DD0EAE28-9F67-15E6-18B5-8F52C2D857C0&ext=pdf on 23.08.2014.

Department of Health (2008). *High Quality Care for All: NHS Next Stage Review Final Report.* London: Department of Health. Downloaded from www.gov.uk/government/uploads/ system/uploads/attachment_data/file/228836/7432.pdf on 50.05.2014.

Fisher, B. (2013). The dangers of marketization. *Health Service Journal*, 23 January. Downloaded from www.hsj.co.uk/comment/the-dangers-of-marketisation/5053782.arti-cle on 09.03.2014.

George, B. (2003). *Authentic Leadership: Rediscovering the Secrets to Creating Lasting Value.* San Francisco, CA: Jossey-Bass.

HSCIC (Health and Social Care Information Centre) (2014a). *Information Governance Toolkit.* London: HSCIC. Downloaded from www.igt.hscic.gov.uk/ on 05.03.2014.

HSCIC (2014b). *Collecting Data.* London: HSCIC. Downloaded from www.hscic.gov.uk/col-lectingdata on 05.03.2014.

HM Government (2014). *The Public Services (Social Value) Act 2012: One Year On.* London: The Stationery Office. Downloaded from www.gov.uk/government/uploads/system/ uploads/attachment_data/file/275719/Public_Services__Social_Value__Act_-_One_ Year_On.pdf on 20.05.2014

James, P. (2009). The centrality and consistency of counselling psychology. *Counselling Psychology Review*, 24(2): 64–73.

Kaffash, J. and Sterling, A. (2013). Majority of new contracts have been put out to competition since April by CCGs. *Pulse.* Downloaded from www.pulsetoday.co.uk/news/commissioning-news/majority-of-new-contracts-have-been-put-out-to-competition-since-april-by-ccgs/20004426.article#.VBK1TvldWSo on 10.09.2014.

Lansley, A. (2014). Address to the NHS Health and Care Innovation Expo 2014, Manchester, UK, 4 March.

Lewis, A.-M. (2012). Organisations adjusting to change: A discussion of the impact of an Improving Access to Psychological Therapies (IAPT) service on the organizational dynamics of an existing psychological therapies department. *Counselling Psychology Review*, 27(1): 22–29.

McLeod, J. and Machin, L. (1998). The context of counselling: A neglected dimension of training research and practice. *British Journal of Guidance and Counselling*, 26(3): 325–336.

National Audit Office (NAO) (2014). *Successful Commissioning Toolkit*. Downloaded from www.nao.org.uk/successful-commissioning/general-principles/value-for-money/assessing-value-for-money/ on 04.09.2014.

NHS Choices (2014). *NHS Core Principles*. Downloaded from the NHS Choices website at www.nhs.uk/NHSEngland/thenhs/about/Pages/nhscoreprinciples.aspx on 09.03.2014.

NHS England Nursing Directorate (2013). *Compassion in Practice – One Year On*. London: NHS Publications.

Oliver, J.J. and Memmott, C. (2006). *Growing Your Own Heroes: The Commonsense Way to Improve Business Performance*. Cork: Oak Tress Press.

Onyett, S. (2007). *New Ways of Working for Applied Psychologists in Health and Social Care: Working Psychologically in Teams*. Leicester: British Psychological Society.

Parpottas, P. (2012). Working with the therapeutic relationship in cognitive behaviour therapy from an attachment theory perspective. *Counselling Psychology Review*, 27(3): 91–99.

Porter, M.E. (2003). What is strategy? In H.E. Mintzberg, J. Lampel, J.B. Quinn and S. Ghoshal (eds), *The Strategy Process*, an imprint of *The Strategy Process: Concepts, Contexts and Cases, Global* (4th edition). Upper Saddle River, NJ: Pearson Custom Printing, pp. 16–22.

Robinson, L. and Foster, J. (2014). *Commissioning Third Sector Counselling: Valuing and Enabling Services*. Lutterworth: British Association of Counselling and Psychotherapy. Downloaded from www.bacp.co.uk/admin/structure/files/pdf/13340_3rd_sector_report_web.pdf on 03.09.2014.

Bates, Wells and Braithwaite and Social Enterprise Coalition (SEC) (2006). *Keeping it Legal: A Guide to Legal Forms for Social Enterprises*. London: Social Enterprise Coalition.

Stockwell, M.S., Westhoff, C., Kharbanda, E.O., Vargas, C.Y., Camargo, S., Vawdrey, D.K. and Castaño, P.M. (2014). Influenza vaccine text message reminders for urban, low-income pregnant women: A randomized controlled trial. *American Journal of Public Health*, 104(S1) January Supplement: e7–e12.

Vermes, C. (2013). *An Introduction to Bidding for Public Sector Contracts for Counselling Psychologists*. Leicester: British Psychological Society.

Walsh, E. and Frankland, A. (2009). Guest editorial. *Counselling Psychology Review*, 24(1): 1–2.

Williams, Z. (2012). *The Shadow State: A Report about Outsourcing of Public Services*. London: Social Enterprise UK. Downloaded from www.socialenterprise.org.uk/advice-services/publications/the-shadow-state-report-about-outsourcing-public-services on 20.05.2014.

38
RESEARCHING ACROSS THE CAREER SPAN
ELAINE KASKET

INTRODUCTION

During a training programme in counselling psychology, the research experience gained is substantial. Graduates should be familiar with several methodologies and will know one in-depth; they will have written at least one research proposal and have negotiated ethical approval; they will have gathered a large amount of potentially complex data; and they will have had to employ sophisticated analytical skills, critical thinking, effective time management, and sound academic writing to produce a research report and perhaps journal articles as well. These skills could serve one well in ongoing professional life, but questions remain about the extent to which they are put to use after qualification.

From the vantage point of a counselling psychologist who has observed scores of others as they progress through their careers, it would seem that relatively few counselling psychologists in the United Kingdom count research among their primary activities. While my observations are anecdotal, more systematically gathered evidence exists, supporting the view that counselling psychologists in the UK typically do not pursue significant continuing research activity after qualification. One literature survey (Gordon and Hanley, 2013) concluded that only 1.4 per cent of qualified UK counselling psychologists had published research articles within the previous three years. Why might this be, and what are the consequences of it?

While those who qualified within the 'doctoral era' of the last ten years are more likely to possess the repertoire of research skills described in the first paragraph of this chapter, more seasoned practitioners may have less research knowledge and fewer research skills. Busy portfolio professionals may lack the interest, time and/or motivation to undertake research, particularly when it is not key to their livelihoods. Even for those who are interested, if one is not associated with a university or employed by another research-supportive organisation, one may struggle to access needed resources: ethical approval structures, funding, research assistance and library databases. Finally, and importantly, some may not appreciate that not all research involves a large, individually produced piece of work on the scale of a doctoral project, but that it can have myriad forms, take place in a variety of contexts and continue to enhance one's profile, working life and employability in a number of ways.

The consequences of low rates of research activity and publication are even more significant for the profession as a whole than they are for individual practitioners. A field that produces little research will naturally have little influence on evolving theory and practice, and minimal impact on policy and guidance such as that produced by the National Institute for Health and Care Excellence (NICE). It does not have to be this way, however, and the intent behind this chapter is to influence the situation for the better.

READERSHIP AND AIMS FOR THIS CHAPTER

This chapter aims to inspire greater interest in and commitment to continuing the research journey beyond qualification, as well as offering practical information to assist qualified counselling psychologists at every stage of their career, working in various settings: academia, the National Health Service and independent practice. While most of the chapter references the UK specifically, counselling psychologists internationally may benefit from considering the contexts in which ongoing research can occur, the forms it can take, the opportunities for collaboration and support that exist, and the potential personal and professional benefits that can result from being research active. Included in this chapter are six first-person accounts, giving voice to a diverse group of UK-based researchers.

RESEARCH WITHIN ACADEMIA

Co-publishing with supervisees

When one extrapolates from Gordon and Hanley's (2013) findings, one can surmise that of the hundreds of theses produced by trainees from all the counselling psychology training programmes in the UK, only a handful are disseminated via published work. Since there is overlap between doctoral theses and journal articles on at least one criterion – that the research contributes something new and valuable to the field – the low publication rate is curious. Either journals are rejecting the work of doctoral researchers or researchers are not submitting articles.

Any permanent or visiting faculty on a doctoral training programme is likely to be involved in supervision. Although supervision may be paid at a similar rate, it could be argued that supervision delivers fewer immediate benefits for the academic than teaching. First, the learning involved in constructing and delivering a new lecture is considerable – research has long shown that one of the most effective learning methods is teaching the material to someone else. By contrast, the provision of a few hours of supervision is unlikely to result in as much new knowledge for the academic. In addition, a prepared lecture becomes something of direct use to the academic; it can be parlayed into other things (e.g. a book chapter, a journal article, a published commentary) or revised and delivered again in a future term. Supervision only results in such tangible benefits if the doctoral work results in a published article on which the supervisor is co-author.

Some supervisors may not realise that articles produced from doctoral work are expected to be joint, with the principal supervisor as second author. If the extent of supervisory input has been negligible (which may be the case with second supervisors or situations where the candidate has been autonomous), the supervisor may not be named as an author at all; on the other end of the spectrum, a supervisor whose supervisee does not wish to write up the work may publish as first author. The British Psychological Society Research Board's *Statement of Policy on Authorship and Publication Credit* (2011) provides specific guidance for supervisors and supervisees about co-authorship.

While other disciplines are unabashed about expecting publication from doctoral research, and unembarrassed about requiring the supervisor to be co-author, it would seem from the numbers cited in Gordon and Hanley (2013) that counselling psychologist supervisors are shy about creating and following through on such expectations, even though (or perhaps because) this would be in the supervisor's interest. Such coyness disadvantages everyone: doctoral researchers, supervisors, the profession and all those who might benefit from research being disseminated.

If you are a supervisor, consider how you might build a situation where you feel like a genuine stakeholder in your supervisees' work. At the point when candidates are choosing their research areas, strive to connect with those candidates who are willing to carry out research in your own interest areas. An eventual publication that falls in line with your own interest and expertise may give you the sense of having more 'ownership', even if the research is primarily produced by your supervisee, the primary author. Once supervision commences, create a culture of expectation from the outset by discussing eventual publication with your supervisees, as described in the following first-person account of one counselling psychologist's experience of co-publishing with supervisees.

First-person account: Co-publishing with supervisees

Professor Martin Milton, C.Psychol., Regent's University

I drop publication into my early conversations with all of my supervisees, saying, 'When it comes time to write up for publication …'. On rare occasions someone has said, 'Oh no, I'm not planning on publishing!' That provokes a serious conversation about where that's coming from, why on earth I would want to supervise this if it were not going to be a contribution, and a review of what the point of doctoral research is. Is it just to show you can do research? You can show that at undergraduate level. Where's the contribution bit?

It's partly an issue of ethics. People expect research to lead to an improvement in something, and participants make the effort because they think it will do someone good in the end. It isn't enough that it does the *student* good in the end, in terms of getting their degree.

On one of my programmes it was explicitly in the supervisory contract that if the student failed to disseminate their doctoral findings, the supervisor could do so. I had no problem with that. I think students like the supervisor to be keen. It adds a different dimension to the doctoral training, a sense of an academic community, not just 'I'm a student, and they're the lecturer who knows everything'.

Sometimes a student is a good researcher but not such a good writer, so I might do a complete rewrite of the phrasing. I become the storyteller, and they're first author. That said, supervisory input alone is enough to warrant second author – the talking, the idea generation, the editing, what works, what doesn't. When someone has written it up independently, I'm very pleased when they ask me to have a look before submission. That's a nice courtesy, and a chance to say, 'I'm pleased that *our* work has a chance of recognition'.

To me, encouraging supervisees towards publication is an extension of what our teaching and our profession are about. It's about working with and developing our colleagues … and ourselves! I've had plenty of students that published interesting and novel research, things I hadn't thought about, and that's quite exciting. Without the pressure of publishing, they might have passed their vivas and their research would just be sitting on the shelf.

Producing 'REF-able' research

The 'publish or perish' culture may seem foreign to many who teach on counselling psychology professional doctorates in the UK. Within some disciplines, however, an ever-growing CV of grants won, research projects undertaken and journal articles published is essential for continued employment and securing new posts. The combined track records of its faculty members is critical for those universities who rely on monies distributed by the Higher Education Funding Council for England (HEFCE). While HEFCE distributes *teaching* funding based on student numbers and on specific costs associated with a university's particular mix of subject areas, their *research* funding is allocated based on the volume, quality and costs of the research taking place at a given university, and funding is targeted where research quality is highest. The newest framework for assessing and funding research is the Research Excellence Framework (REF), the first round of which drew to a close in 2014 with an assessment of research outputs between 2008 and 2013. The results of that assessment will inform allocation of research funding from 2015 until the next REF.

REF2014 divided submissions into 36 subject-linked Units of Assessment (UoAs), of which one was Psychology, Psychiatry and Neuroscience. Theoretically, counselling psychology faculty who had been research active during 2008–2013 could have put their work forward for their university's Psychology UoA, but their eligibility would have been subject to certain provisos. In order for individual staff members to be included in the REF, they were generally required to have had at least four research outputs that were graded at 1* or above in the REF's star system (shown in Table 38.1) and that were considered to have considerable impact (i.e. reach and significance).

Table 38.1   The starred levels of the Research Excellence Framework (REF)

Classification	Descriptors
Four star (4*)	Quality that is world-leading in terms of originality, significance and rigour
Three star (3*)	Quality that is internationally excellent in terms of originality, significance and rigour but that falls short of the highest standards of excellence
Two star (2*)	Quality that is recognised internationally in terms of originality, significance and rigour
One star (1*)	Quality that is recognised nationally in terms of originality, significance and rigour
Unclassified	Quality that falls below the standard of nationally recognised work, or work that does not meet the published definition of research for the purposes of this assessment

Taken from www.ref.ac.uk

The REF defines publication outputs as journal articles, books, conference papers, policy documents and reports. Gordon and Hanley (2013) only surveyed journal articles, although, given the low rate of these between 2010 and 2013, it seems unlikely that many counselling psychologists (CoPs) submitted for REF2014. Because REF is a new system and a complex one, successful submissions need clear prompting, strong leadership and facilitation at the departmental and university levels, and support and education for potential submitters. Universities may focus their REF encouragements towards those departments with more entrenched research cultures and well-established publication records in the 3* and 4* categories. Interested and active counselling psychologist researchers, therefore, may need to proactively liaise with department heads, research degrees offices and other key figures organising submissions for the next cycle of assessment. While many universities have put together their own REF training materials, the official website (www.ref.ac.uk) has a wealth of information on the process.

The new system has not been without its critics, and despite guidance to the contrary, there have nevertheless been worries that some types of research (e.g. smaller-scale qualitative studies) might be unfairly consigned to the unstarred, 'unclassified' slush pile. Nevertheless, it is pragmatic to consider how being 'REF-able' can be valuable for an academic in these straitened times, when universities are understandably concerned about their financial resources. One concern is employability and mobility. If one wishes to change jobs, while REF-starred outputs may not always be highest priority to the counselling psychology team at your hoped-for destination, they may be of considerable import to the higher university powers, who prioritise future research funding and sift through the pool of applicants accordingly. Career advancement within one's current post also cannot be ignored, and the road from lecturer to professor is paved with numerous impactful publications in quality journals of national and international significance. Whatever your opinion of the star system, and whether or not you anticipate submitting for the next REF cycle, it is worth remembering the quality criteria in Table 38.1 when selecting research questions and choosing the journals to which you submit. It will be interesting to observe how all the applied psychologies engage in future REF cycles.

The following first-person account is from a clinical psychologist, but his story is applicable to aspirant REF submitters within counselling psychology.

First-person account: Submitting to the REF

Dr David Gillanders, CPsychol., Doctoral Programme in Clinical Psychology, University of Edinburgh

The 2014 REF was on my horizon for a long time; every year since 2008–2009 the faculty at my university have filled in annual research activity forms, which each school would collate to see who was on target to be REFable. My university has a strategy for the REF; it was considered important and would influence the research funds that we receive for many years to come. From a personal level, the REF felt hugely important to me, in that I wanted to show that I was research active and contributing to the research culture of the university.

Our university had decided well in advance to only submit people with publications of 3* or 4* quality. Two months before the submission date, I looked like I was on target, but it would be a close call. I was being considered by unit number 4: Psychology, Psychiatry and Neuroscience. I don't really know why, but it did appear that in the last few months the definition of quality seemed to suddenly jump up (e.g. increased focus on high impact factor journals). This coincided with a change in panel chair, but there may have been other reasons for what seemed to be a late shift in the goal posts. Ultimately, my research wasn't judged good enough quality to be returned. At the last minute, there was consideration of submitting under unit 22: Social Work and Social Policy. When that panel reviewed my contribution they felt it did not fit well with their existing narrative. My work is about living with chronic ill health and they thought it was too medical for them. So, not good enough quality for neuroscience, too medical for social science!

I've been through the process but don't have the perspective to comment on the bigger picture of whether the REF works. It's hard in psychology programmes with a heavy applied focus; spending most of your time teaching people to do applied work often doesn't lend itself to doing independently funded research. We do have doctoral students doing research with us and they can lead to publications, but the scale and scope of a doctoral project is often not what is required to get really good 3* and 4* outputs. And if you're producing good work that's nationally and internationally recognised, but it's not in the top-quality journals,

(Continued)

(Continued)

you're then not seen as research active. It's a little black and white and those who are already winning get to win, while those who aren't in front don't get much of a chance at the REF. But my school was extremely good in the whole process. Even though I wasn't REFed, they made me feel that I was still very valued, and it was not a barrier to promotion. My Head of School's take was that I only narrowly didn't make it this time, and that from now, I have a good platform on which to build for the next census.

RESEARCH WITHIN THE NATIONAL HEALTH SERVICE (NHS)

The NHS employs increasing numbers of counselling psychologists, and in a Division of Counselling Psychology survey in 2013, 62.7 per cent of the nearly 500 qualified and in-training respondents reported working in the NHS part- or full-time. Although counselling psychologists' training is not funded, and posts within the NHS are not guaranteed, many training programmes require that a certain percentage of placement hours be undertaken within the NHS, and upon graduation many newly qualified counselling psychologists may parlay their placement experience into an NHS post. Services differ widely in terms of their emphasis on research, but those that have formal links with universities – as in the first-person account below – may be strongly supportive of ongoing research activity.

When one thinks of research within the traditionally clinical environment of the NHS, and when one notes the large amount of generally quantitative data that is collected within Improving Access to Psychological Therapies (IAPT) services, one could assume that the research conducted within this setting is primarily quantitative in nature. Certainly, the hierarchy of evidence adhered to places high-quality randomised controlled trials (RCTs) and case-control or cohort studies at the top, and some prominent UK counselling psychologists have advocated for more engagement with and development of RCTs by those in the counselling and counselling psychology professions (Cooper, 2011). At the same time, NICE's agenda promotes hearing service users' perspectives, tailoring interventions and supporting patient choice, and this means that a large range of research methodologies are valued within NHS settings. In the first-person accounts below, the researchers are carrying out smaller-scale, qualitative investigations of patient experience.

First-person account: Researching in an NHS setting

Joanna Omylinska-Thurston, C.Psychol., AFBPsS, Doctoral Researcher

After finishing the Qualification in Counselling Psychology (QCoP), I went on to a top-up doctorate. I had started a new job as a CoP within a research-orientated NHS service that had a partnership with the university. They were keen to sit down with me to set out the agenda for the department, to tell me about things they were interested in, and to hear what I was interested in as a CoP. After lots of conversations and teasing out of agendas, we came up with something workable: a project about helpful and unhelpful factors in working with cancer patients. This was in line with my supervisor's interests, but also on the agenda of the service and the whole cancer research agenda as regards patient experience. Looking into patients' perspectives also very much fitted in with NICE's agenda about tailoring interventions.

I was extremely lucky because I had quite a supportive group of people around me; there was all this research going on in the service, people had experience with IRAS [Integrated Research Application System], and I could always ask for advice. It was a clinical post, though, and as time went on, tensions around that came up, because although the job description did include research, it was not primary for the role. Although clients DNA [do not arrive] and I can do a bit of this and that during the week, I end up spending a lot of my weekends on research.

I would advise people to negotiate research time – from the beginning of your post if possible – and have it agreed as part of your role. You could ask for half a day a week for research activity, or ask that research be counted as CPD, or request unpaid leave. Acceptance that a lot of weekends will still be taken up with research is important, though. Choose a topic that is in your heart and is interesting for you, because it's a long process and needs stamina. If your service has research on its agenda, it can be good to do as a team – it is always more difficult on your own.

It is important to highlight that when working in an NHS service you may become involved in some investigations that do not constitute formal research projects in the eyes of the Health Research Authority (www.hra.nhs.uk). Service evaluations measure current service without reference to any standard and are done purely to define or judge current care in a service. Clinical audits *do* measure current care against an existing, predetermined standard and are designed to see if service delivery meets that standard. (The pamphlet *Defining Research* (Health Research Authority, 2009) provides more detail on differentiating research, service evaluation, and clinical audit.) Although these activities involve the gathering and analysis of data, neither requires scrutiny by a Research Ethics Committee (REC), which means that they do not require application through the Integrated Research Application System (IRAS).

In the case of qualitative and quantitative research studies that aim to generate new knowledge and test hypotheses, however, researchers must gain approval through the IRAS system; this may apply whether the participants are patients or NHS staff. Many avoid projects requiring IRAS, believing that the process is so complex and lengthy as to make research not worth undertaking. The result of such thinking, however, is that much valuable, relevant, practice- and service-applicable research is avoided. In the first-person account below, the researcher acknowledges the challenges and frustrations but ultimately makes a persuasive case for why the research is worth doing.

First-person account: Going through the Integrated Research Application System (IRAS)

Mike Evans, Trainee Counselling Psychologist, University of West of England

I was working in an emerging BPD [borderline personality disorder] unit in the NHS and became aware of the lack of men with the diagnosis and how men were diagnosed and treated differently by mental health professionals, and I decided to do my doctoral research on men's experiences of the diagnosis of BPD. I think that there has been a view that gaining NHS ethical approval is a monstrous task, and my first director of studies hadn't had a trainee complete the process before, so it was a case of seeking information from the local R&D [research and development] team.

The whole process took approximately six months. It is frustrating due to the number of stages you have to achieve before full permissions are granted, but on reflection it was much easier than first anticipated. From the start I put a lot of thought into various scenarios that might arise and what would be needed to remediate the effects. It helped to know the NHS and its views on risk management, safeguarding and crisis management procedures, all of which I included in the application. I think this increased confidence in the ethics panel regarding my research with a very vulnerable clinical population. NHS ethics panels don't necessarily have mental health professionals on them, so it's useful to include a flow chart of who will be contacted and how in the event of participant distress; to show understanding of how safeguarding policies impact clinical research; and to gain the confidence of care co-ordinators and responsible clinicians, to include primary care clinicians. I would also encourage researchers to go on 'good practice in clinical research' training, as ethics panels tend to favour these.

I would, firstly, advise researchers to commit to the process and expect to have to go backwards several times before completion. Secondly, preparation is vital to success, so think about how you will manage difficulties within the research process and play out scenarios with colleagues. Thirdly, go for proportional review [meaning a lower level of scrutiny can be applied to studies with lower ethical risk] if you can, as this will make things a lot easier. Fourthly, get to know IRAS inside out before you submit your proposal. I got caught out by the authorisation process and ended up very frustrated, but in the end it is quite simple, if you follow the system! Finally, the staff at IRAS are super helpful and friendly, so use them. They are experts in the system and requirements!

NHS ethical procedures are time consuming and an added 'task' to an already fraught process, but for me well worth it. I feel that I am investigating a disenfranchised and excluded population. I am passionate about equality and I encountered so many men in practice that have either been excluded from services or just not seen by clinicians because of strong gender associations around the diagnosis of BPD. I am hoping change will come about because of what I discovered through the research process.

RESEARCH AS AN INDEPENDENT PRACTITIONER

A 2013 survey into the employment status of counselling psychologists (Division of Counselling Psychology, 2013) indicated that large numbers of counselling psychologists are in independent practice. Those with employment in the NHS and other clinical contexts, and those employed within academia, have structures for conducting research, which include access to ethical approval mechanisms. For 'pure' independent practitioners, however, research may be a particularly lonely business. This section aims to help practitioners access a greater level of support.

Accessing literature

It is difficult to embark upon research without access to the appropriate literature. While academics might have such literature at their fingertips, independent practitioners might need to work a bit harder, but the resources are available. Increasingly, full-text journal articles are available on an open-access basis and accessible electronically. British Psychological Society and Division of Counselling Psychology members have additional options: privileges at the Senate House library in London, and ability to access EBSCO, a major provider of research databases, e-journals and other scholarly resources. Division of Counselling Psychology members can also download any back issue of *Counselling Psychology Review* from the BPS online shop. Anyone who registers can access the British Library's EThOS database of UK doctoral theses, and a practitioner researcher who is unaffiliated with a university could apply to the British Library for Reading Room privileges, providing access to virtually any English-language academic journal (www.bl.org.uk).

Research within practitioner research networks

Practitioner research networks (PRNs), or practice-research networks, are 'an infrastructure or form of research action in which practitioners and researchers collaborate to co-construct research and build research capacity' (Henton, 2012: 17). In terms of scale, they may be just a few services or a collection of individuals, or they may be regional, national or international/ global. They may be narrow in focus, perhaps united by an interest in a particular form of therapy (such as the international Acceptance and Commitment Therapy PRN), or they may have broader aims. As Henton outlines, PRNs may focus on pure research, clinical audit, benchmarking, or quality improvement, and the American Psychological Association (APA) recommends them as a good infrastructure for psychotherapy research.

One of the points Henton (2012) makes is that despite the potential usefulness and avail-ability of PRNs, and the support that they offer practitioner-researchers within employment and independent practice alike, counselling psychologists do not seem to utilise them much. Unlike the United Kingdom Council for Psychotherapy (UKCP) and the British Association for Counselling and Psychotherapy (BACP), both of which organisations have PRNs, the Division of Counselling Psychology has yet to develop one. This may partly have to do with differences in membership numbers and available resources: the BACP and UKCP are far larger than the Division of Counselling Psychology, and PRNs require a high level of administration, organisation and funding. Even so, as indicated above, a PRN need not be huge and complex – a group of like-minded practitioners with a common interest can pool their resources and begin their own PRN. Below is one counselling psychologist's account of participating in a PRN.

First-person account: Joining a practitioner research network (PRN)

Dr Terry Hanley, C.Psychol., University of Manchester, Practitioner

I was involved with the British Association for Counselling and Psychotherapy's (BACP) Children and Young People Practice Research Network (CYP PRN). It had a mission to promote psychological health and emotional well-being among children and young people in the UK. The BACP approached me directly about joining because of my publications in that area and connections I had made at conferences.

We met approximately monthly, with the BACP funding meetings, transport and travel. A research officer sorted practicalities, organised rooms and developed web presence. The Head of Research at the BACP chaired the meetings, which included about 11 individuals who were core to the PRN. At the beginning we thought about what the group was going to do and achieve, and shared information about our own projects. In terms of outputs, we presented as a group at conferences, and produced a toolkit for collecting outcome measures when working with children and young people (www.bacp.co.uk/admin/structure/files/pdf/12173_cyp-prn_toolkit_final_web.pdf).

Some PRNs are organically developing entities that find their identity, but a time-limited PRN needs clear goals from the outset. I think with this PRN there was actually a goal: getting a good database on school counselling outcomes. At our meetings, though, we talked quite openly about all kinds of research, so it wasn't clear that the goal of the PRN was ultimately about evidence-based practice. So, when you join a PRN it is important to be clear about the direction and expectations of the group, whether that fits with your needs, and whether you're willing to commit time to its development. For me as an academic, there wasn't a great pay-off in terms of publications and strong relationships from which to develop grant proposals. That said, I'm very interested in this area, and networking ended up being the main thing for me; it was useful to have regular meetings with people doing research and practice in a similar area.

Ethical clearance for individual projects

If you are a self-employed practitioner, not involved in a PRN, not associated with a university, and not employed by an organisation, is research still possible? The answer is yes, absolutely.

The British Psychological Society's *Code of Human Research Ethics* (2010) outlines how independent practitioners and researchers can access ethical review for their research proposals. While the *Code* encourages individuals to 'explore the possibility' of obtaining ethical review from a university, a university may not be willing to review a proposal for someone not on their faculty. That said, independent practitioners who are not permanent faculty but who act as visiting lecturers (VLs) or hourly paid lecturers (HPLs), even occasionally, should always investigate whether they can access the ethics procedures at the universities where they have been on payroll as VLs or HPLs.

When ethics approval is not possible via the above route, the *Code* (British Psychological Society, 2010) advises three general principles:

The individual should be able to demonstrate that:

a) their research proposal was reviewed by an independent person or persons competent to judge ethics standards;

b) they believed they had acted within the ethics standards laid down in relevant guidance documentation (such as the *Code of Ethics and Conduct* and this *Code*); and

c) evidence to this effect could be provided if necessary. (British Psychological Society, 2010: 36)

In embarking on independently reviewed research, three elements are important for the independent practitioner. First, it is essential to put together a clear and complete proposal, including all relevant ethical considerations. In an existing research structure, there are likely to be established forms for the research proposal and for ethical approval. When working on one's own, one has to make independent decisions about these matters. Guidance is available on designing an overall proposal (see, for example, Punch, 2006; Robson, 2011), but the researcher should also consult specific ethics resources when putting together a plan for how research will be conducted ethically. Detail how you will ensure you are working within the boundaries of your competence, with appropriate supervision; how you will avoid harm and minimise risk; how you will gain informed consent; how you will ensure confidentiality and anonymity; how your research will benefit others; how you will avoid power issues and dual roles (especially important if you are researching a population with which you work); and how you will maintain honesty, integrity and transparency throughout the research process (see the 'Researching ethically' chapter in Sanders and Wilkins, 2010, for more details). Ensure you include, within your proposal, all of the information that will be given to your research participants.

Second, choice of reviewers is critical when working independently. Note that the guidance within the *Code of Human Research Ethics* (British Psychological Society, 2010: 36) stipulates that you should choose people who are 'competent to judge ethics standards', so always consult people who have had some experience of evaluating proposals for Research Ethics Committees, or who have had solid experience of gaining research ethical clearance themselves. Do not be shy about asking for their CVs. If there were ever a complaint associated with your project, or a question about its ethicality, you would need to demonstrate that you had chosen reviewers who were competent and knowledgeable in this area. Note also that the guidance says 'person *or persons*' (emphasis added). In academia or in the NHS it would never be just one person reviewing an ethics proposal, so it is advisable to take a belt and braces approach and get more than one evaluation. Once you have received feedback on an initial draft, you may need to revise the proposal and have it re-reviewed; because paying for ethical approval 'services' would look questionable, you will also need to choose someone who is happy to give you a reasonable amount of time *gratis*. If you do not know someone within your professional network, try tapping into the various networks associated with the Division of Counselling Psychology, such as the discussion forum on the Division's website, the regular E-letter distributed by the Divisional Committee, or social networking sites such as the counselling psychology Facebook page. You may also wish to contact the current Research Lead(s) of the Divisional Committee for their recommendations.

Third, documenting your research approval is important. Within an ethical approval file, keep copies of all iterations of your research and ethics proposal; all correspondence between you and the reviewers; and the CVs and contact details of your ethical reviewers. Keep a journal of the ethical review process you undertook. Ask your reviewers to provide you with a clear letter stating final ethical approval.

Research funding

Not all research is expensive to carry out, and often researchers will finance their own projects. It is worth considering, however, that funding may be available from a variety of sources, including your workplace and funding bodies ranging from charities and trusts to government departments and research councils. The BPS and the Division of Counselling Psychology make a number of research-related awards and grants annually, and the BPS also maintains a funding database. The companion website resources for this chapter provide links to more information, and Robson (2011) provides a useful encapsulation of funding options in Chapter 15 of his text on real-world research.

While applying for funding through one of the above routes is one option, some entrepreneurial independent practitioners may also approach other organisations about research collaborations and may have the option of securing funding through them. The next section gives a sense of how this might occur.

RESEARCHING WITH ORGANISATIONS AND INDIVIDUALS

Research can be a lonely business. This section of the chapter discusses some of the mechanics and benefits of collaborating with organisations or other individuals on a shared project, towards shared aims.

Collaborating with organisations

As with some of the other research avenues explored in this chapter, collaborating with organisations may not occur to many counselling psychologists. You can respond to requests for tenders by organisations needing research, or take the initiative by approaching organisations about research you can offer them. The following first-person account describes how one counselling psychologist researcher connected with the West Midlands Police to produce a research project of benefit to all parties. In this example, the possibility of funding was mooted, but the researcher offered her services *gratis*.

First-person account: Collaborating with an organisation

Dr Victoria Galbraith, C.Psychol., Registered Counselling Psychologist

Having trained as a CoP and also done a Masters in Forensic Psychology, I was interested in bringing the two together. Within my university I had contacts with a professor of criminology and the lead for our policing degree, and they are often invited along to research forums where West Midlands Police [WMP] give ideas for research they want conducted. There are different universities there, and it's like speed dating! You go round chatting to people to see what areas they want investigating, and we would pop on a Post-it note the interests that we had, and I spoke to a senior officer within WMP who managed officers whose role was dedicated to prostitution and sex work, and the investigation that we are now doing for them is a grounded theory study looking at entry into and out of sex work within the West Midlands area.

Once the police were happy with the work that we intended to do, university ethical approval was sought. We're now networking and building up relationships with other agencies, having discussions about the possibility of working with them. We may go down an IRAS route, as one of the agencies that we're hoping to tap into is within the NHS. We will need to gain ethical clearance with each of the different organisations. Every six weeks or so we meet with the WMP and other agencies at the prostitution forums, keeping them abreast of what we're doing, because they want regular updates. They've said 'as soon as possible', but there hasn't been a specific deadline. They are assisting us as much as they can and we are working collaboratively with them on the project.

There was mention of funding, but this was something I was willing to volunteer my time for because it brings together two disciplines that interest me. It's a therapeutic perspective on a population that may be considered by many to be offenders as opposed to victims or survivors. I wanted to examine what is putting them in this position, what the background might be that leads individuals to engage in this work. It can be glamorised, like in the movies, but these women and men go through really hard times. I also have a view to publish, and

(Continued)

(Continued)

it is good to be doing real-world research, investigating something that is really going on, and that could influence various agencies.

   If you have an area of interest, make sure that you are placing yourself within those networks that could lead to the work that you desire. Have a look at what's going on locally and nationally; locate the agencies that might be doing work in the area. Read the literature, find out what needs to be done, and you can approach an organisation with what you would like to do for them. If there's something that's of interest, go for it! Often we sit back and wait for opportunities, but I think it's good to go out there and grab them. That's one thing that we ought to be doing, particularly when considering the new standards for counselling psychology, which include leadership and influencing change. We need to get out there and make a difference.

Collaborating with other individual(s)

The alternative to collaborating with organisations is joining forces with other individuals, and conferences are a particularly fertile ground for making such connections. Certainly, joint projects may arise with people you meet at general psychology or counselling psychology conferences, but content-specific, multidisciplinary conferences can lead to particularly interesting collaborations. My own research area sits at the interfaces between psychology, thanatology, and computer–human interaction (CHI), and attending death-and-dying orientated conferences has led to joint papers and symposia with lawyers, sociologists and diverse deathwork professionals on topics of shared interest, such as post-mortem privacy considerations in the digital sphere.

   At best, involvement with collaborators decreases 'research isolation', spreads the workload, increases possible sources for funding, expands the amount of data collected on a research project, and results in a rich multi-voiced and possibly interdisciplinary theoretical paper. In order for things to run smoothly, however, there needs to be someone clearly leading the project who can delegate tasks, set deadlines, organise the source(s) of ethical approval, chair meetings, and perhaps take ultimate responsibility for refining the final journal article, or organising conference abstract submissions and panel presentations. Decisions must be made about the order of authors for any publications produced. Group videoconferencing/audioconferencing technology is useful in bringing together collaborators who are geographically far flung.

CONCLUDING THOUGHTS

Increasing research and publication within counselling psychology benefits everyone: the profession, the individuals who practise it and those who utilise their services. The inherently creative and generative nature of research processes brings a different kind of vitality into a practitioner's life. Carrying on with research activity can enhance and solidify one's professional reputation, expand one's skills and career opportunities, introduce a welcome diversity into the working week, and create opportunities for collegial interactions and the sharing of interests and knowledge. This chapter was designed to be both a support to aspiring practitioner-researchers and a call to action. When the future, fifth edition of *The Handbook of Counselling Psychology* reaches the bookshelves, I hope that it will reflect a burgeoning research culture in our field.

REFERENCES

British Psychological Society (2010) *Code of Human Research Ethics*. Leicester: BPS (www.bps.org.uk/sites/default/files/documents/code_of_human_research_ethics.pdf).

British Psychological Society Research Board (2011) *Statement of Policy on Authorship and Publication Credit*. Leicester: BPS (www.bps.org.uk/system/files/images/statement_of_policy_on_authorship_credit.pdf).

Cooper, M. (2011) *Briefing Paper: Development of a Randomised Controlled Trial of Counselling for Depression*. Lutterworth: British Association for Counselling and Psychotherapy (www.bacp.co.uk/admin/structure/files/pdf/7123_development%20of%20a%20rct%20of%20counselling%20for%20depression.pdf).

Division of Counselling Psychology (2013) *Survey into employment status of counselling psychologists*. Leicester: DCoP (http://dcop.bps.org.uk/dcop/news/news_home.cfm) (accessed 5 June 2013).

Gordon, R. and Hanley, T. (2013) 'Where do counselling psychologists based in the UK disseminate their research? A systematic review', *Counselling Psychology Review*, 28(4): 7–17.

Health Research Authority (2009) *Defining Research*. London: HRA (www.hra.nhs.uk/documents/2013/09/defining-research.pdf).

Henton, I. (2012) 'Practice-based research and counselling psychology: A critical review and proposal', *Counselling Psychology Review*, 27(3): 11–28.

Punch, K.F. (2006) *Developing Effective Research Proposals* (2nd edn). London: Sage.

Robson, C. (2011) *Real World Research* (3rd edn). London: John Wiley & Sons.

Sanders, P. and Wilkins, P. (2010) *First Steps in Practitioner Research: A Guide to Understanding and Doing Research in Counselling and Health and Social Care*. Ross-on-Wye: PCCS Books.

CONCLUDING EDITORIAL

This fourth edition of *The Handbook of Counselling Psychology* has adopted a journey metaphor within, and through, counselling psychology; from initial training through to experienced practitioner, researcher, teacher, leader and supervisor. The book has come to a close but the journey goes on for all of us and we hope that you have found the *Handbook* helpful in your own journey. Each reader will probably have found some sections more pertinent than others at any one point in time and, over time, probably different sections will have come into clearer focus and others faded out.

When we start out on this journey of counselling psychology we are given a common navigational map that provides, indeed prescribes, an external framework. This is the set of core competencies that must be achieved by the end of training. Technically, this is what is being worked towards. So the starting point for the journey includes a very basic route map that highlights a few major thoroughfares and necessary 'landmarks' en route. These include what models of therapy will be studied and practised, skills development, finding placements, appropriate supervision arrangements, personal therapy and research methods training.

Yet as we proceed on the journey, with its external structures, it becomes more personal and individualised. This occurs when we begin to critically evaluate the prescribed maps and navigational tools we have been offered, and find ourselves asking not just how to navigate the route but why – what does it actually *mean* to each of us to be a counselling psychologist. We consider the values that underpin the competences and realise that the maps are actually interactive – so 'the journey' becomes 'our journey'. In short, we internalise the structural maps, making them our own and grounding us in the territory we choose to pursue further as counselling psychologists and those we choose to leave for now.

No journey would be possible without pre-, and ongoing, consideration of the resources needed for its undertaking. This fourth edition of *The Handbook of Counselling Psychology* has attempted to offer you some sustenance on your journey within counselling psychology, i.e. food for thought; whether you are at the beginning of your journey, en route, revisiting territories, or contemplating where you want to complete your journey, we think there is something here for you. Reference lists and web resources for each chapter offer possibilities for further exploration and each of us will continue our individual journeys in different ways.

So the journey through counselling psychology is not linear or deterministic. However, we share a respect for enquiry and evidence as well as the value of experiential learning, and our identity is grounded in humanistic values and a belief in a collaborative approach to working with both clients and colleagues. We understand the fundamental value of 'respect for persons' as including a recognition of the ways in which socio-economic circumstances, oppressive social policies and prejudicial attitudes limit potential, and that this implies a commitment to anti-discriminatory practice. It is these shared attitudes and values, together with our core transferable competencies, that provide coherence to our discipline and are manifest in the variety of individual journeys that may be taken through territories as widely divergent as those found in physical and mental health, forensic, educational, occupational and community settings.

INDEX

Page numbers in *italics* refer to figures and tables.